Annual Review of United Nations Affairs

2006/2007

VOLUME III

Edited by
Joachim Müller
and
Karl P. Sauvant

Oceana®
NEW YORK

OXFORD
UNIVERSITY PRESS

Oxford University Press, Inc., publishes works that further Oxford University's objective of excellence in research, scholarship, and education.

Published by Oxford University Press, Inc.
198 Madison Avenue, New York, New York 10016

ISSN: 0066-4340

ISBN: 978-0-19-533730-3 (2006/2007, Volume III)

Note to Readers:

This publication is designed to provide accurate and authoritative information in regard to the subject matter covered. It is based upon sources believed to be accurate and reliable and is intended to be current as of the time it was written. It is sold with the understanding that the publisher is not engaged in rendering legal, accounting, or other professional services. If legal advice or other expert assistance is required, the services of a competent professional person should be sought. Also, to confirm that the information has not been affected or changed by recent developments, traditional legal research techniques should be used, including checking primary sources where appropriate.

(*Based on the Declaration of Principles jointly adopted by a Committee of the American Bar Association and a Committee of Publishers and Associations.*)

SUMMARY TABLE OF CONTENTS

TABLE OF CONTENTS VOLUME III

CHAPTER 2

Security Council *(continued)*

CHAPTER 3

Economic and Social Council

CHAPTER 4

Trusteeship Council

CHAPTER 5

International Court of Justice

CHAPTER 6

Secretariat: Annual Reports

CHAPTER 2

Security Council
(Continued)

2. Resolutions adopted by the Security Council

Resolution 1707 (2006)

Adopted by the Security Council at its 5521st meeting, on 12 September 2006

The Security Council,

Reaffirming its previous resolutions on Afghanistan, in particular its resolutions 1386 (2001) of 20 December 2001, 1413 (2002) of 23 May 2002, 1444 (2002) of 27 November 2002, 1510 (2003) of 13 October 2003, 1563 (2004) of 17 September 2004, 1623 (2005) of 13 September 2005 and 1659 (2006) of 15 February 2006,

Reaffirming its strong commitment to the sovereignty, independence, territorial integrity and national unity of Afghanistan,

Reaffirming also its resolutions 1368 (2001) of 12 September 2001 and 1373 (2001) of 28 September 2001 and reiterating its support for international efforts to root out terrorism in accordance with the Charter of the United Nations,

Recognizing that the responsibility for providing security and law and order throughout the country resides with the Afghans themselves and welcoming the cooperation of the Government of the Islamic Republic of Afghanistan with the International Security Assistance Force (ISAF),

Recognizing once again the interconnected nature of the challenges in Afghanistan, reaffirming that sustainable progress on security, governance and development, as well as on the cross-cutting issue of counter-narcotics, is mutually reinforcing and welcoming the continuing efforts of the Afghan Government and the international community to address these challenges,

Stressing, in this regard, the importance of the Afghanistan Compact and its annexes, launched at the London Conference, which provide the framework for the partnership between the Afghan Government and the international community,

Expressing its concern about the security situation in Afghanistan, in particular the increased violent and terrorist activity by the Taliban, Al-Qaida, illegally armed groups and those involved in the narcotics trade, which has resulted in increased Afghan civilian casualties,

Reiterating its call on all Afghan parties and groups to engage constructively in the peaceful political development of the country and to avoid resorting to violence including through the use of illegal armed groups,

Stressing, in this context, the importance of the security sector reform including further strengthening of the Afghan National Army and Police, disbandment of illegal armed groups, justice sector reform and counter-narcotics,

Expressing, in this context, its support for the Afghan Security Forces, with the assistance of ISAF and the Operation Enduring Freedom (OEF) coalition in contributing to security in Afghanistan and in building the capacity of the Afghan Security Forces, and welcoming the extension of ISAF into Southern Afghanistan, with effect from 31 July 2006, the planned further ISAF expansion into Eastern Afghanistan and the increased coordination between ISAF and the OEF coalition,

Expressing its appreciation to the United Kingdom for taking over the lead from Italy in commanding ISAF, and recognizing with gratitude the contributions of the North Atlantic Treaty Organization (NATO) and many nations to ISAF,

Determining that the situation in Afghanistan still constitutes a threat to international peace and security,

Determined to ensure the full implementation of the mandate of ISAF, in consultation with the Government of the Islamic Republic of Afghanistan,

Acting for these reasons under Chapter VII of the Charter of the United Nations,

1. *Decides* to extend the authorization of the International Security Assistance Force (ISAF), as defined in resolution 1386 (2001) and 1510 (2003), for a period of twelve months beyond 13 October 2006;

2. *Authorizes* the Member States participating in ISAF to take all necessary measures to fulfil its mandate;

3. *Recognizes* the need to further strengthen ISAF, and in this regard calls upon Member States to contribute personnel, equipment and other resources to ISAF, and to make contributions to the Trust Fund established pursuant to resolution 1386 (2001);

4. *Calls* upon ISAF to continue to work in close consultation with the Government of the Islamic Republic of Afghanistan and the Special Representative of the Secretary-General as well as with the OEF coalition in the implementation of the force mandate;

5. *Requests* the leadership of ISAF to provide quarterly reports on implementation of its mandate to the Security Council through the Secretary-General;

6. *Decides* to remain actively seized of this matter.

Resolution 1708 (2006)

Adopted by the Security Council at its 5524th meeting, on 14 September 2006

The Security Council,

Recalling its previous resolutions concerning the situation in Côte d'Ivoire, in particular resolutions 1572 (2004) of 15 November 2004, 1584 (2005) of 1 February 2005, 1633 (2005) of 21 October 2005 and 1643 (2005) of 15 December 2005, and the relevant statements of its President,

Welcoming the ongoing efforts of the Secretary-General, the African Union and the Economic Community of Western African States (ECOWAS) towards re-establishing peace and stability in Côte d'Ivoire,

Recalling the final report (S/2006/735, annex) of the Group of Experts created by the Secretary-General, further to paragraph 9 of resolution 1643 (2005),

Determining that the situation in Côte d'Ivoire continues to constitute a threat to international peace and security in the region,

Acting under Chapter VII of the Charter of the United Nations,

1. *Decides* to extend the mandate of the Group of Experts to 15 December 2006, and requests the Secretary-General to take the necessary administrative measures;

2. *Requests* the Group of Experts to submit a brief written update to the Council, through the Committee established by paragraph 14 of resolution 1572 (2004), before 1 December 2006, on the implementation of the measures imposed by paragraphs 7, 9 and 11 of resolution 1572 (2004) and paragraphs 4 and 6 of resolution 1643 (2005) with recommendations in this regard;

3. *Decides* to remain actively seized of the matter.

Resolution 1709 (2006)

Adopted by the Security Council at its 5532nd meeting, on 22 September 2006

The Security Council,

Recalling its previous resolutions, in particular resolution 1706 (2006) of 31 August 2006, 1679 (2006) of 16 May 2006, 1663 (2006) of 24 March 2006, 1653 of 27 January 2006, 1627 of 23 September 2005 and 1590 (2005) of 24 March 2005, and the statements of its President, in particular that of 3 February 2006 (S/PRST/2006/5), concerning the situation in the Sudan,

Reaffirming its commitment to the sovereignty, unity, independence, and territorial integrity of the Sudan and to the cause of peace,

Noting with deep concern the restrictions placed on movements and materiel of the United Nations Mission in the Sudan and the adverse impact such restrictions have on UNMIS' ability to perform its mandate effectively,

Expressing its grave concern over the continued deterioration of the humanitarian situation in Darfur, and *reiterating* in the strongest terms the need for all parties to the conflict in Darfur to put an end to the violence and atrocities in that region,

Determining that the situation in the Sudan continues to constitute a threat to international peace and security,

1. *Decides* to extend the mandate of UNMIS until 8 October 2006, with the intention to renew it for further periods;

2. *Decides* to remain actively seized of the matter.

Resolution 1710 (2006)

Adopted by the Security Council at its 5540th meeting, on 29 September 2006

The Security Council,

Reaffirming all its previous resolutions and statements pertaining to the situation between Ethiopia and Eritrea (hereinafter referred to as "the parties") and the requirements contained therein, including in particular resolutions 1320 of 15 September 2000, 1430 of

14 August 2002, 1466 of 14 March 2003, 1640 of 23 November 2005 and 1681 of 31 May 2006,

Stressing its unwavering commitment to the peace process, and to the full and expeditious implementation of the Algiers Agreements, and the importance of prompt implementation of the decision of the Eritrea-Ethiopia Boundary Commission (S/2002/423) as a basis for peaceful and cooperative relations between the parties,

Reaffirming the integrity of the Temporary Security Zone (TSZ) as provided for in the Agreement on Cessation of Hostilities of 18 June 2000 (S/2000/601) and recalling the objectives of its establishment and the commitment of the parties to respect the TSZ,

Commending the efforts made by the United Nations Mission in Ethiopia and Eritrea (UNMEE) and its military and civilian personnel to accomplish its duties, despite the difficult circumstances,

Stressing further that the full demarcation of the border between the two parties is vital to lasting peace between Ethiopia and Eritrea as well as in the region, and *recalling* that both parties have agreed to accept the delimitation and demarcation determinations of the Eritrea-Ethiopia Boundary Commission (EEBC) as final and binding,

Expressing its full support for the ongoing process, aimed at implementing the final and binding decision of the EEBC,

Taking note of UNMEE's statement of 25 September 2006 on allegations against UNMEE staff,

Having considered the report of the Secretary-General of 19 September 2006 (S/2006/749),

1. *Decides* to extend the mandate of UNMEE for a period of four months, until 31 January 2007;

2. *Reiterates its demand* expressed in paragraph 1 of resolution 1640 (2005) that Eritrea reverse, without further delay or preconditions, all restrictions on UNMEE's movement and operations, and provide UNMEE with the access, assistance, support and protection required for the performance of its duties, in this regard *expresses its deep concern* at the recent expulsion of UNMEE personnel by Eritrea;

3. *Reiterates its call* expressed in paragraph 2 of resolution 1640 (2005) that the parties show maximum restraint and refrain from any threat or use of force against each other;

4. *Reiterates its demand* expressed in paragraph 5 of resolution 1640 (2005) that Ethiopia accept fully and without delay the final and binding decision of the Eritrea-Ethiopia Boundary Commission and take immediately concrete steps to enable, without preconditions, the Commission to demarcate the border completely and promptly;

5. *Regrets* the lack of progress on demarcation, *calls upon* both parties to cooperate fully with the EEBC, including attending EEBC meetings, *stresses* that the parties have primary responsibility for the implementation of the Algiers Agreements, and *calls again upon* the parties to implement completely and without further delay or preconditions the decision of the EEBC and to take concrete steps to resume the demarcation process;

6. *Demands* that the parties provide UNMEE with the necessary access, assistance, support and protection required for the performance of its duties, including its mandated task to assist the EEBC in the expeditious and orderly implementation of the Delimitation Decision, in accordance with resolutions 1430 (2002) and 1466 (2003) and *demands* that any restrictions be lifted immediately;

7. *Intends* in the event it determines that the parties have not demonstrated progress towards demarcation by 31 January 2007, to transform or reconfigure UNMEE as the Council may decide;

8. *Intends further* to review the situation before 30 November 2006, in order to prepare for possible changes by 31 January 2007, and to that end *requests* the Secretary-General to present updated options for possible changes to UNMEE's mandate;

9. *Expresses* its willingness to reconsider any changes to UNMEE it may make in accordance with paragraph 7 in light of subsequent progress towards demarcation, and its readiness to take further decisions to ensure that UNMEE will be able to facilitate demarcation as progress becomes possible;

10. *Calls* on Member States to provide contributions to the Trust Fund, established pursuant to resolution 1177 (1998) and referred to in Article 4 (17) of the Comprehensive Peace Agreement signed by the Governments of Ethiopia and Eritrea on 12 December 2000, in order to support the demarcation process;

11. *Expresses* its deep appreciation for the contribution and dedication of the troop-contributing countries to the work of UNMEE;

12. *Decides* to remain actively seized of the matter.

Resolution 1711 (2006)

Adopted by the Security Council at its 5541st meeting, on 29 September 2006

The Security Council,

Recalling its resolutions and the statements of its President concerning the Democratic Republic of the Congo, in particular its resolutions 1565 of 1 October 2004, 1592 of 30 March 2005, 1596 of 18 April 2005, 1621 of 6 September 2005, 1628 of 30 September 2005, 1635 of 28 October 2005, 1671 of 25 April 2006, 1693 of 30 June 2006, and its resolutions 1650 of 21 December 2005, 1669 of 10 April 2006 and 1692 of 30 June 2006 relating to the situation in Burundi and in the Great Lakes region of Africa,

Paying tribute again to the citizens of the Democratic Republic of the Congo who, on 30 July 2006, demonstrated their extraordinary commitment to the democratic process by taking part in great numbers, freely and peacefully, in the first stage of democratic elections of historical importance to their nation,

Reaffirming its commitment to respect the sovereignty, territorial integrity and political independence of the Democratic Republic of the Congo as well as all States in the region and its support for the process of the Global and All Inclusive Agreement on the Transition, signed in Pretoria on 17 December 2002,

Underlining the importance of elections as the foundation for longer term restoration of peace and stability, national reconciliation and establishment of the rule of law in the Democratic Republic of the Congo,

Commending the role in support of the electoral process played by the United Nations Organization Mission in the Democratic Republic of the Congo (MONUC), the United Nations Development Programme (UNDP), and other international partners of the Democratic Republic of the Congo who provided support to the electoral process, in particular its African partners, and especially South Africa, as well as the European Union and the Force it has temporarily deployed during this period ("EUFOR R.D.Congo"),

Taking note of the fact that the second round of the presidential elections, as well as the provincial elections, are scheduled for 29 October 2006,

Stressing the primary responsibility of the Government of the Democratic Republic of the Congo for ensuring security during the period encompassing the elections,

Paying tribute to the donor community for the assistance they provide to the Democratic Republic of the Congo, in particular to the electoral process, and *encouraging* them to maintain it,

Deploring again the violence that erupted in Kinshasa on 20 to 22 August 2006 between security forces loyal to the two remaining presidential candidates,

Condemning the continuation of hostilities by militias and foreign armed groups in the eastern part of the Democratic Republic of the Congo, and the threat they pose to the holding of elections,

Deploring the persistence of violations of human rights and international humanitarian law in the Democratic Republic of the Congo, in particular those carried out by these militias and foreign armed groups and by elements of the Armed Forces of the Democratic Republic of the Congo (FARDC), and *stressing* the urgent need for those responsible for these crimes to be brought to justice,

Condemning the continuing illicit flow of weapons within and into the Democratic Republic of the Congo, and *declaring its determination* to continue close monitoring of the implementation of the arms embargo imposed by resolution 1493 and expanded by resolution 1596, and to enforce the measures provided for in paragraphs 13 and 15 of resolution 1596 against persons and entities acting in violation of this embargo,

Bearing in mind that the mandate of the United Nations Operation in Burundi (ONUB) will expire on 31 December 2006,

Taking note of the report of the Secretary-General dated 22 September 2006 (S/2006/759), and of its recommendations,

Noting that the situation in the Democratic Republic of the Congo continues to constitute a threat to international peace and security in the region,

Acting under Chapter VII of the Charter of the United Nations,

1. *Decides* to extend the mandate of MONUC, as contained in resolutions 1565, 1592, 1596, 1621 and 1635 until 15 February 2007;

2 *Decides* to extend until 15 February 2007 the increase in the military and civilian police strength of MONUC authorized by resolutions 1621 and 1635;

3. *Decides* to extend until 31 December 2006 the authorization contained in resolutions 1669 and 1692 for the Secretary-General to redeploy temporarily a maximum of one infantry battalion, a military hospital and 50 military observers from ONUB to MONUC;

4. *Takes note* of the recommendation of the Secretary-General to temporarily maintain until 15 February 2007 the capabilities referred to in paragraph 3 above, and expresses its intention to re-examine this issue before 31 December 2006 with a view to ensuring that MONUC has adequate capabilities to perform its mandate fully until the date referred to in paragraph 1;

5. *Underlines* the temporary character of the provisions of paragraphs 2 and 3 above, and *requests* the Secretary-General to take the necessary steps with a view to downsizing or repatriating this additional strength by 15 February 2007, as long as their presence in the Democratic Republic of the Congo would no longer be vital to the successful completion of the electoral process;

6. *Calls once again* on the Transitional institutions and on all Congolese parties to ensure that free, fair and peaceful elections take place, that the next steps of the timetable for polls developed by the Independent Electoral Commission are scrupulously respected and calls on all candidates, in particular the two remaining presidential candidates, to restate their commitment to the democratic process;

7. *Reiterates* the importance of a cantonment of non-police security forces in the province of Kinshasa and its support for the International Committee in Support of the Transition (CIAT) in this regard, and *takes note* of the Commitment for a weapons-free city-province of Kinshasa signed on 23 September 2006;

8. *Calls* on the Transitional institutions and all Congolese parties to ensure that the security forces exercise restraint and remain impartial while providing security to the electoral process, and to respect the rights of every candidate to conduct a campaign;

9. *Calls* on all Congolese parties to refrain from incitement to hatred and violence and from any threat or use of force to prevent elections, dispute their outcome or subvert the peace process, and to resolve political differences by peaceful means, including through the framework established with the facilitation of MONUC, and in the framework of democratic institutions and the rule of law;

10. *Welcomes* the intention expressed by the Secretary-General to consult closely with the new Congolese authorities on an adjustment of MONUC's mandate and capacities after the completion of the electoral process, requests the Secretary-General to submit recommendations to the Council in this regard by the end of January 2007, and expresses its commitment to continue to contribute to the consolidation of peace and stability in the Democratic Republic of the Congo in the post-transitional period;

11. *Decides* to remain actively seized of the matter.

Resolution 1712 (2006)

Adopted by the Security Council at its 5542nd meeting, on 29 September 2006

The Security Council,

Recalling its previous resolutions and statements by its President concerning the situations in Liberia and the subregion, in particular its resolutions 1509 (2003) of 19 September 2003, 1694 (2006) of 13 July 2006 and 1667 (2006) of 31 March 2006,

Welcoming the Secretary-General's report of 12 September 2006 (S/2006/743),

Further welcoming the steps taken by the Government of Liberia to combat corruption,

Expressing its appreciation for the continuing support of the Economic Community of West African States (ECOWAS) and the African Union (AU) for the Liberian peace process, as well as for financial and other assistance provided by the international community,

Commending the United Nations Mission in Liberia (UNMIL), under the leadership of the Special Representative of the Secretary-General, for the significant part its support has played in restoring peace and stability to Liberia,

Emphasizing that significant challenges remain in completing reintegration and repatriation of ex-combatants and the urgent restructuring of the Liberian security sector, as well as maintaining stability in Liberia and the subregion,

Welcoming UNMIL's deployments in vulnerable areas at Liberia's borders,

Reiterating the continuing need for UNMIL's support for the security of the Special Court for Sierra Leone,

Determining that the situation in Liberia continues to constitute a threat to international peace and security in the region,

Acting under Chapter VII of the Charter of the United Nations,

1. *Decides* that the mandate of the United Nations Mission in Liberia (UNMIL) shall be extended until 31 March 2007;

2. *Reaffirms* its intention to authorize the Secretary-General to redeploy troops between UNMIL and the United Nations Operation in Côte d'Ivoire (UNOCI) on a temporary basis in accordance with the provisions of resolution 1609 (2005), as may be needed;

3. *Endorses* the Secretary-General's recommendations for a phased, gradual consolidation, drawdown and withdrawal of UNMIL's troop contingent, as the situation permits and without compromising the security of Liberia;

4. *Requests* the Secretary-General to monitor progress on the stabilization of Liberia and to continue to keep the Security Council informed, with particular reference to the broad benchmarks laid out in paragraphs 70 to 71 and annex 1 of his report of 12 September 2006, in particular the restructuring of the security sector, the reintegration of former combatants, the facilitation of political and ethnic reconciliation, the consolidation of State authority throughout the country, judicial reform, restoration of effective Government control over the country's natural and mineral resources, and establishment of a stable and secure environment necessary to foster economic growth;

5. *Calls* on the Government of Liberia, in close coordination with UNMIL, to take the necessary steps on its part towards achieving the benchmarks laid out in paragraph 4 above, including ensuring the effective implementation of the Forestry Reform Law, the continuing commitment to the Government and Economic Management Program, and the rapid development of a national security policy and architecture and *encourages* the international community to support these efforts;

6. *Welcomes* the efforts undertaken by UNMIL to implement the Secretary-General's zero tolerance policy on sexual exploitation and abuse and to ensure full compliance of its personnel with the United Nations code of conduct, and *requests* the Secretary-General to take all necessary action in this regard and to keep the Security Council informed, and *urges* troop-contributing countries to take appropriate preventive action, including the conduct of predeployment awareness training, and to take disciplinary and other action to ensure that allegations of sexual exploitation or abuse against their personnel are properly investigated and, if substantiated, punished;

7. *Decides* to remain actively seized of the matter.

Resolution 1713 (2006)

Adopted by the Security Council at its 5543rd meeting, on 29 September 2006

The Security Council,

Recalling its previous resolutions concerning the situation in Sudan, in particular resolutions 1665 (2006) of 29 March 2006, 1651 (2005) of 21 December 2005, 1591 (2005) of 29 March 2005, and 1556 (2004) of 30 July 2004 and statements of its President concerning Sudan,

Stressing again its firm commitment to the cause of peace throughout Sudan, full implementation of the Comprehensive Peace Agreement of 9 January 2005, full implementation of the framework agreed between the parties for a resolution of the conflict in Darfur (the Darfur Peace Agreement), and an end to the violence and atrocities in Darfur,

Urging those parties that have not signed the Darfur Peace Agreement to do so without delay and not act in any way that would impede the implementation of the Agreement, and *further urging* that those that have signed that Agreement implement their obligations without delay,

Deploring the ongoing violence, impunity, and consequent deterioration of the humanitarian situation, and *reiterating* its deep concern about the security of civilians and humanitarian aid workers and about humanitarian access to populations in need, and *calling* upon all parties in Darfur to cease offensive actions immediately and to refrain from further violent attacks,

Commending the efforts of, and reiterating its full support for, the African Union, the Secretary-General, and the leaders of the region to promote peace and stability in Darfur,

Recalling the 25 July 2006 midterm briefing by the Panel of Experts appointed by the Secretary-General pursuant to paragraph 3 (b) of resolution 1591 (2005) and extended by resolutions 1651 (2005) and 1665 (2006), *anticipating* the receipt of the Panel's final report presented on August 31, 2006 to the Committee established pursuant to resolution 1591

(2005) and currently under consideration, and *expressing* its intent to study the Panel's recommendations further and to consider appropriate next steps,

Emphasizing the need to respect the provisions of the Charter concerning privileges and immunities, and the Convention on the Privileges and Immunities of the United Nations, as applicable to United Nations operations and persons engaged in such operations,

Reaffirming its commitment to the sovereignty, unity, independence and territorial integrity of Sudan, and recalling the importance of the principles of good neighbourliness, non-interference and cooperation in the relations among States in the region,

Determining that the situation in Sudan continues to constitute a threat to international peace and security in the region,

Acting under Chapter VII of the Charter of the United Nations,

1. *Decides* to extend until 29 September 2007 the mandate of the Panel of Experts originally appointed pursuant to resolution 1591 (2005) and previously extended by resolutions 1651 (2005) and 1665 (2006), and requests the Secretary-General to appoint a fifth member to enable the Panel to better carry out its mission, and to take the necessary administrative measures;

2. *Requests* the Panel of Experts to provide no later than 29 March 2007 a midterm briefing on its work and no later than 90 days after adoption of this resolution an interim report to the Committee established pursuant to paragraph 3 (a) of resolution 1591 (2005), and a final report no later than 30 days prior to termination of its mandate to the Council with its findings and recommendations;

3. *Urges* all States, relevant United Nations bodies, the African Union and other interested parties, to cooperate fully with the Committee and the Panel of Experts, in particular by supplying any information at their disposal on implementation of the measures imposed by resolution 1591 (2005) and resolution 1556 (2004);

4. *Decides* to remain actively seized of the matter.

Resolution 1714 (2006)

Adopted by the Security Council at its 5545th meeting, on 6 October 2006

The Security Council,

Recalling its previous resolutions, in particular resolutions 1709 (2006) of 22 September 2006, 1706 (2006) of 31 August 2006, 1679 (2006) of 16 May 2006, 1663 (2006) of 24 March 2006, 1653 (2006) of 27 January 2006, 1627 (2005) of 23 September 2005 and 1590 (2005) of 24 March 2005, and the statements of its President, in particular that of 3 February 2006, concerning the situation in the Sudan,

Reaffirming its commitment to the sovereignty, unity, independence, and territorial integrity of the Sudan and to the cause of peace,

Welcoming the progress in implementation of security arrangements by the parties of the Comprehensive Peace Agreement of 9 January 2005, and *calling* upon the parties to urgently accelerate progress on implementing these and other aspects of the Agreement,

Welcoming the full deployment of United Nations forces within the United Nations Mission in the Sudan (UNMIS) in those areas of operation in support of the Comprehensive Peace Agreement, and *acknowledging* the commitment by troop-contributing countries in support of this mission,

Welcoming the improving humanitarian situation in southern Sudan resulting from progress on implementation of the Comprehensive Peace Agreement,

Noting with concern the restrictions placed on UNMIS movements and materiel by the Government of Sudan and the adverse impact such restrictions have on UNMIS' ability to perform its mandate effectively,

Expressing its grave concern over the recruitment and use of children in conflict in the Sudan, particularly by Other Armed Groups in southern Sudan,

Expressing its grave concern over the continued deterioration of the humanitarian situation in Darfur, and reiterating in the strongest terms the need for all parties to the conflict in Darfur, including non-parties to the Darfur Peace Agreement, to put an end to the violence and atrocities in that region,

Welcoming the decision of the 63rd meeting of the African Union Peace and Security Council of 20 September 2006 to extend the mandate of AMIS to 31 December 2006,

Encouraging the efforts of the Secretary-General and the African Union to implement those provisions of resolution 1706 (2006) on United Nations assistance to the African Union Mission in the Sudan (AMIS), and calling upon the parties to the Darfur Peace Agreement and all other parties in Darfur to facilitate this process,

Determining that the situation in the Sudan continues to constitute a threat to international peace and security,

1. *Decides* to extend the mandate of UNMIS until 30 April 2007, with the intention to renew it for further periods;

2. *Requests* the Secretary-General to report to the Council every three months on the implementation of the mandate of UNMIS;

3. *Calls* upon the parties to the Comprehensive Peace Agreement, the Darfur Peace Agreement and the N'djamena Humanitarian Cease-fire Agreement to respect their commitments and implement fully all aspects of the Agreements without delay, and calls upon those parties that have not signed the Darfur Peace Agreement to do so without delay and not to act in any way that would impede implementation of the Agreement;

4. *Decides* to remain actively seized of the matter.

Resolution 1715 (2006)

Adopted by the Security Council at its 5547th (closed) meeting, on 9 October 2006

The Security Council,

Having considered the question of the recommendation for the appointment of the Secretary-General of the United Nations.

Recommends to the General Assembly that Mr. Ban Ki-moon be appointed Secretary-General of the United Nations for a term of office from 1 January 2007 to 31 December 2011.

Resolution 1716 (2006)

Adopted by the Security Council at its 5549th meeting, on 13 October 2006

The Security Council,

Recalling all its relevant resolutions, in particular resolution 1666 of 31 March 2006 (S/RES/1666),

Welcoming the report of the Secretary-General on the activities of the United Nations Observer Mission in Georgia of 28 September 2006,

Supporting the sustained efforts of the Secretary-General and of his Special Representative with the assistance of the Russian Federation in its capacity as facilitator, as well as of the Group of Friends of the Secretary-General and of the OSCE,

Regretting the continued lack of progress on key issues of a comprehensive settlement of the Georgian-Abkhaz conflict,

Acknowledging with concern the observation of the Secretary-General that a new and tense situation has emerged between the Georgian and the Abkhaz sides, in particular as a result of the Georgian special operation in the upper Kodori Valley,

1. *Reaffirms* the commitment of all Member States to the sovereignty, independence and territorial integrity of Georgia within its internationally recognized borders, and *supports* all efforts by the United Nations and the Group of Friends of the Secretary-General which are guided by their determination to promote a settlement of the Georgian-Abkhaz conflict only by peaceful means and within the framework of the Security Council resolutions;

2. *Recalls,* with a view to achieving a lasting and comprehensive settlement, its support for the principles contained in the "Paper on Basic Principles for the Distribution of Competencies between Tbilisi and Sukhumi" and welcomes additional ideas that the sides would be willing to offer with a view to conducting creatively and constructively a political dialogue under the aegis of the United Nations;

3. *Having in mind* the relevant Security Council resolutions containing an appeal to both sides to refrain from any action that might impede the peace process, *expresses* its concern with regard to the actions of the Georgian side in the Kodori Valley in July 2006, and to all violations of the Moscow agreement on ceasefire and separation of forces of 14 May 1994, and other Georgian-Abkhaz agreements concerning the Kodori Valley;

4. *Urges* the Georgian side to ensure that the situation in the upper Kodori Valley is in line with the Moscow agreement and that no troops unauthorized by this agreement are present;

5. *Notes* with satisfaction the resumption of joint patrols in the upper Kodori Valley by UNOMIG and the CIS peacekeeping force and reaffirms that such joint patrols should be conducted on a regular basis;

6. *Urges* both parties to comply fully with previous agreements and understandings regarding ceasefire, non-use of violence and confidence-building measures, and *stresses* the need to strictly observe the Moscow Agreement on Ceasefire and the Separation of Forces in the air, on the sea and on land, including in the Kodori Valley;

7. *Acknowledges* the important role of the CIS peacekeeping force and of UNOMIG in the Georgian-Abkhaz conflict zone, *stresses* the importance of close and effective cooperation between UNOMIG and the CIS peacekeeping force as they currently play a stabilizing role in the conflict zone, *looks* to all sides to continue to extend the necessary cooperation to them and *recalls* that a lasting and comprehensive settlement of the conflict will require appropriate security guarantees;

8. *Once again urges* the Georgian side to address seriously legitimate Abkhaz security concerns, to avoid steps which could be seen as threatening and to refrain from militant rhetoric and provocative actions, especially in upper Kodori Valley;

9. *Urges* the Abkhaz leadership to address seriously the need for a dignified return of IDPs and refugees, including their security and human rights concerns, publicly reassure the local population, particularly in the Gali district, that their residency rights and identity will be respected, and move without delay on implementing past commitments relating to United Nations police advisers, a United Nations human rights sub-office and the language of instruction;

10. *Urges* both parties to finalize without delay the package of documents on the non-use of violence and on the return of refugees and internally displaced persons for the Gali district and to undertake necessary steps to secure the protection and dignity of the civilian population including the returnees;

11. *Commends* the presentation by both sides of ideas as a basis for dialogue and *calls on* the two sides to resume this dialogue by using all existing mechanisms as described in the relevant Security Council resolutions in order to come to a peaceful settlement;

12. *Calls on* both parties to follow up on their expressed readiness for a meeting of their highest authorities without preconditions and to maintain open channels of communication to build confidence, and *encourages* further contacts between representatives of civil society;

13. *Calls* on the Secretary-General to explore with the sides ways and means to build confidence, in particular by improving welfare and security of the inhabitants of Gali and Zugdidi districts;

14. *Supports* all efforts by the Georgian and Abkhaz sides to engage constructively in economic cooperation as envisaged in the Geneva meetings and complemented by the working groups established in Sotchi in March 2003, including, security conditions permitting, the

rehabilitation of infrastructure, and welcomes the intention expressed by Germany to host a meeting on economic cooperation and confidence-building measures, pending progress in the conflict resolution process;

15. *Underlines* that it is the primary responsibility of both sides to provide appropriate security and to ensure the freedom of movement of UNOMIG, the CIS peacekeeping force and other international personnel and *calls on* both sides to fulfil their obligations in this regard;

16. *Welcomes* the efforts being undertaken by UNOMIG to implement the Secretary-General's zero tolerance policy on sexual exploitation and abuse and to ensure full compliance of its personnel with the United Nations code of conduct, *requests* the Secretary-General to continue to take all necessary action in this regard and to keep the Security Council informed, and *urges* troop-contributing countries to take appropriate preventive action including the conduct of predeployment awareness training, and to take disciplinary action and other action to ensure full accountability in cases of such conduct involving their personnel;

17. *Decides* to extend the mandate of UNOMIG for a new period terminating on 15 April 2007;

18. *Requests* the Secretary-General to include detailed information on developments in the Kodori Valley and on the progress on efforts for return of refugees and IDPs particularly to the Gali district into his next report on the situation in Abkhazia, Georgia;

19. *Strongly supports* the efforts of the Special Representative of the Secretary-General and calls on the Group of Friends of the Secretary-General to continue giving him their steadfast and unified support;

20. *Decides* to remain actively seized of the matter.

Resolution 1717 (2006)

Adopted by the Security Council at its 5550th meeting, on 13 October 2006

The Security Council,

Recalling its resolutions 955 (1994) of 8 November 1994, 1165 (1998) of 30 April 1998, 1329 (2000) of 30 November 2000, 1411 (2002) of 17 May 2002, 1431 (2002) of 14 August 2002, 1449 (2002) of 13 December 2002, 1503 (2003) of 28 August 2003 and 1534 (2004) of 26 March 2004,

Recalling that on 25 June 2003, the General Assembly by its decision 57/414 and in accordance with Article 12 ter, paragraph 1 (d) of the International Tribunal for Rwanda's Statute, elected from a list of candidates approved by the Security Council the following eighteen ad litem judges to a four-year term of office beginning on 25 June 2003 and to end on 24 June 2007: Mr. Aydin Sefa Akay (Turkey); Ms. Florence Rita Arrey (Cameroon); Ms. Solomy Balungi Bossa (Uganda); Mr. Robert Fremr (Czech Republic); Ms. Taghrid Hikmet (Jordan); Ms. Karin Hökborg (Sweden); Mr. Vagn Joensen (Denmark); Mr. Gberdao Gustave Kam (Burkina Faso); Ms. Flavia Lattanzi (Italy); Mr. Kenneth Machin (United Kingdom); Mr. Joseph Edward Chiondo Masanche (United Republic of Tanzania); Mr. Tan Sri Dato' Hj. Mohd. Azmi Dato' Hj. Kamaruddin (Malaysia); Mr. Lee Gacuiga Muthoga

(Kenya); Mr. Seon Ki Park (Republic of Korea); Mr. Mparany Mamy Richard Rajohnson (Madagascar); Mr. Emile Francis Short (Ghana); Mr. Albertus Henricus Johannes Swart (Netherlands); and Ms. Aura E. Guerra de Villalaz (Panama),

Recalling that the Security Council by its resolution 1684 (2006) of 13 June 2006 extended the terms of the eleven permanent judges serving at the International Tribunal for Rwanda until 31 December 2008,

Recalling that the Security Council by its resolution 1705 (2006) of 29 August 2006 decided, notwithstanding the provisions of Article 12 ter of the Statute of the International Tribunal for Rwanda, and notwithstanding that Judge Bossa's elected term as an ad litem judge of the International Tribunal will end on 24 June 2007, to authorize her, effective 28 August 2006, to continue to serve as a judge in the *Butare* case until its completion,

Taking note of the letter to the President of the Security Council from the Secretary-General dated 2 October 2006,

1. *Decides* in response to the request by the Secretary-General and notwithstanding the provisions of Article 12 ter of the Statute of the International Tribunal for Rwanda, to extend until 31 December 2008 the term of office of the following ad litem judges of the International Tribunal who were elected on 25 June 2003:

- Mr. Aydin Sefa Akay (Turkey);
- Ms. Florence Rita Arrey (Cameroon);
- Ms. Solomy Balungi Bossa (Uganda);
- Mr. Robert Fremr (Czech Republic);
- Ms. Taghrid Hikmet (Jordan);
- Ms. Karin Hökborg (Sweden);
- Mr. Vagn Joensen (Denmark);
- Mr. Gberdao Gustave Kam (Burkina Faso);
- Ms. Flavia Lattanzi (Italy);
- Mr. Kenneth Machin (United Kingdom);
- Mr. Joseph Edward Chiondo Masanche (United Republic of Tanzania);
- Mr. Tan Sri Dato' Hj. Mohd. Azmi Dato' Hj. Kamaruddin (Malaysia);
- Mr. Lee Gacuiga Muthoga (Kenya);
- Mr. Seon Ki Park (Republic of Korea);
- Mr. Mparany Mamy Richard Rajohnson (Madagascar);
- Mr. Emile Francis Short (Ghana);
- Mr. Albertus Henricus Johannes Swart (Netherlands);
- Ms. Aura E. Guerra de Villalaz (Panama).

2. *Decides* in response to the request by the Secretary-General to allow ad litem Judges Bossa, Arrey, Lattanzi, Muthoga, Short, Hökborg, Hikmet, Kam and Park to serve in the

International Tribunal for Rwanda beyond the cumulative period of service provided for under Article 12 ter of the Statute and until 31 December 2008;

3. *Requests* States to continue to make every effort to ensure that their nationals who were elected as ad litem judges of the International Tribunal for Rwanda remain available to serve until 31 December 2008;

4. *Decides* to remain seized of the matter.

Resolution 1718 (2006)

Adopted by the Security Council at its 5551st meeting, on 14 October 2006

The Security Council,

Recalling its previous relevant resolutions, including resolution 825 (1993), resolution 1540 (2004) and, in particular, resolution 1695 (2006), as well as the statement of its President of 6 October 2006 (S/PRST/2006/41),

Reaffirming that proliferation of nuclear, chemical and biological weapons, as well as their means of delivery, constitutes a threat to international peace and security,

Expressing the gravest concern at the claim by the Democratic People's Republic of Korea (DPRK) that it has conducted a test of a nuclear weapon on 9 October 2006, and at the challenge such a test constitutes to the Treaty on the Non-Proliferation of Nuclear Weapons and to international efforts aimed at strengthening the global regime of non-proliferation of nuclear weapons, and the danger it poses to peace and stability in the region and beyond,

Expressing its firm conviction that the international regime on the non-proliferation of nuclear weapons should be maintained and recalling that the DPRK cannot have the status of a nuclear-weapon state in accordance with the Treaty on the Non-Proliferation of Nuclear Weapons,

Deploring the DPRK's announcement of withdrawal from the Treaty on the Non-Proliferation of Nuclear Weapons and its pursuit of nuclear weapons,

Deploring further that the DPRK has refused to return to the Six-Party talks without precondition,

Endorsing the Joint Statement issued on 19 September 2005 by China, the DPRK, Japan, the Republic of Korea, the Russian Federation and the United States,

Underlining the importance that the DPRK respond to other security and humanitarian concerns of the international community,

Expressing profound concern that the test claimed by the DPRK has generated increased tension in the region and beyond, and *determining* therefore that there is a clear threat to international peace and security,

Acting under Chapter VII of the Charter of the United Nations, and taking measures under its Article 41,

1. *Condemns* the nuclear test proclaimed by the DPRK on 9 October 2006 in flagrant disregard of its relevant resolutions, in particular resolution 1695 (2006), as well as of the

statement of its President of 6 October 2006 (S/PRST/2006/41), including that such a test would bring universal condemnation of the international community and would represent a clear threat to international peace and security;

2. *Demands* that the DPRK not conduct any further nuclear test or launch of a ballistic missile;

3. *Demands* that the DPRK immediately retract its announcement of withdrawal from the Treaty on the Non-Proliferation of Nuclear Weapons;

4. *Demands* further that the DPRK return to the Treaty on the Non-Proliferation of Nuclear Weapons and International Atomic Energy Agency (IAEA) safeguards, and underlines the need for all States Parties to the Treaty on the Non-Proliferation of Nuclear Weapons to continue to comply with their Treaty obligations;

5. *Decides* that the DPRK shall suspend all activities related to its ballistic missile programme and in this context re-establish its pre-existing commitments to a moratorium on missile launching;

6. *Decides* that the DPRK shall abandon all nuclear weapons and existing nuclear programmes in a complete, verifiable and irreversible manner, shall act strictly in accordance with the obligations applicable to parties under the Treaty on the Non-Proliferation of Nuclear Weapons and the terms and conditions of its International Atomic Energy Agency (IAEA) Safeguards Agreement (IAEA INFCIRC/403) and shall provide the IAEA transparency measures extending beyond these requirements, including such access to individuals, documentation, equipments and facilities as may be required and deemed necessary by the IAEA;

7. *Decides* also that the DPRK shall abandon all other existing weapons of mass destruction and ballistic missile programme in a complete, verifiable and irreversible manner;

8. *Decides* that:

(a) All Member States shall prevent the direct or indirect supply, sale or transfer to the DPRK, through their territories or by their nationals, or using their flag vessels or aircraft, and whether or not originating in their territories, of:

(i) Any battle tanks, armoured combat vehicles, large calibre artillery systems, combat aircraft, attack helicopters, warships, missiles or missile systems as defined for the purpose of the United Nations Register on Conventional Arms, or related materiel including spare parts, or items as determined by the Security Council or the Committee established by paragraph 12 below (the Committee);

(ii) All items, materials, equipment, goods and technology as set out in the lists in documents S/2006/814 and S/2006/815, unless within 14 days of adoption of this resolution the Committee has amended or completed their provisions also taking into account the list in document S/2006/816, as well as other items, materials, equipment, goods and technology, determined by the Security Council or the Committee, which could contribute to DPRK's nuclear-related, ballistic missile-related or other weapons of mass destruction-related programmes;

(iii) Luxury goods;

(b) The DPRK shall cease the export of all items covered in subparagraphs (a) (i) and (a) (ii) above and that all Member States shall prohibit the procurement of such items from the DPRK by their nationals, or using their flagged vessels or aircraft, and whether or not originating in the territory of the DPRK;

(c) All Member States shall prevent any transfers to the DPRK by their nationals or from their territories, or from the DPRK by its nationals or from its territory, of technical training, advice, services or assistance related to the provision, manufacture, maintenance or use of the items in subparagraphs (a) (i) and (a) (ii) above;

(d) All Member States shall, in accordance with their respective legal processes, freeze immediately the funds, other financial assets and economic resources which are on their territories at the date of the adoption of this resolution or at any time thereafter, that are owned or controlled, directly or indirectly, by the persons or entities designated by the Committee or by the Security Council as being engaged in or providing support for, including through other illicit means, DPRK's nuclear-related, other weapons of mass destruction-related and ballistic missile-related programmes, or by persons or entities acting on their behalf or at their direction, and ensure that any funds, financial assets or economic resources are prevented from being made available by their nationals or by any persons or entities within their territories, to or for the benefit of such persons or entities;

(e) All Member States shall take the necessary steps to prevent the entry into or transit through their territories of the persons designated by the Committee or by the Security Council as being responsible for, including through supporting or promoting, DPRK policies in relation to the DPRK's nuclear-related, ballistic missile-related and other weapons of mass destruction-related programmes, together with their family members, provided that nothing in this paragraph shall oblige a state to refuse its own nationals entry into its territory;

(f) In order to ensure compliance with the requirements of this paragraph, and thereby preventing illicit trafficking in nuclear, chemical or biological weapons, their means of delivery and related materials, all Member States are called upon to take, in accordance with their national authorities and legislation, and consistent with international law, cooperative action including through inspection of cargo to and from the DPRK, as necessary;

9. *Decides* that the provisions of paragraph 8 (d) above do not apply to financial or other assets or resources that have been determined by relevant States:

(a) To be necessary for basic expenses, including payment for foodstuffs, rent or mortgage, medicines and medical treatment, taxes, insurance premiums, and public utility charges, or exclusively for payment of reasonable professional fees and reimbursement of incurred expenses associated with the provision of legal services, or fees or service charges, in accordance with national laws, for routine holding or maintenance of frozen funds, other financial assets and economic resources, after notification by the relevant States to the Committee of the intention to authorize, where appropriate, access to such funds, other financial assets and economic resources and in the absence of a negative decision by the Committee within five working days of such notification;

(b) To be necessary for extraordinary expenses, provided that such determination has been notified by the relevant States to the Committee and has been approved by the Committee; or

(c) To be subject of a judicial, administrative or arbitral lien or judgement, in which case the funds, other financial assets and economic resources may be used to satisfy that lien or judgement provided that the lien or judgement was entered prior to the date of the present resolution, is not for the benefit of a person referred to in paragraph 8 (d) above or an individual or entity identified by the Security Council or the Committee, and has been notified by the relevant States to the Committee;

10. *Decides* that the measures imposed by paragraph 8 (e) above shall not apply where the Committee determines on a case-by-case basis that such travel is justified on the grounds of humanitarian need, including religious obligations, or where the Committee concludes that an exemption would otherwise further the objectives of the present resolution;

11. *Calls upon* all Member States to report to the Security Council within thirty days of the adoption of this resolution on the steps they have taken with a view to implementing effectively the provisions of paragraph 8 above;

12. *Decides* to establish, in accordance with rule 28 of its provisional rules of procedure, a Committee of the Security Council consisting of all the members of the Council, to undertake the following tasks:

(a) To seek from all States, in particular those producing or possessing the items, materials, equipment, goods and technology referred to in paragraph 8 (a) above, information regarding the actions taken by them to implement effectively the measures imposed by paragraph 8 above of this resolution and whatever further information it may consider useful in this regard;

(b) To examine and take appropriate action on information regarding alleged violations of measures imposed by paragraph 8 of this resolution;

(c) To consider and decide upon requests for exemptions set out in paragraphs 9 and 10 above;

(d) To determine additional items, materials, equipment, goods and technology to be specified for the purpose of paragraphs 8 (a) (i) and 8 (a) (ii) above;

(e) To designate additional individuals and entities subject to the measures imposed by paragraphs 8 (d) and 8 (e) above;

(f) To promulgate guidelines as may be necessary to facilitate the implementation of the measures imposed by this resolution;

(g) To report at least every 90 days to the Security Council on its work, with its observations and recommendations, in particular on ways to strengthen the effectiveness of the measures imposed by paragraph 8 above;

13. *Welcomes and encourages further* the efforts by all States concerned to intensify their diplomatic efforts, to refrain from any actions that might aggravate tension and to facilitate the early resumption of the Six-Party Talks, with a view to the expeditious implementation of the Joint Statement issued on 19 September 2005 by China, the DPRK, Japan, the

Republic of Korea, the Russian Federation and the United States, to achieve the verifiable denuclearization of the Korean Peninsula and to maintain peace and stability on the Korean Peninsula and in north-east Asia;

14. *Calls upon* the DPRK to return immediately to the Six-Party Talks without precondition and to work towards the expeditious implementation of the Joint Statement issued on 19 September 2005 by China, the DPRK, Japan, the Republic of Korea, the Russian Federation and the United States;

15. *Affirms* that it shall keep DPRK's actions under continuous review and that it shall be prepared to review the appropriateness of the measures contained in paragraph 8 above, including the strengthening, modification, suspension or lifting of the measures, as may be needed at that time in light of the DPRK's compliance with the provisions of the resolution;

16. *Underlines* that further decisions will be required, should additional measures be necessary;

17. *Decides* to remain actively seized of the matter.

Resolution 1719 (2006)

Adopted by the Security Council at its 5554th meeting, on 25 October 2006

The Security Council,

Recalling its resolutions and the statements of its President on Burundi, in particular its resolutions 1545 (2004) of 21 May 2004, 1577 (2004) of 1 December 2004, 1602 (2005) of 31 May 2005, 1606 (2005) of 20 June 2005, 1650 (2005) of 21 December 2005 and 1692 (2006) of 30 June 2006,

Reaffirming its strong commitment to the sovereignty, independence, territorial integrity and unity of Burundi, and emphasising the importance of national ownership by Burundi of peacebuilding, security and long-term development,

Congratulating again the people of Burundi on the successful conclusion of the transitional period and the peaceful transfer of authority to a representative and democratically elected Government and institutions,

Welcoming the signature, on 7 September 2006 at Dar-es-Salaam, of a Comprehensive Ceasefire Agreement between the Government of Burundi and the Forces nationales de libération (Palipehutu-FNL),

Paying tribute to the efforts made by the States of the Regional Peace Initiative, in particular Uganda and the United Republic of Tanzania, and the facilitation efforts of South Africa in the service of peace in Burundi, welcoming the continued commitment and engagement of these States, and recalling also the role played by the Burundi Partner's Forum established at the summit meeting on Burundi held in New York on 13 September 2005,

Taking note with concern of reports of a possible attempt to perpetrate a coup d'Etat in Burundi and of the subsequent arrest of a number of political figures,

Reaffirming its support for legitimately elected institutions, and *stressing* that any attempt to seize power by force or derail the democratic process would be deemed unacceptable,

Calling upon the authorities and all political actors in Burundi to persevere in their dialogue on achieving stability and national reconciliation and to promote social harmony in their country, and underscoring the importance of successfully completing the reforms provided for in the Peace and Reconciliation Agreement for Burundi, signed at Arusha on 28 August 2000, in the Comprehensive Ceasefire Agreement signed in Dar-es-Salaam on 16 November 2003 and in the Comprehensive Ceasefire Agreement signed in Dar-es-Salaam on 7 September 2006,

Calling upon the authorities also to persevere in their efforts to promote good governance, including through continued measures to combat corruption,

Emphasizing the need for the United Nations system and the international community to maintain their support for the security and long-term development of Burundi, inter alia by strengthening the capacity of the Burundian Government,

Expressing once again its gratitude to the United Nations Operation in Burundi (ONUB), as well as to the African Mission in Burundi (AMIB) previously deployed by the African Union, for their important contribution to the successful completion of the transition process in Burundi and to peace in the region,

Welcoming the holding on 13 October 2006 of the first country-specific meeting of the Peacebuilding Commission on Burundi and taking note of the Chairman's summary of that meeting,

Having considered the seventh report of the Secretary-General, dated 21 June 2006 (S/2006/429), and the addendum thereto of 14 August 2006 (S/2006/429/Add.1), and welcoming his recommendation on the establishment of a United Nations integrated office in Burundi following the withdrawal of ONUB, with a view to providing continued peacebuilding assistance to the Burundian Government by strengthening national capacity to address the root causes of conflict,

Underscoring the need for a smooth transition from ONUB to the United Nations integrated office and to ensure the proper functioning of that entity,

1. *Requests* the Secretary-General to establish a United Nations Integrated Office in Burundi (Bureau Intégré des Nations Unies au Burundi, BINUB) as recommended in the addendum of his seventh report of 14 August 2006 (S/2006/429/Add.1) for an initial period of 12 months, commencing on 1 January 2007, to support the Government in its effort towards long-term peace and stability throughout the peace consolidation phase in Burundi, including through ensuring coherence and coordination of the United Nations agencies in Burundi, under the leadership of the Executive Representative of the Secretary-General;

2. *Requests* that, once established, BINUB focuses on and supports the Government in the following areas, in coordination with donors and taking account of the Agreement concluded on 24 May 2006 by the Government of Burundi and the Secretary-General and of the role of the Peacebuilding Commission:

Peace consolidation and democratic governance

(a) Strengthening the capacity of national institutions and civil society to address the root causes of conflict and to prevent, manage and resolve internal conflicts, particularly through reforms in the political and administrative spheres;

(b) Strengthening good governance and the transparency and accountability of public institutions;

(c) Promotion of freedom of the press and strengthening the legal and regulatory framework for the media and communications, and enhancing the professionalization of the media;

(d) Consolidation of the rule of law, in particular by strengthening the justice and corrections system, including independence and capacity of the judiciary;

Disarmament, demobilization and reintegration and reform of the security sector

(e) Support for the implementation of the Dar-es-Salaam Comprehensive Ceasefire Agreement of 7 September 2006;

(f) Support for the development of a national plan for reform of the security sector, including human rights training, and provision of technical assistance for its implementation, including training and capacity-building for the Burundi National Police, and technical assistance to enhance the professionalization of the National Defence Force of Burundi;

(g) Support for the completion of the national programme for the demobilization and reintegration of former combatants;

(h) Support for efforts to combat the proliferation of small arms and light weapons;

Promotion and protection of human rights and measures to end impunity

(i) Promotion and protection of human rights, including by building national institutional capacity in that area, particularly with regard to the rights of women, children and other vulnerable groups, by assisting with the design and implementation of a national human rights action plan including the establishment of an independent national human rights commission;

(j) Support for efforts to combat impunity, particularly through the establishment of transitional justice mechanisms, including a truth and reconciliation commission and a special tribunal;

Donor and United Nations agency coordination

(k) Strengthening the partnership between the Government and donors for the implementation of priority, emergency and longer-term activities, within the framework of the Government's Emergency Programme and the Poverty Reduction Strategy Paper, which is being finalized;

(l) Strengthening the Government's capacity for donor coordination, effective communication with donors, and mobilization of resources in line with the Poverty Reduction Strategy Paper, when finalized;

(m) Ensuring effective coordination among the strategies and programmes of the various United Nations agencies, funds and programmes in Burundi;

3. *Urges* BINUB to take account of the rights of women and gender considerations as set out in resolution 1325 (2000) as cross-cutting issues in all the areas outlined in paragraph 2 above, including through consultation with local and international women's group, and

requests the Secretary-General, where appropriate, to include in his reporting to the Security Council progress on gender mainstreaming throughout the Integrated Office and all other aspects relating to the situation of women and girls, especially in relation to the need to protect them from gender-based violence;

4. *Stresses* the need for cooperation, within the limits of their respective capacities and current mandates, between BINUB and the United Nations Organization Mission in the Democratic Republic of the Congo;

5. *Welcomes* the recommendation, in the addendum to the Secretary-General's report, that the Integrated Office should be headed by an Executive Representative of the Secretary-General and that the latter should also serve as the Resident Representative of the United Nations Development Programme and as the United Nations Resident Coordinator and Humanitarian Coordinator;

6. *Takes note* of the benchmarks outlined in the Addendum to the Secretary-General's report for gauging progress made by BINUB during its mandate, in particular as they relate to the priorities mentioned in paragraph 2 above, and of the proposed time frame for the eventual transition to a primarily development-focused engagement, and reaffirms its willingness to adjust as appropriate the United Nations presence in Burundi during the peace consolidation phase, taking all circumstances into account;

7. *Emphasizes* that the Government of Burundi bears the primary responsibility for peacebuilding, security and long-term development in the country, and urges international donors to continue to support the Government's efforts in those areas;

8. *Urges* the authorities and all political actors in Burundi to pursue the reforms agreed upon at Arusha and Dar-es-Salaam and to maintain the spirit of dialogue, consensus-building and inclusiveness that enabled them to achieve a successful transition in their country;

9. *Encourages* the Burundian authorities to continue to cooperate with the Secretary-General, including for the establishment of the mechanisms referred to in Council resolution 1606 (2005);

10. *Calls upon* the Burundian authorities, in their investigations into the alleged attempt to perpetrate a coup d'Etat, to follow due process and to respect the guarantees provided for by law and its international obligations;

11. *Expresses its deep concern* at reports of continuing human rights violations, and urges the Government to investigate all such reports, take the necessary steps to prevent further violations and to ensure that those responsible for such violations are brought to justice;

12. *Calls upon* the Government of Burundi and the Forces nationales de libération (Palipehutu-FNL) to expeditiously implement in good faith the Comprehensive Ceasefire Agreement, which they signed at Dar-es-Salaam on 7 September 2006, and to pursue their efforts to resolve outstanding issues in a spirit of cooperation;

13. *Encourages* the States of the Regional Peace Initiative and the South-African Facilitation to continue to work with the Burundian authorities to consolidate peace in their country and in the region;

14. *Requests* the Secretary-General to keep the Security Council regularly informed of the progress made in establishing the United Nations Integrated Office in Burundi and,

subsequently, to report regularly to the Council on the implementation of the present resolution, including with respect to the security situation and the human rights situation;

15. *Decides* to remain actively seized of the matter.

Resolution 1720 (2006)

Adopted by the Security Council at its 5560th meeting, on 31 October 2006

The Security Council,

Recalling all its previous resolutions on Western Sahara, including resolution 1495 (2003) of 31 July 2003, resolution 1541 (2004) of 29 April 2004, and resolution 1675 (2006) of 28 April 2006,

Reaffirming its strong support for the efforts of the Secretary-General and his Personal Envoy,

Reaffirming its commitment to assist the parties to achieve a just, lasting and mutually acceptable political solution, which will provide for the self-determination of the people of Western Sahara in the context of arrangements consistent with the principles and purposes of the Charter of the United Nations, and noting the role and responsibilities of the parties in this respect,

Reiterating its call upon the parties and States of the region to continue to cooperate fully with the United Nations to end the current impasse and to achieve progress towards a political solution,

Having considered the report of the Secretary-General of 16 October 2006 (S/2006/817),

1. *Reaffirms* the need for full respect of the military agreements reached with MINURSO with regard to the ceasefire;

2. *Calls* on Member States to consider voluntary contributions to fund Confidence Building Measures that allow for increased contact between separated family members, especially family unification visits;

3. *Requests* the Secretary-General provide a report on the situation in the Western Sahara before the end of the mandate period;

4. *Requests* the Secretary-General to continue to take the necessary measures to ensure full compliance in MINURSO with the United Nations zero-tolerance policy on sexual exploitation and abuse and to keep the Council informed, and urges troop-contributing countries to take appropriate preventive action including pre-deployment awareness training, and other action to ensure full accountability in cases of such conduct involving their personnel;

5. *Decides* to extend the mandate of the United Nations Mission for the Referendum in Western Sahara (MINURSO) until 30 April 2007;

6. *Decides* to remain seized of the matter.

Resolution 1721 (2006)

Adoped by the Security Council at its 5561st meeting, on 1 November 2006

The Security Council,

Recalling its previous resolutions and the statements of its President relating to the situation in Côte d'Ivoire,

Reaffirming its strong commitment to the sovereignty, independence, territorial integrity and unity of Côte d'Ivoire, and recalling the importance of the principles of good-neighbourliness, non-interference and regional cooperation,

Recalling that it endorsed the Agreement signed by the Ivorian political forces in Linas-Marcoussis on 24 January 2003 (S/2003/99) (the Linas-Marcoussis Agreement) approved by the Conference of Heads of State on Côte d'Ivoire, held in Paris on 25 and 26 January 2003, the Agreement signed in Accra on 30 July 2004 (the Accra III Agreement) and the Agreement signed in Pretoria on 6 April 2005 (the Pretoria Agreement),

Commending the continued efforts of the African Union, the Economic Community of West African States and the leaders of the region to promote peace and stability in Côte d'Ivoire, and reiterating its full support for them,

Paying tribute to President Thabo Mbeki of the Republic of South Africa for the untiring efforts he has deployed in the service of peace and reconciliation in Côte d'Ivoire, as well as the numerous initiatives he has taken to move forward the peace process, in his capacity as African Union Mediator, driven by his deep commitment to finding African solutions to African problems,

Commending also the constant efforts of the Special Representative of the Secretary-General, Mr. Pierre Schori, and of the High Representative for the Elections, Mr. Gérard Stoudmann, and of the International Working Group (IWG), and reiterating its full support for them,

Reaffirming its support to the impartial forces, namely the United Nations Operation in Côte d'Ivoire (UNOCI) and the French forces which support it,

Having taken note of the decision of the Peace and Security Council of the African Union adopted at its 64th meeting at the level of Heads of State and Government, held on 17 October 2006 in Addis Ababa ("the decision of the Peace and Security Council") (S/2006/829),

Having heard on 25 October 2006 the report by M. Saïd Djinnit, Commissioner of the African Union,

Having taken note of the report of the Secretary-General dated 17 October 2006 (S/2006/821), in particular its paragraphs 68 to 80,

Bearing in mind that the constitutional mandate of President Laurent Gbagbo expired on 30 October 2005 and the mandate of the former National Assembly expired on 16 December 2005,

Expressing its serious concern at the persistence of the crisis and the deterioration of the situation in Côte d'Ivoire, including its grave humanitarian consequences causing large-scale civilian suffering and displacement,

Reiterating its firm condemnation of all violations of human rights and international humanitarian law in Côte d'Ivoire,

Determining that the situation in Côte d'Ivoire continues to pose a threat to international peace and security in the region,

Acting under Chapter VII of the Charter of the United Nations,

1. *Endorses* the decision of the Peace and Security Council, *underlines* that its unfettered implementation requires the full support from the Council, *considers* therefore that the following provisions of the present resolution, based on the decision of the Peace and Security Council, aim at implementing fully the peace process in Côte d'Ivoire and at organizing free, open, fair and transparent elections in this country by 31 October 2007, and *affirms* that such provisions are intended to be applicable during the transition period until a newly elected President takes up his duties and a new National Assembly is elected;

2. *Takes note* of the tenth final communiqué of the IWG dated 8 September 2006;

3. *Takes note* of the impossibility of organizing elections, presidential and legislative, on the scheduled date and of the expiry, on 31 October 2006, of the transition period and of the mandates of President Laurent Gbagbo and Prime Minister, Mr. Charles Konan Banny;

4. *Recalls* paragraphs 5 and 8 of the tenth final communiqué of the IWG dated 8 September 2006, paragraph 10 of the decision of the Peace and Security Council and paragraph 75 (a) of the report of the Secretary-General dated 17 October 2006 (S/2006/821), and, therefore, declares that the full implementation of the present resolution, consistent with paragraphs 13 and 14 of the decision of the Peace and Security Council, and of the peace process led by the Prime Minister requires full compliance by all Ivorian parties and that no legal provisions should be invoked by them to obstruct the process;

5. *Endorses* the decision of the Peace and Security Council that President Laurent Gbagbo should remain Head of State as from 1 November 2006 for a new and final transition period not exceeding 12 months;

6. *Endorses* the decision of the Peace and Security Council to renew the mandate of the Prime Minister, Mr. Charles Konan Banny, as from 1 November 2006 for a new and final transition period not exceeding 12 months, and *endorses* also the decision of the Peace and Security Council that the Prime Minister shall not be eligible to stand for the presidential elections to be organized by 31 October 2007;

7. *Stresses* that the Prime Minister shall have a mandate to implement all the provisions of the road map drawn up by the IWG and of the agreements concluded between the Ivorian parties with a view to holding free, open, fair and transparent elections by 31 October 2007 at the latest, with support from the United Nations and potential donors, and to carry out, in particular:

- The disarmament, demobilization and reintegration (DDR) programme,
- The identification of population and registration of voters in order to compile credible electoral rolls,
- The operations of disarmament and dismantling of militias,

– The restoration of State authority and the redeployment of the administration and public services throughout the territory of Côte d'Ivoire,

– The technical preparations for the elections,

– The restructuring of the armed forces, in accordance with paragraph 17 of the decision of the Peace and Security Council and paragraph 3 article f) of the Linas-Marcoussis Agreement;

8. *Stresses* that the Prime Minister, for the implementation of the mandate set out in paragraph 7 above, must have all the necessary powers, and all appropriate financial, material and human resources, as well as full and unfettered authority, consistent with ECOWAS recommendations dated 6 October 2006 and must be empowered to take all necessary decisions, in all matters, within the Council of Ministers or the Council of Government, by ordinances or decree-laws;

9. *Stresses also* that the Prime Minister, for the implementation of the mandate set out in paragraph 7 above, must also have the necessary authority over the Defence and Security Forces of Côte d'Ivoire;

10. *Recalls* paragraph 10 article (iii) of the decision of the Peace and Security Council of the African Union dated 6 October 2005 (S/2005/639) and the statement of the President of the Council dated 9 December 2005 (S/PRST/2005/60), *reaffirms* the provisions of paragraphs 6 and 7 of resolution 1633 (2005), and *recalls* that the Prime Minister shall have full authority over the Government that he will establish;

11. *Reaffirms* that the DDR and identification processes should be carried out concomitantly, stresses the centrality of both processes to the peace process, urges the Prime Minister to implement them without delay, and *calls upon* all the Ivorian parties to cooperate fully with him in this regard;

12. *Demands* the immediate resumption of the programme for the disarmament and dismantling of militias throughout the national territory, *stresses* that this programme is a key element of the peace process, and *underlines* the individual responsibility of the leaders of the militias in the full implementation of this process;

13. *Urges* the Prime Minister to immediately take all appropriate measures, through the signing of the relevant ordinances in the conditions set out in paragraph 8 above, to expedite the issuance of birth and nationality certificates in the context of the identification process, in a spirit of equity and transparency;

14. *Demands* that all the Ivorian parties concerned, in particular the Armed Forces of Forces Nouvelles and the Armed Forces of Côte d'Ivoire, participate fully and in good faith in the work of the quadripartite commission responsible for overseeing the implementation of the DDR programme and the operations for the disarmament and dismantling of militias;

15. *Invites* the Prime Minister to establish immediately, in liaison with all the Ivorian parties, UNOCI and the French forces which support it, a working group responsible for submitting to him a plan on the restructuring of the Defence and Security Forces and preparing possible seminars on security sector reform to be organized by the African Union and ECOWAS, with a view to rebuilding Defence and Security Forces committed to the values of integrity and republican morality;

16. *Encourages* the African Union and ECOWAS to organize seminars on security sector reform, in collaboration with partners and with the participation of commanding and senior officers from West African countries emerging from conflict, to examine, among other issues, the principles of civilian control of armed forces and personal and individual responsibility for acts of impunity or violation of human rights;

17. *Invites* the Prime Minister to establish immediately, in liaison with all the Ivorian parties concerned and the High Representative for the Elections, a working group responsible for helping him implement the identification of the population and registration of voters, in order to ensure their credibility and transparency;

18. *Encourages* the Prime Minister to seek, as appropriate, the active involvement of civil society in moving the peace process forward, and urges the Ivorian parties, the High Representative for the Elections together with UNOCI to take account of the rights and resources of women and of gender considerations as set out in resolution 1325 (2000) as cross-cutting issues in the implementation of the peace process including through the consultations with local and international women's groups;

19. *Demands* that all Ivorian parties end all incitement to hatred and violence, in radio and television broadcasting as well as in any other media, and urges the Prime Minister to establish and implement without delay a code of conduct for the media, in conformity with the decisions taken at Yamoussoukro on 5 July 2006 and the decision of the Peace and Security Council;

20. *Endorses* the decision of the Peace and Security Council that, to avoid multiple and conflicting mediation efforts, President Denis Sassou Nguesso of the Republic of the Congo ("the Mediator"), in his capacity as Chairperson of the African Union shall lead the mediation efforts, in liaison with the Chairperson of the Commission of the African Union and ECOWAS and, as the need may arise, in liaison with any other African leader willing to make a contribution to the search for peace in Côte d'Ivoire and *underlines* that the representative of the Mediator in Côte d'Ivoire will lead, in liaison with the Special Representative of the Secretary-General, the day-to-day mediation;

21. *Requests* the African Union and the Economic Community of West African States to continue to monitor and follow up closely the implementation of the peace process, and *invites* them to review before 1 February 2007 the progress achieved, and should they deem it appropriate, to review the situation again between that date and 31 October 2007, and *requests* them to report to the Council, through the Secretary-General, on their assessment and, if necessary, to submit to the Council any new recommendations;

22. *Renews* for a period of 12 months the mandate of the High Representative for the Elections laid down in paragraph 7 of resolution 1603 (2005), *underscores* that the Peace and Security Council of the African Union encouraged the High Representative for the Elections to play a greater role in the resolution of disputes linked to the electoral process, or issues arising out of the procedures and processes to be adopted to ensure open, free, fair and transparent elections, and *decides* therefore that, in addition to this mandate, the High Representative for the Elections, in full support of and in consultation with the Prime Minister:

– shall be the sole authority authorized to arbitrate with a view to preventing or resolving any problems or disputes related to the electoral process, in liaison with the Mediator,

– shall certify that all stages of the electoral process, including the process of identification of the population, the establishment of a register of voters and the issuance of voters' cards, provide all the necessary guarantees for the holding of open, free, fair and transparent presidential and legislative elections in accordance with international standards;

23. *Requests* UNOCI, consistent with its mandate in resolution 1609 to protect United Nations personnel, to provide security to the High Representative for the Elections, within its capabilities and its areas of deployment;

24. *Recalls* paragraph 9 above, and stresses therefore that the Prime Minister must have authority over the personnel of the Defence and Security Forces of Côte d'Ivoire who ensure his close protection and provide the security of his offices, including through designating them, without prejudice to the provisions of paragraph 2 (alinea 1) of resolution 1609 (2005);

25. *Recalls* the IWG's role of guarantor and impartial arbitrator of the peace process, and requests the IWG to:

– establish as soon as possible, in liaison with the Prime Minister, a precise timetable for the implementation of the main components of the road map,

– evaluate, monitor and follow up closely the progress achieved in implementing the road map on a monthly basis,

– report to the Council, through the Secretary-General, on its assessment of the progress achieved and on any obstacles encountered by the Prime Minister in carrying out his mandate set out in paragraph 7 above,

– submit as appropriate, to all the Ivorian parties concerned and to the Council, any recommendations it deems necessary;

26. *Demands* that all Ivorian parties refrain from any use of force and violence, including against civilians and foreigners, and from all kinds of disruptive street protests;

27. *Demands* that all Ivorian parties guarantee the security and freedom of movement of all Ivorian nationals throughout the territory of Côte d'Ivoire;

28. *Demands* that all Ivorian parties cooperate fully with the operations of UNOCI and the French forces which support it, as well as United Nations agencies and associated personnel, in particular by guaranteeing the safety, security and freedom of movement of their personnel, as well as associated personnel, throughout the territory of Côte d'Ivoire, and *reaffirms* that any obstacle to their freedom of movement or to the full implementation of their mandates would not be tolerated;

29. *Urges* countries neighbouring Côte d'Ivoire to prevent any cross-border movement of combatants or arms into Côte d'Ivoire;

30. *Reiterates* its serious concern at all violations of human rights and international humanitarian law in Côte d'Ivoire, and urges the Ivorian authorities to investigate these violations without delay in order to put an end to impunity;

31. *Recalls* the individual responsibility of all Ivorian parties, including members of the Ivorian Defence and Security Forces and of the Armed Forces of the Forces Nouvelles, whatever their rank, in the implementation of the peace process;

32. *Underlines* that it is fully prepared to impose targeted measures against persons to be designated by the Committee established by paragraph 14 of resolution 1572 (2004) who are determined to be, among other things, blocking the implementation of the peace process, including by attacking or obstructing the action of UNOCI, of the French forces which support it, of the High Representative for the Elections, of the IWG, of the Mediator or his representative in Côte d'Ivoire, responsible for serious violations of human rights and international humanitarian law committed in Côte d'Ivoire since 19 September 2002, inciting publicly hatred and violence or in violation of the arms embargo, as provided in resolutions 1572 (2004) and 1643 (2005);

33. *Decides* to remain actively seized of the matter.

Resolution 1722 (2006)

Adopted by the Security Council at its 5567th meeting, on 21 November 2006

The Security Council,

Recalling all its previous relevant resolutions concerning the conflicts in the former Yugoslavia and relevant statements of its President, including resolutions 1031 (1995) of 15 December 1995, 1088 (1996) of 12 December 1996, 1423 (2002) of 12 July 2002, 1491 (2003) of 11 July 2003, 1551 (2004) of 9 July 2004, 1575 (2004) of 22 November 2004 and 1639 (2005) of 21 November 2005,

Reaffirming its commitment to the political settlement of the conflicts in the former Yugoslavia, preserving the sovereignty and territorial integrity of all States there within their internationally recognized borders,

Emphasizing its full support for the High Representative's continued role in Bosnia and Herzegovina,

Underlining its commitment to support the implementation of the General Framework Agreement for Peace in Bosnia and Herzegovina and the Annexes thereto (collectively the Peace Agreement, S/1995/999, annex), as well as the relevant decisions of the Peace Implementation Council (PIC),

Recalling all the agreements concerning the status of forces referred to in Appendix B to Annex 1-A of the Peace Agreement, and reminding the parties of their obligation to continue to comply therewith,

Further recalling the provisions of its resolution 1551 (2004) concerning the provisional application of the status of forces agreements contained in Appendix B to Annex 1-A of the Peace Agreement,

Emphasizing its appreciation to the High Representative, the Commander and personnel of the multinational stabilization force (EUFOR), the Senior Military Representative and personnel of the NATO Headquarters Sarajevo, the Organization for Security and Cooperation in Europe (OSCE), the European Union (EU) and the personnel of other international organizations and agencies in Bosnia and Herzegovina for their contributions to the implementation of the Peace Agreement,

Emphasizing that a comprehensive and coordinated return of refugees and displaced persons throughout the region continues to be crucial to lasting peace,

Recalling the declarations of the Ministerial meetings of the Peace Implementation Conference,

Recognizing that full implementation of the Peace Agreement is not yet complete, while *paying tribute* to the achievements of the authorities at State and entity level in Bosnia and Herzegovina and of the international community in the eleven years since the signing of the Peace Agreement,

Emphasizing the importance of Bosnia and Herzegovina's progress towards Euro-Atlantic integration on the basis of the Peace Agreement, while *recognizing* the importance of Bosnia and Herzegovina's transition to a functional, reform-oriented, modern and democratic European country,

Noting the reports of the High Representative, including his latest report of 6 October 2006 (S/2006/810, annex),

Determined to promote the peaceful resolution of the conflicts in accordance with the purposes and principles of the Charter of the United Nations,

Recalling the relevant principles contained in the Convention on the Safety of United Nations and Associated Personnel adopted on 9 December 1994 and the statement of its President on 10 February 2000 (S/PRST/2000/4),

Welcoming and encouraging efforts by the United Nations to sensitize peacekeeping personnel in the prevention and control of HIV/AIDS and other communicable diseases in all its peacekeeping operations,

Taking note of the conclusions of EU Foreign Ministers at their meeting of 12 June 2006, which refer to the requirement for EUFOR to remain in Bosnia and Herzegovina beyond 2006, and confirm the EU's intention to take the steps necessary to that end,

Recalling the letters between the European Union and NATO sent to the Security Council on 19 November 2004 on how those organizations will cooperate together in Bosnia and Herzegovina in which both organizations recognize that the EUFOR will have the main peace stabilization role under the military aspects of the Peace Agreement (S/2004/916; S/2004/915),

Further recalling the confirmation by the Presidency of Bosnia and Herzegovina, on behalf of Bosnia and Herzegovina, including its constituent entities, of the arrangements for EUFOR and the NATO Headquarters presence (S/2004/917),

Welcoming the European Union's increased engagement in Bosnia and Herzegovina and the continued engagement of NATO,

Further welcoming tangible signs of Bosnia and Herzegovina's progress towards the European Union, and, in particular, the progress made in the negotiations of Bosnia and Herzegovina with the EU on a Stabilization and Association Agreement, and *calling* on the authorities in Bosnia and Herzegovina to implement in full their undertakings, including on police reform, as part of that process,

Determining that the situation in the region continues to constitute a threat to international peace and security,

Acting under Chapter VII of the Charter of the United Nations,

1. *Reaffirms* once again its support for the Peace Agreement, as well as for the Dayton Paris Agreement on implementing the Federation of Bosnia and Herzegovina of 10 November 1995 (S/1995/1021, annex) and *calls upon* the parties to comply strictly with their obligations under those Agreements;

2. *Reiterates* that the primary responsibility for the further successful implementation of the Peace Agreement lies with the authorities in Bosnia and Herzegovina themselves and that the continued willingness of the international community and major donors to assume the political, military and economic burden of implementation and reconstruction efforts will be determined by the compliance and active participation by all the authorities in Bosnia and Herzegovina in implementing the Peace Agreement and rebuilding a civil society, in particular in full cooperation with the International Tribunal for the Former Yugoslavia, in strengthening joint institutions, which foster the building of a fully functioning self-sustaining State, able to integrate itself into the European structures and in facilitating returns of refugees and displaced persons;

3. *Reminds* the parties once again that, in accordance with the Peace Agreement, they have committed themselves to cooperate fully with all entities involved in the implementation of this peace settlement, as described in the Peace Agreement, or which are otherwise authorized by the Security Council, including the International Tribunal for the Former Yugoslavia, as it carries out its responsibilities for dispensing justice impartially, and *underlines* that full cooperation by States and entities with the International Tribunal includes, inter alia, the surrender for trial or apprehension of all persons indicted by the Tribunal and provision of information to assist in Tribunal investigations;

4. *Emphasizes* its full support for the continued role of the High Representative in monitoring the implementation of the Peace Agreement and giving guidance to and coordinating the activities of the civilian organizations and agencies involved in assisting the parties to implement the Peace Agreement, and *reaffirms* that under Annex 10 of the Peace Agreement the High Representative is the final authority in theatre regarding the interpretation of civilian implementation of the Peace Agreement and that in case of dispute he may give his interpretation and make recommendations, and make binding decisions as he judges necessary on issues as elaborated by the Peace Implementation Council in Bonn on 9 and 10 December 1997;

5. *Expresses* its support for the declarations of the Ministerial meetings of the Peace Implementation Conference;

6. *Reaffirms* its intention to keep implementation of the Peace Agreement and the situation in Bosnia and Herzegovina under close review, taking into account the reports submitted pursuant to paragraphs 18 and 21 below, and any recommendations those reports might include, and its readiness to consider the imposition of measures if any party fails significantly to meet its obligations under the Peace Agreement;

7. *Recalls* the support of the authorities of Bosnia and Herzegovina for the EU force and the continued NATO presence and their confirmation that both are the legal successors to SFOR for the fulfilment of their missions for the purposes of the Peace Agreement, its Annexes and Appendices and relevant United Nations Security Council resolutions and can take such actions as are required, including the use of force, to ensure compliance with Annexes 1-A and 2 of the Peace Agreement and relevant United Nations Security Council resolutions;

8. Pays *tribute* to those Member States which participated in the multinational stabilization force (EUFOR), and in the continued NATO presence, established in accordance with its resolution 1575 (2004) and extended with its resolution 1639 (2005) of 21 November 2005, and welcomes their willingness to assist the Parties to the Peace Agreement by continuing to deploy a multinational stabilization force (EUFOR) and by maintaining a continued NATO presence;

9. *Welcomes* the EU's intention to maintain an EU military operation to Bosnia and Herzegovina from November 2006;

10. *Authorizes* the Member States acting through or in cooperation with the EU to establish for a further period of 12 months, starting from the date of the adoption of this resolution, a multinational stabilization force (EUFOR) as a legal successor to SFOR under unified command and control, which will fulfil its missions in relation to the implementation of Annex 1-A and Annex 2 of the Peace Agreement in cooperation with the NATO Headquarters presence in accordance with the arrangements agreed between NATO and the EU as communicated to the Security Council in their letters of 19 November 2004, which recognize that the EUFOR will have the main peace stabilization role under the military aspects of the Peace Agreement;

11. *Welcomes* the decision of NATO to continue to maintain a presence in Bosnia and Herzegovina in the form of a NATO Headquarters in order to continue to assist in implementing the Peace Agreement in conjunction with EUFOR and authorizes the Member States acting through or in cooperation with NATO to continue to maintain a NATO Headquarters as a legal successor to SFOR under unified command and control, which will fulfil its missions in relation to the implementation of Annex 1-A and Annex 2 of the Peace Agreement in cooperation with EUFOR in accordance with the arrangements agreed between NATO and the EU as communicated to the Security Council in their letters of 19 November 2004, which recognize that EUFOR will have the main peace stabilization role under the military aspects of the Peace Agreement;

12. *Reaffirms* that the Peace Agreement and the provisions of its previous relevant resolutions shall apply to and in respect of both EUFOR and the NATO presence as they have applied to and in respect of SFOR and that therefore references in the Peace Agreement, in particular in Annex 1-A and its appendices, and relevant resolutions to IFOR and/or SFOR, NATO and the NAC shall be read as applying, as appropriate, to the NATO presence, EUFOR, the European Union and the Political and Security Committee and Council of the European Union respectively;

13. *Expresses* its intention to consider the terms of further authorization as necessary in the light of developments in the implementation of the Peace Agreement and the situation in Bosnia and Herzegovina;

14. *Authorizes* the Member States acting under paragraphs 10 and 11 above to take all necessary measures to effect the implementation of and to ensure compliance with Annexes 1-A and 2 of the Peace Agreement, *stresses* that the parties shall continue to be held equally responsible for the compliance with that Annex and shall be equally subject to such enforcement action by EUFOR and the .NATO presence as may be necessary to ensure implementation of those Annexes and the protection of EUFOR and the NATO presence;

15. *Authorizes* Member States to take all necessary measures, at the request of either EUFOR or the NATO Headquarters, in defence of the EUFOR or NATO presence respectively, and to assist both organizations in carrying out their missions, and *recognizes* the right of both EUFOR and the NATO presence to take all necessary measures to defend themselves from attack or threat of attack;

16. *Authorizes* the Member States acting under paragraphs 10 and 11 above, in accordance with Annex 1-A of the Peace Agreement, to take all necessary measures to ensure compliance with the rules and procedures governing command and control of airspace over Bosnia and Herzegovina with respect to all civilian and military air traffic;

17. *Demands* that the parties respect the security and freedom of movement of EUFOR, the NATO presence, and other international personnel;

18. *Requests* the Member States acting through or in cooperation with the EU and the Member States acting through or in cooperation with NATO to report to the Council on the activity of EUFOR and NATO Headquarters presence respectively, through the appropriate channels and at least at three-monthly intervals;

19. *Invites* all States, in particular those in the region, to continue to *provide* appropriate support and facilities, including transit facilities, for the Member States acting under paragraphs 10 and 11 above;

20. *Reiterates its appreciation* for the deployment by the EU of its Police Mission (EUPM) to Bosnia and Herzegovina since 1 January 2003;

21. *Also requests* the Secretary-General to continue to submit to the Council reports from the High Representative, in accordance with Annex 10 of the Peace Agreement and the conclusions of the Peace Implementation Conference held in London on 4 and 5 December 1996 (S/1996/1012), and later Peace Implementation Conferences, on the implementation of the Peace Agreement and in particular on compliance by the parties with their commitments under that Agreement;

22. *Decides* to remain seized of the matter.

Resolution 1723 (2006)

Adopted by the Security Council at its 5574th meeting on 28 November 2006

The Security Council,

Welcoming the formation of a national unity government in Iraq with a detailed political, economic and security programme and a strong national reconciliation agenda and *looking forward* to the day Iraqi forces assume full responsibility for the maintenance of security and stability in their country, thus allowing the completion of the multinational force mandate and the end of its presence in Iraq,

Welcoming the progress made to date in the training and equipping of Iraqi security forces as well as in the transfer of security responsibilities to those forces in Muthanna and Dhi Qar provinces and *looking forward* to the continuation of that process during 2007,

Recalling all of its previous relevant resolutions on Iraq,

Reaffirming the independence, sovereignty, unity, and territorial integrity of Iraq,

Reaffirming also the right of the Iraqi people freely to determine their own political future and control their own national resources,

Welcoming the continuing work of the Government of Iraq towards a federal, democratic, pluralistic, and unified Iraq, in which there is full respect for human rights,

Welcoming the vital role played by the Government of Iraq in continuing to promote national dialogue and reconciliation in pursuit of an atmosphere in which sectarianism is totally rejected, including the National Reconciliation Plan announced by Iraqi Prime Minister al-Maliki, *stressing* the importance of the rapid implementation of the plan, and *reaffirming* the willingness of the international community to work closely with the Government of Iraq to assist these reconciliation efforts,

Recognizing the International Compact with Iraq, an initiative of the Government of Iraq to create a new partnership with the international community and to build a strong framework for Iraq's continued political, security and economic transformation and integration into the regional and global economy, and *welcoming* the important role that the United Nations is playing by jointly chairing the Compact with the Government of Iraq,

Calling upon the international community, particularly countries in the region and Iraq's neighbours, to support the Iraqi people in their pursuit of peace, stability, security, democracy, and prosperity, and *noting* that the successful implementation of this resolution will contribute to regional stability,

Demanding those who use violence in an attempt to subvert the political process should lay down their arms and participate in the political process, and *encouraging* the Government of Iraq to continue to engage with all those who renounce violence,

Reaffirming that acts of terrorism must not be allowed to disrupt Iraq's political and economic transition, and *further reaffirming* the obligations of Member States under resolution 1618 (2005) of 4 August 2005 and other relevant resolutions and international conventions with respect, inter alia, to terrorist activities in and from Iraq or against its citizens,

Recognizing the request conveyed in the letter of 11 November 2006 from the Prime Minister of Iraq to the President of the Council, which is annexed to this resolution, to retain the presence of the multinational force in Iraq, and *affirming* the common goals therein: Iraqi assumption of recruiting, training, equipping, and arming of the Iraqi Security Forces; Iraqi assumption of command and control over Iraqi forces; and the transfer of responsibility for security to the Government of Iraq,

Recognizing the importance of consent of the sovereign government of Iraq for the presence of the multinational force and of close coordination and partnership between the multinational force and that government,

Welcoming the willingness of the multinational force to continue efforts to contribute to the maintenance of security and stability in Iraq, including participating in the provision of humanitarian and reconstruction assistance, as described in the letter of 17 November 2006 from the United States Secretary of State to the President of the Council, which is annexed to this resolution,

Recognizing the tasks and arrangements set out in letters annexed to resolution 1546 (2004) of 8 June 2004 and the cooperative implementation by the Government of Iraq and the multinational force of those arrangements,

Affirming the importance for all forces promoting the maintenance of security and stability in Iraq to act in accordance with international law, including obligations under international humanitarian law, and to cooperate with the relevant international organizations, and *welcoming* their commitments in this regard,

Recalling the establishment of the United Nations Assistance Mission for Iraq (UNAMI) on 14 August 2003, and *affirming* that the United Nations should continue to play a leading role in assisting the Iraqi people and government with further political and economic development, including advising and supporting the Government of Iraq, providing strong support in developing the International Compact with Iraq, contributing to coordination and delivery of reconstruction, development and humanitarian assistance, and promoting the protection of human rights, national reconciliation, as well as judicial and legal reform in order to strengthen the rule of law in Iraq,

Recognizing that international support for security and stability is essential to the well-being of the people of Iraq as well as the ability of all concerned, including the United Nations, to carry out their work on behalf of the people of Iraq, and *expressing* appreciation for Member State contributions in this regard under resolution 1483 (2003), resolution 1511 (2003), resolution 1546 (2004) and resolution 1637 (2005),

Recognizing that the Government of Iraq will continue to have the primary role in coordinating international assistance to Iraq and *reaffirming* the importance of international assistance and development of the Iraqi economy and the importance of coordinated donor assistance,

Recognizing the significant role of the Development Fund for Iraq and the International Advisory and Monitoring Board in helping the Government of Iraq to ensure that Iraq's resources are being used transparently and equitably for the benefit of the people of Iraq,

Stressing the responsibility of the Iraqi authorities to undertake all appropriate steps to prevent attacks on the diplomatic personnel accredited in Iraq in accordance with the Vienna Convention on Diplomatic Relations of 1961,

Determining that the situation in Iraq continues to constitute a threat to international peace and security,

Acting under Chapter VII of the Charter of the United Nations,

1. *Notes* that the presence of the multinational force in Iraq is at the request of the Government of Iraq and *reaffirms* the authorization for the multinational force as set forth in resolution 1546 (2004) and *decides* to extend the mandate of the multinational force as set forth in that resolution until 31 December 2007, taking into consideration the Iraqi Prime Minister's letter dated 11 November 2006 and the United States Secretary of State's letter dated 17 November 2006;

2. *Decides further* that the mandate for the multinational force shall be reviewed at the request of the Government of Iraq or no later than 15 June 2007, and *declares* that it will terminate this mandate earlier if requested by the Government of Iraq;

3. *Decides* to extend until 31 December 2007 the arrangements established in paragraph 20 of resolution 1483 (2003) for the depositing into the Development Fund for Iraq of proceeds from export sales of petroleum, petroleum products, and natural gas and the arrangements referred to in paragraph 12 of resolution 1483 (2003) and paragraph 24 of resolution 1546 (2004) for the monitoring of the Development Fund for Iraq by the International Advisory and Monitoring Board;

4. *Decides further* that the provisions in the above paragraph for the deposit of proceeds into the Development Fund for Iraq and for the role of the International Advisory and Monitoring Board shall be reviewed at the request of the Government of Iraq or no later than 15 June 2007;

5. *Requests* that the Secretary-General continue to report to the Council on UNAMI operations in Iraq on a quarterly basis;

6. *Requests* that the United States, on behalf of the multinational force, continue to report to the Council on the efforts and progress of this force on a quarterly basis;

7. *Decides* to remain actively seized of the matter.

Annex I
Letter dated 11 November 2006 from the Prime Minister of Iraq addressed to the President of the Security Council

[Original: Arabic and English]

Iraq has taken in the specified time the steps required for the completion of the political process, in particular the drafting of a permanent constitution and the laying of foundations for building its political and legal institutions. In May 2006, the constitutionally elected Council of Representatives formed a Government of national unity. The steps for building a democratic, federal and united Iraq were consolidated by the commitment of the Government to adopt a dialogue and national reconciliation scheme, secure broad political participation, monitor human rights, establish the rule of law and economic development and provide services to citizens.

Establishing security and securing permanent stability are among the highest priorities of the Iraqi Government's programme to realize the desired peace and prosperity for the Iraqi people. However, terrorists and forces hostile to democracy continue to target innocent citizens and the various State institutions.

Security and stability in Iraq are the responsibility of the Iraqi Government. The Security Council affirmed in its resolution 1546 (2004) that Iraqi security forces would play a progressively greater role in enabling the Iraqi Government to assume that responsibility, diminishing and thereby ending the role of the multinational force, when the responsibility for security of the Iraqi security forces increases and expands. From the experience of the past two and a half years, it was established that the Iraqi security forces, which operated under the command of the Iraqi Government, had acquired new experiences and responsibilities and had grown in size, experience and capacity, demonstrated by their increased ability to assume full responsibility in the fields of security and defence.

We started to reap the fruits of success when our forces assumed responsibility for security in the governorates of Al Muthanna and Dhi Qar. In September 2006, the Ministry of Defence assumed the operational command and control of the ground, naval and air force commands. It also assumed operational command and control over two military divisions, indicating an increase in the ability of the Iraqi Army to assume the leadership in providing security to the Iraqi people. The Iraqi Government is also relentlessly working on building the necessary administrative and logistics system to make our Iraqi forces self-sufficient.

It is the intention of the Iraqi Government to continue increasing the number of governorates that fall fully under the control of the Iraqi authorities during 2006, until all 18 are under their control. When the responsibilities for security are transferred to the Iraqi authorities in a certain governorate, the multinational force will be present in its bases and can provide support to Iraqi security forces at the request of the Iraqi authorities, in accordance with an agreement that allocates the authorities and responsibilities between the two sides.

We have agreed on three common goals: first, assumption by Iraq of recruiting, training, equipping and arming of Iraqi security forces; second, assumption by Iraq of command and control over Iraqi forces; and third, transferring responsibility for security to the Government of Iraq. We have formed a high-level working group that will provide recommendations on how best to achieve these goals. It has also been agreed to work towards the Iraqi authorities' assuming the apprehension, detention and imprisonment tasks on the basis of an agreement to be reached between the Government of Iraq and the multinational force.

Hence, the Iraqi Government requests the extension of the mandate of the multinational force in accordance with Security Council resolutions 1546 (2004) and 1637 (2005) and the letters attached thereto for another 12 months starting on 31 December 2006, provided that the extension is subject to a commitment by the Council to end the mandate at an earlier date if the Iraqi Government so requests and that the mandate is subject to periodic review before 15 June 2007. The Iraqi Government requests the termination of the UNMOVIC mission due to the completion of its tasks. The Iraqi Government believes that the time has come to terminate the war compensations that were imposed on Iraq.

The Iraqi Government realizes that the provisions of resolution 1546 (2004) relating to the depositing of revenues in the Development Fund for Iraq and the role of the International Advisory and Monitoring Board help to ensure the use of the natural resources of Iraq for the benefit of the people of Iraq. We recognize that the fund plays an important role in convincing donors and creditors that Iraq is managing its resources and debts in a responsible way for the Iraqi people. This role is vital, especially since Iraq is seeking to form a new partnership with the international community to build a vital network for economic transformation and integration in the economies of the region and the world through the International Compact with Iraq. We ask the Security Council to extend the mandate of the Development Fund for Iraq and the International Advisory and Monitoring Board for another 12 months and to review this mandate based on the request of the Iraqi Government before 15 June 2007.

The people of Iraq are determined to establish a stable and peaceful democracy for themselves and a proper basis for building a vital economy. This vision for the future of Iraq cannot become a reality without the help of the international community.

We realize that the Security Council intends to append the present letter to the special resolution concerning Iraq that is being prepared. Meanwhile, I ask that the present letter be distributed to the members of the Security Council as soon as possible.

(*Signed*) Nuri Kamel **al-Maliki**
Prime Minister of the Republic of Iraq

Annex II
Letter dated 17 November 2006 from the Secretary of State of the United States of America to the President of the Security Council

Having reviewed the request of the Government of Iraq to extend the mandate of the Multinational Force (MNF) in Iraq and following consultations with the Government of Iraq, I am writing to confirm, consistent with this request, that MNF under unified command stands ready to continue to fulfil its mandate as set out in Security Council resolution 1546 (2004) and extended by Security Council resolution 1637 (2005).

The Government of Iraq and MNF in Iraq continue to improve their cooperation through a security partnership to combat the challenges that threaten Iraq's security and stability. This partnership has evolved over time to incorporate the increasing leadership by Iraqi security forces in fighting and deterring terrorism and other violent acts throughout Iraq's 18 provinces. In the context of this partnership, MNF is prepared to continue to undertake a broad range of tasks to contribute to the maintenance of security and stability and to ensure force protection, acting under the authorities set forth in resolution 1546 (2004), including the tasks and arrangements set out in the letters annexed thereto, and in close cooperation with the Government of Iraq. The forces that make up MNF will remain committed to acting consistently with their obligations and rights under international law, including the law of armed conflict.

Iraqi security forces have already made substantial progress this year in developing their capabilities and, as a result, they are shouldering a greater portion of the responsibility for Iraq's security. This progress is most notable in their assumption of security responsibility in Dhi Qar and Muthana and the assumption of operational command and control over the Ground, Naval, and Air Force Commands and two Iraqi military divisions by the Ministry of Defense.

The Government of Iraq and MNF have agreed on three common goals: Iraqi assumption of recruiting, training, equipping and arming of the Iraqi security forces; Iraqi assumption of command and control over Iraqi forces; and transferring responsibility for security to the

Government of Iraq. We look forward to recommendations from the newly formed high-level working group on how these goals can best be achieved. The strong partnership between the Government of Iraq and MNF is a vital factor in fulfilling these goals. Together we will build towards the day when the Iraqi forces assume full responsibility for the maintenance of security and stability in Iraq.

The co-sponsors intend to annex this letter to the resolution on Iraq that is under consideration. In the meantime, I request that you provide copies of the present letter to members of the Council as quickly as possible.

(*Signed*) Condoleezza **Rice**

Resolution 1724 (2006)

Adopted by the Security Council at its 5575th meeting on 29 November 2006

The Security Council,

Reaffirming its previous resolutions and the statements of its President concerning the situation in Somalia, in particular resolution 733 (1992) of 23 January 1992, which established an embargo on all delivery of weapons and military equipment to Somalia (hereinafter referred to as the "arms embargo"), resolution 1519 (2003) of 16 December 2003, resolution 1558 (2004) of 17 August 2004, resolution 1587 (2005) of 15 March 2005, resolution 1630 (2005) of 14 October 2005, and resolution 1676 (2006) of 10 May 2006,

Reaffirming the importance of the sovereignty, territorial integrity, political independence and unity of Somalia,

Stressing the need for the Transitional Federal Institutions to continue working towards establishing effective national governance in Somalia,

Reiterating the urgent need for all Somali leaders to take tangible steps to continue political dialogue,

Commending the efforts of the African Union, the Intergovernmental Authority on Development and the League of Arab States for their continued support for national reconciliation in Somalia, and urging both the Transitional Federal Institutions and the Union of Islamic Courts to recommit to the principles of the 22 June 2006 Khartoum Declaration and the agreements made at the 2-4 September 2006 Khartoum meeting and to engage in the next round of talks without further delays,

Reiterating its strong support for the Special Representative of the Secretary-General,

Taking note of the report of the Monitoring Group dated 21 November 2006 (S/2006/913) submitted pursuant to paragraph 3 (i) of resolution 1676 (2006) and the observations and recommendations contained therein,

Condemning the significant increase in the flow of weapons and ammunition supplies to and through Somalia, which constitutes a violation of the arms embargo and a serious threat to peace and stability in Somalia,

Reiterating its insistence that all Member States, in particular those in the region, should refrain from any action in contravention of the arms embargo and should take all necessary steps to hold violators accountable,

Reiterating and underscoring the importance of enhancing the monitoring of the arms embargo in Somalia through persistent and vigilant investigation into the violations, bearing in mind that strict enforcement of the arms embargo will improve the overall security situation in Somalia,

Determining that the situation in Somalia constitutes a threat to international peace and security in the region,

Acting under Chapter VII of the Charter of the United Nations,

1. *Stresses* the obligation of all Member States to comply fully with the measures imposed by resolution 733 (1992);

2. *Expresses* its intention, in light of the report of the Monitoring Group dated 21 November 2006 (S/2006/913), to consider specific action to improve implementation of and compliance with measures imposed by resolution 733 (1992);

3. *Requests* the Secretary-General, in consultation with the Committee established pursuant to resolution 751 (1992) of 24 April 1992 (hereinafter referred to as "the Committee"), to re-establish within thirty days from the date of the adoption of this resolution, and for a period of six months, the Monitoring Group referred to in paragraph 3 of resolution 1558 (2004), with the following mandate:

(a) to continue the tasks outlined in paragraphs 3 (a) to (c) of resolution 1587 (2005);

(b) to continue to investigate, in coordination with relevant international agencies, all activities, including in the financial, maritime and other sectors, which generate revenues used to commit arms embargo violations;

(c) to continue to investigate any means of transport, routes, seaports, airports and other facilities used in connection with arms embargo violations;

(d) to continue refining and updating information on the draft list of those individuals and entities who violate the measures implemented by Member States in accordance with resolution 733 (1992), inside and outside Somalia, and their active supporters, for possible future measures by the Council, and to present such information to the Committee as and when the Committee deems appropriate;

(e) to continue making recommendations based on its investigations, on the previous reports of the Panel of Experts (S/2003/223 and S/2003/1035) appointed pursuant to resolutions 1425 (2002) of 22 July 2002 and 1474 (2003) of 8 April 2003, and on the previous reports of the Monitoring Group (S/2004/604, S/2005/153, S/2005/625, S/2006/229 and S/2006/913) appointed pursuant to resolutions 1519 (2003) of 16 December 2003, 1558 (2004) of 17 August 2004, 1587 (2005) of 15 March 2005, 1630 (2005) of 14 October 2005, and 1676 (2006) of 10 May 2006;

(f) to work closely with the Committee on specific recommendations for additional measures to improve overall compliance with the arms embargo;

(g) to assist in identifying areas where the capacities of States in the region can be strengthened to facilitate the implementation of the arms embargo;

(h) to provide to the Council, through the Committee, a midterm briefing within 90 days from its establishment, and to submit progress reports to the Committee on a monthly basis;

(i) to submit, for the Security Council's consideration, through the Committee, a final report covering all the tasks set out above, no later than 15 days prior to the termination of the Monitoring Group's mandate;

4. *Further requests* the Secretary-General to make the necessary financial arrangements to support the work of the Monitoring Group;

5. *Reaffirms* paragraphs 4, 5, 7, 8 and 10 of resolution 1519 (2003);

6. *Requests* the Committee, in accordance with its mandate and in consultation with the Monitoring Group and other relevant United Nations entities, to consider the recommendations in the reports of the Monitoring Group dated 5 April and 16 October 2006 and recommend to the Council ways to improve implementation of and compliance with the arms embargo, in response to continuing violations;

7. *Decides* to remain actively seized of the matter.

Resolution 1725 (2006)

Adopted by the Security Council at its 5579th meeting on 6 December 2006

The Security Council,

Recalling its previous resolutions concerning the situation in Somalia, in particular resolution 733 (1992) of 23 January 1992, resolution 1356 (2001) of 19 June 2001, resolution 1425 (2002) of 22 January 2002, and the statements of its President, in particular that of 13 July 2006 (S/PRST/2006/31),

Reaffirming its respect for the sovereignty, territorial integrity, political independence, and unity of Somalia,

Reiterating its commitment to a comprehensive and lasting settlement of the situation in Somalia through the Transitional Federal Charter, and stressing the importance of broad-based and representative institutions and of an inclusive political process, as envisaged in the Transitional Federal Charter,

Reiterating its insistence that all Member States, in particular those in the region, should refrain from any action in contravention of the arms embargo and related measures, and should take all actions necessary to prevent such contraventions,

Emphasizing its willingness to engage with all parties in Somalia who are committed to achieving a political settlement through peaceful and inclusive dialogue, including the Union of Islamic Courts,

Underlining the importance for stability in Somalia of broad-based and representative institutions and of an inclusive political process, *commending* the crucial efforts of the League of Arab States and the Intergovernmental Authority on Development (IGAD) to promote and encourage political dialogue between the Transitional Federal Institutions and the Union of Islamic Courts, *expressing* its full support for these initiatives, and *affirming* its readiness to assist as appropriate an inclusive political process in Somalia,

Urging both the Transitional Federal Institutions and the Union of Islamic Courts to unite behind and continue a process of dialogue, recommit to the principles of the 22 June 2006 Khartoum Declaration and the agreements made at the 2-4 September 2006 Khartoum meeting, and establish a stable security situation inside Somalia,

Calling upon the Union of Islamic Courts to cease any further military expansion and reject those with an extremist agenda or links to international terrorism,

Deploring the bombing in Baidoa on 30 November 2006 and *expressing* the Security Council's concern regarding the continued violence inside Somalia,

Welcoming the agreement reached between the Union of Islamic Courts and the Secretariat of the Intergovernmental Authority on Development dated 2 December 2006, and *encouraging* IGAD to continue discussions with the Transitional Federal Institutions,

Calls upon all parties inside Somalia and all other States to refrain from action that could provoke or perpetuate violence and violations of human rights, contribute to unnecessary tension and mistrust, endanger the ceasefire and political process, or further damage the humanitarian situation,

Taking note of the note verbale dated 16 October 2006 from the Permanent Mission of Kenya to the United Nations to the President of the Security Council transmitting the text of the Deployment Plan for a Peacekeeping Mission of IGAD in Somalia (IGASOM),

Determining that the situation in Somalia continues to constitute a threat to international peace and security in the region,

Acting under Chapter VII of the Charter of the United Nations,

1. *Reiterates* that the Transitional Federal Charter and Institutions offer the only route to achieving peace and stability in Somalia, emphasizes the need for continued credible dialogue between the Transitional Federal Institutions and the Union of Islamic Courts, and affirms therefore that the following provisions of the present resolution, based on the decisions of IGAD and the Peace and Security Council of the African Union, aim solely at supporting peace and stability in Somalia through an inclusive political process and creating the conditions for the withdrawal of all foreign forces from Somalia;

2. *Urges* the Transitional Federal Institutions and the Union of Islamic Courts to fulfil commitments they have made, resume without delay peace talks on the basis of the agreements reached in Khartoum, and adhere to agreements reached in their dialogue, and states its intention to consider taking measures against those that seek to prevent or block a peaceful dialogue process, overthrow the Transitional Federal Institutions by force, or take action that further threatens regional stability;

3. *Decides* to authorize IGAD and Member States of the African Union to establish a protection and training mission in Somalia, to be reviewed after an initial period of six months by the Security Council with a briefing by IGAD, with the following mandate drawing on

the relevant elements of the mandate and concept of operations specified in the Deployment Plan for IGASOM:

(a) To monitor progress by the Transitional Federal Institutions and the Union of Islamic Courts in implementing agreements reached in their dialogue;

(b) To ensure free movement and safe passage of all those involved with the dialogue process;

(c) To maintain and monitor security in Baidoa;

(d) To protect members of the Transitional Federal Institutions and Government as well as their key infrastructure;

(e) To train the Transitional Federal Institutions' security forces to enable them to provide their own security and to help facilitate the re-establishment of national security forces of Somalia;

4. *Endorses* the specification in the IGAD Deployment Plan that those States that border Somalia would not deploy troops to Somalia;

5. *Decides* that the measures imposed by paragraph 5 of resolution 733 (1992) and further elaborated in paragraphs 1 and 2 of resolution 1425 (2002) shall not apply to supplies of weapons and military equipment and technical training and assistance intended solely for the support of or use by the force referred to in paragraph 3 above;

6. *Encourages* Member States to provide financial resources for IGASOM;

7. *Requests* the Secretary-General, in consultation with the Commission of the African Union and the secretariat of IGAD, to report to the Security Council on the implementation of the mandate of IGASOM within thirty (30) days, and every sixty (60) days thereafter;

8. *Emphasizes* the continued contribution made to Somalia's peace and security by the arms embargo, *demands* that all Member States, in particular those of the region, fully comply with it, and *reiterates* its intention to consider urgently ways to strengthen its effectiveness, including through targeted measures in support of the arms embargo;

9. *Decides* to remain actively seized of the matter.

Resolution 1726 (2006)

Adopted by the Security Council at its 5591st meeting, on 15 December 2006

The Security Council,

Recalling its previous resolutions and the statements of its President relating to the situation in Côte d'Ivoire,

Reaffirming its strong commitment to the sovereignty, independence, territorial integrity and unity of Côte d'Ivoire, and recalling the importance of the principles of good-neighbourliness, non-interference and regional cooperation,

Having taken note of the report of the Secretary-General dated 4 December 2006 (S/2006/939),

Reaffirming its support to the impartial forces, namely the United Nations Operation in Côte d'Ivoire (UNOCI) and the French forces which support it,

Expressing its serious concern at the persistence of the crisis and the deterioration of the situation in Côte d'Ivoire, including its grave humanitarian consequences causing large-scale civilian suffering and displacement,

Determining that the situation in Côte d'Ivoire continues to pose a threat to international peace and security in the region,

Acting under Chapter VII of the Charter of the United Nations,

1. *Decides* that the mandate of UNOCI and of the French forces which support it shall be extended until 10 January 2007;

2. *Decides* to remain actively seized of the matter.

Resolution 1727 (2006)

Adopted by the Security Council at is 5592nd meeting, on 15 December 2006

The Security Council,

Recalling its previous resolutions and the statements of its President relating to the situation in Côte d'Ivoire,

Reaffirming its strong commitment to the sovereignty, independence, territorial integrity and unity of Côte d'Ivoire, and recalling the importance of the principles of good-neighbourliness, non-interference and regional cooperation,

Taking note of the reports of the United Nations Panel of Experts on Côte d'Ivoire dated 5 October 2006 (S/2006/735) and 12 December 2006 (S/2006/964),

Expressing its serious concern at the persistence of the crisis and the deterioration of the situation in Côte d'Ivoire, including its grave humanitarian consequences causing large-scale civilian suffering and displacement,

Determining that the situation in Côte d'Ivoire continues to pose a threat to international peace and security in the region,

Acting under Chapter VII of the Charter of the United Nations,

1. *Decides* to renew until 31 October 2007 the provisions of paragraphs 7 to 12 of resolution 1572 (2004) and of paragraph 6 of resolution 1643 (2005);

2. *Demands* that all Ivorian parties, including the transitional Government and the Forces nouvelles, provide unhindered access, particularly to the Group of Experts established pursuant to paragraph 9 of resolution 1643 (2005), to equipment, sites and installations referred to in paragraph 2 (a) of resolution 1584 (2005), and to UNOCI and French forces which support it to enable them to carry out the tasks set out in paragraphs 2 and 12 of resolution 1609 (2005);

3. *Reiterates* that any serious obstacle to the freedom of movement of UNOCI and of the French forces which support it, or any attack or obstruction to the action of UNOCI, of the French forces, of the High Representative for the Elections, of the International Working Group (IWG), of the Mediator mentioned in paragraph 20 of resolution 1721 (2006) or his

representative in Côte d'Ivoire constitutes a threat to the peace and national reconciliation process for purposes of paragraphs 9 and 11 of resolution 1572 (2004);

4. *Requests* the Secretary-General and the French Government to report to it immediately, through the Committee established by paragraph 14 of resolution 1572 (2004) (the Committee), of any serious obstacle to the freedom of movement of UNOCI and of the French forces which support it, including the names of those responsible, and *requests* also the High Representative for the elections, the IWG, the Mediator mentioned in paragraph 20 of resolution 1721 (2006) or his representative in Côte d'Ivoire to report to it immediately, through the Committee, any attack or obstruction to their action;

5. *Requests* all States concerned, in particular those in the region, to report to the Committee, within 90 days from the date of adoption of this resolution, on the practical steps they have taken to implement the measures imposed by paragraphs 7, 9 and 11 of resolution 1572 (2004) and by paragraph 6 of resolution 1643 (2005), and *authorizes* the Committee to request whatever further information it may consider necessary;

6. *Decides* that at the end of the period mentioned in paragraph 1 above, the Security Council shall review the measures imposed by paragraphs 7, 9 and 11 of resolution 1572 (2004), paragraph 6 of resolution 1643 (2005) and reiterated in paragraph 3 above, in the light of progress accomplished in the peace and national reconciliation process in Côte d'Ivoire as referred to in resolution 1721 (2006), and *expresses* its readiness to consider the modification or termination of these measures before the aforesaid period only if the provisions of resolution 1721 (2006) have been fully implemented;

7. *Decides* to extend the mandate of the Group of Experts for a further six months, and *requests* the Secretary-General to take the necessary administrative measures as expeditiously as possible, drawing, as appropriate, on the expertise of the members of the Group of Experts and appointing new members as necessary in consultation with the Committee, this mandate being as follows:

(a) To exchange information with UNOCI and the French forces in the context of their monitoring mandate set out in paragraphs 2 and 12 of resolution 1609 (2005);

(b) To gather and analyse all relevant information in Côte d'Ivoire and elsewhere, in cooperation with the governments of those countries, on flows of arms and related materiel, on provision of assistance, advice or training related to military activities, on networks operating in violation of the measures imposed by paragraph 7 of resolution 1572 (2004), and on the sources of financing, including from the exploitation of natural resources in Côte d'Ivoire, for purchases of arms and related materiel and activities;

(c) To consider and recommend, where appropriate, ways of improving the capabilities of States, in particular those in the region, to ensure the effective implementation of the measures imposed by paragraph 7 of resolution 1572 (2004) and by paragraph 6 of resolution 1643 (2005);

(d) To seek further information regarding the action taken by States with a view to implementing effectively the measures imposed by paragraph 6 of resolution 1643 (2005);

(e) To report to the Security Council in writing before 15 June 2007, through the Committee, on the implementation of the measures imposed by paragraphs 7, 9 and

11 of resolution 1572 (2004) and paragraph 6 of resolution 1643 (2005), with recommendations in this regard;

(f) To keep the Committee regularly updated on its activities;

(g) To provide the Committee in its reports with evidence of any violations of the measures imposed by paragraph 7 of resolution 1572 (2004) and paragraph 6 of resolution 1643 (2005);

(h) To cooperate with other relevant groups of experts, in particular that established on Liberia by resolutions 1521 (2003) and 1579 (2004);

(i) To monitor the implementation of the individual measures set out in paragraphs 9 and 11 of resolution 1572 (2004);

8. *Requests* the Secretary-General to communicate as appropriate to the Security Council, through the Committee, information gathered by UNOCI and, when possible, reviewed by the Group of Experts, about the supply of arms and related materiel to Côte d'Ivoire;

9. *Requests* also the French Government to communicate as appropriate to the Security Council, through the Committee, information gathered by the French forces and, when possible, reviewed by the Group of Experts, about the supply of arms and related materiel to Côte d'Ivoire;

10. *Requests* also the Kimberley Process to communicate as appropriate to the Security Council, through the Committee, information and, when possible, reviewed by the Group of Experts, about the production and illicit export of diamonds;

11. *Urges all* States, relevant United Nations bodies and other organizations and interested parties, including the Kimberley Process, to cooperate fully with the Committee, the Group of Experts, UNOCI and the French forces, in particular by supplying any information at their disposal on possible violations of the measures imposed by paragraphs 7, 9 and 11 of resolution 1572 (2004), paragraph 6 of resolution 1643 (2005) and reiterated in paragraph 3 above;

12. *Underlines* that it is fully prepared to impose targeted measures against persons to be designated by the Committee who are determined to be, among other things:

(a) A threat to the peace and national reconciliation process in Côte d'Ivoire, in particular by blocking the implementation of the peace process as referred to in resolution 1721 (2006);

(b) Attacking or obstructing the action of UNOCI, of the French forces which support it, of the High Representative for the Elections, of the IWG, of the Mediator or his representative in Côte d'Ivoire;

(c) Responsible for obstacles to the freedom of movement of UNOCI and of the French forces which support it;

(d) Responsible for serious violations of human rights and international humanitarian law committed in Côte d'Ivoire;

(e) Inciting publicly hatred and violence;

(f) Acting in violation of the measures imposed by paragraph 7 of resolution 1572 (2004);

13. *Decides* to remain actively seized of the matter.

Resolution 1728 (2006)

Adopted by the Security Council at its 5593rd meeting, on 15 December 2006

The Security Council,

Welcoming the report of the Secretary-General of 1 December 2006 (S/2006/931) on the United Nations operation in Cyprus,

Noting that the Government of Cyprus is agreed that in view of the prevailing conditions in the island it is necessary to keep UNFICYP beyond 15 December 2006,

Taking note of the assessment of the Secretary-General that the security situation on the island continues to be generally stable and that the situation along the Green Line remains calm, and welcoming the decrease in the overall number of incidents involving the two sides,

Urging both sides to avoid any action which could lead to an increase in tension such as military exercises and, in this context, noting with concern that disagreements have arisen over civilian activities in the buffer zone, including farming and construction, and encouraging both sides to engage in consultations with UNFICYP on the demarcation of the buffer zone, respecting UNFICYP's mandate, and to reach an agreed approach to UNFICYP's operations in the buffer zone on the basis of the United Nations 1989 aide-memoire,

Expressing its strong appreciation for the work of Under-Secretary-General Gambari in achieving the 8 July agreement and welcoming the principles and decisions enshrined therein, including recognition that the status quo is unacceptable and that a comprehensive settlement based on a bicommunal, bizonal federation and political equality, as set out in the relevant Security Council resolutions, is both desirable and possible and should not be further delayed, but noting, with regret, the Secretary-General's assessment that continued lack of trust between the parties has so far prevented the implementation of any of those decisions, underlining the need to implement the 8 July agreement without further delay, and expressing the hope that the recent positive reaction of the leaders of both communities to suggestions by the United Nations will result in the finalisation of the preparatory phase as soon as possible in order to prepare the ground for fully-fledged negotiations leading to a comprehensive and durable settlement,

Welcoming continued progress in demining, expressing strong support for UNFICYP's efforts to extend demining operations to Turkish Forces minefields in the rest of the buffer zone, and welcoming the prospect that it could be declared free of mines within two years,

Reiterating its call to the parties to assess and address the humanitarian issue of missing persons with due urgency and seriousness, and welcoming in this regard the resumption of the activities of the Committee on Missing Persons since August 2004, and the progress which has since been made, as well as the appointment by the Secretary-General of a third member,

Welcoming the continuing crossings by Greek Cypriots to the north and Turkish Cypriots to the south which have taken place peacefully, and encouraging early progress on other confidence-building measures, such as the opening of additional crossing points, including at Ledra Street,

Welcoming all efforts to promote bicommunal contacts and events, including, inter alia, on the part of the United Nations, and urging the two sides to promote further bicommunal contacts and to remove any obstacles to such contacts,

Expressing concern, in this respect, that opportunities for constructive public debate about the future of the island, within and between the communities, are becoming fewer, and that this atmosphere is hampering, in particular, efforts to foster bicommunal activities intended to benefit Greek Cypriots and Turkish Cypriots, and to promote reconciliation and build trust in order to facilitate a comprehensive settlement,

Noting the primary role of the United Nations in assisting the parties to bring the Cyprus conflict and division of the island to a comprehensive and durable settlement,

Reaffirming the importance of the Secretary-General continuing to keep the operations of UNFICYP under close review while continuing to take into account developments on the ground and the views of the parties, and reverting to the Council with recommendations as appropriate for further adjustments to UNFICYP's mandate, force levels and concept of operation as soon as warranted,

Echoing the Secretary-General's gratitude to the Government of Cyprus and the Government of Greece for their voluntary contributions to the funding of UNFICYP, and his request for further voluntary contributions from other countries and organizations,

Welcoming and encouraging efforts by the United Nations to sensitize peacekeeping personnel in the prevention and control of HIV/AIDS and other communicable diseases in all its peacekeeping operations,

1. *Welcomes* the observations in the Secretary-General's report on progress since June, and in particular on developments since 8 July, and expresses appreciation for his personal efforts over the last 10 years, and those of his staff, aimed at achieving a comprehensive solution;

2. *Reaffirms* all its relevant resolutions on Cyprus, in particular resolution 1251 (1999) of 29 June 1999 and subsequent resolutions;

3. *Expresses* its full support for UNFICYP, including its mandate in the buffer zone, and decides to extend its mandate for a further period ending 15 June 2007;

4. *Calls on* the Turkish Cypriot side and Turkish forces to restore in Strovilia the military status quo which existed there prior to 30 June 2000;

5. *Expresses* full support for the process agreed by the leaders, *encourages* active participation in bicommunal discussions as described in Under-Secretary-General Gambari's letter of 15 November 2006, under the auspices of the SRSG, and *calls for* early completion of the preparatory phase so that a fully-fledged good offices process may resume as soon as possible;

6. *Requests* the Secretary-General to submit a report on implementation of this resolution by 1 June 2007;

7. *Welcomes* the efforts being undertaken by UNFICYP to implement the Secretary-General's zero tolerance policy on sexual exploitation and abuse and to ensure full compliance of its personnel with the United Nations code of conduct, requests the Secretary-General to continue to take all necessary action in this regard and to keep the Security Council informed, and urges troop-contributing countries to take appropriate preventive action including the conduct of predeployment awareness training, and to take disciplinary action and other action to ensure full accountability in cases of such conduct involving their personnel;

8. *Decides* to remain seized of the matter.

Resolution 1729 (2006)

Adopted by the Security Council at its 5596th meeting, on 15 December 2006

The Security Council,

Having considered the report of the Secretary-General on the United Nations Disengagement Observer Force of 4 December 2006 (S/2006/938), and also reaffirming its resolution 1308 (2000) of 17 July 2000,

1. *Calls upon* the parties concerned to implement immediately its resolution 338 (1973) of 22 October 1973;

2. *Welcomes* the efforts being undertaken by the United Nations Disengagement Observer Force to implement the Secretary-General's zero-tolerance policy on sexual exploitation and abuse and to ensure full compliance of its personnel with the United Nations code of conduct, requests the Secretary-General to continue to take all necessary action in this regard and to keep the Security Council informed, and urges troop-contributing countries to take preventive and disciplinary action to ensure that such acts are properly investigated and punished in cases involving their personnel;

3. *Decides* to renew the mandate of the United Nations Disengagement Observer Force for a period of six months, that is, until 30 June 2007;

4. *Requests* the Secretary-General to submit, at the end of this period, a report on developments in the situation and the measures taken to implement resolution 338 (1973).

Resolution 1730 (2006)

Adopted by the Security Council at its 5599th meeting, on 19 December 2006

The Security Council,

Recalling the statement of its President of 22 June 2006 (S/PRST/2006/28),

Emphasizing that sanctions are an important tool in the maintenance and restoration of international peace and security,

Further emphasizing the obligations placed upon all Member States to implement, in full, the mandatory measures adopted by the Security Council,

Continuing in its resolve to ensure that sanctions are carefully targeted in support of clear objectives and implemented in ways that balance effectiveness against possible adverse consequences,

Committed to ensuring that fair and clear procedures exist for placing individuals and entities on sanctions lists and for removing them, as well as for granting humanitarian exemptions,

1. *Adopts* the de-listing procedure in the document annexed to this resolution and *requests* the Secretary-General to establish within the Secretariat (Security Council Subsidiary Organs Branch), a focal point to receive de-listing requests and to perform the tasks described in the attached annex;

2. *Directs* the sanctions committees established by the Security Council, including those established pursuant to resolution 1718 (2006), 1636 (2005), 1591 (2005), 1572 (2004), 1533 (2004), 1521 (2005), 1518 (2003), 1267 (1999), 1132 (1997), 918 (1994), and 751 (1992) to revise their guidelines accordingly;

3. *Decides* to remain seized of the matter.

De-listing procedure

The Security Council requests the Secretary-General to establish, within the Secretariat (Security Council Subsidiary Organs Branch), a focal point to receive de-listing requests. Petitioners seeking to submit a request for de-listing can do so either through the focal point process outlined below or through their state of residence or citizenship.[1]

The focal point will perform the following tasks:

1. Receive de-listing requests from a petitioner (individual(s), groups, undertakings, and/or entities on the Sanctions Committee's lists).

2. Verify if the request is new or is a repeated request.

3. If it is a repeated request and if it does not contain any additional information, return it to the petitioner.

4. Acknowledge receipt of the request to the petitioner and inform the petitioner on the general procedure for processing that request.

5. Forward the request, for their information and possible comments to the designating government(s) and to the government(s) of citizenship and residence. Those governments are encouraged to consult with the designating government(s) before recommending de-listing. To this end, they may approach the focal point, which, if the designating state(s) so agree(s), will put them in contact with the designating state(s).

6. (a) If, after these consultations, any of these governments recommend de-listing, that government will forward its recommendation, either through the focal point or directly to the Chairman of the Sanctions Committee, accompanied by that government's explanation. The Chairman will then place the de-listing request on the Committee's agenda.

(b) If any of the governments, which were consulted on the de-listing request under paragraph 5 above oppose the request, the focal point will so inform the Committee and provide copies of the de-listing request. Any member of the Committee, which possesses information in support of the de-listing request, is encouraged to share such information with the governments that reviewed the de-listing request under paragraph 5 above.

(c) If, after a reasonable time (3 months), none of the governments which reviewed the de-listing request under paragraph 5 above comment, or indicate that they are working on the de-listing request to the Committee and require an additional definite period of time, the focal point will so notify all members of the Committee and provide copies of the de-listing request. Any member of the Committee may, after consultation with the designating government(s), recommend de-listing by forwarding the request to the Chairman of the Sanctions Committee, accompanied by an explanation. (Only one member of the Committee needs to recommend de-listing in order to place the issue on the Committee's agenda.) If after one month, no Committee member recommends de-listing, then it shall be deemed rejected and the Chairman of the Committee shall inform the focal point accordingly.

7. The focal point shall convey all communications, which it receives from Member States, to the Committee for its information.

8. Inform the petitioner:

(a) Of the decision of the Sanctions Committee to grant the de-listing petition; or

(b) That the process of consideration of the de-listing request within the Committee has been completed and that the petitioner remains on the list of the Committee.

[1] A State can decide, that as a rule, its citizens or residents should address their de-listing requests directly to the focal point. The State will do so by a declaration addressed to the Chairman of the Committee that will be published on the Committee's website.

Resolution 1731 (2006)

Adopted by the Security Council at its 5602nd meeting, on 20 December 2006

The Security Council,

Recalling its previous resolutions and statements by its President on the situation in Liberia and West Africa,

Welcoming the sustained progress made by the Government of Liberia since January 2006, in rebuilding Liberia for the benefit of all Liberians, with the support of the international community,

Recalling its decision not to renew the measures in paragraph 10 of resolution 1521 (2003) regarding round log and timber products originating in Liberia, and stressing that Liberia's progress in the timber sector must continue with the effective implementation and enforcement of the National Forestry Reform Law signed into law on 5 October 2006, including the resolution of land and tenure rights,

Welcoming the Government of Liberia's continuing cooperation with the Kimberley Process Certification Scheme and noting Liberia's progress towards putting in place the necessary internal controls and other requirements in order to satisfy the minimum requirements of the Kimberley Process,

Stressing the continuing importance of the United Nations Mission in Liberia (UNMIL) in improving security through Liberia and helping the new Government establish its authority throughout the country, particularly in the diamond and timber-producing regions, and border areas,

Recognizing the need for newly vetted and trained Liberian security forces to assume greater responsibility for national security, and taking note of the need for Liberian armed forces to procure humanitarian, medical and/or training equipment,

Taking note of the report of the United Nations Panel of Experts on Liberia dated 20 December 2006 (S/2006/976), including on the issues of diamonds, timber, rubber, and arms,

Having reviewed the measures imposed by paragraphs 2, 4, and 6 of resolution 1521 (2003) and paragraph 1 of resolution 1532 (2004) and the progress towards meeting the conditions set out by paragraphs 5 and 7 of resolution 1521 (2003), and concluding that insufficient progress has been made towards that end,

Underlining its determination to support the Government of Liberia in its efforts to meet those conditions, and encouraging donors to do likewise,

Determining that, despite significant progress having been made in Liberia, the situation there continues to constitute a threat to international peace and security in the region,

Acting under Chapter VII of the Charter of the United Nations,

1. *Decides*, on the basis of its assessment of progress made to date towards meeting the conditions for lifting the measures imposed by resolution 1521 (2003):

(a) To renew the measures on arms imposed by paragraph 2 of resolution 1521 (2003) and modified by paragraphs 1 and 2 of resolution 1683 (2006) and to renew the measures on travel imposed by paragraph 4 of resolution 1521 (2003) for a further period of 12 months from the date of adoption of this resolution;

(b) That the measures on arms imposed by paragraph 2 (a) and (b) of resolution 1521 (2003) shall not apply to supplies of non-lethal military equipment, excluding non-lethal weapons and ammunition, as notified in advance to the Committee established by paragraph 21 of resolution 1521 (2003), intended solely for use by members of the Government of Liberia police and security forces who have been vetted and trained since the inception of the United Nations Mission in Liberia (UNMIL) in October 2003;

(c) To renew the measures on diamonds imposed by paragraph 6 of resolution 1521 (2003) and renewed by paragraph 4 of resolution 1689 (2006) for an additional six (6) months with a review by the Council after four (4) months, to allow the Government of Liberia sufficient time to establish an effective Certificate of Origin regime for trade in Liberian rough diamonds that is transparent and internationally verifiable, with a view to joining the Kimberley Process, and calls upon the Government of Liberia to provide the Sanctions Committee, established according to paragraph 21 of resolution 1521 (2003) with a detailed description of the proposed regime;

(d) To review any of the above measures at the request of the Government of Liberia, once the Government reports to the Council that the conditions set out in resolution 1521 (2003) for terminating the measures have been met, and provides the Council with information to justify its assessment;

2. *Notes* that the measures imposed by paragraph 1 of resolution 1532 (2004) remain in force and reconfirms its intention to review these measures at least once a year;

3. *Encourages* the Government of Liberia to benefit from UNMIL's offer to provide joint patrols with the Forestry Development Authority with a view to strengthening Government control in forestry areas;

4. *Decides* to extend the mandate of the current Panel of Experts appointed pursuant to paragraph 5 of resolution 1689 (2006) for a further period until 20 June 2007 to undertake the following tasks:

(a) To conduct a follow-up assessment mission to Liberia and neighbouring States, in order to investigate and compile a report on the implementation, and any violations, of the measures imposed by resolution 1521 (2003) and renewed in paragraphs 1 and 2 above, including any information relevant to the designation by the Committee of the individuals described in paragraph 4 (a) of resolution 1521 (2003) and paragraph 1 of resolution 1532 (2004), and including the various sources of financing, such as from natural resources, for the illicit trade of arms;

(b) To assess the impact of and effectiveness of the measures imposed by paragraph 1 of resolution 1532 (2004), including particularly with respect to the assets of former President Charles Taylor;

(c) To assess the implementation of forestry legislation passed by the Liberian Congress on 19 September 2006 and signed into law by President Johnson-Sirleaf on 5 October 2006 and the progress and humanitarian and socio-economic impact of the measures imposed by paragraphs 2, 4 and 6 of resolution 1521 (2003) and renewed in paragraph 1 of resolution 1647 (2005);

(d) To report to the Council through the Committee by 6 June 2007 on all the issues listed in this paragraph, and to provide informal updates to the Committee as appropriate before that date, especially on progress towards meeting the conditions for lifting the measures imposed by paragraph 6 of resolution 1521 (2003) and on progress in the timber sector since the lifting of paragraph 10 of resolution 1521 (2003) in June 2006;

(e) To cooperate with other relevant groups of experts, in particular that established on Côte d'Ivoire by resolution 1708 (2006) of 14 September 2006, and with the Kimberley Process Certification Scheme;

(f) To identify and make recommendations regarding areas where the capacity of States in the region can be strengthened to facilitate the implementation of the measures imposed by paragraph 4 of resolution 1521 (2003) and paragraph 1 of resolution 1532 (2004);

5. *Requests* the Secretary-General to take the necessary measures, in this exceptional instance, to re-appoint the current members of the Panel of Experts as referred to in his letter to the President of the Security Council dated 27 June 2006 (S/2006/438) and to make the necessary financial and security arrangements to support the work of the Panel;

6. *Calls upon* all States and the Government of Liberia to cooperate fully with the Panel of Experts in all the aspects of its mandate;

7. *Encourages* the Kimberley Process to inform, as appropriate, the Security Council through its Committee about any possible follow-up visit to Liberia and its assessment of progress made by the Liberian Government towards joining the Kimberley Process Certification Scheme;

8. *Decides* to remain actively seized of the matter.

Resolution 1732 (2006)

Adopted by the Security Council at its 5605th meeting, on 21 December 2006

The Security Council,

Welcomes the report of the Informal Working Group on General Issues of Sanctions, established pursuant to paragraph 3 of the note by the President of the Security Council dated 17 April 2000 (S/2000/319).

Decides that the Working Group has fulfilled its mandate as contained in document S/2005/841 dated 29 December 2005, to develop general recommendations on how to improve the effectiveness of United Nations sanctions.

Takes note with interest of the best practices and methods contained in the Working Group's report (S/2006/997) and requests its subsidiary bodies to take note as well.

Resolution 1733 (2006)

Adopted by the Security Council at its 5607th meeting, on 22 December 2006

The Security Council,

Recognizing the central role that Secretary-General Kofi Annan has played in guiding the Organization in the discharge of his responsibilities under the Charter of the United Nations,

Further recognizing his sustained efforts towards finding just and lasting solutions to various disputes and conflicts around the globe,

Commending the reforms that he has initiated and the many proposals that he has made on the restructuring and strengthening of the role and functioning of the United Nations system,

1. *Acknowledges* the contribution of Secretary-General Kofi Annan to international peace, security and development, his exceptional efforts to solve international problems in economic, social and cultural fields, as well as his endeavours to meet humanitarian needs and to promote and encourage respect for human rights and fundamental freedoms for all;

2. *Expresses its deep appreciation* to Secretary-General Kofi Annan for his dedication to the purposes and principles enshrined in the Charter and to the development of friendly relations among nations.

Resolution 1734 (2006)

Adopted by the Security Council at its 5608th meeting, on 22 December 2006

The Security Council,

Recalling its previous resolutions and the statements of its President concerning the situation in Sierra Leone, in particular resolutions 1688 (2006) and 1620 (2005),

Commending the valuable contribution that the United Nations Integrated Office in Sierra Leone (UNIOSIL) has made to the recovery of Sierra Leone from conflict and to the country's peace, security and development,

Considering the report of the Secretary-General of 28 November (S/2006/922) and welcoming his recommendation that the mandate of UNIOSIL is extended for a further 12 months until 31 December 2007 with a view to providing continued peacebuilding assistance to the Government of Sierra Leone and preparing for the general elections in July 2007,

Noting the letter of 27 November from the President of Sierra Leone to the Secretary-General that likewise emphasizes the need for the mandate of UNIOSIL to be extended for a further 12 months,

Stressing that the July 2007 elections and the wide acceptance of their outcome will be a major milestone indicating the sustainability of peace and security in Sierra Leone, which should also help to define UNIOSIL's exit strategy,

Emphasizing the importance of the continued support of the United Nations system and the international community for the long-term peace, security and development of Sierra Leone, particularly through strengthening the capacity of the Government of Sierra Leone,

Taking note of the Peacebuilding Commission country specific meetings of 12 October and 13 December 2006, which discussed four priority areas for peacebuilding efforts in Sierra Leone as well as gaps in those areas, recommended next steps for peacebuilding, and noted the determination of the Government of Sierra Leone to coordinate and prioritize work in country, working with UNIOSIL, donors, international institutions, civil society and the private sector to take forward these priorities in order to help bring about a sustainable peace,

Welcoming the progress made in reforming the security sector in Sierra Leone and, in particular, the developing professionalism of the Sierra Leone armed forces and police, and *urging* further strengthening and rationalizing of the security architecture so that the police and armed forces are sustainable in the long term and able to carry out their tasks effectively, in particular in connection with the elections in July 2007,

Welcoming the launch in July 2006 of the Improved Governance and Accountability Pact (IGAP) agreed between main donors and the Government of Sierra Leone, which sets out ten critical governance commitments, including on anti-corruption, public procurement, civil service reform and democracy, and a further ten donor principles of engagement to improve aid effectiveness,

Reiterating its appreciation for the work of the Special Court for Sierra Leone and its vital contribution to reconciliation and the rule of law in Sierra Leone and the subregion, *stressing* the importance of the forthcoming trial of former Liberian President Charles Taylor by the Court and the progress being made in other trials, *reiterating* its expectation that the Court will finish its work expeditiously, *noting* in this regard the Secretary-General's letter of 27 November, and *calling upon* Member States to contribute generously to the Court,

Encouraging the Member States of the Mano River Union and other regional organizations to continue their dialogue aimed at building regional peace and security,

1. *Decides* to extend the mandate of UNIOSIL, as outlined in resolution 1620 (2005), until 31 December 2007;

2. *Endorses* the increase in the number of personnel of UNIOSIL recommended in paragraph 70 of the report of the Secretary-General of 28 November for a period from 1 January 2007 to 31 October 2007 in order to enhance the support provided by UNIOSIL for the elections and its ability to carry out its functions elsewhere in Sierra Leone;

3. *Calls upon* the Secretary-General to conduct a comprehensive assessment of UNIOSIL's role, closer to the election date, with a view to developing its exit strategy;

4. *Calls upon* all parties in Sierra Leone to demonstrate their full commitment to the democratic process and to ensure that the 2007 presidential and parliamentary elections are peaceful, transparent, free and fair;

5. *Calls upon* the Government of Sierra Leone to provide the necessary support for the electoral institutions and *urges* Member States to provide technical and material support including to address the shortfall in the electoral budget;

6. *Emphasizes* that the Government of Sierra Leone bears the primary responsibility for peacebuilding, security and long-term development in the country, *encourages* the Government of Sierra Leone to continue its close engagement with the Peacebuilding Commission and international donors to continue to provide support to the Government;

7. *Calls upon* the Government of Sierra Leone, UNIOSIL and all other stakeholders in the country to increase their efforts to promote good governance, including through continued measures to combat corruption, improve accountability, promote the development of the private sector to generate wealth and employment opportunities, strengthen the judiciary and promote human rights;

8. *Calls upon* the Government of Sierra Leone to expedite the implementation of the recommendations of the Truth and Reconciliation Commission, and *calls upon* Member States to assist the Government in funding the activities of the National Human Rights Commission;

9. *Emphasizes* the important role of women in the prevention and resolution of conflicts and in peacebuilding, as recognized in resolution 1325 (2000), *underlines* that a gender perspective should be taken into account in implementing all aspects of the mandate of UNIOSIL, *welcomes* in this regard the action plan developed by UNIOSIL, *encourages*

UNIOSIL to work with the Government of Sierra Leone in this area, and *requests* the Secretary-General to ensure there is adequate capacity, expertise and resources within UNIOSIL to carry out this work;

10. *Requests* the Secretary-General, where appropriate, to include in his reporting to the Council progress on gender mainstreaming throughout UNIOSIL and all other aspects relating to the situation of women and girls, especially in relation to the need to protect them from gender-based violence;

11. *Welcomes* the efforts undertaken by UNIOSIL to implement the Secretary-General's zero-tolerance policy on sexual exploitation and abuse to ensure full compliance of its personnel with the United Nations code of conduct;

12. *Requests* the Secretary-General to keep the Council regularly informed of progress made in the implementation of the mandate of UNIOSIL and this resolution;

13. *Decides* to remain actively seized of the matter.

Resolution 1735 (2006)

Adopted by the Security Council at its 5609th meeting, on 22 December 2006

The Security Council,

Recalling its resolutions 1267 (1999) of 15 October 1999, 1333 (2000) of 19 December 2000, 1363 (2001) of 30 July 2001, 1373 (2001) of 28 September 2001, 1390 (2002) of 16 January 2002, 1452 (2002) of 20 December 2002, 1455 (2003) of 17 January 2003, 1526 (2004) of 30 January 2004, 1566 (2004) of 8 October 2004, 1617 (2005) of 29 July 2005, 1624 (2005) of 14 September 2005, and 1699 (2006) of 8 August 2006, and the relevant statements of its President,

Reaffirming that terrorism in all its forms and manifestations constitutes one of the most serious threats to peace and security and that any acts of terrorism are criminal and unjustifiable regardless of their motivations, whenever and by whomsoever committed; and reiterating its unequivocal condemnation of Al-Qaida, Usama bin Laden, the Taliban, and other individuals, groups, undertakings, and entities associated with them, for ongoing and multiple criminal terrorist acts aimed at causing the death of innocent civilians and other victims, destruction of property and greatly undermining stability,

Expressing its deep concern about the increased violent and terrorist activities in Afghanistan of the Taliban and Al-Qaida, and other individuals, groups, undertakings, and entities associated with them,

Reaffirming the need to combat by all means, in accordance with the Charter of the United Nations and international law, threats to international peace and security caused by terrorist acts, stressing in this regard the important role the United Nations plays in leading and coordinating this effort,

Stressing that terrorism can only be defeated by a sustained and comprehensive approach involving the active participation and collaboration of all States, and international and regional organizations to impede, impair, isolate, and incapacitate the terrorist threat,

Emphasizing that dialogue between the Committee established pursuant to resolution 1267 (1999) ("the Committee") and Member States is vital to the full implementation of the measures,

Recognizing that one of the most effective means of dialogue between the Committee and Member States is through direct contact, including country visits,

Welcoming the expanded cooperation with Interpol, including the establishment of "Interpol—UN Security Council Special Notices" and the passage of resolution 1699 (2006), and encouraging Member States to work in the framework of Interpol and other international and regional organizations in order to reinforce the implementation of the measures against Al-Qaida, Usama bin Laden, and the Taliban, and other individuals, groups, undertakings and entities associated with them,

Noting the need for robust implementation of the measures in paragraph 1 of this resolution as a significant tool in combating terrorist activity,

Reiterating that the measures referred to in paragraph 1 below, are preventative in nature and are not reliant upon criminal standards set out under national law,

Underscoring that, in giving effect to the measures in paragraph 1 of resolution 1617 (2005) and other relevant resolutions, full account is to be taken of the provisions regarding exemptions in paragraphs 1 and 2 of resolution 1452 (2002),

Taking note of the Committee's document on the arms embargo (SCA/2/06(20)), which is intended to be a useful tool to assist States in the implementation of the measures in paragraph 1(c) of this resolution,

Expressing its deep concern about criminal misuse of the internet by Al-Qaida, Usama bin Laden, and the Taliban, and other individuals, groups, undertakings, and entities associated with them, in furtherance of terrorist acts,

Noting with concern the changing nature of the threat presented by Al-Qaida, Usama bin Laden and the Taliban, and other individuals, groups, undertakings and entities associated with them, in particular the ways in which terrorist ideologies are promoted,

Stressing the importance of meeting all aspects of the threat that Al-Qaida, Usama bin Laden and the Taliban, and other individuals, groups, undertakings and entities associated with them represent to international peace and security,

Acting under Chapter VII of the Charter of the United Nations,

Measures

1. *Decides* that all States shall take the measures as previously imposed by paragraph 4 (b) of resolution 1267 (1999), paragraph 8 (c) of resolution 1333 (2000), paragraphs 1 and 2 of resolution 1390 (2002), with respect to Al-Qaida, Usama bin Laden, and the Taliban and other individuals, groups, undertakings and entities associated with them, as referred to in the list created pursuant to resolutions 1267 (1999) and 1333 (2000) (the "Consolidated List"):

(a) Freeze without delay the funds and other financial assets or economic resources of these individuals, groups, undertakings and entities, including funds derived from property owned or controlled, directly or indirectly, by them or by persons acting on their behalf or at their direction, and ensure that neither these nor any other funds, financial assets or economic resources are made available, directly or indirectly, for such persons' benefit, or by their nationals or by persons within their territory;

(b) Prevent the entry into or the transit through their territories of these individuals, provided that nothing in this paragraph shall oblige any State to deny entry or require the departure from its territories of its own nationals and this paragraph shall not apply where entry or transit is necessary for the fulfilment of a judicial process or the Committee established pursuant to resolution 1267 (1999) ("the Committee") determines on a case-by-case basis only that entry or transit is justified;

(c) Prevent the direct or indirect supply, sale, or transfer, to these individuals, groups, undertakings and entities from their territories or by their nationals outside their territories, or using their flag vessels or aircraft, of arms and related material of all types including weapons and ammunition, military vehicles and equipment, paramilitary equipment, and spare parts for the aforementioned and technical advice, assistance, or training related to military activities;

2. *Reminds* States of their obligation to freeze without delay the funds and other financial assets or economic resources pursuant to paragraph 1 (a) of this resolution;

3. *Confirms* that the requirements in paragraph 1 (a) of this resolution apply to economic resources of every kind;

4. *Calls upon* States to redouble their efforts to implement the measure in paragraph 1 (b) and 1 (c) of this resolution;

Listing

5. *Decides* that, when proposing names to the Committee for inclusion on the Consolidated List, States shall act in accordance with paragraph 17 of resolution 1526 (2004) and paragraph 4 of resolution 1617 (2005) and provide a statement of case; the statement of case should provide as much detail as possible on the basis(es) for the listing, including: (i) specific information supporting a determination that the individual or entity meets the criteria above; (ii) the nature of the information and (iii) supporting information or documents that can be provided; States should include details of any connection between the proposed designee and any currently listed individual or entity;

6. *Requests* designating States, at the time of submission, to identify those parts of the statement of case which may be publicly released for the purposes of notifying the listed individual or entity, and those parts which may be released upon request to interested States;

7. *Calls upon* States to use the cover sheet attached in Annex I when proposing names for the Consolidated List, in order to ensure clarity and consistency in requests for listing;

8. *Directs* the Committee to encourage the submission of names from Member States for inclusion on the Consolidated List;

9. *Directs* the Committee to encourage States to submit additional identifying and other information on listed individuals and entities, including updates on assets frozen and the movement of listed individuals as such information becomes available;

10. *Decides* that the Secretariat shall, after publication but within two weeks after a name is added to the Consolidated List, notify the Permanent Mission of the country or countries

where the individual or entity is believed to be located and, in the case of individuals, the country of which the person is a national (to the extent this information is known), and include with this notification a copy of the publicly releasable portion of the statement of case, a description of the effects of designation, as set forth in the relevant resolutions, the Committee's procedures for considering delisting requests, and the provisions of resolution 1452 (2002);

11. *Calls upon* States receiving notification as in paragraph 10 to take reasonable steps according to their domestic laws and practices to notify or inform the listed individual or entity of the designation and to include with this notification a copy of the publicly releasable portion of the statement of case, a description of the effects of designation, as provided in the relevant resolutions, the Committee's procedures for considering delisting requests, the provisions of resolution 1452 (2002);

12. *Encourages* States to submit to the Committee for inclusion on the Consolidated List names of individuals and entities participating in the financing or support of acts or activities of Al-Qaida, Usama bin Laden and the Taliban, and other individuals, groups, undertakings and entities associated with them, as described in paragraph 2 of resolution 1617 (2005), by any means, including but not limited to using proceeds derived from illicit cultivation, production, and trafficking of narcotic drugs originating in Afghanistan, and their precursors;

Delisting

13. *Decides* that the Committee shall continue to develop, adopt, and apply guidelines regarding the de-listing of individuals and entities on the Consolidated List;

14. *Decides* that the Committee, in determining whether to remove names from the Consolidated List, may consider, among other things, (i) whether the individual or entity was placed on the Consolidated List due to a mistake of identity, or (ii) whether the individual or entity no longer meets the criteria set out in relevant resolutions, in particular resolution 1617 (2005); in making the evaluation in (ii)above, the Committee may consider, among other things, whether the individual is deceased, or whether it has been affirmatively shown that the individual or entity has severed all association, as defined in resolution 1617 (2005), with Al-Qaida, Usama bin Laden, the Taliban, and their supporters, including all individuals and entities on the Consolidated List;

Exemptions

15. *Decides* to extend the period for consideration by the Committee of notifications submitted pursuant to paragraph 1 (a) of resolution 1452 (2002) from 48 hours to 3 working days;

16. *Reiterates* that the Committee must make a negative decision on notifications submitted pursuant to paragraph 1 (a) of resolution 1452 (2002), in order to prevent the release of funds and other financial assets or economic resources that have been determined by the notifying State(s) to be necessary for basic expenses;

17. *Directs* the Committee to review its guidelines with respect to the provisions of paragraph 1(a) of resolution 1452 (2002) as reiterated in paragraph 15 above;

18. *Encourages* States that submit requests to the Committee, pursuant to paragraph 1 (b) of resolution 1452 (2002), to report in a timely way on the use of such funds, with a view to preventing such funds from being used to finance terrorism;

Measures Implementation

19. *Encourages* States to identify, and if necessary introduce, adequate procedures to fully implement all aspects of the measures described in paragraph 1 of this resolution;

20. *Stresses* that the measures imposed by paragraph 1(a) of this resolution apply to all forms of financial resources, including but not limited to those used for the provision of Internet hosting or related services, used for the support of Al-Qaida, Usama bin Laden, and the Taliban and other individuals, groups, undertakings and entities associated with them;

21. *Directs* the Committee to identify possible cases of non-compliance with the measures pursuant to paragraph 1 above, and requests the Chairman, in his periodic reports to the Council pursuant to paragraph 31 below, to provide progress reports on the Committee's work on this issue;

22. *Requests* States to ensure that the most up to date version of the Consolidated List is promptly made available to relevant Government offices and other relevant bodies, in particular, those offices responsible for the assets freeze and border control;

23. *Requests* the Secretary General to take the necessary steps to increase cooperation between the United Nations and relevant international and regional organisations, including Interpol, ICAO, IATA, and the WCO, in order to provide the Committee with better tools to fulfil its mandate more effectively and to give Member States better tools to implement the measures referred to in paragraph 1 of this resolution;

Taliban

24. *Encourages* States to submit names of individuals and entities currently associated with the Taliban to the Committee for inclusion on the Consolidated List;

25. *Directs* the Committee to encourage States to provide additional identifying and other information on listed Taliban individuals and entities;

26. *Directs* the Committee to work, in accordance with its guidelines, to consider requests for inclusion on the Consolidated List, names of individuals and entities associated with the Taliban, and to consider petitions for the removal of listed members and/or associates of the Taliban who are no longer associated with the Taliban;

Coordination

27. *Reiterates* the need for ongoing close cooperation and exchange of information among the Committee, the Counter Terrorism Committee ("CTC"), and the Committee established pursuant to resolution 1540 (2004), as well as their respective groups of experts, including enhanced information sharing, coordinated visits to countries, technical assistance, and other issues of relevance to all three committees;

Outreach

28. *Further reiterates* the importance of having the Committee follow up via oral and/or written communications with Member States regarding effective implementation of the sanctions measures;

29. *Strongly encourages* Member States to send representatives to meet the Committee for more in-depth discussion of relevant issues;

30. *Requests* the Committee to consider, where and when appropriate, visits to selected countries by the Chairman and/or Committee members to enhance the full and effective implementation of the measures referred to in paragraph 1 above, with a view to encouraging States to comply fully with this resolution and resolutions 1267 (1999), 1333 (2000), 1390 (2002), 1455 (2003), 1526 (2004) and 1617 (2005);

31. *Requests* the Committee to report orally, through its Chairman, at least every 180 days to the Council on the overall work of the Committee and the Analytical Support and Sanctions Monitoring Team ("Monitoring Team"), and, as appropriate, in conjunction with the reports by the Chairmen of the CTC and the Committee established pursuant to resolution 1540 (2004), including briefings for all interested Member States;

Monitoring Team and Reviews

32. *Decides*, in order to assist the Committee in the fulfilment of its mandate, to extend the mandate of the current New York-based Monitoring Team, appointed by the Secretary-General pursuant to paragraph 20 of resolution 1617 (2005), for a further period of 18 months, under the direction of the Committee with the responsibilities outlined in Annex II, and requests the Secretary-General to make the necessary arrangements to this effect;

33. *Decides* to review the measures described in paragraph 1 of this resolution with a view to their possible further strengthening in 18 months, or sooner if necessary;

34. *Decides* to remain actively seized of the matter.

Annex I — Coversheet

Consolidated List: Cover Sheet for Member State Submissions to the Committee

Please complete as many of the following fields as possible:

I. IDENTIFIER INFORMATION — for Individuals							
Where possible, note the nationality or cultural or ethnic sources of names/aliases. Provide all available spellings.		**Surname/ Family Name/ Last Name**	**First Name**	**Additional name (e.g. father's name or middle name), where applicable**	**Additional name (e.g. grandfather's name), where applicable**	**Additional name, where applicable**	**Additional name, where applicable**
Full Name: (in original and Latin script)							
Aliases/"Also Known As" (A.K.A.s): Note whether it is a strong or weak alias.	Current						
	Former						
Other nom de guerre, pseudonym:				**Title:** Honorary, professional, or religious title			
Employment/Occupation: Official title/position				**Nationality/ Citizenship:**			

Date of Birth: (DD/MM/YYYY)		**Passport Details:** (Number, issuing date & country, expiry date)	
Alternative Dates of Birth (if any): (DD/MM/YYYY)		**National Identification Number(s), Type(s):** (e.g. Identity card, Social Security)	
Place of Birth: (provide all known details including city, region, province/state, country)		**Address(es):** (provide all known details, including street address, city, province/state, country)	
Alternative Place(s) of Birth (if any): (city, region, province/state, country)		**Previous Address(es):** (provide all known details, including street address, city, province/state, country)	
Gender:		**Languages spoken:**	
Father's full name:		**Mother's full name:**	
Current location:		**Previous location(s):**	

Undertakings and entities owned or controlled, directly or indirectly by the individual (see UNSCR 1617 (2005), para. 3):	
Website Addresses:	
Other relevant detail: (such as physical description, distinguishing marks and characteristics)	

IDENTIFIER INFORMATION — For Groups, Undertakings, or Entities	
Name:	
Also Known As (A.K.A.s): Where possible, note whether it is a strong or weak A.K.A.	**Now Known As (N.K.A.s)**
	Formerly Known As (F.K.A.s)
Address(es): Headquarters and/or branches. Provide all known details, including street address, city, province/state, country	
Tax Identification Number: (or local equivalent, type)	
Other Identification Number and type:	
Website Addresses:	
Other Information	

II. BASIS FOR LISTING

May the Committee publicly release the following information?	*Yes*	*No*
May the Committee release the following information to Member States?	*Yes*	*No*

Complete one or more of the following:

	(a) participating in the financing, planning, facilitating, preparing, or perpetrating of acts or activities by, in conjunction with, under the name of, on behalf of, or in support of Al-Qaida (AQ), Usama bin Laden (UBL), or the Taliban, or any cell, affiliate, splinter group or derivative thereof.[1] • Names(s) of cell, affiliate, splinter group or derivate thereof: ____________________________________

	(b) supplying, selling or transferring arms and related materiel to AQ, UBL or the Taliban, or any cell, affiliate, splinter group or derivative thereof.[1] • Names(s) of cell, affiliate, splinter group or derivate thereof: ______________________________
	(c) recruiting for AQ, UBL or the Taliban, or any cell, affiliate, splinter group or derivative thereof.[1] • Name(s) of cell, affiliate, splinter group or derivate thereof: ______________________________
	(d) otherwise supporting acts or activities of AQ, UBL or the Taliban, or any cell, affiliate, splinter group or derivative thereof.[1] • Name(s) of cell, affiliate, splinter group or derivate thereof: ______________________________
	(e) Other association with AQ, UBL or the Taliban, or any cell, affiliate, splinter group or derivative thereof. • Briefly explain nature of association and provide name of cell, affiliate, splinter group or derivate thereof: ______________________________
	(f) Entity owned or controlled, directly or indirectly, by, or otherwise supporting, an individual or entity on the Consolidated List.[2] • Name(s) of individual or entity on the Consolidated List: ______________________________
Please attach a Statement of the Case which should provide as much detail as possible on the basis(es) for listing indicated above, including: (1) specific information supporting the association or activities alleged; (2) the nature of the information (e.g., intelligence, law enforcement, judicial, media, admissions by subject, etc.) and (3) supporting information or documents that can be provided. Include details of any connection with a currently listed individual or entity. Indicate what portion(s) of the Statement of Case the Committee may publicly release or release to Member States.	

[1]S/RES/1617 (2005), para. 2.

[2]S/RES/1617 (2005), para. 3.

III. POINT OF CONTACT *The individual(s) below may serve as a point-of-contact for further questions on this case:* (THIS INFORMATION SHALL REMAIN CONFIDENTIAL)	
Name:	*Position/Title:*

Annex II

In accordance with paragraph 32 of this resolution, the Monitoring Team shall operate under the direction of the Committee established pursuant to resolution 1267 (1999) and shall have the following responsibilities:

a. To collate, assess, monitor and report on and make recommendations regarding implementation of the measures, including implementation of the measures in paragraph 1(a) of this resolution as it pertains to preventing the criminal misuse of the internet by Al-Qaida, Usama bin Laden, the Taliban, and other individuals, groups, undertakings, and entities associated with them, to pursue case studies, as appropriate; and to explore in depth any other relevant issues as directed by the Committee;

b. To submit a comprehensive program of work to the Committee for its review and approval, as necessary, in which the Monitoring Team should detail the activities, envisaged in order to fulfil its responsibilities, including proposed travel, based on close coordination with the CTC's Executive Directorate ("CTED") and the 1540 Committee's group of experts to avoid duplication and reinforce synergies;

c. To submit, in writing, two comprehensive, independent reports to the Committee, one by 30 September 2007 and the other by 31 March 2008, on implementation by States of the measures referred to in paragraph 1 of this resolution, including specific recommendations for improved implementation of the measures and possible new measures;

d. To analyze reports submitted pursuant to paragraph 6 of resolution 1455 (2003), the checklists submitted pursuant to paragraph 10 of resolution 1617 (2005), and other information submitted by Member States to the Committee as instructed by the Committee;

e. To work closely and share information with CTED and the 1540 Committee's group of experts to identify areas of convergence and overlap and to help facilitate concrete coordination, including in the area of reporting, among the three Committees;

f. To assist the Committee with its analysis of non-compliance with the measures referred to in paragraph 1 of this resolution by collating information collected from Member States and submitting case studies, both on its own initiative and upon the Committee's request, to the Committee for its review;

g. To present to the Committee recommendations, which could be used by Member States to assist them with the implementation of the measures referred to in paragraph 1 of this resolution and in preparing proposed additions to the Consolidated List;

h. To consult with Member States in advance of travel to selected Member States, based on its program of work as approved by the Committee;

i. To encourage Member States to submit names and additional identifying information for inclusion on the Consolidated List, as instructed by the Committee;

j. To study and report to the Committee on the changing nature of the threat of Al-Qaida and the Taliban and the best measures to confront it, including by developing a dialogue with relevant scholars and academic bodies, in consultation with the Committee;

k. To consult with Member States and other relevant organizations, including regular dialogue with representatives in New York and in capitals, taking into account their comments, especially regarding any issues that might be contained in the Monitoring Team's reports referred to in paragraph c of this annex;

l. To consult with Member States' intelligence and security services, including through regional fora, in order to facilitate the sharing of information and to strengthen enforcement of the measures;

m. To consult with relevant representatives of the private sector, including financial institutions, to learn about the practical implementation of the assets freeze and to develop recommendations for the strengthening of that measure;

n. To work with relevant international and regional organizations in order to promote awareness of, and compliance with, the measures;

o. To assist other subsidiary bodies of the Security Council, and their expert panels, upon request with enhancing their cooperation with Interpol, referred to in resolution 1699 (2006);

p. To report to the Committee, on a regular basis or when the Committee so requests, through oral and/or written briefings on the work of the Monitoring Team, including its visits to Member States and its activities;

q. Any other responsibility identified by the Committee.

Resolution 1736 (2006)

Adopted by the Security Council at its 5610th meeting, on 22 December 2006

The Security Council,

Recalling its resolutions and the statements of its President concerning the situation in the Democratic Republic of the Congo, in Burundi and in the Great Lakes region of Africa,

Paying tribute again to the citizens of the Democratic Republic of the Congo for the remarkable commitment they have demonstrated to the democratic process,

Taking note of the letter of the Secretary-General dated 15 November 2006 (S/2006/892), and of the recommendation it contains,

Noting that the 50 military observers deployed in the Democratic Republic of the Congo under the authorized military strength of the United Nations Operation in Burundi (ONUB) pursuant to resolutions 1669 (2006) and 1692 (2006) have successfully performed observation tasks related to the electoral process and will be repatriated by 31 December 2006,

Condemning the continuation of hostilities by militias and foreign armed groups in the eastern part of the Democratic Republic of the Congo, and the threat they pose to the security of civilians and to the stability of the region,

Deploring the persistence of violations of human rights and international humanitarian law in the Democratic Republic of the Congo, in particular those carried out by these militias and foreign armed groups and by elements of the Armed Forces of the Democratic Republic of the Congo (FARDC), and *stressing* the urgent need for those responsible for these crimes to be brought to justice,

Bearing in mind that the mandates of ONUB and of the United Nations Organization Mission in the Democratic Republic of the Congo (MONUC) will expire respectively on 31 December 2006 and on 15 February 2007,

Looking forward to the Secretary-General's proposals, after close consultations with the new Congolese authorities, regarding MONUC's future mandate, including a review of the Mission's military strength,

Noting that the situation in the Democratic Republic of the Congo continues to constitute a threat to international peace and security in the region,

Acting under Chapter VII of the Charter of the United Nations,

1. *Authorizes*, from 1 January 2007 until the expiry of MONUC's current mandate on 15 February 2007, an increase in the military strength of MONUC of up to 916 military personnel, to allow for the continued deployment to MONUC of the infantry battalion and the military hospital currently authorized under the ONUB mandate and *expresses* its

intention to examine this issue further before 15 February, in the context of the Secretary General's forthcoming proposals, with a view to ensuring that MONUC has adequate capabilities to perform its mandate;

2. *Decides* to remain actively seized of the matter.

Resolution 1737 (2006)

Adopted by the Security Council at its 5612th meeting, on 23 December 2006

The Security Council,

Recalling the Statement of its President, S/PRST/2006/15, of 29 March 2006, and its resolution 1696 (2006) of 31 July 2006,

Reaffirming its commitment to the Treaty on the Non-Proliferation of Nuclear Weapons, and recalling the right of States Party, in conformity with Articles I and II of that Treaty, to develop research, production and use of nuclear energy for peaceful purposes without discrimination,

Reiterating its serious concern over the many reports of the IAEA Director General and resolutions of the IAEA Board of Governors related to Iran's nuclear programme, reported to it by the IAEA Director General, including IAEA Board resolution GOV/2006/14,

Reiterating its serious concern that the IAEA Director General's report of 27 February 2006 (GOV/2006/15) lists a number of outstanding issues and concerns on Iran's nuclear programme, including topics which could have a military nuclear dimension, and that the IAEA is unable to conclude that there are no undeclared nuclear materials or activities in Iran,

Reiterating its serious concern over the IAEA Director General's report of 28 April 2006 (GOV/2006/27) and its findings, including that, after more than three years of Agency efforts to seek clarity about all aspects of Iran's nuclear programme, the existing gaps in knowledge continue to be a matter of concern, and that the IAEA is unable to make progress in its efforts to provide assurances about the absence of undeclared nuclear material and activities in Iran,

Noting with serious concern that, as confirmed by the IAEA Director General's reports of 8 June 2006 (GOV/2006/38), 31 August 2006 (GOV/2006/53) and 14 November 2006 (GOV/2006/64), Iran has not established full and sustained suspension of all enrichment-related and reprocessing activities as set out in resolution 1696 (2006), nor resumed its cooperation with the IAEA under the Additional Protocol, nor taken the other steps required of it by the IAEA Board of Governors, nor complied with the provisions of Security Council resolution 1696 (2006) and which are essential to build confidence, and *deploring* Iran's refusal to take these steps,

Emphasizing the importance of political and diplomatic efforts to find a negotiated solution guaranteeing that Iran's nuclear programme is exclusively for peaceful purposes, and *noting* that such a solution would benefit nuclear nonproliferation elsewhere, and *welcoming* the continuing commitment of China, France, Germany, the Russian Federation, the United Kingdom and the United States, with the support of the European Union's High Representative to seek a negotiated solution,

Determined to give effect to its decisions by adopting appropriate measures to persuade Iran to comply with resolution 1696 (2006) and with the requirements of the IAEA, and also to constrain Iran's development of sensitive technologies in support of its nuclear and missile programmes, until such time as the Security Council determines that the objectives of this resolution have been met,

Concerned by the proliferation risks presented by the Iranian nuclear programme and, in this context, by Iran's continuing failure to meet the requirements of the IAEA Board of Governors and to comply with the provisions of Security Council resolution 1696 (2006), *mindful* of its primary responsibility under the Charter of the United Nations for the maintenance of international peace and security,

Acting under Article 41 of Chapter VII of the Charter of the United Nations,

1. *Affirms* that Iran shall without further delay take the steps required by the IAEA Board of Governors in its resolution GOV/2006/14, which are essential to build confidence in the exclusively peaceful purpose of its nuclear programme and to resolve outstanding questions;

2. *Decides,* in this context, that Iran shall without further delay suspend the following proliferation sensitive nuclear activities:

(a) all enrichment-related and reprocessing activities, including research and development, to be verified by the IAEA; and

(b) work on all heavy water-related projects, including the construction of a research reactor moderated by heavy water, also to be verified by the IAEA;

3. *Decides* that all States shall take the necessary measures to prevent the supply, sale or transfer directly or indirectly from their territories, or by their nationals or using their flag vessels or aircraft to, or for the use in or benefit of, Iran, and whether or not originating in their territories, of all items, materials, equipment, goods and technology which could contribute to Iran's enrichment-related, reprocessing or heavy water-related activities, or to the development of nuclear weapon delivery systems, namely:

(a) those set out in sections B.2, B.3, B.4, B.5, B.6 and B.7 of INFCIRC/254/Rev.8/Part 1 in document S/2006/814;

(b) those set out in sections A.1 and B.1 of INFCIRC/254/Rev.8/Part 1 in document S/2006/814, except the supply, sale or transfer of:

(i) equipment covered by B.1 when such equipment is for light water reactors;

(ii) low-enriched uranium covered by A.1.2 when it is incorporated in assembled nuclear fuel elements for such reactors;

(c) those set out in document S/2006/815, except the supply, sale or transfer of items covered by 19.A.3 of Category II;

(d) any additional items, materials, equipment, goods and technology, determined as necessary by the Security Council or the Committee established by paragraph 18 below (herein "the Committee"), which could contribute to enrichment-related, or reprocessing, or heavy water-related activities, or to the development of nuclear weapon delivery systems;

4. *Decides* that all States shall take the necessary measures to prevent the supply, sale or transfer directly or indirectly from their territories, or by their nationals or using their flag vessels or aircraft to, or for the use in or benefit of, Iran, and whether or not originating in their territories, of the following items, materials, equipment, goods and technology:

(a) those set out in INFCIRC/254/Rev.7/Part2 of document S/2006/814 if the State determines that they would contribute to enrichment-related, reprocessing or heavy water-related activities;

(b) any other items not listed in documents S/2006/814 or S/2006/815 if the State determines that they would contribute to enrichment-related, reprocessing or heavy water-related activities, or to the development of nuclear weapon delivery systems;

(c) any further items if the State determines that they would contribute to the pursuit of activities related to other topics about which the IAEA has expressed concerns or identified as outstanding;

5. *Decides* that, for the supply, sale or transfer of all items, materials, equipment, goods and technology covered by documents S/2006/814 and S/2006/815 the export of which to Iran is not prohibited by subparagraphs 3 (b), 3 (c) or 4 (a) above, States shall ensure that:

(a) the requirements, as appropriate, of the Guidelines as set out in documents S/2006/814 and S/2006/985 have been met; and

(b) they have obtained and are in a position to exercise effectively a right to verify the end-use and end-use location of any supplied item; and

(c) they notify the Committee within ten days of the supply, sale or transfer; and

(d) in the case of items, materials, equipment, goods and technology contained in document S/2006/814, they also notify the IAEA within ten days of the supply, sale or transfer;

6. *Decides* that all States shall also take the necessary measures to prevent the provision to Iran of any technical assistance or training, financial assistance, investment, brokering or other services, and the transfer of financial resources or services, related to the supply, sale, transfer, manufacture or use of the prohibited items, materials, equipment, goods and technology specified in paragraphs 3 and 4 above;

7. *Decides* that Iran shall not export any of the items in documents S/2006/814 and S/2006/815 and that all Member States shall prohibit the procurement of such items from Iran by their nationals, or using their flag vessels or aircraft, and whether or not originating in the territory of Iran;

8. *Decides* that Iran shall provide such access and cooperation as the IAEA requests to be able to verify the suspension outlined in paragraph 2 and to resolve all outstanding issues, as identified in IAEA reports, and calls upon Iran to ratify promptly the Additional Protocol;

9. *Decides* that the measures imposed by paragraphs 3, 4 and 6 above shall not apply where the Committee determines in advance and on a case-by-case basis that such supply, sale, transfer or provision of such items or assistance would clearly not contribute to the development of Iran's technologies in support of its proliferation sensitive nuclear activities and

of development of nuclear weapon delivery systems, including where such items or assistance are for food, agricultural, medical or other humanitarian purposes, provided that:

(a) contracts for delivery of such items or assistance include appropriate end-user guarantees; and

(b) Iran has committed not to use such items in proliferation sensitive nuclear activities or for development of nuclear weapon delivery systems;

10. *Calls upon* all States to exercise vigilance regarding the entry into or transit through their territories of individuals who are engaged in, directly associated with or providing support for Iran's proliferation sensitive nuclear activities or for the development of nuclear weapon delivery systems, and *decides* in this regard that all States shall notify the Committee of the entry into or transit through their territories of the persons designated in the Annex to this resolution (herein "the Annex"), as well as of additional persons designated by the Security Council or the Committee as being engaged in, directly associated with or providing support for Iran's proliferation sensitive nuclear activities and for the development of nuclear weapon delivery systems, including through the involvement in procurement of the prohibited items, goods, equipment, materials and technology specified by and under the measures in paragraphs 3 and 4 above, except where such travel is for activities directly related to the items in subparagraphs 3 (b) (i) and (ii) above;

11. *Underlines* that nothing in the above paragraph requires a State to refuse its own nationals entry into its territory, and that all States shall, in the implementation of the above paragraph, take into account humanitarian considerations as well as the necessity to meet the objectives of this resolution, including where Article XV of the IAEA Statute is engaged;

12. *Decides* that all States shall freeze the funds, other financial assets and economic resources which are on their territories at the date of adoption of this resolution or at any time thereafter, that are owned or controlled by the persons or entities designated in the Annex, as well as those of additional persons or entities designated by the Security Council or by the Committee as being engaged in, directly associated with or providing support for Iran's proliferation sensitive nuclear activities or the development of nuclear weapon delivery systems, or by persons or entities acting on their behalf or at their direction, or by entities owned or controlled by them, including through illicit means, and that the measures in this paragraph shall cease to apply in respect of such persons or entities if, and at such time as, the Security Council or the Committee removes them from the Annex, and *decides further* that all States shall ensure that any funds, financial assets or economic resources are prevented from being made available by their nationals or by any persons or entities within their territories, to or for the benefit of these persons and entities;

13. *Decides* that the measures imposed by paragraph 12 above do not apply to funds, other financial assets or economic resources that have been determined by relevant States:

(a) to be necessary for basic expenses, including payment for foodstuffs, rent or mortgage, medicines and medical treatment, taxes, insurance premiums, and public utility charges or exclusively for payment of reasonable professional fees and reimbursement of incurred expenses associated with the provision of legal services, or fees or service charges, in accordance with national laws, for routine holding or maintenance of frozen funds, other financial assets and economic resources, after notification by the relevant

States to the Committee of the intention to authorize, where appropriate, access to such funds, other financial assets or economic resources and in the absence of a negative decision by the Committee within five working days of such notification;

(b) to be necessary for extraordinary expenses, provided that such determination has been notified by the relevant States to the Committee and has been approved by the Committee;

(c) to be the subject of a judicial, administrative or arbitral lien or judgement, in which case the funds, other financial assets and economic resources may be used to satisfy that lien or judgement provided that the lien or judgement was entered into prior to the date of the present resolution, is not for the benefit of a person or entity designated pursuant to paragraphs 10 and 12 above, and has been notified by the relevant States to the Committee;

(d) to be necessary for activities directly related to the items specified in subparagraphs 3 (b) (i) and (ii) and have been notified by the relevant States to the Committee;

14. *Decides* that States may permit the addition to the accounts frozen pursuant to the provisions of paragraph 12 above of interests or other earnings due on those accounts or payments due under contracts, agreements or obligations that arose prior to the date on which those accounts became subject to the provisions of this resolution, provided that any such interest, other earnings and payments continue to be subject to these provisions and are frozen;

15. *Decides* that the measures in paragraph 12 above shall not prevent a designated person or entity from making payment due under a contract entered into prior to the listing of such a person or entity, provided that the relevant States have determined that:

(a) the contract is not related to any of the prohibited items, materials, equipment, goods, technologies, assistance, training, financial assistance, investment, brokering or services referred to in paragraphs 3, 4 and 6 above;

(b) the payment is not directly or indirectly received by a person or entity designated pursuant to paragraph 12 above;

and after notification by the relevant States to the Committee of the intention to make or receive such payments or to authorize, where appropriate, the unfreezing of funds, other financial assets or economic resources for this purpose, ten working days prior to such authorization;

16. *Decides* that technical cooperation provided to Iran by the IAEA or under its auspices shall only be for food, agricultural, medical, safety or other humanitarian purposes, or where it is necessary for projects directly related to the items specified in subparagraphs 3 (b) (i) and (ii) above, but that no such technical cooperation shall be provided that relates to the proliferation sensitive nuclear activities set out in paragraph 2 above;

17. *Calls upon* all States to exercise vigilance and prevent specialized teaching or training of Iranian nationals, within their territories or by their nationals, of disciplines which would contribute to Iran's proliferation sensitive nuclear activities and development of nuclear weapon delivery systems;

18. *Decides* to establish, in accordance with rule 28 of its provisional rules of procedure, a Committee of the Security Council consisting of all the members of the Council, to undertake the following tasks:

(a) to seek from all States, in particular those in the region and those producing the items, materials, equipment, goods and technology referred to in paragraphs 3 and 4 above, information regarding the actions taken by them to implement effectively the measures imposed by paragraphs 3, 4, 5, 6, 7, 8, 10 and 12 of this resolution and whatever further information it may consider useful in this regard;

(b) to seek from the secretariat of the IAEA information regarding the actions taken by the IAEA to implement effectively the measures imposed by paragraph 16 of this resolution and whatever further information it may consider useful in this regard;

(c) to examine and take appropriate action on information regarding alleged violations of measures imposed by paragraphs 3, 4, 5, 6, 7, 8, 10 and 12 of this resolution;

(d) to consider and decide upon requests for exemptions set out in paragraphs 9, 13 and 15 above;

(e) to determine as may be necessary additional items, materials, equipment, goods and technology to be specified for the purpose of paragraph 3 above;

(f) to designate as may be necessary additional individuals and entities subject to the measures imposed by paragraphs 10 and 12 above;

(g) to promulgate guidelines as may be necessary to facilitate the implementation of the measures imposed by this resolution and include in such guidelines a requirement on States to provide information where possible as to why any individuals and/or entities meet the criteria set out in paragraphs 10 and 12 and any relevant identifying information;

(h) to report at least every 90 days to the Security Council on its work and on the implementation of this resolution, with its observations and recommendations, in particular on ways to strengthen the effectiveness of the measures imposed by paragraphs 3, 4, 5, 6, 7, 8, 10 and 12 above;

19. *Decides* that all States shall report to the Committee within 60 days of the adoption of this resolution on the steps they have taken with a view to implementing effectively paragraphs 3, 4, 5, 6, 7, 8, 10, 12 and 17 above;

20. *Expresses* the conviction that the suspension set out in paragraph 2 above as well as full, verified Iranian compliance with the requirements set out by the IAEA Board of Governors, would contribute to a diplomatic, negotiated solution that guarantees Iran's nuclear programme is for exclusively peaceful purposes, *underlines* the willingness of the international community to work positively for such a solution, *encourages* Iran, in conforming to the above provisions, to re-engage with the international community and with the IAEA, and *stresses* that such engagement will be beneficial to Iran;

21. *Welcomes* the commitment of China, France, Germany, the Russian Federation, the United Kingdom and the United States, with the support of the European Union's High Representative, to a negotiated solution to this issue and encourages Iran to engage with their June 2006 proposals (S/2006/521), which were endorsed by the Security Council in

resolution 1696 (2006), for a long-term comprehensive agreement which would allow for the development of relations and cooperation with Iran based on mutual respect and the establishment of international confidence in the exclusively peaceful nature of Iran's nuclear programme;

22. *Reiterates* its determination to reinforce the authority of the IAEA, strongly supports the role of the IAEA Board of Governors, *commends* and *encourages* the Director General of the IAEA and its secretariat for their ongoing professional and impartial efforts to resolve all remaining outstanding issues in Iran within the framework of the IAEA, *underlines* the necessity of the IAEA continuing its work to clarify all outstanding issues relating to Iran's nuclear programme;

23. *Requests* within 60 days a report from the Director General of the IAEA on whether Iran has established full and sustained suspension of all activities mentioned in this resolution, as well as on the process of Iranian compliance with all the steps required by the IAEA Board and with the other provisions of this resolution, to the IAEA Board of Governors and in parallel to the Security Council for its consideration;

24. *Affirms* that it shall review Iran's actions in the light of the report referred to in paragraph 23 above, to be submitted within 60 days, and:

(a) that it shall suspend the implementation of measures if and for so long as Iran suspends all enrichment-related and reprocessing activities, including research and development, as verified by the IAEA, to allow for negotiations;

(b) that it shall terminate the measures specified in paragraphs 3, 4, 5, 6, 7, 10 and 12 of this resolution as soon as it determines that Iran has fully complied with its obligations under the relevant resolutions of the Security Council and met the requirements of the IAEA Board of Governors, as confirmed by the IAEA Board;

(c) that it shall, in the event that the report in paragraph 23 above shows that Iran has not complied with this resolution, adopt further appropriate measures under Article 41 of Chapter VII of the Charter of the United Nations to persuade Iran to comply with this resolution and the requirements of the IAEA, and underlines that further decisions will be required should such additional measures be necessary;

25. *Decides* to remain seized of the matter.

Annex

A. Entities involved in the nuclear programme

1. Atomic Energy Organisation of Iran
2. Mesbah Energy Company (provider for A40 research reactor — Arak)
3. Kala-Electric (aka Kalaye Electric) (provider for PFEP — Natanz)
4. Pars Trash Company (involved in centrifuge programme, identified in IAEA reports)
5. Farayand Technique (involved in centrifuge programme, identified in IAEA reports)

6. Defence Industries Organisation (overarching MODAFL-controlled entity, some of whose subordinates have been involved in the centrifuge programme making components, and in the missile programme)
7. 7th of Tir (subordinate of DIO, widely recognized as being directly involved in the nuclear programme)

B. Entities involved in the ballistic missile programme

1. Shahid Hemmat Industrial Group (SHIG) (subordinate entity of AIO)
2. Shahid Bagheri Industrial Group (SBIG) (subordinate entity of AIO)
3. Fajr Industrial Group (formerly Instrumentation Factory Plant, subordinate entity of AIO)

C. Persons involved in the nuclear programme

1. Mohammad Qannadi, AEOI Vice President for Research & Development
2. Behman Asgarpour, Operational Manager (Arak)
3. Dawood Agha-Jani, Head of the PFEP (Natanz)
4. Ehsan Monajemi, Construction Project Manager, Natanz
5. Jafar Mohammadi, Technical Adviser to the AEOI (in charge of managing the production of valves for centrifuges)
6. Ali Hajinia Leilabadi, Director General of Mesbah Energy Company
7. Lt Gen Mohammad Mehdi Nejad Nouri, Rector of Malek Ashtar University of Defence Technology (chemistry dept, affiliated to MODALF, has conducted experiments on beryllium)

D. Persons involved in the ballistic missile programme

1. Gen Hosein Salimi, Commander of the Air Force, IRGC (Pasdaran)
2. Ahmad Vahid Dastjerdi, Head of the AIO
3. Reza-Gholi Esmaeli, Head of Trade & International Affairs Dept, AIO
4. Bahmanyar Morteza Bahmanyar, Head of Finance & Budget Dept, AIO

E. Persons involved in both the nuclear and ballistic missile programmes

1. Maj Gen Yahya Rahim Safavi, Commander, IRGC (Pasdaran)

Resolution 1738 (2006)

Adopted by the Security Council at its 5613th meeting, on 23 December 2006

The Security Council,

Bearing in mind its primary responsibility under the Charter of the United Nations for the maintenance of international peace and security, and underlining the importance of taking measures aimed at conflict prevention and resolution,

Reaffirming its resolutions 1265 (1999), 1296 (2000) and 1674 (2006) on the protection of civilians in armed conflict and its resolution 1502 (2003) on protection of United Nations personnel, associated personnel and humanitarian personnel in conflict zones, as well as other relevant resolutions and presidential statements,

Reaffirming its commitment to the Purposes of the Charter of the United Nations as set out in Article 1 (1-4) of the Charter, and to the Principles of the Charter as set out in Article 2 (1-7) of the Charter, including its commitment to the principles of the political independence, sovereign equality and territorial integrity of all States, and respect for the sovereignty of all States,

Reaffirming that parties to an armed conflict bear the primary responsibility to take all feasible steps to ensure the protection of affected civilians,

Recalling the Geneva Conventions of 12 August 1949, in particular the Third Geneva Convention of 12 August 1949 on the treatment of prisoners of war, and the Additional Protocols of 8 June 1977, in particular article 79 of the Additional Protocol I regarding the protection of journalists engaged in dangerous professional missions in areas of armed conflict,

Emphasizing that there are existing prohibitions under international humanitarian law against attacks intentionally directed against civilians, as such, which in situations of armed conflict constitute war crimes, and *recalling* the need for States to end impunity for such criminal acts,

Recalling that the States Parties to the Geneva Conventions have an obligation to search for persons alleged to have committed, or to have ordered to be committed a grave breach of these Conventions, and an obligation to try them before their own courts, regardless of their nationality, or may hand them over for trial to another concerned State provided this State has made out a prima facie case against the said persons,

Drawing the attention of all States to the full range of justice and reconciliation mechanisms, including national, international and "mixed" criminal courts and tribunals and truth and reconciliation commissions, and *noting* that such mechanisms can promote not only individual responsibility for serious crimes, but also peace, truth, reconciliation and the rights of the victims,

Recognizing the importance of a comprehensive, coherent and action-oriented approach, including in early planning, of protection of civilians in situations of armed conflict. *Stressing*, in this regard, the need to adopt a broad strategy of conflict prevention, which addresses the root causes of armed conflict in a comprehensive manner in order to enhance the protection of civilians on a long-term basis, including by promoting sustainable development, poverty eradication, national reconciliation, good governance, democracy, the rule of law and respect for and protection of human rights,

Deeply concerned at the frequency of acts of violence in many parts of the world against journalists, media professionals and associated personnel in armed conflict, in particular deliberate attacks in violation of international humanitarian law,

Recognizing that the consideration of the issue of protection of journalists in armed conflict by the Security Council is based on the urgency and importance of this issue, and recognizing the valuable role that the Secretary-General can play in providing more information on this issue,

1. *Condemns* intentional attacks against journalists, media professionals and associated personnel, as such, in situations of armed conflict, and calls upon all parties to put an end to such practices;

2. *Recalls* in this regard that journalists, media professionals and associated personnel engaged in dangerous professional missions in areas of armed conflict shall be considered as civilians and shall be respected and protected as such, provided that they take no action adversely affecting their status as civilians. This is without prejudice to the right of war correspondents accredited to the armed forces to the status of prisoners of war provided for in article 4.A.4 of the Third Geneva Convention;

3. *Recalls* also that media equipment and installations constitute civilian objects, and in this respect shall not be the object of attack or of reprisals, unless they are military objectives;

4. *Reaffirms* its condemnation of all incitements to violence against civilians in situations of armed conflict, further reaffirms the need to bring to justice, in accordance with applicable international law, individuals who incite such violence, and indicates its willingness, when authorizing missions, to consider, where appropriate, steps in response to media broadcast inciting genocide, crimes against humanity and serious violations of international humanitarian law;

5. *Recalls its demand* that all parties to an armed conflict comply fully with the obligations applicable to them under international law related to the protection of civilians in armed conflict, including journalists, media professionals and associated personnel;

6. *Urges* States and all other parties to an armed conflict to do their utmost to prevent violations of international humanitarian law against civilians, including journalists, media professionals and associated personnel;

7. *Emphasizes* the responsibility of States to comply with the relevant obligations under international law to end impunity and to prosecute those responsible for serious violations of international humanitarian law;

8. *Urges* all parties involved in situations of armed conflict to respect the professional independence and rights of journalists, media professionals and associated personnel as civilians;

9. *Recalls* that the deliberate targeting of civilians and other protected persons, and the commission of systematic, flagrant and widespread violations of international humanitarian and human rights law in situations of armed conflict may constitute a threat to international peace and security, and *reaffirms in this regard its readiness* to consider such situations and, where necessary, to adopt appropriate steps;

10. *Invites* States which have not yet done so to consider becoming parties to the Additional Protocols I and II of 1977 to the Geneva Conventions at the earliest possible date;

11. *Affirms* that it will address the issue of protection of journalists in armed conflict strictly under the agenda item "protection of civilians in armed conflict";

12. *Requests* the Secretary-General to include as a sub-item in his next reports on the protection of civilians in armed conflict the issue of the safety and security of journalists, media professionals and associated personnel.

Resolution 1739 (2007)

Adopted by the Security Council at its 5617th meeting, on 10 January 2007

The Security Council,

Recalling its previous resolutions and the statements of its President relating to the situation in Côte d'Ivoire, in particular its resolution 1721 (2006) on the transition period leading to the holding of free, open, fair and transparent elections in Côte d'Ivoire by 31 October 2007,

Recalling also its resolution 1712 (2006) relating to the situation in Liberia,

Reaffirming its strong commitment to the sovereignty, independence, territorial integrity and unity of Côte d'Ivoire, and recalling the importance of the principles of good-neighbourliness, non-interference and regional cooperation,

Having taken note of the report of the Secretary-General dated 4 December 2006 (S/2006/939),

Reaffirming its support to the United Nations Operation in Côte d'Ivoire (UNOCI) and the French forces which support it,

Expressing its serious concern at the persistence of the crisis and the deterioration of the situation in Côte d'Ivoire, including its grave humanitarian consequences causing large-scale civilian suffering and displacement,

Determining that the situation in Côte d'Ivoire continues to pose a threat to international peace and security in the region,

Acting under Chapter VII of the Charter of the United Nations,

1. *Decides* that the mandates of UNOCI and of the French forces which support it, determined respectively in paragraphs 2 and 8 below, shall be extended until 30 June 2007, and expresses its intention to review by this date their mandates, including their length, and UNOCI's level of troops, in the light of the progress achieved in the implementation of the peace process as referred to in resolution 1721 (2006);

2. *Decides* that UNOCI shall have the following mandate from the date of adoption of this resolution:

(a) Monitoring of the cessation of hostilities and movements of armed groups

– To observe and monitor the implementation of the joint declaration of the end of the war of 6 April 2005 and of the comprehensive ceasefire agreement of 3 May

2003, to prevent, within its capabilities and its areas of deployment, any hostile action, and to investigate violations of the ceasefire,

– To liaise with the National Armed Forces of Côte d'Ivoire (FANCI) and the military elements of the Forces Nouvelles in order to promote, in coordination with the French forces, the re-establishment of trust among all the Ivorian forces involved,

– To assist the Government of Côte d'Ivoire in monitoring the borders, with particular attention to the situation of Liberian refugees and to any cross-border movement of combatants,

(b) Disarmament, demobilization, reintegration, repatriation and resettlement

– To assist the Government of Côte d'Ivoire in undertaking the regrouping of all the Ivorian forces involved and to assist in ensuring the security of their disarmament, cantonment and demobilization sites,

– To support the Government of Côte d'Ivoire, within UNOCI's current capacities, in the implementation of the national programme for the disarmament, demobilization and reintegration of combatants, including through logistical support, in particular for the preparation of cantonment sites, paying special attention to the specific needs of women and children,

– To coordinate closely with the United Nations Mission in Liberia (UNMIL) in the implementation of a voluntary repatriation and resettlement programme for foreign ex-combatants, paying special attention to the specific needs of women and children, in support of the efforts of the Government of Côte d'Ivoire and in cooperation with the Governments concerned, relevant international financial institutions, international development organizations and donor nations,

– To ensure that the national programme for the disarmament, demobilization and reintegration of combatants and that the voluntary repatriation and resettlement programme for foreign ex-combatants take into account the need for a coordinated regional approach,

– To secure, neutralize or destroy any weapons, ammunition or any other military materiel surrendered by the former combatants,

(c) Disarmament and dismantling of militias

– To assist the Prime Minister in formulating and implementing the programme for the immediate disarmament and dismantling of militias consistent with paragraph 12 of resolution 1721 (2006), and to monitor its implementation,

– To secure, neutralize or destroy all weapons, ammunition and other military materiel surrendered by militias,

(d) Operations of identification of the population and registration of voters

– To contribute, in close liaison with the working group mentioned in paragraph 17 of resolution 1721 (2006), to the security of the operations of identification of the population and registration of voters, within its capabilities and its areas of deployment,

(e) Reform of the security sector

– To assist, in close liaison with the working group mentioned in paragraph 15 of resolution 1721 (2006), in formulating a plan on the restructuring of the Defence and Security Forces and in preparing possible seminars on security sector reform to be organized by the African Union and ECOWAS,

(f) Protection of United Nations personnel, institutions and civilians

– To protect United Nations personnel, installations and equipment, ensure the security and freedom of movement of United Nations personnel and, without prejudice to the responsibility of the Government of Côte d'Ivoire, to protect civilians under imminent threat of physical violence, within its capabilities and its areas of deployment,

– To support, in coordination with the Prime Minister, the provision of security for members of the Government of Côte d'Ivoire,

(g) Monitoring of the arms embargo

– To monitor the implementation of the measures imposed by paragraph 7 of resolution 1572 (2004), in cooperation with the Group of Experts established under resolution 1584 (2005) and, as appropriate, with UNMIL and Governments concerned, including by inspecting, as they deem it necessary and without notice, the cargo of aircraft and of any transport vehicle using the ports, airports, airfields, military bases and border crossings of Côte d'Ivoire,

– To collect, as appropriate, arms and any related materiel brought into Côte d'Ivoire in violation of the measures imposed by paragraph 7 of resolution 1572 (2004), and to dispose of such arms and related materiel as appropriate,

(h) Support for humanitarian assistance

– To facilitate the free flow of people, goods and humanitarian assistance, inter alia, by helping to establish the necessary security conditions and taking into account the special needs of vulnerable groups, especially women, children and elderly people,

(i) Support for the redeployment of State administration

– To facilitate, with the assistance of the African Union, ECOWAS and other international partners, the re-establishment by the Government of Côte d'Ivoire of the authority of the State throughout Côte d'Ivoire and of the institutions and public services essential for the social and economic recovery of the country,

(j) Support for the organization of open, free, fair and transparent elections

– To provide all necessary technical assistance to the Prime Minister, his Government, the Independent Electoral Commission and other relevant agencies or institutes, with the support of the African Union, ECOWAS and other international partners, for the organization of open, free, fair and transparent elections, presidential and legislative, by 31 October 2007 at the latest, as referred to in resolution 1721 (2006),

– To provide technical information, advice and assistance as appropriate to the High Representative for the Elections,

– To contribute, within its capabilities and its areas of deployment, to the security of the areas where voting is to take place,

– To provide as necessary, within its capabilities and its areas of deployment, in close cooperation with the United Nations Programme for Development, logistical support for the Independent Electoral Commission, in particular for the transportation of electoral material,

(k) Assistance in the field of human rights

– To contribute to the promotion and protection of human rights in Côte d'Ivoire, with special attention to violence committed against children and women, to monitor and help investigate human rights violations with a view to ending impunity, and to keep the Security Council Committee established pursuant to paragraph 14 of resolution 1572 (2004) (the Committee) regularly informed of developments in this regard,

(l) Public information

– To promote the peace process as referred to in resolution 1721 (2006) throughout the territory of Côte d'Ivoire, through the Mission's public information capacity, in particular its radio broadcasting capability through ONUCI FM,

– To monitor the Ivorian mass media, in particular with regard to any incidents of incitement by the media to hatred, intolerance and violence, and to keep the Committee regularly informed of the situation in this regard,

(m) Law and order

– To assist the Government of Côte d'Ivoire in conjunction with the African Union, ECOWAS and other international organizations in restoring a civilian policing presence throughout Côte d'Ivoire, and to advise the Government of Côte d'Ivoire on the restructuring of the internal security services,

– To assist the Government of Côte d'Ivoire in conjunction with the African Union, ECOWAS and other international organizations in re-establishing the authority of the judiciary and the rule of law throughout Côte d'Ivoire,

– To support the Government of Côte d'Ivoire in ensuring the neutrality and impartiality of public media by providing, as necessary, security of the premises of the Radio Télévision Ivoirienne (RTI);

3. *Decides* to extend the provisions of paragraph 3 of resolution 1609 (2005) and of paragraph 2 of resolution 1682 (2006) for the period specified in paragraph 1 above;

4. *Reaffirms* its intention to authorize the Secretary-General to redeploy on a temporary basis troops between UNMIL and UNOCI as may be needed, in consultation with the Governments concerned and relevant troop-contributing countries, in accordance with the provisions of resolution 1609 (2005);

5. *Authorizes* UNOCI to use all necessary means to carry out its mandate, within its capabilities and its areas of deployment;

6. *Requests* UNOCI to carry out its mandate in close liaison with UNMIL, including especially in the prevention of movements of arms and combatants across shared borders and the implementation of disarmament and demobilization programmes;

7. *Urges* UNOCI to take into account the rights of women and of gender considerations as set out in Security Council resolution 1325 as a cross-cutting issue, including through consultation with local and international women's groups, and requests the Secretary-General, where appropriate, to include in his reporting to the Security Council progress on gender mainstreaming throughout UNOCI and all other aspects relating to the situation of women and girls, especially in relation to the need to protect them from gender-based violence;

8. *Authorizes* from the date of adoption of this resolution the French forces to use all necessary means in order to support UNOCI in accordance with the agreement reached between UNOCI and the French authorities, and in particular to:

(a) Contribute to the general security of the area of activity of the impartial forces,

(b) Intervene at the request of UNOCI in support of its elements whose security may be threatened,

(c) In consultation with UNOCI, intervene against belligerent actions, if the security conditions so require, outside UNOCI's areas of deployment,

(d) Help to protect civilians, in the deployment areas of their units,

(e) Contribute to monitoring the arms embargo established by resolution 1572 (2004),

(f) Contribute to the drawing up of a plan on the restructuring of the Defence and Security Forces and to the preparation of possible seminars on security sector reform to be organized by the African Union and ECOWAS;

9. *Calls upon* all parties to cooperate fully in the deployment and operations of UNOCI and of the French forces which support it, in particular by guaranteeing their safety, security and freedom of movement with unhindered and immediate access, as well as associated personnel, throughout the territory of Côte d'Ivoire, to enable them to carry out fully their mandates;

10. *Decides* to remain actively seized of the matter.

Resolution 1740 (2007)

Adopted by the Security Council at its 5622nd meeting, on 23 January 2007

The Security Council,

Welcoming the signing on 21 November by the Government of Nepal and the Communist Party of Nepal (Maoist) of a Comprehensive Peace Agreement, and the stated commitment of both parties to transforming the existing ceasefire into a permanent and sustainable peace and commending the steps taken to date to implement the Agreement,

Taking note of the request of the parties for United Nations assistance in implementing key aspects of the Agreement, in particular monitoring of arrangements relating to the management of arms and armed personnel of both sides and election monitoring,

Recalling the letter of the Secretary-General of 22 November 2006 (S/2006/920) and the statement of its President of 1 December (S/PRST/2006/49), and welcoming progress made in dispatching an advance deployment of monitors and electoral personnel to Nepal,

Recognizing the strong desire of the Nepalese people for peace and the restoration of democracy and the importance in this respect of the implementation of the Comprehensive Peace Agreement, and encouraging the parties to maintain that momentum,

Recognizing the need to pay special attention to the needs of women, children and traditionally marginalized groups in the peace process, as mentioned in the Comprehensive Peace Agreement,

Welcoming the Secretary-General's report of 9 January 2007 (S/2007/7) and having considered its recommendations, which are based on the request of the signatories of the Comprehensive Peace Agreement and the findings of the technical assessment mission,

Expressing its readiness to support the peace process in Nepal in the timely and effective implementation of the Comprehensive Peace Agreement,

Reaffirming the sovereignty, territorial integrity and political independence of Nepal and its ownership of the implementation of the Comprehensive Peace Agreement,

Expressing appreciation for the efforts of the Secretary-General and his Personal Representative, the United Nations Country Team including the Office of the High Commissioner for Human Rights and other United Nations representatives in Nepal,

1. *Decides* to establish a United Nations political mission in Nepal (UNMIN) under the leadership of a Special Representative of the Secretary-General and with the following mandate based on the recommendations of the Secretary-General in his report:

(a) To monitor the management of arms and armed personnel of both sides, in line with the provisions of the Comprehensive Peace Agreement;

(b) To assist the parties through a Joint Monitoring Coordinating Committee in implementing their agreement on the management of arms and armed personnel of both sides, as provided for in that agreement;

(c) To assist in the monitoring of the ceasefire arrangements;

(d) To provide technical support for the planning, preparation and conduct of the election of a Constituent Assembly in a free and fair atmosphere, in consultation with the parties;

(e) To provide a small team of electoral monitors to review all technical aspects of the electoral process, and report on the conduct of the election;

2. *Decides* that the mandate of UNMIN, in view of the particular circumstances, will be for a period of 12 months from the date of this resolution, and expresses its intention to terminate or further extend that mandate upon request of the Government of Nepal, taking into consideration the Secretary-General's expectation that UNMIN will be a focussed mission of limited duration;

3. *Welcomes* the Secretary-General's proposal that his Special Representative will coordinate the United Nations effort in Nepal in support of the peace process, in close consultation with the relevant parties in Nepal and in close cooperation with other international actors;

4. *Requests* the Secretary-General to keep the Council regularly informed of progress in implementing this resolution;

5. *Requests* the parties in Nepal to take the necessary steps to promote the safety, security and freedom of movement of UNMIN and associated personnel in executing the tasks defined in the mandate;

6. *Decides* to remain seized of the matter.

Resolution 1741 (2007)

Adopted by the Security Council at its 5626th meeting, on 30 January 2007

The Security Council,

Reaffirming all its previous resolutions and statements pertaining to the situation between Ethiopia and Eritrea (hereinafter referred to as "the parties") and the requirements contained therein, including in particular resolutions 1320 (2000), 1430 (2002), 1466 (2003), 1640 (2005), 1681 (2006) and 1710 (2006),

Stressing its unwavering commitment to the peace process, and to the full and expeditious implementation of the Algiers Agreements, and the importance of prompt implementation of the decision of the Eritrea-Ethiopia Boundary Commission (S/2002/423) as a basis for peaceful and cooperative relations between the parties,

Reaffirming the integrity of the Temporary Security Zone (TSZ) as provided for in the Agreement on Cessation of Hostilities of 18 June 2000 (S/2000/601) and recalling the objectives of its establishment and the commitment of the parties to respect the TSZ,

Commending the efforts made by the United Nations Mission in Ethiopia and Eritrea (UNMEE) and its military and civilian personnel to accomplish its duties, despite the difficult circumstances,

Stressing further that the full demarcation of the border between the two parties is vital to lasting peace between Ethiopia and Eritrea as well as in the region, recalling that both parties have agreed to accept the delimitation and demarcation determinations of the Eritrea-Ethiopia Boundary Commission (EEBC) as final and binding, commending the efforts of the EEBC to resume demarcation, and expressing its regret that the EEBC, for reasons beyond its control as explained in the Annexes of the report of the Secretary-General of 22 January 2007 (S/2007/33), has so far been unable to complete demarcation of the boundary as planned,

Expressing its full support for the work of the EEBC and acknowledging the Statement of the Eritrea-Ethiopia Boundary Commission (EEBC) of 27 November 2006,

Having considered the Special report of the Secretary-General of 15 December 2006 (S/2006/992) and the options on the future of UNMEE contained therein, and taking note of the report of the Secretary-General of 22 January 2007 (S/2007/33),

Recalling paragraph 7 of resolution 1710 (2006),

1. *Decides* to extend the mandate of UNMEE for a period of six months, until 31 July 2007;

2. *Approves* the reconfiguration of UNMEE's military component, from the current 2300 to 1700 military personnel, including 230 military observers, in accordance with option I, as described in paragraphs 24 and 25 of the Special report of the Secretary-General (S/2006/992), *decides* to maintain the current mandate and maximum authorized force levels, as stipulated in Resolution 1320 (2000) and further adjusted in Resolutions 1430 (2002) and 1681 (2006), and *stresses* the need to preserve sufficient military capacity for UNMEE to implement its mandate;

3. *Reiterates its demand* expressed in paragraph 5 of resolution 1640 (2005) that Ethiopia accept fully and without delay the final and binding decision of the Eritrea-Ethiopia Boundary Commission and take immediately concrete steps to enable, without preconditions, the Commission to demarcate the border completely and promptly;

4. *Demands* that Eritrea immediately withdraw its troops and equipment from the Temporary Security Zone;

5. *Reiterates its demand* expressed in paragraph 1 of resolution 1640 (2005) that Eritrea reverse, without further delay or preconditions, all restrictions on UNMEE's movement and operations, noting that these include the movement and operations of the acting SRSG, and provide UNMEE with the access, assistance, support and protection required for the performance of its duties;

6. *Reiterates its call* expressed in paragraph 2 of resolution 1640 (2005) that the parties show maximum restraint and refrain from any threat or use of force against each other;

7. *Regrets the lack* of progress on demarcation, *calls upon* both parties to cooperate fully with the EEBC, *stresses* that the parties have primary responsibility for the implementation of the Algiers Agreements, and *calls again upon* the parties to implement completely and without further delay or preconditions the decision of the EEBC and to take concrete steps to resume and complete the demarcation process;

8. *Demands* that the parties provide UNMEE with the necessary access, assistance, support and protection required for the performance of its duties, including its mandated task to assist the EEBC in the expeditious and orderly implementation of the Delimitation Decision, in accordance with Resolutions 1430 (2002) and 1466 (2003) and demands that any restrictions be lifted immediately;

9. *Calls upon* the Secretary-General and the international community to engage with Eritrea and Ethiopia to help them to normalize their relations, to promote stability between the parties, and to lay the foundation for sustainable peace in the region;

10. *Expresses* its willingness to reconsider any changes to UNMEE in light of subsequent progress toward demarcation, and its readiness to take further decisions to ensure that UNMEE will be able to facilitate demarcation as progress becomes possible;

11. *Calls* on Member States to provide contributions to the Trust Fund, established pursuant to Resolution 1177 (1998) and referred to in Article 4 (17) of the Comprehensive Peace Agreement signed by the Governments of Ethiopia and Eritrea on 12 December 2000, in order to support the demarcation process;

12. *Expresses* its deep appreciation for the contribution and dedication of the troop-contributing countries to the work of UNMEE;

13. *Requests* the Secretary-General to include in his next progress report due by the end of April 2007, details of the progress made towards the implementation of this Resolution and the implementation of the EEBC decision;

14. *Decides* to remain actively seized of the matter.

Resolution 1742 (2007)

Adopted by the Security Council at its 5630th meeting, on 15 February 2007

The Security Council,

Recalling its resolutions and the statements of its President concerning the Democratic Republic of the Congo,

Reaffirming its commitment to the sovereignty, territorial integrity and political independence of the Democratic Republic of the Congo,

Recalling the support it provided, in particular through the United Nations Organization Mission in the Democratic Republic of the Congo (MONUC), for the process of the Global and All Inclusive Agreement on the Transition, signed in Pretoria on 17 December 2002, and for the elections that represented the culmination of that process,

Reaffirming its commitment to continue to contribute to the consolidation of peace and stability in the Democratic Republic of the Congo in the post-transition period,

Underlining its attachment to the continuation of a regular political dialogue with the Congolese authorities, and *recalling* the importance it attaches to the consultations undertaken with them by the Secretary-General on possible adjustments to be made to the mandate and capacities of MONUC during this period,

Taking note of the letter addressed to its President on 15 January 2007 by the Permanent Representative of the Democratic Republic of the Congo (S/2007/17),

Noting that the situation in the Democratic Republic of the Congo continues to pose a threat to international peace and security in the region,

Acting under Chapter VII of the Charter of the United Nations,

1. *Decides* to extend the mandate and personnel strength of MONUC, as set out in its resolutions 1565 (2004), 1592 (2005), 1596 (2005), 1621 (2005), 1635 (2005) and 1736 (2006), until 15 April 2007;

2. *Requests* the Secretary-General to report, as soon as possible and not later than 15 March 2007, on his consultations with the Congolese authorities and to submit recommendations on adjustments the Council may consider making to the mandate and capacities of MONUC;

3. *Decides* to remain actively seized of the matter.

Resolution 1743 (2007)

Adopted by the Security Council at its 5631st meeting, on 15 February 2007

The Security Council,

Reaffirming its previous resolutions on Haiti, in particular its resolutions 1702 (2006), 1658 (2006), 1608 (2005), 1576 (2004) and 1542 (2004), as well as relevant statements by its President,

Reaffirming also its strong commitment to the sovereignty, independence, territorial integrity and unity of Haiti,

Welcoming the progress achieved in Haiti's political process, including through the successful holding of national, municipal and local elections in 2006 and reiterating its appeal to the Government of Haiti and all Haitians to continue to pursue all-inclusive political dialogue and national reconciliation in order to strengthen democratic governance,

Recognizing the interconnected nature of the challenges in Haiti, reaffirming that sustainable progress on security, rule of law and institutional reform, national reconciliation, and development are mutually reinforcing, and welcoming the continuing efforts of the Haitian Government and the international community to address these challenges,

Recognizing that respect for human rights, due process and addressing the issue of criminality and credible, competent, and transparent governance are essential to ensuring security in Haiti,

Expressing its appreciation to MINUSTAH, a key actor in the ongoing stabilization of the country, for continuing to assist the Government of Haiti to ensure a secure and stable environment, and welcoming the close collaboration that has developed in this regard,

Emphasizing the role of the regional organizations in the ongoing process of stabilization and reconstruction of Haiti and *calling* on MINUSTAH to continue to work closely with the Organization of the American States (OAS) and the Caribbean Community (CARICOM),

Emphasizing that a combination of measures are necessary to effectively disarm, demobilize, and reintegrate gang members and *encouraging* the Government of Haiti in coordination with the international community, to accelerate efforts towards this end,

Calling on the Haitian Government, in coordination with the international community, to maintain momentum behind security sector reform, in particular the Haitian National Police (HNP) Reform Plan, as well as efforts to reform the judiciary and correctional systems, including by addressing prolonged pretrial detentions and prison overcrowding, and by putting an end to impunity,

Encouraging the development by the Haitian authorities, with the support of donors and regional organizations, of permanent and effective electoral institutions,

Urging the Government of Haiti, in coordination with the international community, to establish a unified justice sector reform strategy encompassing merging of resources and joint planning,

Underlining the need for the quick implementation of highly effective and visible labour-intensive projects that help create jobs and deliver basic social services, and emphasizing the importance of quick-impact projects in the post-electoral phase,

Acknowledging the laudable work done by Haitian authorities and MINUSTAH to respond to the needs of disaster-affected people and welcoming future coordinated actions in this regard,

Expressing gratitude to the troops and police personnel of MINUSTAH and to their countries and paying tribute to those injured or killed in the line of duty,

Stressing that the Haitian people and their Government hold primary responsibility for achieving stability, social and economic development, and law and order in their country, and recognizing the commitment of the Government of Haiti to its people and to international partners,

Determining that the situation in Haiti continues to constitute a threat to international peace and security in the region, despite the progress achieved thus far,

Acting under Chapter VII of the Charter of the United Nations, as described in section 1 of operative paragraph 7 of resolution 1542 (2004),

1. *Decides* to extend the mandate of MINUSTAH as contained in its resolutions 1542 (2004), 1608 (2005) and 1702 (2006) until 15 October 2007 with the intention to renew for further periods;

2. *Welcomes* the Secretary-General's report S/2006/1003 of 19 December 2006, and takes note of its recommendations;

3. *Expresses* its full support for the Special Representative of the Secretary-General, notably in his efforts to improve the security situation in close cooperation with the Government of Haiti, and reaffirms his authority in the coordination and conduct of all activities of United Nations agencies, funds and programmes in Haiti;

4. *Recognizes* the ownership and primary responsibility of the Government of Haiti over all aspects of the country's stabilization and good governance and *recognizes* the role of MINUSTAH in supporting the Government's efforts in this regard, and encourages the Government of Haiti to continue to take full advantage of international support to enhance its capacity;

5. *Reaffirms* its call upon MINUSTAH to support the constitutional and political process under way in Haiti, including through its good offices and, in cooperation with the Government of Haiti, to promote all-inclusive political dialogue and national reconciliation;

6. *Welcomes* the continuing contribution by MINUSTAH to capacity and institution-building at all levels, and *calls upon* MINUSTAH, consistent with its mandate, to expand such support to strengthen State institutions, especially outside Port-au-Prince, including through the provision of specialized expertise to key ministries;

7. *Requests* that MINUSTAH continue the increased tempo of operations in support of the HNP against armed gangs as deemed necessary to restore security, notably in

Port-au-Prince, and encourages MINUSTAH and the Government of Haiti to undertake coordinated deterrent actions to decrease the level of violence;

8. *Requests also* the United Nations country team and calls upon the humanitarian and development actors, to complement security operations undertaken by the Government of Haiti with the support of MINUSTAH with activities aimed at effectively improving the living conditions of the concerned populations;

9. *Requests* MINUSTAH to continue to implement quick-impact projects;

10. *Requests*, in this context, MINUSTAH to accelerate efforts to reorient its disarmament, demobilization and reintegration resources towards a comprehensive community violence reduction programme as decided in resolution 1702 (2006), in close coordination with the Government of Haiti and other relevant actors;

11. *Deplores* and condemns in the strongest terms any attack against personnel from MINUSTAH and *demands* that no acts of intimidation or violence be directed against United Nations and associated personnel and other international and humanitarian organizations engaged in humanitarian, development or peacekeeping work;

12. *Reaffirms* MINUSTAH's mandate to provide operational support to the Haitian coast guard, and invites Member States, in coordination with MINUSTAH, to engage with the Government of Haiti to address cross-border illicit trafficking of drugs and arms, and other illegal activities;

13. *Welcomes* progress in the implementation of the HNP Reform Plan and *requests* MINUSTAH to remain engaged in assisting the Government of Haiti to reform and restructure the HNP, consistent with its mandate, including by increasing momentum behind the monitoring, mentoring, training, vetting of all police personnel and the strengthening of institutional capacities;

14. *Requests* MINUSTAH to provide necessary support for the Haitian authorities' efforts to reform the key elements of justice and the corrections sectors, closely synchronized with the plan for the reform and restructuring of the HNP, consistent with its mandate under resolution 1542 (2004) and as further decided in resolution 1702 (2006), and *encourages* the Government of Haiti to take full advantage of that support;

15. *Reaffirms* MINUSTAH's human rights mandate and calls on the Haitian authorities to continue their efforts to promote and protect human rights;

16. *Welcomes* MINUSTAH's policy to promote and protect the rights of women and to take into account gender considerations as set out in Security Council resolution 1325 as a cross-cutting issue throughout its mandate and keep the Council informed;

17. *Strongly condemns* the grave violations against children affected by armed violence, as well as widespread rape and other sexual abuse of girls;

18. *Underlines* the importance of continued assistance to help address the basic needs of Haiti's population and in that regard takes notes with appreciation of the Joint Communiqué of the International Conference for the Economic and Social Development for Haiti held in Madrid, Spain, on 30 November 2006, and encourages donors to accelerate the disbursement of their pledges as a contribution to development and stability in Haiti;

19. *Calls* on MINUSTAH to continue its efforts to enhance its coordination with the United Nations country team and the various development actors in Haiti in order to ensure greater efficiency in development efforts and to address urgent development problems;

20. *Calls* on the United Nations system and the international community, in particular donor countries, in cooperation with the Haitian authorities, to devise and support a renewed aid coordination system, which would focus on immediate needs as well as on long-term reconstruction and poverty reduction;

21. *Requests* MINUSTAH to maintain a proactive communications and public outreach strategy to improve public understanding of the mandate and the role of MINUSTAH in Haiti;

22. *Requests* the Secretary-General to continue to take the necessary measures to ensure full compliance of all MINUSTAH personnel with the United Nations zero-tolerance policy on sexual exploitation and abuse and to keep the Council informed, and urges troop-contributing countries to ensure that acts involving their personnel are properly investigated and punished;

23. *Requests* the Secretary-General to report to the Council on the implementation of MINUSTAH's mandate semi-annually but not later than 45 days prior to its expiration, and to include in his report a comprehensive assessment of the security risks, challenges and priorities facing Haiti, including specific recommendations on how to accelerate the peace-building process, build institutional capacity in the security and justice sectors, and achieve disarmament, demobilization, and reintegration in Haiti;

24. *Decides* to remain seized of the matter.

Resolution 1744 (2007)

Adopted by the Security Council at its 5633rd meeting,on 20 February 2007

The Security Council,

Recalling its previous resolutions concerning the situation in Somalia, in particular resolution 733 (1992), resolution 1356 (2001), resolution 1425 (2002) and resolution 1725 (2006), the statements of its President, in particular those of 13 July 2006 (S/PRST/2006/31) and 22 December 2006 (S/PRST/2006/59),

Reaffirming its respect for the sovereignty, territorial integrity, political independence and unity of Somalia,

Reiterating its commitment to a comprehensive and lasting settlement of the situation in Somalia through the Transitional Federal Charter, and stressing the importance of broad-based and representative institutions reached through an all-inclusive political process, as envisaged in the Transitional Federal Charter,

Reiterating its strong support for the Special Representative of the Secretary-General, Mr. François Fall,

Reiterating its appreciation of the efforts of the African Union, the League of Arab States and the Intergovernmental Authority on Development to promote peace, stability and reconciliation in Somalia, and *welcoming* their continued engagement in this regard,

Taking note of the communiqué of the African Union Peace and Security Council of 19 January 2007, which states that the African Union shall deploy for a period of six months a mission to Somalia (AMISOM), aimed essentially at contributing to the initial stabilization phase in Somalia, and that the mission will evolve into a United Nations operation that will support the long-term stabilization and post-conflict restoration of Somalia,

Welcoming the African Union's intention to establish a mission in Somalia and *underlining* the urgency of the development,

Welcoming the decision of Ethiopia to withdraw its troops from Somalia, *taking note* of the fact that Ethiopia has already started withdrawing its troops, and *underlining* that the deployment of AMISOM will help avoid a security vacuum and create the conditions for full withdrawal and the lifting of emergency security measures currently in place,

Reiterating its support for Somalia's Transitional Federal Institutions, *underlining* the importance of maintaining and providing stability and security throughout Somalia, and *underscoring* in this regard the importance of disarmament, demobilization and reintegration of militia and ex-combatants in Somalia,

Condemning all acts of violence and extremism inside Somalia, *deploring* the recent bombings in Mogadishu, and *expressing* its concern regarding the continued violence inside Somalia,

Determining that the situation in Somalia continues to constitute a threat to international peace and security in the region,

Acting under Chapter VII of the Charter of the United Nations,

1. *Stresses* the need for broad-based and representative institutions reached through an all-inclusive political process in Somalia, as envisaged in the Transitional Federal Charter, in order to consolidate stability, peace and reconciliation in the country and ensure that international assistance is as effective as possible;

2. *Welcomes* the initiative of the Transitional Federal Institutions to pursue an inclusive intra-Somali political process, particularly the announcement made by President Abdullahi Yusuf Ahmed at the African Union Summit of his intention to convene urgently a national reconciliation congress involving all stakeholders including political leaders, clan leaders, religious leaders, and representatives of civil society, *looks forward* to the sustained and all-inclusive political process that is needed as a result of that commitment and that will help pave the way to democratic elections at the local, regional and national levels as set out in Somalia's Transitional Federal Charter, and *encourages* those in the Transitional Federal Government and the other Transitional Federal Institutions to unite behind efforts to promote such an inclusive dialogue;

3. *Requests* the Secretary-General to assist the Transitional Federal Institutions with the national reconciliation congress, and, more widely, promoting an ongoing all-inclusive political process, working together with the African Union, the League of Arab States and the Intergovernmental Authority on Development, *requests* the Secretary-General to report back to the Security Council within sixty (60) days of adoption of this resolution on progress made by the Transitional Federal Institutions in pursuing an all-inclusive political process and reconciliation, and *reiterates its intention* to consider taking measures against those who seek to prevent or block a peaceful political process, threaten the Transitional

Federal Institutions by force, or take action that undermines stability in Somalia or the region;

4. *Decides* to authorize member States of the African Union to establish for a period of six months a mission in Somalia, which shall be authorized to take all necessary measures as appropriate to carry out the following mandate:

(a) To support dialogue and reconciliation in Somalia by assisting with the free movement, safe passage and protection of all those involved with the process referred to in paragraphs 1, 2 and 3;

(b) To provide, as appropriate, protection to the Transitional Federal Institutions to help them carry out their functions of government, and security for key infrastructure;

(c) To assist, within its capabilities, and in coordination with other parties, with implementation of the National Security and Stabilization Plan, in particular the effective re-establishment and training of all-inclusive Somali security forces;

(d) To contribute, as may be requested and within capabilities, to the creation of the necessary security conditions for the provision of humanitarian assistance;

(e) To protect its personnel, facilities, installations, equipment and mission, and to ensure the security and freedom of movement of its personnel;

5. *Urges* member States of the African Union to contribute to the above mission in order to create the conditions for the withdrawal of all other foreign forces from Somalia;

6. *Decides* that the measures imposed by paragraph 5 of resolution 733 (1992) and further elaborated in paragraphs 1 and 2 of resolution 1425 (2002) shall not apply to:

(a) Supplies of weapons and military equipment, technical training and assistance intended solely for the support of or use by the mission referred to in paragraph 4 above; or

(b) Such supplies and technical assistance by States intended solely for the purpose of helping develop security sector institutions, consistent with the political process set out in paragraphs 1, 2 and 3 above and in the absence of a negative decision by the Committee established pursuant to resolution 751 (1992) within five working days of receiving the notification described in paragraph 7 below;

7. *Decides* that States providing supplies or technical assistance in accordance with paragraph 6 (b) above shall notify the Committee established pursuant to resolution 751 (1992) in advance and on a case-by-case basis;

8. *Urges* Member States to provide personnel, equipment and services if required, for the successful deployment of AMISOM, and *encourages* Member States to provide financial resources for AMISOM;

9. *Requests* the Secretary-General to send a Technical Assessment Mission to the African Union headquarters and Somalia as soon as possible to report on the political and security situation and the possibility of a UN Peacekeeping Operation following the AU's deployment, and to report to the Security Council within sixty (60) days of the adoption of this resolution with recommendations covering the UN's further engagement in support of

peace and security in Somalia, as well as further recommendations on stabilization and reconstruction;

10. *Emphasizes* the continued contribution made to Somalia's peace and security by the arms embargo, *demands* that all Member States, in particular those of the region, fully comply with it, and *reiterates* its intention to consider urgently ways to strengthen its effectiveness, including through targeted measures in support of the arms embargo;

11. *Expresses its deep concern* over the humanitarian situation in Somalia, demands that all parties in Somalia ensure complete and unhindered humanitarian access, as well as providing guarantees for the safety and security of humanitarian aid workers in Somalia, and *welcomes* and *encourages* the ongoing relief efforts in Somalia;

12. *Decides* that, having regard to the establishment of AMISOM, the measures contained in paragraphs 3 to 7 of resolution 1725 (2006) shall no longer apply;

13. *Decides* to remain actively seized of the matter.

Resolution 1745 (2007)

Adopted by the Security Council at its 5634th meeting, on 22 February 2007

The Security Council,

Reaffirming all its previous resolutions and statements on the situation in Timor-Leste, in particular its resolutions 1599 (2005) of 28 April 2005, 1677 (2006) of 12 May 2006, 1690 (2006) of 20 June 2006, 1703 (2006) of 18 August 2006 and 1704 (2006) of 25 August 2006,

Welcoming the report of the Secretary-General of 1 February 2007 (S/2007/50),

Reaffirming its full commitment to the sovereignty, independence, territorial integrity, national unity of Timor-Leste and the promotion of long-term stability in the country,

Commending the people and the Government of Timor-Leste for their continued action to resolve their political challenges and other steps taken towards national dialogue and political reconciliation, and *encouraging* all parties to redouble their efforts in this regard,

Reaffirming the need for respect for the independence of the judiciary and its responsibility and *welcoming* the conviction of the leaders of Timor-Leste on the need for justice and their determination to act against impunity,

Expressing its concern over the still fragile and volatile security, political, social and humanitarian situation in Timor-Leste and *welcoming* initial efforts made in the security sector,

Taking note of a joint letter dated 7 December 2006 addressed to the Secretary-General (S/2006/1022) from President Gusmao, Prime Minister Ramos-Horta and National Parliament President Guterres, requesting that the United Nations Integrated Mission in Timor-Leste (UNMIT) be reinforced with an additional Formed Police Unit (FPU),

Reiterating its view that the forthcoming presidential and parliamentary elections will be a significant step in the process of strengthening democracy in Timor-Leste,

Welcoming the adoption of the laws on the National Commission on Elections, as well as on the Parliamentary and Presidential Elections, and *encouraging* additional steps, including amendments deemed necessary, implementation of an appropriate regulatory framework, and logistical preparations to be undertaken with the assistance of UNMIT,

Further welcoming the passing by the Parliament of Timor-Leste on 9 January 2007, of a resolution, which adopted the recommendations of the Independent Special Commission of Inquiry and the additional recommendations of the Ad Hoc Parliamentary Commission and *noting* the action taken to date by the Government of Timor-Leste, including a number of judicial proceedings in relation to the events of April and May 2006, and *further noting* the need for continued efforts to implement the recommendations of the Commission of Inquiry,

Stressing the need to implement fully the "Arrangement on the Restoration and Maintenance of Public Security in Timor-Leste and Assistance to the Reform, Restructuring and Rebuilding of PNTL and the Ministry of Interior", concluded between the Government of Timor-Leste and UNMIT on 1 December 2006,

Expressing its full support for the continued deployment of the international security force in response to the requests of the Government of Timor-Leste, and their activities to support UNMIT in the restoration and maintenance of law and stability,

Noting with appreciation the signing of a Memorandum of Understanding between the Government of Timor-Leste, the United Nations and the Government of Australia on 26 January 2007 that established a Trilateral Coordination Forum to enhance security activities,

Recalling that, while the manifestations of the current challenges in Timor-Leste are political and institutional in nature, poverty and its associated deprivations also contributed to these challenges, *paying tribute* to Timor-Leste's bilateral and multilateral partners for their invaluable assistance, particularly with regard to institutional capacity-building and social and economic development, and *recognizing* the progress being made in the development of many aspects of governance in Timor-Leste,

Welcoming the Agreement between the Government of Timor-Leste and the United Nations Development Programme to provide, with donor support, technical support for enhancing transparency and anti-corruption measures,

Taking note of the launching on 17 January 2007 of a Consolidated Appeal Process (CAP) to respond to the remaining humanitarian and ongoing protection needs for a period of six months beyond December 2006, including providing humanitarian assistance to internally displaced persons in order to facilitate their return, relocation and reintegration,

Reaffirming its resolutions 1325 (2000) on women, peace and security and 1502 (2003) on the protection of humanitarian and United Nations personnel,

Expressing its appreciation for the efforts of UNMIT and the United Nations Country Team, under the leadership of the Special Representative of the Secretary-General,

1. *Decides* to extend the mandate of UNMIT until 26 February 2008;

2. *Decides* to increase UNMIT's authorized force strength by up to 140 police personnel in order to permit the deployment of an additional formed police unit to supplement the existing FPUs particularly during the pre- and post-electoral period;

3. *Welcomes* the signing of the military technical arrangement between the United Nations and Australia on 25 January 2007 under which the international security force ensures protection of United Nations premises and properties as well as a rapid response capacity for the UNMIT police;

4. *Calls upon* the Government of Timor-Leste, assisted by UNMIT, to continue working on a comprehensive review of future role and needs of the security sector including the Ministry of Interior, PNTL, Ministry of Defence, and F-FDTL;

5. *Emphasizes* the need for regular meetings and information sharing and, in that regard, *welcomes* the establishment of a Trilateral Coordination Forum, with participants from the Government of Timor-Leste, UNMIT and the international security force, in order to maintain coordination;

6. *Calls upon* all parties in Timor-Leste to adhere to the principles of non-violence and to democratic and legal processes to ensure that the upcoming elections have a unifying impact and contribute to bringing the people of Timor-Leste together and *encourages* all Timorese parties to ensure that free, fair and peaceful elections take place and that the timetable for polls developed by the National Commission on Elections is respected;

7. *Takes note* of the work of the United Nations Independent Certification Team, *encourages* the implementation of its key recommendations to ensure credibility of the electoral process, and *further encourages* the international community to assist in this process including through electoral observation;

8. *Calls upon* all parties in Timor-Leste, and in particular political leaders, to continue to work together in a spirit of cooperation and compromise in order to consolidate progress made by Timor-Leste in recent years and to enable the country to move to a peaceful and more prosperous future;

9. *Emphasizes* the importance of ongoing efforts to reach accountability and justice for the events of 1999 and April through May 2006, including follow-up to the Independent Special Commission of Inquiry report and, in this regard, *encourages* UNMIT's sustained efforts to support national dialogue, political reconciliation and the strengthening of the justice system;

10. *Calls upon* UNMIT to continue to cooperate and coordinate with the United Nations agencies, funds and programmes as well as all relevant partners to support the Government of Timor-Leste and relevant institutions and in designing poverty reduction and economic growth policies;

11. *Urges* the development partners including the United Nations agencies and multilateral financial institutions to continue providing resources and assistance for the preparations for the upcoming elections, other projects towards sustainable development and *calls upon* the international donor community to consider contributing generously towards the 2007 Consolidated Appeal for Timor-Leste;

12. *Requests* UNMIT fully to take into account gender considerations as set out in Security Council resolution 1325 as a cross-cutting issue throughout its mandate, and *further requests* the Secretary-General to include in his reporting to the Security Council progress on gender mainstreaming throughout UNMIT and all other aspects relating to the situation of women and girls, especially in relation to the need to protect them from gender-based violence;

13. *Requests* the Secretary-General to continue to take the necessary measures to ensure full compliance in UNMIT with the United Nations zero-tolerance policy on sexual exploitation and abuse and to keep the Council informed, and urges those countries contributing troops and police to take appropriate preventive action and to ensure full accountability in cases of such conduct involving their personnel;

14. *Further requests* the Secretary-General to keep the Council closely and regularly informed of developments on the ground, in particular the state of preparations for the upcoming elections and the security situation and to submit a report which includes recommendations for possible adjustments in UNMIT's mandate and strength to the Security Council within 60 days after the Presidential and Parliamentary elections in Timor-Leste, and to submit a report no later than 45 days before the expiration of the current mandate and to submit further reports as and when he considers appropriate;

15. *Decides* to remain seized of the matter.

Resolution 1746 (2007)

Adopted by the Security Council at its 5645th meeting on 23 March 2007

The Security Council,

Recalling its previous resolutions on Afghanistan, in particular its resolution 1662 (2006) extending through 23 March 2007 the mandate of the United Nations Assistance Mission in Afghanistan (UNAMA) as laid out in the report of the Secretary-General of 7 March 2006 (S/2006/145), and its resolution 1659 (2006) endorsing the Afghanistan Compact, and *recalling also* the report of the Security Council mission to Afghanistan, 11 to 16 November 2006 (S/2006/935),

Reaffirming its strong commitment to the sovereignty, independence, territorial integrity and national unity of Afghanistan,

Reaffirming its continued support for the Government and people of Afghanistan as they rebuild their country, strengthen the foundations of sustainable peace and constitutional democracy and assume their rightful place in the community of nations,

Reaffirming in this context its support for the implementation, under the ownership of the Afghan people, of the Afghanistan Compact, of the Afghanistan National Development Strategy (ANDS) and of the National Drugs Control Strategy, and *noting* that sustained efforts by all relevant actors are required to consolidate progress made towards their implementation and to overcome current challenges,

Recalling that the Afghanistan Compact is based on a partnership between the Afghan Government and the international community, with a central and impartial coordinating role for the United Nations,

Recognizing once again the interconnected nature of the challenges in Afghanistan, *reaffirming* that sustainable progress on security, governance and development, as well as the cross-cutting issue of counter-narcotics is mutually reinforcing and *welcoming* the continuing efforts of the Afghan Government and the international community to address these challenges in a coherent manner through the comprehensive framework provided by the Afghanistan Compact,

Noting, in the context of a comprehensive approach, the synergies in the objectives of UNAMA and of the International Security Assistance Force (ISAF), and *stressing* the need for continued cooperation and coordination, taking due account of their respective designated responsibilities,

Reiterating its concern about the security situation in Afghanistan, in particular the increased violent and terrorist activities by the Taliban, Al-Qaida, illegally armed groups and those involved in the narcotics trade, and the links between terrorism activities and illicit drugs, resulting in threats to the local population, national security forces and international military and civilian personnel, and *stressing* the importance of the security and safety of the United Nations and associated personnel,

Expressing also its concern over the harmful consequences of the insurgency on the capacity of the Afghan Government to provide security and basic services to the Afghan people, and to ensure the full enjoyment of their human rights and fundamental freedoms,

Recalling the importance of the Kabul Declaration of 22 December 2002 on Good-Neighbourly Relations (Kabul Declaration) (S/2002/1416), *welcoming* the New Delhi Declaration adopted at the Second Regional Economic Cooperation Conference on Afghanistan on 19 November 2006, *looking forward* to the Third Regional Economic Cooperation Conference on Afghanistan to be held in Islamabad, Pakistan in 2007, and *stressing* the crucial importance to all parties of advancing regional cooperation as an effective means to promote security, governance and development in Afghanistan,

Recalling its resolutions 1265 (1999), 1296 (2000), 1674 (2006), 1738 (2006) on the protection of civilians in armed conflict and its resolution 1325 (2000) on women and peace and security,

Stressing the central and impartial role that the United Nations continues to play in promoting peace and stability in Afghanistan by leading the efforts of the international community, including, jointly with the Government of Afghanistan, the coordination and monitoring of efforts in implementing the Afghanistan Compact, and *expressing* its appreciation and strong support for the ongoing efforts of the Secretary-General, his Special Representative for Afghanistan and the women and men of UNAMA,

1. *Welcomes* the report of the Secretary-General of 15 March 2007 (S/2007/152);

2. *Expresses its appreciation* for the United Nations long-term commitment to work with the Government and the people of Afghanistan;

3. *Decides* to extend the mandate of UNAMA, as established by resolution 1662 (2006), until 23 March 2008;

4. *Stresses* the role of UNAMA to promote a more coherent international engagement in support of Afghanistan, to extend its good offices through outreach in Afghanistan, to

support regional cooperation in the context of the Afghanistan Compact, to promote humanitarian coordination and to continue to contribute to human rights protection and promotion, including monitoring of the situation of civilians in armed conflict;

5. *Welcomes* UNAMA's expanded presence in the provinces, through regional and provincial offices, which support efforts at the central level to coordinate and monitor the implementation of the Afghanistan Compact and assist the efforts of the Government of Afghanistan and its international partners in improving the delivery of services to Afghan citizens throughout the country, and *encourages* further progress in this regard, including in the southern and eastern provinces, security circumstances permitting;

6. *Reiterates* its call on the Afghan Government, and on all members of the international community and international organizations, to implement the Afghanistan Compact and its annexes in full;

7. *Emphasizes* the importance of meeting the benchmarks and timelines of the Compact for the progress on security, governance and development as well as the cross-cutting issue of counter-narcotics and of increasing the effectiveness and coordination of the assistance to Afghanistan;

8. *Acknowledges* the central role played by the Joint Coordination and Monitoring Board in facilitating and monitoring the implementation of the Compact, stresses the role of the JCMB to support Afghanistan by, inter alia, coordinating international assistance and reconstruction programmes, *encourages* efforts to strengthen the JCMB Secretariat, *welcomes* the results of the JCMB meeting at senior officials level held in Berlin on 30 and 31 January 2007, and *encourages* further efforts to provide appropriate high level political guidance and promote a more coherent international engagement;

9. *Calls* on all Afghan parties and groups to engage constructively in an inclusive political dialogue, within the framework of the Afghan Constitution and Afghan-led reconciliation programmes, and in the social development of the country, and *stresses* the importance of these factors to enhance security and stability;

10. *Stresses* the need for further progress on security sector reform, inter alia in order to advance towards the goal of ethnically balanced Afghan security forces providing security and ensuring the rule of law throughout the country, *welcomes* in this regard the ongoing efforts to increase functionality, professionalism and accountability of the security sector, including the Afghan National Army and the Afghan National Police, including the recent proposed contributions by the United States and other partners, and *calls for* proper monitoring of the deployment of the Auxiliary Police to ensure its accountability to central authorities;

11. *Welcomes* the decision by the European Union to establish a mission in the field of policing with linkages to the wider rule of law and counter narcotics, to assist and enhance current efforts in the area of police reform at central and provincial levels, and looks forward to the early launch of the mission;

12. *Welcomes* the successful conclusion of the disarmament, demobilization and reintegration (DDR) process started in October 2003, as well as the launch of the programme of disbandment of illegal armed groups (DIAG) and the commitments made in this regard at the Second Tokyo Conference on Consolidation of Peace in Afghanistan on 5 July 2006,

calls for determined efforts by the Afghan Government to pursue at all levels the timely implementation of the programme throughout the country, including through the implementation of the newly adopted Action Plan, and *requests* the international community to extend further assistance to these efforts, taking fully into account the guidance by UNAMA;

13. *Stresses* the need for accelerated progress in the implementation of the 10-year strategy for justice reform in the framework of the Afghanistan Compact, including through definition of responsibilities and provision of adequate resources, *invites* the Afghan Government, with the assistance of the international community, to continue to work towards the establishment of a fair and transparent justice system, including the reconstruction and reform of the correctional system, in order to strengthen the rule of law throughout the country and eliminate impunity, and *takes note* with interest of the initiative to organize in Rome a Conference on Rule of Law in Afghanistan to enhance Afghan and international commitment to justice sector reform;

14. *Welcomes* the continued efforts by the Afghan authorities to promote legislative reform, and stresses the importance of international support for capacity-building in such reform and its implementation;

15. *Welcomes* the establishment of the provincial councils in accordance with the Afghan Constitution, *encourages* all institutions to work in a spirit of cooperation, *calls on* the Afghan Government to pursue continued public administrative reform in order to ensure good governance, full representation and accountability at both national and local levels, and *stresses* the need for further international efforts to provide technical assistance in this regard, particularly at the local level;

16. *Calls upon* the Afghan Government, with support from the international community, to begin planning and preparation for Afghanistan's next election cycle, including the establishment of a permanent Civil Voter Registry (CVR) as called for in the Afghanistan Compact, the passage and implementation of an updated Election Law, and financial and political support for the Independent Election Commission (IEC) to ensure that it possesses the resources needed, and to ensure that Afghanistan is set on the path to the creation of affordable and sustainable systems that will contribute to free, fair and transparent elections;

17. *Notes with concern* the effects of widespread corruption on security, good governance and counter-narcotics efforts, and *calls on* the Afghan Government, with the assistance of the international community, to vigorously lead the fight against corruption and to sustain its efforts to establish a more effective, accountable and transparent administration, and *welcomes* recent steps by the Afghan Government in this regard;

18. *Calls for* full respect for human rights and international humanitarian law throughout Afghanistan; *requests* UNAMA, with the support of the Office of the United Nations High Commissioner for Human Rights, to continue to assist in the full implementation of the human rights provisions of the Afghan Constitution and international treaties to which Afghanistan is a state party, in particular those regarding the full enjoyment by women of their human rights; *commends* the Afghan Independent Human Rights Commission for its courageous efforts to monitor respect for human rights in Afghanistan as well as to foster and protect these rights;

19. *Stresses* the importance of the ongoing process of national reconciliation undertaken by the Government of Afghanistan and *encourages* the full and timely implementation, with international support, of the Action Plan on Peace, Justice and Reconciliation in accordance with the Afghanistan Compact, without prejudice to the implementation of measures introduced by the Security Council in its resolution 1267 (1999) of 15 October 1999 and other relevant resolutions of the Security Council;

20. *Welcomes* the cooperation of the Afghan Government and UNAMA with the Security Council's Committee established pursuant to resolution 1267 (1999) with the implementation of resolution 1735 (2006), and *encourages* the continuation of such cooperation;

21. *Welcomes* the progress made in the implementation of the ANDS, stresses the need for continued leadership by the Afghan Government in its implementation, and encourages the participants at the London Conference to continue to fulfil and consider increasing their pledges, including financial assistance for the implementation of the Strategy;

22. *Expresses* its concern at the serious harm that increasing opium cultivation, production and trafficking causes to the security, development and governance of Afghanistan as well as to the region and internationally; *calls on* the Afghan Government, with the assistance of the international community, to pursue effective implementation of the National Drug Control Strategy; and encourages additional international support for the four priorities identified in that Strategy, *including* through contributions to the Counter Narcotics Trust Fund and continued regional cooperation for the fight against the illicit trafficking in drugs and precursors and against money-laundering linked to such trafficking;

23. *Welcomes* the outcome of the Second Ministerial Conference on Drug Trafficking Routes from Afghanistan organized by the Government of the Russian Federation in cooperation with the United Nations Office on Drugs and Crime held in Moscow from 26 to 28 June 2006 (S/2006/598), within the framework of the Paris Pact initiative, and *calls upon* States to strengthen international and regional cooperation to counter the threat to the international community posed by the illicit production and trafficking of drugs originated in Afghanistan;

24. *Calls upon* all Afghan and international parties to continue to cooperate with UNAMA in the implementation of its mandate and in efforts to promote the security and freedom of movement of United Nations and associated personnel throughout the country;

25. *Calls upon* the Afghan Government, with the assistance of the international community, including the International Security Assistance Force and Operation Enduring Freedom coalition, in accordance with their respective designated responsibilities as they evolve, to continue to address the threat to the security and stability of Afghanistan posed by the Taliban, Al-Qaida, other extremist groups and criminal activities, welcomes the completion of ISAF's expansion throughout Afghanistan and *calls upon* all parties to uphold international humanitarian and human rights law and to ensure the protection of civilian life;

26. *Welcomes* the ongoing efforts by the Government of Afghanistan and its neighbouring and regional partners to foster trust and cooperation with each other, stresses the importance of increasing cooperation between Afghanistan and the partners against the Taliban, Al-Qaida and other extremist groups, in promoting peace and prosperity in Afghanistan and in fostering cooperation in the economic and development sectors as a means to achieve the full integration of Afghanistan into regional dynamics and the global economy, and further *welcomes* progress in this regard;

27. *Recognizes* the importance of voluntary, safe, orderly return and sustainable reintegration of the remaining Afghan refugees for the stability of the country and the region, and calls for continued and enhanced international assistance in this regard;

28. *Requests* the Secretary-General to report to the Council every six months on developments in Afghanistan;

29. *Decides* to remain actively seized of the matter.

Resolution 1747 (2007)

Adopted by the Security Council at its 5647th meeting on 24 March 2007

The Security Council,

Recalling the Statement of its President, S/PRST/2006/15, of 29 March 2006, and its resolution 1696 (2006) of 31 July 2006, and its resolution 1737 (2006) of 23 December 2006, and *reaffirming* their provisions,

Reaffirming its commitment to the Treaty on the Non-Proliferation of Nuclear Weapons, the need for all States Party to that Treaty to comply fully with all their obligations, and recalling the right of States Party, in conformity with Articles I and II of that Treaty, to develop research, production and use of nuclear energy for peaceful purposes without discrimination,

Recalling its serious concern over the reports of the IAEA Director General as set out in its resolutions 1696 (2006) and 1737 (2006),

Recalling the latest report by the IAEA Director General (GOV/2007/8) of 22 February 2007 and *deploring* that, as indicated therein, Iran has failed to comply with resolution 1696 (2006) and resolution 1737 (2006),

Emphasizing the importance of political and diplomatic efforts to find a negotiated solution guaranteeing that Iran's nuclear programme is exclusively for peaceful purposes, and *noting* that such a solution would benefit nuclear non-proliferation elsewhere, and *welcoming* the continuing commitment of China, France, Germany, the Russian Federation, the United Kingdom and the United States, with the support of the European Union's High Representative to seek a negotiated solution,

Recalling the resolution of the IAEA Board of Governors (GOV/2006/14), which states that a solution to the Iranian nuclear issue would contribute to global non-proliferation efforts and to realizing the objective of a Middle East free of weapons of mass destruction, including their means of delivery,

Determined to give effect to its decisions by adopting appropriate measures to persuade Iran to comply with resolution 1696 (2006) and resolution 1737 (2006) and with the requirements of the IAEA, and also to constrain Iran's development of sensitive technologies in support of its nuclear and missile programmes, until such time as the Security Council determines that the objectives of these resolutions have been met,

Recalling the requirement on States to join in affording mutual assistance in carrying out the measures decided upon by the Security Council,

Concerned by the proliferation risks presented by the Iranian nuclear programme and, in this context, by Iran's continuing failure to meet the requirements of the IAEA Board of Governors and to comply with the provisions of Security Council resolutions 1696 (2006) and 1737 (2006), *mindful* of its primary responsibility under the Charter of the United Nations for the maintenance of international peace and security,

Acting under Article 41 of Chapter VII of the Charter of the United Nations,

1. *Reaffirms* that Iran shall without further delay take the steps required by the IAEA Board of Governors in its resolution GOV/2006/14, which are essential to build confidence in the exclusively peaceful purpose of its nuclear programme and to resolve outstanding questions, and, in this context, *affirms* its decision that Iran shall without further delay take the steps required in paragraph 2 of resolution 1737 (2006);

2. *Calls upon* all States also to exercise vigilance and restraint regarding the entry into or transit through their territories of individuals who are engaged in, directly associated with or providing support for Iran's proliferation sensitive nuclear activities or for the development of nuclear weapon delivery systems, and *decides* in this regard that all States shall notify the Committee established pursuant to paragraph 18 of resolution 1737 (2006) (herein "the Committee") of the entry into or transit through their territories of the persons designated in the Annex to resolution 1737 (2006) or Annex I to this resolution, as well as of additional persons designated by the Security Council or the Committee as being engaged in, directly associated with or providing support for Iran's proliferation sensitive nuclear activities or for the development of nuclear weapon delivery systems, including through the involvement in procurement of the prohibited items, goods, equipment, materials and technology specified by and under the measures in paragraphs 3 and 4 of resolution 1737 (2006), except where such travel is for activities directly related to the items in subparagraphs 3 (b) (i) and (ii) of that resolution;

3. *Underlines* that nothing in the above paragraph requires a State to refuse its own nationals entry into its territory, and that all States shall, in the implementation of the above paragraph, take into account humanitarian considerations, including religious obligations, as well as the necessity to meet the objectives of this resolution and resolution 1737 (2006), including where Article XV of the IAEA Statute is engaged;

4. *Decides* that the measures specified in paragraphs 12, 13, 14 and 15 of resolution 1737 (2006) shall apply also to the persons and entities listed in Annex I to this resolution;

5. *Decides* that Iran shall not supply, sell or transfer directly or indirectly from its territory or by its nationals or using its flag vessels or aircraft any arms or related materiel, and that all States shall prohibit the procurement of such items from Iran by their nationals, or using their flag vessels or aircraft, and whether or not originating in the territory of Iran;

6. *Calls upon* all States to exercise vigilance and restraint in the supply, sale or transfer directly or indirectly from their territories or by their nationals or using their flag vessels or aircraft of any battle tanks, armoured combat vehicles, large calibre artillery systems, combat aircraft, attack helicopters, warships, missiles or missile systems as defined for the purpose of the United Nations Register on Conventional Arms to Iran, and in the provision to Iran of any technical assistance or training, financial assistance, investment, brokering or other services, and the transfer of financial resources or services, related to the supply,

sale, transfer, manufacture or use of such items in order to prevent a destabilizing accumulation of arms;

7. *Calls upon* all States and international financial institutions not to enter into new commitments for grants, financial assistance, and concessional loans, to the Government of the Islamic Republic of Iran, except for humanitarian and developmental purposes;

8. *Calls upon* all States to report to the Committee within 60 days of the adoption of this resolution on the steps they have taken with a view to implementing effectively paragraphs 2, 4, 5, 6 and 7 above;

9. Expresses the conviction that the suspension set out in paragraph 2 of resolution 1737 (2006) as well as full, verified Iranian compliance with the requirements set out by the IAEA Board of Governors would contribute to a diplomatic, negotiated solution that guarantees Iran's nuclear programme is for exclusively peaceful purposes, *underlines* the willingness of the international community to work positively for such a solution, *encourages* Iran, in conforming to the above provisions, to re-engage with the international community and with the IAEA, and stresses that such engagement will be beneficial to Iran;

10. *Welcomes* the continuous affirmation of the commitment of China, France, Germany, the Russian Federation, the United Kingdom and the United States, with the support of the European Union's High Representative, to a negotiated solution to this issue and *encourages* Iran to engage with their June 2006 proposals (S/2006/521), attached in Annex II to this resolution, which were endorsed by the Security Council in resolution 1696 (2006), and *acknowledges* with appreciation that this offer to Iran remains on the table, for a long-term comprehensive agreement which would allow for the development of relations and cooperation with Iran based on mutual respect and the establishment of international confidence in the exclusively peaceful nature of Iran's nuclear programme;

11. *Reiterates* its determination to reinforce the authority of the IAEA, strongly supports the role of the IAEA Board of Governors, *commends and encourages* the Director General of the IAEA and its secretariat for their ongoing professional and impartial efforts to resolve all outstanding issues in Iran within the framework of the IAEA, *underlines* the necessity of the IAEA, which is internationally recognized as having authority for verifying compliance with safeguards agreements, including the non-diversion of nuclear material for non-peaceful purposes, in accordance with its Statute, to continue its work to clarify all outstanding issues relating to Iran's nuclear programme;

12. *Requests* within 60 days a further report from the Director General of the IAEA on whether Iran has established full and sustained suspension of all activities mentioned in resolution 1737 (2006), as well as on the process of Iranian compliance with all the steps required by the IAEA Board and with the other provisions of resolution 1737 (2006) and of this resolution, to the IAEA Board of Governors and in parallel to the Security Council for its consideration;

13. *Affirms* that it shall review Iran's actions in light of the report referred to in paragraph 12 above, to be submitted within 60 days, and:

(a) that it shall suspend the implementation of measures if and for so long as Iran suspends all enrichment-related and reprocessing activities, including research and development, as verified by the IAEA, to allow for negotiations in good faith in order to reach an early and mutually acceptable outcome;

(b) that it shall terminate the measures specified in paragraphs 3, 4, 5, 6, 7 and 12 of resolution 1737 (2006) as well as in paragraphs 2, 4, 5, 6 and 7 above as soon as it determines, following receipt of the report referred to in paragraph 12 above, that Iran has fully complied with its obligations under the relevant resolutions of the Security Council and met the requirements of the IAEA Board of Governors, as confirmed by the IAEA Board;

(c) that it shall, in the event that the report in paragraph 12 above shows that Iran has not complied with resolution 1737 (2006) and this resolution, adopt further appropriate measures under Article 41 of Chapter VII of the Charter of the United Nations to persuade Iran to comply with these resolutions and the requirements of the IAEA, and underlines that further decisions will be required should such additional measures be necessary;

14. *Decides* to remain seized of the matter.

Annex I
Entities involved in nuclear or ballistic missile activities

1. Ammunition and Metallurgy Industries Group (AMIG) (aka Ammunition Industries Group) (AMIG controls 7th of Tir, which is designated under resolution 1737 (2006) for its role in Iran's centrifuge programme. AMIG is in turn owned and controlled by the Defence Industries Organisation (DIO), which is designated under resolution 1737 (2006))

2. Esfahan Nuclear Fuel Research and Production Centre (NFRPC) and Esfahan Nuclear Technology Centre (ENTC) (Parts of the Atomic Energy Organisation of Iran's (AEOI) Nuclear Fuel Production and Procurement Company, which is involved in enrichment-related activities. AEOI is designated under resolution 1737 (2006))

3. Kavoshyar Company (Subsidiary company of AEOI, which has sought glass fibres, vacuum chamber furnaces and laboratory equipment for Iran's nuclear programme)

4. Parchin Chemical Industries (Branch of DIO, which produces ammunition, explosives, as well as solid propellants for rockets and missiles)

5. Karaj Nuclear Research Centre (Part of AEOI's research division)

6. Novin Energy Company (aka Pars Novin) (Operates within AEOI and has transferred funds on behalf of AEOI to entities associated with Iran's nuclear programme)

7. Cruise Missile Industry Group (aka Naval Defence Missile Industry Group) (Production and development of cruise missiles. Responsible for naval missiles including cruise missiles)

8. Bank Sepah and Bank Sepah International (Bank Sepah provides support for the Aerospace Industries Organisation (AIO) and subordinates, including Shahid Hemmat Industrial Group (SHIG) and Shahid Bagheri Industrial Group (SBIG), both of which were designated under resolution 1737 (2006))

9. Sanam Industrial Group (subordinate to AIO, which has purchased equipment on AIO's behalf for the missile programme)

10. Ya Mahdi Industries Group (subordinate to AIO, which is involved in international purchases of missile equipment)

Iranian Revolutionary Guard Corps entities

1. Qods Aeronautics Industries (Produces unmanned aerial vehicles (UAVs), parachutes, para-gliders, para-motors, etc. Iranian Revolutionary Guard Corps (IRGC) has boasted of using these products as part of its asymmetric warfare doctrine)

2. Pars Aviation Services Company (Maintains various aircraft including MI-171, used by IRGC Air Force)

3. Sho'a' Aviation (Produces micro-lights which IRGC has claimed it is using as part of its asymmetric warfare doctrine)

Persons involved in nuclear or ballistic missile activities

1. Fereidoun Abbasi-Davani (Senior Ministry of Defence and Armed Forces Logistics (MODAFL) scientist with links to the Institute of Applied Physics, working closely with Mohsen Fakhrizadeh-Mahabadi, designated below)

2. Mohsen Fakhrizadeh-Mahabadi (Senior MODAFL scientist and former head of the Physics Research Centre (PHRC). The IAEA have asked to interview him about the activities of the PHRC over the period he was head but Iran has refused)

3. Seyed Jaber Safdari (Manager of the Natanz Enrichment Facilities)

4. Amir Rahimi (Head of Esfahan Nuclear Fuel Research and Production Center, which is part of the AEOI's Nuclear Fuel Production and Procurement Company, which is involved in enrichment-related activities)

5. Mohsen Hojati (Head of Fajr Industrial Group, which is designated under resolution 1737 (2006) for its role in the ballistic missile programme)

6. Mehrdada Akhlaghi Ketabachi (Head of SBIG, which is designated under resolution 1737 (2006) for its role in the ballistic missile programme)

7. Naser Maleki (Head of SHIG, which is designated under resolution 1737 (2006) for its role in Iran's ballistic missile programme. Naser Maleki is also a MODAFL official overseeing work on the Shahab-3 ballistic missile programme. The Shahab-3 is Iran's long range ballistic missile currently in service)

8. Ahmad Derakhshandeh (Chairman and Managing Director of Bank Sepah, which provides support for the AIO and subordinates, including SHIG and SBIG, both of which were designated under resolution 1737 (2006))

Iranian Revolutionary Guard Corps key persons

1. Brigadier General Morteza Rezaie (Deputy Commander of IRGC)

2. Vice Admiral Ali Akbar Ahmadian (Chief of IRGC Joint Staff)

3. Brigadier General Mohammad Reza Zahedi (Commander of IRGC Ground Forces)

4. Rear Admiral Morteza Safari (Commander of IRGC Navy)

5. Brigadier General Mohammad Hejazi (Commander of Bassij resistance force)

6. Brigadier General Qasem Soleimani (Commander of Qods force)

7. General Zolqadr (IRGC officer, Deputy Interior Minister for Security Affairs)

Annex II
Elements of a long-term agreement

Our goal is to develop relations and cooperation with Iran, based on mutual respect and the establishment of international confidence in the exclusively peaceful nature of the nuclear programme of the Islamic Republic of Iran. We propose a fresh start in the negotiation of a comprehensive agreement with Iran. Such an agreement would be deposited with the International Atomic Energy Agency (IAEA) and endorsed in a Security Council resolution.

To create the right conditions for negotiations,

We will:

- Reaffirm Iran's right to develop nuclear energy for peaceful purposes in conformity with its obligations under the Treaty on the Non-Proliferation of Nuclear Weapons (hereinafter, NPT), and in this context reaffirm our support for the development by Iran of a civil nuclear energy programme.
- Commit to support actively the building of new light water reactors in Iran through international joint projects, in accordance with the IAEA statute and NPT.
- Agree to suspend discussion of Iran's nuclear programme in the Security Council upon the resumption of negotiations.

Iran will:

- Commit to addressing all of the outstanding concerns of IAEA through full cooperation with IAEA.
- Suspend all enrichment-related and reprocessing activities to be verified by IAEA, as requested by the IAEA Board of Governors and the Security Council, and commit to continue this during these negotiations.
- Resume the implementation of the Additional Protocol.

Areas of future cooperation to be covered in negotiations on a long-term agreement

1. Nuclear

We will take the following steps:

Iran's rights to nuclear energy

- Reaffirm Iran's inalienable right to nuclear energy for peaceful purposes without discrimination and in conformity with articles I and II of NPT, and cooperate with Iran in the development by Iran of a civil nuclear power programme.
- Negotiate and implement a Euratom/Iran nuclear cooperation agreement.

Light water reactors

- Actively support the building of new light water power reactors in Iran through international joint projects, in accordance with the IAEA statute and NPT, using state-of-the-art technology, including by authorizing the transfer of necessary goods and the provision of advanced technology to make its power reactors safe against earthquakes.
- Provide cooperation with the management of spent nuclear fuel and radioactive waste through appropriate arrangements.

Research and development in nuclear energy

- Provide a substantive package of research and development cooperation, including possible provision of light water research reactors, notably in the fields of radioisotope production, basic research and nuclear applications in medicine and agriculture.

Fuel guarantees

- Give legally binding, multilayered fuel assurances to Iran, based on:
- Participation as a partner in an international facility in Russia to provide enrichment services for a reliable supply of fuel to Iran's nuclear reactors. Subject to negotiations, such a facility could enrich all uranium hexaflouride (UF_6) produced in Iran.
- Establishment on commercial terms of a buffer stock to hold a reserve of up to five years' supply of nuclear fuel dedicated to Iran, with the participation and under supervision of IAEA.
- Development with IAEA of a standing multilateral mechanism for reliable access to nuclear fuel, based on ideas to be considered at the next meeting of the Board of Governors.

Review of moratorium

The long-term agreement would, with regard to common efforts to build international confidence, contain a clause for review of the agreement in all its aspects, to follow:

- Confirmation by IAEA that all outstanding issues and concerns reported by it, including those activities which could have a military nuclear dimension, have been resolved;
- Confirmation that there are no undeclared nuclear activities or materials in Iran and that international confidence in the exclusively peaceful nature of Iran's civil nuclear programme has been restored.

2. Political and economic

Regional security cooperation

Support for a new conference to promote dialogue and cooperation on regional security issues.

International trade and investment

Improving Iran's access to the international economy, markets and capital, through practical support for full integration into international structures, including the World Trade Organization and to create the framework for increased direct investment in Iran and trade with Iran (including a trade and economic cooperation agreement with the European Union). Steps would be taken to improve access to key goods and technology.

Civil aviation

Civil aviation cooperation, including the possible removal of restrictions on United States and European manufacturers in regard to the export of civil aircraft to Iran, thereby widening the prospect of Iran renewing its fleet of civil airliners.

Energy partnership

Establishment of a long-term energy partnership between Iran and the European Union and other willing partners, with concrete and practical applications.

Telecommunications infrastructure

Support for the modernization of Iran's telecommunication infrastructure and advanced Internet provision, including by possible removal of relevant United States and other export restrictions.

High technology cooperation

Cooperation in fields of high technology and other areas to be agreed upon.

Agriculture

Support for agricultural development in Iran, including possible access to United States and European agricultural products, technology and farm equipment.

Resolution 1748 (2007)

Adopted by the Security Council at its 5648th meeting on 27 March 2007

The Security Council,

Recalling all its previous relevant resolutions, in particular resolutions 1595 (2005), 1636 (2005), 1644 (2005), 1664 (2006), 1686 (2006), 1373 (2001) and 1566 (2004),

Reaffirming its strongest condemnation of the 14 February 2005 terrorist bombing, as well as of all other attacks in Lebanon since October 2004, and reaffirming also that those involved in these attacks must be held accountable for their crimes,

Having examined the report of the International Independent Investigation Commission (S/2007/150) ("The Commission"), submitted pursuant to resolutions 1595 (2005), 1636 (2005), 1644 (2005), and 1686 (2006),

Commending the Commission for the outstanding professional work it continues to accomplish under difficult circumstances in assisting the Lebanese authorities in their investigation into all aspects of this terrorist act,

Taking note of the letter of the Prime Minister of Lebanon of 21 February 2007 to the Secretary-General (S/2007/159, Enclosure) requesting that the mandate of the Commission be extended for a further period of up to one year from 15 June 2007 in order to ensure stability and continuity in the investigative process, and noting the concurrent recommendation of the Secretary-General in this regard,

Noting the Commission's conclusion that, in light of its current and planned investigative activities and while significant progress has been made, it is unlikely that the Commission will complete its work before its current mandate expires and that the Commission therefore welcomes the Lebanese request for an extension of its mandate beyond this date,

Willing to continue to assist Lebanon in the search for the truth and in holding all those involved in this terrorist attack accountable,

1. *Welcomes* the report of the Commission;

2. *Decides* to extend the mandate of the Commission until 15 June 2008 and declares its readiness to terminate the mandate earlier if the Commission reports that it has completed the implementation of its mandate;

3. *Requests* the Commission to continue to report to the Council on the progress of the investigation every four months, or at any other time as it deems appropriate;

4. *Decides* to remain seized of the matter.

Resolution 1749 (2007)

Adopted by the Security Council at its 5650th meeting on 28 March 2007

The Security Council,

Recalling its resolutions 918 (1994) of 17 May 1994, 1005 (1995) of 17 July 1995, 1011 (1995) of 16 August 1995, 1013 (1995) of 7 September 1995, 1053 (1996) of 23 April 1996, and 1161 (1998) of 9 April 1998,

Having considered the report of the Security Council Committee established pursuant to resolution 918 (1994) concerning Rwanda of 28 December 2006 (S/2006/1049) and the oral report of the Chairman of the Security Council Committee established pursuant to resolution 918 (1994) concerning Rwanda of 13 March 2007,

Taking note of the letter dated 2 March 2007 from the Permanent Representative of Rwanda to the United Nations addressed to the President of the Security Council (S/2007/121) requesting the termination of the measures imposed by paragraph 11 of resolution 1011 (1995),

Recalling the termination on 1 September 1996 of the restrictions imposed by paragraph 13 of resolution 918 (1994) in accordance with paragraph 8 of resolution 1011 (1995) and reaffirming the measures imposed by paragraphs 9 and 10 of resolution 1011 (1995),

Stressing the importance of the cooperation of all States, in particular those in the region, with the Security Council Committees established pursuant to resolutions 918 (1994) and 1533 (2004) and with the Group of Experts established by resolution 1533 (2004), while carrying out its mandate as renewed by resolution 1698 (2006),

Stressing further the need for States in the region to ensure that arms and related materiel delivered to them are not diverted to or used by illegal armed groups,

Welcoming the positive developments in Rwanda and the Great Lakes Region, particularly the signing of the Pact on Security, Stability and Development in the Great Lakes Region at the Second Summit of the International Conference on the Great Lakes Region in Nairobi, Kenya, on 15 December 2006, and encouraging the signatories to ratify this pact as soon as possible and to provide for its expeditious implementation,

Reiterating its call upon the States of the region to deepen further their cooperation with a view to consolidating peace in the region,

Acting under Chapter VII of the Charter of the United Nations,

1. *Decides* to terminate with immediate effect the measures imposed by paragraph 11 of resolution 1011 (1995);

2. *Decides* to remain actively seized of the matter.

Resolution 1750 (2007)

Adopted by the Security Council at its 5652nd meeting, on 30 March 2007

The Security Council,

Recalling its resolutions and statements by its President concerning the situations in Liberia and the subregion, in particular its resolution 1509 (2003) of 19 September 2003, 1712 (2006) of 29 September 2006, and its resolution 1626 (2005) of 19 September 2005,

Welcoming the Secretary-General's report of 15 March 2007 (S/2007/151),

Further welcoming the continuing steps being taken by the Government of Liberia to improve governance and combat corruption, as well as the significant progress made in regaining government control over Liberia's natural resources,

Expressing its appreciation for the continuing financial and other support provided by the international community, the Economic Community of West African States (ECOWAS) and the African Union (AU) for the Liberian peace consolidation process,

Acknowledging and commending the work of the United Nations Mission in Liberia (UNMIL), under the leadership of the Special Representative of the Secretary-General, for the important role it continues to play in supporting peace and stability in Liberia, and *welcoming* the close cooperation between UNMIL and the United Nations Operation in Côte d'Ivoire (UNOCI), as well as with neighbouring Governments, in coordinating security activities in the border areas in the subregion,

Noting with appreciation the substantial progress made in the reintegration of ex-combatants, and recognizing that further progress will depend on the availability of formal sector employment for ex-combatants,

Welcoming UNMIL's policy to promote and protect the rights of women and *calling on* Liberian authorities to continue their efforts to enhance cooperation with the United Nations country team and civil society, in order to aid in efforts to combat sexual exploitation and abuse,

Recognizing that significant challenges remain in the consolidation of Liberia's post-conflict transition, including massive development and reconstruction needs, the reform of the judiciary, extension of the rule of law throughout the country, the development of the Liberian security forces and security architecture, and consolidation of State authority,

Reiterating the continuing need for UNMIL's support for the security of the Special Court for Sierra Leone,

Determining that the situation in Liberia continues to constitute a threat to international peace and security in the region,

Acting under Chapter VII of the Charter of the United Nations,

1. *Decides* the mandate of the United Nations Mission in Liberia (UNMIL) shall be extended until 30 September 2007;

2. *Reaffirms* its intention to authorize the Secretary-General to redeploy troops, as may be needed, between UNMIL and UNOCI on a temporary basis in accordance with the provisions of resolution 1609 (2005);

3. *Requests* that the Secretary-General present a detailed drawdown plan for the mission in his next report to the Council scheduled for June, which should include specific recommendations on force levels and options for a drawdown, and which should be presented no later than 45 days prior to the expiration of UNMIL's mandate and to continue to inform the Council on progress on the stabilization of Liberia, with reference to the broad benchmarks laid out in his report of 12 September 2006;

4. *Calls on* the Government of Liberia, in close coordination with UNMIL, to take further steps towards achieving those benchmarks with a view to a phased, gradual consolidation, drawdown and withdrawal of UNMIL's troop contingent, as the situation permits and without compromising the security of Liberia;

5. *Notes* the intention of the Special Court for Sierra Leone to reach agreement with the Government of Liberia on carrying out a programme of activities in Liberia, and decides that UNMIL's mandate shall include the following additional element: to provide, within its capabilities and areas of deployment and without prejudice to the performance of its other mandated tasks, administrative and related support and security, on a cost-reimbursable basis, for activities conducted in Liberia by the Special Court for Sierra Leone with the consent of the Government of Liberia;

6. *Decides* to remain actively seized of the matter.

Resolution 1751 (2007)

Adopted by the Security Council at its 5660th meeting, on 13 April 2007

The Security Council,

Recalling its resolutions and the statements of its President concerning the Democratic Republic of the Congo,

Reaffirming its commitment to the sovereignty, territorial integrity and political independence of the Democratic Republic of the Congo, and its commitment to continue to contribute to the consolidation of peace and stability in the Democratic Republic of the Congo in the post-transition period, in particular through the United Nations Organization Mission in the Democratic Republic of the Congo (MONUC),

Noting that the situation in the Democratic Republic of the Congo continues to pose a threat to international peace and security in the region,

Acting under Chapter VII of the Charter of the United Nations,

1. *Decides* to extend the mandate and personnel strength of MONUC, as set out in its resolutions 1565 (2004), 1592 (2005), 1596 (2005), 1621 (2005), 1635 (2005) and 1736 (2006), until 15 May 2007;

2. *Decides* to remain actively seized of the matter.

Resolution 1752 (2007)

Adopted by the Security Council at its 5661st meeting, on 13 April 2007

The Security Council,

Recalling all its relevant resolutions including resolution 1716 of 13 October 2006 (S/RES/1716),

Welcoming the reports of the Secretary-General on the activities of the United Nations Observer Mission in Georgia of 11 January 2007 (S/2007/15) and 3 April 2007,

Supporting the sustained efforts of the Secretary-General and of his Special Representative with the assistance of the Group of Friends of the Secretary-General as well as the Russian Federation in its capacity as facilitator and of the OSCE,

Stressing the importance of close and effective cooperation between UNOMIG and the CIS peacekeeping force as they currently play an important stabilizing role in the conflict zone, and *recalling* that a lasting and comprehensive settlement of the conflict will require appropriate security guarantees,

Stressing that economic development is urgently required in Abkhazia, Georgia to improve the livelihoods of the communities affected by the conflict, in particular the refugees and internally displaced persons,

1. *Reaffirms* the commitment of all Member States to the sovereignty, independence and territorial integrity of Georgia within its internationally recognized borders, and supports all efforts by the United Nations and the Group of Friends of the Secretary-General which are guided by their determination to promote a settlement of the Georgian-Abkhaz conflict only by peaceful means and within the framework of the Security Council resolutions;

2. *Calls on* both sides to resume dialogue, make full use of all existing mechanisms as described in the relevant Security Council resolutions, to comply fully with previous agreements regarding ceasefire and non-use of violence, and to finalize without delay the package of documents on the non-use of violence and on the return of refugees and internally displaced persons;

3. *Recalls*, with a view to achieving a lasting and comprehensive settlement, its support for the principles contained in the "Paper on Basic Principles for the Distribution of Competencies between Tbilisi and Sukhumi" and welcomes additional ideas that the sides would be willing to offer with a view to conducting creatively and constructively a political dialogue under the aegis of the United Nations;

4. *Endorses* the proposals for confidence-building measures presented by the Group of Friends of the Secretary-General during the meeting held in Geneva on 12 and 13 February 2007 under participation of the Georgian and Abkhaz parties, and urges both parties with the assistance of UNOMIG and of international partners and the support of the Group of Friends of the Secretary-General to immediately engage in implementing these measures without conditions;

5. *Welcomes* progress achieved by both sides towards the implementation of resolution 1716 (2006), calls on the Georgian side to ensure that the situation in the upper Kodori valley is in line with the Moscow agreement on ceasefire and separation of forces of 14 May 1994; and *calls on* the Abkhaz side to exercise restraint in connection with the Georgian commitments with regard to the Kodori valley;

6. *Condemns* the attack on villages in the Upper Kodori valley carried out in the night of 11 and 12 March 2007 and urges all sides to extend full support to the ongoing investigation conducted by the Joint Fact Finding Group under the leadership of UNOMIG;

7. *Stresses* that the situation on the ground in the areas of security, return of IDPs and rehabilitation and development must be improved and *calls* on both sides to resume dialogue without preconditions in these areas, using all existing mechanisms, including Quadripartite meetings;

8. *Urges* the sides to address seriously each other's legitimate security concerns, to refrain from any actions which might impede the peace process, and to extend the necessary cooperation to UNOMIG and the CIS peacekeeping force;

9. *Stresses* the urgent need to alleviate the plight of refugees and internally displaced persons and the need for a perspective of life in security and dignity in particular for a new generation growing up outside Abkhazia, Georgia, and recalling the right of return for all internally displaced persons to Abkhazia, Georgia, calls on both sides to implement the UNHCR's *Strategic Directions* for the return in the first instance to the Gali region;

10. *Welcomes* existing and *encourages* further contacts between representatives of civil society of the sides;

11. *Underlines* that it is the primary responsibility of both sides to provide appropriate security and to ensure the freedom of movement of UNOMIG, the CIS peacekeeping force and other international personnel and *calls on* both sides to fulfil their obligations in this regard;

12. *Requests* the Secretary-General to continue to take the necessary measures to ensure full compliance of all UNOMIG personnel with the United Nations zero-tolerance policy on sexual exploitation and abuse and to keep the Council informed, and urges troop-contributing countries to ensure that acts involving their personnel are properly investigated and punished;

13. *Decides* to extend the mandate of UNOMIG for a new period terminating on 15 October 2007;

14. *Requests* the Secretary-General to make use of this extended mandate in order to support the parties in implementing measures to build confidence and to establish an intensive and meaningful dialogue, and to inform the Council in his next report on the situation in Abkhazia, Georgia, on progress made in this respect;

15. *Strongly supports* the efforts of the Special Representative of the Secretary-General and calls on the Group of Friends of the Secretary-General to continue giving him their steadfast and unified support;

16. *Decides* to remain actively seized of the matter.

Resolution 1753 (2007)

Adopted by the Security Council at its 5668th meeting, on 27 April 2007

The Security Council,

Recalling its previous resolutions and statements by its President on the situation in Liberia and West Africa,

Applauding the Government of Liberia's continuing cooperation with the Kimberley Process Certification Scheme and noting Liberia's progress towards putting in place the necessary internal controls and other requirements in order to satisfy the minimum requirements of the Kimberley Process,

Taking note of the letter of the Government of Liberia to the Sanctions Committee, with a detailed description of the proposed Certificate of Origin regime, dated 4 April 2007,

Welcoming the interim report of the United Nations Panel of Experts dated 4 April 2007 and *looking forward* to the submission by 6 June 2007 of the United Nations Panel of Experts final report as requested in paragraph 4 (d) of resolution 1731 (2006),

Having reviewed the measures imposed and conditions set out by paragraphs 6 through 9 of resolution 1521 (2003) and concluding that sufficient progress has been made towards meeting those conditions,

Determining that the situation in Liberia continues to constitute a threat to international peace and security in the region,

Acting under Chapter VII of the Charter of the United Nations,

1. *Decides* to terminate the measures on diamonds imposed by paragraph 6 of resolution 1521 (2003) and renewed by paragraph 1 of resolution 1731 (2006);

2. *Encourages* the Kimberley Process to report in ninety (90) days to the Council, through the Committee established pursuant to resolution 1521 (2003), on Liberia's application to the Kimberley Process and calls on the Government of Liberia to carry out the recommendations of the expert mission identified for the period following admission to the Kimberley Process Certification Scheme;

3. *Decides* to review the termination of the measures in paragraph 6 of resolution 1521 (2003) after consideration of the report of the United Nations Panel of Experts as requested in paragraph 4 (d) of resolution 1731 (2006) and of the report of the Kimberley Process encouraged in paragraph two (2), with a particular focus on the compliance of Liberia with the Kimberley Process Certification Scheme;

4. *Decides* to remain actively seized of the matter.

Resolution 1754 (2007)

Adopted by the Security Council at its 5669th meeting, on 30 April 2007

The Security Council,

Recalling all its previous resolutions on Western Sahara,

Reaffirming its strong support for the efforts of the Secretary-General and his Personal Envoy,

Reaffirming its commitment to assist the parties to achieve a just, lasting and mutually acceptable political solution, which will provide for the self-determination of the people of Western Sahara in the context of arrangements consistent with the principles and purposes of the Charter of the United Nations, and noting the role and responsibilities of the parties in this respect,

Reiterating its call upon the parties and States of the region to continue to cooperate fully with the United Nations and with each other to end the current impasse and to achieve progress towards a political solution,

Taking note of the Moroccan proposal presented on 11 April 2007 to the Secretary-General and welcoming serious and credible Moroccan efforts to move the process forward towards resolution; *also taking note* of the Polisario Front proposal presented on 10 April 2007 to the Secretary-General,

Having considered the report of the Secretary-General of 13 April 2007 (S/2007/202),

1. *Reaffirms* the need for full respect of the military agreements reached with MINURSO with regard to the ceasefire;

2. *Calls upon* the parties to enter into negotiations without preconditions in good faith, taking into account the developments of the last months, with a view to achieving a just, lasting and mutually acceptable political solution, which will provide for the self-determination of the people of Western Sahara;

3. *Requests* the Secretary-General to set up these negotiations under his auspices and invites Member States to lend appropriate assistance to such talks;

4. *Requests* the Secretary-General to provide a report by 30 June 2007 on the status and progress of these negotiations under his auspices, and expresses its intention to meet to receive and discuss this report;

5. *Requests* the Secretary-General to provide a report on the situation in Western Sahara before the end of the mandate period;

6. *Calls on* Member States to consider voluntary contributions to fund Confidence Building Measures that allow for increased contact between separated family members, especially family unification visits;

7. *Requests* the Secretary-General to continue to take the necessary measures to ensure full compliance in MINURSO with the United Nations zero-tolerance policy on sexual exploitation and abuse and to keep the Council informed, and urges troop-contributing countries to take appropriate preventive action including pre-deployment awareness training, and other action to ensure full accountability in cases of such conduct involving their personnel;

8. *Decides* to extend the mandate of the United Nations Mission for the Referendum in Western Sahara (MINURSO) until 31 October 2007;

9. *Decides* to remain seized of the matter.

Resolution 1755 (2007)

Adopted by the Security Council at its 5670th meeting, on 30 April 2007

The Security Council,

Recalling its previous resolutions, in particular resolutions 1714 (2006) of 6 October 2006, 1709 (2006) of 22 September 2006, 1706 (2006) of 31 August 2006, 1679 (2006) of 16 May 2006, 1663 (2006) of 24 March 2006, 1653 (2006) of 27 January 2006, 1627 (2005) of 23 September 2005, and 1590 (2005) of 24 March 2005,

Recalling also its previous resolutions 1674 (2006) of 28 April 2006 on the protection of civilians in armed conflict, which reaffirms, inter alia, the relevant provisions of the United Nations World Summit Outcome document, 1612 (2005) of 26 July 2005 on children in armed conflict, 1502 (2003) of 26 August 2003 on the protection of humanitarian and United Nations personnel, and 1325 (2000) of 31 October 2000 on women, peace and security,

Reaffirming its commitment to the sovereignty, unity, independence and territorial integrity of the Sudan and to the cause of peace,

Welcoming the progress in implementation of elements of the Comprehensive Peace Agreement of 9 January 2005, in particular overall compliance with the ceasefire this year, the progress made in the establishment of the institutional framework provided for in the power-sharing protocol, the adoption of a budget by the authorities of Southern Sudan and introduction of a new currency of the Sudan,

Recalling the commitment of the international community to support the Comprehensive Peace Agreement process, including through development aid; *taking note* of the meeting of the Sudan Consortium that was held from 19 to 21 March 2007 in Khartoum and Juba; and *calling upon* donors to continue to support the implementation of the Comprehensive Peace Agreement,

Stressing that elections and force redeployment will be important milestones in Comprehensive Peace Agreement implementation, that meeting commitments against both in 2007 will be central to Comprehensive Peace Agreement credibility, and that urgent action is needed to accelerate preparations for elections,

Calling upon the Government of National Unity and the international community to support a successful elections process,

Welcoming the first organized returns of internally displaced persons from Khartoum to Southern Kordofan and Southern Sudan,

Welcoming the full deployment in Southern Sudan of the United Nations Mission in the Sudan (UNMIS) in support of the Comprehensive Peace Agreement, and *acknowledging* the continued commitment by troop-contributing countries in support of this mission,

Reiterating its concern over the restrictions and bureaucratic impediments placed on UNMIS movements and materiel, and the adverse impact such restrictions and impediments have on UNMIS' ability to perform its mandate effectively and on the ability of the humanitarian community to reach affected persons; and *calling upon* the Government of National Unity to abide by its international obligations, in this regard, as well as those set out in the Status of Forces Agreement,

Expressing its grave concern over the continued deterioration of the humanitarian situation in Darfur and the impact on the region; *condemning* continued violent attacks on civilians, including displaced persons, refugees, women, children, the elderly and humanitarian workers; and *reiterating* in the strongest terms the need for all parties to the conflict in Darfur, including non-parties to the Darfur Peace Agreement, to put an end to the violence and atrocities in Darfur and the region,

Expressing its concern over the information about the treatment following the 19 January 2007 arrests and detentions of personnel from the United Nations, African Union Mission in the Sudan (AMIS), and international non-governmental organizations in Nyala, South Darfur; and *calling for* the Government of National Unity to respect its commitment to cooperate with the United Nations in the investigation of this incident,

Welcoming the communiqué signed between the United Nations and the Government of National Unity in Khartoum on 28 March 2007, to support, protect and facilitate all humanitarian operations in Darfur; and *calling for* its immediate implementation,

Commending the efforts of the African Union for successful deployment of AMIS, despite exceptionally difficult circumstances, and *condemning* the recent fatal attacks on AMIS,

Expressing full support for the coordinated efforts of United Nations and African Union Envoys for Darfur and other leaders to broaden support for and move forward implementation of the Darfur Peace Agreement,

Noting its concern that armed attacks by Other Armed Groups threaten the successful implementation of the Comprehensive Peace Agreement, *welcoming* the agreement between the Government of Uganda and the Lord's Resistance Army to extend the cessation of hostilities agreement and resume peace talks in Juba on 26 April 2007, *commending* the efforts of United Nations Special Envoy Chissano to bring this progress about, and *calling upon* both sides to meet their commitments under this process,

Taking note of the report of the Secretary-General on the Sudan dated 17 April 2007 (S/2007/213),

Determining that the situation in the Sudan continues to constitute a threat to international peace and security,

1. *Decides* to extend the mandate of UNMIS until 31 October 2007, with the intention to renew it for further periods;

2. *Requests* the Secretary-General to appoint urgently a new Special Representative for the Sudan and to report to the Council every three months on the implementation of the mandate of UNMIS;

3. *Calls upon* the parties to the Comprehensive Peace Agreement to accelerate urgently progress on implementing all their commitments, in particular to carry out the establishment of Joint Integrated Units and other aspects of the security sector reforms; to re-energize the process of disarmament, demobilization and reintegration of combatants; to complete the full and verified redeployment of forces by 9 July 2007; to demarcate precisely the 1 January 1956 North/South borderline, consistent with the Machakos Protocol of 20 July 2002; to resolve the Abyei problem and urgently establish an administration there; and to take the necessary steps to hold national elections according to the agreed time frame;

4. *Calls upon* the parties to the Comprehensive Peace Agreement, the Darfur Peace Agreement, the N'Djamena Humanitarian Ceasefire Agreement, the Eastern Sudan Peace Agreement and the communiqué of 28 March 2007 to respect their commitments and implement fully all aspects of those agreements without delay; and calls upon those parties that have not signed the Darfur Peace Agreement to do so without delay and not to act in any way that would impede the implementation of the Agreement;

5. *Requests* the Secretary-General to continue to take the necessary measures to ensure full compliance in UNMIS with the United Nations zero-tolerance policy on sexual exploitation and abuse and to keep the Council informed, and urges troop-contributing countries to take appropriate preventive action, including predeployment accountability in cases of such conduct involving their personnel;

6. *Decides* to remain actively seized of the matter.

Resolution 1756 (2007)

Adopted by the Security Council at its 5674th meeting, on 15 May 2007

The Security Council,

Recalling its resolutions and the statements of its President concerning the Democratic Republic of the Congo,

Reaffirming its commitment to respect the sovereignty, territorial integrity and political independence of the Democratic Republic of the Congo,

Recalling the support it provided, in particular through the United Nations Organization Mission in the Democratic Republic of the Congo (MONUC), for the process of the Global and All-Inclusive Agreement on the Transition, signed in Pretoria on 17 December 2002, and for the elections that represented the culmination of that process, and *reaffirming* its commitment to continue to contribute to the consolidation of peace and stability in the Democratic Republic of the Congo in the post-transition period,

Stressing the primary responsibility of the Government of the Democratic Republic of the Congo for ensuring security in its territory and protecting its civilians with respect for the rule of law, human rights and international humanitarian law,

Deploring again the violence and loss of lives which occurred in late January and early February 2007 in the province of Bas-Congo and from 22 to 25 March 2007 in Kinshasa, *encouraging* the Congolese authorities and MONUC to continue and complete the necessary investigations into these events, *regretting* the use of violence, instead of dialogue, to resolve disputes, and *urging* all Congolese stakeholders to pursue negotiated solutions to their differences with respect for the constitutional framework and the law,

Paying tribute to the international community for the assistance provided to the Democratic Republic of the Congo, *encouraging* the maintenance of that assistance, and *underlining* its commitment to the continuation of a regular political dialogue with the Congolese authorities,

Recalling the importance of elections, including the forthcoming local elections, as a milestone for the longer term restoration of peace and stability, national reconciliation and establishment of the rule of law in the Democratic Republic of the Congo,

Recalling also the importance of urgently carrying out security sector reform and of disarming, demobilizing, resettling or repatriating, as appropriate, and reintegrating Congolese and foreign armed groups for the long-term stabilization of the Democratic Republic of the Congo, and the contribution made by international partners in this field,

Reiterating its grave concern at the presence of armed groups and militias in the eastern part of the Democratic Republic of the Congo, particularly in the Ituri district and in North and South Kivu, which perpetuate a climate of insecurity in the whole region,

Deploring again the persistence of violations of human rights and international humanitarian law in the Democratic Republic of the Congo, in particular those carried out by these militias and armed groups and by elements of the Armed Forces of the Democratic Republic of the Congo (FARDC), the Congolese National Police (PNC) and other security and intelligence services, and *stressing* the urgent need for those responsible for these crimes to be brought to justice,

Recalling its resolution 1612 (2005) on children in armed conflict and the subsequent conclusions of the Security Council Working Group on Children and Armed Conflict pertaining to parties in the armed conflict of the Democratic Republic of Congo (S/2006/724),

Calling attention to the grave humanitarian situation that persists in the Democratic Republic of the Congo, and *calling on* Member States to continue to provide assistance in that regard,

Taking note with satisfaction of the adoption of the programme of the Government, in particular the governance contract included therein, *calling on* the Government to ensure the full implementation of the contract and *welcoming* the Country Assistance Framework Process as a common strategic approach for assistance to the DRC and as a mechanism to implement the priorities set out in the DRC's Poverty Reduction Strategy Paper for 2007-2010,

Condemning the continuing illicit flow of weapons within and into the Democratic Republic of the Congo, and *declaring its determination* to closely monitor implementation of the arms embargo imposed by resolution 1493 (2003) and expanded by resolution 1596 (2005), and to continue enforcing the measures provided for in paragraphs 13 and 15 of resolution 1596 (2005), in paragraph 2 of resolution 1649 (2005) and in paragraph 13 of resolution 1698 (2006),

Recognizing the link between the illegal exploitation of natural resources, the illicit trade in such resources and the proliferation and trafficking of arms as one of the factors fuelling and exacerbating conflicts in the Great Lakes region of Africa, and in particular in the Democratic Republic of the Congo, and *urging* all States, especially those in the region, to take appropriate steps to end these illegal activities,

Welcoming the signing in Nairobi on 15 December 2006 of the Pact on Security, Stability and Development in the Great Lakes Region, the first meeting of parliamentarians of the Great Lakes region held in Kinshasa from 26 to 28 February 2007, and the resumption of the activities of the Economic Community of the countries of the Great Lakes region (CEPGL),

Taking note of the twenty-third report of the Secretary-General on MONUC, dated 20 March 2007 (S/2007/156), and of its recommendations,

Noting that the situation in the Democratic Republic of the Congo continues to pose a threat to international peace and security in the region,

Acting under Chapter VII of the Charter of the United Nations,

1. Decides to extend the deployment of MONUC until 31 December 2007 and authorizes the continuation until that date of up to 17,030 military personnel, 760 military observers, 391 police trainers and 750 personnel of formed police units;

2. Decides that MONUC will have the mandate, within the limits of its capabilities and in its areas of deployment, to assist the Government of the Democratic Republic of the Congo in establishing a stable security environment in the country, and, to that end, to:

Protection of civilians, humanitarian personnel and United Nations personnel and facilities

(a) Ensure the protection of civilians, including humanitarian personnel, under imminent threat of physical violence;

(b) Contribute to the improvement of the security conditions in which humanitarian assistance is provided, and assist in the voluntary return of refugees and internally displaced persons;

(c) Ensure the protection of United Nations personnel, facilities, installations and equipment;

(d) Ensure the security and freedom of movement of United Nations and associated personnel;

(e) Carry out joint patrols with the riot control units of the national police to improve security in the event of civil disturbance;

Territorial security of the Democratic Republic of the Congo

(f) Observe and report in a timely manner on the position of armed movements and groups and the presence of foreign military forces in the key areas of volatility, especially by monitoring the use of landing strips and the borders, including on the lakes;

(g) Monitor the implementation of the measures imposed by paragraph 20 of resolution 1493 (2003) as amended and expanded by paragraph 1 of resolution 1596 (2005), in cooperation, as appropriate, with the Governments concerned and with the Group of Experts established by resolution 1533 (2004), including by inspecting, as it deems necessary and without notice, the cargo of aircraft and of any transport vehicle using the ports, airports, airfields, military bases and border crossings in North and South Kivu and in Ituri;

(h) Seize or collect, as appropriate, the arms and any related materiel whose presence in the territory of the Democratic Republic of the Congo violates the measures imposed by paragraph 20 of resolution 1493 (2003) as amended and expanded by paragraph 1 of resolution 1596 (2005), and to dispose of such arms and related materiel as appropriate;

(i) Provide assistance, where it has a permanent presence, to the competent customs authorities of the Democratic Republic of the Congo in implementing the provisions of paragraph 10 of resolution 1596 (2005);

(j) Assist the Government in enhancing its demining capacity;

Disarmament and demobilization of foreign and Congolese armed groups

(k) Deter any attempt at the use of force to threaten the political process from any armed group, foreign or Congolese, particularly in the Eastern part of the Democratic Republic of the Congo, including by using cordon and search tactics to prevent attacks on civilians and disrupt the military capability of illegal armed groups that continue to use violence in those areas;

(l) Support operations led by the FARDC integrated brigades deployed in the eastern part of the Democratic Republic of the Congo, including by undertaking the steps listed in paragraph 75, subparagraphs (b), (c), (d) and (e) of the Secretary-General's third special report on MONUC (S/2004/650), in accordance with internationally recognized standards and norms on human rights and international humanitarian law, with a view to:

- Disarming the recalcitrant local armed groups in order to ensure their participation in the disarmament, demobilization and reintegration process and the release of children associated with those armed groups;
- Disarming the foreign armed groups in order to ensure their participation in the disarmament, demobilization, repatriation, resettlement and reintegration process and the release of children associated with those armed groups;
- Preventing the provision of support to illegal armed groups, including support derived from illicit economic activities;

(m) Facilitate the voluntary demobilization and repatriation of disarmed foreign combatants and their dependants;

(n) Contribute to the implementation of the national programme of disarmament, demobilization and reintegration (DDR) of Congolese combatants and their dependants, with particular attention to children, by monitoring the disarmament process and providing as appropriate security in some sensitive locations, as well as supporting reintegration efforts pursued by the Congolese authorities in cooperation with the United Nations Country Team and bilateral and multilateral partners;

Security sector reform

(o) Provide in the short term basic training, including in the area of human rights, international humanitarian law, child protection and the prevention of gender-based violence, to various members and units of the FARDC integrated brigades deployed in the eastern part of the Democratic Republic of the Congo with a view to enhancing their capacity to carry out the missions referred to in subparagraph (l) above;

(p) In coordination with international partners, continue to develop the capacities of the Congolese national police and related law enforcement agencies in accordance with internationally recognized standards and norms on human rights, proportionate use of force and criminal justice, including the prevention, investigation and prosecution of cases of gender-based violence, by providing technical assistance, training and mentoring support;

(q) In coordination with international partners, advise the Government in strengthening the capacity of the judicial and correctional systems, including the military justice system;

(r) In coordination with international partners, contribute to the efforts of the international community to assist the Government in the initial planning process of the reform of the security sector;

3. Decides that MONUC will also have the mandate, in close cooperation with the Congolese authorities, the United Nations country team and donors, to support the strengthening of democratic institutions and the rule of law in the Democratic Republic of the Congo and, to that end, to:

(a) Provide advice to strengthen democratic institutions and processes at the national, provincial, regional and local levels;

(b) Promote national reconciliation and internal political dialogue, including through the provision of good offices, and support the strengthening of civil society;

(c) Assist in the promotion and protection of human rights, with particular attention to women, children and vulnerable persons, investigate human rights violations with a view to putting an end to impunity, assist in the development and implementation of a transitional justice strategy, and cooperate in national and international efforts to bring to justice perpetrators of grave violations of human rights and international humanitarian law;

(d) In close coordination with international partners and the United Nations Country Team, provide preliminary assistance to the Congolese authorities, including the National Independent Electoral Commission, in the organization, preparation and conduct of local elections, including the provision of advice, technical assistance and logistical support, and keep the Security Council closely informed of progress in this regard, including in the framework of the Secretary-General's periodic reports on MONUC;

(e) Assist in the establishment of a secure and peaceful environment for the holding of free and transparent elections;

(f) Contribute to the promotion of good governance and respect for the principle of accountability;

4. *Authorizes* MONUC to use all necessary means, within the limits of its capacity and in the areas where its units are deployed, to carry out the tasks listed in paragraph 2, subparagraphs (a) to (e), (g), (h), (k), (l) and (n), and in paragraph 3, subparagraph (e) above;

5. *Exhorts* the democratically elected authorities to respect the space and role conferred on the opposition parties by the Constitution in order to ensure their effective participation in the national political debate and *encourages* all parties to remain committed to the political process and national reconciliation in accordance with the constitutional framework and the law;

6. *Encourages* the Government and the principal partners of the Democratic Republic of the Congo to establish an effective arrangement for regular consultations promoting a political dialogue aimed at enhancing understanding by key partners of the goals and initiatives of the Government, the continuation of international involvement and concerted efforts by the country's international partners to prevent or respond to crises;

7. *Urges* the Government of the Democratic Republic of the Congo to strengthen its efforts, with the support of the international community, including specialized international organizations, with a view to effectively extending the State's authority throughout its territory, establishing its control over the exploitation and export of natural resources, and improving the transparency of the management of the revenues from the exploitation of those natural resources;

8. *Requests* the Government, with the support of the international community, to develop as a matter of urgency a national security strategy and to plan and carry out security sector reform in order to establish professional security organizations in the areas of defence, police and the administration of justice that are well managed, protect civilians and act in accordance with the Constitution and with respect for the rule of law, human rights and international humanitarian law;

9. *Calls on* the donor community to continue to be firmly committed to the provision of the urgent assistance needed for the integration, training and equipping of the Armed Forces and of the National Police of the Democratic Republic of the Congo as well as for the reform of the administration of justice and *urges* the Government and its partners, in particular the European Union, to agree promptly on ways to coordinate their efforts and to carry out security sector reform by building on the results already achieved;

10. *Demands* that the militias and armed groups that are still present in the eastern part of the Democratic Republic of the Congo lay down their arms and engage voluntarily and without any further delay or preconditions in their demobilization, repatriation or resettlement, and reintegration;

11. *Urgently requests* the Government to develop in close coordination with MONUC, as a matter of priority as part of its effort to extend its authority throughout the Democratic Republic of the Congo, a plan to ensure security in the eastern part of the country, particularly by carrying out the disarmament, demobilization, repatriation or resettlement, as appropriate, and reintegration of foreign and Congolese combatants, and by promoting national reconciliation, recovery and development in the region;

12. *Reiterates its call* upon the Congolese authorities to put an end to impunity, including by bringing to justice without delay perpetrators of grave violations of human rights and of international humanitarian law, and to take into account when they select candidates for official positions, including key posts in the armed forces, national police and other security services, the candidates' past actions in terms of respect for international humanitarian law and human rights;

13. *Recalling* its resolution 1502 of 26 August 2003, *reaffirms* the obligation of all parties to comply fully with the relevant rules and principles of international humanitarian law relating to the protection of humanitarian and United Nations personnel, and *also demands* that all parties concerned grant immediate, full and unimpeded access by humanitarian personnel to all persons in need of assistance, as provided for in applicable international law;

14. *Encourages* the Congolese authorities to continue their efforts, with the support of their international partners, to exercise effective, transparent and comprehensive control over State finances in order to put an end to impunity for those responsible for acts of embezzlement or corruption;

15. *Urges* all States, especially those in the region, including the Democratic Republic of the Congo itself, to take appropriate steps to end the illicit trade in natural resources, including if necessary through judicial means, and, where necessary, to report to the Council, and calls upon the international financial institutions to assist the Government of the DRC in establishing effective and transparent control over the exploitation of natural resources;

16. *Demands* that all parties cooperate fully with the operations of MONUC and that they ensure the security of as well as unhindered and immediate access for United Nations and associated personnel in carrying out their mandate, throughout the territory of the Democratic Republic of the Congo, *demands* in particular that all parties provide full access to MONUC military observers, including in all ports, airports, airfields, military bases and border crossings, and, in addition, that MONUC human rights observers are granted access to prisons, and *requests* the Secretary-General to report without delay any failure to comply with these demands;

17. *Encourages* the international community to continue its support for the peace consolidation process in the Democratic Republic of the Congo;

18. *Further urges* all Governments in the region, in particular those of Burundi, the Democratic Republic of the Congo, Rwanda and Uganda, to resolve in a constructive manner their shared security and border problems and to prevent the use of their respective territories in support of violations of the arms embargo imposed by resolutions 1493 and 1596 or in support of activities of armed groups present in the region, in particular through the Tripartite Plus Joint Commission and through the implementation of the Security, Stability and Development Pact for the Great Lakes Region which they signed on

15 December 2006, and *calls on* the signatories to ratify the Pact at the earliest possible opportunity and to take the necessary measures for its prompt implementation;

19. *Welcomes* MONUC's policy to promote and protect the rights of women and to take into account gender considerations as set out in its resolution 1325 (2000) as a cross-cutting issue throughout its mandate and to keep the Council informed;

20. *Requests* the Secretary-General, through his Special Representative for the Democratic Republic of the Congo, to continue to coordinate all the activities of the United Nations system in the Democratic Republic of the Congo;

21. *Requests* the Secretary-General to ensure that his Special Representative for the Democratic Republic of the Congo, his Executive Representative for Burundi and his Special Representative for the Sudan coordinate the activities of MONUC, the United Nations Integrated Office in Burundi (BINUB) and the United Nations Mission in the Sudan (UNMIS), within their respective mandates, inter alia:

- By sharing military information at their disposal, especially information concerning cross-border movements of armed elements and arms trafficking;
- By pooling their logistic and administrative resources, to an extent that does not prejudice the ability of these two Missions and the Office to carry out their respective mandates, in order to ensure their maximum efficiency and cost-effectiveness;
- By coordinating, as appropriate, the implementation of national disarmament, demobilization, repatriation, reintegration, resettlement and reintegration programmes;

22. *Expressing* grave concern at the allegations of sexual exploitation and violence by civilian and military personnel of MONUC, *taking note* of the measures taken by MONUC to address instances of sexual exploitation and abuse and of the zero tolerance policy reiterated by the Secretary General during his recent visit to the Democratic Republic of the Congo, *requests* the Secretary-General to continue to fully investigate these allegations, to take the appropriate measures set out in the Secretary-General's bulletin on special measures for protection from sexual exploitation and sexual abuse (ST/SGB/2003/13), and to keep the Council informed, *underlines* the importance of MONUC conducting training for the personnel concerned in order to ensure full compliance with its Code of Conduct regarding sexual misconduct, and *urges* troop-contributing countries to take appropriate disciplinary and other action to ensure full accountability in cases of such misconduct involving their personnel;

23. *Requests* the Secretary-General to keep it informed periodically of developments in the situation in the Democratic Republic of the Congo, and to submit to the Council by 15 November 2007 a report containing benchmarks and an indicative timetable for the gradual drawdown of MONUC;

24. *Decides* to remain actively seized of the matter.

Resolution 1757 (2007)

Adopted by the Security Council at its 5685th meeting, on 30 May 2007

The Security Council,

Recalling all its previous relevant resolutions, in particular resolutions 1595 (2005) of 7 April 2005, 1636 (2005) of 31 October 2005, 1644 (2005) of 15 December 2005, 1664 (2006) of 29 March 2006 and 1748 (2007) of 27 March 2007,

Reaffirming its strongest condemnation of the 14 February 2005 terrorist bombings as well as other attacks in Lebanon since October 2004,

Reiterating its call for the strict respect of the sovereignty, territorial integrity, unity and political independence of Lebanon under the sole and exclusive authority of the Government of Lebanon,

Recalling the letter of the Prime Minister of Lebanon to the Secretary-General of 13 December 2005 (S/2005/783) requesting inter alia the establishment of a tribunal of an international character to try all those who are found responsible for this terrorist crime, and the request by this Council for the Secretary-General to negotiate an agreement with the Government of Lebanon aimed at establishing such a Tribunal based on the highest international standards of criminal justice,

Recalling further the report of the Secretary-General on the establishment of a special tribunal for Lebanon on 15 November 2006 (S/2006/893) reporting on the conclusion of negotiations and consultations that took place between January 2006 and September 2006 at United Nations Headquarters in New York, the Hague, and Beirut between the Legal Counsel of the United Nations and authorized representatives of the Government of Lebanon, and the letter of its President to the Secretary-General of 21 November 2006 (S/2006/911) reporting that the Members of the Security Council welcomed the conclusion of the negotiations and that they were satisfied with the Agreement annexed to the Report,

Recalling that, as set out in its letter of 21 November 2006, should voluntary contributions be insufficient for the Tribunal to implement its mandate, the Secretary-General and the Security Council shall explore alternate means of financing the Tribunal,

Recalling also that the Agreement between the United Nations and the Lebanese Republic on the establishment of a Special Tribunal for Lebanon was signed by the Government of Lebanon and the United Nations respectively on 23 January and 6 February 2007,

Referring to the letter of the Prime Minister of Lebanon to the Secretary-General of the United Nations (S/2007/281), which recalled that the parliamentary majority has expressed its support for the Tribunal, and asked that his request that the Special Tribunal be put into effect be presented to the Council as a matter of urgency,

Mindful of the demand of the Lebanese people that all those responsible for the terrorist bombing that killed former Lebanese Prime Minister Rafiq Hariri and others be identified and brought to justice,

Commending the Secretary-General for his continuing efforts to proceed, together with the Government of Lebanon, with the final steps for the conclusion of the Agreement as requested in the letter of its President dated 21 November 2006 and referring in this regard to the briefing by the Legal Counsel on 2 May 2007, in which he noted that the establishment of the Tribunal through the Constitutional process is facing serious obstacles, but noting also that all parties concerned reaffirmed their agreement in principle to the establishment of the Tribunal,

Commending also the recent efforts of parties in the region to overcome these obstacles,

Willing to continue to assist Lebanon in the search for the truth and in holding all those involved in the terrorist attack accountable and reaffirming its determination to support Lebanon in its efforts to bring to justice perpetrators, organizers and sponsors of this and other assassinations,

Reaffirming its determination that this terrorist act and its implications constitute a threat to international peace and security,

1. *Decides*, acting under Chapter VII of the Charter of the United Nations, that:

(a) The provisions of the annexed document, including its attachment, on the establishment of a Special Tribunal for Lebanon shall enter into force on 10 June 2007, unless the Government of Lebanon has provided notification under Article 19 (1) of the annexed document before that date;

(b) If the Secretary-General reports that the Headquarters Agreement has not been concluded as envisioned under Article 8 of the annexed document, the location of the seat of the Tribunal shall be determined in consultation with the Government of Lebanon and be subject to the conclusion of a Headquarters Agreement between the United Nations and the State that hosts the Tribunal;

(c) If the Secretary-General reports that contributions from the Government of Lebanon are not sufficient to bear the expenses described in Article 5 (b) of the annexed document, he may accept or use voluntary contributions from States to cover any shortfall;

2. *Notes* that, pursuant to Article 19 (2) of the annexed document, the Special Tribunal shall commence functioning on a date to be determined by the Secretary-General in consultation with the Government of Lebanon, taking into account the progress of the work of the International Independent Investigation Commission;

3. *Requests* the Secretary-General, in coordination, when appropriate, with the Government of Lebanon, to undertake the steps and measures necessary to establish the Special Tribunal in a timely manner and to report to the Council within 90 days and thereafter periodically on the implementation of this resolution;

4. *Decides* to remain actively seized of the matter.

Annex
Agreement between the United Nations and the Lebanese Republic on the establishment of a Special Tribunal for Lebanon

Whereas the Security Council, in its resolution 1664 (2006) of 29 March 2006, which responded to the request of the Government of Lebanon to establish a tribunal of an international character to try all those who are found responsible for the terrorist crime which killed the former Lebanese Prime Minister Rafiq Hariri and others, recalled all its previous resolutions, in particular resolutions 1595 (2005) of 7 April 2005, 1636 (2005) of 31 October 2005 and 1644 (2005) of 15 December 2005,

Whereas the Security Council has requested the Secretary-General of the United Nations (hereinafter "the Secretary-General") "to negotiate an agreement with the Government of Lebanon aimed at establishing a tribunal of an international character based on the highest international standards of criminal justice", taking into account the recommendations of the Secretary-General's report of 21 March 2006 (S/2006/176) and the views that have been expressed by Council members,

Whereas the Secretary-General and the Government of the Lebanese Republic (hereinafter "the Government") have conducted negotiations for the establishment of a Special Tribunal for Lebanon (hereinafter "the Special Tribunal" or "the Tribunal"),

Now therefore the United Nations and the Lebanese Republic (hereinafter referred to jointly as the "Parties") have agreed as follows:

Article 1
Establishment of the Special Tribunal

1. There is hereby established a Special Tribunal for Lebanon to prosecute persons responsible for the attack of 14 February 2005 resulting in the death of former Lebanese Prime Minister Rafiq Hariri and in the death or injury of other persons. If the tribunal finds that other attacks that occurred in Lebanon between 1 October 2004 and 12 December 2005, or any later date decided by the Parties and with the consent of the Security Council, are connected in accordance with the principles of criminal justice and are of a nature and gravity similar to the attack of 14 February 2005, it shall also have jurisdiction over persons responsible for such attacks. This connection includes but is not limited to a combination of the following elements: criminal intent (motive), the purpose behind the attacks, the nature of the victims targeted, the pattern of the attacks (modus operandi) and the perpetrators.

2. The Special Tribunal shall function in accordance with the Statute of the Special Tribunal for Lebanon. The Statute is attached to this Agreement and forms an integral part thereof.

Article 2
Composition of the Special Tribunal and appointment of judges

1. The Special Tribunal shall consist of the following organs: the Chambers, the Prosecutor, the Registry and the Defence Office.

2. The Chambers shall be composed of a Pre-Trial Judge, a Trial Chamber and an Appeals Chamber, with a second Trial Chamber to be created if, after the passage of at least six months from the commencement of the functioning of the Special Tribunal, the Secretary-General or the President of the Special Tribunal so requests.

3. The Chambers shall be composed of no fewer than eleven independent judges and no more than fourteen such judges, who shall serve as follows:

(a) A single international judge shall serve as a Pre-Trial Judge;

(b) Three judges shall serve in the Trial Chamber, of whom one shall be a Lebanese judge and two shall be international judges;

(c) In the event of the creation of a second Trial Chamber, that Chamber shall be likewise composed in the manner contained in subparagraph (b) above;

(d) Five judges shall serve in the Appeals Chamber, of whom two shall be Lebanese judges and three shall be international judges; and

(e) Two alternate judges, of whom one shall be a Lebanese judge and one shall be an international judge.

4. The judges of the Tribunal shall be persons of high moral character, impartiality and integrity, with extensive judicial experience. They shall be independent in the performance of their functions and shall not accept or seek instructions from any Government or any other source.

5. (a) Lebanese judges shall be appointed by the Secretary-General to serve in the Trial Chamber or the Appeals Chamber or as an alternate judge from a list of twelve persons presented by the Government upon the proposal of the Lebanese Supreme Council of the Judiciary;

(b) International judges shall be appointed by the Secretary-General to serve as Pre-Trial Judge, a Trial Chamber Judge, an Appeals Chamber Judge or an alternate judge, upon nominations forwarded by States at the invitation of the Secretary-General, as well as by competent persons;

(c) The Government and the Secretary-General shall consult on the appointment of judges;

(d) The Secretary-General shall appoint judges, upon the recommendation of a selection panel he has established after indicating his intentions to the Security Council. The selection panel shall be composed of two judges, currently sitting on or retired from an international tribunal, and the representative of the Secretary-General.

6. At the request of the presiding judge of a Trial Chamber, the President of the Special Tribunal may, in the interest of justice, assign alternate judges to be present at each stage of the trial and to replace a judge if that judge is unable to continue sitting.

7. Judges shall be appointed for a three-year period and may be eligible for reappointment for a further period to be determined by the Secretary-General in consultation with the Government.

8. Lebanese judges appointed to serve in the Special Tribunal shall be given full credit for their period of service with the Tribunal on their return to the Lebanese national judiciaries from which they were released and shall be reintegrated at a level at least comparable to that of their former position.

Article 3
Appointment of a Prosecutor and a Deputy Prosecutor

1. The Secretary-General, after consultation with the Government, shall appoint a Prosecutor for a three-year term. The Prosecutor may be eligible for reappointment for a further period to be determined by the Secretary-General in consultation with the Government.

2. The Secretary-General shall appoint the Prosecutor, upon the recommendation of a selection panel he has established after indicating his intentions to the Security Council. The selection panel shall be composed of two judges, currently sitting on or retired from an international tribunal, and the representative of the Secretary-General.

3. The Government, in consultation with the Secretary-General and the Prosecutor, shall appoint a Lebanese Deputy Prosecutor to assist the Prosecutor in the conduct of the investigations and prosecutions.

4. The Prosecutor and the Deputy Prosecutor shall be of high moral character and possess the highest level of professional competence and extensive experience in the conduct of investigations and prosecutions of criminal cases. The Prosecutor and the Deputy Prosecutor shall be independent in the performance of their functions and shall not accept or seek instructions from any Government or any other source.

5. The Prosecutor shall be assisted by such Lebanese and international staff as may be required to perform the functions assigned to him or her effectively and efficiently.

Article 4
Appointment of a Registrar

1. The Secretary-General shall appoint a Registrar who shall be responsible for the servicing of the Chambers and the Office of the Prosecutor, and for the recruitment and administration of all support staff. He or she shall also administer the financial and staff resources of the Special Tribunal.

2. The Registrar shall be a staff member of the United Nations. He or she shall serve a three-year term and may be eligible for reappointment for a further period to be determined by the Secretary-General in consultation with the Government.

Article 5
Financing of the Special Tribunal

1. The expenses of the Special Tribunal shall be borne in the following manner:

(a) Fifty-one per cent of the expenses of the Tribunal shall be borne by voluntary contributions from States;

(b) Forty-nine per cent of the expenses of the Tribunal shall be borne by the Government of Lebanon.

2. It is understood that the Secretary-General will commence the process of establishing the Tribunal when he has sufficient contributions in hand to finance the establishment of the Tribunal and twelve months of its operations plus pledges equal to the anticipated expenses of the following 24 months of the Tribunal's operation. Should voluntary contributions be insufficient for the Tribunal to implement its mandate, the Secretary-General and the Security Council shall explore alternate means of financing the Tribunal.

Article 6
Management Committee

The parties shall consult concerning the establishment of a Management Committee.

Article 7
Juridical capacity

The Special Tribunal shall possess the juridical capacity necessary:

(a) To contract;

(b) To acquire and dispose of movable and immovable property;

(c) To institute legal proceedings;

(d) To enter into agreements with States as may be necessary for the exercise of its functions and for the operation of the Tribunal.

Article 8
Seat of the Special Tribunal

1. The Special Tribunal shall have its seat outside Lebanon. The location of the seat shall be determined having due regard to considerations of justice and fairness as well as security and administrative efficiency, including the rights of victims and access to witnesses, and subject to the conclusion of a headquarters agreement between the United Nations, the Government and the State that hosts the Tribunal.

2. The Special Tribunal may meet away from its seat when it considers it necessary for the efficient exercise of its functions.

3. An Office of the Special Tribunal for the conduct of investigations shall be established in Lebanon subject to the conclusion of appropriate arrangements with the Government.

Article 9
Inviolability of premises, archives and all other documents

1. The Office of the Special Tribunal in Lebanon shall be inviolable. The competent authorities shall take appropriate action that may be necessary to ensure that the Tribunal shall not be dispossessed of all or any part of the premises of the Tribunal without its express consent.

2. The property, funds and assets of the Office of the Special Tribunal in Lebanon, wherever located and by whomsoever held, shall be immune from search, seizure, requisition, confiscation, expropriation and any other form of interference, whether by executive, administrative, judicial or legislative action.

3. The archives of the Office of the Special Tribunal in Lebanon, and in general all documents and materials made available, belonging to or used by it, wherever located and by whomsoever held, shall be inviolable.

Article 10
Funds, assets and other property

The Office of the Special Tribunal, its funds, assets and other property in Lebanon, wherever located and by whomsoever held, shall enjoy immunity from every form of legal process, except insofar as in any particular case the Tribunal has expressly waived its immunity. It is understood, however, that no waiver of immunity shall extend to any measure of execution.

Article 11
Privileges and immunities of the judges, the Prosecutor, the Deputy Prosecutor,the Registrar and the Head of the Defence Office

1. The judges, the Prosecutor, the Deputy Prosecutor, the Registrar and the Head of the Defence Office, while in Lebanon, shall enjoy the privileges and immunities, exemptions and facilities accorded to diplomatic agents in accordance with the Vienna Convention on Diplomatic Relations of 1961.

2. Privileges and immunities are accorded to the judges, the Prosecutor, the Deputy Prosecutor, the Registrar and the Head of the Defence Office in the interest of the Special Tribunal and not for the personal benefit of the individuals themselves. The right and the duty to waive the immunity in any case where it can be waived without prejudice to the purposes for which it is accorded shall lie with the Secretary-General, in consultation with the President of the Tribunal.

Article 12
Privileges and immunities of international and Lebanese personnel

1. Lebanese and international personnel of the Office of the Special Tribunal, while in Lebanon, shall be accorded:

(a) Immunity from legal process in respect of words spoken or written and all acts performed by them in their official capacity. Such immunity shall continue to be accorded after termination of employment with the Office of the Special Tribunal;

(b) Exemption from taxation on salaries, allowances and emoluments paid to them.

2. International personnel shall, in addition thereto, be accorded:

(a) Immunity from immigration restriction;

(b) The right to import free of duties and taxes, except for payment for services, their furniture and effects at the time of first taking up their official duties in Lebanon.

3. The privileges and immunities are granted to the officials of the Office of the Special Tribunal in the interest of the Tribunal and not for their personal benefit. The right and the duty to waive the immunity in any case where it can be waived without prejudice to the purpose for which it is accorded shall lie with the Registrar of the Tribunal.

Article 13
Defence counsel

1. The Government shall ensure that the counsel of a suspect or an accused who has been admitted as such by the Special Tribunal shall not be subjected, while in Lebanon, to any measure that may affect the free and independent exercise of his or her functions.

2. In particular, the counsel shall be accorded:

(a) Immunity from personal arrest or detention and from seizure of personal baggage;

(b) Inviolability of all documents relating to the exercise of his or her functions as a counsel of a suspect or accused;

(c) Immunity from criminal or civil jurisdiction in respect of words spoken or written and acts performed in his or her capacity as counsel. Such immunity shall continue to be accorded after termination of his or her functions as a counsel of a suspect or accused;

(d) Immunity from any immigration restrictions during his or her stay as well as during his or her journey to the Tribunal and back.

Article 14
Security, safety and protection of persons referred to in this Agreement

The Government shall take effective and adequate measures to ensure the appropriate security, safety and protection of personnel of the Office of the Special Tribunal and other persons referred to in this Agreement, while in Lebanon. It shall take all appropriate steps, within its capabilities, to protect the equipment and premises of the Office of the Special Tribunal from attack or any action that prevents the Tribunal from discharging its mandate.

Article 15
Cooperation with the Special Tribunal

1. The Government shall cooperate with all organs of the Special Tribunal, in particular with the Prosecutor and defence counsel, at all stages of the proceedings. It shall facilitate access of the Prosecutor and defence counsel to sites, persons and relevant documents required for the investigation.

2. The Government shall comply without undue delay with any request for assistance by the Special Tribunal or an order issued by the Chambers, including, but not limited to:

(a) Identification and location of persons;

(b) Service of documents;

(c) Arrest or detention of persons;

(d) Transfer of an indictee to the Tribunal.

Article 16
Amnesty

The Government undertakes not to grant amnesty to any person for any crime falling within the jurisdiction of the Special Tribunal. An amnesty already granted in respect of any such persons and crimes shall not be a bar to prosecution.

Article 17
Practical arrangements

With a view to achieving efficiency and cost-effectiveness in the operation of the Special Tribunal:

(a) Appropriate arrangements shall be made to ensure that there is a coordinated transition from the activities of the International Independent Investigation Commission, established by the Security Council in its resolution 1595 (2005), to the activities of the Office of the Prosecutor;

(b) Judges of the Trial Chamber and the Appeals Chamber shall take office on a date to be determined by the Secretary-General in consultation with the President of the Special Tribunal. Pending such a determination, judges of both Chambers shall be convened on an ad hoc basis to deal with organizational matters and serving, when required, to perform their duties.

Article 18
Settlement of disputes

Any dispute between the Parties concerning the interpretation or application of this Agreement shall be settled by negotiation or by any other mutually agreed upon mode of settlement.

Article 19
Entry into force and commencement of the functioning of the Special Tribunal

1. This Agreement shall enter into force on the day after the Government has notified the United Nations in writing that the legal requirements for entry into force have been complied with.

2. The Special Tribunal shall commence functioning on a date to be determined by the Secretary-General in consultation with the Government, taking into account the progress of the work of the International Independent Investigation Commission.

Article 20
Amendment

This Agreement may be amended by written agreement between the Parties.

Article 21
Duration of the Agreement

1. This Agreement shall remain in force for a period of three years from the date of the commencement of the functioning of the Special Tribunal.

2. Three years after the commencement of the functioning of the Special Tribunal the Parties shall, in consultation with the Security Council, review the progress of the work of the Special Tribunal. If at the end of this period of three years the activities of the Tribunal have not been completed, the Agreement shall be extended to allow the Tribunal to complete its work, for a further period(s) to be determined by the Secretary-General in consultation with the Government and the Security Council.

3. The provisions relating to the inviolability of the funds, assets, archives and documents of the Office of the Special Tribunal in Lebanon, the privileges and immunities of those referred to in this Agreement, as well as provisions relating to defence counsel and the protection of victims and witnesses, shall survive termination of this Agreement.

In witness whereof, the following duly authorized representatives of the United Nations and of the Lebanese Republic have signed this Agreement.

Done at __________ on __________ 2006, in three originals in the Arabic, French and English languages, all texts being equally authentic.

For the United Nations: For the Lebanese Republic:

______________________ ______________________

Attachment

Statute of the Special Tribunal for Lebanon

Having been established by an Agreement between the United Nations and the Lebanese Republic (hereinafter "the Agreement") pursuant to Security Council resolution 1664 (2006) of 29 March 2006, which responded to the request of the Government of Lebanon to establish a tribunal of an international character to try all those who are found responsible for the terrorist crime which killed the former Lebanese Prime Minister Rafiq Hariri and others, the Special Tribunal for Lebanon (hereinafter "the Special Tribunal") shall function in accordance with the provisions of this Statute.

Section I
Jurisdiction and applicable law

Article 1
Jurisdiction of the Special Tribunal

The Special Tribunal shall have jurisdiction over persons responsible for the attack of 14 February 2005 resulting in the death of former Lebanese Prime Minister Rafiq Hariri and in the death or injury of other persons. If the Tribunal finds that other attacks that occurred in Lebanon between 1 October 2004 and 12 December 2005, or any later date decided by the Parties and with the consent of the Security Council, are connected in accordance with the principles of criminal justice and are of a nature and gravity similar to the attack of 14 February 2005, it shall also have jurisdiction over persons responsible for such attacks. This connection includes but is not limited to a combination of the following elements: criminal intent (motive), the purpose behind the attacks, the nature of the victims targeted, the pattern of the attacks (modus operandi) and the perpetrators.

Article 2
Applicable criminal law

The following shall be applicable to the prosecution and punishment of the crimes referred to in article 1, subject to the provisions of this Statute:

(a) The provisions of the Lebanese Criminal Code relating to the prosecution and punishment of acts of terrorism, crimes and offences against life and personal integrity, illicit associations and failure to report crimes and offences, including the rules regarding the material elements of a crime, criminal participation and conspiracy; and

(b) Articles 6 and 7 of the Lebanese law of 11 January 1958 on "Increasing the penalties for sedition, civil war and interfaith struggle".

Article 3
Individual criminal responsibility

1. A person shall be individually responsible for crimes within the jurisdiction of the Special Tribunal if that person:

(a) Committed, participated as accomplice, organized or directed others to commit the crime set forth in article 2 of this Statute; or

(b) Contributed in any other way to the commission of the crime set forth in article 2 of this Statute by a group of persons acting with a common purpose, where such contribution is intentional and is either made with the aim of furthering the general criminal activity or purpose of the group or in the knowledge of the intention of the group to commit the crime.

2. With respect to superior and subordinate relationships, a superior shall be criminally responsible for any of the crimes set forth in article 2 of this Statute committed by subordinates under his or her effective authority and control, as a result of his or her failure to exercise control properly over such subordinates, where:

(a) The superior either knew, or consciously disregarded information that clearly indicated that the subordinates were committing or about to commit such crimes;

(b) The crimes concerned activities that were within the effective responsibility and control of the superior; and

(c) The superior failed to take all necessary and reasonable measures within his or her power to prevent or repress their commission or to submit the matter to the competent authorities for investigation and prosecution.

3. The fact that the person acted pursuant to an order of a superior shall not relieve him or her of criminal responsibility, but may be considered in mitigation of punishment if the Special Tribunal determines that justice so requires.

Article 4
Concurrent jurisdiction

1. The Special Tribunal and the national courts of Lebanon shall have concurrent jurisdiction. Within its jurisdiction, the Tribunal shall have primacy over the national courts of Lebanon.

2. Upon the assumption of office of the Prosecutor, as determined by the Secretary-General, and no later than two months thereafter, the Special Tribunal shall request the national judicial authority seized with the case of the attack against Prime Minister Rafiq Hariri and others to defer to its competence. The Lebanese judicial authority shall refer to the Tribunal the results of the investigation and a copy of the court's records, if any. Persons detained in connection with the investigation shall be transferred to the custody of the Tribunal.

3. (a) At the request of the Special Tribunal, the national judicial authority seized with any of the other crimes committed between 1 October 2004 and 12 December 2005, or a later date decided pursuant to article 1, shall refer to the Tribunal the results of the investigation and a copy of the court's records, if any, for review by the Prosecutor;

(b) At the further request of the Tribunal, the national authority in question shall defer to the competence of the Tribunal. It shall refer to the Tribunal the results of the investigation and a copy of the court's records, if any, and persons detained in connection with any such case shall be transferred to the custody of the Tribunal;

(c) The national judicial authorities shall regularly inform the Tribunal of the progress of their investigation. At any stage of the proceedings, the Tribunal may formally request a national judicial authority to defer to its competence.

Article 5
Non bis in idem

1. No person shall be tried before a national court of Lebanon for acts for which he or she has already been tried by the Special Tribunal.

2. A person who has been tried by a national court may be subsequently tried by the Special Tribunal if the national court proceedings were not impartial or independent, were designed to shield the accused from criminal responsibility for crimes within the jurisdiction of the Tribunal or the case was not diligently prosecuted.

3. In considering the penalty to be imposed on a person convicted of a crime under this Statute, the Special Tribunal shall take into account the extent to which any penalty imposed by a national court on the same person for the same act has already been served.

Article 6
Amnesty

An amnesty granted to any person for any crime falling within the jurisdiction of the Special Tribunal shall not be a bar to prosecution.

Section II
Organization of the Special Tribunal

Article 7
Organs of the Special Tribunal

The Special Tribunal shall consist of the following organs:

(a) The Chambers, comprising a Pre-Trial Judge, a Trial Chamber and an Appeals Chamber;

(b) The Prosecutor;

(c) The Registry; and

(d) The Defence Office.

Article 8
Composition of the Chambers

1. The Chambers shall be composed as follows:

(a) One international Pre-Trial Judge;

(b) Three judges who shall serve in the Trial Chamber, of whom one shall be a Lebanese judge and two shall be international judges;

(c) Five judges who shall serve in the Appeals Chamber, of whom two shall be Lebanese judges and three shall be international judges;

(d) Two alternate judges, one of whom shall be a Lebanese judge and one shall be an international judge.

2. The judges of the Appeals Chamber and the judges of the Trial Chamber, respectively, shall elect a presiding judge who shall conduct the proceedings in the Chamber to which he or she was elected. The presiding judge of the Appeals Chamber shall be the President of the Special Tribunal.

3. At the request of the presiding judge of the Trial Chamber, the President of the Special Tribunal may, in the interest of justice, assign the alternate judges to be present at each stage of the trial and to replace a judge if that judge is unable to continue sitting.

Article 9
Qualification and appointment of judges

1. The judges shall be persons of high moral character, impartiality and integrity, with extensive judicial experience. They shall be independent in the performance of their functions and shall not accept or seek instructions from any Government or any other source.

2. In the overall composition of the Chambers, due account shall be taken of the established competence of the judges in criminal law and procedure and international law.

3. The judges shall be appointed by the Secretary-General, as set forth in article 2 of the Agreement, for a three-year period and may be eligible for reappointment for a further period to be determined by the Secretary-General in consultation with the Government.

Article 10
Powers of the President of the Special Tribunal

1. The President of the Special Tribunal, in addition to his or her judicial functions, shall represent the Tribunal and be responsible for its effective functioning and the good administration of justice.

2. The President of the Special Tribunal shall submit an annual report on the operation and activities of the Tribunal to the Secretary-General and to the Government of Lebanon.

Article 11
The Prosecutor

1. The Prosecutor shall be responsible for the investigation and prosecution of persons responsible for the crimes falling within the jurisdiction of the Special Tribunal. In the interest of proper administration of justice, he or she may decide to charge jointly persons accused of the same or different crimes committed in the course of the same transaction.

2. The Prosecutor shall act independently as a separate organ of the Special Tribunal. He or she shall not seek or receive instructions from any Government or from any other source.

3. The Prosecutor shall be appointed, as set forth in article 3 of the Agreement, by the Secretary-General for a three-year term and may be eligible for reappointment for a further period to be determined by the Secretary-General in consultation with the Government. He or she shall be of high moral character and possess the highest level of professional competence, and have extensive experience in the conduct of investigations and prosecutions of criminal cases.

4. The Prosecutor shall be assisted by a Lebanese Deputy Prosecutor and by such other Lebanese and international staff as may be required to perform the functions assigned to him or her effectively and efficiently.

5. The Office of the Prosecutor shall have the power to question suspects, victims and witnesses, to collect evidence and to conduct on-site investigations. In carrying out these tasks, the Prosecutor shall, as appropriate, be assisted by the Lebanese authorities concerned.

Article 12
The Registry

1. Under the authority of the President of the Special Tribunal, the Registry shall be responsible for the administration and servicing of the Tribunal.

2. The Registry shall consist of a Registrar and such other staff as may be required.

3. The Registrar shall be appointed by the Secretary-General and shall be a staff member of the United Nations. He or she shall serve for a three-year term and may be eligible for reappointment for a further period to be determined by the Secretary-General in consultation with the Government.

4. The Registrar shall set up a Victims and Witnesses Unit within the Registry. This Unit shall provide, in consultation with the Office of the Prosecutor, measures to protect the safety, physical and psychological well-being, dignity and privacy of victims and witnesses, and such other appropriate assistance for witnesses who appear before the Special Tribunal and others who are at risk on account of testimony given by such witnesses.

Article 13
The Defence Office

1. The Secretary-General, in consultation with the President of the Special Tribunal, shall appoint an independent Head of the Defence Office, who shall be responsible for the appointment of the Office staff and the drawing up of a list of defence counsel.

2. The Defence Office, which may also include one or more public defenders, shall protect the rights of the defence, provide support and assistance to defence counsel and to the persons entitled to legal assistance, including, where appropriate, legal research, collection of evidence and advice, and appearing before the Pre-Trial Judge or a Chamber in respect of specific issues.

Article 14
Official and working languages

The official languages of the Special Tribunal shall be Arabic, French and English. In any given case proceedings, the Pre-Trial Judge or a Chamber may decide that one or two of the languages may be used as working languages as appropriate.

Section III
Rights of defendants and victims

Article 15
Rights of suspects during investigation

A suspect who is to be questioned by the Prosecutor shall not be compelled to incriminate himself or herself or to confess guilt. He or she shall have the following rights of which he or she shall be informed by the Prosecutor prior to questioning, in a language he or she speaks and understands:

(a) The right to be informed that there are grounds to believe that he or she has committed a crime within the jurisdiction of the Special Tribunal;

(b) The right to remain silent, without such silence being considered in the determination of guilt or innocence, and to be cautioned that any statement he or she makes shall be recorded and may be used in evidence;

(c) The right to have legal assistance of his or her own choosing, including the right to have legal assistance provided by the Defence Office where the interests of justice so require and where the suspect does not have sufficient means to pay for it;

(d) The right to have the free assistance of an interpreter if he or she cannot understand or speak the language used for questioning;

(e) The right to be questioned in the presence of counsel unless the person has voluntarily waived his or her right to counsel.

Article 16
Rights of the accused

1. All accused shall be equal before the Special Tribunal.

2. The accused shall be entitled to a fair and public hearing, subject to measures ordered by the Special Tribunal for the protection of victims and witnesses.

3. (a) The accused shall be presumed innocent until proved guilty according to the provisions of this Statute;

(b) The onus is on the Prosecutor to prove the guilt of the accused;

(c) In order to convict the accused, the relevant Chamber must be convinced of the guilt of the accused beyond reasonable doubt.

4. In the determination of any charge against the accused pursuant to this Statute, he or she shall be entitled to the following minimum guarantees, in full equality:

(a) To be informed promptly and in detail in a language which he or she understands of the nature and cause of the charge against him or her;

(b) To have adequate time and facilities for the preparation of his or her defence and to communicate without hindrance with counsel of his or her own choosing;

(c) To be tried without undue delay;

(d) Subject to the provisions of article 22, to be tried in his or her presence, and to defend himself or herself in person or through legal assistance of his or her own choosing; to be informed, if he or she does not have legal assistance, of this right; and to have legal assistance assigned to him or her, in any case where the interests of justice so require and without payment by him or her in any such case if he or she does not have sufficient means to pay for it;

(e) To examine, or have examined, the witnesses against him or her and to obtain the attendance and examination of witnesses on his or her behalf under the same conditions as witnesses against him or her;

(f) To examine all evidence to be used against him or her during the trial in accordance with the Rules of Procedure and Evidence of the Special Tribunal;

(g) To have the free assistance of an interpreter if he or she cannot understand or speak the language used in the Special Tribunal;

(h) Not to be compelled to testify against himself or herself or to confess guilt.

5. The accused may make statements in court at any stage of the proceedings, provided such statements are relevant to the case at issue. The Chambers shall decide on the probative value, if any, of such statements.

Article 17
Rights of victims

Where the personal interests of the victims are affected, the Special Tribunal shall permit their views and concerns to be presented and considered at stages of the proceedings determined to be appropriate by the Pre-Trial Judge or the Chamber and in a manner that is not prejudicial to or inconsistent with the rights of the accused and a fair and impartial trial. Such views and concerns may be presented by the legal representatives of the victims where the Pre-Trial Judge or the Chamber considers it appropriate.

Section IV
Conduct of proceedings

Article 18
Pre-Trial proceedings

1. The Pre-Trial Judge shall review the indictment. If satisfied that a prima facie case has been established by the Prosecutor, he or she shall confirm the indictment. If he or she is not so satisfied, the indictment shall be dismissed.

2. The Pre-Trial Judge may, at the request of the Prosecutor, issue such orders and warrants for the arrest or transfer of persons, and any other orders as may be required for the conduct of the investigation and for the preparation of a fair and expeditious trial.

Article 19
Evidence collected prior to the establishment of the Special Tribunal

Evidence collected with regard to cases subject to the consideration of the Special Tribunal, prior to the establishment of the Tribunal, by the national authorities of Lebanon or by the

International Independent Investigation Commission in accordance with its mandate as set out in Security Council resolution 1595 (2005) and subsequent resolutions, shall be received by the Tribunal. Its admissibility shall be decided by the Chambers pursuant to international standards on collection of evidence. The weight to be given to any such evidence shall be determined by the Chambers.

Article 20
Commencement and conduct of trial proceedings

1. The Trial Chamber shall read the indictment to the accused, satisfy itself that the rights of the accused are respected, confirm that the accused understands the indictment and instruct the accused to enter a plea.

2. Unless otherwise decided by the Trial Chamber in the interests of justice, examination of witnesses shall commence with questions posed by the presiding judge, followed by questions posed by other members of the Trial Chamber, the Prosecutor and the Defence.

3. Upon request or *proprio motu*, the Trial Chamber may at any stage of the trial decide to call additional witnesses and/or order the production of additional evidence.

4. The hearings shall be public unless the Trial Chamber decides to hold the proceedings in camera in accordance with the Rules of Procedure and Evidence.

Article 21
Powers of the Chambers

1. The Special Tribunal shall confine the trial, appellate and review proceedings strictly to an expeditious hearing of the issues raised by the charges, or the grounds for appeal or review, respectively. It shall take strict measures to prevent any action that may cause unreasonable delay.

2. A Chamber may admit any relevant evidence that it deems to have probative value and exclude such evidence if its probative value is substantially outweighed by the need to ensure a fair trial.

3. A Chamber may receive the evidence of a witness orally or, where the interests of justice allow, in written form.

4. In cases not otherwise provided for in the Rules of Procedure and Evidence, a Chamber shall apply rules of evidence that will best favour a fair determination of the matter before it and are consonant with the spirit of the Statute and the general principles of law.

Article 22
Trials in absentia

1. The Special Tribunal shall conduct trial proceedings in the absence of the accused, if he or she:

(a) Has expressly and in writing waived his or her right to be present;

(b) Has not been handed over to the Tribunal by the State authorities concerned;

(c) Has absconded or otherwise cannot be found and all reasonable steps have been taken to secure his or her appearance before the Tribunal and to inform him or her of the charges confirmed by the Pre-Trial Judge.

2. When hearings are conducted in the absence of the accused, the Special Tribunal shall ensure that:

(a) The accused has been notified, or served with the indictment, or notice has otherwise been given of the indictment through publication in the media or communication to the State of residence or nationality;

(b) The accused has designated a defence counsel of his or her own choosing, to be remunerated either by the accused or, if the accused is proved to be indigent, by the Tribunal;

(c) Whenever the accused refuses or fails to appoint a defence counsel, such counsel has been assigned by the Defence Office of the Tribunal with a view to ensuring full representation of the interests and rights of the accused.

3. In case of conviction in absentia, the accused, if he or she had not designated a defence counsel of his or her choosing, shall have the right to be retried in his or her presence before the Special Tribunal, unless he or she accepts the judgement.

Article 23
Judgement

The judgement shall be rendered by a majority of the judges of the Trial Chamber or of the Appeals Chamber and shall be delivered in public. It shall be accompanied by a reasoned opinion in writing, to which any separate or dissenting opinions shall be appended.

Article 24
Penalties

1. The Trial Chamber shall impose upon a convicted person imprisonment for life or for a specified number of years. In determining the terms of imprisonment for the crimes provided for in this Statute, the Trial Chamber shall, as appropriate, have recourse to international practice regarding prison sentences and to the practice of the national courts of Lebanon.

2. In imposing sentence, the Trial Chamber should take into account such factors as the gravity of the offence and the individual circumstances of the convicted person.

Article 25
Compensation to victims

1. The Special Tribunal may identify victims who have suffered harm as a result of the commission of crimes by an accused convicted by the Tribunal.

2. The Registrar shall transmit to the competent authorities of the State concerned the judgement finding the accused guilty of a crime that has caused harm to a victim.

3. Based on the decision of the Special Tribunal and pursuant to the relevant national legislation, a victim or persons claiming through the victim, whether or not such victim had

been identified as such by the Tribunal under paragraph 1 of this article, may bring an action in a national court or other competent body to obtain compensation.

4. For the purposes of a claim made under paragraph 3 of this article, the judgement of the Special Tribunal shall be final and binding as to the criminal responsibility of the convicted person.

Article 26
Appellate proceedings

1. The Appeals Chamber shall hear appeals from persons convicted by the Trial Chamber or from the Prosecutor on the following grounds:

(a) An error on a question of law invalidating the decision;

(b) An error of fact that has occasioned a miscarriage of justice.

2. The Appeals Chamber may affirm, reverse or revise the decisions taken by the Trial Chamber.

Article 27
Review proceedings

1. Where a new fact has been discovered that was not known at the time of the proceedings before the Trial Chamber or the Appeals Chamber and that could have been a decisive factor in reaching the decision, the convicted person or the Prosecutor may submit an application for review of the judgement.

2. An application for review shall be submitted to the Appeals Chamber. The Appeals Chamber may reject the application if it considers it to be unfounded. If it determines that the application is meritorious, it may, as appropriate:

(a) Reconvene the Trial Chamber;

(b) Retain jurisdiction over the matter.

Article 28
Rules of Procedure and Evidence

1. The judges of the Special Tribunal shall, as soon as practicable after taking office, adopt Rules of Procedure and Evidence for the conduct of the pre-trial, trial and appellate proceedings, the admission of evidence, the participation of victims, the protection of victims and witnesses and other appropriate matters and may amend them, as appropriate.

2. In so doing, the judges shall be guided, as appropriate, by the Lebanese Code of Criminal Procedure, as well as by other reference materials reflecting the highest standards of international criminal procedure, with a view to ensuring a fair and expeditious trial.

Article 29
Enforcement of sentences

1. Imprisonment shall be served in a State designated by the President of the Special Tribunal from a list of States that have indicated their willingness to accept persons convicted by the Tribunal.

2. Conditions of imprisonment shall be governed by the law of the State of enforcement subject to the supervision of the Special Tribunal. The State of enforcement shall be bound by the duration of the sentence, subject to article 30 of this Statute.

Article 30
Pardon or commutation of sentences

If, pursuant to the applicable law of the State in which the convicted person is imprisoned, he or she is eligible for pardon or commutation of sentence, the State concerned shall notify the Special Tribunal accordingly. There shall only be pardon or commutation of sentence if the President of the Tribunal, in consultation with the judges, so decides on the basis of the interests of justice and the general principles of law.

Resolution 1758 (2007)

Adopted by the Security Council at its 5696th meeting, on 15 June 2007

The Security Council,

Welcoming the report of the Secretary-General of 4 June 2007 (S/2007/328) on the United Nations operation in Cyprus,

Noting that the Government of Cyprus is agreed that in view of the prevailing conditions in the island it is necessary to keep UNFICYP beyond 15 June 2007,

Echoing the Secretary-General's firm belief that the responsibility of finding a solution lies first and foremost with the Cypriots themselves and noting the primary role of the United Nations in assisting the parties to bring the Cyprus conflict and division of the island to a comprehensive and durable settlement,

Taking note of the assessment of the Secretary-General that the security situation on the island and along the Green Line remains generally stable, but noting with concern the increase in the overall number of violations of the buffer zone, and urging both sides to avoid any action which could lead to an increase in tension,

Underlining that activity in the buffer zone should not be at the expense of stability and security, and noting the Secretary-General's firm belief that the situation in the buffer zone would be improved if both sides accepted the 1989 aidememoire used by the United Nations,

Welcoming the principles and decisions enshrined in the 8 July 2006 Agreement, stressing that a comprehensive settlement based on a bicommunal, bizonal federation and political equality, as set out in the relevant Security Council resolutions, is both desirable and possible and should not be further delayed,

Noting, with regret, the failure to date to implement the 8 July 2006 Agreement, and urging the leaders of both communities to act to start the process without delay in order to prepare the ground for fully-fledged negotiations leading to a comprehensive and durable settlement,

Regretting that demining activity in the buffer zone has stalled, welcoming the provision by the European Union of funds to support these activities, and urging the Turkish Forces and the Turkish Cypriot side to allow the resumption of demining activities,

Reiterating its call to the parties to assess and address the humanitarian issue of all missing persons with due urgency and seriousness, and welcoming in this regard the progress and continuation of the important activities of the Committee on Missing Persons; expressing the hope that this process will promote reconciliation between the communities,

Welcoming the continuing crossings of the Green Line by Cypriots and encouraging further progress on other confidence-building measures, such as the opening of additional crossing points including, but not limited to, at Ledra Street, taking into account the arrangements already in place at existing crossing points,

Welcoming all efforts to promote bicommunal contacts and events, including, inter alia, on the part of all United Nations bodies on the island urging the two sides to promote the active engagement of civil society and the encouragement of cooperation between economic and commercial bodies and to remove all obstacles to such contacts,

Expressing concern, in this respect, that opportunities for constructive public debate about the future of the island, within and between the communities, are becoming fewer, and that this atmosphere is hampering, in particular, efforts to foster bicommunal activities intended to benefit all Cypriots, and to promote reconciliation and build trust in order to facilitate a comprehensive settlement,

Reaffirming the importance of the Secretary-General continuing to keep the operations of UNFICYP under close review while continuing to take into account developments on the ground and the views of the parties, and reverting to the Council with recommendations as appropriate for further adjustments to UNFICYP's mandate, force levels and concept of operation as soon as warranted,

Noting the unacceptable accommodation conditions endured by many UNFICYP troops, and welcoming the recent commitment by the Republic of Cyprus to address this issue without delay,

Echoing the Secretary-General's gratitude to the Government of Cyprus and the Government of Greece for their voluntary contributions to the funding of UNFICYP, and his request for further voluntary contributions from other countries and organizations,

Welcoming and encouraging efforts by the United Nations to sensitize peacekeeping personnel in the prevention and control of HIV/AIDS and other communicable diseases in all its peacekeeping operations,

1. *Welcomes* the observations in the Secretary-General's report;

2. *Expresses* full support for the 8 July process, notes with concern the lack of progress, and calls upon all parties to immediately engage constructively with the United Nations efforts, as described in Under-Secretary-General Gambari's letter of 15 November 2006, to demonstrate measurable progress in order to allow fully-fledged negotiations to begin, and to cease mutual recriminations;

3. *Reaffirms* all its relevant resolutions on Cyprus, in particular resolution 1251 (1999) of 29 June 1999 and subsequent resolutions;

4. *Reaffirms* that the status quo is unacceptable, that time is not on the side of a settlement, and that negotiations on a final political solution to the Cyprus problem have been at an impasse for too long;

5. *Expresses* its full support for UNFICYP and decides to extend its mandate for a further period ending 15 December 2007;

6. *Calls on* both sides to engage, as a matter of urgency and while respecting UNFICYP's mandate, in consultations with UNFICYP on the demarcation of the buffer zone, in particular in relation to the Ledra Street crossing point, with a view to reaching agreement on the United Nations 1989 aide-memoire;

7. *Calls on* the Turkish Cypriot side and Turkish forces to restore in Strovilia the military status quo which existed there prior to 30 June 2000;

8. *Requests* the Secretary-General to submit a report on implementation of this resolution by 1 December 2007;

9. *Welcomes* the efforts being undertaken by UNFICYP to implement the Secretary-General's zero tolerance policy on sexual exploitation and abuse and to ensure full compliance of its personnel with the United Nations code of conduct, requests the Secretary-General to continue to take all necessary action in this regard and to keep the Security Council informed, and urges troop-contributing countries to take appropriate preventive action including the conduct of predeployment awareness training, and to take disciplinary action and other action to ensure full accountability in cases of such conduct involving their personnel;

10. *Decides* to remain seized of the matter.

Resolution 1759 (2007)

Adopted by the Security Council at its 5698th meeting, on 20 June 2007

The Security Council,

Having considered the report of the Secretary-General on the United Nations Disengagement Observer Force of 5 June 2007 (S/2007/331), and also reaffirming its resolution 1308 (2000) of 17 July 2000,

1. *Calls upon* the parties concerned to implement immediately its resolution 338 (1973) of 22 October 1973;

2. *Welcomes* the efforts being undertaken by the United Nations Disengagement Observer Force to implement the Secretary-General's zero-tolerance policy on sexual exploitation and abuse and to ensure full compliance of its personnel with the United Nations code of conduct, requests the Secretary-General to continue to take all necessary action in this regard and to keep the Security Council informed, and urges troop-contributing countries to take preventive and disciplinary action to ensure that such acts are properly investigated and punished in cases involving their personnel;

3. *Decides* to renew the mandate of the United Nations Disengagement Observer Force for a period of six months, that is, until 31 December 2007;

4. *Requests* the Secretary-General to submit, at the end of this period, a report on developments in the situation and the measures taken to implement resolution 338 (1973).

Resolution 1760 (2007)

Adopted by the Security Council at its 5699th meeting, on 20 June 2007

The Security Council,

Recalling its previous resolutions and statements by its President on the situation in Liberia and West Africa,

Welcoming the sustained progress made by the Government of Liberia since January 2006, in rebuilding Liberia for the benefit of all Liberians, with the support of the international community,

Recalling its decision not to renew the measures in paragraph 10 of resolution 1521 (2003) regarding round log and timber products originating in Liberia, and stressing that Liberia's progress in the timber sector must continue with the effective implementation and enforcement of the National Forestry Reform Law signed into law on 5 October 2006, including the resolution of land and tenure rights,

Applauding the Government of Liberia's recent admission as a participant in the Kimberley Process Certification Scheme,

Anticipating the Kimberley Process report to the Council, through the Committee established pursuant to resolution 1521 (2003), as encouraged in paragraph 2 of resolution 1753 (2007),

Stressing the continuing importance of the United Nations Mission in Liberia (UNMIL) in improving security through Liberia and helping the new Government establish its authority throughout the country, particularly in the diamond and timber-producing regions, and border areas,

Taking note of the report of the United Nations Panel of Experts on Liberia dated 24 May 2007 (S/2007/340, annex),

Having reviewed the measures imposed by paragraphs 2 and 4 of resolution 1521 (2003) and paragraph 1 of resolution 1532 (2004) and the progress towards meeting the conditions set out by paragraph 5 of resolution 1521 (2003), and concluding that insufficient progress has been made towards that end,

Underlining its determination to support the Government of Liberia in its efforts to meet those conditions, and encouraging donors to do likewise,

Determining that, despite significant progress having been made in Liberia, the situation there continues to constitute a threat to international peace and security in the region,

Acting under Chapter VII of the Charter of the United Nations,

1. *Requests* the Secretary-General to establish, within one month from the date of adoption of this resolution, in consultation with the Committee, for a period of six months, a Panel of Experts consisting of up to three members, with the range of expertise necessary to fulfil the Panel's mandate described in this paragraph, drawing as much as possible on the expertise of the members of the Panel of Experts reappointed pursuant to resolution 1731 (2006), to undertake the following tasks:

(a) To conduct a follow-up assessment mission to Liberia and neighbouring States, in order to investigate and compile a report on the implementation, and any violations, of the measures imposed by resolution 1521 (2003), including any information relevant to the designation by the Committee of the individuals described in paragraph 4 (a) of resolution 1521 (2003) and paragraph 1 of resolution 1532 (2004), and including the various sources of financing, such as from natural resources, for the illicit trade of arms;

(b) To assess the impact of and effectiveness of the measures imposed by paragraph 1 of resolution 1532 (2004), including particularly with respect to the assets of former President Charles Taylor;

(c) To assess the implementation of forestry legislation passed by the Liberian Congress on 19 September 2006 and signed into law by President Johnson Sirleaf on 5 October 2006, recalling that resolution 1689 (2006) decided not to renew the measure in paragraph 10 of resolution 1521 (2003) that obligated Member States to prevent the import into their territories of all round log and timber products originating in Liberia;

(d) To assess the Government of Liberia's compliance with the Kimberley Process Certification Scheme, recalling that resolution 1753 (2007) decided to terminate the measures on diamonds imposed by paragraph 6 of resolution 1521 (2003) and renewed by paragraph 1 of resolution 1731 (2006);

(e) To report to the Council through the Committee by 6 December 2007 on all the issues listed in this paragraph, and to provide informal updates to the Committee as appropriate before that date;

(f) To cooperate with other relevant groups of experts, in particular that established on Côte d'Ivoire by resolution 1708 (2006) of 14 September 2006;

(g) To identify and make recommendations regarding areas where the capacity of States in the region can be strengthened to facilitate the implementation of the measures imposed by paragraph 4 of resolution 1521 (2003) and paragraph 1 of resolution 1532 (2004);

2. *Calls upon* all States and the Government of Liberia to cooperate fully with the Panel of Experts in all the aspects of its mandate;

3. *Decides* to remain actively seized of the matter.

Resolution 1761 (2007)

Adopted by the Security Council at its 5700th meeting, on 20 June 2007

The Security Council,

Recalling its previous resolutions concerning the situation in Côte d'Ivoire, in particular resolution 1727 (2006) of 15 December 2006, and the relevant statements of its President,

Recalling the final report (S/2007/349) of the Group of Experts whose mandate has been extended pursuant to resolution 1727 (2006),

Determining that the situation in Côte d'Ivoire continues to constitute a threat to international peace and security in the region,

Acting under Chapter VII of the Charter of the United Nations,

1. *Decides* to extend the mandate of the Group of Experts, as set out in resolution 1727 (2006), until 31 October 2007, and requests the Secretary-General to take the necessary administrative measures;

2. *Requests* the Group of Experts to submit a written update to the Council, through the Committee established by paragraph 14 of resolution 1572 (2004), before 15 October 2007, on the implementation of the measures imposed by paragraphs 7, 9 and 11 of resolution 1572 (2004) and paragraphs 4 and 6 of resolution 1643 (2005) with recommendations in this regard;

3. *Decides* to remain actively seized of the matter.

Resolution 1762 (2007)

Adopted by the Security Council at its 5710th meeting, on 29 June 2007

The Security Council,

Recalling its previous relevant resolutions, including resolutions 661 (1990) of 6 August 1990, 687 (1991) of 3 April 1991, 699 (1991) of 17 June 1991, 707 (1991) of 15 August 1991, 715 (1991) of 11 October 1991, 1051 (1996) of 27 March 1996, 1284 (1999) of 17 December 1999, 1441 (2002) of 8 November 2002, 1483 (2003) of 22 May 2003, 1540 (2004) of 28 April 2004 and 1546 (2004) of 8 June 2004,

Expressing gratitude to the United Nations Monitoring, Verification and Inspection Commission (UNMOVIC) and the International Atomic Energy Agency (IAEA) for their important and comprehensive contributions under the relevant resolutions, *noting* the accumulation of expertise, experience and maintenance of a roster of experts during UNMOVIC's mandate, and *encouraging* Member States to maintain similar expertise for the future,

Acknowledging that a democratically elected and constitutionally based Government of Iraq is now in place, *noting* the Government of Iraq's declaration of support for the international non-proliferation regime, and *welcoming* the concrete steps taken in this regard, including the commitment enshrined in the Permanent Constitution and the establishment of the National Monitoring Directorate with responsibility for import/export control,

Recalling Iraq's disarmament obligations under relevant resolutions, its obligations under the Treaty on the Non-Proliferation of Nuclear Weapons, its IAEA Safeguards Agreement, The Convention on the Prohibition of the Development, Production and Stockpiling of Bacteriological (Biological) and Toxin Weapons and on their Destruction and the Geneva Protocol, *noting* Iraq's commitment to detect, deter, prevent and combat, including through international cooperation when necessary, the illicit trafficking and brokering in nuclear, chemical and biological weapons and their means of delivery and related materials, in accordance with its legal authorities and legislation and consistent with international law, and *urging* its adherence to all applicable disarmament and non-proliferation treaties, notably the Convention on the Prohibition of the Development, Production, Stockpiling and Use of Chemical Weapons, and an Additional Protocol to the IAEA Safeguards Agreement,

Noting disarmament efforts regarding Iraq since 1991, and *further noting* the joint US-UK letter dated 28 June 2007 and the Government of Iraq letter to the Security Council dated 8 April 2007 annexed to this resolution,

Recognizing that the continued operations of UNMOVIC and the IAEA's Iraq Nuclear Verification Office (INVO) are no longer necessary to verify Iraqi compliance with its obligations under the relevant resolutions,

Acting under Chapter VII of the Charter of the United Nations,

1. *Decides* to terminate immediately the mandates of UNMOVIC and the IAEA under the relevant resolutions;

2. *Reaffirms* Iraq's disarmament obligations under relevant resolutions, acknowledges Iraq's constitutional commitment to the non-proliferation, non-development, non-production and non-use of nuclear, chemical, and biological weapons and associated equipment, material, and technologies for use in the development, manufacture, production and use of such weapons, as well as delivery systems, and urges Iraq to continue to implement this commitment and to adhere to all applicable disarmament and non-proliferation treaties and related international agreements;

3. *Invites* the Government of Iraq to report to the Security Council within one year on progress made in adhering to all applicable disarmament and non-proliferation treaties and related international agreements, notably the Convention on the Prohibition of the Development, Production, Stockpiling and Use of Chemical Weapons, an Additional Protocol to its Safeguards Agreement, and on progress made by the National Monitoring Directorate and the Government of Iraq with regard to dual-use controls and harmonizing Iraqi export legislation with international standards;

4. *Takes note* of the summary briefings provided by UNMOVIC/UNSCOM and IAEA on their respective activities in Iraq since 1991, and expresses appreciation for their dedicated work;

5. *Requests* the Secretary-General to take all necessary measures to provide for the appropriate disposition of UNMOVIC's archives and other property under arrangements ensuring, in particular, that sensitive proliferation information or information provided in confidence by Member States is kept under strict control, and further requests that the Secretary-General inform the Security Council within three months on steps taken in this regard;

6. *Requests* the Secretary-General to transfer to the Government of Iraq through the Development Fund for Iraq not later than three months from the date of this resolution, all remaining unencumbered funds in the account established pursuant to paragraph 8 (e) of resolution 986 (1995), after returning to Member States at their request contributions made by them pursuant to paragraph 4 of resolution 699 (1991);

7. *Decides* to remain actively seized of the matter.

Annex I
Letter from the Secretary of State for Foreign and Commonwealth Affairs of the United Kingdom of Great Britain and Northern Ireland and Secretary of State of the United States of America to the United Nations addressed to the President of the Security Council

The United States of America and the United Kingdom of Great Britain and Northern Ireland wish to inform the Security Council of the steps that have been taken with regard to ensuring Iraqi compliance with its disarmament obligations, as called for in Council resolution 1483 (2003).

Together with the Government of Iraq and other Member States, the United States and the United Kingdom, pursuant to the letter dated 8 May 2003 from their Permanent Representatives to the United Nations addressed to the President of the Security Council (S/2003/538), have been working since March 2003 with the objective of locating and securing, removing, disabling, rendering harmless, eliminating or destroying weapons of mass destruction, ballistic missiles and related delivery systems and programmes in Iraq developed under the regime of Saddam Hussein.

We wish to inform the Security Council that all appropriate steps have been taken to secure, remove, disable, render harmless, eliminate or destroy (a) all of Iraq's known weapons of mass destruction and ballistic missiles with a range of greater than 150 kilometres and (b) all known elements of Iraq's programmes established to research, develop, design, manufacture, produce, support, assemble and employ such weapons and delivery systems, subsystems and components thereof.

Furthermore, we wish to draw the attention of the Security Council to the conclusions of the report issued by the Special Advisor to the United States Director of Central Intelligence on Iraq's Weapons of Mass Destruction ("the Duelfer Report") following a review of Iraq's weapons of mass destruction programmes, undertaken by drawing upon information received from former Iraqi officials, other Iraqi citizens, suspected weapon sites and both technical and procurement-related documents. In the course of their investigation, Iraq Survey Group analysts visited suspected weapons-related sites and searched through documents. The report and its addenda are available from the following website: https://www.cia.gov/library/reports/general-reports-1/iraq_wmd_2004/index.html.

The letter dated 24 April 2007 from the Minister for Foreign Affairs of Iraq to the President of the Security Council (S/2007/236, annex) outlines additional actions that Iraq has taken and other actions that it intends to take in the near future to demonstrate and affirm to the international community its belief that it is now in full compliance with its disarmament obligations under the relevant Council resolutions.

(*Signed*) Condoleezza **Rice**
Secretary of State
United States of America

Signed 27 June 2007

(*Signed*) Margaret **Beckett**
Secretary of State for
Foreign and Commonwealth Affairs
United Kingdom of Great Britain and Northern Ireland

Signed 22 June 2007

Annex II
Letter dated 8 April 2007 from the Minister for Foreign Affairs of Iraq addressed to the President of the Security Council

[Original: Arabic]

I have the honour to address the present letter to you, and through you to the other members of the Security Council, requesting, on behalf of the Government of Iraq, that the Council consider terminating the mandates of the United Nations Monitoring, Verification and Inspection Commission (UNMOVIC) and the Iraq Action Team of the International Atomic Energy Agency (IAEA) established by the Security Council resolutions on the elimination and removal of former Iraqi weapons of mass destruction, as there are no longer any legal or technical grounds for continuing their mandate and we are certain that Iraq currently has none of the programmes or weapons in question. In this connection, please note the following:

1. Today Iraq has a democratically elected Government and a new Parliament in addition to a Constitution that has been approved by the Iraqis. Today it declares that it is joining the global democratic community in its support for the international non-proliferation regime.

2. Article 9 (e) of the Permanent Constitution of the Government of Iraq states that: "The Iraqi Government shall respect and implement Iraq's international obligations regarding the non-proliferation, non-development, non-production and non-utilization of nuclear, chemical and biological weapons, and shall prohibit associated equipment, materiel, technologies and communication systems for use in the development, manufacture, production and utilization of such weapons". This Constitution was approved by the Iraqi people in the national referendum held in 2005.

3. As Security Council members know, the Iraqi Government has cooperated fully with the Iraq Survey Group (ISG) in respect of the former regime's weapons programme.

4. Today the Iraqi Government affirms its full commitment to the relevant Security Council resolutions and, in that connection, reiterates the request that it made to the President of the Council in March 2005, as well as the letter from the Iraqi Prime Minister of 11 November 2006 calling for the termination of the mandates of UNMOVIC and the IAEA Iraq Action Team.

5. The Iraqi Government reiterates its commitment to the Treaty on the Non-Proliferation of Nuclear Weapons, the safeguards agreement of the International Atomic Energy Agency, the Biological Weapons Convention and the 1925 Geneva Protocol for the Prohibition of the Use in War of Asphyxiating, Poisonous or Other Gases, and of Bacteriological Methods of Warfare. The provisional Iraqi Government announced previously in July 2004 its commitment to all the agreements and conventions on the prevention of proliferation. The Iraqi technical authorities have elaborated a draft law on Iraq's accession to the Chemical Weapons Convention, which is currently before the Parliament — the country's legislative branch — with a view to its adoption and preparations are under way for accession to the Model Additional Protocol of the International Atomic Energy Agency's safeguards regime.

6. With regard to coordination with IAEA on a code of conduct on the safety and security of radioactive sources in Iraq, Iraq has set up an agency responsible for identifying radioactive sources in Iraq and guaranteeing their security, namely, the Iraqi Radioactive Sources Regulatory Authority. Since the fall of the previous regime, IAEA has made four successful

verification visits to the Tuwaitha site — in June 2003, August 2004, September 2005 and, most recently, in November 2006.

7. The Iraqi National Monitoring Directorate is overseeing the transfer of dual-use substances and is now making every effort to harmonize Iraqi export legislation with international standards. Iraq has submitted its national report in accordance with its obligations under Security Council resolution 1540 (2004).

8. The Iraqi Government has undertaken to guarantee the security of its borders by strengthening controls in cooperation with the multinational force.

The Government and people of my country hope that the Security Council will make a serious and objective assessment of the situation in Iraq — namely, the absence of weapons of mass destruction and related programmes — and take the appropriate decision to terminate the mandate of UNMOVIC and the IAEA Iraq Action Team and transfer the balance in the Iraq account opened by the United Nations to the Development Fund for Iraq, for the purposes of investment.

I should be grateful if you would have the text of the present letter circulated to the members of the Security Council as a document of the Security Council.

(*Signed*) Hoshyar **Zebari**
Minister for Foreign Affairs of Iraq 8 April 2007

Resolution 1763 (2007)

Adopted by the Security Council at its 5711th meeting, on 29 June 2007

The Security Council,

Recalling its previous resolutions and the statements of its President relating to the situation in Côte d'Ivoire,

Reaffirming its strong commitment to the sovereignty, independence, territorial integrity and unity of Côte d'Ivoire, and recalling the importance of the principles of good-neighbourliness, non-interference and regional cooperation,

Reaffirming its support to the impartial forces, namely the United Nations Operation in Côte d'Ivoire (UNOCI) and the French forces which support it,

Recalling its endorsement of the political Agreement signed on 4 March 2007 in Ouagadougou by President Laurent Gbagbo and Mr. Guillaume Soro under the facilitation of the Chairperson of the Economic Community of West African States, President Blaise Compaoré,

Reaffirming its readiness to take further steps, in the light of the progress achieved, in order to help the parties in implementing their commitments and to support the peace process in Côte d'Ivoire, in particular the electoral process,

Having taken note of the report of the Secretary-General dated 14 May 2007 (S/2007/275),

Determining that the situation in Côte d'Ivoire continues to pose a threat to international peace and security in the region,

Acting under Chapter VII of the Charter of the United Nations,

1. *Decides* that the mandate of UNOCI and of the French forces which support it shall be extended until 16 July 2007;

2. *Decides* to remain actively seized of the matter.

Resolution 1764 (2007)

Adopted by the Security Council at its 5713th meeting, on 29 June 2007

The Security Council,

Recalling all its previous relevant resolutions,

Recalling also the General Framework Agreement for Peace in Bosnia and Herzegovina and the Annexes thereto (collectively the Peace Agreement, S/1995/999, Annex), and the conclusions of the Peace Implementation Conferences held in Bonn on 9 and 10 December 1997 (S/1997/979, Annex), Madrid on 16 and 17 December 1998 (S/1999/139, appendix) and Brussels on 23 and 24 May 2000 (S/2000/586, Annex) as well as the Declaration by the Steering Board of the Peace Implementation Council on 19 June 2007,

1. *Welcomes* and agrees to the designation by the Steering Board of the Peace Implementation Council on 19 June 2007 of Mr. Miroslav Laj ák as High Representative in succession to Mr. Christian Schwarz-Schilling;

2. *Pays tribute* to the efforts of Mr. Christian Schwarz-Schilling in his work as High Representative;

3. *Reaffirms* the importance it attaches to the role of the High Representative in pursuing the implementation of the Peace Agreement and giving guidance to and coordinating the activities of the civilian organizations and agencies involved in assisting the parties to implement the Peace Agreement;

4. *Reaffirms* also the final authority of the High Representative in theatre regarding the interpretation of Annex 10 on civilian implementation of the Peace Agreement;

5. *Takes note* of the decision of the Steering Board of the Peace Implementation Council on 19 June 2007 that the Office of the High Representative will remain in place and continue to carry out its mandate and that the aim is closure of the Office of the High Representative by 30 June 2008;

6. *Decides* to remain seized of the matter.

Resolution 1765 (2007)

Adopted by the Security Council at its 5716th meeting, on 16 July 2007

The Security Council,

Recalling its previous resolutions, in particular resolution 1739 (2007), and the statements of its President relating to the situation in Côte d'Ivoire,

Reaffirming its strong commitment to the sovereignty, independence, territorial integrity and unity of Côte d'Ivoire, and recalling the importance of the principles of good-neighbourliness, non-interference and regional cooperation,

Recalling that it endorsed the Agreement signed by President Laurent Gbagbo and Mr. Guillaume Soro in Ouagadougou on 4 March 2007 ("the Ouagadougou political Agreement", S/2007/144), and that it has supported the appointment of Mr. Guillaume Soro as Prime Minister,

Paying tribute to the Chairperson of the Economic Community of West African States (ECOWAS) President Blaise Compaoré for his continued efforts of facilitation of the inter-Ivorian direct dialogue that enabled in particular the signing of the Ouagadougou political Agreement, and to other leaders of the region, *commending* and *encouraging* the continued efforts of the African Union and ECOWAS to promote peace and stability in Côte d'Ivoire, and *reiterating* its full support for them,

Reiterating its strong condemnation of any attempt to destabilize the peace process by force, in particular the attack committed on 29 June 2007 in Bouaké against the Prime Minister of the Republic of Côte d'Ivoire, Mr. Guillaume Soro, that resulted in several deaths, and *stressing* that the perpetrators of such criminal acts must be brought to justice,

Having taken note of the report of the Secretary-General dated 14 May 2007 (S/2007/275),

Reiterating its firm condemnation of all violations of human rights and international humanitarian law in Côte d'Ivoire,

Recalling its resolutions 1460 (2003) and 1612 (2005) on children and armed conflict and the subsequent conclusions of the Security Council Working Group on Children and Armed Conflict pertaining to parties in the armed conflict of Côte d'Ivoire (S/2007/93),

Recalling also its resolution 1325 (2000) on Women, Peace and Security, *Determining* that the situation in Côte d'Ivoire continues to pose a threat to international peace and security in the region,

Acting under Chapter VII of the Charter of the United Nations,

1. *Decides* to renew the mandates of the United Nations Operation in Côte d'Ivoire (UNOCI) and of the French forces which support it until 15 January 2008, in order to support the organization in Côte d'Ivoire of free, open, fair and transparent elections within the time frame set out in the Ouagadougou political Agreement, and expresses its readiness to renew them further as appropriate;

2. *Endorses* the recommendations contained in paragraphs 42 to 72 and 75 to 83 of the report of the Secretary-General dated 14 May 2007, which adapt UNOCI's role to the new phase of the peace process in Côte d'Ivoire as set out in the Ouagadougou political Agreement, and, accordingly, requests UNOCI, within its existing resources, to support the full implementation of the Ouagadougou political Agreement, including by supporting the integrated command centre, the restoration of State administration throughout the country, the identification and voter registration processes, the electoral process, persons affected by the conflict, efforts to create a positive political environment, protection and promotion of human rights, and the economic recovery process of Côte d'Ivoire;

3. *Calls upon* all concerned parties to ensure that the protection of women and children is addressed in the implementation of the Ouagadougou political Agreement as well as the post-conflict reconstruction and recovery phases, including continued monitoring and reporting of the situation of women and children;

4. *Also invites* the signatories of the Ouagadougou political Agreement to take the necessary steps to protect vulnerable civilian populations, including by guaranteeing the voluntary return, reinstallation, reintegration and security of displaced persons, with the support of the United Nations system, and to fulfil in this regard their commitments in accordance with the Ouagadougou political Agreement and their obligations under international humanitarian law;

5. *Expresses* its intention to review by 15 October 2007 the mandates of UNOCI and the French forces which support it, as well as the level of troops of UNOCI, in the light of the progress achieved in the implementation of the key steps of the peace process, and requests the Secretary-General to provide to it a report on these key steps before this date;

6. *Decides* to terminate the mandate of the High Representative for the Elections, decides therefore that the Special Representative of the Secretary-General in Côte d'Ivoire shall certify that all stages of the electoral process provide all the necessary guarantees for the holding of open, free, fair and transparent presidential and legislative elections in accordance with international standards, and requests the Secretary-General to take all the necessary steps so that the Special Representative has at his disposal a support cell providing him all the appropriate assistance to fulfil this task;

7. *Commends* the High Representative for the Elections, Mr. Gérard Stoudmann, whose tireless efforts permitted progress in the implementation of the peace process and the preparation of the elections;

8. *Recalls* the importance of the provisions of the Ouagadougou political Agreement, including paragraph 8.1, and urges the Ivorian political forces to rely on the mediation by the Facilitator, for any major difficulty concerning the electoral process;

9. *Supports* the establishment, as agreed by the parties at the meeting of the evaluation and monitoring committee of 11 May 2007 and the Facilitator, of an international consultative organ including the Special Representative of the Secretary-General, of the resident coordinator of the United Nations system, of the representatives of the World Bank, the International Monetary Fund, the European Union, the African Union, the African Development Bank, ECOWAS and France, to accompany the Ivorian political forces and the Facilitator in the implementation of the Ouagadougou political Agreement, and notes that this organ shall participate in the meetings of the evaluation and monitoring committee, as an observer, and may be consulted at any time by the Facilitator;

10. *Encourages* the Facilitator, President Blaise Compaoré, to continue to support the process to settle the crisis in Côte d'Ivoire, welcomes his decision to appoint a special representative in Abidjan to follow up on the Ouagadougou political Agreement, and requests UNOCI to assist him in the conduct of the facilitation, including by helping him, as appropriate and upon his request, to carry out his arbitration role according to the provisions of paragraph 8.1 of the Ouagadougou political Agreement;

11. *Decides* to remain actively seized of the matter.

Resolution 1766 (2007)

Adopted by the Security Council at its 5720th meeting, on 23 July 2007

The Security Council,

Reaffirming its previous resolutions and the statements of its President concerning the situation in Somalia, in particular resolution 733 (1992) of 23 January 1992, which established an embargo on all delivery of weapons and military equipment to Somalia (hereinafter referred to as the "arms embargo"), resolution 1519 (2003) of 16 December 2003, resolution 1558 (2004) of 17 August 2004, resolution 1587 (2005) of 15 March 2005, resolution 1630 (2005) of 14 October 2005, resolution 1676 (2006) of 10 May 2006, resolution 1724 (2006) of 29 November 2006 and resolution 1744 (2007) of 20 February 2007,

Recalling that, as set out in its resolution 1744 (2007), the arms embargo on Somalia does not apply to supplies and technical assistance by States intended solely for the purpose of helping develop security sector institutions, consistent with the political process set out in that resolution and in the absence of a negative decision by the Committee established pursuant to resolution 751 (1992),

Reaffirming the importance of the sovereignty, territorial integrity, political independence and unity of Somalia,

Stressing the need for the Transitional Federal Institutions to continue working towards establishing effective national governance in Somalia,

Reiterating the urgent need for all Somali leaders to take tangible steps to continue political dialogue,

Commending the efforts of the African Union, the Intergovernmental Authority on Development and the League of Arab States for their continued support for national reconciliation in Somalia, and urging the Transitional Federal Institutions, clans, business leaders, civil society, religious leaders and other Somali political leaders to work together to ensure an effective National Reconciliation Congress and to guarantee security for it in order to make progress in the political process in Somalia,

Reiterating its strong support for the Special Representative of the Secretary-General,

Taking note of the report of the Monitoring Group dated 17 July 2007 (S/2007/436) submitted pursuant to paragraph 3 (i) of resolution 1724 (2006) and the observations and recommendations contained therein,

Condemning flows of weapons and ammunition supplies to and through Somalia in violation of the arms embargo as a serious threat to peace and stability in Somalia,

Reiterating its insistence that all Member States, in particular those in the region, should refrain from any action in contravention of the arms embargo and should take all necessary steps to hold violators accountable,

Reiterating and underscoring the importance of enhancing the monitoring of the arms embargo in Somalia through persistent and vigilant investigation into the violations, bearing in mind that strict enforcement of the arms embargo will improve the overall security situation in Somalia,

Determining that the situation in Somalia continues to constitute a threat to international peace and security in the region,

Acting under Chapter VII of the Charter of the United Nations,

1. *Stresses* the obligation of all Member States to comply fully with the measures imposed by resolution 733 (1992);

2. *Expresses* its intention, in light of the report of the Monitoring Group dated 17 July 2007 (S/2007/436), to consider specific action to improve implementation of and compliance with measures imposed by resolution 733 (1992);

3. *Decides* to extend the mandate of the Monitoring Group referred to in paragraph 3 of resolution 1558 (2004) and requests the Secretary-General to take the necessary administrative measures as expeditiously as possible to re-establish the Monitoring Group for a further six months, drawing, as appropriate, on the expertise of the members of the Monitoring Group established pursuant to resolution 1724 (2006) and appointing new members as necessary in consultation with the Committee established pursuant to resolution 751 (1992) (hereinafter referred to as "the Committee"), this mandate being as follows:

(a) to continue the tasks outlined in paragraphs 3 (a) to (c) of resolution 1587 (2005);

(b) to continue to investigate, in coordination with relevant international agencies, all activities, including in the financial, maritime and other sectors, which generate revenues used to commit arms embargo violations;

(c) to continue to investigate any means of transport, routes, seaports, airports and other facilities used in connection with arms embargo violations;

(d) to continue refining and updating information on the draft list of those individuals and entities who violate the measures implemented by Member States in accordance with resolution 733 (1992), inside and outside Somalia, and their active supporters, for possible future measures by the Council, and to present such information to the Committee as and when the Committee deems appropriate;

(e) to continue making recommendations based on its investigations, on the previous reports of the Panel of Experts (S/2003/223 and S/2003/1035) appointed pursuant to resolutions 1425 (2002) of 22 July 2002 and 1474 (2003) of 8 April 2003, and on the previous reports of the Monitoring Group (S/2004/604, S/2005/153, S/2005/625, S/2006/229, S/2006/913 and S/2007/436) appointed pursuant to resolutions 1519 (2003) of 16 December 2003, 1558 (2004) of 17 August 2004, 1587 (2005) of 15 March 2005, 1630 (2005) of 14 October 2005, 1676 (2006) of 10 May 2006, and 1724 (2006) of 29 November 2006;

(f) to work closely with the Committee on specific recommendations for additional measures to improve overall compliance with the arms embargo;

(g) to assist in identifying areas where the capacities of States in the region can be strengthened to facilitate the implementation of the arms embargo;

(h) to provide to the Council, through the Committee, a midterm briefing within 90 days from its establishment, and to submit progress reports to the Committee on a monthly basis;

(i) to submit, for the Security Council's consideration, through the Committee, a final report covering all the tasks set out above, no later than 15 days prior to the termination of the Monitoring Group's mandate;

4. *Further requests* the Secretary-General to make the necessary financial arrangements to support the work of the Monitoring Group;

5. *Reaffirms* paragraphs 4, 5, 7, 8 and 10 of resolution 1519 (2003);

6. *Requests* the Committee, in accordance with its mandate and in consultation with the Monitoring Group and other relevant United Nations entities, to consider the recommendations in the reports of the Monitoring Group dated 5 April, 16 October 2006, and 17 July 2007 and recommend to the Council ways to improve implementation of and compliance with the arms embargo, in response to continuing violations;

7. *Decides* to remain actively seized of the matter.

Resolution 1767 (2007)

Adopted by the Security Council at its 5725th meeting, on 30 July 2007

The Security Council,

Reaffirming all its previous resolutions and statements pertaining to the situation between Ethiopia and Eritrea (hereinafter referred to as "the parties") and the requirements contained therein, including in particular resolutions 1320 (2000), 1430 (2002), 1466 (2003), 1640 (2005), 1681 (2006), 1710 (2006) and 1741 (2007),

Stressing once again its unwavering commitment to the peace process, and to the full and expeditious implementation of the Algiers Agreements, and the importance of prompt implementation of the delimitation decision of the Eritrea-Ethiopia Boundary Commission (EEBC) (S/2002/423) as a basis for peaceful and cooperative relations between the parties,

Reaffirming the integrity of the Temporary Security Zone (TSZ) as provided for in the Agreement on Cessation of Hostilities of 18 June 2000 (S/2000/601) and recalling the objectives of its establishment and the commitment of the parties to respect the TSZ, and in this regard, *expressing deep concern* over the continuing serious violations of the TSZ,

Underlining that the Security Council remains committed to its role, in particular helping to ensure that the parties respect the commitments they made in the Agreement on Cessation of Hostilities,

Commending the efforts made by the United Nations Mission in Ethiopia and Eritrea (UNMEE) and its military and civilian personnel to accomplish its duties, despite the difficult circumstances,

Stressing further that the full demarcation of the border between the two parties is vital to lasting peace between Ethiopia and Eritrea as well as in the region, *recalling* that both parties under the Peace Agreement of 12 December 2000 have agreed to cooperate with the EEBC in the delimitation and demarcation process and that they also agreed that the delimitation and demarcation determinations of the EEBC will be final and binding, *commending* the efforts of the EEBC to resume demarcation, and *expressing* its regret that the EEBC, for reasons beyond its control as explained in the Annexes of the report of the Secretary-General of 22 January 2007 (S/2007/33), has so far been unable to demarcate the boundary as planned,

Acknowledging the Statement of the EEBC of 27 November 2006,

Reaffirming its full support for the work of the EEBC and *welcoming* the decision of the EEBC to convene a meeting with the parties on 6 September 2007 in New York,

Expressing its deep concern over the continued delay in the demarcation of the border and over the continued tense and potentially unstable security situation in the Temporary Security Zone and the adjacent areas, and *stressing* that it is the primary responsibility of the Parties to end this situation by fulfilling their obligations expeditiously under the Algiers agreements,

Having considered the report of the Secretary-General of 18 July 2007 (S/2007/440),

1. *Decides* to extend the mandate of UNMEE for a period of six months, until 31 January 2008;

2. *Calls on* the parties to maintain their full commitment to the Agreement on Cessation of Hostilities and to de-escalate the situation, including by returning to the 16 December 2004 levels of deployment and by avoiding provocative military activities;

3. *Reiterates its call* expressed in paragraph 2 of resolution 1640 (2005) that the parties show maximum restraint and refrain from any threat or use of force against each other and reiterates its call to put an end to the exchange of hostile statements;

4. *Reiterates* its demands that Eritrea immediately withdraw its troops and heavy military equipment from the TSZ;

5. *Calls on* Ethiopia to reduce the number of additional military forces recently introduced in certain areas adjacent to the TSZ;

6. *Regrets* the lack of progress on demarcation, and stresses that the parties have the primary responsibility for the implementation of the Algiers Agreements, and again calls upon the parties to implement completely and without further delay or preconditions the delimitation decision of the EEBC and to take concrete steps to resume and complete the demarcation process, including agreeing on a time frame for possible next steps;

7. *Stresses* the need for progress on demarcation and reiterates its call upon both parties to cooperate fully with the EEBC, including participating constructively and with sufficient authority in the meeting to be convened by the EEBC on 6 September in New York, and underlines the importance of this meeting;

8. *Welcomes* the letter dated 8 June 2007 from the Minister for Foreign Affairs of Ethiopia to the President of Security Council, reiterating that his Government had accepted the delimitation decision of the EEBC without preconditions, and reiterates its demand, expressed in paragraph 5 of Security Council resolution 1640 (2005), that Ethiopia immediately take concrete steps to enable, without preconditions, the EEBC to demarcate the border expeditiously;

9. *Demands* that the parties provide UNMEE with the necessary access, assistance, support and protection required for the performance of its duties, including its mandated task to assist the EEBC in the expeditious and orderly implementation of the Delimitation Decision, in accordance with resolutions 1430 (2002) and 1466 (2003) and *demands* that any restrictions be lifted immediately, including those restrictions specified in the report S/2007/440;

10. *Reiterates its demand* expressed in paragraph 1 of resolution 1640 (2005) that Eritrea reverse, without further delay or preconditions, all restrictions on UNMEE's movement and operations, and provide UNMEE with the cooperation, access, protection and support required for the performance of its duties;

11. *Reiterates its call* to both parties to fully cooperate with UNMEE with a view to urgently reactivating the work of the Military Coordination Commission which remains a unique forum to discuss pressing military and security issues;

12. *Expresses* its willingness to reconsider any changes to UNMEE in light of subsequent progress toward demarcation, and its readiness to take further decisions to ensure that UNMEE will be able to facilitate demarcation as progress becomes possible;

13. *Welcomes and looks forward* to the continuation of the ongoing efforts by the Secretary-General and the international community to engage with Eritrea and Ethiopia to help them to normalize their relations, to promote stability between the parties, and to lay the foundation for sustainable peace in the region;

14. *Welcomes* the ongoing efforts by the Secretary-General towards the earliest appointment of a Special Representative;

15. *Calls* on Member States to provide contributions to the Trust Fund, established pursuant to resolution 1177 (1998) and referred to in Article 4 (17) of the Comprehensive Peace Agreement signed by Ethiopia and Eritrea on 12 December 2000, in order to support the demarcation process;

16. *Expresses* its deep appreciation for the contribution and dedication of the troop-contributing countries to the work of UNMEE;

17. *Decides* to remain actively seized of the matter.

Resolution 1768 (2007)

Adopted by the Security Council at its 5726th meeting, on 31 July 2007

The Security Council,

Recalling its previous resolutions, in particular resolution 1756 (2007),

Taking note of the final report (S/2007/423) of the Group of Experts on the Democratic Republic of the Congo established pursuant to resolution 1698 (2006),

Condemning the continuing illicit flow of weapons within and into the Democratic Republic of the Congo, and *declaring its determination* to continue close monitoring of the implementation of the arms embargo imposed by resolution 1493 (2003) and expanded by resolution 1596 (2005), and to enforce the measures provided for in paragraphs 13 and 15 of resolution 1596 against persons and entities acting in violation of this embargo, as amended and expanded by resolution 1649 (2005) and resolution 1698 (2006),

Reiterating its serious concern regarding the presence of armed groups and militias in the eastern part of the Democratic Republic of the Congo, particularly in the provinces of North and South Kivu and the Ituri district, which perpetuate a climate of insecurity in the whole region,

Taking note of the report of the Security Council mission which visited Kinshasa on 20 June 2007 (S/2007/421),

Noting that the situation in the Democratic Republic of the Congo continues to constitute a threat to international peace and security in the region,

Acting under Chapter VII of the Charter of the United Nations,

1. *Decides* to extend until 10 August 2007 the measures on arms imposed by paragraph 20 of resolution 1493 (2003) as amended and expanded by paragraph 1 of resolution 1596 (2005);

2. *Decides* to extend, for the period specified in paragraph 1 above, the measures on transport imposed by paragraphs 6, 7 and 10 of resolution 1596;

3. *Decides* to extend, for the period specified in paragraph 1 above, the financial and travel measures imposed by paragraphs 13 and 15 of resolution 1596, paragraph 2 of resolution 1649 (2005), and paragraph 13 of resolution 1698;

4. *Decides* to extend, for the period specified in paragraph 1 above, the mandate of the Group of Experts referred to in paragraph 3 of resolution 1698;

5. *Decides* to remain actively seized of the matter.

Resolution 1769 (2007)

Adopted by the Security Council at its 5727th meeting, on 31 July 2007

The Security Council,

Recalling all its previous resolutions and presidential statements concerning the situation in Sudan,

Reaffirming its strong commitment to the sovereignty, unity, independence and territorial integrity of Sudan, and to the cause of peace, and *expressing its determination* to work with the Government of Sudan, in full respect of its sovereignty, to assist in tackling the various problems in Darfur, Sudan,

Recalling the conclusions of the Addis Ababa high-level consultation on the situation in Darfur of 16 November 2006 as endorsed in the communiqué of the 66th meeting of the Peace and Security Council of the African Union held in Abuja on 30 November 2006 as well as the communiqué of 79th meeting of the Peace and Security Council of the African Union on 22 June 2007, *recalling* the statement of its President of 19 December 2006 endorsing the Addis Ababa and Abuja agreements, *welcoming* the progress made so far and *calling* for them to be fully implemented by all parties without delay and for all parties to facilitate the immediate deployment of the United Nations Light and Heavy Support packages to the African Union Mission in the Sudan (AMIS) and a Hybrid operation in Darfur, for which back-stopping and command and control structures will be provided by the United Nations, and *recalling* that co-operation between the UN and the regional arrangements in matters relating to the maintenance of peace and security is an integral part of collective security as provided for in the Charter of the United Nations,

Re-affirming also its previous resolutions 1325 (2000) on women, peace and security, 1502 (2003) on the protection of humanitarian and United Nations personnel, 1612 (2005) on children and armed conflict and the subsequent conclusions of the Security Council Working Group on Children in Armed Conflict pertaining to parties to the armed conflict in Sudan (S/2006/971), and 1674 (2006) on the protection of civilians in armed conflict, as well as *recalling* the report of its Mission to Addis Ababa and Khartoum from 16 to 17 June 2007,

Welcoming the report of the Secretary-General and the Chairperson of the African Union Commission of 5 June 2007,

Commending in this regard the agreement of Sudan that the Hybrid operation shall be deployed in Darfur, as detailed in the conclusions of the high-level AU/UN consultations with the Government of Sudan in Addis Ababa on 12 June 2007 and confirmed in full during the Council's meeting with the President of Sudan on 17 June in Khartoum,

Recalling the Addis Ababa Agreement that the Hybrid operation should have a predominantly African character and the troops should, as far as possible, be sourced from African countries,

Commending the efforts of the African Union for the successful deployment of AMIS, as well as the efforts of member states and regional organisations that have assisted it in its deployment, *stressing* the need for AMIS, as supported by the United Nations Light and Heavy Support Packages, to assist implementation of the Darfur Peace Agreement until the end of its mandate, *calling upon* the Government of Sudan to assist in removing all obstacles to the proper discharge by AMIS of its mandate; and *recalling* the communiqué of the 79th meeting of the Peace and Security Council of the African Union of 22 June to extend the mandate of AMIS for an additional period not exceeding six months until 31 December 2007,

Stressing the urgent need to mobilise the financial, logistical and other support and assistance required for AMIS,

Welcoming the ongoing preparations for the Hybrid operation, including the putting in place of logistical arrangements in Darfur, at United Nations Headquarters and the African Union Commission Headquarters, force and police generation efforts and on-going joint efforts by the Secretary General and the Chairperson of the African Union to finalise essential operational policies, and *further welcoming* action taken so that appropriate financial and administrative mechanisms are established to ensure the effective management of the Hybrid,

Re-iterating its belief in the basis provided by the Darfur Peace Agreement for a lasting political solution and sustained security in Darfur, *deploring* that the Agreement has not been fully implemented by the signatories and not signed by all parties to the conflict in Darfur, *calling* for an immediate cease-fire, *urging* all parties not to act in any way that would impede the implementation of the Agreement, and *recalling* the communiqué of the second international meeting on the situation in Darfur convened by the African Union and United Nations Special Envoys in Tripoli from 15-16 July 2007,

Noting with strong concern on-going attacks on the civilian population and humanitarian workers and continued and widespread sexual violence, including as outlined in the Report of the Secretary-General and the Chairperson of the African Union Commission on the Hybrid Operation in Darfur and the report of the Secretary-General of 23 February 2007, *emphasising* the need to bring to justice the perpetrators of such crimes and *urging* the Government of Sudan to do so, and *reiterating* in this regard its condemnation of all violations of human rights and international humanitarian law in Darfur,

Reiterating its deep concern for the security of humanitarian aid workers and their access to populations in need, *condemning* those parties to the conflict who have failed to ensure the full, safe and unhindered access of relief personnel to all those in need in Darfur as well as the delivery of humanitarian assistance, in particular to internally displaced persons and refugees, and *recognising* that, with many citizens in Darfur having been displaced, humanitarian efforts remain a priority until a sustained cease-fire and inclusive political process are achieved,

Demanding that there should be no aerial bombings and the use of United Nations markings on aircraft used in such attacks,

Reaffirming its concern that the ongoing violence in Darfur might further negatively affect the rest of Sudan as well as the region, *stressing* that regional security aspects must be addressed to achieve long-term peace in Darfur, and *calling* on the Governments of Sudan and Chad to abide by their obligations under the Tripoli Agreement of 8 February 2006 and subsequent bilateral agreements,

Determining that the situation in Darfur, Sudan continues to constitute a threat to international peace and security,

1. *Decides*, in support of the early and effective implementation of the Darfur Peace Agreement and the outcome of the negotiations foreseen in paragraph 18, to authorise and mandate the establishment, for an initial period of 12 months, of an AU/UN Hybrid operation in Darfur (UNAMID) as set out in this resolution and pursuant to the report of the Secretary-General and the Chairperson of the African Union Commission of 5 June 2007, and further decides that the mandate of UNAMID shall be as set out in paragraphs 54 and 55 of the report of the Secretary General and the Chairperson of the African Union Commission of 5 June 2007;

2. *Decides* that UNAMID, which shall incorporate AMIS personnel and the UN Heavy and Light Support Packages to AMIS, shall consist of up to 19,555 military personnel, including 360 military observers and liaison officers, and an appropriate civilian component including up to 3,772 police personnel and 19 formed police units comprising up to 140 personnel each;

3. *Welcomes* the appointment of the AU-UN Joint Special Representative for Darfur Rodolphe Adada and Force Commander Martin Agwai, and calls on the Secretary-General to immediately begin deployment of the command and control structures and systems necessary to ensure a seamless transfer of authority from AMIS to UNAMID;

4. *Calls* on all parties to urgently facilitate the full deployment of the UN Light and Heavy Support Packages to AMIS and preparations for UNAMID, and further calls on member states to finalise their contributions to UNAMID within 30 days of the adoption of this resolution and on the Secretary-General and the Chairperson of the African Union Commission to agree the final composition of the military component of UNAMID within the same time period;

5. *Decides* that:

(a) no later than October 2007, UNAMID shall establish an initial operational capability for the headquarters, including the necessary management and command and control structures, through which operational directives will be implemented, and shall establish financial arrangements to cover troops costs for all personnel deployed to AMIS;

(b) as of October 2007, UNAMID shall complete preparations to assume operational command authority over the Light Support Package, personnel currently deployed to AMIS, and such Heavy Support Package and hybrid personnel as may be deployed by that date, in order that it shall perform such tasks under its mandate as its resources and capabilities permit immediately upon transfer of authority consistent with sub-paragraph (c) below;

(c) as soon as possible and no later than 31 December 2007, UNAMID having completed all remaining tasks necessary to permit it to implement all elements of its mandate, will assume authority from AMIS with a view to achieving full operational capability and force strength as soon as possible thereafter;

6. *Requests* the Secretary General to report to the Council within 30 days of the passage of this resolution and every 30 days thereafter, on the status of UNAMID's implementation of the steps specified in paragraph 5, including on the status of financial, logistical, and administrative arrangements for UNAMID and on the extent of UNAMID's progress toward achieving full operational capability;

7. *Decides* that there will be unity of command and control which, in accordance with basic principles of peacekeeping, means a single chain of command, *further decides* that command and control structures and backstopping will be provided by the United Nations, and, in this context, *recalls* the conclusions of the Addis Ababa high level consultation on the situation in Darfur of 16 November;

8. *Decides* that force and personnel generation and administration shall be conducted as set out in paragraphs 113-115 of the report of the Secretary-General and the Chairperson of the African Union Commission of 5 June 2007, and *requests* the Secretary-General to put in place without delay the practical arrangements for deploying UNAMID including submitting to the General Assembly recommendations on funding and effective financial management and oversight mechanisms;

9. *Decides* that UNAMID shall monitor whether any arms or related material are present in Darfur in violation of the Agreements and the measures imposed by paragraphs 7 and 8 of resolution 1556 (2004);

10. *Calls on* all Member States to facilitate the free, unhindered and expeditious movement to Sudan of all personnel, as well as equipment, provisions, supplies and other goods, including vehicles and spare parts, which are for the exclusive use of UNAMID in Darfur;

11. *Stresses* the urgent need to mobilise the financial, logistical and other support required for AMIS, and calls on member states and regional organisations to provide further assistance, in particular to permit the early deployment of two additional battalions during the transition to UNAMID;

12. *Decides* that the authorised strength of UNMIS shall revert to that specified in resolution 1590 (2005) upon the transfer of authority from AMIS to UNAMID pursuant to paragraph 5(c);

13. *Calls* on all the parties to the conflict in Darfur to immediately cease all hostilities and commit themselves to a sustained and permanent cease-fire;

14. *Demands* an immediate cessation of hostilities and attacks on AMIS, civilians and humanitarian agencies, their staff and assets and relief convoys, and further demands that all parties to the conflict in Darfur fully co-operate with AMIS, civilians and humanitarian agencies, their staff and assets and relief convoys, and give all necessary assistance to the deployment of the United Nations Light and Heavy Support Packages to AMIS, and to UNAMID;

15. Acting under Chapter VII of the Charter of the United Nations:

(a) *decides* that UNAMID is authorised to take the necessary action, in the areas of deployment of its forces and as it deems within its capabilities in order to:

(i) protect its personnel, facilities, installations and equipment, and to ensure the security and freedom of movement of its own personnel and humanitarian workers,

(ii) support early and effective implementation of the Darfur Peace Agreement, prevent the disruption of its implementation and armed attacks, and protect civilians, without prejudice to the responsibility of the Government of Sudan;

(b) *requests* that the Secretary-General, in consultation with the Chairperson of the African Union Commission, and the Government of Sudan conclude within 30 days a status-of-forces agreement with respect to UNAMID, taking into consideration General Assembly resolution 58/82 on the scope of legal protection under the Convention on the Safety of United Nations and Associated Personnel and General Assembly resolution 61/133 on the Safety and Security of Humanitarian Personnel and the Protection of United Nations Personnel, and *decides* that pending the conclusion of such an agreement the model status-of-forces agreement dated 9 October 1990 (A/45/594) shall provisionally apply with respect to UNAMID personnel operating in that country;

16. *Requests* the Secretary-General to take the necessary measures to achieve actual compliance in UNAMID with the United Nations zero-tolerance policy on sexual exploitation and abuse, including the development of strategies and appropriate mechanisms to prevent, identify and respond to all forms of misconduct, including sexual exploitation and abuse, and the enhancement of training for personnel to prevent misconduct and ensure full compliance with the United Nations code of conduct, and to further take all necessary action in accordance with the Secretary-General's Bulletin on special measures for protection from sexual exploitation and sexual abuse (ST/SGB/2003/13) and to keep the Council informed, and urges troop-contributing countries to take appropriate preventive action including the conduct of pre-deployment awareness training and, in the case of forces previously deployed under AU auspices, post-deployment awareness training, and to take disciplinary action

and other action to ensure full accountability in cases of such conduct involving their personnel;

17. *Calls* on all concerned parties to ensure that the protection of children is addressed in the implementation of the Darfur Peace Agreement, and requests the Secretary-General to ensure continued monitoring and reporting of the situation of children and continued dialogue with parties to the conflict towards the preparations of time-bound action plans to end recruitment and use of child soldiers and other violations against children;

18. *Emphasises* there can be no military solution to the conflict in Darfur, *welcomes* the commitment expressed by the Government of Sudan and some other parties to the conflict to enter into talks and the political process under the mediation, and in line with the deadlines set out in the roadmap, of the United Nations Special Envoy for Darfur and the African Union Special Envoy for Darfur, who have its full support, looks forward to these parties doing so, calls on the other parties to the conflict to do likewise, and urges all the parties, in particular the non-signatory movements, to finalise their preparations for the talks;

19. *Welcomes* the signature of a Joint Communiqué between the Government of Sudan and the United Nations on Facilitation of Humanitarian Activities in Darfur, and calls for it to be fully implemented and on all parties to ensure, in accordance with relevant provisions of international law, the full, safe and unhindered access of relief personnel to all those in need and delivery of humanitarian assistance, in particular to internally displaced persons and refugees;

20. *Emphasises* the need to focus, as appropriate, on developmental initiatives that will bring peace dividends on the ground in Darfur, including in particular, finalising preparations for reconstruction and development, return of IDPs to their villages, compensation and appropriate security arrangements;

21. *Requests* the Secretary-General to report to the Council for its consideration no later than every 90 days after the adoption of this resolution on progress being made on, and immediately as necessary on any obstacles to:

(a) the implementation of the Light and Heavy Support Packages and UNAMID,

(b) the implementation of the Joint Communiqué between the Government of Sudan and the United Nations on Facilitation of Humanitarian Activities in Darfur,

(c) the political process,

(d) the implementation of the Darfur Peace Agreement and the parties' compliance with their international obligations and their commitments under relevant agreements, and

(e) the cease-fire and the situation on the ground in Darfur;

22. *Demands* that the parties to the conflict in Darfur fulfil their international obligations and their commitments under relevant agreements, this resolution and other relevant Council resolutions;

23. *Recalls* the reports of the Secretary-General of 22 December 2006 (S/2006/1019) and 23 February 2007 (S/2007/97) which detail the need to improve the security of civilians in the regions of eastern Chad and north-eastern Central African Republic, expresses its readiness to support this endeavour, and looks forward to the Secretary-General reporting on his recent consultations with the Governments of Chad and CAR;

24. *Emphasises* its determination that the situation in Darfur shall significantly improve so that the Council can consider, in due course and as appropriate, and taking into consideration recommendations of the Secretary-General and the Chairperson of the African Union, the drawing down and eventual termination of UNAMID;

25. *Decides* to remain seized of the matter.

Resolution 1770 (2007)

Adopted by the Security Council at its 5729th meeting, on 10 August 2007

The Security Council,

Recalling all its previous relevant resolutions on Iraq, in particular 1500 (2003) of 14 August 2003, 1546 (2004) of 8 June 2004, 1557 (2004) of 12 August 2004, 1619 (2005) of 11 August 2005 and 1700 (2006) of 10 August 2006,

Reaffirming the independence, sovereignty, unity and territorial integrity of Iraq,

Emphasizing the importance of the stability and security of Iraq for the people of Iraq, the region, and the international community,

Acknowledging that a democratically elected and constitutionally based Government of Iraq is now in place,

Underscoring the need for all communities in Iraq to reject sectarianism, participate in the political process, and engage in an inclusive political dialogue and national reconciliation for the sake of Iraq's political stability and unity,

Reaffirming the importance of the United Nations, in particular the United Nations Assistance Mission for Iraq (UNAMI), in supporting the efforts of the Iraqi people and Government to strengthen institutions for representative government, promote political dialogue and national reconciliation, engage neighbouring countries, assist vulnerable groups, including refugees and internally displaced persons, and promote the protection of human rights and judicial and legal reform,

Expressing concern for the humanitarian issues confronting the Iraqi people and stressing the need for a coordinated response and adequate resources to address these issues,

Underscoring the sovereignty of the Government of Iraq and reaffirming that all parties should take all feasible steps to ensure the protection of affected civilians, and should create conditions conducive to the voluntary, safe, dignified, and sustainable return of refugees and internally displaced persons,

Urging all those concerned as set forth in international humanitarian law, including the Geneva Conventions and the Hague Regulations, to allow full unimpeded access by humanitarian personnel to all people in need of assistance, and to make available, as far as possible, all necessary facilities for their operations, and to promote the safety, security and freedom of movement of humanitarian personnel and United Nations and its associated personnel and their assets,

Welcoming the formal launch of the International Compact with Iraq on 3 May 2007 as well as the expanded Neighbours Conference on 4 May 2007 and resultant working groups, and underscoring the importance of continued regional and international support for Iraq's development,

Acknowledging with appreciation past contributions by Member States to the United Nations Assistance Mission for Iraq (UNAMI) and recalling the need for UNAMI to have the necessary resources to fulfil its mission,

Welcoming the letter of 6 August 2007 from the Minister for Foreign Affairs of Iraq to the Secretary-General (S/2007/481, annex), expressing the view of the Government of Iraq requesting the United Nations Assistance Mission for Iraq (UNAMI) to assist Iraqi efforts to build a productive and prosperous nation at peace with itself and its neighbours,

1. *Decides to* extend the mandate of UNAMI for another period of twelve months from the date of this resolution;

2. *Decides further* that, as circumstances permit, the Special Representative of the Secretary-General and UNAMI, at the request of the Government of Iraq, shall:

(a) Advise, support, and assist:

(i) The Government and people of Iraq on advancing their inclusive, political dialogue and national reconciliation;

(ii) The Government of Iraq and the Independent High Electoral Commission on the development of processes for holding elections and referendums;

(iii) The Government of Iraq and the Council of Representatives on Constitutional review and the implementation of constitutional provisions, as well as on the development of processes acceptable to the Government of Iraq to resolve disputed internal boundaries;

(iv) The Government of Iraq on facilitating regional dialogue, including on issues of border security, energy, and refugees;

(v) The Government of Iraq at an appropriate time and in connection with progress on reconciliation efforts, on planning, funding and implementing reintegration programmes for former members of illegal armed groups;

(vi) The Government of Iraq on initial planning for the conduct of a comprehensive census;

(b) Promote, support, and facilitate, in coordination with the Government of Iraq:

(i) The coordination and delivery of humanitarian assistance and the safe, orderly, and voluntary return, as appropriate, of refugees and displaced persons;

(ii) The implementation of the International Compact with Iraq, including coordination with donors and international financial institutions;

(iii) The coordination and implementation of programmes to improve Iraq's capacity to provide essential services for its people and continue active donor coordination of critical reconstruction and assistance programmes through the International Reconstruction Fund Facility for Iraq (IRFFI);

(iv) Economic reform, capacity-building and the conditions for sustainable development, including through coordination with national and regional organizations and, as appropriate, civil society, donors, and international financial institutions;

(v) The development of effective civil, social and essential services, including through training and conferences in Iraq when possible;

(vi) The contributions of United Nations agencies, funds, and programmes to the objectives outlined in this resolution under a unified leadership of the Secretary-General through his Special Representative for Iraq;

(c) And also promote the protection of human rights and judicial and legal reform in order to strengthen the rule of law in Iraq;

3. *Recognizes* the important role of the Multi-National Force Iraq (MNF-I) in supporting UNAMI, including security and logistical support, and further recognizes that security is essential for UNAMI to carry out its work on behalf of the people of Iraq;

4. *Calls on* Member States to continue providing UNAMI with the necessary financial, logistical and security resources and support to fulfil its mission;

5. *Expresses* its intention to review the mandate of UNAMI in twelve months or sooner, if requested by the Government of Iraq;

6. *Requests* the Secretary-General to report to the Council within three months from the date of this resolution on UNAMI operations in Iraq, and on a quarterly basis thereafter on the progress made towards the fulfilment of all UNAMI's responsibilities; and

7. *Decides* to remain seized of the matter.

Resolution 1771 (2007)

Adopted by the Security Council at its 5730th meeting, on 10 August 2007

The Security Council,

Recalling its previous resolutions, in particular resolution 1756 (2007), and the statements by its President concerning the Democratic Republic of the Congo, in particular on 23 July 2007,

Reaffirming its commitment to respect the sovereignty, territorial integrity and political independence of the Democratic Republic of the Congo as well as all States in the region,

Welcoming the establishment in the Democratic Republic of the Congo of democratically elected institutions, and *reaffirming* the sovereign authority of the elected government to establish effective security and control throughout the national territory,

Taking note with satisfaction of the adoption of the programme of the Government, in particular the governance contract included therein,

Taking note of the final report (S/2007/423) of the Group of Experts on the Democratic Republic of the Congo established pursuant to resolution 1698 (2006),

Condemning the continuing illicit flow of weapons within and into the Democratic Republic of the Congo, *declaring* its determination to continue close monitoring of the implementation of the arms embargo imposed by resolution 1493 (2003) and expanded by resolution 1596 (2005), and to enforce the measures provided for in resolution 1596 against persons and entities acting in violation of this embargo, as amended and expanded by resolutions 1649 (2005) and resolution 1698, and recognizing the linkage between the illegal exploitation of natural resources, illicit trade in such resources and the proliferation and trafficking of arms as one of the factors fuelling and exacerbating conflicts in the Great Lakes region of Africa,

Recalling its resolution 1612 (2005) and its previous resolutions on children and armed conflict, and once again strongly condemning the continued recruitment and use of children in violation of applicable international law, in the hostilities in the Democratic Republic of the Congo,

Reiterating its serious concern regarding the presence of armed groups and militias in the Eastern part of the Democratic Republic of the Congo, particularly in the provinces of North and South Kivu and the Ituri district, which perpetuate a climate of insecurity in the whole region,

Taking note of the report of the Security Council mission which visited Kinshasa on 20 June 2007 (S/2007/421),

Recalling the importance of urgently carrying out security sector reform and of disarming, demobilizing, resettling or repatriating, as appropriate, and reintegrating Congolese and foreign armed groups for the long-term stabilization of the Democratic Republic of the Congo,

Noting that the situation in the Democratic Republic of the Congo continues to constitute a threat to international peace and security in the region,

Acting under Chapter VII of the Charter of the United Nations,

1. *Decides* to renew until 15 February 2008 the measures on arms imposed by paragraph 20 of resolution 1493 as amended and expanded by paragraph 1 of resolution 1596;

2. *Reaffirms* paragraph 21 of resolution 1493 and paragraph 2 of resolution 1596, and *recalls* in particular that the measures referred to in paragraph 1 above shall not apply to supplies of arms and related materiel or technical training and assistance intended solely for support of or use by units of the army and police of the Democratic Republic of the Congo, provided that the said units:

(a) Have completed the process of their integration, or

(b) Operate under the command, respectively, of the état-major intégré of the Armed Forces or of the National Police of the Democratic Republic of the Congo, or

(c) Are in the process of their integration, in the territory of the Democratic Republic of the Congo outside the provinces of North and South Kivu and the Ituri district;

3. *Decides* further that the measures referred to in paragraph 1 above shall not apply to technical training and assistance agreed to by the Government and intended solely for support of units of the army and police of the Democratic Republic of the Congo that are in the process of their integration in the provinces of North and South Kivu and the Ituri district;

4. *Decides that the conditions specified* in paragraph 4 of resolution 1596, as now applied to the Government, shall apply to supplies of arms and related materiel as well as technical

training and assistance which are consistent with such exemptions noted in paragraph 2 and 3 above and notes in this regard that States have an obligation to notify such supplies in advance to the Committee referred to in paragraph 7;

5. *Decides to renew,* for the period specified in paragraph 1 above, the measures on transport imposed by paragraphs 6, 7 and 10 of resolution 1596;

6. *Decides* to renew, for the period specified in paragraph 1 above the financial and travel measures imposed by paragraphs 13 and 15 of resolution 1596, paragraph 2 of resolution 1649, and paragraph 13 of resolution 1698, and reaffirms the provisions of paragraph 14 and 16 of resolution 1596, and paragraph 3 of resolution 1698;

7. *Recalls* the mandate of the Committee established pursuant to paragraph 8 of resolution 1533 (2004), as expanded pursuant to paragraph 18 of resolution 1596, paragraph 4 of resolution 1649 and paragraph 14 of resolution 1698;

8. *Calls upon* all States, in particular those of the region, to support the implementation of the arms embargo and to cooperate fully with the Committee in carrying out its mandate;

9. *Requests* the Secretary-General to re-establish for a period expiring on 15 February 2008 the Group of Experts established pursuant to paragraph 10 of resolution 1533 and expanded pursuant to paragraph 21 of resolution 1596;

10. *Requests* the Group of Experts to fulfil its mandate as defined in paragraph 5 and 17 of resolution 1698, to update the Committee on its work as appropriate, and to report to the Council in writing, through the Committee, by 15 January 2008;

11. *Requests* MONUC, within its existing capabilities and without prejudice to the performance of its current mandate, and the Group of Experts referred to in paragraph 9 above to continue to focus their monitoring activities in North and South Kivu and in Ituri;

12. *Reaffirms its demand,* expressed in paragraph 19 of resolution 1596, that all parties and all States cooperate fully with the work of the Group of Experts, and that they ensure:

- the safety of its members,
- unhindered and immediate access, in particular to persons, documents and sites the Group of Experts deems relevant to the execution of its mandate;

13. *Further demands* that all parties and all States ensure the cooperation with the Group of Experts of individuals and entities within their jurisdiction or under their control, and calls on all States in the region to implement fully their obligations under paragraph 12 above;

14. *Decides* that, no later than 15 February 2008, it shall review the measures set forth in paragraphs 1, 5 and 6 above, with a view to adjusting them, as appropriate, in the light of consolidation of the security situation in the Democratic Republic of the Congo, in particular progress in security sector reform including the integration of the armed forces and the reform of the national police, and in disarming, demobilizing, resettling or repatriating, as appropriate, and reintegrating Congolese and foreign armed groups;

15. *Decides* to remain actively seized of the matter.

Resolution 1772 (2007)

Adopted by the Security Council at its 5732nd meeting, on 20 August 2007

The Security Council,

Recalling its previous resolutions concerning the situation in Somalia, in particular resolution 733 (1992), resolution 1356 (2001), resolution 1425 (2002), resolution 1725 (2006) and resolution 1744 (2007), the statements of its President, in particular those of 13 July 2006 (S/PRST/2006/31), 22 December 2006 (S/PRST/2006/59), 30 April 2007 (S/PRST/2007/13) and 14 June 2007 (S/PRST/2007/19),

Reaffirming its respect for the sovereignty, territorial integrity, political independence and unity of Somalia,

Reiterating its commitment to a comprehensive and lasting settlement of the situation in Somalia through the Transitional Federal Charter, and stressing the importance of broad-based and representative institutions reached through an all-inclusive political process, as envisaged in the Transitional Federal Charter,

Reiterating its strong support for the Special Representative of the Secretary-General, Mr. François Fall,

Reiterating its appreciation of the efforts of the international community, in particular the African Union, as well as the League of Arab States, the Intergovernmental Authority on Development and the European Union, to promote peace, stability and reconciliation in Somalia, and *welcoming* their continued engagement,

Welcoming the communiqué of the African Union Peace and Security Council of 18 July 2007, which states that the African Union will extend the mandate of its mission to Somalia (AMISOM) for an additional six months, and *noting* that the communiqué calls for the United Nations to deploy a peacekeeping operation to Somalia that will support the long-term stabilization and post-conflict restoration in the country,

Taking note of the letter of the Chairperson of the African Union Commission dated 4 August 2007 to the Secretary-General (S/2007/499), which requested that experts from the African Union Commission and the United Nations Secretariat meet as soon as possible to discuss what further support might be provided to AMISOM,

Taking note of the Secretary-General's report on Somalia of 25 June 2007 (S/2007/381), in particular paragraph 30 on the deployment of a team of 10 military, police, and civilian experts to African Union headquarters to support its mission planning and management capacity structure, and *expressing* its appreciation for this support of AMISOM,

Recalling that cooperation between the United Nations and the regional arrangements in matters relating to the maintenance of peace and security, as are appropriate for regional action, is an integral part of collective security as provided for in the Charter of the United Nations,

Taking note of paragraph 27 of the Secretary-General's report referred to above communicating the offer of the International Contact Group of its "Good Offices" to facilitate the process of genuine political reconciliation in Somalia, and *encouraging* the International Contact Group to continue the implementation of this offer,

Reiterating its support for Somalia's Transitional Federal Institutions, *underlining* the importance of providing and maintaining stability and security throughout Somalia, and *underscoring* the importance of disarmament, demobilization and reintegration of militia and ex-combatants in Somalia,

Condemning all acts of violence and extremism inside Somalia, and *expressing* its concern regarding the continued violence inside Somalia,

Stressing its concern at the upsurge in piracy off the Somali coast described in paragraph 51 of the Secretary-General's report, and *taking note* of the joint communiqué of the International Maritime Organization and the World Food Programme of 10 July 2007,

Emphasizing the contribution that AMISOM and its Ugandan contingents are making to lasting peace and stability in Somalia, *condemning* any hostility towards them, and *urging* all parties in Somalia and the region to support and cooperate with AMISOM,

Underlining that the full deployment of AMISOM will help avoid a security vacuum and help create the conditions for full withdrawal of other foreign forces from Somalia,

Determining that the situation in Somalia continues to constitute a threat to international peace and security in the region,

Acting under Chapter VII of the Charter of the United Nations,

1. *Stresses* the need for broad-based and representative institutions reached through an all-inclusive political process in Somalia, as envisaged in the Transitional Federal Charter, in order to consolidate stability, peace and reconciliation in the country and to ensure that international assistance is as effective as possible;

2. *Welcomes* the convening of the National Reconciliation Congress (NRC) at the initiative of the Transitional Federal Institutions, and *urges* all parties to support the NRC and participate in the political process;

3. *Stresses* the need for the NRC to be an all-inclusive intra-Somali political process involving all stakeholders including all political leaders, clan leaders, religious leaders, the business community, and representatives of civil society such as women's groups;

4. *Urges* the Transitional Federal Institutions and all parties in Somalia to respect the conclusions of the NRC and to sustain an equally inclusive ongoing political process thereafter, and *encourages* them to unite behind the efforts to promote such an inclusive dialogue;

5. *Reiterates* the need for the ongoing political process to both agree on a comprehensive and lasting cessation of hostilities and to produce a road map for a comprehensive peace process, including democratic elections at the local, regional and national levels as set out in Somalia's Transitional Federal Charter;

6. *Requests* the Secretary-General to continue and intensify his efforts to strengthen the NRC and, more widely, promote an ongoing all-inclusive political process, including by assisting the Transitional Federal Institutions' role in delivering both and by working together with the African Union, the League of Arab States, the Intergovernmental Authority on Development, the European Union, and the International Contact Group on Somalia, and *requests* the Secretary-General to report, pursuant to the timetable set out in paragraph

17 below, on the efforts of the Transitional Federal Institutions, on progress made in the NRC and the subsequent political process, and on any obstacles to the success of either;

7. *Requests* the Secretary-General to provide in the same reports an assessment of further measures that may be required to strengthen the ability of the United Nations Political Office for Somalia (UNPOS) to fulfil the role envisaged in paragraph 6 above, including the possibility of relocation from Nairobi to Mogadishu and any security measures that might be necessary for such a move;

8. *States its intention,* following the Secretary-General's reports referred to in paragraph 6 above, to take measures against those who seek to prevent or block the NRC or a peaceful political process, or those who threaten the Transitional Federal Institutions or AMISOM by force, or take action that undermines stability in Somalia or the region;

9. *Decides* to authorize member States of the African Union to maintain a mission in Somalia for a further period of six months, which shall be authorized to take all necessary measures as appropriate to carry out the following mandate:

(a) To support dialogue and reconciliation in Somalia by assisting with the free movement, safe passage and protection of all those involved with the process referred to in paragraphs 1 to 5;

(b) To provide, as appropriate, protection to the Transitional Federal Institutions to help them carry out their functions of government, and security for key infrastructure;

(c) To assist, within its capabilities, and in coordination with other parties, with implementation of the National Security and Stabilization Plan, in particular the effective re-establishment and training of all-inclusive Somali security forces;

(d) To contribute, as may be requested and within capabilities, to the creation of the necessary security conditions for the provision of humanitarian assistance;

(e) To protect its personnel, facilities, installations, equipment and mission, and to ensure the security and freedom of movement of its personnel;

10. *Urges* member States of the African Union to contribute to the above mission in order to help create the conditions for the withdrawal of all other foreign forces from Somalia;

11. *Decides* that the measures imposed by paragraph 5 of resolution 733 (1992) and further elaborated upon in paragraphs 1 and 2 of resolution 1425 (2002) shall not apply to:

(a) Supplies of weapons and military equipment, technical training and assistance intended solely for the support of or use by the mission referred to in paragraph 9 above; or

(b) Such supplies and technical assistance by States intended solely for the purpose of helping develop security sector institutions, consistent with the political process set out in paragraphs 1 to 5 above and in the absence of a negative decision by the Committee established pursuant to resolution 751 (1992) within five working days of receiving the notification described in paragraph 12 below;

12. *Decides* that States providing supplies or technical assistance in accordance with paragraph 11 (b) above shall notify the Committee established pursuant to resolution 751 (1992) in advance and on a case-by-case basis;

13. *Emphasizes* the continued contribution made to Somalia's peace and security by the arms embargo, *demands* that all Member States, in particular those of the region, fully comply with it, *reiterates* its intention to consider urgently ways to strengthen its effectiveness, including through targeted measures in support of the arms embargo, and requests that the Committee established pursuant to resolution 751 (1992) report to the Council within 60 days of the adoption of this resolution on possible measures that might be taken and how they might be implemented;

14. *Urges* Member States to provide financial resources, personnel, equipment and services for the full deployment of AMISOM;

15. *Requests* the Secretary-General to consult with the African Union Commission on what further support might be provided to AMISOM and report back to the Council on any progress, pursuant to the timetable set out in paragraph 17 below;

16. *Requests* the Secretary-General, further to the observations in his report on Somalia of 25 June 2007 referred to above, to continue to develop the existing contingency planning for the possible deployment of a United Nations Peacekeeping Operation replacing AMISOM including:

(a) Sending a further Technical Assessment Mission to the region as soon as possible;

(b) Further contact with potential troop-contributing countries;

(c) Identifying what further action the United Nations and the international community should take to help create the conditions necessary for, and to overcome potential obstacles to, the deployment and success of a United Nations peacekeeping mission in Somalia, including specifying measures, indicators and time frames for review of progress that will assist the Security Council's decision on the appropriateness of and objectives for a United Nations mission;

17. *Requests* that the Secretary-General report to the Council within 30 days after the adoption of this resolution, and then again within a further 30 days, on the status of the further development of the plans outlined in paragraph 16 above, as well as the political aspects in paragraphs 6 and 7 above;

18. *Encourages* Member States whose naval vessels and military aircraft operate in international waters and airspace adjacent to the coast of Somalia to be vigilant to any incident of piracy therein and to take appropriate action to protect merchant shipping, in particular the transportation of humanitarian aid, against any such act, in line with relevant international law;

19. *Reaffirms* its previous resolutions 1325 (2000) on women, peace and security, and 1674 (2006) and 1738 (2006) on the protection of civilians in armed conflict, and *stresses* the responsibility of all parties and armed groups in Somalia to take appropriate steps to protect the civilian population in the country, consistent with international humanitarian, human rights and refugee law, in particular by avoiding any indiscriminate attacks on populated areas;

20. *Strongly supports and encourages* the ongoing relief efforts in Somalia, recalls its resolution 1502 (2003) on the protection of humanitarian and United Nations personnel, *calls* on all parties and armed groups in Somalia to take appropriate steps to ensure the safety

and security of AMISOM and humanitarian personnel, and grant timely, safe and unhindered access for the delivery of humanitarian assistance to all those in need, and *urges* the countries in the region to facilitate the provision of humanitarian assistance by land or via air and sea ports;

21. *Reaffirms* its previous resolution 1612 (2005) on children and armed conflict and *recalls* the subsequent conclusions of the Security Council Working Group on Children in Armed Conflict pertaining to parties to the armed conflict in Somalia (S/AC.51/2007/14);

22. *Decides* to remain actively seized of the matter.

Resolution 1773 (2007)

Adopted by the Security Council at its 5733rd meeting, on 24 August 2007

The Security Council,

Recalling all its previous resolutions on Lebanon, in particular resolutions 425 (1978), 426 (1978), 1559 (2004), 1680 (2006) and 1701 (2006), as well as the statements of its President on the situation in Lebanon, in particular the statement of 3 August 2007 (S/PRST/2007/29),

Recalling also the report of the Secretary-General of 28 June 2007 (S/2007/392) and the letter from the Secretary-General to its President of 2 August 2007 (S/2007/470),

Reaffirming its strong commitment to the sovereignty, territorial integrity, unity and political independence of Lebanon within its internationally recognized borders and under the sole and exclusive authority of its Government,

Reiterating its strong support for full respect for the cessation of hostilities and the Blue Line in its entirety,

Reaffirming its attachment to the full implementation of all provisions of resolution 1701 (2006), and *aware* of its responsibilities to help secure a permanent ceasefire and a long-term solution as envisioned in the resolution,

Emphasizing the need to address the causes of the conflict, including that the abducted Israeli soldiers have not been released, nor has proof of life been provided, and calling once again for their immediate and unconditional return,

Encouraging the efforts aimed at urgently settling the issue of the Lebanese prisoners detained in Israel,

Welcoming the steps taken by the Government of Lebanon to extend its authority over its territory, through its own legitimate armed forces, such that there will be no weapons without the consent of the Government of Lebanon and no authority other than that of the Government of Lebanon, and *encouraging* it to continue its efforts in this regard,

Welcoming also the tripartite arrangements referred to in the aforementioned report, and *encouraging* the parties to coordinate further with the United Nations Interim Force in Lebanon (UNIFIL), notably to visibly mark the Blue Line and reach an agreement on the northern part of Ghajar,

Condemning in the strongest terms all terrorist attacks against UNIFIL and *emphasizing* the need for further coordination between UNIFIL and the Lebanese Armed Forces in particular regarding the establishment between the Blue Line and the Litani river of an area free of any armed personnel, assets and weapons other than those of the Government of Lebanon and of UNIFIL, and for UNIFIL to enhance its investigative capacities in response to these attacks,

Underlining the importance of continued efforts to clear unexploded ordnance from Southern Lebanon and calling on all parties to support these efforts,

Reaffirming UNIFIL's authority to take all necessary action in areas of deployment of its forces and as it deems within its capabilities, to ensure that its area of operations is not utilized for hostile activities of any kind and to resist attempts by forceful means to prevent it from discharging its mandate,

Recalling the relevant principles contained in the Convention on the Safety of United Nations and Associated Personnel,

Commending the active role and dedication of the personnel of UNIFIL, notably of its Commander, as well as of the Special Coordinator of the United Nations for Lebanon,

Expressing its strong appreciation to Member states that contribute to UNIFIL and underlining the necessity that UNIFIL have at its disposal all necessary means and equipment to carry out its mandate,

Responding to the request of the Government of Lebanon to extend the mandate of UNIFIL for a new period of one year without amendment presented in the letter from the Lebanese Prime Minister to the Secretary-General of 25 June 2007 (S/2007/396),

Determining that the situation in Lebanon continues to constitute a threat to international peace and security,

1. *Decides* to extend the present mandate of UNIFIL until 31 August 2008;

2. *Commends* the positive role of UNIFIL, whose deployment together with the Lebanese Armed Forces has helped to establish a new strategic environment in southern Lebanon, and *looks forward* to its increased cooperation with the LAF in the discharge of its mandate;

3. *Calls upon* all parties concerned to respect the cessation of hostilities and the Blue Line in its entirety;

4. *Urges* all parties to cooperate fully with the United Nations and UNIFIL and to abide scrupulously by their obligation to respect the safety of the UNIFIL and other United Nations personnel, including by avoiding any course of action which endangers United Nations personnel and by ensuring UNIFIL is accorded full freedom of movement within its area of operation;

5. *Calls* upon all parties to cooperate fully with the Security Council and the Secretary-General to achieve a permanent ceasefire and a long-term solution as envisioned in resolution 1701 (2006), and *emphasizes* the need for greater progress in this regard;

6. *Reiterates* its intention to consider further steps to contribute to the implementation of a permanent ceasefire and a long-term solution;

7. *Welcomes* the efforts being undertaken by UNIFIL to implement the Secretary-General's zero-tolerance policy on sexual exploitation and abuse and to ensure full compliance of its personnel with the United Nations code of conduct, requests the Secretary-General to continue to take all necessary action in this regard and to keep the Security Council informed, and urges troop-contributing countries to take preventive and disciplinary action to ensure that such acts are properly investigated and punished in cases involving their personnel;

8. *Requests* the Secretary-General to continue to report to the Council on the implementation of resolution 1701 (2006) every four months, or at any time as he deems appropriate;

9. *Stresses* the importance of, and the need to achieve, a comprehensive, just and lasting peace in the Middle East, based on all its relevant resolutions including its resolutions 242 (1967) of 22 November 1967, 338 (1973) of 22 October 1973, and 1515 (2003) of 19 November 2003;

10. *Decides* to remain actively seized of the matter.

Resolution 1774 (2007)

Adopted by the Security Council at its 5741st meeting, on 14 September 2007

The Security Council,

Recalling its resolution 1505 (2003) of 4 September 2003,

Having regard to Article 15 (4) of the Statute of the International Criminal Tribunal for Rwanda (ICTR) as adopted by the Council in its resolution 1503 (2003),

Having considered the nomination by the Secretary-General of Mr. Hassan Bubacar Jallow for reappointment as Prosecutor of the International Criminal Tribunal for Rwanda (S/2007/539),

Recalling that resolution 1503 (2003) of 28 August 2003 called upon the International Criminal Tribunal for Rwanda to take all possible measures to complete all trial activities at first instance by the end of 2008, and to complete all work in 2010 (ICTR completion strategy),

Recalling also its resolution 1534 (2004) of 26 March 2004 which emphasized the importance of fully implementing the International Tribunal's completion strategy and urges the Tribunal to plan and act accordingly,

Decides to reappoint Mr. Hassan Bubacar Jallow as Prosecutor of the International Criminal Tribunal for Rwanda with effect from 15 September 2007 for a four-year term, which is subject to an earlier termination by the Security Council upon completion of the work of the International Tribunal.

Resolution 1775 (2007)

Adopted by the Security Council at its 5742nd meeting, on 14 September 2007

The Security Council,

Recalling its resolution 1504 (2003) of 4 September 2003,

Having regard to Article 16 (4) of the Statute of the International Criminal Tribunal for the former Yugoslavia,

Aware that the term of office for Ms. Carla Del Ponte as Prosecutor for the International Criminal Tribunal for the former Yugoslavia expires on 14 September 2007,

Noting the need to ensure a smooth transition between the departure of Ms. Carla Del Ponte and the assumption of office of her successor,

Having considered the request of the Secretary-General to extend the appointment of Ms. Del Ponte from 15 September 2007 to 31 December 2007 (S/2007/538),

Noting the intention of the Secretary-General to submit the name of his nominee for the position of Prosecutor of the International Criminal Tribunal for the former Yugoslavia,

Decides, notwithstanding the provisions of article 16 (4) of the Statute, to extend for a final period the appointment of Ms. Carla Del Ponte as Prosecutor of the International Criminal Tribunal for the former Yugoslavia with effect from 15 September 2007 until 31 December 2007.

CHAPTER 3

Economic and Social Council

1. Report of the Economic and Social Council for 2006 (A/61/3)

Chapter I

Matters calling for action by or brought to the attention of the General Assembly

1. In 2006, the Economic and Social Council adopted resolutions and decisions that call for action by or that are to be brought to the attention of the General Assembly. The relevant paragraphs of those resolutions and decisions are summarized below.

Adoption of the agenda and other organizational matters (item 1)

Enlargement of the Executive Committee of the Programme of the United Nations High Commissioner for Refugees

2. By **decision 2006/237**, the Council recommended that the General Assembly, at its sixty-first session, decide on the question of enlarging the membership of the Executive Committee of the Programme of the United Nations High Commissioner for Refugees from 70 to 72 States.

Special economic, humanitarian and disaster relief assistance(item 5)

Strengthening of the coordination of emergency humanitarian assistance of the United Nations

3. By **resolution 2006/5**, the Council requested the Secretary-General to continue to develop more systematic links with Member States offering military assets for natural disaster response in order to identify the availability of such assets and to report to the General Assembly through the Council in that regard and reiterated its request to the Secretary-General to report to the Assembly through the Council on progress achieved in developing and improving mechanisms for the use of emergency standby capacities.

4. In the same resolution, the Council re-emphasized that the discussions of humanitarian policies and activities by the General Assembly and the Council should be continuously revitalized by Member States with a view to enhancing their relevance, efficiency and impact and recommended that the Assembly, in order to have a more focused discussion on humanitarian issues, explore the possibility at its sixty-first session of reallocating to the plenary of the Assembly the sub-items of its agenda related to the strengthening of the coordination of humanitarian and disaster relief assistance of the United Nations currently considered by the Second Committee. The Council also encouraged Member States to continue to strengthen cooperation and coordination between the Assembly and the Council on humanitarian issues, based on their respective mandates and taking into account comparative advantages and existing complementarities of the two bodies, and requested the Secretary-General to reflect the progress made in the implementation of and follow-up to the resolution in his next report to the Council and the Assembly on the strengthening of the coordination of emergency humanitarian assistance of the United Nations.

Implementation of and follow-up to major United Nations conferences and summits (item 6)

Follow-up to the World Summit on the Information Society and review of the Commission on Science and Technology for Development

5. By **resolution 2006/46**, the Council decided to keep the General Assembly apprised, through its annual report, on progress made in the implementation of and follow-up to the outcomes of the World Summit on the Information Society, taking into account the work of the Commission on Science and Technology for Development (see also under sub-item 13 (b)).

Coordination, programme and other questions (item 7)

Tobacco or health (sub-item 7 (h))

Smoke-free United Nations premises

6. By **resolution 2006/42**, the Council recommended that the General Assembly, at its sixty-first session, consider the implementation of a complete ban on smoking at all United Nations indoor premises, at Headquarters as well as at regional and country offices throughout the United Nations system, and the implementation of a complete ban on sales of tobacco products at all United Nations premises, and also recommended that the Assembly request the Secretary-General to submit a report on the implementation of the resolution to the Council at its substantive session of 2008.

Economic and social repercussions of the Israeli occupation on the living conditions of the Palestinian people in the Occupied Palestinian Territory, including East Jerusalem, and the Arab population in the occupied Syrian Golan (item 11)

Economic and social repercussions of the Israeli occupation on the living conditions of the Palestinian people in the Occupied Palestinian Territory, including East Jerusalem, and the Arab population in the occupied Syrian Golan

7. By **resolution 2006/43**, the Council requested the Secretary-General to submit to the General Assembly at its sixty-first session, through the Council, a report on the implementation of the resolution and to continue to include in the report of the United Nations Special Coordinator for the Middle East Peace Process and Personal Representative of the Secretary-General to the Palestine Liberation Organization and the Palestinian Authority, an update on the living conditions of the Palestinian people, in collaboration with relevant United Nations agencies.

Economic and environmental questions (item 13)

Science and technology for development (sub-item 13 (b))

Follow-up to the World Summit on the Information Society and review of the Commission on Science and Technology for Development

8. By **resolution 2006/46**, the Council decided to keep the General Assembly apprised, through its annual report, on progress made in the implementation of and follow-up to the

outcomes of the World Summit on the Information Society, taking into account the work of the Commission on Science and Technology for Development (see also under item 6).

Human settlements (sub-item 13 (d))

Human settlements

9. By **decision 2006/247**, the Council took note of the report of the Secretary-General on the coordinated implementation of the Habitat Agenda (E/2006/71) and decided to transmit the report to the General Assembly for consideration at its sixty-first session.

Population and development (sub-item 13 (f))

Report of the Commission on Population and Development on its thirty-ninth session and provisional agenda for the fortieth session of the Commission

10. By **decision 2006/233**, the Council took note of the report of the Commission on Population and Development on its thirty-ninth session (E/2006/25) and decided to transmit the report to the High-level Dialogue on International Migration and Development, to be held during the sixty-first session of the General Assembly.

United Nations Forum on Forests (sub-item 13 (i))

Proclamation of an International Year of Forests

11. By **decision 2006/230**, the Council, recognizing the need to raise awareness of forest-related issues, decided to recommend that the General Assembly, at its sixty-first session, proclaim 2011 as the International Year of Forests.

Social and human rights questions (item 14)

Advancement of women (sub-item 14 (a))

High-level panel discussion on the gender dimensions of international migration held by the Commission on the Status of Women

12. By **decision 2006/234**, the Council decided to transmit to the General Assembly the summary, submitted by the Chairperson of the Commission on the Status of Women, on the high-level panel discussion on the gender dimensions of international migration held during the Commission's fiftieth session (see E/2006/27 and Corr.1, chap. I, sect. A).

Crime prevention and criminal justice (sub-item 14 (c))

Strengthening the United Nations Crime Prevention and Criminal Justice Programme and the role of the Commission on Crime Prevention and Criminal Justice as its governing body

13. By **decision 2006/256**, the Council decided to transmit to the General Assembly the draft resolution contained therein.

International cooperation in the prevention, combating and elimination of kidnapping and in providing assistance to victims

14. By **resolution 2006/19**, the Council recommended to the General Assembly the adoption of the draft resolution contained therein.

---

* The present report is a preliminary version of those sections of the report of the Economic and Social Council relating to the organizational and resumed organizational sessions for 2006 and the substantive session of 2006. The section relating to the resumed substantive session will be issued as an addendum to the present report. The entire report will be issued in final form as *Official Records of the General Assembly, Sixty-first Session, Supplement No. 3* (A/61/3/Rev.1).

The resolutions and decisions adopted by the Council at the organizational and resumed organizational sessions for 2006 and the substantive session of 2006 are being issued initially in documents E/2006/INF/2 and Add.1. Those adopted at the resumed substantive session will be issued in document E/2006/INF/2/Add.2. The resolutions and decisions will be issued in final form as *Official Records of the Economic and Social Council, 2006, Supplement No. 1* (E/2006/99).

Chapter II

Special high-level meeting of the Council with the Bretton Woods institutions, the World Trade Organization and the United Nations Conference on Trade and Development

1. In its resolution 60/188, and in accordance with paragraph 88 of annex I to its resolution 50/227, the General Assembly resolved to continue to make full use of the existing institutional arrangement for reviewing the implementation of the Monterrey Consensus of the International Conference on Financing for Development,[1] as set out in paragraph 69 of the Monterrey Consensus and in line with its resolution 57/270 B, including the high-level dialogues convened by the Assembly and the spring meetings of the Council with the Bretton Woods institutions, the World Trade Organization and the United Nations Conference on Trade and Development. Pursuant thereto, the Council held a special high-level meeting with the Bretton Woods institutions, the World Trade Organization and the United Nations Conference on Trade and Development at its 6th and 7th meetings, on 24 April 2006. An account of the proceedings is contained in the relevant summary records (E/2006/SR.6 and 7). The Council had before it a note by the Secretary-General on coherence, coordination and cooperation in the context of the implementation of the Monterrey Consensus and the 2005 World Summit Outcome (E/2006/48 and Corr.1).

2. At the 6th meeting, on 24 April, the President of the Council made an introductory statement.

3. The Secretary-General of the United Nations addressed the meeting.

4. At the same meeting, the President of the Council introduced the following panellists from intergovernmental organizations who made statements: the Chairman of the Development Committee, the President of the Trade and Development Board of the United Nations Conference on Trade and Development, the Deputy Managing Director of the International Monetary Fund and the Deputy Director-General of the World Trade Organization.

5. After the presentations, the Council adjourned the 6th meeting and moved on to round tables A, B, C and D.

Round tables

6. Round table A was co-chaired by Maria Luiza Viotti, Director-General, Humanitarian and Social Themes, Ministry of External Relations of Brazil, and Tom Scholar (United Kingdom of Great Britain and Northern Ireland), Executive Director of the International Monetary Fund and the World Bank.

7. Round table B was co-chaired by Eckhard Deutscher (Germany), Executive Director of the World Bank, and Ransford Smith, President, Trade and Development Board of the United Nations Conference on Trade and Development.

8. Round table C was co-chaired by Sri Mulyani, Minister of Finance of Indonesia, and Willy Kiekens (Belgium), Senior Executive Director of the International Monetary Fund.

9. Round table D was co-chaired by Mohamed Nouri Jouini, Minister of Development and International Cooperation of Tunisia, and Leire Pajin, Vice-Minister, Secretary of State for International Cooperation of Spain.

10. At its 7th meeting, on 24 April, the Council heard a briefing by the Director-General for Development Cooperation of the Ministry for Foreign Affairs of Sweden and member of the High-level Panel on United Nations System-wide Coherence in the Areas of Development, Humanitarian Assistance and Environment.

11. At the same meeting, the Council resumed the special high-level meeting with the Bretton Woods institutions, the World Trade Organization and the United Nations Conference on Trade and Development, and heard oral reports from the Director-General, Humanitarian and Social Themes, Ministry of External Relations of Brazil (round table A), the Executive Director of the World Bank (Germany) (round table B), the Senior Executive Director of the International Monetary Fund (Belgium) (round table C) and the Vice-Minister, Secretary of State for International Cooperation of Spain (round table D), on the outcome of the four round tables.

Statements by representatives of the civil society and the business sector

12. At the 7th meeting, on 24 April, the Council heard statements by the representative of civil society (Ecumenical Coordinator for the Millennium Development Goals, All Africa Conference of Churches and Global Call to Action Against Poverty) and a representative of the business sector (Chief Executive Officer and Managing Partner of INVESCO Private Capital).

Exchange of views among participants

13. At the 7th meeting, on 24 April, the representatives of Austria (on behalf of the European Union, the acceding countries Bulgaria and Romania, the candidate countries Croatia, the former Yugoslav Republic of Macedonia and Turkey, and the countries of the stabilization and association process and potential candidates Bosnia and Herzegovina, Montenegro and Serbia, as well as Ukraine and the Republic of Moldova) and the Republic of Korea made statements.

14. At the same meeting, the representative of the Economic and Social Commission for Asia and the Pacific made a statement on behalf of the regional commissions.

15. The proceedings of the special high-level meeting of the Council with the Bretton Woods institutions, the World Trade Organization and the United Nations Conference on Trade and Development were summarized by the President of the Council (see A/61/81-E/2006/73).

Closing of the meeting

16. At the 7th meeting, the President of the Council, after having made a preliminary summary of the meeting, declared the special high-level meeting of the Council with the Bretton Woods institutions, the World Trade Organization and the United Nations Conference on Trade and Development closed.

Chapter III

High-level segment

Creating an environment at the national and international levels conducive to generating full and productive employment and decent work for all, and its impact on sustainable development

Opening of the session

1. The high-level segment of the substantive session of 2006 of the Council was held at its 12th to 16th meetings, from 3 to 5 July 2006. An account of the proceedings is contained in the relevant summary records (E/2006/SR.12-16). In accordance with Council decision 2005/313 of 21 October 2005, the theme for the high-level segment was "Creating an environment at the national and international levels conducive to generating full and productive employment and decent work for all, and its impact on sustainable development (agenda item 2). The Council had before it the following documents:

(a) Relevant part of the report of the Committee for Development Policy on its eighth session (E/2006/33);[2]

(b) Relevant part of the report of the Secretary-General on regional cooperation in the economic, social and related fields (E/2006/15);

(c) Relevant part of the addendum to the report of the Secretary-General on regional cooperation in the economic, social and related fields: matters calling for action by the Economic and Social Council or brought to its attention (E/2006/15/Add.1);

(d) World Economic and Social Survey 2006: Diverging Growth and Development: overview (E/2006/50);

(e) Letter dated 10 April 2006 from the Chairperson of the Commission on the Status of Women to the President of the Economic and Social Council (E/2006/52);

(f) Report of the Secretary-General on creating an environment at the national and international levels conducive to generating full and productive employment and decent work for all, and its impact on sustainable development (E/2006/55);

(g) Draft ministerial declaration of the high-level segment submitted by the President of the Council on the basis of informal consultations (E/2006/L.8);

(h) Conference room paper on the theme of the 2006 high-level segment (E/2006/CRP.2) (English only);

(i) World economic situation and prospects as of mid-May 2006 (E/2006/CRP.3) (English only);

(j) Summary by the President of the Council of the informal preparatory meeting held on 4 and 5 April 2006 on the theme of the 2006 high-level segment (E/2006/CRP.6) (English only);

(k) Note by the Secretariat on creating an environment at the national and international levels conducive to generating full and productive employment and decent work for all, and its impact on sustainable development (E/CN.6/2006/CRP.4) (all languages);

(l) Statement submitted by Foundation for Research on Technology Migration and Integration, a non-governmental organization in consultative status with the Economic and Social Council (E/2006/NGO/1);

(m) Statement submitted by Hadassah-Women's Zionist Organization of America, a non-governmental organization in consultative status with the Economic and Social Council (E/2006/NGO/2);

(n) Statement submitted by Institute of International Social Development, a non-governmental organization in consultative status with the Economic and Social Council (E/2006/NGO/3);

(o) Statement submitted by Droit à l'energie SOS futur, a non-governmental organization in consultative status with the Economic and Social Council (E/2006/NGO/4);

(p) Statement submitted by Comité de Apoyo a los Trabajadores Agrícolas, a non-governmental organization in consultative status with the Economic and Social Council (E/2006/NGO/5);

(q) Statement submitted by Soroptimist International, a non-governmental organization in consultative status with the Economic and Social Council (E/2006/NGO/6);

(r) Statement submitted by International Indian Treaty Council, a non-governmental organization in consultative status with the Economic and Social Council (E/2006/NGO/7);

(s) Statement submitted by World Family Organization, a non-governmental organization in consultative status with the Economic and Social Council (E/2006/NGO/8);

(t) Statement submitted by Mulchand and Parpati Thadhani Foundation, a non-governmental organization in consultative status with the Economic and Social Council (E/2006/NGO/9);

(u) Statement submitted by Maryknoll Fathers and Brothers and Maryknoll Sisters of St. Dominic, non-governmental organizations in consultative status with the Economic and Social Council (E/2006/NGO/10);

(v) Statement submitted by New Humanity, a non-governmental organization in consultative status with the Economic and Social Council (E/2006/NGO/11);

(w) Statement submitted by Association de volontaires pour le service international, a non-governmental organization in consultative status with the Economic and Social Council (E/2006/NGO/12);

(x) Statement submitted by Tamana Association, a non-governmental organization in consultative status with the Economic and Social Council (E/2006/NGO/13);

(y) Statement submitted by World Society for the Protection of Animals, a non-governmental organization in consultative status with the Economic and Social Council (E/2006/NGO/14);

(z) Statement submitted by Help Handicapped International, a non-governmental organization in consultative status with the Economic and Social Council (E/2006/NGO/15);

(aa) Statement submitted by International Association of Applied Psychology, a non-governmental organization in consultative status with the Economic and Social Council (E/2006/NGO/16);

(bb) Statement submitted by Brahma Kumaris World Spiritual University, a non-governmental organization in consultative status with the Economic and Social Council (E/2006/NGO/17);

(cc) Statement submitted by the African Youth Network for Sustainable Development, Association algérienne d'alphabétisation, Association algérienne de solidarité aux maladies respiratoires, Association algérienne pour la planification familiale, Association d'aide aux enfants cancéreux, Association nationale de soutien aux enfants en difficulté et en institution, Association nationale de volontariat "Touiza", Comité algérien des droits de l'homme et des peuples, Comité national d'entraide de la jeunesse et de l'enfance, Croissant-Rouge algérien, Federation of Associations of Motor-Disabled Persons, Fondation pour la promotion de la santé et le développement de la recherche, SOS femmes en détresse et Scouts musulmans algériens, non-governmental organizations in consultative status with the Economic and Social Council (E/2006/NGO/18);

(dd) Statement submitted by Partnership for Indigenous Peoples Environment, a non-governmental organization in consultative status with the Economic and Social Council (E/2006/NGO/19);

(ee) Statement submitted by International Telecommunication Academy, a non-governmental organization in consultative status with the Economic and Social Council (E/2006/NGO/20);

(ff) Statement submitted by Hope for the Nations, a non-governmental organization in consultative status with the Economic and Social Council (E/2006/NGO/21);

(gg) Statement submitted by W. Haywood Burns Environmental Education Centre, a non-governmental organization in consultative status with the Economic and Social Council (E/2006/NGO/22);

(hh) Statement submitted by Foundation Alvaralice, a non-governmental organization in consultative status with the Economic and Social Council (E/2006/NGO/23);

(ii) Statement submitted by Peoples Decade for Human Rights Education, a non-governmental organization in consultative status with the Economic and Social Council (E/2006/NGO/24);

(jj) Statement submitted by IUS PRIMI VIRI International Association, a non-governmental organization in consultative status with the Economic and Social Council (E/2006/NGO/25);

(kk) Statement submitted by United Nations Association of China, a non-governmental organization in consultative status with the Economic and Social Council (E/2006/NGO/26);

(ll) Statement submitted by International Institute for Non-Aligned Studies, a non-governmental organization in consultative status with the Economic and Social Council (E/2006/NGO/27);

(mm) Statement submitted by Legiào da Boa Vontade, a non-governmental organization in consultative status with the Economic and Social Council (E/2006/NGO/28);

(nn) Statement submitted by Indian Social Institute, a non-governmental organization in consultative status with the Economic and Social Council (E/2006/NGO/29);

(oo) Statement submitted by non-governmental organizations participating in the Economic and Social Council Non-Governmental Organizations Forum (Part I) (E/2006/NGO/30);

(pp) Statement submitted by non-governmental organizations participating in the Economic and Social Council Non-Governmental Organizations Forum (Part II) (E/2006/NGO/31);

(qq) Statement submitted by Mumbai Educational Trust, a non-governmental organization in consultative status with the Economic and Social Council (E/2006/NGO/32);

(rr) Statement submitted by National Association of Housing and Redevelopment Officials, a non-governmental organization in consultative status with the Economic and Social Council (E/2006/NGO/33);

(ss) Statement submitted by Institute for the Development of Education, Arts and Leisure, a non-governmental organization in consultative status with the Economic and Social Council (E/2006/NGO/34);

(tt) Statement submitted by Osservatorio per la Comunicazione Culturale e l'Audiovisivo nel Mediterraneo e nel Mondo, a non-governmental organization in consultative status with the Economic and Social Council (E/2006/NGO/35);

(uu) Statement submitted by Jigyansu Tribal Research Centre, a non-governmental organization in consultative status with the Economic and Social Council (E/2006/NGO/36).

2. At the 12th meeting, on 3 July, the President of the Council opened the session and made a statement.

3. At the same meeting, the Deputy Secretary-General of the United Nations addressed the Council.

Working out of poverty

4. At its 12th meeting, on 3 July, the Council heard statements by Shaukat Aziz, Prime Minister of Pakistan; Jens Stoltenberg, Prime Minister of Norway; Luísa Dias Diogo, Prime Minister of Mozambique; Chadli Laroussi, Minister of Labour and Youth Employment of Tunisia; and Juan Somavía, Director-General of the International Labour Organization, on the theme "Working out of poverty".

High-level policy dialogue and discussion on important developments in the world economy and international economic cooperation with the executive heads of financial and trade institutions of the United Nations system

5. At its 12th meeting, on 3 July, the Council held a high-level policy dialogue and discussion on important developments in the world economy and international economic cooperation with the executive heads of financial and trade institutions of the United Nations system.

6. At the same meeting, the Council heard opening remarks by the Under-Secretary-General for Economic and Social Affairs as well as the panellists: Supachai Panitchpakdi, Secretary-General of the United Nations Conference on Trade and Development; Valentine Rugwabiza, Deputy Director-General of the World Trade Organization; François Bourguignon, Chief Economist and Senior Vice-President of the World Bank; and Reinhard H. Munzberg, Special Representative of the International Monetary Fund to the United Nations.

7. Also at the 12th meeting, the representative of the Economic and Social Commission for Asia and the Pacific made a statement.

8. At the same meeting, during the exchange of views, statements were made by the representatives of South Africa (on behalf of the Group of 77 and China), Brazil, Thailand and the Russian Federation and the observers for Finland (on behalf of the European Union and the Dominican Republic).

9. Also at the 12th meeting, the representatives of the World Trade Organization and the International Monetary Fund responded to queries raised by delegations.

Creating an environment at the national and international levels conducive to generating full and productive employment and decent work for all, and its impact on sustainable development

Opening of the high-level segment (general debate)

10. At its 13th meeting, on 4 July, the Council began its consideration of agenda item 2 and heard introductory statements by the Under-Secretary-General for Economic and Social Affairs and the Vice-Chairperson of the Committee for Development Policy.

11. At the same meeting, statements were made by: M. Mdladlana, Minister of Labour of South Africa (on behalf of the Group of 77 and China); Tarja Filatov, Minister of Labour of Finland (on behalf of the European Union); Ali bin Abdulah Al Ka'abi, Minister of Labour of the United Arab Emirates; Gilbert Ondongo, Minister of Labour, Employment and Social Security of the Congo; Madan M. Dulloo, Minister for Foreign Affairs, International Trade and Cooperation of Mauritius; Mohamed Ould Abed, Minister for Economic Affairs and Development of Mauritania; Rubén Ramírez Lezcano, Vice-Minister for Economic Relations and Integration of Paraguay; A. Yakovenko, Deputy Minister for Foreign Affairs

of the Russian Federation; Cestmir Sajda, Deputy Minister of Labour and Social Affairs of the Czech Republic; María Pilar Hernández, Vice-Minister of External Relations of the Bolivarian Republic of Venezuela; Carmen Elisa Sosa de Callejas, Vice-Minister of Labour of El Salvador; Goran Bankov, Deputy Minister of Labour and Social Policy of Bulgaria; Hamayetuddin, Foreign Secretary, Ministry of Foreign Affairs of Bangladesh; Esteban Rodríguez, Director-General of Labour, Ministry of Social Affairs and Labour of Spain; Clyde Mascoll, Minister of State, Ministry of Finance of Barbados; and Choi Hyuck, Permanent Representative of the Republic of Korea to the United Nations Office at Geneva.

12. Also at the 13th meeting, the Secretary-General of the World Tourism Organization made a statement.

13. At the same meeting, statements were made by the representatives of the following non-governmental organizations in consultative status with the Council: Conference of Non-Governmental Organizations in Consultative Relationship with the United Nations, World Federation of United Nations Associations, and Chinese People's Association for Peace and Disarmament.

14. At the 14th meeting, on 4 July, statements were made by Athauda Seneviratne, Minister of Labour Relations and Foreign Employment of Sri Lanka; Ivan Sahan, Minister of Labour and Social Policy of Ukraine; Norberto Ciavarino, Chef de Cabinet, Ministry of Labour, Employment and Social Security of Argentina; Walter Fust, Director-General, Ministry of Foreign Affairs of Switzerland; Kazimierz Kuberski, Under-Secretary of State, Ministry of Labour and Social Policy of Poland; Labeed M. Abbawi, Under-Secretary, Ministry of Foreign Affairs of Iraq; Valdas Rupšys, Under-Secretary, Ministry of Social Affairs and Labour of Lithuania; and K. C. Singh, Additional Secretary, International Organisations Division, Ministry of External Affairs of India.

15. At the same meeting, statements were also made by the representatives of the following non-governmental organizations in consultative status with the Council: Hope for the Nations, World Family Organization and Droit à l'énergie SOS futur.

16. At the 15th meeting, on 5 July, statements were made by Hassan Lawal, Minister for Labour and Productivity of Nigeria; Alpheus Naruseb, Minister of Labour and Social Welfare of Namibia; Jean-Max Bellerive, Minister of Planning and External Cooperation of Haiti; Richard T. Miller, Head of Delegation of the United States of America; Adelaine Mwau, Assistant Minister, Ministry of Labour and Human Resource Development of Kenya; Gordan Markotić, Permanent Representative of Croatia to the United Nations Office at Geneva; Hjálmar Hannesson, Permanent Representative of Iceland to the United Nations in New York; Caroline Jane Millar, Head of Delegation of Australia; Jean-Maurice Ripert, Permanent Representative of France to the United Nations Office at Geneva; Ronaldo Sardenberg, Permanent Representative of Brazil to the United Nations in New York; and Gusti Agung Wesaka Puja, Permanent Representative of Indonesia to the United Nations Office at Geneva.

17. At the same meeting, the European Commissioner for Employment, Social Affairs and Equal Opportunity made a statement.

18. Also at the 15th meeting, statements were made by the representative of the International Association of Economic and Social Councils and Similar Institutions and the Secretary-General of the IUS PRIMI VIRI International Association.

19. At the 16th meeting, on 5 July, statements were made by Clemencia Forero Ucros, Permanent Representative of Colombia to the United Nations Office at Geneva; Matern Y. Lumbanga, Permanent Representative of the United Republic of Tanzania to the United Nations Office at Geneva; Elchin Amirbayov, Permanent Representative of Azerbaijan to the United Nations Office at Geneva; Sha Zukang, Permanent Representative of China to the United Nations Office at Geneva; Virgilio Marques Faria, Director for International Organizations, Foreign Ministry of Angola; Chaiyong Satjipanon, Permanent Representative of Thailand to the United Nations Office at Geneva; Boubacar Diallo, Permanent Representative of Guinea to the United Nations Office at Geneva; Ali Reza Moaiyeri, Permanent Representative of the Islamic Republic of Iran to the United Nations Office at Geneva; Manuel Rodríguez Cuadros, Permanent Representative of Peru to the United Nations Office at Geneva; Sergeí Aleinik, Permanent Representative of Belarus to the United Nations Office at Geneva; Elisabet Borsiin Bonnier, Permanent Representative of Sweden to the United Nations Office at Geneva; Shigeru Endo, Deputy Permanent Representative of Japan to the United Nations Office at Geneva; and Pablo Macedo, Deputy Permanent Representative of Mexico to the United Nations Office at Geneva; and Mgr. Silvano M. Tomasi, Permanent Observer for the Holy See to the United Nations Office at Geneva.

20. At the same meeting, statements were also made by the President, International Fund for Agricultural Development (also on behalf of the Food and Agriculture Organization of the United Nations and the World Food Programme); the Director-General, International Organization for Migration; the Chairperson, Development Commission of the International Federation of Red Cross and Red Crescent Societies; the Deputy Executive Director, United Nations Population Fund; the Director, United Nations Educational, Scientific and Cultural Organization Liaison Office, Geneva; and the Deputy Executive Director, United Nations Office on Drugs and Crime.

21. Also at the 16th meeting, the Under-Secretary-General and High Representative for the Least Developed Countries, Landlocked Developing Countries and Small Island Developing States made a statement.

22. Statements were also made by the Chairman of the inter-State Committee of the Commonwealth of Independent States and the representative of the International Confederation of Free Trade Unions (on behalf of the Global Unions Coalition).

High-level round tables

23. The high-level round tables (1 to 4) on the theme of the high-level segment were held simultaneously on 5 July 2006.

Round table 1

Creating decent work opportunities with productivity growth

24. Round table 1 was chaired by Chadli Laroussi, Minister of Labour and Youth Employment of Tunisia, and co-moderated by José Luis Machinea, Executive Secretary of the Economic Commission for Latin America and the Caribbean, and José Manuel Salazar-Xirinachs, Executive Director for Employment of the International Labour Organization.

25. The Chairman made an opening statement.

26. The co-moderator, José Luis Machinea, Executive Secretary of the Economic Commission for Latin America and the Caribbean, opened the discussion of round table 1 and made a statement.

27. Statements were made by the following panellists: Membathisi Mdladlana, Minister of Labour of South Africa; Aart-Jan de Geus, Minister for Social Affairs and Employment of the Netherlands; Walter Fust, Director-General of the Swiss Agency for Development and Cooperation; Marc Blondel, Former General Secretary of Force Ouvrière of France; and Daniel Funes de Rioja, Vice-Chair of the International Labour Organization Governing Body and President of the Argentinian Employers Federation.

28. Interventions were made by the representatives of Spain, Sri Lanka, Nigeria and Costa Rica and the representative of the Food and Agriculture Organization of the United Nations.

29. The panellists made concluding remarks and the co-moderator, José Manuel Salazar-Xirinachs, Executive Director for Employment of the International Labour Organization, summarized the discussion of round table 1.

30. The Chairman of round table 1 made concluding remarks.

Round table 2

Meeting the challenges of employment creation in Africa and the least developed countries

31. Round table 2 was chaired by Seydou Bouda, Minister of Economy and Development of Burkina Faso, and co-moderated by Legwaila Joseph Legwaila, Under-Secretary-General and Special Adviser on Africa, and Anwarul K. Chowdhury, Under-Secretary-General and High Representative for the Least Developed Countries, Landlocked Developing Countries and Small Island Developing States.

32. Statements were made by the following panellists: Keat Chhon, Minister of Finance and Economy of Cambodia; Aisha Abdel Hadi, Chair of the African Union Labour and Social Affairs Commission and Minister of Manpower and Immigration of Egypt; Abdoulie Janneh, Executive Secretary of the Economic Commission for Africa; Kim Hak-Su, Executive Secretary of the Economic and Social Commission for Asia and the Pacific; and Alhaji Bamanga Tukur, President of the African Business Roundtable and Chairperson of the Business Group of the New Partnership for Africa's Development.

33. Interventions were made by the representatives of Guinea, the United States of America, Guinea-Bissau, Haiti, Japan and Namibia, the observers for Burkina Faso and Cape Verde, the representatives of the Food and Agriculture Organization of the United Nations, the International Labour Organization and the United Nations Human Settlements Programme (UN-Habitat) and the representatives of the Committee of Action for Children's and Women's Rights in Africa (CADEF), the United States Committee for Refugees and Immigrants, and the Legion of Good Will.

34. The panellists responded to comments made and questions raised by the participants and the Chairman made concluding remarks.

Round table 3

Globalization and labour migration

35. Round table 3 was chaired by Athauda Seneviratne, Minister of Labour Relations and Foreign Employment of Sri Lanka, and co-moderated by Brunson McKinley, Director-General of the International Organization for Migration, and Juan Somavía, Director-General of the International Labour Organization.

36. Following a statement by the co-moderator, Brunson McKinley, statements were made by the following panellists: Murat Basesgioglu, Minister of Employment and Social Security of Turkey; Supachai Panitchpakdi, Secretary-General of the United Nations Conference on Trade and Development; Axumite Gebre-Egziabher, Director, United Nations Human Settlements Programme (UN-Habitat), New York Office; Vladimír Špidla, European Commissioner for Employment, Social Affairs and Equal Opportunity; and Sharan Burrow, member of the Global Commission on International Migration.

37. Interventions were made by the representatives of India, South Africa, Australia, Nigeria, Belgium, Pakistan, Poland, Canada, Indonesia and Mexico and the observer for Finland.

38. The co-moderator, Juan Somavía, made concluding remarks.

Round table 4

Innovation at work: national strategies to achieve gender equality in employment

39. Round table 4 was chaired by Nicole Ameline, Special Ambassador for Social and Gender Issues in International Relations and former Minister for Gender of France.

40. The co-moderator, Rachel Mayanja, Assistant Secretary-General and Special Adviser on Gender Issues and Advancement of Women, made an introductory statement.

41. Presentations were made by the following panellists: Anne Kathrine Slungård, Marketing Director, Entra Realestate and Chair, Statoil Board of Elections of Norway; Shanti Chadha, Managing Director, Nepal Woman Crafts; Barbara Byers, Executive Vice-President, Canadian Labour Congress and member of the International Labour Organization Governing Body; and Awa Wade, Deputy General Secretary, National Union of Educators, Senegal.

42. The co-moderator, Mari Simonen, Deputy Executive Director, United Nations Population Fund, opened the floor for discussion.

43. Interventions were made by the representatives of the Bureau of Gender Equality of the International Labour Organization, the International Federation of University Women, the United Nations Development Fund for Women, Gender in Trade Development, the Ministry of Finance of Kenya and the Bureau for Workers' Activities of the International Labour Organization.

44. The panellists responded to comments made and questions posed by the participants and the Chairperson made concluding remarks.

Action taken by the Council

45. At the 16th meeting, on 5 July, the President of the Council introduced the draft ministerial declaration of the high-level segment (E/2006/L.8), submitted by him on the basis of informal consultations, and entitled "Creating an environment at the national and international levels conducive to generating full and productive employment and decent work for all, and its impact on sustainable development".

46. At the same meeting, before the adoption of the draft ministerial declaration, statements were made by the representatives of the Bolivarian Republic of Venezuela, Mexico, Finland (on behalf of the European Union), Cuba and the Russian Federation.

47. Also at the 16th meeting, the observer for Barbados, as facilitator of the draft ministerial declaration, made a statement of clarification.

48. The Council then adopted the ministerial declaration contained in document E/2006/L.8 (English only), as orally corrected.

49. At the same meeting, the representative of South Africa (on behalf of the Group of 77 and China) and the observer for Finland (on behalf of the European Union) made statements.

50. The text of the ministerial declaration read as follows:

> **"Ministerial declaration**
>
> **"Creating an environment at the national and international levels conducive to generating full and productive employment and decent work for all, and its impact on sustainable development**
>
> *"We, the Ministers and Heads of Delegations participating in the high-level segment of the substantive session of 2006 of the Economic and Social Council, held in Geneva from 3 to 5 July 2006,*
>
> "*Having considered* the theme 'Creating an environment at the national and international levels conducive to generating full and productive employment and decent work for all, and its impact on sustainable development', as well as the report of the Secretary-General on the subject,[1]
>
> "*Recalling* the internationally agreed development goals, including the Millennium Development Goals, and the outcomes of the major United Nations conferences and summits in the economic, social and related fields,
>
> "*Recalling also* the 2005 World Summit Outcome,[2]
>
> *"Having considered World Economic and Social Survey, 2006: Diverging Growth and Development,*[3]
>
> "*Recognizing* that the total number of people unemployed worldwide reached a new high in 2005, even though the global unemployment rate remained unchanged, and that half of the world's workers, most of them women, are unable to earn enough to lift themselves and their family members out of poverty, and hence emphasizing the dual challenge of creating new productive jobs and improving the quality of existing ones,
>
> "*Have adopted* the following declaration:
>
> "1. We are convinced of the urgent need to create an environment at the national and international levels that is conducive to the attainment of full and productive employment and decent work for all as a foundation for sustainable development. An environment that

supports investment, growth and entrepreneurship is essential to the creation of new job opportunities. Opportunities for men and women to obtain productive work in conditions of freedom, equity, security and human dignity are essential to ensuring the eradication of hunger and poverty, the improvement of the economic and social well-being for all, the achievement of sustained economic growth and sustainable development of all nations, and a fully inclusive and equitable globalization.

"2. We recognize that full and productive employment and decent work for all, which encompass social protection, fundamental principles and rights at work and social dialogue, are key elements of sustainable development for all countries, and therefore a priority objective of international cooperation.

"3. We recognize the decent work agenda of the International Labour Organization as an important instrument for achieving the objective of full and productive employment and decent work for all.

"4. We strongly support fair globalization and resolve to make the goals of full and productive employment and decent work for all, including women and young people, a central objective of our relevant national and international policies and our national development strategies, including poverty reduction strategies, as part of our efforts to achieve the internationally agreed development goals, including the Millennium Development Goals. These measures should also encompass the elimination of the worst forms of child labour, as defined in International Labour Organization Convention No. 182, and forced labour. We also resolve to ensure full respect for fundamental principles and rights at work.

"5. We resolve to promote full and productive employment and decent work for all, inter alia, by:

"(a) Respecting, promoting and realizing the principles contained in the International Labour Organization Declaration on Fundamental Principles and Rights at Work and its follow-up, recognizing the central role of the International Labour Organization in this regard;

"(b) Making continued efforts towards ratifying — where Member States have not done so — and fully implementing the International Labour Organization conventions concerning respect for fundamental principles and rights at work, namely, freedom of association and the effective recognition of the right to organize and bargain collectively, and the elimination of all forms of forced or compulsory labour, as well as the effective elimination of child labour and discrimination in respect of employment and occupation;

"(c) Considering the ratification and full implementation of other International Labour Organization conventions concerning the employment rights of women, youth, persons with disabilities, migrants and indigenous people.

"6. We reaffirm that an employment strategy that aims to promote full, freely chosen and productive employment, as well as decent work for all, with full respect for fundamental principles and rights at work under conditions of equity, equality, security and dignity, should constitute a fundamental component of any development strategy. We further reaffirm that macroeconomic policies should, inter alia, support employment creation. The social impact and dimension of globalization should be taken fully into account.

"7. We reaffirm our determination to promote gender equality and the empowerment of women and girls, recognizing that these are critical for achieving sustainable development and for efforts to combat hunger, poverty and disease. We are determined to implement our commitments to promoting and protecting all women's human rights by, inter alia, ensuring equal access to full and productive employment and decent work.

“8. We recognize that violence against women and girls is a serious obstacle to the achievement of full and productive employment and decent work for all, and of sustainable development, and reaffirm our commitment to elaborating and implementing strategies and policies, including targeted measures, in order to fulfil the obligation to exercise due diligence so as to prevent all forms of violence against women and girls, provide protection to victims, and investigate, prosecute and punish perpetrators of such violence.

“9. We underline the need for the consistent use of a gender mainstreaming strategy for the creation of an enabling environment for women’s participation in development that requires multisectoral, integrated approaches and a range of measures, including political commitment at the highest levels; institutional and organizational change; the adoption and implementation of sector-specific policies and programmes; the establishment and enforcement of legislative frameworks in line with any obligations undertaken under international human rights instruments, such as the Convention on the Elimination of All Forms of Discrimination against Women[4] and International Labour Organization conventions; adequate resources and gender-responsive budget initiatives; accountability and monitoring mechanisms; and capacity-building and public awareness-raising.

“10. We affirm our commitment to developing and implementing strategies that give persons with disabilities everywhere equal opportunities to full access and productive employment and decent work on an equal basis with others and without any kind of discrimination, including by promoting a labour market and a work environment that are open, inclusive and accessible to all and by ensuring just and favourable conditions of work.

“11. We reaffirm our commitment to developing and implementing strategies that give youth everywhere a real and equal opportunity to find full and productive employment and decent work. In this respect, noting that almost half of the unemployed people in the world are young people, we are determined to mainstream youth employment into national development strategies and agendas; to develop policies and programmes for enhancing the employability of youth, including through education, training and lifelong learning that meet labour-market requirements; and to promote access to work through integrated policies that enable the creation of new and quality jobs for young people and facilitate access to those jobs, including through information and training initiatives.

“12. We recognize the importance of the work of the Youth Employment Network as a peer exchange, support and review mechanism, and invite Member States, the United Nations and partner organizations to strengthen and expand the Network at the national, regional and international levels.

“13. We stress the important nexus between international migration and development and look forward to the High-level Dialogue on International Migration and Development to be held on 14 and 15 September 2006 during the sixty-first session of the General Assembly as an opportunity to discuss the multidimensional aspects of international migration and development in order to identify appropriate ways and means to maximize their development benefits and minimize their negative impacts.

“14. We reaffirm the importance of promoting and attaining the goals of universal and equitable access to quality education, the highest attainable standards of physical and mental health and the access of all to primary health care as part of the effort to eradicate poverty, promote full and productive employment and foster social integration. We recognize the continued need to address the impact of HIV/AIDS, malaria and tuberculosis, and other major infectious diseases, on social and economic development.

"15. We emphasize that good governance at the international level is fundamental for achieving sustainable development. In order to ensure a dynamic and enabling international economic environment, it is important to promote global economic governance through addressing the international finance, trade, technology and investment patterns that have an impact on the development prospects of developing countries. To this effect, the international community should take all necessary and appropriate measures, including ensuring support for structural and macroeconomic reform, a comprehensive solution to the external debt problem and increasing the market access of developing countries.

"16. We call upon all countries to promote good governance, which is essential for sustainable development, and reaffirm that sound economic policies, solid democratic institutions that are responsive to the needs of the people and improved infrastructure are the basis for sustained economic growth, poverty eradication and employment creation, and that freedom, peace and security, domestic stability, respect for human rights, including the right to development, the rule of law, gender equality, market-oriented policies and an overall commitment to just and democratic societies are also essential and mutually reinforcing.

"17. We recognize that appropriate institutions and regulation, including frameworks for social dialogue, are important elements for the effective and fair functioning of labour markets. This includes the adoption and implementation of labour laws that protect workers rights.

"18. We encourage Governments and other relevant institutions, where appropriate, to consider the impact of their policies on employment and decent work for all, including ensuring coherence of policies.

"19. We recognize that, in the context of globalization, countries need to devise policies that enable them to pursue both economic efficiency and social security and develop systems of social protection with broader and effective coverage, which should be guided by each country's needs and circumstances, and in this regard invite the international community, including the international financial institutions and the International Labour Organization, to work together to assist, as appropriate and upon request, the developing countries in their efforts.

"20. We reaffirm that, with three quarters of the world's poor living in rural and agricultural regions mostly in developing countries, rural and agricultural development should be an integral part of national and international development policies, and that working out of poverty requires urgent efforts to improve productivity and raise incomes in rural farm and non-farm sectors, given the importance of livelihood security for subsistence farmers in developing countries. This should include substantial improvement in market access; reductions of, with a view to phasing out, all forms of export subsidies; substantial reductions in trade-distorting domestic support; and increased investment, including foreign direct investment, in physical infrastructure and product diversification, as well as increasing the value-added content of exports. We call for enhanced support for agricultural development and trade capacity-building in the agricultural sector in developing countries, including by the international community and the United Nations system, and encourage support for commodity development projects, especially market-based projects, and for their preparation under the Second Account of the Common Fund for Commodities.

"21. We re-emphasize that rural and urban areas are economically, socially and environmentally interdependent and that cities and towns are engines of growth that contribute to the development of both rural and urban human settlements. Integrated physical planning and balanced attention to rural and urban living conditions are of crucial importance for all nations. Full advantage must be taken of the complementary contributions of and linkages between rural and urban areas by giving appropriate attention to their different economic, social and environmental requirements. While addressing urban poverty, it is also essential to eradicate rural poverty and to improve living conditions, as well as to create employment and educational opportunities in rural settlements and small and medium-sized cities and towns.

"22. We reaffirm that the eradication of hunger and poverty, changing unsustainable patterns of production and consumption, and protecting and managing the natural resource base of economic and social development are overarching objectives of and essential requirements for sustainable development, and invite all countries to promote sustainable consumption and production patterns, with the developed countries taking the lead and all countries benefiting from the process, taking into account the Rio principles, including, inter alia, that of common but differentiated responsibilities as set out in principle 7 of the Rio Declaration on Environment and Development,[5] as called for in the Plan of Implementation of the World Summit on Sustainable Development ('Johannesburg Plan of Implementation').[6]

"23. We recognize that the increasing interdependence of national economies in a globalizing world and the emergence of rule-based regimes for international economic relations have meant that the space for national economic policy, that is to say the scope for domestic policies, especially in the areas of trade, investment and industrial development, is now often framed by international disciplines, commitments and global market considerations. It is for each Government to evaluate the trade-off between the benefits of accepting international rules and commitments and the constraints posed by the loss of policy space. It is particularly important for developing countries, bearing in mind development goals and objectives, that all countries take into account the need for an appropriate balance between national policy space and international disciplines and commitments.

"24. We resolve to encourage greater direct investment, including foreign direct investment, in developing countries and countries with economies in transition in order to support their development activities and to enhance the benefits they can derive from such investments.

"25. We further resolve to continue to support efforts by developing countries and countries with economies in transition to create a domestic environment conducive to attracting investments through, inter alia, achieving a transparent, stable and predictable investment climate with proper contract enforcement and respect for property rights and the rule of law and pursuing appropriate policy and regulatory frameworks that encourage business formation.

"26. We commit ourselves to promoting and facilitating, as appropriate, access to and the development, transfer and diffusion of technologies, including environmentally sound technologies and corresponding know-how, to developing countries and countries with economies in transition, on favourable terms, including on concessional and preferential terms, as mutually agreed.

"27. We acknowledge the vital role the private sector can play in generating new investments, employment and financing for development.

"28. We encourage Governments to continue to pursue the creation of a conducive environment for enterprise development in both rural and urban areas. Particular attention should be given to policies that promote microenterprises and small and medium-sized enterprises and women's participation and entrepreneurship in formal and informal sectors through, inter alia, simplified and improved administrative regimes for the registration of small businesses access to microcredit, social security systems and information on markets and new technology, as well as better regulations. Such policies should contribute to the integration of informal economic activity into the mainstream economy.

"29. We stress the importance of promoting corporate responsibility and accountability. We encourage responsible business practices such as those promoted by the Global Compact and call upon the private sector to take into account not only the economic and financial but also the developmental, social, human rights, gender and environmental implications of their undertakings. In this context, we underline the importance of the International Labour Organization Tripartite Declaration of Principles concerning Multinational Enterprises and Social Policy.

"30. We call for increased national investment and international development funding and investment flows to developing countries and countries with economies in transition that are targeted to sectors of the economy with greater potential to generate productive employment and decent work for all. Such development funding could include, as appropriate, debt-for-sustainable development swaps aimed at creating employment and decent work for all, particularly youth and women.

"31. We also acknowledge the important role the public sector can play as an employer and in developing an environment that enables the effective generation of full and productive employment and decent work for all.

"32. We underline the important contribution that employment generation can make to post-conflict reconstruction and development. We stress the urgency of generating employment opportunities for men and women whose livelihoods have been destroyed by the impact of conflict or disaster. We call upon all international organizations, civil society groups and the private sector to complement national efforts towards employment generation when addressing the impact of such emergencies.

"33. We strongly encourage multilateral and bilateral donor and inter-agency cooperation and coordination, in the pursuit of the goals of full and productive employment and decent work for all. To this end, we invite all the relevant international organizations, at the request of national Governments and relevant stakeholders, to contribute, through their programmes, policies and activities, to the goals of full and productive employment and decent work for all in accordance with national development strategies.

"34. We request the funds, programmes and agencies of the United Nations system and invite financial institutions to support efforts to mainstream the goals of full and productive employment and decent work for all in their policies, programmes and activities. In this regard, we invite stakeholders to duly take account of the International Labour Organization decent work country programmes in order to achieve a more coherent and pragmatic United Nations approach to development at the national level on a voluntary basis.

"35. We also request the functional and regional commissions to consider how their activities contribute, or could contribute, to the goals of full employment and decent work for all.

"36. We also encourage all relevant organizations to collaborate actively in the development of the toolkit for promoting decent work that is currently being developed by the

International Labour Organization at the request of the United Nations System Chief Executives Board for Coordination.

"37. We call upon the International Labour Organization to focus on the implementation of commitments regarding the promotion of full and productive employment and decent work for all at the major United Nations conferences and summits, including those contained in the outcomes of the 2005 World Summit and the World Summit for Social Development, in order to achieve significant progress in both policy and operational programmes, and in this regard we request the International Labour Organization to consider developing time-bound action plans to 2015, in collaboration with all relevant parties, for the achievement of this goal.

"38. We commit ourselves to the implementation of the present declaration and invite all relevant actors, including the Bretton Woods institutions and other multilateral banks, to join our efforts in this regard.

"39. We decide to keep the implementation of the present declaration under review, including through the subsidiary bodies of the Economic and Social Council, and underline that the Council should ensure the coordination and coherence of the relevant programmes of United Nations entities.

"40. We request the Secretary-General to include, in his annual report on the follow-up to the outcomes of the major United Nations conferences and summits, a review of the progress achieved in creating an environment at the national and international levels conducive to generating full and productive employment and decent work for all, and its impact on sustainable development, at both the policy and the operational levels."

"[1] E/2006/55.

"[2] See General Assembly resolution 60/1.

"[3] United Nations publication, Sales No. E.06.II.C.I.

"[4] United Nations, *Treaty Series*, vol. 1249, No. 20378.

"[5] *Report of the United Nations Conference on Environment and Development, Rio de Janeiro, 3-14 June 1992,* vol. I, *Resolutions Adopted by the Conference* (United Nations publication, Sales No. E.93.I.8 and corrigendum), resolution 1, annex I.

"[6] *Report of the World Summit on Sustainable Development, Johannesburg, South Africa, 26 August-4 September 2002* (United Nations publication, Sales No. E.03.II.A.1 and corrigendum), chap. I, resolution 1, annex.

Documents considered by the Council in connection with its high-level segment

51. At its 16th meeting, on 5 July, on the proposal of the President of the Council, the Council took note of documents submitted under agenda item 2. See Council **decision 2006/219**.

Closure of the high-level segment

52. At its 16th meeting, on 5 July, the Assistant Secretary-General for Policy Coordination and Inter-Agency Affairs made a statement.

53. At the same meeting, the President of the Council made a concluding statement and declared closed the high-level segment of the substantive session of 2006 of the Council.

Chapter IV

Operational activities segment

Operational activities of the United Nations for international development cooperation

1. The Council considered the question of operational activities of the United Nations for international development cooperation (agenda item 3) at its 23rd to 26th and 40th meetings, from 11 to 13 and on 26 July 2006. An account of the discussion is contained in the relevant summary records (E/2006/SR.23-26 and 40). It had before it the report of the Secretary-General on the review of trends and perspectives in funding for development cooperation (E/2006/60).

2. At its 23rd meeting, on 11 July, the Council held a panel discussion on the comprehensive review of trends and perspectives in funding for development cooperation. Introductory remarks were made by the Vice-President of the Council, Léo Mérorès (Haiti), and the moderator of the panel, José Antonio Ocampo, Under-Secretary-General for Economic and Social Affairs. The following panellists made presentations: Bambang Widianto, Deputy Minister of Planning, State Ministry of Planning/National Development Planning Agency (BAPPENAS), Indonesia; Luiz Henrique Pereira Fonseca, Director, Brazilian Cooperation Agency; Mr. Hannu Kyröläinen, Director-General, Department for Global Affairs, Ministry for Foreign Affairs, Finland; Hyun Cho, Deputy Permanent Representative of the Republic of Korea to the United Nations in New York and former Director-General for International Economic Affairs, Ministry of Foreign Affairs and Trade; Jeroen Steeghs, Minister Plenipotentiary, Head, Economic and Social Affairs Section, Permanent Mission of the Netherlands to the United Nations in New York; and Bruce Jenks, Assistant Secretary-General and Director, Bureau for Resources and Strategic Partnerships, United Nations Development Programme. The presentations were followed by an exchange of views with delegations.

3. At its 25th meeting on 12 July, the Council held a panel discussion with members of the United Nations country team from Indonesia on the role of United Nations development cooperation in pursuit of employment creation and decent work: results, coherence and system-wide support through the United Nations Development Assistance Framework. The Vice-President of the Council, Léo Mérorès (Haiti), made an opening statement. The following panellists made presentations: Bambang Widianto, Deputy Minister of Planning, State Ministry of Planning/National Development Planning Agency (BAPPENAS), Indonesia; Bo Asplund, United Nations System Resident Coordinator/ Humanitarian Coordinator and United Nations Development Programme Resident Representative; Gwi-Yeop Son, Country Director, United Nations Development Programme (Indonesia); Peter Rademaker, International Labour Organization Deputy Director, Indonesia Office; and Masayoshi Matsushita, representative of the United Nations Industrial Development Organization. The presentations were followed by an exchange of views with delegations.

A. Follow-up to policy recommendations of the General Assembly and the Council

4. At its 26th meeting, on 13 July 2006, the Council held a general discussion on agenda item 3 (a), entitled "Follow-up to policy recommendations of the General Assembly and the Council". It had before it the following documents:

(a) Report of the Secretary-General on the comprehensive statistical data on operational activities for development for 2003 (A/60/74-E/2005/57);

(b) Report of the Secretary-General on the comprehensive statistical data on operational activities for development for 2004 (A/61/77-E/2006/59);

(c) Report of the Secretary-General on the funding options and modalities for financing operational activities for development on the United Nations system (A/60/83-E/2005/72);

(d) Report of the Secretary-General on the progress in the implementation of General Assembly resolution 59/250 (E/2006/58);

(e) Note by the Secretary-General on the review of trends and perspectives in funding for development cooperation (E/2006/60);

(f) Consolidated list of issues related to the coordination of operational activities for development, 2006 (E/2006/CRP.1).

5. At the same meeting, an introductory statement was made by the Assistant Secretary-General for Policy Coordination and Inter-Agency Affairs.

6. Also at the 26th meeting, statements were made by the representatives of South Africa (on behalf of the Group of 77 and China), the United States of America, the Russian Federation, Australia (on behalf of Canada, Australia and New Zealand), China, Bangladesh, Indonesia, India, Guinea, Guinea-Bissau, Benin and Thailand and the observers for Finland (on behalf of the European Union and the acceding countries Bulgaria and Romania, the candidate countries Croatia, the former Yugoslav Republic of Macedonia and Turkey, and the countries of the stabilization and association process and potential candidates Albania, Bosnia and Herzegovina and Serbia, as well as Ukraine and the Republic of Moldova), Azerbaijan, Norway, Switzerland and Belarus. Statements were also made by the representatives of the Food and Agriculture Organization of the United Nations (FAO) and the World Health Organization (WHO).

B. Reports of the Executive Boards of the United Nations Development Programme/ United Nations Population Fund, the United Nations Children's Fund and the World Food Programme

7. The Council held a discussion on agenda item 3 (b), entitled "Reports of the Executive Boards of the United Nations Development Programme/United Nations Population Fund, the United Nations Children's Fund and the World Food Programme", at its 24th and 40th meetings, on 12 and 26 July 2006. It had before it the following documents:

(a) Report of the Executive Board of the United Nations Development Programme and of the United Nations Population Fund on the first regular session of 2006 (20 to 27 January 2006, New York) (DP/2006/15);[3]

(b) Decisions adopted by the Executive Board of the United Nations Development Programme and of the United Nations Population Fund at its first regular session of 2006 (20 to 27 January) (DP/2006/16);[3]

(c) Report of the Executive Board of the United Nations Children's Fund on the first, second and annual sessions of 2005 (E/2005/34/Rev.1);[4]

(d) Report of the Executive Board of the United Nations Development Programme/ United Nations Population Fund on its work during 2005 (E/2005/35);[5]

(e) Joint report of the Administrator of the United Nations Development Programme and the Executive Director of the United Nations Population Fund to the Economic and Social Council (E/2006/5);

(f) Annual report of the Executive Director of the United Nations Children's Fund to the Economic and Social Council (E/2006/6-E/ICEF/2006/3);

(g) Note by the Secretary-General transmitting the annual report of the Executive Director of the World Food Programme for 2005 (E/2006/14);

(h) Report of the Executive Board of the United Nations Children's Fund on the work of its 2006 first regular session (16-20 and 23 January 2006) (E/2006/34 (Part I)-E/ ICEF/2006/5 (Part I));[6]

(i) Addendum to the report of the Executive Board of the United Nations Children's Fund on the work of its first regular session of 2006 (16-20 and 23 January 2006): Joint meeting of the Executive Boards of the United Nations Development Programme/United Nations Population Fund, the United Nations Children's Fund and the World Food Programme (E/2006/34 (Part I)/Add.1-E/ICEF/2006/5 (Part I)/Add.1);[6]

(j) Report of the Executive Board of the World Food Programme on the first and second regular sessions and annual session of 2005 (E/2006/36);[7]

(k) Extract from the report of the Executive Board of the United Nations Children's Fund on its 2006 annual session (5-9 June 2006) (E/2006/L.6);[6]

(l) Decisions of the Executive Board of the United Nations Development Programme/ United Nations Population Fund on its annual session of 2006 (E/2006/CRP.8).[3]

8. At its 24th meeting, on 12 July, the Council held a dialogue with heads of United Nations funds and programmes. The Vice-President of the Council, Léo Mérorès (Haiti), made an opening statement. Presentations were made by the Administrator of the United Nations Development Programme, on behalf of the United Nations Development Group; the Executive Director of the United Nations Children's Fund; the Executive Director of the United Nations Population Fund; the Executive Director of the World Food Programme; and the Associate Administrator of the United Nations Development Programme. The presentations were followed by an exchange of views with delegations.

Action taken by the Council

9. Under agenda item 3 (a), the Council adopted **resolution 2006/14**. Under agenda item 3 (b), the Council adopted **decision 2006/236**.

Progress in the implementation of General Assembly resolution 59/250 on the triennial comprehensive policy review of operational activities for development of the United Nations system

10. At its 40th meeting, on 26 July, the Council had before it a draft resolution (E/2006/L.28) entitled "Progress in the implementation of General Assembly resolution 59/250 on the triennial comprehensive policy review of operational activities for development of the United Nations system", submitted by the Vice-President of the Council, Léo Mérorès (Haiti), on the basis of informal consultations.

11. At the same meeting, the observer for Switzerland, as facilitator of the draft resolution, made oral corrections to the text (see E/2006/SR.40).

12. Also at the 40th meeting, the representative of the United States of America made a statement in which he requested a vote on the draft resolution.

13. At the same meeting, the Council adopted the draft resolution, as orally corrected, by a show of hands of 40 to 1, with no abstentions. See Council **resolution 2006/14**.

14. A statement in explanation of vote before the vote was made by the representative of South Africa (on behalf of the Group of 77 and China). Statements in explanation of vote after the vote were made by the representatives of the United States of America and Canada.

15. Subsequently, a statement was made by the observer for Finland (on behalf of the European Union).

Documents considered by the Council in connection with the follow-up to policy recommendations of the General Assembly and the Council

16. At its 40th meeting, on 26 July, on the proposal of the Vice-President, Léo Mérorès (Haiti), the Council took note of several documents submitted under agenda item 3 (b). See Council **decision 2006/236**.

Chapter V

Coordination segment

Sustained economic growth for social development, including the eradication of poverty and hunger

1. The Council held a discussion on "Sustained economic growth for social development, including the eradication of poverty and hunger" (agenda item 4) at its 18th to 21st and 29th meetings, on 6, 7, 10 and 17 July 2006. It had before it the report of the Secretary-General on sustained economic growth for social development, including poverty eradication and hunger (E/2006/56). An account of the discussion is contained in the relevant summary records (E/2006/SR.18-21 and 29).

General discussion

2. At its 18th meeting, on 6 July, the Council held a general discussion on agenda item 4 and heard an opening statement by the Vice-President of the Council, Hjálmar W. Hannesson (Iceland), and an introductory statement by the Assistant Secretary-General for Policy Coordination and Inter-Agency Affairs (see E/2006/SR.18).

3. At the same meeting, statements were made by the representatives of South Africa (on behalf of the Group of 77 and China), the United States of America, the Russian Federation, Pakistan, China, Brazil, India and Guinea-Bissau. Statements were also made by the observers for Finland (on behalf of the European Union, the acceding countries Bulgaria and Romania, the candidate countries Croatia and Turkey, and the countries of the stabilization and association process and potential candidates Albania, Bosnia and Herzegovina and Serbia, as well as Ukraine and the Republic of Moldova), Switzerland and Norway.

4. Also at the 18th meeting, a statement was made by the representative of the Association of World Citizens, a non-governmental organization in consultative status with the Council.

Panel discussion: "Sustained economic growth for social development, including the eradication of poverty and hunger: (a) the normative and policy dimension; and (b) the programme and operational dimension"

5. At its 19th meeting, on 7 July, the Council held a panel discussion on the theme "Sustained economic growth for social development, including the eradication of poverty and hunger: (a) the normative and policy dimension; and (b) the programme and operational dimension". The Vice-President of the Council, Hjálmar W. Hannesson (Iceland), opened the panel discussion and made a statement.

6. The following panellists made presentations: Semakula Kiwanuka, Minister of State for Finance, Uganda; Jim Harvey, Department for International Development, United Kingdom of Great Britain and Northern Ireland; Nora Lustig, Leader, Poverty Group, Bureau for Development Policy, United Nations Development Programme; and Yash Tandon, Director, South Centre, Geneva. The presentations were followed by an interactive debate.

7. Interventions were made by the representatives of Guinea, Nigeria, Mauritania, the United States of America and Benin and the observers for the Bolivarian Republic of Venezuela and Finland.

8. The panellists responded to queries raised and the Vice-President of the Council, Hjálmar W. Hannesson (Iceland), made a statement.

Panel discussion with the Chairpersons of the functional commissions and other subsidiary bodies of the Council on the theme "Sustained economic growth for social development, including the eradication of poverty and hunger"

9. At its 20th meeting, on 7 July, the Council held a panel discussion with the Chairpersons of the functional commissions and other subsidiary bodies of the Council on the theme "Sustained economic growth for social development, including the eradication of poverty and hunger". Opening remarks were made by the Vice-President of the Council, Hjálmar

W. Hannesson (Iceland) and the Assistant Secretary-General for Policy Coordination and Inter-Agency Affairs.

10. Presentations were made by the Deputy Permanent Representative of Mexico, on behalf of the Chairman of the Statistical Commission; the Vice-Chairman of the Commission on Population and Development, on behalf of the Chairman of the Commission; the Chairman of the Commission for Social Development; the Chairperson of the Commission on the Status of Women; the Chairman of the Commission on Crime Prevention and Criminal Justice; the observer for Egypt, on behalf of the Chairman of the Commission on Science and Technology for Development; the Chairman of the Bureau of the United Nations Forum on Forests; and the Chairperson of the Permanent Forum on Indigenous Issues. The presentations were followed by an interactive debate.

11. Interventions were made by the representatives of Guinea-Bissau, Mauritania, Guinea, the Democratic Republic of the Congo, the United States of America and Nigeria and the observer for Finland.

12. The panellists responded to comments and queries addressed to them and concluding remarks were made by the Assistant Secretary-General for Policy Coordination and Inter-Agency Affairs and the Vice-President of the Council, Hjálmar W. Hannesson (Iceland).

Special event on Avian influenza: a global emergency

13. At its 21st meeting, on 10 July, the Council held a special event on the theme "Avian influenza: a global emergency". The President of the Council made an opening statement.

14. Presentations were made by the following panellists: David Harcharik, Deputy Director-General, Food and Agriculture Organization of the United Nations; Dr. Margaret Chan, Assistant Director-General for Communicable Diseases and the Director-General's Representative for Pandemic Influenza, World Health Organization; Joseph Ingram, Special Representative of the World Bank, Geneva; Peter Batchelor, Team Leader, Bureau for Crisis Prevention and Recovery, United Nations Development Programme, Geneva; Katherine Rooney, representative of the International Civil Aviation Organization; Amr Abdel-Ghaffar, Programme Coordinator and Focal Point for Avian Flu, World Tourism Organization; and Richard Blewitt, Director, Movement Cooperation Division, International Federation of Red Cross and Red Crescent Societies.

15. An interactive dialogue ensued in which statements were made by the representatives of China, the Russian Federation, Bangladesh, Nigeria, Thailand, the United States of America, Indonesia, Australia, Guinea-Bissau, France, the Democratic Republic of the Congo and Turkey and the observers for Finland and El Salvador.

16. Statements were also made by the representatives of the United Nations Environment Programme and the United Nations Children's Fund, as well as the World Organization for Animal Health, an intergovernmental organization.

17. At the conclusion of the panel discussion, David Nabarro, Senior United Nations System Coordinator for Avian and Human Influenza, summarized the discussion.

Action taken by the Council

18. Under agenda item 4, the Council adopted **resolution 2006/4** and **decision 2006/220.**

Sustained economic growth for social development, including the eradication of poverty and hunger

19. At its 29th meeting, on 17 July, the Council had before it a draft resolution (E/2006/L.14), entitled "Sustained economic growth for social development, including the eradication of poverty and hunger", submitted by the Vice-President of the Council, Hjálmar W. Hannesson (Iceland), on the basis of informal consultations.

20. At the same meeting, the Council adopted the draft resolution. See Council **resolution 2006/4**.

Multi-year work programme for the coordination segment and the document considered under the item

21. At the 29th meeting on 17 July, on the proposal of the President of the Council, the Council, bearing in mind paragraph (c) of its decision 2005/221, decided to defer to a resumed session the finalization of the multi-year work programme for the coordination segment and took note of the document submitted under item 4 (E/2006/56). See Council **decision 2006/220**.

Conclusion of the coordination segment

22. At its 29th meeting, on 17 July, the Council concluded its coordination segment.

Chapter VI

Humanitarian affairs segment

Special economic, humanitarian and disaster relief assistance

1. The Council considered the question of special economic, humanitarian and disaster relief assistance (agenda item 5) at its 27th to 30th meetings, on 14, 17 and 18 July 2006. An account of the discussion is contained in the relevant summary records (E/2006/SR.27-30).

2. For its consideration of agenda item 5, the Council had before it the following documents:

(a) Report of the Secretary-General on humanitarian assistance and rehabilitation for El Salvador and Guatemala (A/61/78-E/2006/61);

(b) Report of the Secretary-General on strengthening emergency relief, rehabilitation, reconstruction and prevention in the aftermath of the South Asian earthquake disaster — Pakistan (A/61/79-E/2006/67);

(c) Report of the Secretary-General on the strengthening of the coordination of emergency humanitarian assistance of the United Nations (A/61/85-E/2006/81);

(d) Report of the Secretary-General on strengthening emergency relief, rehabilitation, reconstruction, recovery and prevention in the aftermath of the Indian Ocean tsunami disaster (A/61/87-E/2006/77).

General discussion

3. At the 27th meeting, on 14 July, the Vice-President of the Council, Prasad Kariyawasam (Sri Lanka), made an opening statement. An introductory statement was made by the Under-Secretary-General for Humanitarian Affairs and Emergency Relief Coordinator. A statement was also made by the Deputy Special Envoy of the Secretary-General for Tsunami Recovery.

4. At the same meeting, statements were made by the representatives of South Africa (on behalf of the Group of 77 and China), the United States of America, the Russian Federation, France, Canada, Australia, Pakistan, Japan, the United Republic of Tanzania and China and the observers for Finland (on behalf of the European Union, the acceding countries Bulgaria and Romania, the candidate countries Croatia, the former Yugoslav Republic of Macedonia and Turkey, and the countries of the stabilization and association process and potential candidates Albania, Bosnia and Herzegovina and Serbia, as well as the Ukraine and the Republic of Moldova) and Norway.

5. Also at the 27th meeting, statements were made by the observer for the Sovereign Military Order of Malta and the representatives of the International Federation of Red Cross and Red Crescent Societies and the World Health Organization.

Panel discussion: "Gender-based violence inhumanitarian emergencies"

6. At its 28th meeting, on 17 July, the Council held a panel discussion on gender-based violence in humanitarian emergencies. Introductory statements were made by the Vice-President of the Council, Prasad Kariyawasam (Sri Lanka), and the moderator of the panel, Erika Feller, Assistant High Commissioner, Office of the United Nations High Commission for Refugees.

7. The following panellists made presentations: Nicolas Michel, Under-Secretary-General for Legal Affairs, the Legal Counsel; François Ngendahayo, Minister of National Solidarity, Human Rights and Gender, Burundi; Gabrielle Nanchen, member, Assembly of the International Committee of the Red Cross; and Lois Lewis Bruthus, Director, Association of Female Lawyers of Liberia. The presentations were followed by an exchange of views with delegations.

8. Interventions were made by the representatives of Guinea, the Democratic Republic of the Congo, Bangladesh, the United States of America, Haiti, the Russian Federation and Australia and the observers for Finland (on behalf of the European Union), the Sudan and the Islamic Republic of Iran.

9. The panellists responded to comments and queries addressed to them and the Vice-President of the Council, Prasad Kariyawasam (Sri Lanka), made concluding remarks.

Panel discussion: "Chronically underfunded emergencies"

10. At its 30th meeting, on 18 July, the Council held a panel discussion on chronically underfunded emergencies. Introductory statements were made by the Vice-President of the Council, Prasad Kariyawasam (Sri Lanka), and the moderator of the panel, Jan Egeland, Under-Secretary-General for Humanitarian Affairs and Emergency Relief Coordinator.

11. The following panellists made presentations: Antonio Cavaco, Director-General, European Commission, Humanitarian Aid Department (ECHO); Abdi Ali Raghe, Chief Executive Office, Africa Rescue Committee; and Dennis McNamara, Special Adviser to the Emergency Relief Coordinator on Internal Displacement. The presentations were followed by an exchange of views with delegations.

12. Interventions were made by the representatives of Guinea-Bissau, Guinea, the United States of America, the United Kingdom of Great Britain and Northern Ireland and Canada and the observers for Finland (on behalf of the European Union), the Islamic Republic of Iran and the Netherlands.

13. Statements were also made by the representatives of the World Food Programme, the World Health Organization and the United Nations Human Settlements Programme (UN-Habitat).

14. The panellists responded to comments and queries addressed to them and the Vice-President of the Council, Prasad Kariyawasam (Sri Lanka), made concluding remarks.

Action taken by the Council

15. Under agenda item 5, the Council adopted **resolution 2006/5**.

Strengthening of the coordination of emergency humanitarian assistance of the United Nations

16. At its 30th meeting, on 18 July, the Council had before it a draft resolution (E/2006/L.13) entitled "Strengthening of the coordination of emergency humanitarian assistance of the United Nations", submitted by the Vice-President of the Council, Prasad Kariyawasam (Sri Lanka), on the basis of informal consultations.

17. At the same meeting, the Secretary orally corrected the text of preambular paragraph 3 and of operative paragraph 15.

18. Also at the 30th meeting, the Council adopted the draft resolution, as orally corrected. See Council **resolution 2006/5**.

Chapter VII

General segment

A. Implementation of and follow-up to major United Nations conferences and summits

1. The Council considered the question of the implementation of and follow-up to major United Nations conferences and summits (agenda item 6) jointly with economic and environmental questions: science and technology for development (agenda item 13 (b)) at its 22nd and 43rd meetings, on 10 and 28 July 2006. The Council also considered agenda item 6 jointly with the question of the implementation of General Assembly resolutions 50/227, 52/12 B and 57/270 B (agenda item 8) at its 31st and 43rd meetings, on 19 and 28 July 2006.

An account of the discussions is contained in the relevant summary records (E/2006/SR.22, 31 and 43).

2. The Council considered the question of the follow-up to the International Conference on Financing for Development (agenda item 6 (a)) jointly with the question of the review and coordination of the implementation of the Programme of Action for the Least Developed Countries for the Decade 2001-2010 (agenda item 6 (b)) at its 32nd, 33rd, 42nd and 43rd meetings, on 20, 27 and 28 July.

3. For its consideration of item 6, the Council had before it the following documents:

(a) Updated report of the Secretary-General on the role of the Economic and Social Council in the integrated and coordinated implementation of the outcomes of and follow-up to major United Nations conferences and summits, in the light of General Assembly resolutions 50/227, 52/12 B and 57/270 B (A/61/90-E/2006/84) (see also under item 8 and the chapeau of items 13 and 14);

(b) Report of the Secretary-General on the modalities of the inter-agency coordination of the implementation of the outcomes of the World Summit on the Information Society, including recommendations on the follow-up process (E/2006/85 and A/60/1005/Corr.1-E/2006/85/Corr.1);

(c) Synopsis of the review of the methods of work undertaken by the functional commissions and other relevant subsidiary bodies of the Economic and Social Council (E/2006/CRP.7) (English only) (see also under item 8 and the chapeau of items 13 and 14);

Follow-up to the International Conference on Financing for Development (agenda item 6 (a))

(d) Summary by the President of the Economic and Social Council of the special high-level meeting of the Council with the Bretton Woods institutions, the World Trade Organization and the United Nations Conference on Trade and Development (New York, 24 April 2006) (A/61/81-E/2006/73);

Review and coordination of the implementation of the Programme of Action for the Least Developed Countries for the Decade 2001-2010 (agenda item 6 (b))

(e) Annual progress report of the Secretary-General on the implementation of the Programme of Action for the Least Developed Countries for the Decade 2001-2010 (A/61/82-E/2006/74 and Corr.1).

4. At the 22nd meeting, on 10 July, the President of the Council opened the general segment of the substantive session of 2006 of the Council.

5. At the same meeting, the Council heard an introductory statement by the Assistant Secretary-General for Policy Coordination and Inter-Agency Affairs and a keynote address by Jamaludin Jarjis, Minister of Science, Technology and Innovation of Malaysia. The Deputy Secretary-General of the United Nations Conference on Trade and Development also made a statement (under agenda items 6 and 13 (b)).

6. At its 31st meeting, on 19, the Council heard an introductory statement by the Director of the Office for ECOSOC Support and Coordination (under agenda items 6 and 8).

7. At its 32nd meeting, on 20 July, the Council heard an introductory statement by the Under-Secretary-General and High Representative for the Least Developed Countries, Landlocked Developing Countries and Small Island Developing States (under agenda item 6 (b)).

Action taken by the Council

8. Under agenda items 6, 8, 13 and 14, the Council adopted **resolution 2006/44**. Under agenda items 6 and 13 (b), the Council adopted **resolution 2006/46**. For action taken by the Council jointly under these items, see sect. VII.H below.

Role of the Economic and Social Council in the integrated and coordinated implementation of the outcomes of and follow-up to major United Nations conferences and summits, in the light of General Assembly resolutions 50/227, 52/12 B and 57/270 B

9. At its 43rd meeting, on 28 July 2006, the Vice-President of the Council, Dalius Čekuolis (Lithuania), introduced a draft resolution (E/2006/L.35) entitled "Role of the Economic and Social Council in the integrated and coordinated implementation of the outcomes of and follow-up to major United Nations conferences and summits, in the light of General Assembly resolutions 50/227, 52/12 B and 57/270 B", submitted on the basis of informal consultations.

10. At the same meeting, the Council was informed that the draft resolution had no programme budget implications.

11. Also at the 43rd meeting, the Council adopted draft resolution E/2006/L.35, under agenda items 6, 8, 13 and 14. See Council **resolution 2006/44**.

1. Follow-up to the International Conference on Financing for Development

Action taken by the Council

12. Under agenda item 6 (a), the Council adopted **resolution 2006/45**.

Follow-up to the International Conference on Financing for Development

13. At its 43rd meeting, on 28 July, the Council had before it a draft resolution (E/2006/L.34) entitled "Follow-up to the International Conference on Financing For Development", submitted by the Vice-President of the Council, Dalius Čekuolis (Lithuania), on the basis of informal consultations.

14. At the same meeting, the Council was informed that the draft resolution had no programme budget implications.

15. Also at the 43rd meeting, the Council adopted the draft resolution. See Council **resolution 2006/45**.

2. Review and coordination of the implementation of the Programme of Action for the Least Developed Countries for the Decade 2001-2010

Panel discussion on "Mobilizing resources and creating an enabling environment for poverty eradication in the least developed countries: implementation of the 2004 ministerial declaration"

16. At its 33rd meeting, on 20 July, the Council held a panel discussion, under item 6 (b), entitled "Mobilizing resources and creating an enabling environment for poverty

eradication in the least developed countries: implementation of the 2004 ministerial declaration". The panel was chaired by the Vice-President of the Council, Dalius Čekuolis (Lithuania).

17. At the same meeting, introductory statements were made by the Under-Secretary-General and High Representative for the Least Developed Countries, Landlocked Developing Countries and Small Island Developing States and the moderator, Mandeep Bains, Senior Policy Adviser for the United Nations Millennium Campaign.

18. Also at the 33rd meeting, the following panellists made presentations: Simon Scott, Principal Administrator and Head, Statistics and Monitoring Division, Development Assistance Committee (DAC) secretariat; Seidou Imorou Mako, Director of Housing and Sanitation in the Ministry of Environment, Habitat and Urban Planning of Benin; and Arjun K. Karki, President of LDC Watch.

19. At the same meeting, an exchange of views ensued during which interventions were made by the representatives of Bangladesh, Guinea-Bissau, the United Republic ofTanzania and Benin.

20. The panellists responded to queries raised and the Under-Secretary-General and High Representative for the Least Developed Countries, Landlocked Developing Countries and Small Island Developing States made concluding remarks.

Action taken by the Council

21. Under agenda item 6 (b), the Council adopted **resolution 2006/41**.

Implementation of the Programme of Action for the Least DevelopedCountries for the Decade 2001-2010

22. At the 33rd meeting, on 20 July, following a statement by the representative of South Africa (on behalf of the Group of 77 and China), the representative of Benin introduced a draft resolution (E/2006/L.15) entitled "Implementation of the Programme of Action for the Least Developed Countries for the Decade 2001-2010", which read as follows:

"*The Economic and Social Council*,

"*Recalling* the Brussels Declaration and the Programme of Action for the Least Developed Countries for the Decade 2001-2010,

"*Recalling also* its decision 2001/320 of 24 October 2001, in which it decided to establish, under the regular agenda item entitled 'Integrated and coordinated implementation of and follow-up to the major United Nations conferences and summits', a regular sub-item entitled 'Review and coordination of the implementation of the Programme of Action for the Least Developed Countries for the Decade 2001-2010',

"*Recalling further* its resolution 2005/44 of 27 July 2005,

"*Recalling* General Assembly resolution 60/228 of 23 December 2005 and Assembly decision 60/556 of 16 May 2006,

"1. *Takes note* of the annual progress report of the Secretary-General on the implementation of the Programme of Action for the Least Developed Countries for the Decade 2001-2010;

"2. *Reiterates* its deep concern over the insufficient progress achieved in the implementation of the Programme of Action;

"3. *Stresses* the need to address the areas of weaknesses in the implementation of the Programme of Action and urges the least developed countries and their bilateral and multilateral development partners to undertake increased efforts and to adopt speedy measures with a view to meeting the goals and targets of the Programme of Action in a timely manner;

"4. *Also stresses* the need to assess the implementation of the Programme of Action sector by sector and in this regard invites all relevant organizations, consistent with their respective mandates, to report on the progress made in its implementation using quantifiable criteria and indicators to be measured against the goals and targets of the Programme of Action;

"5. *Urges* the high-level meeting on the midterm comprehensive global review of the implementation of the Programme of Action for the Least Developed Countries for the Decade 2001-2010, to be held in New York on 18 and 19 September 2006, to take results-based measures so as to speed up progress in the implementation of the Programme of Action;

"6. *Requests* the Secretary-General to submit an annual progress report on the implementation of the Programme of Action in an analytical and results-oriented way, by placing emphasis on the progress achieved in its implementation by the least developed countries and their development partners."

23. At its 42nd meeting, on 27 July, the Council had before it a draft resolution (E/2006/L.29) entitled "Implementation of the Programme of Action for the Least Developed Countries for the Decade 2001-2010", submitted by the Vice-President of the Council, Dalius čekuolis (Lithuania), on the basis of informal consultations held on draft resolution E/2006/L.15.

24. At the same meeting, the representative of Benin orally corrected the text as follows:

(a) In preambular paragraph 3, the words "the ministerial declaration adopted by the Economic and Social Council at the high-level segment" were replaced by the words "the ministerial declaration of the high-level segment";

(b) Operative paragraph 6, which had read:

"6. *Requests* the Secretary-General to submit an annual progress report on the implementation of the Programme of Action in an analytical and results-oriented way, by placing emphasis on the progress achieved in its implementation by the least developed countries and their development partners therein";

was revised to read:

"6. *Requests* the Secretary-General to submit an annual progress report on the implementation of the Programme of Action in a more analytical and results-oriented way, by placing greater emphasis on the progress achieved by the least developed countries and their development partners in its implementation".

25. Also at its 42nd meeting, the Council was informed that the draft resolution had no programme budget implications.

26. At the same meeting, the Council adopted draft resolution E/2006/L.29, as orally corrected. See Council **resolution 2006/41**.

27. In the light of the adoption of draft resolution E/2006/L.29, draft resolution E/2006/L.15 was withdrawn by its sponsor.

B. Coordination, programme and other questions

28. The Council held a discussion on coordination, programme and other questions (agenda item 7) at its 36th to 39th and 41st to 43rd meetings, on 24 to 28 July 2006. An account of the discussion is contained in the relevant summary records (E/2006/SR.36-39 and 41-43). It had before it the following documents:

Reports of coordination bodies (agenda item 7 (a))

(a) Annual overview report of the United Nations System Chief Executives Board for Coordination for 2005/06 (E/2006/66);

Proposed programme budget for the biennium 2006-2007

(agenda item 7 (b))

(b) Relevant programmes of the proposed strategic framework for the period 2008-2009 (relevant fascicles of A/61/6);

International cooperation in the field of informatics (agenda item 7 (c))

(c) Report of the Secretary General on international cooperation in the field of informatics (E/2006/79);

Long-term programme of support for Haiti (agenda item 7 (d))

(d) Report of the Economic and Social Council Ad Hoc Advisory Group on Haiti (E/2006/69 and Corr.1);

(e) Letter dated 29 June 2006 from the Permanent Representative of Haiti to the United Nations addressed to the President of the Economic and Social Council (E/2006/88);

Mainstreaming a gender perspective into all policies and programmes in the United Nations system (agenda item 7 (e))

(f) Report of the Secretary-General on the follow-up to the Fourth World Conference on Women and progress made in the implementation of the Beijing Declaration and Platform for Action and the outcome of the twenty-third special session of the General Assembly (E/2006/65) (see also under item 14 (a));

(g) Report of the Secretary-General on the United Nations system-wide policy and strategy on gender mainstreaming (E/2006/83);

Information and Communication Technologies Task Force

(agenda item 7 (f))

(h) Note by the Secretary-General transmitting the fourth annual report of the Information and Communication Technologies Task Force (E/2006/63);

Ad hoc advisory groups on African countries emerging from conflict(agenda item 7 (g))

(i) Report of the Secretary-General on the assessment of the ad hoc advisory groups of the Economic and Social Council on African countries emerging from conflict (E/2006/64);

(j) Report of the Economic and Social Council Ad Hoc Advisory Group on Burundi (E/2006/53);

(k) Report of the Ad Hoc Advisory Group on Guinea-Bissau (E/2006/8);

Tobacco or health (agenda item 7 (h))

(l) Report of the Secretary-General on the Ad Hoc Inter-Agency Task Force on Tobacco Control (E/2006/62).

29. At the 36th meeting, on 24 July, an introductory statement was made by the Assistant Secretary-General for Policy Coordination and Inter-Agency Affairs, Department of Economic and Social Affairs (under agenda items 7 (a) and (b)) and the Director of the Office for ECOSOC Support and Coordination (under agenda items 7 (c) and (f)).

30. At the 37th meeting, on 24 July, an introductory statement was made by the Director of the Tobacco Free Initiative, World Health Organization (under agenda item 7 (h)).

31. At the 38th meeting, on 25 July, introductory statements were made by the Assistant Secretary-General and Special Adviser on Gender Issues and Advancement of Women and the Director of the Division for the Advancement of Women (under agenda items 7 (e), 13 (l) and 14 (a)).

32. At the 39th meeting, on 26 July, introductory statements were made by the Chairman of the Ad Hoc Advisory Group on Haiti (under agenda item 7 (d)) and the representative of South Africa, on behalf of the Chairman of the Ad Hoc Advisory Groups on Guinea-Bissau and Burundi and the United Nations Resident Coordinator in Guinea-Bissau (under agenda item 7 (g)).

33. At the same meeting, an introductory statement was also made by the Assistant Secretary-General for Policy Coordination and Inter-Agency Affairs, Department of Economic and Social Affairs (under agenda item 7 (g)).

Action taken by the Council

34. Under agenda item 7, the Council adopted **resolutions 2006/10** to **2006/13**, **2006/35, 2006/36** and **2006/42** and **decisions 2006/227, 2006/248** and **2006/251**.

1. Reports of coordination bodies

Document considered by the Council in connection with agenda item 7 (a)

35. At its 36th meeting, on 24 July, on the proposal of the Vice-President of the Council, Dalius Čekuolis (Lithuania), the Council took note of the annual overview report of the United Nations System Chief Executives Board for Coordination for 2005/06 (E/2006/66). See Council **decision 2006/227**.

2. Proposed strategic framework for the biennium 2008-2009

36. At its 36th meeting, on 24 July, the Council considered agenda item 7 (b). No action was taken by the Council under this item.

3. International cooperation in the field of informatics

The need to harmonize and improve United Nations informatics systems for optimal utilization and accessibility by all States

37. At its 41st meeting, on 27 July, the Council had before it a resolution (E/2006/L.22) entitled "The need to harmonize and improve United Nations informatics systems for optimal utilization and accessibility by all States", submitted by the Vice-President of the Council, Dalius Čekuolis (Lithuania), on the basis of informal consultations.

38. At the same meeting, the Secretary of the Council orally corrected operative paragraph 1 by replacing the words "States Members" with the words "Member States".

39. Also at the 41st meeting, the Council was informed that the draft resolution had no programme budget implications.

40. At the same meeting, the Council adopted the draft resolution, as orally corrected. See Council **resolution 2006/35**.

4. Long-term programme of support for Haiti

Ad Hoc Advisory Group on Haiti

41. At the 39th meeting, on 26 July, the representative of Canada, on behalf of Benin, Brazil, Canada, Haiti, Spain, Trinidad and Tobago[8] and Tunisia, introduced a draft resolution entitled "Ad hoc Advisory Group on Haiti" (E/2006/L.11). Subsequently, Belize and Guyana joined in sponsoring the draft resolution.

42. At the same meeting, the Secretary of the Council read out a statement of the programme budget implications of the draft resolution.

43. Also at the 39th meeting, the Council adopted the draft resolution. See Council **resolution 2006/10**.

44. After the adoption of the draft resolution, statements were made by the representatives of Haiti and Brazil.

5. Mainstreaming a gender perspective into all policies and programmes in the United Nations system

Mainstreaming a gender perspective into all policies and programmes in the United Nations system

45. At its 41st meeting, on 27 July, the Council had before it a draft resolution (E/2006/L.30) entitled "Mainstreaming a gender perspective into all policies and programmes in the United Nations system", submitted by the Vice-President of the Council, Dalius Čekuolis (Lithuania), on the basis of informal consultations.

46. At the same meeting, the representative of Mexico, as facilitator of the draft resolution, orally revised the text as follows:

(a) After the existing fourth preambular paragraph, a new preambular paragraph was inserted, which read:

"*Recognizing* that training is critical for increasing awareness, knowledge, commitment and the capacity of staff to mainstream a gender perspective into the United Nations policies and programmes and that the provision of effective gender training requires adequate financial and human resources";

(b) In the chapeau of operative paragraph 4, the words "other existing training budgets" were replaced by the words "other existing United Nations training budgets, without prejudice to the achievement of other training priorities".

47. At the same meeting, the Council adopted the draft resolution, as orally revised. See Council **resolution 2006/36**.

Documents considered by the Council in connection with agendaitem 7 (e)

48. At its 41st meeting, on 27 July, on the proposal of the Vice-President, the Council took note of the following documents:

(a) Report of the Secretary-General on the follow-up to the Fourth World Conference on Women and progress made in the implementation of the Beijing Declaration and Platform for Action and the outcome of the twenty-third special session of the General Assembly (document E/2006/65);

(b) Report of the Secretary-General on the United Nations system-wide policy and strategy on gender mainstreaming (E/2006/83).

49. See Council **decision 2006/227**.

6. Information and Communication Technologies Task Force

Information and Communication Technologies Task Force

50. At its 43rd meeting, on 28 July, the Council had before it a draft decision entitled "United Nations Information and Communication Technologies (ICT) Task Force" (E/2006/L.33), submitted by the Vice-President of the Council, Dalius Čekuolis (Lithuania), on the basis of informal consultations.

51. At the same meeting, the Council was informed that the draft decision had no programme budget implications.

52. Also at the 43rd meeting, the Council adopted the draft decision. See Council **decision 2006/251**.

7. Ad hoc advisory groups on African countries emerging from conflict

Ad Hoc Advisory Group on Guinea-Bissau

53. At its 39th meeting, on 26 July, the Council had before it a draft resolution (E/2006/L.21) entitled "Ad Hoc Advisory Group on Guinea-Bissau", submitted by the Vice-President of the Council, Dalius Čekuolis (Lithuania), on the basis of informal consultations.

54. At the same meeting, the Council adopted the draft resolution. See Council **resolution 2006/11**.

Ad Hoc Advisory Group on Burundi

55. At its 39th meeting, on 26 July, the Council had before it a draft resolution (E/2006/L.19) entitled "Ad Hoc Advisory Group on Burundi", submitted by the Vice-President of the Council, Dalius Čekuolis (Lithuania), on the basis of informal consultations.

56. At the same meeting, the Council adopted the draft resolution. See Council **resolution 2006/12**.

Assessment of the ad hoc advisory groups of the Economic and SocialCouncil on African countries emerging from conflict

57. At its 39th meeting, on 26 July, the Council had before it a draft resolution (E/2006/L.20) entitled "Assessment of the ad hoc advisory groups of the Economic and Social Council on African countries emerging from conflict", submitted by the Vice-President of the Council, Dalius Čekuolis (Lithuania), on the basis of informal consultations.

58. At the same meeting, the Council adopted the draft resolution. See Council **resolution 2006/13**.

8. Tobacco or health

Smoke-free United Nations premises

59. At the 36th meeting on 24 July, the representative of India introduced a draft resolution (E/2006/L.10) entitled "Smoke-free United Nations premises", which read as follows:

> "*The Economic and Social Council,*
>
> "*Noting with appreciation* the report of the Secretary-General on the Ad Hoc Inter-Agency Task Force on Tobacco Control,
>
> "*Further noting with* concern the serious harmful impact of second-hand smoke on the health of non-smokers,
>
> "*Acknowledging* that second-hand smoke at the workplace is a fully preventable occupational health hazard,

"*Recognizing* that second-hand smoke has a variety of psychological and social aspects at the workplace that can lead, at the individual level, to disease, disability and death, higher risk of fire, increased family or social problems, stigmatization and discrimination,

"*Recalling* article 8, 'Protection from exposure to tobacco smoke', of the World Health Organization Framework Convention on Tobacco Control, which states that each party shall adopt and implement measures to provide 'protection from exposure to tobacco smoke in indoor workplaces, public transport, indoor places and, as appropriate, other public places',

"*Emphasizing* the importance of protecting the well-being of individuals in their working environments,

"*Recognizing* the need to approach the issue from an occupational safety and health perspective with the aim of protecting the health of United Nations staff,

"1. *Requests* the Secretary-General to implement a complete ban on smoking at United Nations premises, at Headquarters as well as regional and country offices;

"2. *Also requests* the Secretary-General to implement a ban on the sale of tobacco products at United Nations premises;

"3. *Calls upon* the Secretary-General to submit at its substantive session of 2007 a brief report confirming the implementation of the present resolution."

60. At its 41st meeting, on 27 July, the Council had before it a revised draft resolution (E/2006/L.10/Rev.1) entitled "Smoke-free United Nations premises", submitted by Australia, Austria, Canada, Finland,[1] France, Germany, Hungary,[1] Iceland, India, Ireland,[1] Italy, Jordan,[1] Latvia,[1] Lithuania, Malta,[1] the Netherlands,[1] Poland, Portugal,[1] the Republic of Korea, South Africa, Spain and the United Kingdom of Great Britain and Northern Ireland. Subsequently, the Czech Republic, Romania,[1] Slovenia,[1] Turkey and the United Republic of Tanzania joined in sponsoring the revised draft resolution.

61. At the same meeting, statements were made by the representatives of France and the Russian Federation.

62. At the 42nd meeting, on 27 July, the Council adopted the revised draft resolution. See Council **resolution 2006/42**.

Report of the Secretary-General on the Ad Hoc Inter-Agency Task Force on Tobacco Control

63. At the 41st meeting, on 27 July, the representative of India, on behalf of Brazil and India, introduced a draft decision (E/2006/L.32) entitled "Report of the Secretary-General on the Ad Hoc Inter-Agency Task Force on Tobacco Control".

64. At the same meeting, statements were made by the representatives of France and the Russian Federation.

65. At the 42nd meeting, on 27 July, the Council adopted the draft decision. See Council **decision 2006/248**.

C. Implementation of General Assembly resolutions 50/227, 52/12 B and 57/270 B

66. The Council held a discussion on the implementation of General Assembly resolutions 50/227, 52/12 B and 57/270 B (agenda item 8) jointly with the question of the implementation of and follow-up to major United Nations conferences and summits (agenda item 6) at its 31st and 43rd meetings, on 19 and 28 July 2006. An account of the discussion is contained in the relevant summary records (E/2006/SR.31 and 43).

67. For its consideration of agenda item 8, the Council had before it the following documents:

(a) Updated report of the Secretary-General on the role of the Economic and Social Council in the integrated and coordinated implementation of the outcomes of and follow-up to major United Nations conferences and summits, in the light of General Assembly resolutions 50/227, 52/12 B and 57/270 B (A/61/90-E/2006/84) (see also under chapeaux of items 6, 13 and 14);

(b) Synopsis of the review of the methods of work undertaken by the functional commissions and other relevant subsidiary bodies of the Economic and Social Council (E/2006/CRP.7) (English only) (see also under item 6 and the chapeaux of items 13 and 14).

Action taken by the Council

68. Under agenda item 8, jointly with items 6, 13 and 14, the Council adopted **resolution 2006/44** (see chap. VII, sect. A).

D. Implementation of the Declaration on the Granting of Independence to Colonial Countries and Peoples by the specialized agencies and the international institutions associated with the United Nations

69. The Council held a discussion on the implementation of the Declaration on the Granting of Independence to Colonial Countries and Peoples by the specialized agencies and the international institutions associated with the United Nations (agenda item 9) at its 36th, 39th and 41st meetings, on 24, 26 and 27 July 2006. An account of the discussion is contained in the relevant summary records (E/2006/SR.36, 39 and 41). The Council had before it the following documents:

(a) Letter dated 16 May 2006 from the Permanent Representative of Saint Lucia to the United Nations addressed to the Secretary-General, transmitting the Plan of Implementation of the Decolonization Mandate 2006-07 (A/60/853-E/2006/75) (see also under items 10 and 13 (c));

(b) Report of the Secretary-General on the implementation of the Declaration on the Granting of Independence to Colonial Countries and Peoples by the specialized agencies and the international institutions associated with the United Nations (A/61/62);

(c) Report of the Secretary-General on assistance to the Palestinian people (A/61/80-E/2006/72);

(d) Report of the President of the Council on consultations held with the Chairman of the Special Committee on the Situation with regard to the Implementation of the Declaration on the Granting of Independence to Colonial Countries and Peoples (E/2006/47).

70. At the 36th meeting, on 24 July, an introductory statement was made by the representative of Cuba, on behalf of the Special Committee.

Action taken by the Council

71. Under agenda item 9, the Council adopted **resolution 2006/37**.

Support to Non-Self-Governing Territories by the specialized agenciesand the international institutions associated with the United Nations

72. At the 39th meeting, on 26 July, the representative of Cuba, on behalf of Antigua and Barbuda,[1] Bolivia,[1] China, Cuba, Dominica,[1] Fiji,[1] Grenada,[1] the Libyan Arab Jamahiriya,[1] Malaysia,[1] Namibia, Papua New Guinea,[1] Saint Lucia,[1] Saint Vincent and the Grenadines,[1] the Sudan,[1] the Syrian Arab Republic,[1] Venezuela (Bolivarian Republic of)[1] and Zambia,[1] introduced a draft resolution (E/2006/L.27) entitled "Support to Non-Self-Governing Territories by the specialized agencies and international institutions associated with the United Nations". Subsequently, Belize joined in sponsoring the draft resolution.

73. At the 41st meeting, on 27 July, South Africa joined in sponsoring the draft resolution.

74. At the same meeting, the Council adopted the draft resolution by a recorded vote of 29 to none, with 20 abstentions. See Council **resolution 2006/37**. The voting was as follows:[9]

In favour:

> Angola, Armenia, Bangladesh, Belize, Benin, Brazil, China, Colombia, Costa Rica, Cuba, Guinea, Guyana, Haiti, India, Indonesia, Madagascar, Mauritania, Mexico, Namibia, Nigeria, Pakistan, Paraguay, Saudi Arabia, South Africa, Sri Lanka, Thailand, Tunisia, United Arab Emirates, United Republic of Tanzania.

Against:

> None.

Abstaining:

> Albania, Australia, Austria, Belgium, Canada, Czech Republic, France, Germany, Iceland, Italy, Japan, Lithuania, Mauritius, Poland, Republic of Korea, Russian Federation, Spain, Turkey, United Kingdom of Great Britain and Northern Ireland, United States of America.

75. Before the draft resolution was adopted, a statement was made by the representative of the United States of America. A statement in explanation of vote before the vote was made by the representative of the Russian Federation. A statement was made by the observer for Finland (on behalf of the European Union and the acceding countries Bulgaria and Romania, the candidate countries Croatia, the former Yugoslav Republic of Macedonia and Turkey, and the countries of the stabilization and association process and potential candidates Albania, Bosnia and Herzegovina and Serbia, as well as Ukraine and the Republic of Moldova).

E. Regional cooperation

76. The Council considered the question of regional cooperation (agenda item 10) at its 17th, 35th, 36th and 41st meetings, on 6, 21, 24 and 27 July 2006. An account of the discussion is contained in the relevant summary records (E/2004/SR.17, 35, 36 and 41). It had before it the following documents:

(a) Letter dated 16 May 2006 from the Permanent Representative of Saint Lucia to the United Nations addressed to the Secretary-General, transmitting the Plan of Implementation of the Decolonization Mandate 2006-07 (A/60/853-E/2006/75) (see also under items 9 and 13 (c));

(b) Report of the Secretary-General on regional cooperation in the economic, social and related fields (E/2006/15);

(c) Addendum to the report of the Secretary-General on regional cooperation in the economic, social and related fields: matters calling for action by the Economic and Social Council or brought to its attention (E/2006/15/Add.1);

(d) Summary of the economic trends, as well as risks and opportunities, for the economies in the Economic Commission for Europe region (E/2006/16);

(e) Overview of the Economic Report on Africa, 2006: "Recent economic trends in Africa and prospects for 2006" (E/2006/17);

(f) Summary of the economic and social survey of Asia and the Pacific, 2006 (E/2006/18);

(g) Summary of the economic situation and outlook, 2005-2006, of Latin America and the Caribbean (E/2006/19);

(h) Summary of the survey of economic and social developments in the Economic and Social Commission for Western Asia region, 2005-2006 (E/2006/20).

Interactive dialogue with the Executive Secretaries of the regional commissions on the following theme: "The regional dimension of creating an environment conducive to generating full and productive employment and decent work for all, and its impact on sustainable development"

77. At its 17th meeting, on 6 July, the Council held a dialogue with the Executive Secretaries of the regional commissions. The Executive Secretary of the Economic and Social Commission for Asia and the Pacific, Kim Hak-Su, made an introductory statement, followed by a presentation.

78. At the same meeting, presentations were also made by the Executive Secretary of the Economic Commission for Europe, Marek Belka, on "How unique were the labour-market changes during the transition?"; the Executive Secretary of the Economic Commission for Latin America and the Caribbean, José Luis Machinea, on "Labour markets and social protection"; the Executive Secretary of the Economic Commission for Africa, Abdoulie Janneh, on "Growth and employment for inclusive development in Africa"; and the Executive Secretary of the Economic and Social Commission for Western Asia, Mervat Tallawy, on "Youth unemployment: challenges and prospects".

79. At the same meeting, statements were made by the representatives of Brazil, Finland (on behalf of the European Union), Guinea-Bissau, Pakistan, Nigeria, the Russian Federation, Barbados, the United States of America, Japan, Guinea, Norway and China. The Executive Secretaries responded to comments and queries addressed to them.

Action taken by the Council

80. Under item 10, the Council adopted **resolutions 2006/38** to **2006/40** and **decision 2006/246**.

Recommendations contained in the addendum to the report of the Secretary-General on regional cooperation in the economic, social and related fields

Workplan on reform of the Economic Commission for Europe and revised terms of reference of the Commission

81. At its 41st meeting, on 27 July, the Council adopted draft resolution I entitled "Workplan on reform of the Economic Commission for Europe and revised terms of reference of the Commission", recommended by the Economic Commission for Europe (see E/2006/15/Add.1, sect. I.A). See Council **resolution 2006/38**.

Admission of Japan as a member of the Economic Commission for Latin America and the Caribbean

82. At its 41st meeting, on 27 July, the Council adopted draft resolution I entitled "Admission of Japan as a member of the Economic Commission for Latin America and the Caribbean", recommended by the Economic Commission for Latin America and the Caribbean (see E/2006/15/Add.1, sect. I.B). See Council **resolution 2006/39**.

Venue of the thirty-second session of the Economic Commission for Latin America and the Caribbean

83. At its 41st meeting, on 27 July, the Council adopted draft resolution II entitled "Venue of the thirty-second session of the Economic Commission for Latin America and the Caribbean", recommended by the Economic Commission for Latin America and the Caribbean (see E/2006/15/Add.1, sect. I.B). See Council **resolution 2006/40**.

Documents considered by the Economic and Social Council in connection with regional cooperation

84. At the same meeting, on the proposal of the Vice-President of the Council, Dalius Čekuolis (Lithuania), the Council took note of several reports considered in connection with the question of regional cooperation. See Council **decision 2006/246**.

F. Economic and social repercussions of the Israeli occupation on the living conditions of the Palestinian people in the occupied Palestinian territory, including Jerusalem, and the Arab population in the occupied Syrian Golan

85. The Council held a discussion on the economic and social repercussions of the Israeli occupation on the living conditions of the Palestinian people in the occupied Palestinian territory, including Jerusalem, and the Arab population in the occupied Syrian Golan (agenda item 11) at its 35th, 36th and 42nd meetings, on 21, 24 and 27 July 2006. An account of the discussion is contained in the relevant summary records (E/2006/SR.35, 36 and 42).

The Council had before it a note by the Secretary-General (A/61/67-E/2006/13) transmitting the report prepared by the Economic and Social Commission for Western Asia on the economic and social repercussions of the Israeli occupation on the living conditions of the Palestinian people in the occupied Palestinian territory, including Jerusalem, and of the Arab population in the occupied Syrian Golan.

86. At the 35th meeting, on 21 July, the Chief of the Regional Commissions New York Office made an introductory statement.

Action taken by the Council

87. Under agenda item 11, the Council adopted **resolution 2006/43** and **decision 2006/249**.

Economic and social repercussions of the Israeli occupation on the living conditions of the Palestinian people in the Occupied Palestinian Territory, including East Jerusalem, and the Arab population in the occupied Syrian Golan

88. At the 36th meeting, on 24 July, the representative of Saudi Arabia, on behalf of Algeria,[1] Azerbaijan,[1] Bahrain,[1] Bangladesh, Chad, Cuba, Indonesia, Jordan,[1] Malaysia,[1] Mauritania, Morocco,[1] Pakistan, Saudi Arabia, South Africa, Tunisia, the United Arab Emirates and Palestine,[10] introduced a draft resolution (E/2006/L.17) entitled "Economic and social repercussions of the Israeli occupation on the living conditions of the Palestinian people in the Occupied Palestinian Territory, including East Jerusalem, and the Arab population in the occupied Syrian Golan", which read as follows:

"*The Economic and Social Council*,

"*Recalling* General Assembly resolution 60/183 of 22 December 2005,

"*Also recalling* its resolution 2005/51 of 27 July 2005,

"*Guided* by the principles of the Charter of the United Nations affirming the inadmissibility of the acquisition of territory by force and recalling relevant Security Council resolutions, including resolutions 242 (1967) of 22 November 1967, 252 (1968) of 21 May 1968, 338 (1973) of 22 October 1973 and 497 (1981) of 17 December 1981,

"*Recalling* the resolutions of the tenth emergency special session of the General Assembly, including ES-10/13 of 21 October 2003, ES-10/14 of 8 December 2003 and ES-10/15 of 20 July 2004,

"*Reaffirming* the applicability of the Geneva Convention relative to the Protection of Civilian Persons in Time of War, of 12 August 1949 to the Occupied Palestinian Territory, including East Jerusalem, and other Arab territories occupied by Israel since 1967,

"*Stressing* the importance of the revival of the Middle East peace process on the basis of Security Council resolutions 242 (1967), 338 (1973), 425 (1978), 1397 (2002), 1515 (2003) and 1544 (2004) and the principle of land for peace as well as compliance with the agreements reached between the Government of Israel and the Palestine Liberation Organization, the representative of the Palestinian people,

"*Reaffirming* the principle of the permanent sovereignty of peoples under foreign occupation over their natural resources,

"*Convinced* that the Israeli occupation has gravely impeded the efforts to achieve sustainable development and a sound economic environment in the Occupied Palestinian Territory, including East Jerusalem, and in the occupied Syrian Golan,

"*Gravely concerned* about the deterioration of the economic and living conditions of the Palestinian people in the Occupied Palestinian Territory, including East Jerusalem, and of the Arab population of the occupied Syrian Golan and the exploitation by Israel, the occupying Power, of their natural resources,

"*Gravely concerned also* by the formidable impact on the economic and social conditions of the Palestinian people caused by Israel's construction of the wall and its associated regime inside the Occupied Palestinian Territory, including in and around East Jerusalem, and the resulting violation of their economic and social rights, including the right to work, to health, to education and to an adequate standard of living,

"*Recalling* in this regard the International Covenant on Civil and Political Rights, the International Covenant on Economic, Social and Cultural Rights and the Convention on the Rights of the Child, and affirming that these human rights instruments must be respected in the Occupied Palestinian Territory, including East Jerusalem, as well as in the occupied Syrian Golan,

"*Gravely concerned* at the extensive destruction by Israel, the occupying Power, of agricultural land and orchards in the Occupied Palestinian Territory, including East Jerusalem, and in particular as a result of its unlawful construction of the wall in the Occupied Palestinian Territory, especially in and around East Jerusalem,

"*Recalling* the advisory opinion rendered on 9 July 2004 by the International Court of Justice on the *Legal Consequences of the Construction of a Wall in the Occupied Palestinian Territory*, recalling also General Assembly resolution ES-10/15, and stressing the need to comply with the obligations mentioned therein,

"*Extremely concerned* at the dire humanitarian crisis and the dangerous situation in the Occupied Palestinian Territory as a result of current Israeli military operations, the economic siege imposed on the Palestinian people, and Israel's withholding of Palestinian tax revenues,

"*Expressing grave concern* at the escalating indiscriminate Israeli attacks against Palestinian civilians, which have led to many deaths and injuries, including of children,

"*Commending* the important work being done by the United Nations and the specialized agencies in support of the economic and social development of the Palestinian people, as well as the assistance being provided in the humanitarian field,

"*Conscious* of the urgent need for the reconstruction of the economic and social infrastructure of the Occupied Palestinian Territory, including East Jerusalem, as well as the urgent need to address the dire humanitarian crisis facing the Palestinian people,

"1. *Calls for* the lifting of the economic siege imposed on the Palestinian people and for other urgent measures to be taken to alleviate the desperate humanitarian situation in the Occupied Palestinian Territory;

"2. *Demands* that Israel transfer urgently Palestinian tax revenues to the Palestinian Authority in compliance with the Paris Economic Agreement of 1994;

"3. *Stresses* the need to preserve the national unity and the territorial integrity of the Occupied Palestinian Territory, including East Jerusalem, and to guarantee the freedom of movement of persons and goods in the Territory, including the removal of restrictions on going into and from East Jerusalem, and the freedom of movement to and from the outside world;

"4. *Deplores* the continuous Israeli destruction of vital infrastructure in the occupied Gaza Strip, including the only power station, water networks, schools, bridges, the airport, the seaport and Palestinian ministries and institutions, which aggravates the harsh humanitarian and socio-economic conditions therein;

"5. *Demands* that Israel, the occupying Power, ensure the passage of foodstuffs and other essential supplies through commercial crossings and lift forthwith the restrictions on the movement and access of United Nations agencies to and within the Occupied Palestinian Territory;

"6. *Demands also* that Israel, the occupying Power, put an immediate end to its military operations in the Occupied Palestinian Territory and refrain from imposing collective punishment on the Palestinian people;

"7. *Affirms* that ending the Israeli occupation of the Palestinian Territory, including East Jerusalem, and of the Syrian Golan is a prerequisite for economic and social development therein;

"8. *Reaffirms* the inalienable right of the Palestinian people and the Arab population of the occupied Syrian Golan to all their natural and economic resources, and calls upon Israel, the occupying Power, not to exploit, endanger or cause loss or depletion of these resources;

"9. *Calls upon* Israel, the occupying Power, to cease the dumping of all kinds of waste materials in the Occupied Palestinian Territory, including East Jerusalem, and in the occupied Syrian Golan, which gravely threaten their natural resources, namely the water and land resources, and pose an environmental hazard and health threat to the civilian populations;

"10. *Reaffirms* that Israeli settlements in the Occupied Palestinian Territory, including East Jerusalem, and the occupied Syrian Golan, are illegal and an obstacle to economic and social development, and calls for the full implementation of the relevant Security Council resolutions;

"11. *Stresses* that the wall being constructed at an accelerated pace by Israel in the Occupied Palestinian Territory, including in and around East Jerusalem, is contrary to international law and is isolating East Jerusalem, dividing up the West Bank and seriously debilitating to the economic and social development of the Palestinian people, and calls in this regard for full compliance with the legal obligations mentioned in the 9 July 2004 advisory opinion of the International Court of Justice and in General Assembly resolution ES-10/15;

"12. *Emphasizes* the importance of the work of the organizations and agencies of the United Nations and of the United Nations Special Coordinator for the Middle East Peace Process and Personal Representative of the Secretary-General to the Palestine Liberation Organization and the Palestinian Authority;

"13. *Requests* the Secretary-General to submit to the General Assembly at its sixty-first session, through the Economic and Social Council, a report on the implementation of the present resolution and to continue to include in the report of the United Nations Special Coordinator an update on the living conditions of the Palestinian people, in collaboration with relevant United Nations agencies;

"14. *Decides* to include the item entitled 'Economic and social repercussions of the Israeli occupation on the living conditions of the Palestinian people in the Occupied Palestinian Territory, including East Jerusalem, and the Arab population in the occupied Syrian Golan' in the agenda of its substantive session of 2007."

89. At its 42nd meeting, on 27 July, the Council had before it a revised draft resolution (E/2006/L.17/Rev.1) entitled "Economic and social repercussions of the Israeli occupation on the living conditions of the Palestinian people in the Occupied Palestinian Territory, including East Jerusalem, and the Arab population in the occupied Syrian Golan", introduced by the representative of Saudi Arabia, on behalf of the sponsors of draft resolution E/2006/L.17 as well as Egypt.[1] The Bolivarian Republic of Venezuela[1] subsequently joined in sponsoring the draft resolution.

90. At the same meeting, the Council adopted the revised draft resolution by a roll-call vote of 45 to 3, with 3 abstentions. See Council **resolution 2006/43**. The voting was as follows:

In favour:

Albania, Armenia, Austria, Bangladesh, Belgium, Belize, Benin, Brazil, Chad, China, Colombia, Costa Rica, Cuba, Denmark, France, Germany, Guinea, Guyana, Haiti, Iceland, India, Indonesia, Italy, Japan, Lithuania, Madagascar, Mauritania, Mauritius, Mexico, Namibia, Nigeria, Pakistan, Panama, Paraguay, Republic of Korea, Russian Federation, Saudi Arabia, South Africa, Spain, Sri Lanka, Thailand, Tunisia, Turkey, United Arab Emirates, United Republic of Tanzania.

Against:

Australia, Canada, United States of America.

Abstaining:

Czech Republic, Poland, United Kingdom of Great Britain and Northern Ireland.

91. Before the adoption of the draft resolution, a statement was made by the representative of the United States of America and the observer for Finland (on behalf of the European Union and the acceding countries Bulgaria and Romania, the candidate countries Croatia, the former Yugoslav Republic of Macedonia and Turkey and the countries of the stabilization and association process and potential candidates Albania, Bosnia and Herzegovina and Serbia, as well as Ukraine and the Republic of Moldova). A statement in explanation of vote before the vote was made by the representative of Costa Rica. Statements in explanation of vote after the vote were made by the representatives of the United States of America, the Russian Federation, Japan, India and Canada. Statements were made by the observer for the Syrian Arab Republic and the observer for Palestine.

Document considered by the Council in connection with agenda item 11

92. At its 42nd meeting, on 27 July, on the proposal of the President of the Council, the Council took note of the note by the Secretary-General transmitting the report prepared by the Economic and Social Commission for Western Asia (A/61/67-E/2006/13) on the economic and social repercussions of the Israeli occupation on the living conditions of the Palestinian people in the occupied Palestinian Territory, including Jerusalem, and of the Arab population in the occupied Syrian Golan. See Council **decision 2006/249**.

G. Non-governmental organizations

93. The Council held a discussion on non-governmental organizations (agenda item 12) at its 34th and 35th meetings, on 21 July 2006. An account of the discussion is contained in the relevant summary records (E/2006/SR.34 and 35). It had before it the following documents:

(a) Report of the Committee on Non-Governmental Organizations on its 2006 regular session (E/2006/32 (Part I));[11]

(b) Excerpt from the Report of the Committee on Non-Governmental Organizations on its resumed 2006 session (E/2006/L.7).[11]

Action taken by the Council

94. Under agenda item 12, the Council adopted **decisions 2006/221** to **2006/226** and **2006/253**.

Recommendations contained in the report of the Committee on Non-Governmental Organizations on its 2006 regular session

Applications for consultative status and requests for reclassification received from non-governmental organizations

95. At its 34th meeting, on 21 July, the Council adopted draft decision I entitled "Applications for consultative status and requests for reclassification received from non-governmental organizations", recommended by the Committee (see E/2006/32 (Part I), chap. I, sect. A), with the exception of the application of the non-governmental organization Geneva Call, which the Council decided to refer back to the Committee for its further consideration. See Council **decision 2006/221**.

Application of the International Lesbian and Gay Association

96. At its 34th meeting, on 21 July, the Council had before it draft decision II entitled "Application of the International Lesbian and Gay Association", recommended by the Committee (see E/2006/32 (Part I), chap. I, sect. A).

97. At the same meeting, the representative of Germany (on behalf of the European Union) proposed an oral amendment to the draft decision.

98. Also at the 34th meeting, the representative of the Russian Federation proposed a motion requiring that no decision be taken on the proposal of the representative of Germany, in accordance with rule 67, paragraph 2, of the rules of procedure of the Council.

99. At the same meeting, the representatives of Guinea-Bissau and Mauritania made statements in favour of the motion.

100. Also at the 34th meeting, the representatives of Germany and Brazil made statements against the motion.

101. At the same meeting, the Council proceeded to a roll-call vote on the motion requiring that no decision be taken on the proposal made by Germany. The motion was carried by a vote of 25 to 21, with 5 abstentions. The voting was as follows:

In favour:

Angola, Benin, China, Costa Rica, Cuba, Democratic Republic of the Congo, Guinea, Guinea-Bissau, Haiti, Indonesia, Madagascar, Mauritania, Mauritius, Namibia, Nigeria, Pakistan, Russian Federation, Saudi Arabia, South Africa, Sri Lanka, Thailand, Tunisia, United Arab Emirates, United Republic of Tanzania, United States of America.

Against:

Albania, Armenia, Australia, Austria, Belgium, Brazil, Canada, Colombia, Czech Republic, Denmark, France, Germany, Iceland, Italy, Japan, Lithuania, Mexico, Panama, Republic of Korea, Spain, United Kingdom of Great Britain and Northern Ireland.

Abstaining:

Belize, Guyana, India, Paraguay, Turkey.

Voting process on draft decision II

102. At its 34th meeting, on 21 July, the Council adopted draft decision II by a roll-call vote of 22 to 19, with 9 abstentions. See Council **decision 2006/222**. The voting was as follows:

In favour:

Angola, Australia, Benin, China, Costa Rica, Democratic Republic of the Congo, Guinea, Guinea-Bissau, Haiti, Madagascar, Mauritania, Mauritius, Namibia, Nigeria, Pakistan, Russian Federation, Saudi Arabia, South Africa, Tunisia, United Arab Emirates, United Republic of Tanzania, United States of America.

Against:

Albania, Armenia, Austria, Belgium, Brazil, Canada, Colombia, Czech Republic, Denmark, France, Germany, Iceland, Italy, Japan, Lithuania, Mexico, Panama, Spain, United Kingdom of Great Britain and Northern Ireland.

Abstaining:

Belize, Guyana, India, Indonesia, Paraguay, Republic of Korea, Sri Lanka, Thailand, Turkey.

103. Before the vote, a statement in explanation of vote was made by the representative of Brazil. Statements in explanation of vote after the vote were made by the representatives of the United Republic of Tanzania, South Africa and Guinea-Bissau.

Application of the Danish National Association for Gays and Lesbians

104. At its 34th meeting, on 21 July, the Council had before it draft decision III entitled "Application of the Danish National Association for Gays and Lesbians", recommended by the Committee (see E/2006/32 (Part I), chap. I, sect. A).

105. At the same meeting, the representative of Germany (on behalf of the European Union) proposed an oral amendment to the draft decision.

106. Also at the 34th meeting, the representative of the Russian Federation proposed a motion requiring that no decision be taken on the proposal of the representative of Germany, in accordance with rule 67, paragraph 2, of the rules of procedure of the Council.

107. At the same meeting, the Council proceeded to a roll-call vote on the motion requiring that no decision be taken on the proposal made by Germany. The motion was carried by a vote of 23 to 21, with 5 abstentions. The voting was as follows:

In favour:

Angola, Benin, China, Cuba, Democratic Republic of the Congo, Guinea, Guinea-Bissau, Haiti, Indonesia, Madagascar, Mauritania, Mauritius, Namibia, Nigeria, Pakistan, Russian Federation, Saudi Arabia, South Africa, Sri Lanka, Thailand, Tunisia, United Arab Emirates, United Republic of Tanzania.

Against:

Armenia, Australia, Austria, Belgium, Brazil, Canada, Colombia, Czech Republic, Denmark, France, Germany, Iceland, Italy, Japan, Lithuania, Mexico, Panama, Republic of Korea, Spain, United Kingdom of Great Britain and Northern Ireland, United States of America.

Abstaining:

Belize, Costa Rica, Guyana, India, Paraguay, Turkey.

Voting process on draft decision III

108. At its 34th meeting, on 21 July, based on a proposal by the representative of Germany, the Council rejected draft decision III by a roll-call vote of 19 to 22, with 9 abstentions. The voting was as follows:

In favour:

Angola, Benin, China, Democratic Republic of the Congo, Guinea, Guinea-Bissau, Haiti, Madagascar, Mauritania, Mauritius, Namibia, Nigeria, Pakistan, Russian Federation, Saudi Arabia, South Africa, Tunisia, United Arab Emirates, United Republic of Tanzania.

Against:

Albania, Armenia, Australia, Austria, Belgium, Brazil, Canada, Colombia, Czech Republic, Denmark, France, Germany, Iceland, Italy, Japan, Lithuania, Mexico, Panama, Republic of Korea, Spain, United Kingdom of Great Britain and Northern Ireland, United States of America.

Abstaining:

Belize, Costa Rica, Guyana, India, Indonesia, Paraguay, Sri Lanka, Thailand, Turkey.

109. Statements in explanation of vote after the vote were made by the representatives of South Africa and Haiti.

110. At the same meeting, the representative of Guinea-Bissau proposed that the Council decide to refer the application of the Danish National Association for Gays and Lesbians back to the Committee for its reconsideration.

111. At the 35th meeting, on 21 July, the proposal by the representative of Guinea-Bissau was rejected by a roll-call vote of 20 to 20, with 9 abstentions. The voting was as follows:

In favour:

Angola, Armenia, Benin, China, Cuba, Guinea, Guinea-Bissau, Haiti, Indonesia, Madagascar, Mauritania, Namibia, Nigeria, Pakistan, Russian Federation, Saudi Arabia, South Africa, Tunisia, United Arab Emirates, United Republic of Tanzania.

Against:

Albania, Australia, Austria, Belgium, Brazil, Canada, Colombia, Czech Republic, Denmark, France, Germany, Iceland, Italy, Lithuania, Mexico, Panama, Republic of Korea, Spain, United Kingdom of Great Britain and Northern Ireland, United States of America.

Abstaining:

Belize, Costa Rica, Guyana, India, Japan, Paraguay, Sri Lanka, Thailand, Turkey.

112. At the same meeting, statements were made before the vote by the representatives of Armenia and Sri Lanka.

113. Also at the 35th meeting, the representative of Germany, on behalf of the European Union, proposed that the Council decide to grant consultative status to the Danish National Association for Gays and Lesbians.

114. At the same meeting, the representative of Mauritania proposed a motion, under rule 50 of the rules of procedure of the Council, of adjournment of debate on the proposal made by the representative of Germany until later in the session.

115. Also at the 35th meeting, the representatives of the Russian Federation and Pakistan made statements in favour of the motion.

116. At the same meeting, the representatives of Germany and Brazil made statements against the motion.

117. Also at the 35th meeting, the Council proceeded to a roll-call vote on the motion for adjournment of debate until later in the session. The motion was carried by a vote of 28 to 20, with 4 abstentions. The voting was as follows:

In favour:

Angola, Armenia, Bangladesh, Benin, China, Cuba, Democratic Republic of the Congo, Guinea, Guinea-Bissau, Guyana, Haiti, India, Indonesia, Madagascar, Mauritania, Mauritius, Namibia, Nigeria, Pakistan, Paraguay, Russian Federation, Saudi Arabia, South Africa, Sri Lanka, Thailand, Tunisia, United Arab Emirates, United Republic of Tanzania.

Against:

Albania, Australia, Austria, Belgium, Brazil, Canada, Colombia, Czech Republic, Denmark, France, Germany, Iceland, Italy, Lithuania, Mexico, Panama, Republic of Korea, Spain, United Kingdom of Great Britain and Northern Ireland, United States of America.

Abstaining:

Belize, Costa Rica, Japan, Turkey.

Application of the non-governmental organization People in Need

118. At its 35th meeting, on 21 July, the Council proceeded to a roll-call vote on draft decision IV entitled "Application of the non-governmental organization People in Need", recommended by the Committee (see E/2006/32 (Part I), chap. I, sect. A).

119. The Council adopted draft decision IV by a roll-call vote of 25 to 18, with 6 abstentions. See Council **decision 2006/223**. The voting was as follows:

In favour:

Angola, Bangladesh, Benin, Brazil, China, Colombia, Cuba, Democratic Republic of the Congo, Guinea, Guinea-Bissau, Haiti, India, Indonesia, Mauritania, Mexico, Namibia, Nigeria, Pakistan, Panama, Russian Federation, Saudi Arabia, South Africa, Sri Lanka, United Arab Emirates, United Republic of Tanzania.

Against:

Albania, Australia, Austria, Belgium, Canada, Costa Rica, Czech Republic, Denmark, France, Germany, Iceland, Italy, Japan, Lithuania, Republic of Korea, Spain, United Kingdom of Great Britain and Northern Ireland, United States of America.

Abstaining:

Armenia, Belize, Guyana, Paraguay, Thailand, Turkey.

120. At the same meeting, statements in explanation of vote after the vote were made by the representatives of South Africa, the Czech Republic and Guinea.

Withdrawal of status of the Islamic African Relief Agency

121. At its 35th meeting, on 21 July, the Council adopted draft decision V entitled "Withdrawal of status of the Islamic African Relief Agency", recommended by the Council (see E/2006/32 (Part I), chap. I, sect. A). See Council **decision 2006/224**.

Report of the Committee on Non-Governmental Organizations on its 2006 regular session

122. At its 35th meeting, on 21 July, the Council decided to adjourn to a later stage action on draft decision VI entitled "Report of the Committee on Non-Governmental Organizations on its 2006 regular session", recommended by the Committee (see E/2006/32 (Part I), chap. I. sect. A).

Recommendations contained in the excerpt from the report of the Committee on Non-Governmental Organizations on its resumed 2006 session

Applications for consultative status and requests for reclassification received from non-governmental organizations

123. At its 35th meeting, on 21 July, the Council adopted draft decision I, entitled "Applications for consultative status and requests for reclassification received from non-governmental organizations", recommended by the Committee (see E/2006/L.7, chap. I, sect. A). See Council **decision 2006/225**.

Application of the Lesbian and Gay Federation in Germany

124. At its 35th meeting, on 21 July, the Council had before it draft decision II entitled "Application of the Lesbian and Gay Federation in Germany", recommended by the Committee (see E/2006/L.7, chap. I, sect. A).

125. At the same meeting, the Council rejected the draft decision by a roll-call vote of 20 to 23 against, with 7 abstentions. The voting was as follows:

In favour:

Angola, Bangladesh, Benin, China, Democratic Republic of the Congo, Guinea, Guinea-Bissau, Haiti, Indonesia, Madagascar, Mauritania, Namibia, Nigeria, Pakistan, Russian Federation, Saudi Arabia, South Africa, Tunisia, United Arab Emirates, United Republic of Tanzania.

Against:

Albania, Armenia, Australia, Austria, Belgium, Brazil, Canada, Colombia, Costa Rica, Czech Republic, Denmark, France, Germany, Iceland, Italy, Japan, Lithuania, Mexico, Panama, Republic of Korea, Spain, United Kingdom of Great Britain and Northern Ireland, United States of America.

Abstaining:

Belize, Guyana, India, Paraguay, Sri Lanka, Thailand, Turkey.

126. At the same meeting, the representative of the Russian Federation proposed that the Council decide to refer the application of the Lesbian and Gay Federation in Germany back to the Committee for its reconsideration.

127. On the basis of a statement by the representative of Germany, the Council adjourned consideration of the proposal to a later stage.

Application of the International Lesbian and Gay Association — Europe

128. At its 35th meeting, on 21 July, the Council had before it draft decision III entitled "Application of the International Lesbian and Gay Association — Europe", recommended by the Committee (see E/2006/L.7, chap. I, sect. A).

129. At the same meeting, the Council rejected the draft decision by a roll-call vote of 22 to 22, with 6 abstentions. The voting was as follows:

In favour:

Angola, Bangladesh, Benin, China, Costa Rica, Democratic Republic of the Congo, Guinea, Guinea-Bissau, Haiti, India, Indonesia, Madagascar, Mauritania, Namibia,

Nigeria, Pakistan, Russian Federation, Saudi Arabia, South Africa, Tunisia, United Arab Emirates, United Republic of Tanzania.

Against:

Albania, Armenia, Australia, Austria, Belgium, Brazil, Canada, Colombia, Czech Republic, Denmark, France, Germany, Iceland, Italy, Japan, Lithuania, Mexico, Panama, Republic of Korea, Spain, United Kingdom of Great Britain and Northern Ireland, United States of America.

Abstaining:

Belize, Guyana, Paraguay, Sri Lanka, Thailand, Turkey.

130. Also at the 35th meeting, statements in explanation of vote after the vote were made by the representatives of the Russian Federation, South Africa and Guinea-Bissau.

131. At the same meeting, the representative of the Russian Federation proposed that the Council decide to refer the application of the International Lesbian and Gay Association — Europe back to the Committee for its reconsideration.

132. Also at the 35th meeting, the Council decided to postpone consideration of the proposal to a later stage.

Dates of the 2007 session of the Committee on Non-Governmental Organizations and provisional agenda

133. At the 35th meeting, on 21 July, the Council adopted draft decision IV entitled "Dates of the 2007 session of the Committee on Non-Governmental Organizations and provisional agenda", recommended by the Committee (see E/2006/L.7, chap. I, sect. A). See Council **decision 2006/226**.

Report of the Committee on Non-Governmental Organizations

134. At its 43rd meeting, on 28 July, the Council decided to defer the consideration of pending issues under this agenda item until its resumed substantive session. See **decision 2006/252**.

H. Economic and environmental questions

135. The Council held a discussion on economic and environmental questions (agenda item 13) at its 22nd, 37th, 38th, 41st and 43rd meetings, on 10, 24, 25, 27 and 28 July 2006. An account of the discussion is contained in the relevant summary records (E/2006/SR.22, 37, 38, 41 and 43). The Council had before it the following documents:

(a) Updated report of the Secretary-General on the role of the Economic and Social Council in the integrated and coordinated implementation of the outcomes of and follow-up to major United Nations conferences and summits, in the light of General Assembly resolutions 50/227, 52/12 B and 57/270 B (A/61/90-E/2006/84) (see also under chapeau of item 6, item 8 and chapeau of item 14);

(b) Synopsis of the review of methods of work undertaken by the functional commissions and other relevant subsidiary bodies of the Economic and Social Council (E/2006/CRP.7) (English only) (see also under chapeau of item 6, item 8 and chapeau of item 14).

136. At the 22nd meeting, on 10 July, an introductory statement was made by the Assistant Secretary-General for Policy Coordination and Inter-Agency Affairs, Department of Economic and Social Affairs (under item 13 (b)).

137. At the 37th meeting, on 24 July, introductory statements were made by the Chairperson of the Committee for Development Policy (under item 13 (a)) and the Director, United Nations Human Settlements Programme (UN-Habitat) New York Office (under item 13 (d)).

138. At the same meeting, introductory statements were made by the Director of the Division for Public Administration and Development Management, Department of Economic and Social Affairs (under item 13 (g)) and the Chairperson of the Committee of Experts on International Cooperation in Tax Matters (under item 13 (h)).

139. At the 38th meeting, on 25 July, introductory statements were made by the Assistant Secretary-General and Special Adviser on Gender Issues and Advancement of Women and the Director, Division for the Advancement of Women (under items 7 (e), 13 (l) and 14 (a)).

Action taken by the Council

140. Under agenda item 13, jointly with items 6, 8 and 14, the Council adopted **resolution 2006/44** (see chap. VII, sect. A).

1. Sustainable development

141. The Council held a discussion on sustainable development (agenda item 13 (a)) at its 37th and 43rd meetings, on 24 and 28 July. An account of the discussion is contained in the relevant summary records (E/2006/SR.37 and 43). The Council had before it the following documents:

(a) Letter dated 21 April 2006 from the Permanent Representative of Samoa to the United Nations addressed to the Secretary-General, transmitting the final report of the Pacific Regional Meeting to follow up implementation of the Mauritius Strategy, held in Apia from 17 to 19 October 2005 (A/61/72-E/2006/54);

(b) Letter dated 13 April 2006 from the Permanent Representative of Seychelles to the United Nations addressed to the Secretary-General, transmitting the final report of the Atlantic, Indian Ocean, Mediterranean and South China Seas Regional Meeting to follow up on implementation of the Mauritius Strategy, held in Baie Lazare, Seychelles, from 26 to 28 October 2006 (A/61/75-E/2006/49);

(c) Letter dated 13 April 2006 from the Permanent Representative of Saint Kitts and Nevis to the United Nations addressed to the Secretary-General, transmitting the final report of the Caribbean Regional Meeting to follow up implementation of the Mauritius Strategy, held in Frigate Bay, Saint Kitts and Nevis from 5 to 7 October 2005 (A/61/76-E/2006/51);

(d) Report of the Commission on Sustainable Development on its fourteenth session (E/2006/29);[12]

(e) Report of the Committee for Development Policy on its eighth session (E/2006/33) (see also under item 2);[13]

(f) Note verbale dated 21 July 2006 from the Permanent Mission of Samoa to the United Nations transmitting a letter from the Prime Minister of Samoa addressed to the President of the Economic and Social Council (E/2006/90);

(g) Letter dated 21 July 2006 from the Permanent Representative of Papua New Guinea to the United Nations addressed to the Secretariat (E/2006/91).

Action taken by the Council

142. Under agenda item 13 (a), the Council adopted **decisions 2006/228** and **2006/253**.

Recommendations contained in the report of the Commission on Sustainable Development on its fourteenth session

Report of the Commission on Sustainable Development on its fourteenth session and provisional agenda for the fifteenth session of the Commission

143. At its 37th meeting, on 24 July, the Council adopted the draft decision entitled "Report of the Commission on Sustainable Development on its fourteenth session and provisional agenda for the fifteenth session of the Commission", recommended by the Commission (see E/2006/29, chap. I). See Council **decision 2006/228**.

Report of the Committee for Development Policy on its eighth session

144. At the 43rd meeting, on 28 July, the Council decided to defer consideration of the report of the Committee for Development Policy on its eighth session to its resumed substantive session. See Council **decision 2006/253**.

2. Science and technology for development

145. The Council held a discussion on science and technology for development (agenda item 13 (b)) at its 22nd and 43rd meetings, on 10 and 28 July. An account of the discussion is contained in the relevant summary records (E/2006/SR.22 and 43). The Council had before it the report of the Commission on Science and Technology for Development on its ninth session (E/2006/31).[14]

Action taken by the Council

146. Under agenda items 13 (b) and 6, the Council adopted **resolution 2006/46** and **decision 2006/254**.

Follow-up to the World Summit on the Information Society and review of the Commission on Science and Technology for Development

147. At its 43rd meeting, on 28 July, the Council had before it the draft resolution (E/2006/L.37) entitled "Follow-up to the World Summit on the Information Society and review of the Commission on Science and Technology for Development", submitted by the Vice-President of the Council, Dalius Čekuolis (Lithuania), on the basis of informal consultations.

148. At the same meeting, the representative of Latvia, as facilitator of the draft resolution, orally corrected operative paragraph 15 (b), by inserting the words "including the private sector" after the words "business-sector entities".

149. The Secretary of the Council read out a statement of the programme budget implications of the draft resolution.

150. Also at the 43rd meeting, the Council adopted the draft resolution, as orally corrected. See Council **resolution 2006/46**.

151. After the adoption of the draft resolution, statements were made by the representatives of the Russian Federation, the United States of America and Canada and the observer for Finland (on behalf of the European Union).

Report of the Commission on Science and Technology for Development on its ninth session

152. At its 43rd meeting, on 28 July, the Council decided to defer consideration of the report of the Commission on Science and Technology for Development on its ninth session to the Council's resumed substantive session. See Council **decision 2006/254**.

3. Statistics

153. The Council held a discussion on statistics (agenda item 13 (c)) at its 37th meeting, on 24 July. An account of the discussion is contained in the relevant summary record (E/2006/SR.37). It had before it the following documents:

(a) Letter dated 16 May 2006 from the Permanent Representative of Saint Lucia to the United Nations addressed to the Secretary-General, transmitting the Plan of Implementation of the Decolonization Mandate 2006-07 (A/60/853-E/2006/75) (see also under items 9 and 10);

(b) Report of the Statistical Commission on its thirty-seventh session (E/2006/24).[15]

Action taken by the Council

154. Under agenda item 13 (c), the Council adopted **resolution 2006/6** and **decision 2006/232**.

Recommendations contained in the report of the Statistical Commission on its thirty-seventh session

Strengthening statistical capacity

155. At its 37th meeting, on 24 July, the Council adopted the draft resolution entitled "Strengthening statistical capacity", recommended by the Commission (see E/2006/24, chap. I, sect. A). See Council **resolution 2006/6**.

Report of the Statistical Commission on its thirty-seventh session and provisional agenda, dates and documentation for the thirty-eighth session of the Commission

156. At its 37th meeting, on 24 July, the Council adopted the draft decision entitled "Report of the Statistical Commission on its thirty-seventh session and provisional agenda, dates and documentation for the thirty-eighth session of the Commission", recommended by the Commission (see E/2006/24, chap. I, sect. B). See Council **decision 2006/232**.

4. Human settlements

157. The Council held a discussion on human settlements (agenda item 13 (d)) at its 37th and 41st meetings, on 24 and 27 July. An account of the discussion is contained in the

relevant summary records (E/2006/SR.37 and 41). The Council had before it the report of the Secretary-General on the coordinated implementation of the Habitat Agenda (E/2006/71).

Action taken by the Council

158. Under agenda item 13 (d), the Council adopted **decision 2006/247**.

Human settlements

159. At the 37th meeting, on 24 July, the representative of South Africa (on behalf of the States Members of the United Nations that are members of the Group of 77 and China) introduced a draft decision (E/2006/L.16) entitled "Human settlements".

160. At its 41st meeting, on 27 July, the Council adopted the draft decision. See Council **decision 2006/247**.

5. Environment

161. The Council held a discussion on environment (agenda item 13 (e)) at its 37th meeting, on 24 July. An account of the discussion is contained in the relevant summary record (E/2006/SR.37). The Council had before it the report of the United Nations Environment Programme Governing Council/Global Ministerial Environment Forum on its ninth special session (A/61/25).[16]

Action taken by the Council

162. Under agenda item 13 (e), the Council adopted **decision 2006/229**.

Document considered in connection with environment

163. At its 37th meeting, on 24 July, the Council, on the proposal of the Vice-President of the Council, Dalius Čekuolis (Lithuania), took note of the report of the United Nations Environment Programme Governing Council/Global Ministerial Environment Forum on its ninth special session. See Council **decision 2006/229**.

6. Population and development

164. The Council held a discussion on population (agenda item 13 (f)) at its 37th meeting, on 24 July. An account of the discussion is contained in the relevant summary record (E/2006/SR.37). The Council had before it the report of the Commission on Population and Development on its thirty-ninth session (E/2006/25).[17]

Action taken by the Council

165. Under agenda item 13 (f), the Council adopted **decision 2006/233**.

Recommendation contained in the report of the Commission on Population and Development on its thirty-ninth session

Report of the Commission on Population and Development on its thirty-ninth session and provisional agenda for the fortieth session of the Commission

166. At its 37th meeting, on 24 July, the Council adopted the draft decision entitled "Report of the Commission on Population and Development on its thirty-ninth session and provisional agenda for the fortieth session of the Commission", recommended by the Commission (see E/2006/25, chap. I, sect. A). See Council **decision 2006/233**.

7. Public administration and development

167. The Council held a discussion on public administration and development (agenda item 13 (g)) at its 37th and 43rd meetings, on 24 and 28 July. An account of the discussion is contained in the relevant summary records (E/2006/SR.37 and 43). The Council had before it the report of the Committee of Experts on Public Administration on its fifth session (E/2006/44).[18]

Action taken by the Council

168. Under agenda item 13 (g), the Council adopted **resolution 2006/47**.

Report of the Committee of Experts on Public Administration on its fifth session and dates, venue and provisional agenda for the sixth session of the Committee

169. At its 43rd meeting, on 28 July, the Council had before it a draft resolution (E/2006/L.31) entitled "Report of the Committee of Experts on Public Administration on its fifth session and dates, venue and provisional agenda for the sixth session of the Committee", submitted by the Vice-President of the Council, Dalius Čekuolis (Lithuania), on the basis of informal consultations held on the draft resolution contained in the report of the Committee of Experts on Public Administration on its fifth session (see E/2006/44, chap. I).

170. At the same meeting, the Council adopted the draft resolution. See Council **resolution 2006/47**.

8. International cooperation in tax matters

171. The Council held a discussion on international cooperation in tax matters (agenda item 13 (h)) at its 37th, 38th and 43rd meetings, on 24, 25 and 28 July. An account of the discussion is contained in the relevant summary records (E/2006/SR.37, 38 and 43). The Council had before it the report of the Committee of Experts on International Cooperation in Tax Matters on its first session (E/2005/45).[19]

Action taken by the Council

172. Under agenda item 13 (h), the Council adopted **resolution 2006/48**.

Committee of Experts on International Cooperation in Tax Matters

173. At the 38th meeting, on 25 July, the representative of South Africa, on behalf of States Members of the United Nations that are members of the Group of 77 and China, introduced a draft resolution (E/2006/L.12) entitled "Committee of Experts on International Cooperation in Tax Matters", which read:

"*The Economic and Social Council,*

"*Recalling* its resolution 2004/69 of 11 November 2004, in which the Council decided that the Ad Hoc Group of Experts on International Cooperation in Tax Matters should be renamed the Committee of Experts on International Cooperation in Tax Matters,

"*Recognizing* the call made in the Monterrey Consensus of the International Conference on Financing for Development for the strengthening of international tax cooperation through enhanced dialogue among national tax authorities and greater coordination of the work of the concerned multilateral bodies and relevant regional organizations, giving special attention to the needs of developing countries and countries with economies in transition,

"*Taking note* of the report of the Secretary-General on the implementation of and follow-up to commitments and agreements made at the International Conference on Financing for Development and the recommendations contained therein,

"*Recognizing* the need for an inclusive, participatory and broad-based dialogue on international cooperation in tax matters,

"*Noting* the activities developing within the concerned multilateral bodies and relevant regional organizations,

"1. *Takes note* with appreciation of the report of the Committee of Experts on International Cooperation in Tax Matters on its first session;

"2. *Recognizes* that the Committee agreed to create, as necessary, ad hoc subcommittees composed of experts and observers who would work throughout the year to prepare and determine the supporting documentation for the agenda items, including requests for papers by independent experts, for consideration at its regular session;

"3. *Also recognizes* that four subcommittees on substantial matters, namely, treaty abuses, mutual assistance in collecting tax debts, definition of permanent establishment, and exchange of information, and two working groups, on international tax arbitration and the Manual for the Negotiation of Bilateral Tax Treaties between Developed and Developing Countries, were created at the first session;

"4. *Acknowledges* that the efficient operation of the subcommittees indicated above may require some face-to-face meetings in order that issues relating to the agenda may be dealt with on a continuous basis;

"5. *Invites* the Committee to organize training workshops for developing countries as part of the work required to carry out its mandate to make recommendations on capacity-building and provide technical assistance;

"6. *Requests* the Secretary-General to establish a trust fund to supplement regular budget resources, which would receive contributions from Member States and other institutions interested in providing financing for the Committee's activities in supporting international cooperation in tax matters, including support for the participation of experts from developing countries;

"7. *Decides* that the second session of the Committee shall be convened in Geneva from 30 October to 3 November 2006;

"8. *Approves* the provisional agenda for the second session of the Committee, as contained in paragraph 122 of its report on its first session."

174. At its 43rd meeting, on 28 July, the Council had before it the draft resolution (E/2006/L.36) entitled "Committee of Experts on International Cooperation in Tax Matters", submitted by the Vice-President of the Council, Dalius Čekuolis (Lithuania), on the basis of informal consultations held on draft resolution E/2006/L.12.

175. At the same meeting, the Council adopted the draft resolution E/2006/L.36. See Council **resolution 2006/48**.

176. In the light of the adoption of draft resolution E/2006/L.36, draft resolution E/2006/L.12 was withdrawn by its sponsors.

9. United Nations Forum on Forests

177. The Council held a discussion on the United Nations Forum on Forests (agenda item 13 (i)) at its 37th and 43rd meetings, on 24 and 28 July. An account of the discussion is contained in the relevant summary records (E/2006/SR.37 and 43). The Council had before it the report of the United Nations Forum on Forests on its sixth session (E/2006/42 and Corr.1 and 2).[20]

Action taken by the Council

178. Under agenda item 13 (i), the Council adopted **resolution 2006/49** and **decisions 2006/230**, **2006/231** and **2006/255**.

Recommendations contained in the report of the United Nations Forum on Forests on its sixth session

Outcome of the sixth session of the United Nations Forum on Forests

179. At its 43rd meeting, on 28 July, the Council considered the draft resolution entitled "Outcome of the sixth session of the United Nations Forum on Forests", recommended by the Commission (see E/2006/42 and Corr.1 and 2, chap. I, sect. A).

180. At the same meeting, the representative of Australia orally amended operative paragraph 29 by replacing the words "ad hoc working group" with the words "ad hoc expert group".

181. Also at the 43rd meeting, the Secretary of the Council read out a statement on the programme budget implications of the draft resolution.

182. At the same meeting, the Council adopted the draft resolution, as orally amended. See Council **resolution 2006/49**.

183. After the adoption of the draft resolution, a statement was made by the representative of the Russian Federation.

Proclamation of an International Year of Forests

184. At the 37th meeting, on 24 July, the Vice-President of the Council, Dalius Čekuolis (Lithuania), introduced draft decision I entitled "Proclamation of an International Year of Forests", recommended by the Forum (see E/2006/42 and Corr.1 and 2, chap. I, sect. B).

185. At the same meeting, the Vice-President of the Council, Dalius Čekuolis (Lithuania), amended the text of the draft decision by replacing the year "2010" with the year "2011".

186. Also at the 37th meeting, the Council adopted the draft decision, as orally amended. See Council **decision 2006/230**.

Dates and venue for the seventh session of the Forum

187. At its 37th meeting, on 24 July, the Council adopted draft decision II entitled "Dates and venue for the seventh session of the Forum", recommended by the Forum (see E/2006/42 and Corr.1 and 2, chap. I, sect. B). See Council **decision 2006/231**.

Report of the United Nations Forum on Forests on its sixth session and provisional agenda for its seventh session

188. At its 43rd meeting, on 28 July, the Council adopted draft decision III entitled "Report of the United Nations Forum on Forests on its sixth session and provisional agenda for its seventh session", recommended by the Forum (see E/2006/42 and Corr.1 and 2, chap. I, sect. B). See Council **decision 2006/255**.

10. Assistance to third States affected by the application of sanctions

189. The Council considered the question of assistance to third States affected by the application of sanctions (agenda item 13 (j)) at its 37th meeting, on 24 July. An account of the discussion is contained in the relevant summary record (E/2006/ SR.37).

Action taken by the Council

190. The Council took no action under the sub-item.

11. Cartography

191. The Council held a discussion on cartography (agenda item 13 (k)) at its 37th meeting, on 24 July. An account of the discussion is contained in the relevant summary record (E/2006/SR.37). The Council had before it the report of the United Nations Group of Experts on Geographical Names on the work of its twenty-third session (Vienna, 28 March-4 April 2006) (E/2006/57).

Action taken by the Council

192. Under agenda item 13 (k), the Council adopted **decision 2006/229**.

Document considered by the Council in connection with agenda item 13 (k)

193. At its 37th meeting, on 24 July, on the proposal of the Vice-President of the Council, Dalius Čekuolis (Lithuania), the Council took note of the report of the United Nations Group of Experts on Geographical Names on the work of its twenty-third session (E/2006/57). See Council **decision 2006/229**.

12. Women and development

194. The Council considered the question of women and development (agenda item 13 (l)) jointly with that of mainstreaming a gender perspective into all policies and programmes in the United Nations system (agenda item 7 (e)) and that of the advancement of women (agenda item 14 (a)) at its 38th meeting, on 25 July. An account of the discussion is contained in the relevant summary record (E/2006/SR.38). The Council had before it the relevant sections of the report of the Commission on the Status of Women on its fiftieth session (E/2006/27 and Corr.1).[21]

I. Social and human rights questions

195. The Council considered social and human rights questions (agenda item 14 (a) to (h)) at its 38th and 40th to 43rd meetings, on 25 to 28 July. An account of the discussion is contained in the relevant summary records (E/2006/SR.38 and 40-43).

196. Under agenda item 14 as a whole, the Council had before it the following documents:

(a) Updated report of the Secretary-General on the role of the Economic and Social Council in the integrated and coordinated implementation of the outcomes of and follow-up to major United Nations conferences and summits, in the light of General Assembly resolutions 50/227, 52/12 B and 57/270 B (A/61/90-E/2006/84) (see also under chapeau of item 6, item 8 and chapeau of item 13);

(b) Synopsis of the review of the methods of work undertaken by the functional commissions and other relevant subsidiary bodies of the Economic and Social Council (E/2006/CRP.7) (see also under chapeau of item 6, item 8 and chapeau of item 13).

Action taken by the Council

197. Under agenda item 14, jointly with items 6, 8 and 13, the Council adopted **resolution 2006/44** (see chap. VII, sect. A). Under agenda item 14, the Council adopted **decision 2006/250**.

Documents considered by the Council in connection with social and human rights questions

198. At its 41st, 42nd and 43rd meetings, on 27 and 28 July, the Council took note of a number of documents submitted under agenda items 14 (a), (d) and (g). See Council **decision 2006/250**.

1. Advancement of women

199. The Council held a discussion on the advancement of women (agenda item 14 (a)) at its 38th and 42nd meetings, on 25 and 27 July. An account of the discussion is contained in the relevant summary records (E/2006/SR.38 and 42). The Council had before it the following documents:

(a) Report of the Commission on the Status of Women on its fiftieth session (E/2006/27);[21]

(b) Report of the Secretary-General on the follow-up to the Fourth World Conference on Women and progress made in the implementation of the Beijing Declaration and Platform for Action and the outcome of the twenty-third special session of the General Assembly (E/2006/65) (see also under item 7 (e));

(c) Report of the Executive Board of the United Nations International Research and Training Institute for the Advancement of Women on the work of its third session (18 May 2006) (E/2006/80);

(d) Results of the thirty-fourth and thirty-fifth sessions of the Committee on the Elimination of Discrimination against Women: note by the Secretary-General (E/2006/CRP.4).

200. At its 38th meeting, on 25 July, the Council considered the question of the advancement of women jointly with that of mainstreaming a gender perspective into all policies and programmes in the United Nations system (agenda item 7 (e)) and that of women and development (agenda item 13 (l)). Introductory statements were made by the Assistant Secretary-General and Special Adviser on Gender Issues and Advancement of

Women and the Director, Division for the Advancement of Women (under agenda items 7 (e), 13 (l) and 14 (a)).

Action taken by the Council

201. Under agenda item 14 (a), the Council adopted **resolutions 2006/7** to **2006/9** and **decisions 2006/234, 2006/235** and **2006/250**.

Recommendations contained in the report of the Commission on the Status of Women on its fiftieth session (E/2006/27 and Corr.1)

High-level panel discussion on the gender dimensions of international migration

202. At its 38th meeting, on 25 July, the Council decided to transmit to the General Assembly, at the High-level Dialogue on International Migration and Development, to be held in New York on 14 and 15 September 2006, the summary submitted by the Chairperson of the Commission entitled "High-level panel discussion on the gender dimensions of international migration", as contained in chapter I, section A, of the report of the Commission on its fiftieth session. See Council **decision 2006/234**.

Situation of women and girls in Afghanistan

203. At its 38th meeting, on 25 July, the Council adopted draft resolution I, entitled "Situation of women and girls in Afghanistan", recommended by the Commission (see E/2006/27 and Corr.1, chap. I, sect. B). See Council **resolution 2006/7**.

Situation of and assistance to Palestinian women

204. At the 38th meeting, on 25 July, the Council adopted draft resolution II, entitled "Situation of and assistance to Palestinian women", recommended by the Commission (see E/2006/27 and Corr.1, chap. I, sect. B) by a roll-call vote of 38 to 2, with 1 abstention. See Council **resolution 2006/8**. The voting was as follows:[22]

In favour:

Albania, Angola, Austria, Belgium, Belize, Benin, China, Colombia, Costa Rica, Cuba, Czech Republic, France, Germany, Guyana, Iceland, India, Indonesia, Italy, Japan, Lithuania, Madagascar, Mauritania, Mexico, Namibia, Nigeria, Pakistan, Panama, Paraguay, Republic of Korea, Russian Federation, Saudi Arabia, South Africa, Spain, Sri Lanka, Thailand, Tunisia, Turkey, United Kingdom of Great Britain and Northern Ireland.

Against:

Australia, United States of America.

Abstaining:

Haiti.

205. A statement in explanation of vote after the vote was made by the representative of Australia.

206. A statement was made by the representative of the United States of America.

Future organization and methods of work of the Commission on the Status of Women

207. At its 38th meeting, on 25 July, the Council adopted draft resolution III, entitled "Future organization and methods of work of the Commission on the Status of Women", recommended by the Commission (see E/2006/27 and Corr.1, chap. I, sect. B). See Council **resolution 2006/9**.

Report of the Commission on the Status of Women on its fiftieth session and provisional agenda and documentation for the fifty-first session of the Commission

208. At its 38th meeting, on 25 July, the Council adopted the draft decision entitled "Report of the Commission on the Status of Women on its fiftieth session and provisional agenda and documentation for the fifty-first session of the Commission", recommended by the Commission (see E/2006/27 and Corr.1, chap. I, sect. B). See Council **decision 2006/235**.

Document considered by the Council under agenda item 14 (a)

209. At its 42nd meeting, on 27 July, the Council took note of the report of the Executive Board of the United Nations International Research and Training Institute for the Advancement of Women on the work of its third session (E/2006/80). See Council **decision 2006/250**.

2. Social development

210. The Council held a discussion on social development (agenda item 14 (b)), at its 40th meeting, on 26 July. An account of the discussion is contained in the relevant summary record (E/2006/SR.40). The Council had before it the following documents:

(a) Letter dated 30 June 2005 from the Director-General of the International Labour Organization addressed to the Secretary-General (E/2006/11);

(b) Report of the Commission for Social Development on its forty-fourth session (E/2006/26);[23]

(c) Letter dated 29 June 2006 from the Executive Director for Fundamental Principles and Rights at Work of the International Labour Office at Geneva addressed to the President of the Economic and Social Council (E/2006/89).

Action taken by the Council

211. Under this item, the Council adopted **resolutions 2006/15** to **2006/18** and **decision 2006/238**.

Recommendations contained in the report of the Commission for Social Development on its forty-third session

Promoting youth employment

212. At its 40th meeting, on 26 July, the Council adopted draft resolution I, entitled "Promoting youth employment", recommended by the Commission (see E/2006/26, chap. I, sect. A). See Council **resolution 2006/15**.

Comprehensive and integral international convention to protect and promote the rights and dignity of persons with disabilities

213. At its 40th meeting, on 26 July, the Council adopted draft resolution II, entitled "Comprehensive and integral international convention to protect and promote the rights and dignity of persons with disabilities", recommended by the Commission (see E/2006/26, chap. I, sect. A). See Council **resolution 2006/16**.

Social dimensions of the New Partnership for Africa's Development

214. At its 40th meeting, on 26 July, the Council adopted draft resolution III, entitled "Social dimensions of the New Partnership for Africa's Development", recommended by the Commission (see E/2006/26, chap. I, sect. A). See Council **resolution 2006/17**.

Future organization and methods of work of the Commission for Social Development

215. At its 40th meeting, on 26 July, the Council adopted draft resolution IV entitled "Future organization and methods of work of the Commission for Social Development", recommended by the Commission (see E/2006/26, chap. I, sect. A). See Council **resolution 2006/18**.

Report of the Commission for Social Development on its forty-fourth session and provisional agenda and documentation for the forty-fifth session of the Commission

216. At its 40th meeting, on 26 July, the Council adopted a draft decision, entitled "Report of the Commission for Social Development on its forty-fourth session and provisional agenda and documentation for the forty-fifth session", recommended by the Commission (see E/2006/26, chap. I, sect. B). See Council **decision 2006/238**.

3. Crime prevention and criminal justice

217. The Council held a discussion on crime prevention and criminal justice (agenda item 14 (c)) at its 40th, 41st and 43rd meetings, on 26 to 28 July. An account of the discussion is contained in the relevant summary records (E/2006/SR.40, 41 and 43). The Council had before it the report of the Commission on Crime Prevention and Criminal Justice on its fifteenth session (E/2006/30).[24]

218. At the 40th meeting, on 26 July, a statement was made by the Secretary of the Council on the programme budget implications of draft resolution I entitled "Strengthening the United Nations Crime Prevention and Criminal Justice Programme and the role of the Commission on Crime Prevention and Criminal Justice as its governing body", recommended by the Commission for approval by the Council for adoption by the General Assembly (see E/2006/30, chap. I, sect. A) and draft decision I entitled "Report of the Commission on Crime Prevention and Criminal Justice on its fifteenth session and provisional agenda and documentation for the sixteenth session", recommended by the Commission (see E/2006/30, chap. I, sect. C). A statement was also made by the representative of the United States of America.

Action taken by the Council

219. Under agenda item 14 (c), the Council adopted **resolutions 2006/19** to **2006/29**, and **decisions 2006/239, 2006/240** and **2006/256**.

Recommendations contained in the report of the Commission on Crime Prevention and Criminal Justice on its fifteenth session

Strengthening the United Nations Crime Prevention and Criminal Justice Programme and the role of the Commission on Crime Prevention and Criminal Justice as its governing body

220. At its 40th meeting, on 26 July, the Council considered draft resolution I entitled "Strengthening the United Nations Crime Prevention and Criminal Justice Programme and the role of the Commission on Crime Prevention and Criminal Justice as its governing body", recommended by the Commission (see E/2006/30, chap. I, sect. A).

221. At the same meeting, the Secretary of the Council read out a statement of programme budget implications in connection with the draft resolution.

222. Also at the 40th meeting, a statement was made by the representative of the United States of America.

223. At the 41st meeting, on 27 July, the Secretary of the Council responded to points made by the representative of the United States of America and the observer for Finland (on behalf of the European Union).

224. At the 43rd meeting, on 28 July, a statement was made by the observer for Finland (on behalf of the European Union).

225. At the same meeting, the Council took note of the draft resolution and decided to transmit it to the General Assembly. See Council **decision 2006/256**.

International cooperation in the prevention, combating and elimination of kidnapping and in providing assistance to victims

226. At its 41st meeting, on 27 July, the Council approved draft resolution II entitled "International cooperation in the prevention, combating and elimination of kidnapping and in providing assistance to victims" for adoption by the General Assembly (see E/2006/30, chap. I, sect. A). See Council **resolution 2006/19**.

United Nations standards and norms in crime prevention

227. At its 41st meeting, on 27 July, the Council adopted draft resolution I entitled "United Nations standards and norms in crime prevention", recommended by the Commission (see E/2006/30, chap. I, sect. B). See Council **resolution 2006/20**.

Implementation of the Programme of Action, 2006-2010, on strengthening the rule of law and the criminal justice systems in Africa

228. At its 41st meeting, on 27 July, the Council adopted draft resolution II entitled "Implementation of the Programme of Action, 2006-2010, on strengthening the rule of law and the criminal justice systems in Africa", recommended by the Commission (see E/2006/30, chap. I, sect. B). See Council **resolution 2006/21**.

Providing technical assistance for prison reform in Africa and the development of viable alternatives to imprisonment

229. At its 41st meeting, on 27 July, the Council adopted draft resolution III entitled "Providing technical assistance for prison reform in Africa and the development of viable alternatives to imprisonment", recommended by the Commission (see E/2006/30, chap. I, sect. B). See Council **resolution 2006/22**.

Strengthening basic principles of judicial conduct

230. At its 41st meeting, on 27 July, the Council adopted draft resolution IV entitled "Strengthening basic principles of judicial conduct", recommended by the Commission (see E/2006/30, chap. I, sect. B). See Council **resolution 2006/23**.

International cooperation in the fight against corruption

231. At its 41st meeting, on 27 July, the Council adopted draft resolution V entitled "International cooperation in the fight against corruption", recommended by the Commission (see E/2006/30, chap. I, sect. B). See Council **resolution 2006/24**.

Strengthening the rule of law and the reform of criminal justice institutions, including in post-conflict reconstruction

232. At its 41st meeting, on 27 July, the Council adopted draft resolution VI entitled "Strengthening the rule of law and the reform of criminal justice institutions, including in post-conflict reconstruction", recommended by the Commission (see E/2006/30, chap. I, sect. B). See Council **resolution 2006/25**.

Follow-up to the Eleventh United Nations Congress on Crime Prevention and Criminal Justice

233. At its 41st meeting, on 27 July, the Council adopted draft resolution VII entitled "Follow-up to the Eleventh United Nations Congress on Crime Prevention and Criminal Justice", recommended by the Commission (see E/2006/30, chap. I, sect. B). See Council **resolution 2006/26**.

Strengthening international cooperation in preventing and combating trafficking in persons and protecting victims of such trafficking

234. At its 41st meeting, on 27 July, the Council adopted draft resolution VIII entitled "Strengthening international cooperation in preventing and combating trafficking in persons and protecting victims of such trafficking", recommended by the Commission (see E/2006/30, chap. I, sect. B). See Council **resolution 2006/27**.

International Permanent Observatory on Security Measures during Major Events

235. At its 41st meeting, on 27 July, the Council adopted draft resolution IX entitled "International Permanent Observatory on Security Measures during Major Events", recommended by the Commission (see E/2006/30, chap. I, sect. B). See Council **resolution 2006/28**.

Crime prevention and criminal justice responses to violence against women and girls

236. At its 41st meeting, on 27 July, the Council adopted draft resolution X entitled "Crime prevention and criminal justice responses to violence against women and girls",

recommended by the Commission (see E/2006/30, chap. I, sect. B). See Council **resolution 2006/29**.

Report of the Commission on Crime Prevention and Criminal Justice on its fifteenth session and provisional agenda and documentation for its sixteenth session

237. At its 41st meeting, on 27 July, the Council adopted draft decision I entitled "Report of the Commission on Crime Prevention and Criminal Justice on its fifteenth session and provisional agenda and documentation for its sixteenth session", recommended by the Commission (see E/2006/30, chap. I, sect. C). See Council **decision 2006/239**.

Appointment of a member of the Board of Trustees of the United Nations Interregional Crime and Justice Research Institute

238. At its 41st meeting, on 27 July, the Council adopted draft decision II entitled "Appointment of a member of the Board of Trustees of the United Nations Interregional Crime and Justice Research Institute", recommended by the Commission (see E/2006/30, chap. I, sect. C). See Council **decision 2006/240**.

4. Narcotic drugs

239. The Council held a discussion on narcotic drugs (agenda item 14 (d)) at its 40th and 41st meetings, on 26 and 27 July. An account of the discussion is contained in the relevant summary records (E/2006/SR.40 and 41). The Council had before it the following documents:

(a) Report of the Commission on Narcotic Drugs on its forty-ninth session (E/2006/28);[25]

(b) Summary of the report of the International Narcotics Control Board for 2005.[26]

240. At the 40th meeting, on 26 July, the President of the International Narcotics Control Board made an introductory statement.

Action taken by the Council

241. Under agenda item 14 (d), the Council adopted **resolutions 2006/30** to **2006/34** and **decisions 2006/241** and **2006/250**.

Recommendations contained in the report of the Commission on Narcotic Drugs on its forty-ninth session

Baku Accord on Regional Cooperation against Illicit Drugs and Related Matters: a Vision for the Twenty-first Century

242. At its 41st meeting, on 27 July, the Council adopted draft resolution I entitled "Baku Accord on Regional Cooperation against Illicit Drugs and Related Matters: a Vision for the Twenty-first Century", recommended by the Commission (see E/2006/28, chap. I, sect. A). See Council **resolution 2006/30**.

Using alternative development programmes to reduce the cultivation of cannabis plants

243. At its 41st meeting, on 27 July, the Council adopted draft resolution II entitled "Using alternative development programmes to reduce the cultivation of cannabis plants",

recommended by the Commission (see E/2006/28, chap. I, sect. A). See Council **resolution 2006/31**.

Support for the National Drug Control Strategy of the Government of Afghanistan

244. At its 41st meeting, on 27 July, the Council adopted draft resolution III entitled "Support for the National Drug Control Strategy of the Government of Afghanistan", recommended by the Commission (see E/2006/28, chap. I, sect. A). See Council **resolution 2006/32**.

Strengthening international cooperation for alternative development, including preventive alternative development, with due regard for environmental protection

245. At its 41st meeting, on 27 July, the Council adopted draft resolution IV entitled "Strengthening international cooperation for alternative development, including preventive alternative development, with due regard for environmental protection", recommended by the Commission (see E/2006/28, chap. I, sect. A). See Council **resolution 2006/33**.

The need for a balance between demand for and supply of opiates used to meet medical and scientific needs

246. At its 41st meeting, on 27 July, the Council adopted draft resolution V entitled "The need for a balance between demand for and supply of opiates used to meet medical and scientific needs", recommended by the Commission (see E/2006/28, chap. I, sect. A). See Council **resolution 2006/34**.

Report of the Commission on Narcotic Drugs on its forty-ninth session and provisional agenda and documentation for the fiftieth session of the Commission

247. At its 41st meeting, on 27 July, the Council adopted draft decision I entitled "Report of the Commission on Narcotic Drugs on its forty-ninth session and provisional agenda and documentation for the fiftieth session of the Commission", recommended by the Commission (see E/2006/28, chap. I, sect. B). See Council **decision 2006/241**.

Document considered by the Council in connection with agenda item 14 (d): report of the International Narcotics Control Board

248. At its 41st meeting, on 27 July, the Council adopted draft decision II entitled "Report of the International Narcotics Control Board", recommended by the Commission (see E/2006/28, chap. I, sect. B). See Council **decision 2006/250**.

5. United Nations High Commissioner for Refugees

249. The Council held a discussion on the United Nations High Commissioner for Refugees (agenda item 14 (e)) at its 40th and 42nd meetings, on 26 and 27 July. An account of the discussion is contained in the relevant summary records (E/2006/SR.40 and 42). The Council had before it the following documents:

(a) Letter dated 8 March 2006 from the Deputy Permanent Representative of Costa Rica to the United Nations addressed to the Secretary-General (E/2006/3);

(b) Letter dated 30 May 2006 from the Permanent Representative of Estonia to the United Nations addressed to the Secretary-General (E/2006/82).

250. At the 40th meeting, on 26 July, two oral reports were presented by the Assistant High Commissioner for Refugees.

Action taken by the Council

251. Under agenda item 14 (e), the Council adopted **decision 2006/237**.

Enlargement of the Executive Committee of the Programme of the United Nations High Commissioner for Refugees

252. At the 40th meeting, on 26 July, the representative of Costa Rica and the observer for Estonia[1] introduced a draft decision (E/2006/L.9) entitled "Enlargement of the Executive Committee of the Programme of the United Nations High Commissioner for Refugees".

253. At the same meeting, the Council adopted the draft decision. See Council **decision 2006/237**.

6. Comprehensive implementation of and follow-up to the Durban Declaration and Programme of Action

254. No proposals were submitted under this sub-item.

7. Human rights

255. The Council considered the question of human rights (agenda item 14 (g)) at its 40th, 41st and 43rd meetings, on 26 to 28 July. An account of the discussion is contained in the relevant summary records (E/2006/SR.40, 41 and 43). The Council had before it the following documents:

(a) Report of the Committee on the Rights of the Child (A/61/41);[27]

(b) Report of the Committee on Economic, Social and Cultural Rights on its thirty-fourth and thirty-fifth sessions (E/2006/22);[28]

(c) Report of the Commission on Human Rights on its sixty-second session (E/2006/23);[29]

(d) Report of the United Nations High Commissioner for Human Rights (E/2006/86).

256. At the 40th meeting, on 26 July, an introductory statement was made by the Director of the Human Rights Procedures Division, Office of the United Nations High Commissioner for Human Rights.

Action taken by the Council

257. Under agenda item 14 (g), the Council adopted **decisions 2006/242** and **2006/250**.

258. At its 41st meeting, on 27 July, the Council decided to defer its consideration of the report of the Committee on the Rights of the Child (A/61/41) to its resumed substantive session. See Council **decision 2006/242**.

Documents considered under agenda item 14 (g)

259. At the same meeting, the Council took note of the report of the Commission on Human Rights on its sixty-second session (E/2006/23). See Council **decision 2006/250**.

260. At its 43rd meeting, on 28 July, on the proposal of the President of the Council, the Council took note of the report of the Committee on Economic, Social and Cultural Rights on its thirty-fourth and thirty-fifth sessions. See Council **decision 2006/250**.

8. Permanent Forum on Indigenous Issues

261. The Council considered agenda item 14 (h) at its 40th and 41st meetings, on 26 and 27 July. An account of the discussion is contained in the relevant summary records (E/2006/SR.40 and 41). The Council had before it the report of the Permanent Forum on Indigenous Issues on its fifth session (E/2006/43).[30]

Action taken by the Council

262. Under agenda item 14 (h), the Council adopted **decision 2006/243**.

Recommendations contained in the report of the Permanent Forum on Indigenous Issues on its fifth session

263. At the 41st meeting, on 27 July, the Secretary of the Council made a statement on the programme budget implications of the recommendations contained in the report of the Permanent Forum on Indigenous Issues on its fifth session (E/2006/L.18), specifically those related to draft decisions I and III (see E/2006/43, chap. I, sect. A).

264. At the same meeting, the Council decided to defer consideration of draft decisions I, II, III and IV, recommended by the Permanent Forum (see E/2006/43, chap. I, sect. A), to its resumed substantive session. See Council **decision 2006/243**.

Chapter VIII

Elections, nominations, confirmations and appointments

1. The Council considered the question of elections, nominations, confirmations and appointments at its organizational and resumed organizational sessions (agenda item 4) and its substantive session (agenda item 1). The question was considered by the Council at its 2nd, 9th to 11th and 41st meetings, on 7 February, 10 and 12 May and 27 July 2006. An account of the proceedings is contained in the relevant summary records (E/2006/SR.2, 9-11 and 41). The Council had before it the following documents:

(a) Annotated agenda for the organizational and resumed organizational sessions for 2006 (E/2006/2 and Add.1 and Add.1/Corr.1);

(b) Note by the Secretary-General on the election of members of the functional commissions of the Council (E/2006/9);

(c) Note by the Secretary-General on the election of 19 members of the Committee on Non-Governmental Organizations (E/2006/9/Add.1);

(d) Note by the Secretary-General on the election of 13 members of the Intergovernmental Working Group of Experts on International Standards of Accounting and Reporting (E/2006/9/Add.2);

(e) Note by the Secretary-General on the election of 14 members of the Executive Board of the United Nations Children's Fund (E/2006/9/Add.3);

(f) Note by the Secretary-General on the election of 14 members of the Executive Board of the United Nations Development Programme/United Nations Population Fund (E/2006/9/Add.4);

(g) Note by the Secretary-General on the election of six members of the Executive Board of the World Food Programme (E/2006/9/Add.5);

(h) Note by the Secretary-General on the election of 10 members of the Committee for the United Nations Population Award (E/2006/9/Add.6);

(i) Note by the Secretary-General on the election of 10 members of the Executive Board of the International Research and Training Institute for the Advancement of Women (E/2006/9/Add.7);

(j) Note by the Secretary-General on the election of nine members of the Programme Coordination Board of the Joint United Nations Programme on HIV/AIDS (UNAIDS) (E/2006/9/Add.8);

(k) Note by the Secretary-General on the election of 20 members of the Governing Council of the United Nations Human Settlements Programme (UN-Habitat) (E/2006/9/Add.9);

(l) Note by the Secretary-General on the appointment of a new member to the Committee of Experts on International Cooperation in Tax Matters (E/2006/9/Add.10);

(m) Note by the Secretary-General on the election of five members of the International Narcotics Control Board from among candidates nominated by Governments (E/2006/9/Add.11);

(n) Note by the Secretary-General on the election of five members of the International Narcotics Control Board from among candidates nominated by Governments: biographical information on candidates (E/2006/9/Add.12);

(o) Note by the Secretary-General on the election of two members of the International Narcotics Control Board under the provisions of article 9, paragraph 1 (a), of the Single Convention on Narcotic Drugs, 1961, as amended by the 1972 Protocol (E/2006/9/Add.13);

(p) Note by the Secretary-General on the nomination of 24 members of the Committee for Development Policy (E/2006/9/Add.14);

(q) Note by the Secretary-General on the nomination of seven members of the Committee for Programme and Coordination (E/2006/9/Add.15);

(r) Note by the Secretary-General on the election of nine members of the Committee on Economic, Social and Cultural Rights (E/2006/9/Add.16);

(s) Note by the Secretary-General on the election of nine members of the Committee on Economic, Social and Cultural Rights: biographical information on candidates (E/2006/9/Add.17).

Action taken by the Council

2. Under the item on elections, nominations, confirmations and appointments, the Council adopted **decisions 2006/201 A, B** and **C**.

Chapter IX

Organizational matters

1. The Council held its organizational session for 2006 at United Nations Headquarters on 17 January, 7 and 10 February, 14 and 22 March and 8 May 2006 (1st to 5th and 8th meetings); its resumed organizational session at United Nations Headquarters on 10 and 12 May 2006 (9th to 11th meetings); its special high-level meeting with the Bretton Woods institutions, the World Trade Organization and the United Nations Conference on Trade and Development at United Nations Headquarters on 24 April 2006 (6th and 7th meetings); its substantive session at the United Nations Office at Geneva from 3 to 28 July 2006 (12th to 43rd meetings); and its resumed substantive session at United Nations Headquarters ____ ____________ (____ to ____ meetings).

A. Organizational session

Opening of the Council

2. The 1st meeting, on 17 January 2006, was opened by the President of the Council for 2005, Munir Akram (Pakistan). Upon election, the President of the Council for 2006, Ali Hachani (Tunisia), made a statement.

Election of the Bureau

3. At its 1st and 5th meetings, on 17 January and 22 March, pursuant to paragraph 2 (k) of its resolution 1988/77, the Council elected by acclamation the following persons as Vice-Presidents of the Council for 2006: Dalius Čekuolis (Lithuania); Hjálmar W. Hannesson (Iceland); Prasad Kariyawasam (Sri Lanka); and Léo Mérorès (Haiti).

Agenda

4. At its 1st meeting, on 17 January, the Council considered the agenda of its organizational session. It had before it the annotated provisional agenda (E/2006/2).

5. At the same meeting, the Council adopted the agenda of the organizational session (see annex I).

Action taken by the Council

6. At its organizational session for 2006, the Council adopted 3 resolutions and 14 decisions concerning organizational matters. See Council **resolutions 2006/1** to **2006/3** and **decisions 2006/202** to **2006/215**.

Report of the Committee for Development Policy on its seventh session

7. At its 2nd meeting, on 7 February, the Council took note of the report of the Committee for Development Policy on its seventh session (E/2005/33) and endorsed the request of the Committee to be informed by the Secretary-General during the transition period on the implementation of the transition strategy of graduating countries and on their development progress, as laid out in General Assembly resolution 59/209, in order to enable the Committee to carry out the function assigned to it in paragraph 12 of that resolution. The Council requested the Committee to continue developing a consistent set of criteria that

could be applied to all recommendations regarding the inclusion and graduation from the list of least developed countries. See Council **resolution 2006/1**.

Implementation of General Assembly resolution 60/251

8. At its 5th meeting, on 22 March, the Council, having recalled its resolution 5 (I) of 16 February 1946, by which it had established the Commission on Human rights, and its subsequent relevant resolutions relating to the mandate of the Commission, and having also recalled General Assembly resolution 60/251 of 15 March 2006, requested the Commission to conclude its work at its sixty-second session, which should be short and procedural, and to transmit its final report to the Council; and decided to abolish the Commission with effect on 16 June 2006. See Council **resolution 2006/2**.

Membership of the Economic and Social Council on the Organizational Committee of the Peacebuilding Commission pursuant to paragraph 4 (b) of General Assembly resolution 60/180 and of Security Council resolution 1645 (2005)

9. At its 8th meeting, on 8 May, the Economic and Social Council, having recalled General Assembly resolution 60/180 of 20 December 2005 and Security Council resolution 1645 (2005) concurrently establishing the Peacebuilding Commission on 20 December 2005, decided that the distribution of the seven seats allocated to the Economic and Social Council on the Organizational Committee of the Peacebuilding Commission should be as follows:

(a) One seat for each of the five regional groups, namely, African States, Asian States, Eastern European States, Latin American and Caribbean States and Western European and other States;

(b) For the purpose of the first election, the two remaining seats should be allocated to the regional groups of African States and Asian States.

10. The Economic and Social Council also decided that members of the Council should be elected to the Organizational Committee for a two-year term with the possibility, as applicable, of sharing the term within the concerned regional group for the seats allocated to it, subject to the concurrence of the Council, and that elections from among its members to the Organizational Committee should be held every other year;

11. The Council further decided that the rules of procedure and established practice of the Council for the election of members of its subsidiary bodies should apply to the election of members of the Organizational Committee by the Council, and decided to hold the first election at a meeting of its organizational session for 2006. See Council **resolution 2006/3**.

Date of the special high-level meeting of the Economic and Social Council with the Bretton Woods institutions, the World Trade Organization and the United Nations Conference on Trade and Development

12. At its 2nd meeting, on 7 February, the Council decided that its special high-level meeting with the Bretton Woods institutions, the World Trade Organization and the United Nations Conference on Trade and Development would be held at Headquarters on 24 April 2006. See Council **decision 2006/202**.

Change of dates for the fifth session of the Committee of Experts on Public Administration

13. At its 2nd meeting, on 7 February, the Council decided to approve the change in dates for the holding of the fifth session of the Committee of Experts on Public Administration from 3 to 7 April 2006 to 27 to 31 March 2006. See Council **decision 2006/203**.

Participation of intergovernmental organizations in the work of the Council

14. At its 2nd meeting, on 7 February, Council decided to approve the request of the Inter-American Institute for Cooperation on Agriculture to participate as an observer in the work of the Council. See Council **decision 2006/204**.

Regional commissions: Economic Commission for Africa

15. At its 2nd meeting, on 7 February, the Council decided to approve the request that the thirty-ninth session of the Economic Commission for Africa be held in Ouagadougou from 10 to 14 May 2006. See Council **decision 2006/205**.

Adapting the work of the Economic and Social Council

16. At its 3rd meeting, on 10 February, the Council decided that, as soon as possible after the adoption by the General Assembly of its draft resolution in pursuance of paragraphs 155 and 156 of the 2005 World Summit Outcome, the President of the Council should convene consultations of the Council, on an as-available basis, to adapt its organization of work, agenda and current methods of work in pursuance of paragraphs 155 and 156 of the World Summit Outcome and the related Assembly resolution in that regard, with a view to having implementation begin in 2007. See Council **decision 2006/206**.

Request to reactivate the consideration of the inclusion of an item entitled "Observance by the Government of Myanmar of the International Labour Organization Forced Labour Convention, 1930 (No. 29)" in the agenda of the 2006 substantive session of the Council

17. At its 3rd meeting, on 10 February, the Council decided that the letter of the Director-General of the International Labour Organization of 30 June 2006 addressed to the Secretary-General (E/2006/11) should be placed under agenda item 14 (b) of the provisional agenda of the 2006 substantive session, entitled "Social development", for appropriate consideration by the Council. See Council **decision 2006/207**.

Provisional agenda for the substantive session of 2006 of the Economic and Social Council

18. At its 3rd meeting, on 10 February, the Council, having considered the document E/2006/1 containing its proposed basic programme of work for 2006 and 2007, approved the provisional agenda and documentation for its substantive session of 2006. See Council **decision 2006/208**.

Basic programme of work of the Economic and Social Council for 2007

19. At its 3rd meeting, on 10 February, the Council took note of the list of questions for inclusion in the programme of work of the Council for 2007. See Council **decision 2006/209**.

Working arrangements for the 2006 substantive session of the Economic and Social Council

20. At its 3rd meeting, on 10 February, the Council decided on the following working arrangements for its substantive session of 2006:

(a) The high-level segment would be held from 3 to 5 July 2006;

(b) Dialogue with the Executive Secretaries of the regional commissions would be held on 6 July 2006;

(c) The coordination segment would be held from 6 to 10 July 2006;

(d) The operational activities segment would be held from 11 to 13 July 2006;

(e) The humanitarian affairs segment would be held from 14 to 19 July 2006;

(f) The general segment would be held from 19 to 27 July 2006;

(g) The conclusion of the work of the Council would be held on 27 and 28 July 2006.

See Council **decision 2006/210**.

Theme for the item on regional cooperation of the substantive session of 2006 of the Economic and Social Council

21. At its 3rd meeting, on 10 February, the Council decided that the theme for the item on regional cooperation at its substantive session of 2006 would be "The regional dimension of creating an environment conducive to generating full and productive employment, and decent work for all, and its impact on sustainable development". See Council **decision 2006/211**.

Promoting an integrated approach to rural development in developing countries for poverty eradication and sustainable development

22. At its 3rd meeting, on 10 February, the Council decided to consider, at its regular organizational session in February 2007, the proposal to include a discussion on promoting an integrated approach to rural development in developing countries for poverty eradication and sustainable development at a future substantive session of the Council. See Council **decision 2006/212**.

International cooperation in tax matters

23. At its 3rd meeting, on 10 February, the Council decided to defer consideration of the report of the first session of the Committee of Experts on International Cooperation in Tax Matters (E/2005/45) to its 2006 substantive session in Geneva, under item 13 (h), entitled "Economic and environmental questions: international cooperation in tax matters", of the general segment. See Council **decision 2006/213**.

Theme for the humanitarian affairs segment of the substantive session of 2006 of the Economic and Social Council

24. At its 4th meeting, on 14 March, the Council decided:

(a) That the theme for the humanitarian affairs segment of its substantive session of 2006 would be: "Strengthening of the coordination of United Nations humanitarian assistance: implementing improved humanitarian response at all levels, including strengthening capacity, with particular attention to recent humanitarian emergencies including severe natural disasters";

(b) That it would convene two panels, the themes of which would be:

(i) "Gender-based violence in humanitarian emergencies";

(ii) "Chronically under-funded emergencies".

See Council **decision 2006/214**.

Operational activities segment of the substantive session of 2006 of the Economic and Social Council

25. At its 5th meeting, on 22 March, the Council decided that the work of the operational activities segment of its substantive session of 2006 should be devoted to examining the operational activities of the United Nations system in order to evaluate the implementation of General Assembly resolution 59/250 of 22 December 2004, with a view to ensuring its full implementation, including through a comprehensive review of trends and perspectives in funding for development cooperation, and in that context decided to apply Assembly decision 60/545 of 22 December 2005. See Council **decision 2006/215**.

B. Resumed organizational session

Agenda

26. At its 9th and 11th meetings, on 10 and 12 May 2006, the Council had before it the agenda of its resumed organizational session (E/2006/2/Add.1 and Add.1/Corr.1).

Action taken by the Council

27. At its resumed organizational session for 2006, the Council adopted 2 decisions concerning organizational matters. See Council **decisions 2006/216** and **2006/217**.

Participation of intergovernmental organizations in the work of the Economic and Social Council

28. At its 11th meeting, on 12 May, the Council decided to include in the agenda of its substantive session of 2006 the applications for observer status of two intergovernmental organizations: the Convention on Wetlands (E/2006/21) and the South Centre (E/2006/68). See Council **decision 2006/216**.

Economic and Social Council event to discuss relief to development

29. At its 11th meeting, on 12 May, the Council decided that the Council event to discuss relief to development, to be held in the morning of 14 July 2006, would be as follows: (a) the title of the event would be "Economic and Social Council event to discuss relief to development"; (b) the event would be an informal half-day activity; and (c) there would be no negotiated outcome. See Council **decision 2006/217**.

C. Substantive session

Action taken by the Council

30. At its substantive session of 2006, the Council adopted 4 decisions concerning organizational matters. See Council **decisions 2006/218, 2006/220, 2006/244** and **2006/245**.

Agenda

31. At its 12th meeting, on 3 July, the Council considered the agenda and organization of work of its substantive session of 2006. It had before it the following documents:

(a) Annotated provisional agenda for the substantive session of 2006 (E/2006/100);

(b) Proposed programme of work for the substantive session of 2006 (E/2006/L.4);

(c) Note by the Secretariat on the status of documentation for the session (E/2006/L.5);

(d) Updated status of documentation for the substantive session of the Economic and Social Council for 2006 (E/2006/CRP.5).

32. At the same meeting, the Council adopted the agenda for its substantive session of 2006 (see annex I) and approved the programme of work of the session; and, on the recommendation of the Committee on Non-Governmental Organizations, approved the requests made by non-governmental organizations to be heard by the Council at its substantive session of 2006 under agenda item 2 (E/2006/78). See Council **decision 2006/218**.

Requests from non-governmental organizations for hearings

33. See Council **decision 2006/218** (para. 32 above).

Multi-year work programme for the coordination segment and document considered under the item

34. At its 29th meeting, on 17 July, the Council decided to defer to a resumed session the finalization of the multi-year work programme for the coordination segment and to take note of the report of the Secretary-General on sustained economic growth for social development, including poverty eradication and hunger (E/2006/56). See Council **decision 2006/220**.

Applications of intergovernmental organizations for observer status with the Economic and Social Council

35. At its 41st meeting, on 27 July, the Council decided:

(a) To grant observer status to the Intergovernmental Forum on Mining, Minerals, Metals and Sustainable Development and the South Centre;

(b) To defer consideration of the application of the Ramsar Convention and the International Emergency Management Organization to its resumed substantive session.

See Council **decision 2006/244**.

World Tourism Organization

36. At its 41st meeting, on 27 July, the Council decided to defer to its resumed session the consideration of the Convention on the Privileges and Immunities of the Specialized Agencies: draft text relating to the World Tourism Organization. See Council **decision 2006/245**.

---

[1] *Report of the International Conference on Financing for Development, Monterrey, Mexico, 18-22 March 2002* (United Nations publication, Sales No. E.02.II.A.7), chap. I, resolution 1, annex.

[2] Official Records of the Economic and Social Council, 2006, Supplement No. 13 (E/2006/33).
[3] To be issued in *Official Records of the Economic and Social Council, 2006, Supplement No. 15* (E/2006/35).
[4] *Official Records of the Economic and Social Council, 2005, Supplement No. 14* (E/2005/34/Rev.1).
[5] Ibid., *Supplement No. 15* (E/2005/35).
[6] To be issued in *Official Records of the Economic and Social Council, 2006, Supplement No. 14* (E/2006/34/Rev.1).
[7] *Official Records of the Economic and Social Council, 2006, Supplement No. 16* (E/2006/36).
[8] In accordance with rule 72 of the rules of procedure of the Council.
[9] The delegation of Denmark subsequently indicated that, had it been present during the vote, its vote would have been recorded as an abstention.
[10] In accordance with General Assembly resolution 52/250.
[11] The complete report of the Committee on Non-Governmental Organizations on its 2006 regular session will be issued as *Official Records of the Economic and Social Council, 2006, Supplement No. 12* (E/2006/32).
[12] *Official Records of the Economic and Social Council, 2006, Supplement No. 9* (E/2006/29).
[13] Ibid., *Supplement No. 13* (E/2006/33).
[14] Ibid., *Supplement No. 11* (E/2006/31).
[15] Ibid., *Supplement No. 4* (E/2006/24).
[16] *Official Records of the General Assembly, Sixty-first Session, Supplement No. 25* (A/61/25).
[17] *Official Records of the Economic and Social Council, 2006, Supplement No. 5* (E/2006/25).
[18] Ibid., *Supplement No. 24* (E/2006/44).
[19] Ibid., *2005, Supplement No. 25* (E/2005/45).
[20] Ibid., *2006, Supplement No. 22* (E/2006/42 and Corr.1 and 2).
[21] Ibid., *Supplement No. 7* (E/2006/27 and Corr.1).
[22] The delegation of Canada subsequently indicated that, had it been present during the vote, it would have voted against the draft resolution. The delegations of Armenia, Brazil, Denmark, Guinea, Poland, the United Arab Emirates and the United Republic of Tanzania subsequently indicated that, had they been present, they would have voted in favour of the draft resolution.
[23] *Official Records of the Economic and Social Council, 2006, Supplement No. 6* (E/2006/26).
[24] Ibid., *Supplement No. 10* (E/2006/30).
[25] Ibid., *Supplement No. 8* (E/2006/28), chap. I, sect. C.
[26] United Nations publication, Sales No. E.06.XI.2.
[27] *Official Records of the General Assembly, Sixty-first Session, Supplement No. 41* (A/61/41).
[28] *Official Records of the Economic and Social Council, 2006, Supplement No. 2* (E/2006/22).
[29] Ibid., *Supplement No. 3* (E/2006/23).
[30] Ibid., *Supplement No. 23* (E/2006/43).
[31] The text of rule 79, entitled "Participation of other intergovernmental organizations", reads as follows: "Representatives of intergovernmental organizations accorded permanent observer status by the General Assembly and of other intergovernmental organizations designated on an ad hoc or a continuing basis by the Council on the recommendation of the Bureau may participate, without the right to vote, in the deliberations of the Council on questions within the scope of the activities of the organizations".
[32] Superseding the Organization of African Unity.

Annex I

Agendas of the organizational and resumed organizational sessions for 2006 and the substantive session of 2006

Agenda of the organizational and resumed organizational sessions for 2006 (E/2006/2 and Add.1 and Add.1/Corr.1)

Adopted by the Council at its 1st meeting, on 17 January 2006

1. Election of the Bureau.
2. Adoption of the agenda and other organizational matters.
3. Basic programme of work of the Council.
4. Elections, nominations, confirmations and appointments.

Agenda of the substantive session of 2006 (E/2006/100)

Adopted by the Council at its 12th meeting, on 3 July 2006

1. Adoption of the agenda and other organizational matters.

High-level segment

2. Creating an environment at the national and international levels conducive to generating full and productive employment and decent work for all, and its impact on sustainable development.

Operational activities of the United Nations for international development cooperation segment

3. Operational activities of the United Nations for international development cooperation:

   (a) Follow-up to policy recommendations of the General Assembly and the Council;

   (b) Reports of the Executive Boards of the United Nations Development Programme/ United Nations Population Fund, the United Nations Children's Fund and the World Food Programme.

Coordination segment

4. Sustained economic growth for social development, including the eradication of poverty and hunger.

Humanitarian affairs segment

5. Special economic, humanitarian and disaster relief assistance.

General segment

6. Implementation of and follow-up to major United Nations conferences and summits:

   (a) Follow-up to the International Conference on Financing for Development;

   (b) Review and coordination of the implementation of the Programme of Action for the Least Developed Countries for the Decade 2001-2010.

7. Coordination, programme and other questions:

(a) Reports of coordination bodies;

(b) Proposed strategic framework for the biennium 2008-2009;

(c) International cooperation in the field of informatics;

(d) Long-term programme of support for Haiti;

(e) Mainstreaming a gender perspective into all policies and programmes in the United Nations system;

(f) Information and Communication Technologies Task Force;

(g) Ad hoc advisory groups on African countries emerging from conflict;

(h) Tobacco or health.

8. Implementation of General Assembly resolutions 50/227, 52/12 B and 57/270 B.

9. Implementation of the Declaration on the Granting of Independence to Colonial Countries and Peoples by the specialized agencies and the international institutions associated with the United Nations.

10. Regional cooperation.

11. Economic and social repercussions of the Israeli occupation on the living conditions of the Palestinian people in the occupied Palestinian territory, including Jerusalem, and the Arab population in the occupied Syrian Golan.

12. Non-governmental organizations.

13. Economic and environmental questions:

(a) Sustainable development;

(b) Science and technology for development;

(c) Statistics;

(d) Human settlements;

(e) Environment;

(f) Population and development;

(g) Public administration and development;

(h) International cooperation in tax matters;

(i) United Nations Forum on Forests;

(j) Assistance to third States affected by the application of sanctions;

(k) Cartography;

(l) Women and development.

14. Social and human rights questions:

(a) Advancement of women;

(b) Social development;

(c) Crime prevention and criminal justice;

(d) Narcotic drugs;

(e) United Nations High Commissioner for Refugees;

(f) Comprehensive implementation of and follow-up to the Durban Declaration and Programme of Action;

(g) Human rights;

(h) Permanent Forum on Indigenous Issues.

Annex II

Intergovernmental organizations designated by the Council under rule 79 of the rules of procedure[31] for participation in the deliberations of the Council on questions within the scope of their activities

Organizations and other entities accorded permanent observer status by the General Assembly

African, Caribbean and Pacific Group of States (General Assembly resolution 36/4)

African Development Bank (General Assembly resolution 42/10)

African Union[32] (General Assembly resolution 2011 (XX) and Assembly decision 56/475)

Agency for the Prohibition of Nuclear Weapons in Latin America and the Caribbean (General Assembly resolution 43/6)

Andean Community (General Assembly resolution 52/6)

Asian-African Legal Consultative Organization (General Assembly resolution 35/2)

Asian Development Bank (General Assembly resolution 57/30)

Association of Caribbean States (General Assembly resolution 53/5)

Black Sea Economic Cooperation Organization (General Assembly resolution 54/5)

Caribbean Community (General Assembly resolution 46/8)

Central American Integration System (General Assembly resolution 50/2)

Commonwealth of Independent States (General Assembly resolution 48/237)

Commonwealth Secretariat (General Assembly resolution 31/3)

Community of Portuguese-speaking Countries (General Assembly resolution 54/10)

Community of Sahelo-Saharan States (General Assembly resolution 56/92)

Council of Europe (General Assembly resolution 44/6)

Customs Cooperation Council (General Assembly resolution 53/216)

East African Community (General Assembly resolution 58/86)

Economic Community of Central African States (General Assembly resolution 55/161)

Economic Cooperation Organization (General Assembly resolution 48/2)

Eurasian Economic Community (General Assembly resolution 58/84)

European Community (General Assembly resolution 3208 (XXIX))

GUUAM (General Assembly resolution 58/85)

Holy See (General Assembly resolution 58/314)

Inter-American Development Bank (General Assembly resolution 55/160)

International Centre for Migration Policy Development (General Assembly resolution 57/31)

International Committee of the Red Cross (General Assembly resolution 45/6)

International Criminal Police Organization (Interpol) (General Assembly resolution 51/1)

International Development Law Institute (General Assembly resolution 56/90)

International Federation of the Red Cross and Red Crescent Societies (General Assembly resolution 49/2)

International Hydrographic Organization (General Assembly resolution 56/91)

International Institute for Democracy and Electoral Assistance in the General Assembly (General Assembly resolution 58/83)

International Organization for Migration (General Assembly resolution 47/4)

International Organization of la Francophonie (General Assembly resolution 33/18)

International Seabed Authority (General Assembly resolution 51/6)

International Tribunal for the Law of the Sea (General Assembly resolution 51/204)

International Union for the Conservation of Nature and Natural Resources (General Assembly resolution 54/195)

Inter-Parliamentary Union (General Assembly resolution 57/32)

Latin American Economic System (SELA) (General Assembly resolution 35/3)

Latin American Parliament (General Assembly resolution 48/4)

League of Arab States (General Assembly resolution 477 (V))

Organization for Economic Cooperation and Development (General Assembly resolution 53/6)

Organization for Security and Cooperation in Europe (General Assembly resolution 48/5)

Organization of American States (General Assembly resolution 253 (III))

Organization of the Islamic Conference (General Assembly resolution 3369 (XXX))

Pacific Islands Forum (General Assembly resolution 49/1)

Palestine (General Assembly resolution 52/250)

Partners in Population and Development (General Assembly resolution 57/29)

Permanent Court of Arbitration (General Assembly resolution 48/3)

Sovereign Military Order of Malta (General Assembly resolution 48/265)

Organizations designated by the Economic and Social Council

Participation on a continuing basis

African Regional Centre for Technology (Council decision 1980/151)

Asian and Pacific Development Centre (Council decision 2000/213)

Asian Productivity Organization (APO) (Council decision 1980/114)

Common Fund for Commodities (Council decision 2003/221)

Council of Arab Economic Unity (Council decision 109 (LIX))

Global Water Partnership (Council decision 2005/233)

Helsinki Commission (Council decision 2003/312)

Institution for the Use of Micro-alga Spirulina against Malnutrition (Council decision 2003/212)

Intergovernmental Forum on Mining, Minerals, Metals and Sustainable Development (Council decision 2006/244)

International Association of Economic and Social Councils and Similar Institutions (IAESCSI) (Council decision 2001/318)

International Centre for Genetic Engineering and Biotechnology (Council decision 1997/215)

International Centre for Public Enterprises in Developing Countries (ICPE) (Council decision 1980/114)

Islamic Development Bank (Council decision 2003/221)

Islamic Educational, Scientific and Cultural Organization (Council decision 2003/221)

Latin American Energy Organization (OLADE) (Council decision 1980/114)

Organization of Ibero-American States for Education, Science and Culture (Council decision 1986/156)

Organization of Petroleum Exporting Countries (Council decision 109 (LIX))

Regional Organization for the Protection of the Marine Environment (Council decision 1992/265)

South Centre (Council decision 2006/244)

Union économique et monétaire ouest africaine (Council decision 2005/233)

Union of Economic and Social Councils of Africa (Council decision 1996/225)

World Deserts Foundation (Council decision 2004/231)

World Tourism Organization (Council decision 109 (LIX))

Participation on an ad hoc basis

African Accounting Council (Council decision 1987/161)

African Cultural Institute (Council decision 1987/161)

Arab Security Studies and Training Centre (Council decision 1989/165)

Council of Arab Ministers of the Interior (Council decision 1987/161)

International Bauxite Association (Council decision 1987/161)

International Civil Defence Organization (Council decision 109 (LIX))

Latin American Faculty of Social Sciences (Council decision 239 (LXII))

Annex III

Composition of the Council and its subsidiary and related bodies

ECONOMIC AND SOCIAL COUNCIL
(54 members; three-year term)

Membership in 2006	*Membership in 2007*[a]	*Term expires on 31 December*
Albania	Albania	2007
Angola	Angola	2008
Armenia	Australia	2007
Australia	Austria	2008
Austria	Benin	2008
Bangladesh	Brazil	2007
Belgium	Chad	2007
Belize	China	2007
Benin	Costa Rica	2007
Brazil	Cuba	2008
Canada	Czech Republic	2008
Chad	Democratic Republic of the Congo	2007
China	Denmark	2007
Colombia	France	2008
Costa Rica	Germany	2008
Cuba	Guinea	2007
Czech Republic	Guinea-Bissau	2008
Democratic Republic of the Congo	Guyana	2008
Denmark	Haiti	2008
France	Iceland	2007
Germany	India	2007
Guinea	Japan	2008
Guinea-Bissau	Lithuania	2007

Membership in 2006	Membership in 2007[a]	Term expires on 31 December
Guyana	Madagascar	2008
Haiti	Mauritania	2008
Iceland	Mexico	2007
India	Pakistan	2007
Indonesia	Paraguay	2008
Italy	Russian Federation	2007
Japan	Saudi Arabia	2008
Lithuania	South Africa	2007
Madagascar	Spain	2008
Mauritania	Sri Lanka	2008
Mauritius	Thailand	2007
Mexico	Turkey	2008
Namibia	United Kingdom of Great Britain and Northern Ireland	2007
Nigeria		
Pakistan		
Panama		
Paraguay		
Poland		
Republic of Korea		
Russian Federation		
Saudi Arabia		
South Africa		
Spain		
Sri Lanka		
Thailand		
Tunisia		
Turkey		
United Arab Emirates		
United Kingdom of Great Britain and Northern Ireland		
United Republic of Tanzania		
United States of America		

FUNCTIONAL COMMISSIONS AND SUBCOMMISSIONS
STATISTICAL COMMISSION
(24 members; four-year term)

Membership in 2006	Membership in 2007	Term expires on 31 December
Canada	Canada	2009
Cape Verde	Cape Verde	2007
China	China	2008

Membership in 2006	*Membership in 2007*	*Term expires on 31 December*
Colombia	Colombia	2008
Croatia	Croatia	2007
Cuba	Cuba	2007
Democratic Republic of the Congo	Democratic Republic of the Congo	2009
Finland	Finland	2009
France	France	2009
Germany	Germany	2008
Hungary	Hungary	2008
Iran (Islamic Republic of)	Iran (Islamic Republic of)	2007
Jamaica	Jamaica	2009
Japan	Japan	2008
Kenya	Kenya	2007
Mauritania	Mauritania	2009
Mexico	Mexico	2008
Netherlands	Netherlands	2008
Republic of Korea	Republic of Korea	2007
Russian Federation	Russian Federation	2009
South Africa	South Africa	2009
Ukraine	Ukraine	2007
United Kingdom of Great Britain and Northern Ireland	United Kingdom of Great Britain and Northern Ireland	2008
United States of America	United States of America	2007

COMMISSION ON POPULATION AND DEVELOPMENT[b]
(47 members; four-year term)

Membership of the thirty-ninth session	*Membership of the fortieth session*	*Term expires at close of session in the year*
Armenia	Armenia	2008
Bangladesh	Bangladesh	2009
Belgium	Belgium	2009
Bolivia	Bolivia	2007
Botswana	Brazil	2009
Brazil	Bulgaria	2009
Bulgaria	Cameroon	2009
Cameroon	Canada	2009
Canada	China	2010
China	Comoros	2009
Comoros	Democratic Republic of the Congo	2007
Democratic Republic of the Congo	El Salvador	2007
El Salvador	France	2008

Membership of the thirty-ninth session	*Membership of the fortieth session*	*Term expires at close of session in the year*
France	Gambia	2010
Gambia	Germany	2009
Germany	Guyana	2009
Guyana	Haiti	2008
Haiti	Hungary	2007
Hungary	India	2010
India	Indonesia	2009
Indonesia	Iran (Islamic Republic of)	2007
Iran (Islamic Republic of)	Jamaica	2010
Ireland	Japan	2008
Jamaica	Kenya	2008
Japan	Lebanon	2010
Kenya	Libyan Arab Jamahiriya	2008
Lebanon	Luxembourg	2007
Libyan Arab Jamahiriya	Madagascar	2008
Luxembourg	Malaysia	2009
Madagascar	Mauritania	2007
Malaysia	Mexico	2010
Mauritania	Morocco	2009
Mexico	Netherlands	2008
Morocco	Oman	2010
Netherlands	Pakistan	2008
Nicaragua	Peru	2009
Nigeria	Philippines	2007
Pakistan	Russian Federation	2010
Peru	Sierra Leone	2010
Philippines	South Africa	2010
Poland	Sweden	2010
Russian Federation	Switzerland	2009
Sweden	Ukraine	2010
Switzerland	United Kingdom of Great Britain and Northern Ireland	2010
Thailand	United States of America	2010
United States of America	Uruguay	2010
Zambia	Zambia	2010

COMMISSION FOR SOCIAL DEVELOPMENT[c]
(46 members; four-year term)

Membership of the forty-fourth and forty-fifth sessions	*Term expiresat closeof session inthe year*
Angola	2009
Argentina	2007
Bangladesh	2009
Bolivia	2009
Central African Republic	2007
Chile	2008
China	2009
Côte d'Ivoire	2008
Czech Republic	2009
Democratic People's Republic of Korea	2009
Democratic Republic of the Congo	2009
Dominican Republic	2007
Ethiopia	2008
Finland	2009
France	2008
Germany	2008
Haiti	2008
India	2007
Indonesia	2008
Iran (Islamic Republic of)	2007
Italy	2009
Japan	2008
Libyan Arab Jamahiriya	2007
Mali	2008
Malta	2007
Monaco	2009
Myanmar	2009
Netherlands	2009
Pakistan	2007
Paraguay	2009
Peru	2008
Republic of Korea	2008
Republic of Moldova	2008
Romania	2007
Russian Federation	2008
Senegal	2007
Spain	2007
South Africa	2009
Suriname	2007
Tunisia	2008
Turkey	2007
Ukraine	2009

Membership of the forty-fourth and forty-fifth sessions	*Term expiresat closeof session inthe year*
United Republic of Tanzania	2009
United States of America	2008
Venezuela (Bolivarian Republic of)	2009
Zambia	2007

COMMISSION ON HUMAN RIGHTS[d]
(53 members)

Membership of the sixty-second session (2006)

Argentina	India
Armenia	Indonesia
Australia	Italy
Austria	Japan
Azerbaijan	Kenya
Bangladesh	Malaysia
Bhutan	Mauritania
Botswana	Mexico
Brazil	Morocco
Cameroon	Nepal
Canada	Netherlands
China	Nigeria
Congo	Pakistan
Costa Rica	Peru
Cuba	Qatar
Dominican Republic	Republic of Korea
Ecuador	Romania
Egypt	Russian Federation
Eritrea	Saudi Arabia
Ethiopia	South Africa
Finland	Sudan
France	Togo
Germany	United Kingdom of Great Britain and Northern Ireland
Guatemala	United States of America
Guinea	Venezuela (Bolivarian Republic of)
Honduras	Zimbabwe
Hungary	

COMMISSION ON THE STATUS OF WOMEN[e]
(45 members; four-year term)

Membership of the fiftieth session	*Membership of the fifty-first session*	*Term expires at close of session in the year*
Algeria	Algeria	2007
Armenia	Armenia	2007
Belgium	Belgium	2007
Belize	Belize	2009
Bolivia	Bolivia	2007
Botswana	Brazil	2010
Burkina Faso	Cameroon	2010
Canada	Canada	2007
China	China	2008
Congo	Congo	2007
Croatia	Croatia	2009
Cuba	Djibouti	2010
Dominican Republic	Dominican Republic	2008
El Salvador	Ecuador	2010
Gabon	El Salvador	2008
Germany	Germany	2009
Ghana	Ghana	2008
Guatemala	Hungary	2008
Hungary	Iceland	2008
Iceland	India	2007
India	Indonesia	2010
Indonesia	Iran (Islamic Republic of)	2010
Iran (Islamic Republic of)	Japan	2009
Japan	Kazakhstan	2008
Kazakhstan	Lesotho	2010
Malaysia	Malaysia	2010
Mali	Mali	2009
Mauritius	Mauritius	2008
Morocco	Mexico	2010
Netherlands	Morocco	2009
Nicaragua	Netherlands	2009
Nigeria	Nigeria	2007
Peru	Peru	2009
Qatar	Qatar	2009
Republic of Korea	Republic of Korea	2010
Russian Federation	Russian Federation	2007
South Africa	Suriname	2008
Sudan	Thailand	2007
Suriname	Togo	2010
Thailand	Turkey	2007
Turkey	United Arab Emirates	2010

Membership of the fiftieth session	*Membership of the fifty-first session*	*Term expires at close of session in the year*
United Arab Emirates	United Kingdom of Great Britain and Northern Ireland	2009
United Kingdom of Great Britain and Northern Ireland	United Republic of Tanzania	2009
United Republic of Tanzania	Unites States of America	2008
United States of America	Zambia	2010

COMMISSION ON NARCOTIC DRUGS
(53 members; four-year term)

Membership in 2006 and 2007	*Term expires on 31 December*
Algeria	2007
Argentina	2007
Australia	2009
Austria	2007
Belgium	2009
Bolivia	2009
Bosnia and Herzegovina	2007
Brazil	2007
Cameroon	2007
Canada	2009
Chile	2007
Colombia	2009
Croatia	2007
Cuba	2007
Democratic Republic of the Congo	2007
France	2007
Germany	2007
Guatemala	2007
Hungary	2007
India	2007
Iran (Islamic Republic of)	2007
Israel	2007
Italy	2007
Jamaica	2009
Japan	2009
Lao People's Democratic Republic	2007
Lebanon	2007
Madagascar	2007
Malaysia	2007
Mexico	2009

Membership in 2006 and 2007	Term expires on 31 December
Myanmar	2007
Namibia	2009
Niger	2009
Nigeria	2009
Norway	2007
Peru	2007
Poland	2009
Republic of Korea	2009
Russian Federation	2009
Saudi Arabia	2009
Senegal	2009
Sudan	2007
Sweden	2007
Switzerland	2007
Tajikistan	2009
Thailand	2007
Turkey	2009
Uganda	2007
Ukraine	2009
United Arab Emirates	2007
United Kingdom of Great Britain and Northern Ireland	2009
United States of America	2007
Zambia	2007

COMMISSION ON CRIME PREVENTION AND CRIMINAL JUSTICE
(40 members; three-year term)

Membership in 2006	Membership in 2007	Term expires on 31 December
Armenia	Argentina	2009
Austria	Armenia	2008
Bolivia	Austria	2008
Botswana	Bolivia	2008
Brazil	Brazil	2009
Burundi	Cameroon	2009
Canada	Canada	2009
Chile	Chile	2008
China	China	2008
Comoros	Colombia	2009
Costa Rica	Comoros	2008
Cuba	Costa Rica	2008

Membership in 2006	Membership in 2007	Term expires on 31 December
Czech Republic	Democratic Republic of the Congo	2008
Democratic Republic of the Congo	Germany	2008
Egypt	Guatemala	2009
Finland	India	2009
Germany	Indonesia	2009
India	Iran (Islamic Republic of)	2009
Indonesia	Italy	2008
Iran (Islamic Republic of)	Jamaica	2009
Italy	Japan	2008
Jamaica	Libyan Arab Jamahiriya	2008
Japan	Namibia	2008
Libyan Arab Jamahiriya	Niger	2008
Mexico	Nigeria	2009
Namibia	Pakistan	2008
Niger	Republic of Korea	2008
Nigeria	Republic of Moldova	2009
Pakistan	Russian Federation	2008
Paraguay	Saudi Arabia	2009
Republic of Korea	Senegal	2008
Russian Federation	Sierra Leone	2009
Saudi Arabia	South Africa	2009
Senegal	Turkey20	2009
Thailand	Uganda	2008
Uganda	Ukraine	2009
Ukraine	United Arab Emirates	2009
United Kingdom of Great Britain and Northern Ireland	United Kingdom of Great Britain and Northern Ireland	2009
United Republic of Tanzania[f]	United Republic of Tanzania	2008
United States of America	United States of America	2009

COMMISSION ON SUSTAINABLE DEVELOPMENTG
(53 members; three-year term)

Membership of the fourteenth session	Membership of the fifteenth session	Term expires at close of session in the year
Algeria	Algeria	2007
Australia	Antigua and Barbuda	2009
Austria	Australia	2009
Belarus	Austria	2007
Belgium	Belarus	2008
Belize	Belgium	2008
Bolivia	Belize	2008

Membership of the fourteenth session	Membership of the fifteenth session	Term expires at close of session in the year
Brazil	Bolivia	2008
Burkina Faso	Brazil	2007
Cameroon	Burkina Faso	2007
Canada	Cameroon	2008
China	Canada	2008
Colombia	Chile	2009
Cuba	China	2008
Democratic People's Republic of Korea	Colombia	2007
Democratic Republic of the Congo	Cuba	2008
Ethiopia	Czech Republic	2009
Fiji	Democratic People's Republic of Korea	2008
Finland	Democratic Republic of the Congo	2008
France	Djibouti	2009
Georgia	Finland	2007
Germany	France	2007
Ghana	Georgia	2007
Guinea-Bissau	Germany	2008
Honduras	Ghana	2007
Hungary	Indonesia	2009
Iran (Islamic Republic of)	Iran (Islamic Republic of)	2007
Israel	Israel	2008
Italy	Italy	2008
Jamaica	Kazakhstan	2007
Japan	Kuwait	2009
Kazakhstan	Luxembourg	2007
Luxembourg	Mexico	2008
Mexico	Pakistan	2007
Netherlands	Paraguay	2007
Pakistan	Peru	2009
Paraguay	Qatar	2007
Qatar	Republic of Korea	2009
Republic of Korea	Russian Federation	2009
Russian Federation	Saudi Arabia	2008
Saint Lucia	Senegal	2009
Saudi Arabia	Serbia	2008
Serbia and Montenegro	Sierra Leone	2007
Sierra Leone	Spain	2009
Sudan	Sudan	2009
Thailand	Thailand	2008
The former Yugoslav Republic of Macedonia	The former Yugoslav Republic of Macedonia	2007

Membership of the fourteenth session	*Membership of the fifteenth session*	*Term expires at close of session in the year*
Tunisia	Tunisia	2008
Uganda	United Kingdom of Great Britain and Northern Ireland	2009
United Kingdom of Great Britain and Northern Ireland	United Republic of Tanzania	2009
United States of America	United States of America	2009
Zambia	Zambia	2008
Zimbabwe	Zimbabwe	2008

COMMISSION ON SCIENCE AND TECHNOLOGY FOR DEVELOPMENT
(33 members; four-year term)

Membership in 2006	*Membership in 2007*[h]	*Term expires on 31 December*
Angola	Angola	2008
Austria	Austria	2008
Bangladesh	Belarus	2010
Belarus	Brazil	2008
Belgium	China	2010
Bolivia	Cuba	2010
Brazil	Democratic Republic of the Congo	2008
Chile	Dominican Republic	2010
China	El Salvador	2010
Democratic Republic of the Congo	Eritrea	2010
Ethiopia	France	2010
Gambia	Gambia	2008
Germany	Germany	2010
Greece	India	2010
India	Iran (Islamic Republic of)	2010
Iran (Islamic Republic of)	Italy	2008
Italy	Jamaica	2008
Jamaica	Jordan	2008
Jordan	Latvia	2010
Lesotho	Lesotho	2010
Morocco	Malaysia	2010
Oman	Oman	2008
Pakistan	Pakistan	2008
Paraguay	Peru	2008
Peru	Russian Federation	2008
Romania	Sierra Leone	2008
Russian Federation	Slovakia	2008

Membership in 2006	*Membership in 2007*[h]	*Term expires on 31 December*
Sierra Leone	Switzerland	2008
Slovakia	Tunisia	2010
Sudan	Uganda	2010
Switzerland[i]	United Kingdom of Great Britain and Northern Ireland	2008
Turkey		
United Kingdom of Great Britain and Northern Ireland		

United Nations Forum on Forests

The membership of the Forum comprises all States Members of the United Nations and States members of the specialized agencies (see Council resolution 2000/35).

REGIONAL COMMISSIONS
ECONOMIC COMMISSION FOR AFRICA*
(53 members)

Algeria	Libyan Arab Jamahiriya
Angola	Madagascar
Benin	Malawi
Botswana	Mali
Burkina Faso	Mauritania
Burundi	Mauritius
Cameroon	Morocco
Cape Verde	Mozambique
Central African Republic	Namibia
Chad	Niger
Comoros	Nigeria
Congo	Rwanda
Côte d'Ivoire	Sao Tome and Principe
Democratic Republic of the Congo	Senegal
Djibouti	Seychelles
Egypt	Sierra Leone
Equatorial Guinea	Somalia
Eritrea	South Africa
Ethiopia	Sudan
Gabon	Swaziland
Gambia	Togo
Ghana	Tunisia
Guinea	Uganda
Guinea-Bissau	United Republic of Tanzania

Kenya	Zambia
Lesotho	Zimbabwe
Liberia	

* Switzerland participates in a consultative capacity in the work of the Commission by virtue of Council resolution 925 (XXXIV) of 6 July 1962.

ECONOMIC COMMISSION FOR EUROPE* (56 members)

Albania	Liechtenstein
Andorra	Lithuania
Armenia	Luxembourg
Austria	Malta
Azerbaijan	Monaco
Belarus	Montenegro[j]
Belgium	Netherlands
Bosnia and Herzegovina	Norway
Bulgaria	Poland
Canada	Portugal
Croatia	Republic of Moldova
Cyprus	Romania
Czech Republic	Russian Federation
Denmark	San Marino
Estonia	Serbia[j]
Finland	Slovakia
France	Slovenia
Georgia	Spain
Germany	Sweden
Greece	Switzerland
Hungary	Tajikistan
Iceland	The former Yugoslav Republic of Macedonia
Ireland	Turkey
Israel	Turkmenistan
Italy	Ukraine
Kazakhstan	United Kingdom of Great Britain and Northern Ireland
Kyrgyzstan	United States of America
Latvia	Uzbekistan

* The Holy See participates in the work of the Commission in accordance with Commission decision N (XXXI) of 5 April 1976.

ECONOMIC COMMISSION FOR LATIN AMERICA AND THE CARIBBEAN*
(43 members)

Antigua and Barbuda	Honduras
Argentina	Italy
Bahamas	Jamaica
Barbados	Japan[k]
Belize	Mexico
Bolivia	Netherlands
Brazil	Nicaragua
Canada	Panama
Chile	Paraguay
Colombia	Peru
Costa Rica	Portugal
Cuba	Saint Kitts and Nevis
Dominica	Saint Lucia
Dominican Republic	Saint Vincent and the Grenadines
Ecuador	Spain
El Salvador	Suriname
France	Trinidad and Tobago
Germany	
Grenada	United Kingdom of Great Britain and Northern Ireland
Guatemala	United States of America
Guyana	Uruguay
Haiti	Venezuela (Bolivarian Republic of)

Associate members (8)

Anguilla	Netherlands Antilles
Aruba	Puerto Rico
British Virgin Islands	Turks and Caicos Islands[l]
Montserrat	United States Virgin Islands

* Germany and Switzerland participate in a consultative capacity in the work of the Commission by virtue of Council resolutions 632 (XXII) of 19 December 1956 and 861 (XXXII) of 21 December 1961, respectively.

ECONOMIC AND SOCIAL COMMISSION FOR ASIA AND THE PACIFIC*
(53 members)

Afghanistan	Nauru
Armenia	Nepal
Australia	Netherlands
Azerbaijan	New Zealand
Bangladesh	Pakistan

Bhutan	Palau
Brunei Darussalam	Papua New Guinea
Cambodia	Philippines
China	Republic of Korea
Democratic People's Republic of Korea	Russian Federation
Fiji	Samoa
France	Singapore
Georgia	Solomon Islands
India	Sri Lanka
Indonesia	Tajikistan
Iran (Islamic Republic of)	Thailand
Japan	Timor-Leste
Kazakhstan	Tonga
Kiribati	Turkey
Kyrgyzstan	Turkmenistan
Lao People's Democratic Republic	Tuvalu
Malaysia	
Maldives	United Kingdom of Great Britain and Northern Ireland
Marshall Islands	United States of America
Micronesia (Federated States of)	Uzbekistan
Mongolia	Vanuatu
Myanmar	Viet Nam
Associate members (9)	
American Samoa	Guam
Commonwealth of the Northern Mariana Islands	Hong Kong, China
	Macau, China
Cook Islands	New Caledonia
French Polynesia	Niue

* Switzerland participates in a consultative capacity in the work of the Commission by virtue of Council resolution 860 (XXXII) of 21 December 1961.

ECONOMIC AND SOCIAL COMMISSION FOR WESTERN ASIA (13 members)

Bahrain	Palestine
Egypt	Qatar
Iraq	Saudi Arabia
Jordan	Syrian Arab Republic
Kuwait	United Arab Emirates
Lebanon	Yemen
Oman	

STANDING COMMITTEES
COMMITTEE FOR PROGRAMME AND COORDINATION
(34 members; three-year term)

Membership in 2006[m]	*Membership in 2007*[m,n]	*Term expires on 31 December*
Algeria	Algeria	2007
Argentina	Argentina	2008
Armenia	Armenia	2008
Bahamas	Belarus	2008
Belarus	Benin	2008
Benin	Brazil	2008
Brazil	Bulgaria	2008
Bulgaria	Central African Republic	2008
Central African Republic	China	2007
China	Cuba	2008
Comoros	Ghana	2007
Cuba	India	2008
France	Indonesia	2008
Ghana	Iran (Islamic Republic of)	2008
India	Israel	2008
Indonesia	Italy	2008
Iran (Islamic Republic of)	Jamaica 2007	2007
Israel[o]	Japan	2007
Italy	Kenya	2007
Jamaica	Pakistan	2008
Japan	Portugal	2008
Kenya	Republic of Korea	2007
Mexico	Senegal	2008
Pakistan	South Africa	2008
Portugal	Switzerland	2008
Republic of Korea	Uruguay	2008
Russian Federation		
Senegal		
South Africa		
Switzerland		
United States of America		
Uruguay		
Zimbabwe		

COMMITTEE ON NON-GOVERNMENTAL ORGANIZATIONS
(19 members; four-year term)

Membership in 2006	*Membership from 1 January 2007 to 31 December 2010*
Cameroon	Angola
Chile	Burundi
China	China
Colombia	Colombia
Côte d'Ivoire	Cuba
Cuba	Dominica
France	Egypt
Germany	Guinea
India	India
Iran (Islamic Republic of)	Israel
Pakistan	Pakistan
Peru	Peru
Romania	Qatar
Russian Federation	Romania
Senegal	Russian Federation
Sudan	Sudan
Turkey	Turkey
United States of America	
Zimbabwe	United Kingdom of Great Britain and Northern Ireland
	United States of America

EXPERT BODIES

COMMITTEE OF EXPERTS ON THE TRANSPORT OF DANGEROUS GOODS AND ON THE GLOBALLY HARMONIZED SYSTEM OF CLASSIFICATION AND LABELLING OF CHEMICALS

SUBCOMMITTEE OF EXPERTS ON THE TRANSPORT OF DANGEROUS GOODS
(27 members)

Argentina	Japan
Australia	Mexico
Austria	Morocco
Belgium	Netherlands
Brazil	Norway
Canada	Poland
China	Portugal
Czech Republic	Russian Federation
Finland	South Africa
France	Spain
Germany	Sweden
India	
Iran (Islamic Republic of)	United Kingdom of Great Britain and Northern Ireland
Italy	United States of America

SUBCOMMITTEE OF EXPERTS ON THE GLOBALLY HARMONIZED SYSTEM OF CLASSIFICATION AND LABELLING OF CHEMICALS

(32 members)

Argentina	Japan
Australia	Netherlands
Austria	New Zealand
Belgium	Norway
Brazil	Poland
Canada	Portugal
China	Qatar
Czech Republic	Senegal
Denmark	Serbia
Finland	South Africa
France	Spain
Germany	Sweden
Greece	Ukraine
Iran (Islamic Republic of)	
Ireland	United Kingdom of Great Britain and Northern Ireland
Italy	United States of America
	Zambia

INTERGOVERNMENTAL WORKING GROUP OF EXPERTS ON INTERNATIONAL STANDARDS OF ACCOUNTING AND REPORTING

(34 members; three-year term)

Membership in 2006[p]	*Membership in 2007*[p,q]	*Term expires on 31 December*
Argentina	Benin	2009
Benin	Burundi	2009
Brazil	China	2008
Burundi	Cyprus	2009
China	Germany	2008
Cyprus	Italy	2008
Czech Republic	Lebanon	2008
Germany	Malta	2008
Italy	Namibia	2008
Lebanon	Nigeria	2009
Malaysia	Panama	2008
Malta	Poland	2009
Mexico	Portugal	2008
Namibia	Russian Federation	2008
Nigeria	Senegal	2008
Pakistan	Slovakia	2009
Panama	South Africa	2008
Portugal	Sri Lanka	2008

Poland	Sweden	2008
Russian Federation	Tunisia	2009
Senegal	Uganda	2008
South Africa	United Kingdom of Great Britain and Northern Ireland	
Sri Lanka[f]	United Republic of Tanzania	2008
Sweden		2008
Thailand		
Tunisia		
Uganda		
United Kingdom of Great Britain and Northern Ireland		
United Republic of Tanzania		

COMMITTEE FOR DEVELOPMENT POLICY

(24 members; three-year term)

Membership in 2006

N'Dri Thérèse Assié-Lumumba (Côte d'Ivoire)
Iskra Beleva (Bulgaria)
Patricia Bifani-Richard (Chile-Italy)
Albert Binger (Jamaica)
Olav Bjerkholt (Norway)
Gui Ying Cao (China)
Eugenio B. Figueroa (Chile)
Leonid M. Grigoriev (Russian Federation)
Heba Handoussa (Egypt)
Hiroya Ichikawa (Japan)
Willene Johnson (United States of America)
Marju Lauristin (Estonia)
P. Jayendra Nayak (India)
Milivoje Pani (United Kingdom of Great Britain and Northern Ireland)
Carola Pessino (Argentina)
Suchitra Punyaratabandhu (Thailand)
Sylvia Saborio (Costa Rica)
Nasser Hassan Saidi (Lebanon)
Udo Ernst Simonis (Germany)
Funmi Togonu-Bickersteth (Nigeria)
Geedreck Usvatte-Aratchi (Sri Lanka)
Samuel Wangwe (United Republic of Tanzania)
Kerfalla Yansane (Guinea)

Membership in 2007

The Economic and Social Council postponed the appointment of 24 experts to the Committee for a three-year term beginn ing on 1 January 2007 (see Council decision 2006/201 B).

COMMITTEE OF EXPERTS ON PUBLIC ADMINISTRATION
(24 members; three-year term)

Membership from 1 January 2006 through 31 December 2009

Peter Anyang' Nyong'o (Kenya)
Ousmane Batoko (Benin)
Marie-Françoise Bechtel (France)
Rachid Benmokhtar Benabdellah (Morocco)
Emilia Boncodin (Philippines)
Jocelyne Bourgon (Canada)
Luiz Carlos Bresser-Pereira (Brazil)
Mario P. Chiti (Italy)
Mikhail Dmitriev (Russian Federation)
Geraldine Fraser-Moleketi (South Africa)
Edgar Alfonso González Salas (Colombia)
Werner Jann (Germany)
Taher Kannan (Jordan)
Pan Suk Kim (Republic of Korea)
Barbara Kudrycka (Poland)
Florin Lupescu (Romania)
Anthony Makrydemetres (Greece)
Jose Oscar Monteiro (Mozambique)
Siripurapu Kesava Rao (India)
Dennis Rondinelli (United States of America)
Prijono Tjiptoherijanto (Indonesia)
Luis Aguilar Villanueva (Mexico)
Gwendoline Williams (Trinidad and Tobago)
Wang Xiaochu (China)

COMMITTEE ON ECONOMIC, SOCIAL AND CULTURAL RIGHTS
(18 members; four-year term)

Membership in 2006	*Term expires on31 December*
Mohamed Ezzeldin Abdel-Moneim (Egypt)	2008
Clément Atangana (Cameroon)	2006
Rocío Barahona Riera (Costa Rica)	2008
Virginia Bonoan-Dandan (Philippines)	2006
Maria Virginia Brás Gomes (Portugal)	2006
Arundhati Ghose (India)	2006
Azzouz Kerdoun (Algeria)	2006
Yuri Kolosov (Russian Federation)	2006
Giorgio Malinverni (Switzerland)	2008
Jaime Marchán Romero (Ecuador)	2006
Sergei N. Martynov (Belarus)	2008
Ariranga Govindasamy Pillay (Mauritius)	2008
Eibe Riedel (Germany)	2006

Membership in 2006	*Term expires on31 December*
Andrzej Rzeplinski (Poland)	2008
Waleed M. Sa'di (Jordan)	2008
Shen Yongxiang (China)	2008
Philippe Texier (France)	2008
Alvaro Tirado Mejía (Colombia)	2006

Membership in 2007	*Term expires on31 December*
Mohamed Ezzeldin Abdel-Moneim (Egypt)	2008
Clément Atangana (Cameroon)	2010
Rocío Barahona Riera (Costa Rica)	2008
Virginia Bonoan-Dandan (Philippines)	2010
Maria Virginia Brás Gomes (Portugal)	2010
Chandrashekhar Dasgupta (India)	2010
Azzouz Kerdoun (Algeria)	2010
Yuri Kolosov (Russian Federation)	2010
Giorgio Malinverni (Switzerland)	2008
Jaime Marchán Romero (Ecuador)	2010
Sergei N. Martynov (Belarus)	2008
Ariranga Govindasamy Pillay (Mauritius)	2008
Eibe Riedel (Germany)	2010
Andrzej Rzeplinski (Poland)	2008
Waleed M. Sa'di (Jordan)	2008
Shen Yongxiang (China)	2008
Philippe Texier (France)	2008
Alvaro Tirado Mejía (Colombia)	2010

PERMANENT FORUM ON INDIGENOUS ISSUES
(16 members; three-year term)

Membership from 1 January 2005 through 31 December 2007

Eight experts elected by the Council
Eduardo Aguiar de Almeida (Brazil)
Yuri Boychenko (Russian Federation)
Merike Kokajev (Estonia)
William Ralph Joey Langeveldt (South Africa)
Otilia Lux de Coti (Guatemala)
Liliana Muzangi Mbela (Democratic Republic of the Congo)
Ida Nicolaisen (Denmark)
Qin Xiaomei (China)
Eight experts appointed by the President of the Council
Hassan Id Balkassm (Morocco)
Michael Dodson (Australia)
Wilton Littlechild (Canada)
Aqqaluk Lynge (Denmark)
Pavel Sulyandziga (Russian Federation)

Membership from 1 January 2005 through 31 December 2007

Parshuram Tamang (Nepal)
Victoria Tauli-Corpuz (Philippines)
Nina Pacari Vega (Ecuador)

COMMITTEE OF EXPERTS ON INTERNATIONAL COOPERATION INTAX MATTERS

(25 members; four-year term)

Membership through 30 June 2009

Moftah Jassim Al-Moftah (Qatar)
Bernell L. Arrindell (Barbados)
Noureddine Bensouda (Morocco)
Rowena G. Bethel (Bahamas)
Patricia A. Brown (United States of America)
José Antonio Bustos Buiza (Spain)
Nahil L. Hirsh Carrillo (Peru)
Danies Kawama Chisenda (Zambia)
Paolo Ciocca (Italy)
Andrew Dawson (United Kingdom of Great Britain and Northern Ireland)
Talmon de Paula Freitas (Brazil)
Harry Msamire Kitillya (United Republic of Tanzania)
Frank Mullen (Ireland)
Kyung Geun Lee (Republic of Korea)
Tizhong Liao (China)[r]
Habiba Louati (Tunisia)
Ronald Peter van der Merwe (South Africa)
Dmitry Vladimirovich Nikolaev (Russian Federation)
Pascal Saint-Amans (France)
Serafin U. Salvador, Jr. (Philippines)
Erwin Silitonga (Indonesia)
Stig B. Sollund (Norway)
Yoshiki Takeuchi (Japan)
Robert Waldburger (Switzerland)
Armando Lara Yaffar (Mexico)

RELATED BODIES

EXECUTIVE BOARD OF THE UNITED NATIONS CHILDREN'S FUND

(36 members; three-year term)

Membership in 2006	*Membership in 2007*	*Term expires on 31 December*
Algeria	Argentina	2007
Argentina	Australia	2007
Australia	Bahamas	2009
Austria	Belgium[s]	2007

Bangladesh	Bolivia	2007
Belarus	Burkina Faso	2008
Bolivia	Cameroon	2009
Burkina Faso	Central African Republic	2009
Burundi	China	2007
Canada	Colombia	2008
China	Croatia	2009
Colombia	Democratic People's Republic of Korea	2007
Democratic People's Republic of Korea	Denmark	2008
Denmark	Ethiopia	2009
Djibouti	Guatemala	2008
El Salvador	India	2009
Finland	Ireland	2009
Germany	Japan	2007
Guatemala	Malaysia	2009
Italy	Mali	2009
Japan	Mauritania	2009
Lebanon	Mozambique	2007
Malawi	Myanmar	2009
Mozambique	Netherlands	2007
Myanmar	Pakistan	2008
Netherlands	Portugal	2009
Pakistan	Republic of Korea	2008
Republic of Korea	Russian Federation	2007
Russian Federation	Rwanda	2008
Rwanda	Serbia 2	2008
Senegal	Sweden	2009
Serbia	Switzerland[s]	2008
Spain	Turkey[s]	2008
Sweden	Ukraine	2007
Ukraine	United Kingdom of Great Britain and Northern Ireland	2009
	United States of America	2008

EXECUTIVE COMMITTEE OF THE PROGRAMME OF THE UNITED NATIONS HIGH COMMISSIONER FOR REFUGEES

(70 members)

Algeria	Lesotho
Argentina	Madagascar
Australia	Mexico
Austria	Morocco
Bangladesh	Mozambique
Belgium	Namibia
Brazil	Netherlands

Canada	New Zealand
Chile	Nicaragua
China	Nigeria
Colombia	Norway
Côte d'Ivoire	Pakistan
Cyprus	Philippines
Democratic Republic of the Congo	Poland
Denmark	Portugal[t]
Ecuador	Republic of Korea
Egypt	Romania
Ethiopia	Russian Federation
Finland	Serbia
France	Somalia
Germany	South Africa
Ghana	Spain
Greece	Sudan
Guinea	Sweden
Holy See	Switzerland
Hungary	Thailand
India	Tunisia
Iran (Islamic Republic of)	Turkey
Ireland	Uganda
Israel	United Kingdom of Great Britain and Northern Ireland
Italy	United Republic of Tanzania
Japan	United States of America
Jordan[t]	Venezuela (Bolivarian Republic of)
Kenya	Yemen
Lebanon	Zambia

EXECUTIVE BOARD OF THE UNITED NATIONS DEVELOPMENT PROGRAMME/UNITED NATIONS POPULATION FUND

(36 members; three-year term)

Membership in 2006	*Membership in 2007*	*Term expires on 31 December*
Algeria	Algeria	2008
Bangladesh	Angola	2009
Belarus	Antigua and Barbuda	2009
Benin	Bangladesh	2008
Botswana	Belarus	2007
Cameroon	Belgium[u]	2008
Canada	Benin	2008
China	Bhutan	2009
Congo	Canada	2007
Cuba	Central African Republic	2009
Democratic People's Republic of Korea	China	2009
Denmark	Democratic People's Republic of Korea	2007

Ecuador	Ecuador	2008
Eritrea	Germany	2009
France	Greece	2009
Gambia	Guatemala	2007
Guatemala	Guyana	2007
Guyana	India	2009
Indonesia	Italy[u]	2007
Iran (Islamic Republic of)	Jamaica	2008
Jamaica	Japan	2008
Japan	Kazakhstan	2007
Kazakhstan	Malawi	2009
Netherlands	Norway	2008
New Zealand	Pakistan	2008
Norway	Portugal	2007
Pakistan	Russian Federation	2008
Poland	Senegal	2009
Portugal	Serbia	2009
Russian Federation	Somalia	2009
Sweden	Spain	2009
Turkey	Sweden	2009
Uganda	Uganda	2007
Ukraine	Ukraine	2007
United Kingdom of Great Britain and Northern Ireland	United Kingdom of Great Britain and Northern Ireland	2008
United States of America	United States of America	2007

EXECUTIVE BOARD OF THE WORLD FOOD PROGRAMME[v]

(36 members; three-year term)

Membership in 2006

Members elected by the Economic and Social Council	*Term expires on 31 December*	*Members elected by the FAO Council*	*Term expires on 31 December*
Australia	2007	Algeria	2008
China	2007	Angola	2006
Cuba	2007	Austria	2008
Denmark	2006	Bangladesh	2006
Ethiopia	2007	Canada	2007
France	2006	Colombia	2008
India	2006	Congo	2007
Indonesia	2008	Germany	2007
Japan	2008	Guatemala[w]	2006
Mexico	2008	Haiti	2007
Norway	2007	Kuwait[x]	2007
Pakistan	2006	Netherlands	2006

Membership in 2006

Members elected by the Economic and Social Council	*Term expires on 31 December*	*Members elected by the FAO Council*	*Term expires on 31 December*
Russian Federation	2006	Niger	2007
Senegal	2006	Slovenia	2008
Tunisia	2007	Switzerland	2008
Ukraine	2008	Syrian Arab Republic	2006
United Kingdom of Great Britain and Northern Ireland	2008	United Republic of Tanzania	2008
Zimbabwe	2008	United States of America	2006

Membership in 2007

Members elected by the Economic and Social Council	*Term expires on 31 December*	*Members elected by the FAO Council*[b]	*Term expires on 31 December*
Australia	2007	Algeria	2008
Cape Verde	2009	Austria	2008
China	2007	Canada	2007
Cuba	2007	Colombia	2008
Ethiopia	2007	Congo	2007
India	2009	Germany	2007
Indonesia	2008	Haiti	2007
Iran (Islamic Republic of)	2009	Kuwait	2007
Japan	2008	Niger	2007
Mexico	2008	Slovenia	2008
New Zealand	2009	Switzerland	2008
Norway	2007	United Republic of Tanzania	2008
Russian Federation	2009		
Sweden	2009		
Tunisia	2007		
Ukraine	2008		
United Kingdom of Great Britain and Northern Ireland	2008		
Zimbabwe	2008		

INTERNATIONAL NARCOTICS CONTROL BOARD

(13 members; five-year term)

MEMBERS ELECTED BY THE ECONOMIC AND SOCIAL COUNCIL TO SERVE ON THE BOARD AS CONSTITUTED UNDER THE 1972 PROTOCOL AMENDING THE SINGLE CONVENTION ON NARCOTIC DRUGS, 1961

Membership in 2006-2007	*Term expires on 1 March*
Joseph Bediako Asare (Ghana)	2010
Sevil Atasoy (Turkey)	2010

Madan Mohan Bhatnagar (India)	2007
Elisaldo Carlini (Brazil)	2007
Tatiana Borisovna Dmitrieva (Russian Federation)	2010
Philip O. Emafo (Nigeria)	2010
Gilberto Gerra (Italy)	2007
Hamid A. Ghodse (Islamic Republic of Iran)	2007
Camilo Uribe Granja (Colombia)	2010
Melvyn Levitsky (United States of America)	2007
Robert Lousberg (Netherlands)	2007
Rainer Wolfgang Schmid (Austria)	2007
Brian Watters (Australia)	2010

Membership from 2 March 2007	*Term expires on 1 March*
Joseph Bediako Asare (Ghana)	2010
Sevil Atasoy (Turkey)	2010
Tatiana Borisovna Dmitrieva (Russian Federation)	2010
Philip O. Emafo (Nigeria)	2010
Hamid A. Ghodse (Islamic Republic of Iran)	2012
Camilo Uribe Granja (Colombia)	2010
Carola Lander (Germany)	2012
Melvyn Levitsky (United States of America)	2012
María Elena Medina-Mora Icaza (Mexico)	2012
Sri Suryawati (Indonesia)	2012
Brian Watters (Australia)	2010
Raymond Yans (Belgium)	2012
Xin Yu (China)	2012

EXECUTIVE BOARD OF THE INTERNATIONAL RESEARCH AND TRAINING INSTITUTE FOR THE ADVANCEMENT OF WOMEN

(10 members; three-year term)

Membership through 31 December 2006[z]
Burkina Faso
El Salvador
Iran (Islamic Republic of)
Italy
Mexico
Nigeria
Philippines
Romania
Spain

Membership through 31 December 2006[z]
Grenada
Honduras
Spain

COMMITTEE FOR THE UNITED NATIONS POPULATION AWARD[BB]

(10 members; three-year term)

Membership through 31 December 2006

Algeria
Bangladesh
Belarus
Cameroon
Guyana
Haiti
Iran (Islamic Republic of)
Kenya
Netherlands
Peru

Membership from 1 January 2007 through 31 December 2009[cc]

Bangladesh
Haiti
Iran (Islamic Republic of)
Peru
Sweden

PROGRAMME COORDINATION BOARD OF THE JOINT UNITED NATIONS PROGRAMME ON HUMAN IMMUNODEFICIENCY VIRUS/ACQUIRED IMMUNODEFICIENCY SYNDROME (UNAIDS)

(22 members; three-year term)

Membership in 2006	*Membership in 2007[dd]*	*Term expires on 31 December*
Australia	Australia	2008
Bahamas	Belgium	2009
Belgium[ee]	Brazil	2007
Brazil	Democratic Republic of the Congo	2008
Cape Verde	El Salvador	2009
China	Germany	2007
Czech Republic	Grenada	2008
Democratic Republic of the Congo	India	2007
Finland[ff]	Japan	2009
Germany	Kenya	2007
Grenada	Libyan Arab Jamahiriya	2007
India	Myanmar	2009
Italy	Nepal	2007
Japan	Norway	2008
Kenya	Russian Federation	2007
Libyan Arab Jamahiriya	Senegal	2009

Membership in 2006	*Membership in 2007dd*	*Term expires on 31 December*
Nepal	Slovakia	2009
Netherlands[ee]	Thailand	2008
Norway[ff]	United States of America	2007
Russian Federation	Zambia	2009
Swaziland		
Sweden		
Thailand[i]		
United States of America		

GOVERNING COUNCIL OF THE UNITED NATIONS HUMAN SETTLEMENTS PROGRAMME (UN-HABITAT)

(58 members; four-year term)

Membership in 2006[gg]	*Membership in 2007[gg,hh]*	*Term expires on 31 December*
Antigua and Barbuda	Antigua and Barbuda	2008
Argentina	Bangladesh	2008
Bangladesh	Belarus	2007
Belarus	Belgium	2008
Belgium	Bulgaria	2007
Brazil	Burundi	2010
Bulgaria	Canada	2008
Burkina Faso	China	2008
Burundi	Congo	2007
Canada	Costa Rica	2007
Chile	Czech Republic	2008
China	Equatorial Guinea	2010
Congo	Finland	2010
Costa Rica	France	2008
Czech Republic	Germany	2007
Democratic Republic of the Congo	Ghana	2008
Ecuador	Greece	2007
France	Grenada	2010
Germany	Haiti	2008
Ghana	India	2007
Greece	Indonesia	2010
Haiti	Iran (Islamic Republic of)	2010
India	Israel	2007
Indonesia	Japan	2010
Iran (Islamic Republic of)	Jordan	2007
Israel	Kenya	2007
Japan	Libyan Arab Jamahiriya	2008
Jordan	Mauritania	2010
Kenya	Mexico	2007

Membership in 2006[gg]	Membership in 2007[gg,hh]	Term expires on 31 December
Libyan Arab Jamahiriya	Netherlands	2010
Malawi	Niger	2010
Mexico	Nigeria	2007
Netherlands	Norway	2008
Nigeria	Pakistan	2010
Norway	Paraguay	2007
Pakistan	Philippines	2007
Paraguay	Poland	2010
Philippines	Russian Federation	2010
Poland	Rwanda	2008
Russian Federation	Saudi Arabia	2007
Rwanda	Senegal	2010
Saudi Arabia	Slovakia	2008
Senegal	South Africa	2007
Sierra Leone	Spain	2007
Slovakia	Sri Lanka	2007
South Africa	Swaziland	2007
Spain	Sweden	2008
Sri Lanka	Trinidad and Tobago	2008
Swaziland	Uganda	2008
Sweden	United Arab Emirates	2008
Trinidad and Tobago	United Republic of Tanzania	2008
Turkey	United States of America	2010
Uganda	Zimbabwe	2010
United Arab Emirates		
United Kingdom of Great Britain and Northern Ireland		
United Republic of Tanzania		
United States of America		

OTHER COMMISSIONS

ORGANIZATIONAL COMMITTEE OF THE PEACEBUILDING COMMISSION[ii]

(31 members; two-year term, as applicable)[jj]

Membership in 2006
Seven members selected by the Security Council
China
Denmark
France
Russian Federation
United Kingdom of Great Britain and Northern Ireland
United Republic of Tanzania
United States of America

Seven members elected by the General Assembly
Burundi
Chile
Croatia
Egypt
El Salvador
Fiji
Jamaica

Seven members elected by the Economic and Social Council
Angola
Belgium
Brazil
Guinea-Bissau
Indonesia
Poland
Sri Lanka

Five top providers of assessed contributions to United Nations budgets and of voluntary contributions to the United Nations funds, programmes and agencies, including a standing peacebuilding fund (selected by and from among the top 10 providers)
Germany
Italy
Japan
Netherlands
Norway

Five top providers of military personnel and civilian police to United Nations missions (selected by and from among the 10 top providers)
Bangladesh
Ghana
India
Nigeria
Pakistan

[a] The remaining 18 seats are to be filled by the General Assembly at its sixty-first session.

[b] At its 9th meeting, on 10 May 2006, the Council elected the following four members to the Commission on Population and Development for a four-year term beginning at the first meeting, in 2007, of the Commission's forty-first session and expiring at the close of the Commission's forty-fourth session in 2011: Benin, Equatorial Guinea, Iran (Islamic Republic of) and Poland. At the same meeting, the Council postponed the election of one member from Asian States, two members from Latin American and Caribbean States and one member from Western European and other States for a four-year term beginning at the first meeting, in 2007, of the Commission's forty-first session and expiring at the close of the Commission's forty-fourth session in 2011 (decision 2006/201 B).

[c] At its 9th and 41st meetings, on 10 May and 27 July 2006, respectively, the Council elected the following 12 members to the Commission for Social Development for a four-year term beginning at the first meeting, in 2007, of the Commission's forty-sixth session and expiring at the close of the Commission's forty-ninth session in 2011: Andorra, Benin, Cameroon, Cuba, Egypt, India, Jamaica, Mexico, Namibia, Nepal, Spain and the United Arab Emirates (decisions 2006/201 B and C). At its

41st meeting, the Council postponed the election of one member from Eastern European States and one member from Western European and other States for a four-year term beginning at the first meeting, in 2007, of the Commission's forty-sixth session and expiring at the close of the Commission's forty-ninth session in 2011 (decision 2006/201 C).

[d] In accordance with Council resolution 2006/2 of 22 March 2006, the Commission on Human Rights concluded its work at its sixty-second session and was abolished on 16 June 2006.

[e] At its 9th meeting, on 10 May 2006, the Council elected the following 11 members to the Commission on the Status of Women for a four-year term beginning at the first meeting, in 2007, of the Commission's fifty-second session and expiring at the close of the Commission's fifty-fifth session in 2011: Armenia, Azerbaijan, Belgium, Cambodia, Gabon, Namibia, the Niger, Pakistan, Paraguay, Spain and Turkey (decision 2006/201 B).

[f] Elected at the 9th meeting, on 10 May 2006, for a term beginning on the date of election to fill a postponed vacancy (decision 2006/201 B).

[g] At its 9th and 41st plenary meetings, on 10 May and 27 July 2006, the Council elected the following 17 members to the Commission on Sustainable Development for a three-year term beginning at the organizational meeting, in 2007, of the Commission's sixteenth session and expiring at the close of the Commission's eighteenth session in 2010: Bahrain, Cape Verde, Costa Rica, Croatia, France, the Gambia, Guatemala, Guinea, Haiti, India, the Islamic Republic of Iran, Japan, Monaco, the Netherlands, Poland, South Africa and Sweden (decisions 2006/201 B and C).

[h] At its 9th meeting, on 10 May 2006, the Council postponed the election of two members from Western European and other States for a four-year term beginning on 1 January 2007 (decision 2006/201 B).

[i] Elected at the 2nd meeting, on 7 February 2006, for a term beginning on the date of election to fill a postponed vacancy (decision 2006/201 A).

[j] The Member State formerly known as Serbia and Montenegro was renamed Serbia. Montenegro was admitted as a Member State of the United Nations on 28 June 2006 by General Assembly resolution 60/264.

[k] At its 41st meeting, on 27 July 2006, the Council amended the terms of reference of the Commission to reflect the admission of Japan as a member of the Commission (Council resolution 2006/39).

[l] Admitted as an associate member of the Economic Commission for Latin American and the Caribbean in March 2006 (see Commission resolution 628 (XXXI)).

[m] At its 2nd meeting, on 7 February 2006, the Council postponed the nomination of one member from Western European and other States for election by the General Assembly for a term beginning on the date of election and expiring on 31 December 2008 (decision 2006/201 A).

[n] At its 9th and 41st meetings, on 10 May and 27 July 2006, the Council nominated five Member States for election by the General Assembly at its sixty-first session for a three-year term beginning on 1 January 2007 (decisions 2006/201 B and C) and postponed the nomination of two members from Western European and other States for the same term of office (decision 2006/201 C).

[o] Nominated by the Council at its 2nd meeting, on 7 February 2006 (decision 2006/201 A), and elected by the General Assembly at its 74th plenary meeting, on 27 March 2006.

[p] At its 9th meeting, on 10 May 2006, the Council postponed the election of two members from Latin American and Caribbean States and three members from Western European and other States for a term beginning on the date of election and expiring on 31 December 2008 (decision 2006/201 B).

[q] At its 9th meeting, on 10 May 2006, the Council postponed the election of three members from Asian States and three members from Latin American and Caribbean States for a three-year term beginning on 1 January 2007 (decision 2006/201 B).

[r] Elected at the 9th meeting, on 10 May 2006, to fill a vacancy arising from the resignation of Zhiyong Zhang (China) (decision 2006/201 B).

[s] At its 9th meeting, on 10 May 2006, the Council elected Belgium, Switzerland and Turkey for a term beginning on 1 January 2007 to replace Germany, Spain and Canada, respectively (decision 2006/201 B).

[t] Elected at the 9th meeting, on 10 May 2006, in accordance with General Assembly resolution 60/127 of 16 December 2005 (decision 2006/201 B).

[u] At its 9th meeting, on 10 May 2006, the Council elected Belgium and Italy for a term beginning on 1 January 2007 to replace New Zealand and Turkey, respectively (decision 2006/201 B).

[v] Pursuant to General Assembly resolution 50/8 of 1 November 1995, the Economic and Social Council and the Council of the Food and Agriculture Organization of the United Nations elect 18 members each from among the States Members of the United Nations or the States members of the Food and Agriculture Organization of the United Nations, according to the pattern set out in that resolution. The members of the Executive Board were elected from five lists set out in the Basic Texts of the World Food Programme and reproduced in document E/2006/9/Add.5.

[w] Replacing Nicaragua, which resigned effective 31 December 2005.

[x] Replacing Thailand, which resigned effective 31 December 2005.

[y] The remaining six seats are to be filled by the Council of the Food and Agriculture Organization of the United Nations at its session to be held in November 2006.

[z] The Council postponed the election of one member from Eastern European States for a term beginning on the date of election and expiring on 31 December 2006 to fill a vacancy arising from the resignation of the Czech Republic (decision 2006/201 B).

[aa] The Council postponed the election of two members from African States, two members from Asian States, two members from Eastern European States and one member from Western European and other States for a three-year term beginning on 1 January 2007 (decision 2006/201 C).

[bb] For the regulations governing the Award, see General Assembly resolution 36/201 and Assembly decision 41/445.

[cc] The Council postponed the election of three members from African States, one member from Asian States and one member from Eastern European States for a three-year term beginning on 1 January 2007 (decision 2006/201 B).

[dd] The Council postponed the election of two members from Western European and other States for a three-year term beginning on 1 January 2007 (decision 2006/201 B).

[ee] At the 2nd meeting, on 7 February 2006, the Council elected Belgium for a term beginning on the date of election to replace the Netherlands (decision 2006/201 A).

[ff] At the 9th meeting, on 10 May 2006, the Council elected Norway for a term beginning on 1 June 2006, to replace Finland (decision 2006/201 B).

[gg] The Council postponed the election of one member from Asian States for a term beginning on the date of election and expiring on 31 December 2008 (decision 2005/201 B).

[hh] At its organizational session for 2005, the Council, at its 4th meeting, on 31 March 2005, postponed the election of one member from Asian States for a term beginning on the date of election, and expiring on 31 December 2008. At its 41st meeting, on 27 July 2006, the Council postponed the election of three members from Latin American and Caribbean States and one member from Western European and other States for a four-year term beginning on 1 January 2007.

[ii] Established as an intergovernmental advisory body pursuant to General Assembly resolution 60/180 and Security Council resolutions 1645 (2005) and 1646 (2005) of 20 December 2005.

[jj] For guidelines regarding membership in the Organizational Committee, see paras. 4, 5 and 6 of General Assembly resolution 60/180 and of Security Council resolution 1645 (2005) and para. 1 of Security Council resolution 1646 (2005).

CHAPTER 4

Trusteeship Council

1. Trusteeship Council

Status

The Trusteeship Council suspended operation on 1 November 1994, with the independence of Palau, the last remaining United Nations trust territory, on 1 October 1994. By a resolution adopted on 25 May 1994, the Council amended its rules of procedure to drop the obligation to meet annually and agreed to meet as occasion required—by its decision or the decision of its President, or at the request of a majority of its members or the General Assembly or the Security Council.

Background

In setting up an International Trusteeship System, the Charter established the Trusteeship Council as one of the main organs of the United Nations and assigned to it the task of supervising the administration of Trust Territories placed under the Trusteeship System. Major goals of the System were to promote the advancement of the inhabitants of Trust Territories and their progressive development towards self-government or independence. The Trusteeship Council is made up of the five permanent members of the Security Council—China, France, Russian Federation, United Kingdom and United States.

The aims of the Trusteeship System have been fulfilled to such an extent that all Trust Territories have attained self-government or independence, either as separate States or by joining neighbouring independent countries.

Functions and powers

Under the Charter, the Trusteeship Council is authorized to examine and discuss reports from the Administering Authority on the political, economic, social and educational advancement of the peoples of Trust Territories and, in consultation with the Administering Authority, to examine petitions from and undertake periodic and other special missions to Trust Territories.

CHAPTER 5

International Court of Justice

1. Report of the International Court of Justice (A/61/4), 1 August 2005-31 July 2006

Note

Symbols of United Nations documents are composed of capital letters combined with figures. Mention of such a symbol indicates a reference to a United Nations document.

I. Summary

1. The International Court of Justice, principal judicial organ of the United Nations, consists of 15 judges elected for a term of nine years by the General Assembly and the Security Council. Every three years one third of the seats fall vacant. The last elections to fill such vacancies were held on 7 November 2005. Sitting Judge Thomas Buergenthal (United States of America) was re-elected with effect from 6 February 2006; Messrs. Mohamed Bennouna (Morocco), Kenneth Keith (New Zealand), Bernardo Sepúlveda-Amor (Mexico) and Leonid Skotnikov (Russian Federation) were elected with effect from 6 February 2006.

On the latter date the Court, in its new composition, elected Judge Rosalyn Higgins (United Kingdom) as its President and Judge Awn Shawkat Al-Khasawneh (Jordan) as its Vice-President for a term of three years.

2. As from 6 February 2006, the composition of the Court is consequently as follows: President: Rosalyn Higgins (United Kingdom); Vice-President: Awn Shawkat Al-Khasawneh (Jordan); Judges: Raymond Ranjeva (Madagascar), Shi Jiuyong (China), Abdul G. Koroma (Sierra Leone), Gonzalo Parra-Aranguren (Venezuela), Thomas Buergenthal (United States of America), Hisashi Owada (Japan), Bruno Simma (Germany), Peter Tomka (Slovakia), Ronny Abraham (France), Kenneth Keith (New Zealand), Bernardo Sepúlveda-Amor (Mexico), Mohamed Bennouna (Morocco) and Leonid Skotnikov (Russian Federation).

3. The Registrar of the Court, elected for a term of seven years on 10 February 2000, is Mr. Philippe Couvreur; the Deputy-Registrar, re-elected on 19 February 2001, also for a term of seven years, is Mr. Jean-Jacques Arnaldez.

4. It should furthermore be noted that the number of judges *ad hoc* chosen by States parties during the period under review was 24, with these functions being carried out by 20 individuals (the same person is on occasion appointed to sit as judge *ad hoc* in more than one different case).

5. As the Assembly will be aware, the International Court of Justice, which celebrated its sixtieth anniversary in April last, is the only international court of a universal character with general jurisdiction. That jurisdiction is twofold.

6. In the first place, the Court has to decide upon disputes freely submitted to it by States in the exercise of their sovereignty. In this respect, it should be noted that, as at 31 July 2006, 192 States were parties to the Statute of the Court and that 67 of them had deposited with the Secretary-General a declaration of acceptance of the Court's compulsory jurisdiction

in accordance with Article 36, paragraph 2, of the Statute. Further, some 300 bilateral or multilateral treaties provide for the Court to have jurisdiction in the resolution of disputes arising out of their application or interpretation. Finally, States may submit a specific dispute to the Court by way of special agreement, as a number have done recently.

7. Secondly, the Court may also be consulted, on any legal question, by the General Assembly or the Security Council, and, on legal questions arising within the scope of their activities, by other organs of the United Nations and specialized agencies having been so authorized by the General Assembly.

8. Over the past year, the number of cases pending before the Court has remained high. The Court decided two cases during the period under review and issued an order on a request for the indication of provisional measures. It further held heavy hearings in the *Genocide* case instituted by Bosnia and Herzegovina against Serbia and Montenegro[1]. The number of cases on the docket now stands at 12[2].

9. The contentious cases come from all over the world: currently four are between European States, four others between Latin American States, two between African States, one between Asian States, whilst one is of an intercontinental character. This regional diversity illustrates the Court's universality.

10. The subject-matter of these cases is extremely varied. As well as "classic" territorial and maritime delimitation disputes and disputes relating to the treatments of nationals by other States, the Court is seized today of cases concerning more "cutting-edge" issues, such as allegations of massive human rights violations, including genocide, the use of force, or the management of shared natural resources.

11. The Court's docket increasingly includes fact-intensive cases in which the Court must carefully examine and weigh the evidence. No longer can it focus solely on legal questions. Such cases have raised a whole swathe of new procedural issues for the Court.

12. In the run-up to the *Bosnia and Herzegovina* v. *Serbia and Montenegro* case, the Court anticipated many issues likely to arise concerning witness evidence and examination. Special arrangements had to be made for the hearing of experts and witnesses including the translation of statements, questions and replies from and into languages other than English and French as well as with the Press.

13. At the same time, many cases have been rendered more complex as a result of preliminary objections to jurisdiction or admissibility and of counter-claims, as well as requests for the indication of provisional measures, which have to be dealt with as a matter of urgency.

14. During the period under review the Court, on 19 December 2005, handed down its Judgment on the merits in the case concerning *Armed Activities on the Territory of the Congo (Democratic Republic of the Congo* v. *Uganda)*.[3] In respect of the claims by the Democratic Republic of the Congo (DRC), the Court found in that Judgment that, *inter alia*, Uganda, by engaging in military activities against the DRC on the latter's territory, by occupying Ituri and by actively extending support to irregular forces having operated on Congolese territory, had violated the principle of non-use of force in international relations and the principle of non-intervention. The Court further found that Uganda had violated its

obligations under international human rights law and international humanitarian law and had violated other obligations it bore under international law, notably the obligation as an occupying Power in Ituri district to prevent acts of looting, plundering and exploitation of Congolese natural resources. In light of the conclusions reached, the Court found that Uganda had an obligation to make reparation for the injury caused. It considered appropriate the DRC's request for the nature, form and amount of the reparation owed to it to be determined by the Court, failing agreement between the Parties, in a subsequent phase of the proceedings. The Court further found that Uganda had failed to comply with the Order indicating provisional measures handed down by the Court on 1 July 2000.

15. In respect of Uganda's counter-claims, the Court held Uganda's first claim to be admissible but did not uphold it, considering the evidence insufficient to prove that Uganda had been the target of armed rebel groups based in the DRC and supported by its Government. The Court held the second counter-claim admissible in part and found that, by virtue of the conduct of its armed forces, which attacked the Ugandan embassy in Kinshasa and maltreated diplomats and other persons on the embassy premises, as well as Ugandan diplomats at Ndjili International Airport, the DRC had breached its obligations under Articles 22 and 29 of the Vienna Convention on Diplomatic Relations. The Court further held that the removal of property and archives from the Ugandan embassy was in violation of the rules of international law on diplomatic relations. It pointed out however that it would only be in a subsequent phase of the proceedings that, failing agreement between the Parties, the specific circumstances of these violations, the precise damage suffered by Uganda and the extent of the reparation to which it was entitled would have to be demonstrated.

16. On 3 February 2006 the Court handed down its Judgment on its jurisdiction and the admissibility of the DRC's Application in the case concerning *Armed Activities on the Territory of the Congo (New Application: 2002) (Democratic Republic of the Congo* v. *Rwanda)*. The DRC offered some eleven bases for jurisdiction in its seizing of the Court in 2002: Article 30, paragraph 1, of the Convention against Torture; Article 9 of the Convention on Privileges and Immunities; the doctrine of *forum prorogatum*; the Order concerning the indication of provisional measures handed down by the Court on 10 July 2002; Article IX of the Genocide Convention; Article 22 of the Convention on Racial Discrimination; Article 29, paragraph 1, of the Convention on Discrimination Against Women; Article 75 of the WHO Constitution; Article XIV, paragraph 2, of the Unesco Constitution; Article 14, paragraph 1, of the Montreal Convention and Article 66 of the Vienna Convention on the Law of Treaties. The Court examined each such basis in its Judgment and concluded that none could found its jurisdiction in the case. It did however reiterate that there was a fundamental distinction between the acceptance by States of the Court's jurisdiction and the conformity of their acts with international law. Thus, the Court added, whether or not States have accepted the jurisdiction of the Court, they are required to fulfil their obligations under the United Nations Charter and the other rules of international law, including international humanitarian and human rights law, and they remain responsible for acts attributable to them which are contrary to international law.

17. On 13 July 2006 the Court rendered an Order on the request for the indication of provisional measures submitted by Argentina in the case concerning *Pulp Mills on the River Uruguay (Argentina* v. *Uruguay)*. Argentina had requested the Court to indicate provisional measures requiring Uruguay, first, to suspend the authorizations for the construction of two

pulp mills on the River Uruguay and halt building work on them pending a final decision by the Court and, second, to co-operate with Argentina to protect and preserve the aquatic environment of the River Uruguay, to refrain from taking any further unilateral action with respect to construction of the mills which did not comply with the 1975 Statute (a treaty signed by the two States on 26 February 1975 with a view to establishing the joint machinery necessary for the optimum and rational utilization of that part of the river constituting their joint boundary) and to refrain as well from any other action which might aggravate the dispute or render its settlement more difficult. The Court found that "the circumstances, as they now present themselves to the Court, are not such as to require the exercise of its power under Article 41 of the Statute to indicate provisional measures".

18. The judicial year 2005-2006 has been particularly busy, with the holding of nine weeks of hearings, including the calling of witnesses, witness-experts and experts, in the case concerning *Application of the Convention on the Prevention and Punishment of the Crime of Genocide (Bosnia and Herzegovina* v. *Serbia and Montenegro)*.[4] The judicial year 2006-2007 will also be a busy one. In this connection the Court has already announced the opening dates for the oral proceedings in the case concerning *Ahmadou Sadio Diallo (Republic of Guinea* v. *Democratic Republic of the Congo), Preliminary Objections*, and in the case concerning *Maritime Delimitation between Nicaragua and Honduras in the Caribbean Sea (Nicaragua* v. *Honduras), Merits*.

19. In order to cope with the heavy workload, the Court had already in 1997 taken various measures to rationalize the work of the Registry, to make greater use of information technology, to improve its own working methods and to secure greater collaboration from the parties to proceedings. An account of these various measures was set out in the report submitted to the General Assembly in response to Assembly resolution 52/161 of 15 December 1997 (see Appendix 1 to the Report of the Court for the period 1 August 1997 to 31 July 1998). These efforts have been continued. The Court has also taken steps to shorten and simplify proceedings. In December 2000, it revised certain provisions of its Rules (Arts. 79-80). As of October 2001, it adopted various Practice Directions (see pp. 98 and 99 of the Annual Report for 2001-2002). The Court welcomes the co-operation it has received from some parties to cases who have taken steps to reduce both the number and volume of written pleadings as well as the length of their oral arguments, and who in some cases provided the Court with their pleadings in both of its official languages. In April 2002, the Court reviewed again its working methods; they are subject to constant re-examination. In July 2004, it adopted further measures which mostly concern the internal functioning of the Court and are aimed at increasing the number of decisions rendered each year, thereby shortening the period between the closure of written proceedings and the opening of oral proceedings. In addition, the Court seeks better compliance by parties with its previous decisions aimed at accelerating proceedings and it intends to apply these decisions more strictly. The Court amended existing Practice Direction V and promulgated new Practice Directions X, XI and XII (for the text of these Practice Directions, see pages 46 to 47 of the Annual Report for 2003-2004). Finally, in April and September 2005, it again amended provisions of the Rules of Court (Arts. 52 and 43, respectively).

20. With respect to its budget for the biennium 2006-2007, the Court was pleased that its requests for the creation of two posts were granted. The presence of a highly qualified officer, grade P-4, heading the IT Division will from now on enable the Court to make

enhanced use of advanced technologies, as desired by the General Assembly. Further, the President of the Court, who must perform many diplomatic and administrative tasks in addition to her judicial duties, now enjoys the assistance of an officer in grade P-3.

21. However, there are only five law clerks available to carry out research for the other 14 Members of the Court and the 22 judges *ad hoc* chosen in the 12 cases pending before the Court. Given the Court's sustained activity and the need to respond as rapidly as possible to pending cases, the question of increasing the number of law clerks presents itself in ever more acute terms. The Court is of the view that, like members of all leading international courts and national courts, its Members are entitled to individualized legal assistance so that they can work more rapidly and efficiently in their deliberating and adjudicatory tasks. A request to increase the number of law clerks from five to 14 will be included in the Court's budget submission for the biennium 2008-2009.

22. In conclusion, the International Court of Justice welcomes the reaffirmed confidence that States have shown in the Court's ability to resolve their disputes. The Court will give the same meticulous and impartial attention to cases coming before it in the forthcoming year as it has during the 2005-2006 session.

II. Organization of the Court

A. Composition

23. The present composition of the Court is as follows: President: Rosalyn Higgins; Vice-President: Awn Shawkat Al-Khasawneh; Judges: Raymond Ranjeva, Shi Jiuyong, Abdul G. Koroma, Gonzalo Parra-Aranguren, Thomas Buergenthal, Hisashi Owada, Bruno Simma, Peter Tomka, Ronny Abraham, Kenneth Keith, Bernardo Sepúlveda-Amor, Mohamed Bennouna and Leonid Skotnikov.

24. The Registrar of the Court is Mr. Philippe Couvreur. The Deputy-Registrar is Mr. Jean-Jacques Arnaldez.

25. In accordance with Article 29 of the Statute, the Court forms annually a Chamber of Summary Procedure, which is constituted as follows:

Members

President Higgins

Vice-President Al-Khasawneh

Judges Parra-Aranguren, Buergenthal and Skotnikov

Substitute Members

Judges Koroma and Abraham.

26. In the case concerning *Application of the Convention on the Prevention and Punishment of the Crime of Genocide (Bosnia and Herzegovina* v. *Serbia and Montenegro),*[5] Bosnia and Herzegovina chose Sir Elihu Lauterpacht and Serbia and Montenegro Mr. Milenko Kreća to sit as judges *ad hoc*. Following the resignation of Sir Elihu Lauterpacht, Bosnia and Herzegovina chose Mr. Ahmed Mahiou to sit as judge *ad hoc*.

27. In the case concerning the *Gabčíkovo-Nagymaros Project (Hungary/Slovakia)*, Judge Tomka being unable to sit in the case, Slovakia chose Mr. Krzysztof J. Skubiszewski to sit as judge *ad hoc*.

28. In the case concerning *Ahmadou Sadio Diallo (Republic of Guinea* v. *Democratic Republic of the Congo)*, Guinea chose Mr. Mohammed Bedjaoui and the Democratic Republic of the Congo Mr. Auguste Mampuya Kanunk'a Tshiabo to sit as judges *ad hoc*. Following the resignation of Mr. Bedjaoui, Guinea chose Mr. Ahmed Mahiou to sit as judge *ad hoc*.

29. In the case concerning *Armed Activities on the Territory of the Congo (Democratic Republic of the Congo* v. *Uganda)*, the Democratic Republic of the Congo chose Mr. Joe Verhoeven and Uganda Mr. James L. Kateka to sit as judges *ad hoc*.

30. In the case concerning *Application of the Convention on the Prevention and Punishment of the Crime of Genocide (Croatia* v. *Serbia and Montenegro)*,[6] Croatia chose Mr. Budislav Vukas and Serbia and Montenegro Mr. Milenko Kreća to sit as judges *ad hoc*.

31. In the case concerning *Maritime Delimitation between Nicaragua and Honduras in the Caribbean Sea (Nicaragua* v. *Honduras)*, Nicaragua chose Mr. Giorgio Gaja and Honduras Mr. Julio González Campos to sit as judges *ad hoc*.

32. In the case concerning *Territorial and Maritime Dispute (Nicaragua* v. *Colombia)*, Nicaragua chose Mr. Mohammed Bedjaoui and Colombia Mr. Yves L. Fortier to sit as judges *ad hoc*. Mr. Bedjaoui resigned from his duties in May 2006.

33. In the case concerning *Armed Activities on the Territory of the Congo (New Application: 2002) (Democratic Republic of the Congo* v. *Rwanda)*, the Democratic Republic of the Congo chose Mr. Jean-Pierre Mavungu and Rwanda Mr. Christopher J. R. Dugard to sit as judges *ad hoc*.

34. In the case concerning *Certain Criminal Proceedings in France (Republic of the Congo* v. *France)*, the Republic of the Congo chose Mr. Jean-Yves de Cara to sit as judge *ad hoc*. Judge Abraham being unable to sit in the case, France chose Mr. Gilbert Guillaume to sit as judge *ad hoc*.

35. In the case concerning *Sovereignty over Pedra Branca/Pulau Batu Puteh, Middle Rocks and South Ledge (Malaysia/Singapore)*, Malaysia chose Mr. Christopher J. R. Dugard and Singapore Mr. Pemmaraju Sreenevasa Rao to sit as judges *ad hoc*.

36. In the case concerning *Maritime Delimitation in the Black Sea (Romania* v. *Ukraine)*, Romania chose Mr. Jean-Pierre Cot and Ukraine Mr. Bernard H. Oxman to sit as judges *ad hoc*.

37. In the case concerning *Dispute regarding Navigational and Related Rights (Costa Rica* v. *Nicaragua)*, Costa Rica chose Mr. Antônio Augusto Cançado Trindade and Nicaragua Mr. Gilbert Guillaume to sit as judges *ad hoc*.

38. In the case concerning *Pulp Mills on the River Uruguay (Argentina v. Uruguay)*, Argentina chose Mr. Raúl Emilio Vinuesa and Uruguay Mr. Santiago Torres Bernárdez to sit as judges *ad hoc*.

B. Privileges and Immunities

39. Article 19 of the Statute provides: "The Members of the Court, when engaged on the business of the Court, shall enjoy diplomatic privileges and immunities."

40. In the Netherlands, pursuant to an exchange of correspondence between the President of the Court and the Minister for Foreign Affairs, dated 26 June 1946, they enjoy, in a general way, the same privileges, immunities, facilities and prerogatives as Heads of Diplomatic Missions accredited to Her Majesty the Queen of the Netherlands (*I.C.J. Acts and Documents No. 5*, pp. 201-207). In addition, in accordance with the terms of a letter dated 26 February 1971 from the Minister for Foreign Affairs of the Netherlands, the President of the Court takes precedence over the Heads of Mission, including the Dean of the Diplomatic Corps; the Dean, who ranks after the President, is immediately followed by the Vice-President of the Court and thereafter the precedence proceeds alternately between Heads of Mission and Members of the Court (*ibid.*, pp. 207-213).

41. By resolution 90 (I) of 11 December 1946 (*ibid.*, pp. 206-211), the General Assembly of the United Nations approved the agreements concluded with the Government of the Netherlands in June 1946 and recommended that

> "if a judge, for the purpose of holding himself permanently at the disposal of the Court, resides in some country other than his own, he should be accorded diplomatic privileges and immunities during the period of his residence there",

and that

> "judges should be accorded every facility for leaving the country where they may happen to be, for entering the country where the Court is sitting, and again for leaving it. On journeys in connection with the exercise of their functions, they should, in all countries through which they may have to pass, enjoy all the privileges, immunities and facilities granted by these countries to diplomatic envoys."

42. The same resolution also contains a recommendation calling upon Members of the United Nations to recognize and accept United Nations laissez-passer issued to the judges by the Court. Such laissez-passer have been issued since 1950. They are similar in form to those issued by the Secretary-General of the United Nations.

43. Furthermore, Article 32, paragraph 8, of the Statute provides that the "salaries, allowances and compensation" received by judges "shall be free of all taxation".

III. Jurisdiction of the Court

A. Jurisdiction of the Court in contentious cases

44. On 31 July 2006, the 192 States Members of the United Nations were parties to the Statute of the Court.

45. Sixty-seven States have now made declarations (many with reservations) recognizing as compulsory the jurisdiction of the Court, as contemplated by Article 36, paragraphs 2

and 5, of the Statute. They are: Australia, Austria, Barbados, Belgium, Botswana, Bulgaria, Cambodia, Cameroon, Canada, Commonwealth of Dominica, Costa Rica, Côte d'Ivoire, Cyprus, Democratic Republic of the Congo, Denmark, Djibouti, Dominican Republic, Egypt, Estonia, Finland, Gambia, Georgia, Greece, Guinea, Guinea-Bissau, Haiti, Honduras, Hungary, India, Japan, Kenya, Lesotho, Liberia, Liechtenstein, Luxembourg, Madagascar, Malawi, Malta, Mauritius, Mexico, Nauru, Netherlands, New Zealand, Nicaragua, Nigeria, Norway, Pakistan, Panama, Paraguay, Peru, Philippines, Poland, Portugal, Senegal, Serbia and Montenegro,[7] Slovakia, Somalia, Spain, Sudan, Suriname, Swaziland, Sweden, Switzerland, Togo, Uganda, United Kingdom of Great Britain and Northern Ireland and Uruguay. The texts of the declarations filed by the above States will appear in Chapter IV, Section II, of the *I.C.J. Yearbook 2005-2006*.

46. Lists of treaties and conventions which provide for the jurisdiction of the Court will appear in Chapter IV, Section III, of the *I.C.J. Yearbook 2005-2006*. There are currently in force approximately 130 such multilateral conventions and approximately 180 such bilateral conventions. These lists include treaties or conventions in force providing for reference to the Permanent Court of International Justice (Statute, Art. 37).

B. Jurisdiction of the Court in advisory proceedings

47. In addition to United Nations organs (General Assembly, Security Council, Economic and Social Council, Trusteeship Council, Interim Committee of the General Assembly), the following organizations are at present authorized to request advisory opinions of the Court on legal questions arising within the scope of their activities:

International Labour Organisation;

Food and Agriculture Organization of the United Nations;

United Nations Educational, Scientific and Cultural Organization;

International Civil Aviation Organization;

World Health Organization;

World Bank;

International Finance Corporation;

International Development Association;

International Monetary Fund;

International Telecommunication Union;

World Meteorological Organization;

International Maritime Organization;

World Intellectual Property Organization;

International Fund for Agricultural Development;

United Nations Industrial Development Organization;

International Atomic Energy Agency.

48. The international instruments that make provision for the advisory jurisdiction of the Court will be listed in Chapter IV, Section I, of the *I.C.J. Yearbook 2005-2006*.

IV. Functioning of the Court

A. Committees of the Court

49. The committees constituted by the Court to facilitate the performance of its administrative tasks met a number of times during the period under review; they are composed as follows:

(a) the Budgetary and Administrative Committee: the President of the Court (Chair), the Vice-President of the Court and Judges Ranjeva, Buergenthal, Owada and Tomka;

(b) the Library Committee: Judge Buergenthal (Chair), Judges Simma, Tomka, Keith and Bennouna.

50. The Rules Committee, constituted by the Court in 1979 as a standing body, is composed of Judge Owada (Chair), Judges Simma, Abraham, Keith, Sepúlveda-Amor, Bennouna and Skotnikov.

B. The Registry of the Court

51. The Court is the only principal organ of the United Nations to have its own administration (see Art. 98 of the Charter). The Registry is the permanent administrative organ of the Court. Its role is defined by the Statute and the Rules (in particular Arts. 22-29 of the Rules). Since the Court is both a judicial body and an international institution, the role of the Registry is both to provide judicial support and to act as an international secretariat. Thus its work is, on the one hand, judicial and diplomatic, while, on the other, it corresponds to that of the legal, administrative, financial, conference and information departments of an international organization. The organization of the Registry is prescribed by the Court on proposals submitted by the Registrar and its duties are worked out in instructions drawn up by the Registrar and approved by the Court (see Rules, Art. 28, paras. 2 and 3). The Instructions for the Registry were drawn up in October 1946. An organizational chart of the Registry is appended to this Report.

52. Registry officials are appointed by the Court on proposals by the Registrar or, for General Service staff, by the Registrar with the approval of the President. Short-term staff are appointed by the Registrar. Working conditions are laid down in Staff Regulations adopted by the Court (see Art. 28 of the Rules of Court). Registry officials enjoy, generally, the same privileges and immunities as members of diplomatic missions in The Hague of comparable rank. They enjoy a status, remuneration and pension rights corresponding to those of secretariat officials of the equivalent category or grade.

53. Over the last 15 years, the Registry's workload, notwithstanding its adaptation to new technologies, has grown considerably following the substantial increase in the number of cases brought before the Court.

54. Taking into account the creation of two professional posts in the 2006-2007 biennium, the staffing chart for the Registry shows at present a total of 100 staff members as follows: 47 staff members in the professional and higher category (of which 35 hold established posts and 12 temporary posts), and 53 staff members in the General Service category (of which 51 hold established posts and two temporary posts).

55. In order further to enhance the Registry's efficiency and in accordance with the views expressed by the General Assembly, a performance appraisal system was established for Registry staff, effective 1 January 2004.

The Registrar and Deputy-Registrar

56. The Registrar is the regular channel of communications to and from the Court and in particular effects all communications, notifications and transmissions of documents required by the Statute or by the Rules; he keeps a General List of all cases, entered and numbered in the order in which the documents instituting proceedings or requesting an advisory opinion are received in the Registry; he is present in person, or represented by his deputy, at meetings of the Court, and of the Chambers, and is responsible for the preparation of minutes of such meetings; he makes arrangements for such provision or verification of translations and interpretations into the Court's official languages (French and English) as the Court may require; he signs all judgments, advisory opinions and orders of the Court as well as the minutes; he is responsible for the administration of the Registry and for the work of all its departments and divisions, including the accounts and financial administration in accordance with the financial procedures of the United Nations; he assists in maintaining the Court's external relations, in particular with other organs of the United Nations and with other international organizations and States and is responsible for information concerning the Court's activities and for the Court's publications (official publications of the Court, press releases, etc.); finally, he has custody of the seals and stamps of the Court, of the archives of the Court, and of such other archives as may be entrusted to the Court (including the archives of the Nuremberg Tribunal).

57. The Deputy-Registrar assists the Registrar and acts as Registrar in the latter's absence; he has since 1998 been entrusted with wider administrative responsibilities, including direct supervision of the Archives, IT and General Assistance Divisions.

58. The Registrar and the Deputy-Registrar, when acting for the Registrar, are, pursuant to the exchange of correspondence mentioned in paragraph 40 above, accorded the same privileges and immunities as Heads of Diplomatic Missions in The Hague.

The Registry's substantive divisions and units

Department of Legal Matters

59. This Department, composed of eight posts in the Professional category and one in the General Service category, is responsible for all legal matters within the Registry. In particular, its task is to assist the Court in the exercise of its judicial functions. It prepares the minutes of meetings of the Court and acts as secretariat to the drafting committees which prepare the Court's draft decisions, and also as secretariat to the Rules Committee. It carries out research in international law, examining judicial and procedural precedents, and prepares studies and notes for the Court and the Registrar as required. It also prepares for signature by the Registrar all correspondence in pending cases and, more generally, diplomatic correspondence relating to the application of the Statute or the Rules of Court. It is also responsible for monitoring the Headquarters agreements with the host country. Finally, the Department may be consulted on all legal questions relating to the terms of employment of Registry staff.

60. Also attached to the Department is a pool of five law clerks, in the Professional category, whose task it is to undertake legal research at the request of Members of the Court.

Department of Linguistic Matters

61. This Department, currently composed of 17 posts in the Professional category and one in the General Service category, is responsible for the translation of documents to and from the Court's two official languages and provides support to Members of the Court (editing of notes, opinions, etc.). Documents translated include case pleadings and other communications from States parties, verbatim records of Court hearings, the Court's judgments, advisory opinions and orders, together with their drafts and working documents, judges' Notes, minutes of Court and committee meetings, internal reports, notes, studies, memoranda and directives, speeches by the President and judges to outside bodies, reports and communications to the Secretariat, etc. The Department also provides interpretation at private and public meetings of the Court and, as required, at meetings held by the President and Members of the Court with agents of the parties and other official visitors.

62. As a result of the growth of the Department since the 2002-2003 biennium, recourse to outside translators has been substantially reduced. However, outside translation assistance is still necessary on occasion, in particular for Court hearings. Outside interpreters are also still regularly required, notably for Court hearings and deliberations. The Department has attempted to use remote translation by sharing resources with other linguistic departments within the United Nations system but, so far, those departments approached have not been in a position to offer effective assistance. The Court will pursue its efforts in this regard.

Information Department

63. This Department, composed of three posts in the Professional category and one in the General Service category, plays an important part in the Court's external relations. Its duties consist of: preparing all documents or sections of documents containing general information on the Court (in particular the Annual Report of the Court to the General Assembly, the sections concerning the Court in various United Nations documents, the *Yearbook*, and documents for the general public); arranging for the dissemination of printed publications and public documents issued by the Court; encouraging and assisting the press, radio and television to report on the work of the Court (in particular by preparing press releases); replying to all requests for information on the Court; keeping Members of the Court abreast of information in the press or on the Internet concerning pending or possible cases; and organizing the public sittings of the Court and all other official events, in particular a large number of visits, including those by distinguished guests. The Department is also responsible for keeping the Court's website up to date.

Technical Divisions

Personnel Division

64. This Division, currently composed of one post in the Professional category and one in the General Service category, is responsible for various duties related to staff management and administration, including: planning and implementation of recruitment, appointment, promotion, training and separation of staff. In administering staff, it ensures observance of the Staff Regulations for the Registry and of those United Nations Staff Regulations and Rules which the Court determines to be applicable. As part of the recruitment process, the Division prepares vacancy announcements, reviews applications, arranges interviews for selection of candidates and prepares job offers for successful candidates, and provides

introduction, orientation and briefing to new staff members. The Division also administers and monitors staff entitlements and benefits, handles the relevant personnel actions and liaises with the Office of Human Resources Management (OHRM) and the United Nations Joint Staff Pension Fund (UNJSPF).

Finance Division

65. This Division, composed of two posts in the Professional category and three in the General Service category, is responsible for financial matters. Its financial duties include *inter alia*: preparation of the budget; financial accounting and reporting; procurement and inventory control; vendor payments; payroll and payroll-related operations (allowances/ overtime), and travel.

Publications Division

66. This Division, composed of three posts in the Professional category, is responsible for preparation of manuscripts, proofreading and correction of proofs, study of estimates and choice of printing firms in relation to the following official publications of the Court: *(a)* Reports of Judgments, Advisory Opinions and Orders; *(b)* Pleadings, Oral Arguments, Documents (former "Series C"); *(c)* Bibliographies; *(d)* Yearbooks. It is also responsible for various other publications as instructed by the Court or the Registrar ("Blue Book" (handbook on the Court for the general public), "White Book" (composition of the Court and the Registry)). Moreover, as the actual printing of the Court's publications is outsourced, the Division is also responsible for the preparation, conclusion and implementation of contracts with printers, including control of all invoices. (For the Court's publications, see Chapter VIII below.)

Documents Division Library of the Court

67. This Division, composed of two posts in the Professional category and three in the General Service category, has as its main task the acquisition, conservation and classification of leading works on international law, as well as a significant number of periodicals and other relevant documents. The Division operates in close collaboration with the Peace Palace Library of the Carnegie Foundation. It prepares bibliographies for Members of the Court as required and compiles an annual bibliography of all publications concerning the Court. It also has to make good the lack of a reference service for translators. The Division strives to incorporate new technologies, in particular by promoting the use of various databases, including those of the United Nations, thus following the Secretary-General's instructions in paragraph 66 of his report A/57/289 promoting electronic document management. It recently acquired new library management software which will afford the Court and the Registry online access to various catalogues and other services.

68. The Library of the Court is also responsible for the Archives of the Nuremberg Military Tribunal (including paper documents, gramophone records, films and some objects). Further to decisions taken by the Court and the Registry concerning the conservation of the Archives, the Library has implemented a focused conservation plan. First, the paper documents were moved in April 2006 in order to undergo disacidification by specialists. The next stage will be the digitization of those documents and the creation of a database through which they can be easily accessed. Research has also been undertaken with a view to digitizing the metal gramophone records containing the sound recordings made of the trial hearings. Although conservation measures were taken in respect of the films in 1987,

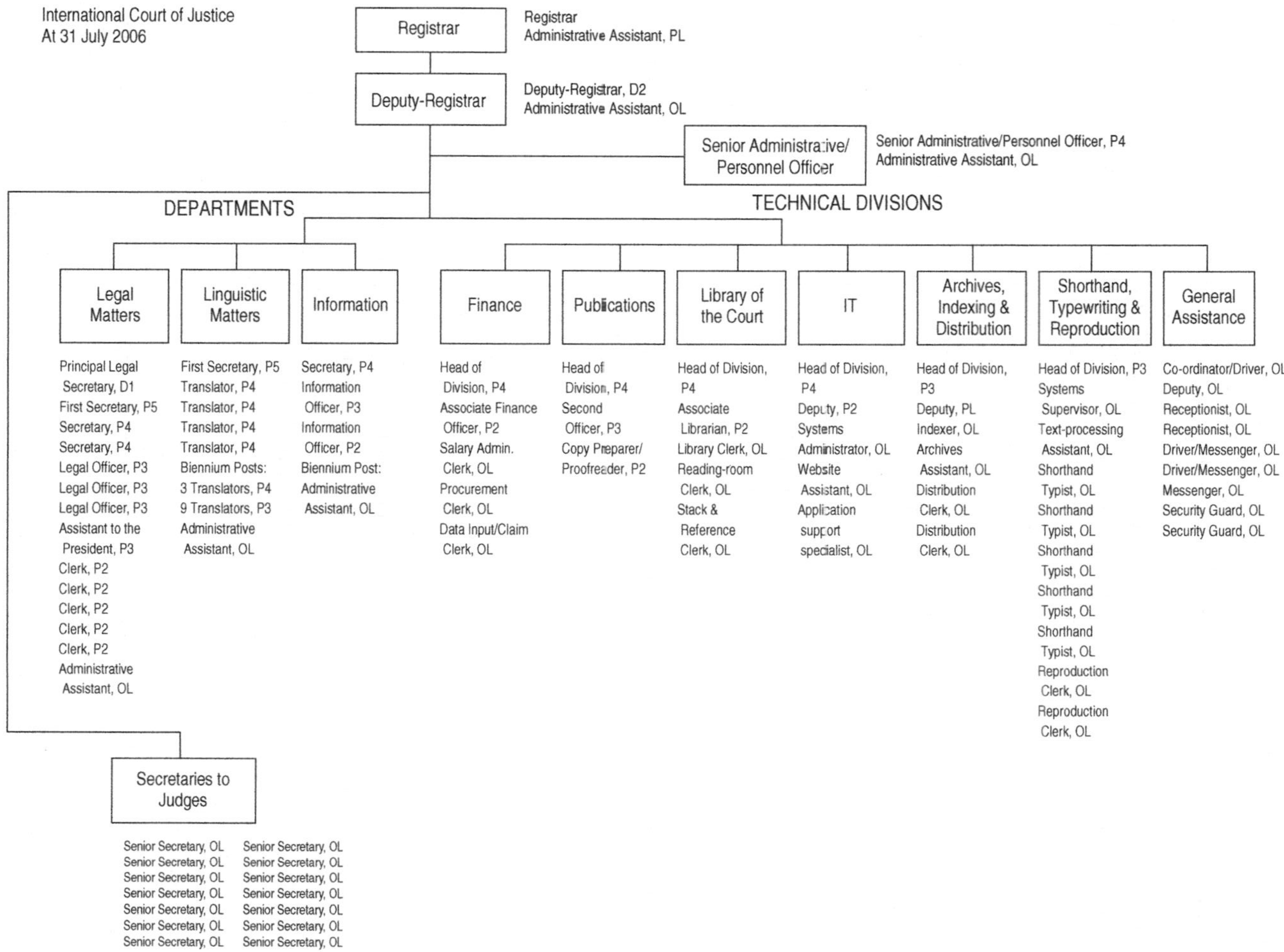
International Court of Justice
At 31 July 2006
Registrar
Registrar
Administrative Assistant, PL
Deputy-Registrar
Deputy-Registrar, D2
Administrative Assistant, OL
Senior Administrative/ Personnel Officer
Senior Administrative/Personnel Officer, P4
Administrative Assistant, OL
DEPARTMENTS
TECHNICAL DIVISIONS
Legal Matters
Principal Legal Secretary, D1
First Secretary, P5
Secretary, P4
Secretary, P4
Legal Officer, P3
Legal Officer, P3
Legal Officer, P3
Assistant to the President, P3
Clerk, P2
Clerk, P2
Clerk, P2
Clerk, P2
Clerk, P2
Administrative Assistant, OL
Linguistic Matters
First Secretary, P5
Translator, P4
Translator, P4
Translator, P4
Translator, P4
Biennium Posts:
3 Translators, P4
9 Translators, P3
Administrative Assistant, OL
Information
Secretary, P4
Information Officer, P3
Information Officer, P2
Biennium Post:
Administrative Assistant, OL
Finance
Head of Division, P4
Associate Finance Officer, P2
Salary Admin. Clerk, OL
Procurement Clerk, OL
Data Input/Claim Clerk, OL
Publications
Head of Division, P4
Second Officer, P3
Copy Preparer/ Proofreader, P2
Library of the Court
Head of Division, P4
Associate Librarian, P2
Library Clerk, OL
Reading-room Clerk, OL
Stack & Reference Clerk, OL
IT
Head of Division, P4
Deputy, P2
Systems Administrator, OL
Website Assistant, OL
Application support specialist, OL
Archives, Indexing & Distribution
Head of Division, P3
Deputy, PL
Indexer, OL
Archives Assistant, OL
Distribution Clerk, OL
Distribution Clerk, OL
Shorthand, Typewriting & Reproduction
Head of Division, P3
Systems Supervisor, OL
Text-processing Assistant, OL
Shorthand Typist, OL
Shorthand Typist, OL
Shorthand Typist, OL
Shorthand Typist, OL
Shorthand Typist, OL
Reproduction Clerk, OL
Reproduction Clerk, OL
General Assistance
Co-ordinator/Driver, OL
Deputy, OL
Receptionist, OL
Receptionist, OL
Driver/Messenger, OL
Driver/Messenger, OL
Messenger, OL
Security Guard, OL
Security Guard, OL
Secretaries to Judges
Senior Secretary, OL
Senior Secretary, OL
Senior Secretary, OL
Senior Secretary, OL
Senior Secretary, OL
Senior Secretary, OL
Senior Secretary, OL
Senior Secretary, OL
Senior Secretary, OL
Senior Secretary, OL
Senior Secretary, OL
Senior Secretary, OL
Senior Secretary, OL
Senior Secretary, OL

the Library is also looking into the possibility of digitizing them. Measures for conserving the objects are also under way.

IT Division

69. The IT Division, composed of two posts in the Professional category and three in the General Service category, is responsible for the efficient functioning and continued development of information technology at the Court. It is charged with the administration and functioning of the Court's local area networks and all other computer and technical equipment. It is also responsible for the implementation of new software and hardware projects, and assists and trains computer users in all aspects of information technology. Finally, the IT Division is responsible for the technical development and management of the ICJ website.

Archives, Indexing and Distribution Division

70. This Division, composed of one post in the Professional category and five in the General Service category, is responsible for indexing and classifying all correspondence and documents received or sent by the Court, and for the subsequent retrieval of any such item on request. The duties of this Division include in particular the keeping of an up-to-date index of correspondence, incoming and outgoing, as well as of all documents, both official and other, held on file. It is also responsible for checking, distributing and filing all internal documents, some of which are strictly confidential. A new computerized system for managing both internal and external documents will become operational within the Division in the course of this biennium.

71. The Archives, Indexing and Distribution Division also handles the despatch of official publications to Members of the United Nations, as well as to numerous institutions and individuals.

Shorthand, Typewriting and Reproduction Division

72. This Division, composed of one post in the Professional category and nine in the General Service category, carries out all the typing work of the Registry and, as necessary, the reproduction of typed texts.

73. The Division is responsible in particular for the typing and reproduction of the following documents in addition to correspondence proper: translations of written pleadings and annexes, verbatim records of hearings and their translations, translations of judges' Notes and judges' amendments, judgments, advisory opinions and orders, translations of judges' opinions. In addition, it is responsible for checking documents and references, re-reading and page layout.

Judges' Secretaries

74. The work done by the 15 judges' secretaries is manifold and varied. As a general rule, the secretaries type Notes, amendments and opinions, as well as all correspondence of judges and judges *ad hoc*. They also check the references in Notes and opinions and provide other assistance as required.

General Assistance Division

75. The General Assistance Division, composed of nine posts in the General Service category, provides general assistance to Members of the Court and Registry staff in regard to messenger, transport, reception and telephone services. It is also responsible for security.

C. Seat

76. The seat of the Court is established at The Hague (Netherlands); this, however, does not prevent the Court from sitting and exercising its functions elsewhere whenever the Court considers it desirable to do so (Statute, Art. 22, para. 1; Rules, Art. 55).

77. The Court occupies, in the Peace Palace at The Hague, the premises formerly occupied by the Permanent Court of International Justice as well as a new wing built at the expense of the Netherlands Government and inaugurated in 1978. An extension of that new wing, as well as a number of newly constructed offices on the third floor of the Peace Palace, were inaugurated in 1997.

78. An agreement of 21 February 1946 between the United Nations and the Carnegie Foundation, which is responsible for the administration of the Peace Palace, determines the conditions under which the Court uses these premises. The agreement was approved by the General Assembly of the United Nations in resolution 84 (I) of 11 December 1946 and has undergone subsequent alterations. The agreement provides for the payment to the Carnegie Foundation of an annual contribution, which presently amounts to US$1,146,978.

D. Peace Palace Museum

79. On 17 May 1999, the Secretary-General of the United Nations, H.E. Mr. Kofi Annan, inaugurated the museum created by the International Court of Justice and situated in the south wing of the Peace Palace.

80. Its collection presents an overview of the theme "Peace through Justice", highlighting the history of the Hague Peace Conferences of 1899 and 1907, the creation at that time of the Permanent Court of Arbitration, the subsequent construction of the Peace Palace as a seat for international justice, as well as the establishment and the functioning of the Permanent Court of International Justice and the present Court (different displays showcase the genesis of the United Nations, the Court and its Registry; the judges on the Bench; the provenance of judges and cases; the procedure of the Court; the world's legal systems; the case law of the Court; prominent visitors).

V. Judicial work of the Court

81. During the period under review 14 contentious cases were pending; the number currently pending is 12.[8]

82. Over this period the Court was seized of three new cases: *Dispute regarding Navigational and Related Rights (Costa Rica* v. *Nicaragua)*; *Status vis-à-vis the Host State of a Diplomatic Envoy to the United Nations (Commonwealth of Dominica* v. *Switzerland)*; and *Pulp Mills on the River Uruguay (Argentina* v. *Uruguay)*.

83. An Application was also filed with the Court on 9 January 2006 by the Republic of Djibouti concerning a dispute with France regarding the alleged violation by the latter of its "international obligations in respect of mutual assistance in criminal matters" in the context of the investigation into the death of the French Judge Bernard Borrel in Djibouti in 1995. In its Application, Djibouti explained that the subject of the dispute specifically concerned "the refusal by the French governmental and judicial authorities to execute an international letter rogatory regarding the transmission to the judicial authorities in Djibouti of the record relating to the investigation in the 'Case against X for the murder of Bernard Borrel'". Djibouti maintains that this refusal constitutes a violation of France's international obligations under the Treaty of Friendship and Co-operation signed by the two States on 27 June 1977 and the Convention on Mutual Assistance in Criminal Matters between France and Djibouti, dated 27 September 1986. Djibouti further asserts in its Application that, in summoning certain internationally protected nationals of Djibouti (including the Head of State) as *témoins assistés* [legally represented witnesses] in connection with a criminal complaint for subornation of perjury against X in the Borrel case, France violated its obligation to prevent attacks on the person, freedom or dignity of persons enjoying such protection. The Republic of Djibouti seeks to found the jurisdiction of the Court on Article 38, paragraph 5, of the Rules of Court and is "confident that the French Republic will agree to submit to the jurisdiction of the Court to settle the present dispute". Under that paragraph:

> "When the applicant State proposes to found the jurisdiction of the Court upon a consent thereto yet to be given or manifested by the State against which such application is made, the application shall be transmitted to that State. It shall not however be entered in the General List, nor any action be taken in the proceedings, unless and until the State against which such application is made consents to the Court's jurisdiction for the purposes of the case."

84. Pursuant to this provision, the Republic of Djibouti's Application was transmitted to the French Government. However, as of 31 July 2006, France had yet to accept the jurisdiction of the Court in this case; in consequence, no further documents have been transmitted and no procedural act has been undertaken.

85. The Court held public hearings in the following cases: *Application of the Convention for the Prevention and Punishment of the Crime of Genocide (Bosnia and Herzegovina* v. *Serbia and Montenegro)*;[9] *Pulp Mills on the River Uruguay (Argentina* v. *Uruguay)*.

86. The Court rendered judgment on the merits in the case concerning *Armed Activities on the Territory of the Congo (Democratic Republic of the Congo* v. *Uganda*), and on the preliminary objections to its jurisdiction and the admissibility of the Application raised by the Respondent in the case concerning *Armed Activities on the Territory of the Congo (New Application: 2002) (Democratic Republic of the Congo* v. *Rwanda*).

87. In the case concerning *Pulp Mills on the River Uruguay (Argentina* v. *Uruguay)*, the Court made an Order with respect to the request for provisional measures submitted by Argentina.

88. The Court also made Orders fixing or extending time-limits for the filing of pleadings in the following cases: *Dispute regarding Navigational and Related Rights (Costa Rica* v. *Nicaragua)*; *Certain Criminal Proceedings in France (Republic of the Congo* v. *France)*;

Maritime Delimitation in the Black Sea (Romania v. *Ukraine)*. It further made an Order providing for the removal from the List of the case concerning *Status vis-à-vis the Host State of a Diplomatic Envoy to the United Nations (Commonwealth of Dominica* v. *Switzerland)*.

89. The Court also amended Article 43 of its Rules.

A. Cases before the Court

1. Application of the Convention on the Prevention and Punishment of the Crime of Genocide (Bosnia and Herzegovina v. Serbia and Montenegro)

90. On 20 March 1993, Bosnia and Herzegovina filed an Application instituting proceedings against Serbia and Montenegro (then known as the Federal Republic of Yugoslavia)[10] in respect of a dispute concerning alleged violations of the Convention on the Prevention and Punishment of the Crime of Genocide, adopted by the General Assembly of the United Nations on 9 December 1948 (hereinafter called the "Genocide Convention"). As basis for the jurisdiction of the Court, Bosnia and Herzegovina invokes Article IX of that Convention.

91. In its Application, Bosnia and Herzegovina, among other claims, requested the Court to adjudge and declare that Serbia and Montenegro, through its agents and surrogates, "has killed, murdered, wounded, raped, robbed, tortured, kidnapped, illegally detained, and exterminated the citizens of Bosnia and Herzegovina", that it must cease immediately this practice of so-called "ethnic cleansing" and pay reparations.

92. On 20 March 1993 Bosnia and Herzegovina also submitted a request for provisional measures. Public hearings were held on 1 and 2 April 1993, and by an Order dated 8 April 1993 the Court indicated that Serbia and Montenegro "should immediately . . . take all measures within its power to prevent commission of the crime of genocide" and that both Serbia and Montenegro and Bosnia and Herzegovina "should not take any action and should ensure that no action is taken which may aggravate or extend the existing dispute . . . or render it more difficult of solution". The Court limited its provisional measures to requests falling within the jurisdiction conferred on it by the Genocide Convention.

93. On 27 July 1993 Bosnia and Herzegovina filed a second request for provisional measures, which was followed on 10 August 1993 by a request for provisional measures from Serbia and Montenegro. Public hearings were held on 25 and 26 August 1993, and by an Order dated 13 September 1993 the Court reaffirmed the measures indicated earlier, adding that they should be immediately and effectively implemented.

94. On 5 August 1993 the President of the Court addressed a message to both Parties, referring to Article 74, paragraph 4, of the Rules of Court, which enables him, pending the meeting of the Court, "to call upon the parties to act in such a way as will enable any order the Court may make on the request for provisional measures to have its appropriate effects".

95. The Memorial of Bosnia and Herzegovina was filed within the extended time-limit of 15 April 1994.

96. On 26 June 1995, within the extended time-limit for the deposit of its Counter-Memorial, Serbia and Montenegro filed preliminary objections to the jurisdiction of the Court and the

admissibility of the Application; the proceedings on the merits were accordingly suspended (Art. 79 of the Rules of Court). After Bosnia and Herzegovina had filed a written statement on the preliminary objections within the time-limit of 14 November 1995 fixed by the Court' s Order of 14 July 1995, public hearings were held between 29 April and 3 May 1996. On 11 July 1996, the Court delivered its Judgment, rejecting the objections of Serbia and Montenegro; finding that, on the basis of Article IX of the Genocide Convention, it had jurisdiction to deal with the case; dismissing the additional basis of jurisdiction invoked by Bosnia and Herzegovina; and finding that the Application was admissible.

97. In the Counter-Memorial filed on 22 July 1997, Serbia and Montenegro submitted counter-claims requesting the Court to adjudge and declare that "Bosnia and Herzegovina [was] responsible for the acts of genocide committed against the Serbs in Bosnia and Herzegovina" and that it "ha[d] the obligation to punish the persons held responsible" for these acts. It also asked the Court to rule that "Bosnia and Herzegovina [was] bound to take necessary measures so that the said acts would not be repeated in future" and "to eliminate all consequences of the violation of the obligations established by the . . . [Genocide] Convention".

98. By letter of 28 July 1997 Bosnia and Herzegovina informed the Court that "the Applicant [was] of the opinion that the Counter-Claim submitted by the Respondent . . . [did] not meet the criterion of Article 80, paragraph 1, of the Rules of Court and should therefore not be joined to the original proceedings".

99. After each Party had filed written observations, the Court, by an Order of 17 December 1997, held that Serbia and Montenegro's counter-claims were "admissible as such" and that they formed "part of the current proceedings" in the case; the Court also directed the Parties to submit further written pleadings on the merits of their respective claims and fixed time-limits for the filing of a Reply by Bosnia and Herzegovina and of a Rejoinder by Serbia and Montenegro. Those time-limits having been extended at the request of each of the Parties, the Reply of Bosnia and Herzegovina was eventually filed on 23 April 1998 and the Rejoinder of Serbia and Montenegro on 22 February 1999. In these pleadings, each of the Parties contested the allegations made by the other.

100. Subsequently several exchanges of letters took place concerning further procedural difficulties in the case.

101. By an Order of 10 September 2001 the President of the Court placed on record the withdrawal by Serbia and Montenegro of the counter-claims submitted by that State in its Counter-Memorial. The Order was made after Serbia and Montenegro had informed the Court that it intended to withdraw its counter-claims and Bosnia and Herzegovina had indicated to the latter that it had no objection to that withdrawal.

102. It is recalled that, on 3 February 2003, the Court rendered its Judgment in the case concerning *Application for Revision of the Judgment of 11 July 1996 in the Case concerning* Application of the Convention on the Prevention and Punishment of the Crime of Genocide (Bosnia and Herzegovina *v.* Yugoslavia), Preliminary Objections *(Yugoslavia* v. *Bosnia and Herzegovina)*, by which it found that the request for revision was inadmissible.

103. It is further recalled that, on 4 May 2001, Serbia and Montenegro (then known as the Federal Republic of Yugoslavia) submitted a document to the Court, entitled "Initiative to

the Court to reconsider ex officio Jurisdiction over Yugoslavia". The submissions presented in that document were, first, that the Court had no jurisdiction *ratione personae* over Serbia and Montenegro and, secondly, that the Court should "suspend proceedings regarding the merits of the case until a decision on this Initiative", i.e. on the jurisdictional issue, had been rendered. In a letter dated 12 June 2003, the Registrar informed the Parties in the case that the Court had decided that it could not effect such a suspension of the proceedings in the circumstances of the case.

104. Public hearings on the merits of the case were held from 27 February 2006 to 9 May 2006. At the conclusion of those hearings, the Parties presented the following final submissions to the Court.

For Bosnia and Herzegovina:

"Bosnia and Herzegovina requests the Court to adjudge and declare:

1. That Serbia and Montenegro, through its organs or entities under its control, has violated its obligations under the Convention on the Prevention and Punishment of the Crime of Genocide by intentionally destroying in part the non-Serb national, ethnical or religious group within, but not limited to, the territory of Bosnia and Herzegovina, including in particular the Muslim population, by:

— killing members of the group;

— causing serious bodily or mental harm to members of the group;

— deliberately inflicting on the group conditions of life calculated to bring about its physical destruction in whole or in part;

— imposing measures intended to prevent births within the group;

— forcibly transferring children of the group to another group;

2. Subsidiarily:

(i) that Serbia and Montenegro has violated its obligations under the Convention on the Prevention and Punishment of the Crime of Genocide by complicity in genocide as defined in paragraph 1, above; and/or

(ii) that Serbia and Montenegro has violated its obligations under the Convention on the Prevention and Punishment of the Crime of Genocide by aiding and abetting individuals, groups and entities engaged in acts of genocide, as defined in paragraph 1 above;

3. That Serbia and Montenegro has violated its obligations under the Convention on the Prevention and Punishment of the Crime of Genocide by conspiring to commit genocide and by inciting to commit genocide, as defined in paragraph 1 above;

4. That Serbia and Montenegro has violated its obligations under the Convention on the Prevention and Punishment of the Crime of Genocide for having failed to prevent genocide;

5. That Serbia and Montenegro has violated and is violating its obligations under the Convention on the Prevention and Punishment of the Crime of Genocide for having failed and for failing to punish acts of genocide or any other act prohibited by the Convention on the Prevention and Punishment of the Crime of Genocide, and for having failed and for failing to transfer individuals accused of genocide or any other act prohibited by the Convention to the International Criminal Tribunal for the former Yugoslavia and to co-operate fully with this Tribunal;

6. That the violations of international law set out in submissions 1 to 5 constitute wrongful acts attributable to Serbia and Montenegro which entail its international responsibility, and, accordingly,

(*a*) that Serbia and Montenegro shall immediately take effective steps to ensure full compliance with its obligation to punish acts of genocide under the Convention on the Prevention and Punishment of the Crime of Genocide or any other act prohibited by the Convention and to transfer individuals accused of genocide or any other act prohibited by the Convention to the International Criminal Tribunal for the former Yugoslavia and to fully co-operate with this Tribunal;

(*b*) that Serbia and Montenegro must redress the consequences of its international wrongful acts and, as a result of the international responsibility incurred for the above violations of the Convention on the Prevention and Punishment of the Crime of Genocide, must pay, and Bosnia and Herzegovina is entitled to receive, in its own right and as *parens patriae* for its citizens, full compensation for the damages and losses caused. That, in particular, the compensation shall cover any financially assessable damage which corresponds to:

(i) damage caused to natural persons by the acts enumerated in Article III of the Convention, including non-material damage suffered by the victims or the surviving heirs or successors and their dependants;

(ii) material damage caused to properties of natural or legal persons, public or private, by the acts enumerated in Article III of the Convention;

(iii) material damage suffered by Bosnia and Herzegovina in respect of expenditures reasonably incurred to remedy or mitigate damage flowing from the acts enumerated in Article III of the Convention;

(*c*) that the nature, form and amount of the compensation shall be determined by the Court, failing agreement thereon between the Parties one year after the Judgment of the Court, and that the Court shall reserve the subsequent procedure for that purpose;

(d) that Serbia and Montenegro shall provide specific guarantees and assurances that it will not repeat the wrongful acts complained of, the form of which guarantees and assurances is to be determined by the Court;

7. That in failing to comply with the Orders for indication of provisional measures rendered by the Court on 8 April 1993 and 13 September 1993 Serbia and Montenegro has been in breach of its international obligations and is under an obligation to Bosnia and Herzegovina to provide for the latter violation symbolic compensation, the amount of which is to be determined by the Court."

For Serbia and Montenegro:

"In accordance with Article 60, paragraph 2, of the Rules of Court, Serbia and Montenegro asks the Court to adjuge and declare:

— that this Court has no jurisdiction because the Respondent had no access to the Court at the relevant moment; or, in the alternative

— that this Court has no jurisdiction over the Respondent because the Respondent never remained or became bound by Article IX of the Convention on the Prevention and Punishment of the Crime of Genocide, and because there is no other ground on which jurisdiction over the Respondent could be based.

In case the Court determines that jurisdiction exists Serbia and Montenegro asks the Court to adjudge and declare:

—"That the requests in paragraphs 1 to 6 of the Submissions of Bosnia and Herzegovina relating to alleged violations of the obligations under the Convention on the Prevention and Punishment of the Crime of Genocide be rejected as lacking a basis either in law or in fact.

— In any event, that the acts and/or omissions for which the respondent State is alleged to be responsible are not attributable to the respondent State. Such attribution would necessarily involve breaches of the law applicable in these proceedings.

— Without prejudice to the foregoing, that the relief available to the applicant State in these proceedings, in accordance with the appropriate interpretation of the Convention on the Prevention and Punishment of the Crime of Genocide, is limited to the rendering of a declaratory judgment.

— Further, without prejudice to the foregoing, that any question of legal responsibility for alleged breaches of the Orders for the indication of provisional measures, rendered by the Court on 8 April 1993 and 13 September 1993, does not fall within the competence of the Court to provide appropriate remedies to an applicant State in the context of contentious proceedings, and, accordingly, the request in paragraph 7 of the Submissions of Bosnia and Herzegovina should be rejected."

105. At the time of preparation of this Report, the Court was deliberating its Judgment.

2. Gabčíkovo-Nagymaros Project (Hungary/Slovakia)

106. On 2 July 1993, Hungary and Slovakia jointly notified to the Court a Special Agreement, signed between them on 7 April 1993, for the submission of certain issues arising out of differences regarding the implementation and the termination of the Budapest Treaty of 16 September 1977 on the construction and operation of the Gabčíkovo-Nagymaros barrage system.

In Article 2 of the Special Agreement:

"(1) The Court is requested to decide on the basis of the Treaty and rules and principles of general international law, as well as such other treaties as the Court may find applicable,

(a) whether the Republic of Hungary was entitled to suspend and subsequently abandon, in 1989, the works on the Nagymaros Project and on the part of the Gabčíkovo Project for which the Treaty attributed responsibility to the Republic of Hungary;

(b) whether the Czech and Slovak Federal Republic was entitled to proceed, in November 1991, to the 'provisional solution' and to put into operation from October 1992 this system, described in the Report of the Working Group of Independent Experts of the Commission of the European Communities, the Republic of Hungary and the Czech and Slovak Federal Republic dated 23 November 1992 (damming up of the Danube at river kilometre 1851.7 on Czechoslovak territory and resulting consequences on water and navigation course);

(c) what are the legal effects of the notification, on 19 May 1992, of the termination of the Treaty by the Republic of Hungary.

(2) The Court is also requested to determine the legal consequences, including the rights and obligations for the Parties, arising from its Judgment on the questions in paragraph (1) of this Article."

107. Each of the Parties filed a Memorial, a Counter-Memorial and a Reply within respective time-limits of 2 May 1994, 5 December 1994 and 20 June 1995, as fixed by the Court or its President.

108. Hearings in the case were held between 3 March and 15 April 1997. From 1 to 4 April 1997, the Court paid a site visit (the first ever in its history) to the Gabčíkovo-Nagymaros Project by virtue of Article 66 of the Rules of Court.

109. In its Judgment of 25 September 1997, the Court found that both Hungary and Slovakia had breached their legal obligations. It called on both States to negotiate in good faith in order to ensure the achievement of the objectives of the 1977 Budapest Treaty, which it declared was still in force, while taking account of the factual situation that had developed since 1989.

110. On 3 September 1998 Slovakia filed in the Registry of the Court a request for an additional judgment in the case. Such an additional judgment was necessary, according to Slovakia, because of the unwillingness of Hungary to implement the Judgment delivered by the Court in that case on 25 September 1997.

111. In its request, Slovakia stated that the Parties had conducted a series of negotiations on the modalities for executing the Court's Judgment and had initialled a draft Framework Agreement, which had been approved by the Government of Slovakia on 10 March 1998. Slovakia contended that on 5 March 1998 Hungary had postponed its approval and, upon the accession of its new Government following the May elections, it had proceeded to disavow the draft Framework Agreement and was further delaying the implementation of the Judgment. Slovakia indicated that it wanted the Court to determine the modalities for executing the Judgment.

112. As the basis for its request, Slovakia invokes Article 5 (3) of the Special Agreement signed at Brussels on 7 April 1993 by itself and Hungary with a view to the joint submission of their dispute to the Court.

113. Hungary filed a written statement of its position on the request for an additional judgment made by Slovakia within the time-limit of 7 December 1998 fixed by the President of the Court.

114. The Parties have subsequently resumed negotiations and have informed the Court on a regular basis of the progress made.

3. Ahmadou Sadio Diallo (Republic of Guinea v. Democratic Republic of the Congo)

115. On 28 December 1998 the Republic of Guinea instituted proceedings against the Democratic Republic of the Congo by filing an "Application for purposes of diplomatic protection", in which it requested the Court to find that "the Democratic Republic of the Congo is guilty of serious breaches of international law committed upon the person of a Guinean national", Mr. Ahmadou Sadio Diallo.

116. According to Guinea, Mr. Ahmadou Sadio Diallo, a businessman who had been a resident of the Democratic Republic of the Congo for 32 years, was "unjustly imprisoned by the authorities of that State" for two and a half months, "despoiled of his sizable investments, business, movable and immovable property and bank accounts, and then", on 2 February 1996, "expelled from the country", because he had sought the payment of debts owed to him by the Democratic Republic of the Congo (in particular by Gécamines, a State undertaking with a monopoly over mining) and by oil companies established in that country (Zaire Shell, Zaire Mobil and Zaire Fina) under contracts with companies owned by him, namely Africom-Zaire and Africacontainers-Zaire.

117. As basis for the Court's jurisdiction, Guinea invokes the declarations whereby the Democratic Republic of the Congo and itself accepted the compulsory jurisdiction of the Court on, respectively, 8 February 1989 and 11 November 1998.

118. Guinea filed its Memorial within the time-limit as extended by the Court. On 3 October 2002, within the time-limit for the deposit of its Counter-Memorial as extended, the Democratic Republic of the Congo filed certain preliminary objections to the Court's

jurisdiction and the admissibility of the Application; the proceedings on the merits were accordingly suspended (Article 79 of the Rules of Court).

119. By an Order of 7 November 2002 the Court fixed 7 July 2003 as the time-limit within which Guinea might present a written statement of its observations and submissions on the preliminary objections raised by the Democratic Republic of the Congo. That written statement was filed within the time-limit thus fixed.

120. The Court has set 27 November 2006 as the date for the opening of hearings on the preliminary objections.

4. Armed Activities on the Territory of the Congo (Democratic Republic of the Congo v. Uganda)[11]

121. On 23 June 1999 the Democratic Republic of the Congo filed an Application instituting proceedings against Uganda for "acts of armed aggression perpetrated in flagrant violation of the United Nations Charter and of the Charter of the OAU".

122. In its Application, the Democratic Republic of the Congo contended that "such armed aggression . . . ha[d] involved *inter alia* violation of the sovereignty and territorial integrity of the [Democratic Republic of the Congo], violations of international humanitarian law and massive human rights violations". The Democratic Republic of the Congo sought "to secure the cessation of the acts of aggression directed against it, which constitute a serious threat to peace and security in central Africa in general and in the Great Lakes region in particular"; it also sought

> "compensation from Uganda in respect of all acts of looting, destruction, removal of property and persons and other unlawful acts attributable to [it], in respect of which the [Democratic Republic of the Congo] reserves the right to determine at a later date the precise amount of the damage suffered, in addition to its claim for the restitution of all property removed".

123. Consequently, the Democratic Republic of the Congo requested the Court to adjudge and declare that Uganda was guilty of an act of aggression contrary to Article 2, paragraph 4, of the United Nations Charter; that it was committing repeated violations of the Geneva Convention of 1949 and the Additional Protocols of 1977 and also guilty of massive human rights violations in defiance of the most basic customary law; that more specifically, by taking forcible possession of the Inga hydroelectric dam, and deliberately and regularly causing massive electrical power cuts, Uganda had rendered itself responsible for very heavy losses of life among the 5 million inhabitants of the city of Kinshasa and the surrounding area; and that by shooting down, on 9 October 1998 at Kindu, a Boeing 727 the property of Congo Airlines, thereby causing the death of 40 civilians, Uganda had also violated certain conventions concerning international civil aviation. The Democratic Republic of the Congo further asked the Court to adjudge and declare that all Ugandan armed forces and Ugandan nationals, both natural and legal persons, should be withdrawn from Congolese territory; and that the Democratic Republic of the Congo was entitled to compensation.

124. The Democratic Republic of the Congo invokes as basis for the Court's jurisdiction the declarations whereby both States have accepted the compulsory jurisdiction of the Court in relation to any other State accepting the same obligation (Art. 36, para. 2, of the Statute of the Court).

125. Taking into account the agreement of the Parties, the Court, by an Order of 21 October 1999, fixed 21 July 2000 as the time-limit for the filing of a Memorial by the Congo and 21 April 2001 for the filing of a Counter-Memorial by Uganda. The Memorial of the Democratic Republic of the Congo was filed within the time-limit thus prescribed.

126. On 19 June 2000 the Democratic Republic of the Congo filed a request for the indication of provisional measures, stating that "since 5 June [2000], the resumption of fighting between the armed troops of . . . Uganda and another foreign army ha[d] caused considerable damage to the Congo and to its population", and "these tactics ha[d] been unanimously condemned, in particular by the United Nations Security Council". By letters of the same date, the President of the Court, acting in conformity with Article 74, paragraph 4, of the Rules of Court, drew "the attention of both Parties to the need to act in such a way as to enable any Order the Court will make on the request for provisional measures to have its appropriate effects".

127. Public hearings on the request for the indication of provisional measures were held on 26 and 28 June 2000. At a public sitting held on 1 July 2000, the Court rendered its Order, by which it unanimously found that both Parties must

> "forthwith, prevent and refrain from any action, and in particular any armed action, which might prejudice the rights of the other Party in respect of whatever judgment the Court may render in the case, or which might aggravate or extend the dispute before the Court or make it more difficult to resolve";
>
> "forthwith, take all measures necessary to comply with all of their obligations under international law, in particular those under the United Nations Charter and the Charter of the Organization of African Unity, and with United Nations Security Council resolution 1304 (2000) of 16 June 2000"; and
>
> "forthwith, take all measures necessary to ensure full respect within the zone of conflict for fundamental human rights and for the applicable provisions of humanitarian law".

128. Within the time-limit of 21 April 2001 fixed by the Court's Order of 21 October 1999, Uganda filed its Counter-Memorial. The Counter-Memorial contained three counter-claims. The first concerned alleged acts of aggression against it by the Democratic Republic of the Congo; the second related to attacks on Ugandan diplomatic premises and personnel in Kinshasa and on Ugandan nationals for which the Democratic Republic of the Congo was alleged to be responsible; and the third dealt with alleged violations by the Democratic Republic of the Congo of the Lusaka Agreement. Uganda asked that the issue of reparation be reserved for a subsequent stage of the proceedings. By an Order of 29 November 2001 the Court found that the first two of the counter-claims submitted by Uganda against the Democratic Republic of the Congo were "admissible as such and [formed] part of the

current proceedings", but that the third was not. In view of these findings, the Court considered it necessary for the Democratic Republic of the Congo to file a Reply and Uganda a Rejoinder, addressing the claims of both Parties, and fixed 29 May 2002 as the time-limit for the filing of the Reply and 29 November 2002 for the filing of the Rejoinder. Further, in order to ensure strict equality between the Parties, the Court reserved the right of the Democratic Republic of the Congo to present its views in writing a second time on the Ugandan counter-claims, in an additional pleading to be the subject of a subsequent Order. The Reply was filed within the time-limit fixed. By an Order of 7 November 2002, the Court extended the time-limit for the filing by Uganda of its Rejoinder and fixed 6 December 2002 as the new time-limit. The Rejoinder was filed within the time-limit as thus extended.

129. By an Order of 29 January 2003, the Court authorized the submission by the Democratic Republic of the Congo of an additional pleading relating solely to the counter-claims submitted by Uganda, and fixed 28 February 2003 as the time-limit for its filing. That written pleading was filed within the time-limit fixed.

130. The Court had initially fixed 10 November 2003 as the date for the opening of the hearings. However, by a letter dated 5 November 2003, the Democratic Republic of the Congo raised the question whether the hearings might be adjourned to a later date, in April 2004, in order to enable the diplomatic negotiations engaged by the Parties to be conducted in an atmosphere of calm. By a letter of 6 November 2003, Uganda indicated that it supported the proposal and adopted the request of the Congo.

131. By a letter dated 6 November 2003, the Registrar informed the Parties that the Court, acting under Article 54, paragraph 1, of the Rules of Court, and taking account of the representations made to it by the Parties, had decided that the opening of the oral proceedings would be postponed but had also decided that it was impossible to fix a date in April 2004 for the adjourned hearings. As the Court's judicial calendar until well into 2004 had been adopted some time before, providing for the hearing of, and deliberation on, a number of other cases, a new date for the opening of oral proceedings in this case would have to be fixed subsequently.

132. Public hearings on the merits of the case were held from 11 to 29 April 2005. At the conclusion of those hearings the Parties presented the following final submissions to the Court.

> *For the Democratic Republic of the Congo (with respect to its claims):*
>
> "The Democratic Republic of the Congo requests the Court to adjudge and declare:
>
> 1. That the Republic of Uganda, by engaging in military and paramilitary activities against the Democratic Republic of the Congo, by occupying its territory and by actively extending military, logistic, economic and financial support to irregular forces operating there, and having operated there, has violated the following principles of conventional and customary law:
>
> — the principle of non-use of force in international relations, including the prohibition of aggression;

— the obligation to settle international disputes exclusively by peaceful means so as to ensure that international peace and security, as well as justice, are not placed in jeopardy;

— respect for the sovereignty of States and the rights of peoples to self-determination, and hence to choose their own political and economic system freely and without outside interference;

— the principle of non-interference in matters within the domestic jurisdiction of States, including refraining from extending any assistance to the parties to a civil war operating on the territory of another State.

2. That the Republic of Uganda, by committing acts of violence against nationals of the Democratic Republic of the Congo, by killing and injuring them or despoiling them of their property, by failing to take adequate measures to prevent violations of human rights in the DRC by persons under its jurisdiction or control, and/or failing to punish persons under its jurisdiction or control having engaged in the above-mentioned acts, has violated the following principles of conventional and customary law:

— the principle of conventional and customary law imposing an obligation to respect, and ensure respect for, fundamental human rights, including in times of armed conflict, in accordance with international humanitarian law;

— the principle of conventional and customary law imposing an obligation, at all times, to make a distinction in an armed conflict between civilian and military objectives;

— the right of Congolese nationals to enjoy the most basic rights, both civil and political, as well as economic, social and cultural.

3. That the Republic of Uganda, by engaging in the illegal exploitation of Congolese natural resources, by pillaging its assets and wealth, by failing to take adequate measures to prevent the illegal exploitation of the resources of the DRC by persons under its jurisdiction or control, and/or failing to punish persons under its jurisdiction or control having engaged in the above-mentioned acts, has violated the following principles of conventional and customary law:

— the applicable rules of international humanitarian law;

— respect for the sovereignty of States, including over their natural resources;

— the duty to promote the realization of the principle of equality of peoples and of their right of self-determination, and consequently to refrain from exposing peoples to foreign subjugation, domination or exploitation;

— the principle of non-interference in matters within the domestic jurisdiction of States, including economic matters.

4. *(a)* That the violations of international law set out in submissions 1, 2 and 3 constitute wrongful acts attributable to Uganda which engage its international responsibility;

(b) That the Republic of Uganda shall cease forthwith all continuing internationally wrongful acts, and in particular its support for irregular forces operating in the DRC and its exploitation of Congolese wealth and natural resources;

(c) That the Republic of Uganda shall provide specific guarantees and assurances that it will not repeat the wrongful acts complained of;

(d) That the Republic of Uganda is under an obligation to the Democratic Republic of the Congo to make reparation for all injury caused to the latter by the violation of the obligations imposed by international law and set out in submissions 1, 2 and 3 above;

(e) That the nature, form and amount of the reparation shall be determined by the Court, failing agreement thereon between the Parties, and that the Court shall reserve the subsequent procedure for that purpose.

5. That the Republic of Uganda has violated the Order of the Court on provisional measures of 1 July 2000, in that it has failed to comply with the following provisional measures:

'(1) Both Parties must, forthwith, prevent and refrain from any action, and in particular any armed action, which might prejudice the rights of the other Party in respect of whatever judgment the Court may render in the case, or which might aggravate or extend the dispute before the Court or make it more difficult to resolve;

(2) Both Parties must, forthwith, take all measures necessary to comply with all of their obligations under international law, in particular those under the United Nations Charter and the Charter of the Organization of African Unity, and with United Nations Security Council resolution 1304 (2000) of 16 June 2000;

(3) Both Parties must, forthwith, take all measures necessary to ensure full respect within the zone of conflict for fundamental human rights and for the applicable provisions of humanitarian law.'"

For the Republic of Uganda (with respect to the claims of the Democratic Republic of the Congo and to its own counter-claims):

"The Republic of Uganda requests the Court:

1. To adjudge and declare in accordance with international law:

(A) That the requests of the Democratic Republic of the Congo relating to the activities or situations involving the Republic of Rwanda or her agents are inadmissible for the reasons set forth in Chapter XV of the Counter-Memorial and reaffirmed in the oral pleadings;

(B) That the requests of the Democratic Republic of the Congo that the Court adjudge and declare that the Republic of Uganda is responsible for various breaches of international law, as alleged in the Memorial, the Reply and/or the oral pleadings are rejected; and

(C) That Uganda's counter-claims presented in Chapter XVIII of the Counter-Memorial, and reaffirmed in Chapter VI of the Rejoinder as well as the oral pleadings be upheld.

2. To reserve the issue of reparation in relation to Uganda's counter-claims for a subsequent stage of the proceedings."

For the Democratic Republic of the Congo (with respect to the counter-claims of Uganda):

"The Congo requests the Court to adjudge and declare:

As regards the *first counter-claim submitted by Uganda,*

1. To the extent that it relates to the period before Laurent-Désiré Kabila came to power, Uganda's claim is inadmissible because Uganda had previously renounced its right to lodge such a claim: in the alternative, the claim is unfounded because Uganda has failed to establish the facts on which it is based;

2. To the extent that it relates to the period from the time when Laurent-Désiré Kabila came to power to the time when Uganda launched its armed attack, Uganda's claim is unfounded in fact because Uganda has failed to establish the facts on which it is based;

3. To the extent that it relates to the period subsequent to the launching of Uganda's armed attack, Uganda's claim is unfounded both in fact and in law because Uganda has failed to establish the facts on which it is based and, in any event, from 2 August 1998 the DRC was in a situation of self-defence.

As regards the *second counter-claim submitted by Uganda:*

1. To the extent that it now relates to the interpretation and application of the Vienna Convention of 1961 on Diplomatic Relations, the claim submitted by Uganda radically changes the subject-matter of the dispute, contrary to the Statute and to the Rules of Court; that part of the claim must therefore be dismissed from the present proceedings;

2. That part of the claim relating to the alleged mistreatment of certain Ugandan nationals remains inadmissible because Uganda has still failed to show that the requirements laid down by international law for the exercise of its diplomatic protection were satisfied; in the alternative, that part of the claim is unfounded because Uganda is still unable to establish the factual and legal bases of its claims.

3. That part of the claim relating to the alleged expropriation of Uganda's public property is unfounded because Uganda is still unable to establish the factual and legal bases of its claims."

133. On 19 December 2005, the Court rendered its Judgment. The operative paragraph of the Judgment reads as follows:

> "For these reasons,
>
> THE COURT,
>
> (1) By sixteen votes to one,
>
> *Finds* that the Republic of Uganda, by engaging in military activities against the Democratic Republic of the Congo on the latter's territory, by occupying Ituri and by actively extending military, logistic, economic and financial support to irregular forces having operated on the territory of the DRC, violated the principle of non-use of force in international relations and the principle of non-intervention;
>
> IN FAVOUR:
> *President* Shi; *Vice-President* Ranjeva; *Judges* Koroma, Vereshchetin, Higgins, Parra-Aranguren, Kooijmans, Rezek, Al-Khasawneh, Buergenthal, Elaraby, Owada, Simma, Tomka, Abraham; *Judge* ad hoc Verhoeven;
>
> AGAINST:
> *Judge* ad hoc Kateka;
>
> (2) Unanimously,
>
> *Finds* admissible the claim submitted by the Democratic Republic of the Congo relating to alleged violations by the Republic of Uganda of its obligations under international human rights law and international humanitarian law in the course of hostilities between Ugandan and Rwandan military forces in Kisangani;
>
> (3) By sixteen votes to one,
>
> *Finds* that the Republic of Uganda, by the conduct of its armed forces, which committed acts of killing, torture and other forms of inhumane treatment of the Congolese civilian population, destroyed villages and civilian buildings, failed to distinguish between civilian and military targets and to protect the civilian population in fighting with other combatants, trained child soldiers, incited ethnic conflict and failed to take measures to put an end to such conflict; as well as by its failure, as an occupying Power, to take measures to respect and ensure respect for human rights and international humanitarian law in Ituri district, violated its obligations under international human rights law and international humanitarian law;
>
> IN FAVOUR:
> *President* Shi; *Vice-President* Ranjeva; *Judges* Koroma, Vereshchetin, Higgins, Parra-Aranguren, Kooijmans, Rezek, Al-Khasawneh, Buergenthal, Elaraby, Owada, Simma, Tomka, Abraham; *Judge* ad hoc Verhoeven;
>
> AGAINST:
> *Judge* ad hoc Kateka

(4) By sixteen votes to one,

Finds that the Republic of Uganda, by acts of looting, plundering and exploitation of Congolese natural resources committed by members of the Ugandan armed forces in the territory of the Democratic Republic of the Congo and by its failure to comply with its obligations as an occupying Power in Ituri district to prevent acts of looting, plundering and exploitation of Congolese natural resources, violated obligations owed to the Democratic Republic of the Congo under international law;

IN FAVOUR:

President Shi; *Vice-President* Ranjeva; *Judges* Koroma, Vereshchetin, Higgins, Parra-Aranguren, Kooijmans, Rezek, Al-Khasawneh, Buergenthal, Elaraby, Owada, Simma, Tomka, Abraham; *Judge* ad hoc Verhoeven;

AGAINST:

Judge ad hoc Kateka;

(5) Unanimously,

Finds that the Republic of Uganda is under obligation to make reparation to the Democratic Republic of the Congo for the injury caused;

(6) Unanimously,

Decides that, failing agreement between the Parties, the question of reparation due to the Democratic Republic of the Congo shall be settled by the Court, and reserves for this purpose the subsequent procedure in the case;

(7) By fifteen votes to two,

Finds that the Republic of Uganda did not comply with the Order of the Court on provisional measures of 1 July 2000;

IN FAVOUR:

President Shi; *Vice-President* Ranjeva; *Judges* Koroma, Vereshchetin, Higgins, Parra-Aranguren, Rezek, Al-Khasawneh, Buergenthal, Elaraby, Owada, Simma, Tomka, Abraham; *Judge* ad hoc Verhoeven;

AGAINST:

Judge Kooijmans; *Judge* ad hoc Kateka;

(8) Unanimously,

Rejects the objections of the Democratic Republic of the Congo to the admissibility of the first counter-claim submitted by the Republic of Uganda;

(9) By fourteen votes to three,

Finds that the first counter-claim submitted by the Republic of Uganda cannot be upheld;

IN FAVOUR:

President Shi; *Vice-President* Ranjeva; *Judges* Koroma, Vereshchetin, Higgins, Parra-Aranguren, Rezek, Al-Khasawneh, Buergenthal, Elaraby, Owada, Simma, Abraham; *Judge* ad hoc Verhoeven;

AGAINST:

Judges Kooijmans, Tomka; *Judge* ad hoc Kateka;

(10) Unanimously,

Rejects the objection of the Democratic Republic of the Congo to the admissibility of the part of the second counter-claim submitted by the Republic of Uganda relating to the breach of the Vienna Convention on Diplomatic Relations of 1961;

(11) By sixteen votes to one,

Upholds the objection of the Democratic Republic of the Congo to the admissibility of the part of the second counter-claim submitted by the Republic of Uganda relating to the maltreatment of individuals other than Ugandan diplomats at Ndjili International Airport on 20 August 1998;

IN FAVOUR:
President Shi; *Vice-President* Ranjeva; *Judges* Koroma, Vereshchetin, Higgins, Parra-Aranguren, Kooijmans, Rezek, Al-Khasawneh, Buergenthal, Elaraby, Owada, Simma, Tomka, Abraham; *Judge ad hoc* Verhoeven;

AGAINST:
Judge ad hoc Kateka;

(12) Unanimously,

Finds that the Democratic Republic of the Congo, by the conduct of its armed forces, which attacked the Ugandan Embassy in Kinshasa, maltreated Ugandan diplomats and other individuals on the Embassy premises, maltreated Ugandan diplomats at Ndjili International Airport, as well as by its failure to provide the Ugandan Embassy and Ugandan diplomats with effective protection and by its failure to prevent archives and Ugandan property from being seized from the premises of the Ugandan Embassy, violated obligations owed to the Republic of Uganda under the Vienna Convention on Diplomatic Relations of 1961;

(13) Unanimously,

Finds that the Democratic Republic of the Congo is under obligation to make reparation to the Republic of Uganda for the injury caused;

(14) Unanimously,

Decides that, failing agreement between the Parties, the question of reparation due to the Republic of Uganda shall be settled by the Court, and reserves for this purpose the subsequent procedure in the case."

134. Judge Koroma appended a declaration to the Judgment; Judges Parra-Aranguren, Kooijmans, Elar aby and Simma appended separate opinions; Judge Tomka and Judge *ad hoc* Verhoeven appended declarations; Judge *ad hoc* Kateka appended a dissenting opinion.

5. Application of the Convention on the Prevention and Punishment of the Crime of Genocide (Croatia v. Serbia and Montenegro)

135. On 2 July 1999 the Republic of Croatia instituted proceedings against Serbia and Montenegro (then known as the Federal Republic of Yugoslavia)[12] for violations of the 1948 Convention on the Prevention and Punishment of the Crime of Genocide alleged to have been committed between 1991 and 1995.

136. In its Application, Croatia contended that

> "by directly controlling the activity of its armed forces, intelligence agents, and various paramilitary detachments, on the territory of . . . Croatia, in the Knin region, eastern and western Slavonia, and Dalmatia, [Serbia and Montenegro] is liable for the 'ethnic cleansing' of Croatian citizens from these areas . . . as well as extensive property destruction—and is required to provide reparation for the resulting damage".

Croatia further claims that

> "in addition, by directing, encouraging, and urging Croatian citizens of Serb ethnicity in the Knin region to evacuate the area in 1995, as . . . Croatia reasserted its legitimate governmental authority . . . [Serbia and Montenegro] engaged in conduct amounting to a second round of 'ethnic cleansing'".

137. Accordingly, Croatia requested the Court to adjudge and declare that Serbia and Montenegro "has breached its legal obligations" to Croatia under the Genocide Convention and that it

> "has an obligation to pay to . . . Croatia, in its own right and as *parens patriae* for its citizens, reparations for damages to persons and property, as well as to the Croatian economy and environment caused by the foregoing violations of international law in a sum to be determined by the Court".

138. As basis for the jurisdiction of the Court, Croatia invokes Article IX of the Genocide Convention, to which it stated that both itself and Serbia and Montenegro were parties.

139. On 14 March 2001, within the time-limit as extended by the Court, Croatia filed its Memorial. On 11 September 2002, within the extended time-limit for the filing of its Counter-Memorial, Serbia and Montenegro filed certain preliminary objections to jurisdiction and admissibility. The proceedings on the merits were accordingly suspended (Art. 79 of the Rules of Court).

140. Following a request from the Government of Bosnia and Herzegovina, the Court, after ascertaining the views of the Parties pursuant to Article 53, paragraph 1, of the Rules of Court, made copies of the pleadings and annexed documents available to Bosnia and Herzegovina.

141. On 25 April 2003, within the time-limit fixed by an Order of the Court of 14 November 2002, Croatia filed a written statement of its observations and submissions on the preliminary objections raised by Serbia and Montenegro.

6. Maritime Delimitation between Nicaragua and Honduras in the Caribbean Sea (Nicaragua v. Honduras)

142. On 8 December 1999 the Republic of Nicaragua filed an Application instituting proceedings against the Republic of Honduras in respect of a dispute concerning the delimitation of the maritime zones appertaining to each of those States in the Caribbean Sea.

143. In its Application, Nicaragua stated *inter alia* that it had for decades "maintained the position that its maritime Caribbean border with Honduras has not been determined", whereas Honduras's position was that

> "there in fact exists a delimitation line that runs straight easterly on the parallel of latitude from the point fixed [in an Arbitral Award of 23 December 1906 made by the King of Spain concerning the land boundary between Nicaragua and Honduras, which was found valid and binding by the International Court of Justice on 18 November 1960] on the mouth of the Coco river".

According to Nicaragua, the "position adopted by Honduras . . . has brought about repeated confrontations and mutual capture of vessels of both nations in and around the general border area". Nicaragua further states that "[d]iplomatic negotiations have failed".

144. Nicaragua therefore requested the Court

> "to determine the course of the single maritime boundary between areas of territorial sea, continental shelf and exclusive economic zone appertaining respectively to Nicaragua and Honduras, in accordance with equitable principles and relevant circumstances recognized by general international law as applicable to such a delimitation of a single maritime boundary".

145. As basis for the Court's jurisdiction, Nicaragua invokes Article XXXI of the American Treaty on Pacific Settlement (officially known as the "Pact of Bogotá"), signed on 30 April 1948, as well as the declarations under Article 36, paragraph 2, of the Statute of the Court, by which both States have accepted the compulsory jurisdiction of the Court.

146. By an Order of 21 March 2000 the Court fixed 21 March 2001 and 21 March 2002 as respective time-limits for the filing of a Memorial by Nicaragua and a Counter-Memorial by Honduras. Those pleadings were duly filed within the prescribed time-limits.

147. Copies of the pleadings and documents annexed were requested by the Governments of Colombia, Jamaica and El Salvador. In accordance with Article 53, paragraph 1, of its Rules, the Court ascertained the views of the Parties and, taking account of the views expressed by them, acceded to the first two countries' requests, but not to that of the third.

148. By an Order of 13 June 2002, the Court authorized the submission of a Reply by Nicaragua and a Rejoinder by Honduras and fixed the following time-limits for the filing of these pleadings: 13 January 2003 for the Reply and 13 August 2003 for the Rejoinder. The Reply of Nicaragua and the Rejoinder of Honduras were filed within the time-limits thus fixed.

149. By letters dated 19 October 2005 the Registrar, in accordance with Article 63, paragraph 1, of the Statute, notified all States parties to the United Nations Convention on the Law of the Sea, to which reference had been made by the Parties in their written pleadings; he also sent to the European Union, which is a party to the Convention, the notification provided for in Article 43, paragraph 2, of the Rules of Court as adopted on 29 September 2005, and asked that organization whether it intended to make written observations under this provision. By a letter dated 12 December 2005 Mr. Javier Solana, Secretary-General of the Council of the European Union, informed the Court that the European Union did not intend to submit written observations on the case.

150. The Court has set 5 March 2007 as the date for the opening of hearings in the case.

7. Territorial and Maritime Dispute (Nicaragua v. Colombia)

151. On 6 December 2001 Nicaragua filed an Application instituting proceedings against Colombia in respect of a dispute concerning "a group of related legal issues subsisting" between the two States "concerning title to territory and maritime delimitation" in the western Caribbean.

152. In its Application, Nicaragua requested the Court to adjudge and declare:

> "First, that . . . Nicaragua has sovereignty over the islands of Providencia, San Andres and Santa Catalina and all the appurtenant islands and keys, and also over the Roncador, Serrana, Serranilla and Quitasueño keys (in so far as they are capable of appropriation);
>
> Second, in the light of the determinations concerning title requested above, the Court is asked further to determine the course of the single maritime boundary between the areas of continental shelf and exclusive economic zone appertaining respectively to Nicaragua and Colombia, in accordance with equitable principles and relevant circumstances recognized by general international law as applicable to such a delimitation of a single maritime boundary."

153. Nicaragua further indicated that it "reserves the right to claim compensation for elements of unjust enrichment consequent upon Colombian possession of the Islands of San Andres and Providencia as well as the keys and maritime spaces up to the 82 meridian, in the absence of lawful title". It also "reserves the right to claim compensation for interference with fishing vessels of Nicaraguan nationality or vessels licensed by Nicaragua".

154. As basis for the Court's jurisdiction, Nicaragua invokes Article 36, paragraph 2, of the Statute of the Court and Article XXXI of the American Treaty on Pacific Settlement (officially known as the "Pact of Bogotá"), signed on 30 April 1948, to which both Nicaragua and Colombia are parties.

155. Copies of the pleadings and documents annexed were requested by the Governments of Honduras, Jamaica, Chile and Peru. Pursuant to Article 53, paragraph 1, of its Rules, the Court ascertained the view of the Parties and, taking account of the views expressed by them, acceded to those requests.

156. By an Order of 26 February 2002, the Court fixed 28 April 2003 and 28 June 2004 as the time-limits for the filing of a Memorial by Nicaragua and of a Counter-Memorial by Colombia. The Memorial of Nicaragua was filed within the time-limit thus fixed.

157. On 21 July 2003, within the time-limit for the submission of its Counter-Memorial, Colombia filed preliminary objections to the jurisdiction of the Court. The proceedings on the merits were accordingly suspended (Rules, Art. 79). Within the time-limit of 26 January 2004, as fixed by the Court in its Order of 24 September 2003, Nicaragua filed a written statement of its observations and submissions on the preliminary objections raised by Colombia.

8. Armed Activities on the Territory of the Congo (New Application: 2002) (Democratic Republic of the Congo v. Rwanda)

158. On 28 May 2002, the Democratic Republic of the Congo filed an Application instituting proceedings against Rwanda in respect of a dispute concerning: "massive, serious and flagrant violations of human rights and of international humanitarian law" resulting "from acts of armed aggression perpetrated by Rwanda on the territory of the Democratic Republic of the Congo in flagrant breach of the sovereignty and territorial integrity of the [latter], as guaranteed by the United Nations and OAU Charters".

159. In its Application, the Democratic Republic of the Congo stated that Rwanda had been guilty of "armed aggression" from August 1998 until the date of filing. According to the Applicant, that aggression had resulted in "large-scale human slaughter" in South Kivu, Katanga Province and the Eastern Province, "rape and sexual assault of women", "assassinations and kidnapping of political figures and human rights activists", "arrests, arbitrary detentions, inhuman and degrading treatment", "systematic looting of public and private institutions, seizure of property belonging to civilians", "human rights violations committed by the invading Rwandan troops and their 'rebel' allies in the major towns in the East" of the Democratic Republic of the Congo, and "destruction of fauna and flora" of the country.

160. In consequence, the Democratic Republic of the Congo requested the Court to adjudge and declare that, by violating the human rights which are the goal pursued by the United Nations through the maintenance of international peace and security, Rwanda had violated and was violating the United Nations Charter as well as Articles 3 and 4 of the OAU Charter; that it further had violated a number of instruments protecting human rights; that, by shooting down a Boeing 727 owned by Congo Airlines on 9 October 1998 at Kindu, thereby causing the death of 40 civilians, Rwanda had also violated certain conventions concerning international civil aviation; and that, by engaging in killing, slaughter, rape, throat-slitting, and crucifying, Rwanda was guilty of genocide against more than 3,500,000 Congolese, including the victims of the recent massacres in the city of Kisangani, and had violated the sacred right to life provided for in certain instruments protecting human rights as well as the Genocide Convention. It further asked the Court to adjudge and declare that all Rwandan armed forces should be withdrawn from Congolese territory; and that the Democratic Republic of the Congo was entitled to compensation.

161. In its Application the Democratic Republic of the Congo, in order to found the jurisdiction of the Court, relied on a number of compromissory clauses in treaties.

162. On the same day, 28 May 2002, the Democratic Republic of the Congo submitted a request for the indication of provisional measures. Public hearings on the request for provisional measures were held on 13 and 14 June 2002. On 10 July 2002, the Court delivered its Order, by which, having found that it had no prima facie jurisdiction, it rejected the request of the Democratic Republic of the Congo. In that Order the Court also rejected the submissions by the Rwandese Republic seeking the removal of the case from the Court's List.

163. By an Order of 18 September 2002, the Court decided, in accordance with Article 79, paragraphs 2 and 3, of the revised Rules of Court, that the written pleadings would first be addressed to the questions of the jurisdiction of the Court and the admissibility of the Application and fixed 20 January 2003 as the time-limit for the filing of a Memorial by

Rwanda and 20 May 2003 for the filing of a Counter-Memorial by the Democratic Republic the Congo. Those pleadings were filed within the time-limits thus fixed.

164. Public hearings addressed to the questions of the jurisdiction of the Court and the admissibility of the Application were held from 4 to 8 July 2005. At the conclusion of those hearings the Parties presented the following final submissions to the Court.

> *For Rwanda:*
>
> "[T]he Republic of Rwanda requests the Court to adjudge and declare that:
>
> 1. it lacks jurisdiction over the claims brought against the Republic of Rwanda by the Democratic Republic of the Congo; and
>
> 2. in the alternative, the claims brought against the Republic of Rwanda by the Democratic Republic of the Congo are inadmissible."
>
> *For the Democratic Republic of the Congo:*
>
> "May it please the Court,
>
> 1. to find that the objections to jurisdiction and admissibility raised by Rwanda are unfounded;
>
> 2. consequently, to find that the Court has jurisdiction to entertain the case on the merits and that the Application of the Democratic Republic of the Congo is admissible as submitted;
>
> 3. to decide to proceed with the case on the merits."

165. On 3 February 2006, the Court delivered its Judgment. The operative paragraph of the Judgment reads as follows:

> "For these reasons,
>
> THE COURT,
>
> By fifteen votes to two,
>
> *Finds* that it has no jurisdiction to entertain the Application filed by the Democratic Republic of the Congo on 28 May 2002.
>
> IN FAVOUR:
> *President* Shi; *Vice-President* Ranjeva; *Judges* Vereshchetin, Higgins, Parra-Aranguren, Kooijmans, Rezek, Al-Khasawneh, Buergenthal, Elaraby, Owada, Simma, Tomka, Abraham; *Judge* ad hoc Dugard;
>
> AGAINST:
> *Judge* Koroma; *Judge* ad hoc Mavungu."

166. Judge Koroma appended a dissenting opinion to the Judgment of the Court; Judges Higgins, Kooijmans, Elaraby, Owada and Simma appended a joint separate opinion; Judge Kooijmans appended a declaration; Judge Al-Khasawneh appended a separate opinion; Judge Elaraby appended a declaration; Judge *ad hoc* Dugard appended a separate opinion; Judge *ad hoc* Mavungu appended a dissenting opinion.

9. Certain Criminal Proceedings in France (Republic of the Congo v. France)

167. On 9 December 2002, the Republic of the Congo filed an Application instituting proceedings against France seeking the annulment of the investigation and prosecution measures taken by the French judicial authorities further to a complaint for crimes against humanity and torture filed by various associations against the President of the Republic of the Congo, Mr. Denis Sassou Nguesso, the Congolese Minister of the Interior, Mr. Pierre Oba, and other individuals including General Norbert Dabira, Inspector-General of the Congolese Armed Forces. The Application further stated that, in connection with these proceedings, an investigating judge of the Meaux *Tribunal de grande instance* had issued a warrant for the President of the Republic of the Congo to be examined as witness.

168. The Republic of the Congo contends that, by "attributing to itself universal jurisdiction in criminal matters and by arrogating to itself the power to prosecute and try the Minister of the Interior of a foreign State for crimes allegedly committed by him in connection with the exercise of his powers for the maintenance of public order in his country", France violated "the principle that a State may not, in breach of the principle of sovereign equality among all Members of the United Nations . . . exercise its authority on the territory of another State". The Republic of the Congo further submitted that, in issuing a warrant instructing police officers to examine the President of the Republic of the Congo as witness in the case, France violated "the criminal immunity of a foreign Head of State, an international customary rule recognized by the jurisprudence of the Court".

169. In its Application, the Republic of the Congo indicated that it sought to found the jurisdiction of the Court, pursuant to Article 38, paragraph 5, of the Rules of Court, "on the consent of the French Republic, which will certainly be given". In accordance with this provision, the Application by the Republic of the Congo was transmitted to the French Government and no further action was taken in the proceedings at that stage.

170. By a letter dated 8 April 2003 and received on 11 April 2003 in the Registry, the French Republic stated that it "consent[ed] to the jurisdiction of the Court to entertain the Application pursuant to Article 38, paragraph 5". This consent made it possible to enter the case in the Court's List and to open the proceedings. In its letter, France added that its consent to the Court's jurisdiction applied strictly within the limits "of the claims formulated by the Republic of the Congo" and that "Article 2 of the Treaty of Co-operation signed on 1 January 1974 by the French Republic and the People's Republic of the Congo, to which the latter refers in its Application, does not constitute a basis of jurisdiction for the Court in the present case".

171. The Application of the Republic of the Congo was accompanied by a request for the indication of a provisional measure "seek[ing] an order for the immediate suspension of the proceedings being conducted by the investigating judge of the Meaux *Tribunal de grande instance*".

172. Taking into account the consent given by France and in accordance with Article 74, paragraph 3, of the Rules of Court, the President of the Court fixed 28 April 2003 as the date for the opening of the public hearings on the request for the indication of a provisional measure submitted by the Republic of the Congo.

173. After those hearings had been held, from 28 to 29 April 2003, the President of the Court, on 17 June 2003, read the Order, by which the Court found, by fourteen votes to one,

that the circumstances, as they presented themselves to the Court, were not such as to require the exercise of its power under Article 41 of the Statute to indicate provisional measures.

174. Judges Koroma and Vereshchetin appended a joint separate opinion to the Order, and Judge *ad hoc* de Cara a dissenting opinion.

175. By an Order of 11 July 2003, the President of the Court fixed 11 December 2003 as the time-limit for the Memorial of the Republic of the Congo and 11 May 2004 as the time-limit for the Counter-Memorial of France. The Memorial and the Counter-Memorial were duly filed within the time-limits fixed.

176. By an Order of 17 June 2004, the Court, taking account of the agreement of the Parties and of the particular circumstances of the case, authorized the submission of a Reply by the Republic of the Congo and a Rejoinder by France, and fixed 10 December 2004 and 10 June 2005 as respective time-limits for the filing of those pleadings. By Orders of 8 and 29 December 2004, of 11 July 2005 and of 11 January 2006, the President of the Court, taking account of the reasons given by the Republic of the Congo and of the agreement of the Parties, successively extended these time-limits to, respectively, 10 January and 10 August 2005, then to 11 July 2005 and 11 August 2006, then to 11 January 2006 and 10 August 2007, and finally to 11 July 2006 and 11 August 2008. The Reply was duly filed within the time-limit as so extended.

10. Sovereignty over Pedra Branca/Pulau Batu Puteh, Middle Rocks and South Ledge (Malaysia/Singapore)

177. On 24 July 2003 Malaysia and Singapore jointly notified the Court of a Special Agreement, which was signed between them on 6 February 2003 at Putrajaya and entered into force on 9 May 2003.

> In Article 2 of that Special Agreement, the parties requested the Court
>
> "to determine whether sovereignty over:
>
> *(a)* Pedra Branca/Pulau Batu Puteh;
>
> *(b)* Middle Rocks;
>
> *(c)* South Ledge,
>
> belongs to Malaysia or the Republic of Singapore".
>
> In Article 6, the Parties "agree to accept the Judgment of the Court . . . as final and binding upon them".

The Parties further set out their views on the procedure to be followed.

178. By an Order of 1 September 2003, the President of the Court, taking into account the provisions of Article 4 of the Special Agreement, fixed 25 March 2004 and 25 January 2005 as respective time-limits for the filing by each of the Parties of a Memorial and a Counter-Memorial. The Memorials and Counter-Memorials were duly filed within the time-limits fixed.

179. By an Order of 1 February 2005, the Court, taking into account the provisions of the Special Agreement, fixed 25 November 2005 as the time-limit for the filing of a Reply by each of the Parties. The Replies were duly filed within the time-limit fixed.

180. By a joint letter of 23 January 2006 the Parties informed the Court that they had agreed that there was no need for an exchange of Rejoinders in the case. The Court itself subsequently decided that no further pleadings were necessary, and that the written proceedings were accordingly now closed.

11. Maritime delimitation in the Black Sea (Romania v. Ukraine)

181. On 16 September 2004, Romania filed an Application instituting proceedings against Ukraine in respect of a dispute concerning "the establishment of a single maritime boundary between the two States in the Black Sea, thereby delimiting the continental shelf and the exclusive economic zones appertaining to them."

182. In its Application Romania explained that, "following a complex process of negotiations", Ukraine and itself signed on 2 June 1997 a Treaty on Relations of Co-operation and Good-Neighbourliness, and concluded an Additional Agreement by exchange of letters between their respective Ministers for Foreign Affairs. Both instruments entered into force on 22 October 1997. By these agreements, "the two States assumed the obligation to conclude a Treaty on the State Border Régime between them, as well as an Agreement for the delimitation of the continental shelf and the exclusive economic zones . . . in the Black Sea". At the same time, "the Additional Agreement provided for the principles to be applied in the delimitation of the above-mentioned areas, and set out the commitment of the two countries that the dispute could be submitted to the ICJ, subject to the fulfilment of certain conditions". Between 1998 and 2004, 24 rounds of negotiations were held. However, according to Romania, "no result was obtained and an agreed delimitation of the maritime areas in the Black Sea was not accomplished". Romania brought the matter before the Court "in order to avoid the indefinite prolongation of discussions that, in [its] opinion, obviously cannot lead to any outcome".

183. Romania requested the Court "to draw in accordance with international law, and specifically the criteria laid down in Article 4 of the Additional Agreement, a single maritime boundary between the continental shelf and the exclusive economic zone of the two States in the Black Sea".

184. As basis for the Court's jurisdiction Romania invoked Article 4 *(h)* of the Additional Agreement, which provides:

> "If these negotiations [referred to above] shall not determine the conclusion of the above-mentioned agreement [on the delimitation of the continental shelf and the exclusive economic zones in the Black Sea] in a reasonable period of time, but not later than 2 years since their initiation, the Government of Romania and the Government of Ukraine have agreed that the problem of delimitation of the continental shelf and the exclusive economic zones shall be solved by the UN International Court of Justice, at the request of any of the parties, provided that the Treaty on the regime of the State border between Romania and Ukraine has entered into force. However, should the International Court of Justice consider that the delay

> of the entering into force of the Treaty on the regime of the State border is the result of the other Party's fault, it may examine the request concerning the delimitation of the continental shelf and the exclusive economic zones before the entering into force of this Treaty."

185. Romania contends that the two conditions set out in Article 4 *(h)* of the Additional Agreement had been fulfilled, since the negotiations had by far exceeded two years and the Treaty on the Romanian-Ukrainian State Border Régime had entered into force on 27 May 2004.

186. In its Application Romania further provided an overview of the applicable law for solving the dispute, citing a number of provisions of the Additional Agreement of 1997, as well as the 1982 Montego Bay United Nations Convention on the Law of the Sea, to which both Ukraine and Romania were parties, together with other relevant instruments binding the two countries.

187. By an Order of 19 November 2004, the Court, taking into account the views of the Parties, fixed 19 August 2005 and 19 May 2006 as time-limits for the filing of a Memorial by Romania and a Counter-Memorial by Ukraine. The Memorial and Counter-Memorial were duly filed within the time-limits fixed.

188. By Order of 30 June 2006 the Court authorized the filing of a Reply by Romania and a Rejoinder by Ukraine and fixed 22 December 2006 and 15 June 2007 as respective time-limits for the filing of these pleadings.

12. Dispute regarding Navigational and Related Rights (Costa Rica v. Nicaragua)

189. On 29 September 2005 Costa Rica filed an Application instituting proceedings against Nicaragua in a dispute concerning navigational and related rights of Costa Rica on the San Juan River.

190. In its Application Costa Rica stated that it sought "the cessation of the [Nicaraguan] conduct which prevents the free and full exercise and enjoyment of the rights that Costa Rica possesses on the San Juan River, and which also prevents Costa Rica from fulfilling its responsibilities" under certain agreements between itself and Nicaragua. Costa Rica further requested the Court to determine the reparation which must be made by Nicaragua. Costa Rica contended that "Nicaragua has in particular since the late 1990s imposed a number of restrictions on the navigation of Costa Rica's boats and their passengers on the San Juan River", in violation of "Article VI of the Treaty of Limits [signed in 1858 between Costa Rica and Nicaragua, which] granted to Nicaragua sovereignty over the waters of the San Juan River, recognizing at the same time important rights to Costa Rica". Costa Rica maintains that these rights were confirmed and interpreted by an arbitral award issued by the President of the United States of America, Mr. Grover Cleveland, on 28 march 1888, and by a judgment of the Central American Court of Justice of 1916, as well as by the "Agreement Supplementary to Article IV of the [1949] Pact of Amity". Costa Rica further contends that "these restrictions are of a continuing character".

191. As basis of jurisdiction Costa Rica invokes the declarations of acceptance of the Court's jurisdiction made by the Parties under Article 36, paragraph 2, of the Statute, as well as the Tovar-Caldera Agreement signed between the Parties on 26 September 2002.

Costa Rica also relies on Article 36, paragraph 1, of the Statute of the Court by virtue of the operation of Article XXXI of the "Pact of Bogotá" of 13 April 1948.

192. By Order of 29 November 2005, the Court fixed 29 August 2006 as the time-limit for the filing of a Memorial by Costa Rica and 29 May 2007 as the time-limit for the filing of a Counter-Memorial by Nicaragua.

13. Status vis-à-vis the Host State of a Diplomatic Envoy to the United Nations (Commonwealth of Dominica v. Switzerland)

193. On 26 April 2006 the Commonwealth of Dominica filed an Application instituting proceedings against Switzerland concerning alleged violations by the latter of the Vienna Convention on Diplomatic Relations, as well of other international instruments and rules, with respect to a diplomatic envoy of Dominica to the United Nations in Geneva.

194. In its Application Dominica stated that the diplomat in question, Mr. Roman Lakschin, had been accredited to the United Nations and its Specialized Agencies and to the World Trade Organization (WTO) since March 1996 as a member of the Permanent Mission of Dominica to the United Nations in Geneva (first as Counsellor, later as *Chargé d'affaires* and Deputy Permanent Representative with the rank of Ambassador). Dominica emphasized that this accreditation was "effected to the organisations and not to Switzerland", but that, nevertheless, Switzerland had "claimed the right to withdraw the accreditation" of the said envoy, "stating that [he] is a 'businessman' and [that] as such he would have no right to be a diplomat". Dominica contended that Switzerland could not be allowed to "control a small State like Dominica, which has a population of merely some 70,000 people and thus is severely restricted in the selection of foreign envoys". It further stated that it "has the right to send whichever envoy [it] considers appropriate to the United Nations in Geneva in [its] attempt to better [its] tourism, prospects and [its] economy". Dominica maintained that Switzerland had deprived it of "welcome and competent assistance in establishing and running a Mission in Geneva and thereby impeded the efforts of Dominica to develop trade and investment".

195. As basis for the Court's jurisdiction, Dominica invoked the declarations of acceptance of the Court's jurisdiction under Article 36, paragraph 2, of its Statute made by Dominica on 17 March 2006 and by Switzerland on 28 July 1948, as well as Article 1 of the Optional Protocol to the Vienna Convention for the Compulsory Settlement of Disputes, to which both parties have adhered.

196. By letter of 15 May 2006, a faxed copy of which was received in the Registry on 24 May and the original on 6 June 2006, the Prime Minister of the Commonwealth of Dominica informed the Court that his Government "did not wish to go on with the proceedings instituted against Switzerland" and requested the Court to make an Order "officially recording [their] unconditional discontinuance" and "directing the removal of the case from the General List". By letter of 24 May 2006, the Swiss Ambassador in The Hague advised the Court that he had informed the competent Swiss authorities of the discontinuance as thus notified.

197. Accordingly, on 9 June 2006 the Court made an Order in which, after noting that the Government of the Swiss Confederation had not taken any step in the proceedings in the case, it recorded the discontinuance of the proceedings by the Commonwealth of Dominica and ordered that the case be removed from the List.

14. Pulp Mills on the River Uruguay (Argentina v. Uruguay)

198. On 4 May 2006 Argentina filed an Application instituting proceedings against Uruguay concerning alleged breaches by Uruguay of obligations incumbent upon it under the Statute of the River Uruguay, a treaty signed between the two States on 26 February 1975 (hereinafter "the 1975 Statute") for the purpose of establishing the joint machinery necessary for the optimum and rational utilization of that part of the river which constitutes their joint boundary.

199. In its Application Argentina charged the Government of Uruguay with having unilaterally authorized the construction of two pulp mills on the River Uruguay without complying with the obligatory prior notification consultation procedures under the Statute. Argentina claims that these mills pose a threat to the river and its environment, are likely to impair the quality of the river's waters and to cause significant transboundary damage to Argentina.

200. As basis for the Court's jurisdiction, Argentina cites the first paragraph of Article 60 of the 1975 Statute, which provides that any dispute concerning the interpretation or application of that Statute which cannot be settled by direct negotiations may be submitted by either party to the Court.

201. Argentina's Application was accompanied by a request for the indication of provisional measures, whereby Argentina asked that Uruguay be ordered to suspend the authorizations for construction of the mills and all building works pending a final decision by the Court, and to co-operate with Argentina with a view to protecting and conserving the aquatic environment of the River Uruguay, as well as to refrain from taking any further unilateral action with respect to construction of the two mills incompatible with the 1975 Statute, and from any other action which might aggravate the dispute or render its settlement more difficult.

202. Public hearings were held on the request for the indication of provisional measures on 8 and 9 June 2006, and on 13 July 2006, at a public sitting, the President of the Court read an Order whereby the Court, by 14 votes to one, found that the circumstances, as they now presented themselves to the Court, were not such as to require the exercise of its power under Article 41 of the Statute to indicate provisional measures.

203. By Order of 13 July 2006 the Court fixed 15 January 2007 as the time-limit for the filing of a Memorial by Argentina and 20 July 2007 as the time-limit for the filing of a Counter-Memorial by Uruguay.

B. Amendment to Article 43 of the Rules of Court

204. As part of the ongoing review of its procedures and working methods, in September 2005 the Court adopted amendments to Article 43 of its Rules (Subsection 1. Institution of Proceedings) regarding the notifications to be sent by the Court to those not directly involved in a case who are parties to a convention whose construction may be in question in the proceedings.

205. Two new paragraphs have been added to the Article, in order to cover the case of international organizations parties to such conventions and to establish an appropriate procedural framework for this purpose. Until now, the Court has sent notifications in these circumstances only to States parties to such conventions.

206. The text of Article 43 of the Rules, as amended, is reproduced below:

"Article 43*

> 1. Whenever the construction of a convention to which States other than those concerned in the case are parties may be in question within the meaning of Article 63, paragraph 1, of the Statute, the Court shall consider what directions shall be given to the Registrar in the matter.
> 2. Whenever the construction of a convention to which a public international organization is a party may be in question in a case before the Court, the Court shall consider whether the Registrar shall so notify the public international organization concerned. Every public international organization notified by the Registrar may submit its observations on the particular provisions of the convention the construction of which is in question in the case.
> 3. If a public international organization sees fit to furnish its observations under paragraph 2 of this Article, the procedure to be followed shall be that provided for in Article 69, paragraph 2, of these Rules."

VI. Sixtieth anniversary of the Court

A. Colloquium organized in co-operation with UNITAR

207. On 10 and 11 April 2006 the Court, in co-operation with UNITAR (United Nations Institute for Training and Research), organized a colloquium at the Peace Palace in The Hague to mark its sixtieth anniversary. This colloquium, held under "Chatham House" rules (i.e., the ideas expressed may be cited, but on an unattributed basis), was attended by some hundred practitioners. It addressed issues of the Court's jurisdiction, rules of procedure and access.

208. The proceedings of the colloquium are due to be published later this year.

B. Solemn commemorative sitting

209. On 12 April 2006, at the Peace Palace, the Court held a solemn sitting in the presence of Her Majesty the Queen of the Netherlands to celebrate the sixtieth anniversary of its inaugural sitting.

210. Also present at the ceremony were the United Nations Secretary-General, His Excellency Mr. Kofi Annan, the President of the General Assembly, His Excellency Mr. Jan Eliasson, and the Minister for Foreign Affairs of the Netherlands, Mr. Bernard Bot. Other guests included members of the diplomatic corps, representatives of the Dutch Parliament and Government and of other Dutch institutions, and senior members of international organizations based in The Hague, such as the Permanent Court of Arbitration (PCA), the Iran-United States Claims Tribunal, the International Criminal Tribunal for the former Yugoslavia (ICTY) and the International Criminal Court (ICC).

211. In his address the Secretary-General observed that the rules of international law "play an increasing role in our global society . . . They reflect the reality, but also the promise, of our international order" and "show the world not only as it is, but as it ought to be". Mr. Annan encouraged "all States that have not yet done so to consider recognizing the

compulsory jurisdiction of the Court", inviting those who "are not yet prepared to [do so] to consider submitting their disputes to the Court by Special Agreements".

212. For his part, the President of the General Assembly emphasized that "the fact that Member States have, year after year, repeated their desire to see more use of the Court in settling disputes between States is strong evidence of the confidence Member States have in this World Court". Mr. Eliasson also reaffirmed the "full trust" of the General Assembly in the Court.

213. The Netherlands Foreign Minister stated that his country would also "help strengthen that jurisdiction wherever possible and will urge other countries to recognize it". Mr. Bot stated that it was his "firm conviction that strengthening the jurisdiction of the Court will make a major contribution to promoting the international legal order and the international rule of law".

214. Judge Bruno Simma, Member of the Court, then presented a summary of the conclusions of the colloquium held by the Court, in co-operation with UNITAR, on 10 and 11 April 2006.

215. In her closing address Judge Rosalyn Higgins, President of the Court, stressed that the International Court of Justice "is not only the principal judicial organ of the United Nations, but it is also the only international judicial body to possess general jurisdiction". Recognizing that "very important work" is being done by the more recently established international criminal courts and tribunals, she emphasized her belief that, by "carefully balancing continuity and change, the Court will remain the lighthouse beacon in our ever-expanding system of international law". "This is a challenge for the period ahead", she concluded.

VII. Visits

A. Official visit of the President of the Russian Federation

216. On 2 November 2005 His Excellency Mr. Vladimir Putin, President of the Russian Federation, was received by the Court. At a solemn sitting held in the Great Hall of Justice and attended by the diplomatic corps and by representatives of the Dutch authorities, the Iran-United States Claims Tribunal, the International Criminal Tribunal for the former Yugoslavia, the International Criminal Court and other international institutions located in The Hague, the President of the Court made a speech, to which the President of the Russian Federation replied.

217. President Shi recalled "the fundamental contribution that Russia has made to the development of various crucial currents of thought in international law", and highlighted the work of some of the eminent Russian scholars and judges "that have helped make the Court what it is today". He paid particular homage to Professor Fedor Martens, who played "a prominent role" in the international peace movement of the nineteenth century. "His dream of a temple of peace indeed inspired the creation of this Peace Palace", said the President of the Court, recalling that Martens "took an especially active part", as a member of the Russian delegation, in the work of the two peace conferences held in The Hague in 1899 and 1907 on Tsar Nicolas II's initiative. "Among other instruments, The Hague Conferences led to the signing of the Convention on the Laws and Customs of Land Warfare and the Convention for the Pacific Settlement of International Disputes" and led to the

unanimous agreement for the establishment of a permanent court of arbitration, President Shi explained. President Shi also highlighted Russia's role in the establishment of the United Nations and the International Court of Justice as its principal judicial organ, adding that the United Nations Charter was signed by the prominent Russian jurist, Sergei Krylov, who was subsequently elected a Member of the Court. President Putin's visit, said President Shi, "bears witness to [Russia's] long-standing attachment to the cause of law and international justice". He quoted Russia's Foreign Minister Lavrov, who recently noted that the decisions of the Court "enjoy high authority" and serve "as an important instrument of peaceful settlement of disputes". The Court "welcomes this encouragement in the fulfilment of [its] task", concluded the President.

218. In reply, President Putin stated that, as a participant in the 2005 World Summit of the United Nations, Russia had "confirmed its commitment to the primacy of international law". "Russia", said the President, "is in favour of strengthening the Court's role and to this end supported the inclusion in the final document of the 2005 Summit of the provisions confirming the obligation of States to settle their disputes by peaceful means, including through the ICJ". The President stressed that "the judgments and advisory opinions of the ICJ play an extremely important role in strengthening and developing international legal principles and rules". "Thus", added the President, "the Court influences in a positive way the process of universalization of international law [and] serves to bolster the stability and legitimacy of the United Nations". President Putin concluded by stressing the ICJ's "vital role in the prevention of international conflicts and in the peaceful resolution of existing disputes . . . thereby facilitating the proper functioning of international justice". "Such a role", stated the President, "has become possible due to the independence of the Court and its unique composition".

B. Other visits

219. During the period under review the President and Court Members, as well as the Registrar and Registry staff, received a large number of visitors, including members of governments, diplomats, parliamentary delegations, presidents and members of judicial bodies and other senior officials.

220. There were also many visits by groups of researchers, academics, lawyers and others.

VIII. Awards

221. On 6 April 2006 the Court was presented with the "Fray Francisco Vitoria" medal, awarded by the municipality of Vitoria (birthplace of the famous Spanish "founding father of international law") and the University of the Basque Country. A ceremony was organised for the occasion in Vitoria, at which speeches were delivered by the Mayor of the city, Mr. Alfonso Alonso, the Rector of the University of the Basque Country, Mr. Juan Ignacio Pérez Iglesias, and the President of the Court, Judge Rosalyn Higgins.

222. "I wish to reiterate how honoured my colleagues and I are to receive this distinguished award on behalf of the International Court of Justice, in recognition of the Court's crucial role as a guardian of the respect of the international law", stated Judge Higgins, who was accompanied by a delegation of Court Members. "The Court will pursue its efforts to prove worthy of the hopes that have been placed on it and to fulfil the mission that was attributed to it 60 years ago by the draftsmen of the United Nations Charter", she added.

223. The "Fray Francisco Vitoria" medal is a prestigious award created by the city of Vitoria at the suggestion of the Advisory Scientific Board of the Vitora-Gasteiz international law and international relations courses, organized under the aegis of the University of the Basque Country. It is intended to honour individuals and institutions having made a notable contribution to the establishment of peace and the promotion of understanding within the international community.

IX. Addresses on the work of the Court

224. During the period covered by this Report, the President of the Court, Judge Shi, on 27 October 2005 addressed the 39th Plenary Meeting of the Sixtieth Session of the General Assembly on the occasion of the presentation of the Court's Annual Report. On 28 October 2005, he also gave an address to the Sixth Committee of the General Assembly.

225. On 3 February 2006 President Shi made a statement to the press following the public reading of the Judgment of the Court in the case concerning *Armed Activities on the Territory of the Congo (New Application: 2002) (Democratic Republic of the Congo* v. *Rwanda)*; this statement was intended as an explanatory comment on the Court's Judgment.

226. On 22 June 2006 the President of the Court, Judge Higgins, made a speech in the course of the public debate organized by the Security Council on the theme, "Strengthening International Law".

227. On 13 July 2006 President Higgins made a statement to the press following the public reading of the Court's Order on Argentina's request for the indication of provisional measures in the case concerning *Pulp Mills on the River Uruguay (Argentina* v. *Uruguay)*.

228. On 25 July 2006, at its fifty-eighth session, President Higgins addressed the International Law Commission on the work of the Court.

X. Publications, documents and website of the Court

229. The publications of the Court are distributed to the Governments of all States entitled to appear before the Court, and to the major law libraries of the world. The sale of those publications is organized chiefly by the Sales and Marketing Sections of the United Nations Secretariat in New York and Geneva, which are in contact with specialized booksellers and distributors throughout the world. A catalogue (together with a price list) published in English and French is distributed free of charge. A revised and updated version of the Catalogue was published in 2004; an addendum will appear at the end of 2006.

230. The publications of the Court consist of several series, three of which are published annually: *Reports of Judgments, Advisory Opinions and Orders* (published in separate fascicles and as a bound volume), a *Yearbook* (in the French version: *Annuaire*) and a *Bibliography* of works and documents relating to the Court. At the time of preparation of this Report, the fascicles in the *Reports* series for the period under review have either been printed or are in preparation for printing. The bound volume of *I.C.J. Reports 2003* has been printed, while the volume for 2004 will appear as soon as the Index has been printed. The *I.C.J. Yearbook 2003-2004* is at press and those for 2004-2005 and 2005-2006 are in preparation.

231. The Court also prepares bilingual printed versions of the instruments instituting proceedings in a case before it (applications instituting proceedings and special agreements), as well as requests for an advisory opinion. In the period under review, the Court received three Applications: *Dispute regarding Navigational and Related Rights (Costa Rica* v. *Nicaragua)*; *Status vis-à-vis the Host State of a Diplomatic Envoy to the United Nations (Commonwealth of Dominica* v. *Switzerland)*; *Pulp Mills on the River Uruguay (Argentina* v. *Uruguay)*. All are in the process of being printed.

232. Before the termination of a case, the Court may, pursuant to Article 53 of the Rules of Court, and after ascertaining the views of the parties, make the pleadings and annexed documents available on request to the government of any State entitled to appear before the Court. The Court may also, having ascertained the views of the parties, make copies of those pleadings and documents accessible to the public on or after the opening of the oral proceedings. The written pleadings in each case (in the format in which the parties produce them) are published by the Court after the end of the proceedings, in the series *Pleadings, Oral Arguments, Documents*. The annexes to the pleadings and the correspondence in cases are now published only exceptionally, as far as they are essential for the understanding of the decisions taken by the Court. The following documents have been published or are at various stages of production in the reporting period: *Frontier Dispute (Burkina Faso/ Republic of Mali)* (4 volumes of text due for publication in September 2006); *Maritime Delimitation in the Area between Greenland and Jan Mayen (Denmark* v. *Norway)* (3 volumes in final preparation); *Aerial Incident of 10 August 1999 (Pakistan* v. *India)* (1 volume, in press); *Legality of the Use by a State of Nuclear Weapons in Armed Conflict* and *Legality of the Threat or Use of Nuclear Weapons* (to be published together) (5 volumes in preparation); *East Timor (Portugal* v. *Australia)* (3-4 volumes in final preparation).

233. In the series *Acts and Documents concerning the Organization of the Court*, the Court also publishes the instruments governing its functioning and practice. The latest edition, No. 5, was published in 1989 and has been reprinted since that date, most recently in 1996. A new, totally updated edition has been prepared and will appear before the end of the year. An offprint of the Rules of Court, as amended on 5 December 2000, is available in English and French. Unofficial Arabic, Chinese, German, Russian and Spanish translations of the Rules (without the amendments of 5 December 2000) are also available.

234. The Court distributes press releases, summaries of its decisions, background notes and a handbook in order to keep lawyers, university teachers and students, government officials, the press and the general public informed about its work, functions and jurisdiction. The fifth edition of the handbook ("Blue Book") came out in January 2006 in the Court's two official languages, French and English. Arabic, Chinese, Russian and Spanish translations of the previous version (published on the occasion of the fortieth anniversary of the Court in 1986) were issued in 1990. Arabic, Chinese, Dutch, English, French, Russian and Spanish editions of a general information booklet on the Court, produced in co-operation with the Department of Public Information of the United Nations, and intended for the general public, have also been published.

235. A special Illustrated Book of the Court ("Coffee Table Book"), in French and English, has been prepared and will appear in the second half of 2006, year of the Court's sixtieth anniversary. As well as this special publication, the Court will also be publishing the

proceedings of the colloquium organized by it on 10 and 11 April 2006 to commemorate that anniversary (see para. 207 above).

236. In order to increase and expedite the availability of ICJ documents and reduce communication costs, the Court launched a website on the Internet on 25 September 1997, both in English and in French. The site is currently being totally reconstructed, with presentation and content being updated so as to improve user-friendliness and coverage and facilitate navigation between subject-headings and languages. The new site is due to be launched later this year.

237. It has already been possible since 1997, on the current site, to view the full text of Judgments, Advisory Opinions and Orders (posted on the day they are issued); summaries of earlier decisions; most of the relevant documents in pending cases (Application or Special Agreement; written pleadings (without annexes) as soon as they become accessible to the public, and oral pleadings); unpublished pleadings for earlier cases; press releases; some basic documents (United Nations Charter and the Statute and Rules of the Court); declarations accepting the Court's compulsory jurisdiction and a list of treaties and other agreements relating to that jurisdiction; general information on the Court's history and procedure; and biographies of the judges, as well as a catalogue of publications. The website can be visited at the following address: http://www.icj-cij.org.

238. Since March 1999 the Court has been offering individuals and institutions interested in its work an e-mail notification service for press releases posted on its website.

XI. Finances of the Court

A. Method of covering expenditure

239. Article 33 of the Statute of the Court provides: "The expenses of the Court shall be borne by the United Nations in such a manner as shall be decided by the General Assembly." As the budget of the Court has consequently been incorporated in the budget of the United Nations, Member States participate in the expenses of both in the same proportion, in accordance with the scale of assessments determined by the General Assembly.

240. States which are not Members of the United Nations but which are parties to the Statute pay, in accordance with the undertaking into which they entered when they became parties to the Statute, a contribution the amount of which is fixed from time to time by the General Assembly in consultation with them.

241. If a State which is not a party to the Statute but to which the Court is open is a party to a case, the Court will fix the amount which that party is to contribute towards the expenses of the Court (Statute, Art. 35, para. 3). Payment is then made by the State concerned to the account of the United Nations.

242. The contributions of States which are not Members of the United Nations are taken into account as miscellaneous income received by the Organization. Under an established rule, sums derived from staff assessment, sales of publications (dealt with by the Sales Sections of the Secretariat), bank interest, etc., are also recorded as United Nations income.

B. Drafting of the budget

243. In accordance with the Instructions for the Registry (Arts. 26-30), a preliminary draft budget is prepared by the Registrar. This preliminary draft is submitted for the consideration of the Budgetary and Administrative Committee of the Court and then, for approval, to the Court itself.

244. When it has been approved, the draft budget is forwarded to the Secretariat of the United Nations for incorporation in the draft budget of the United Nations. It is then examined by the United Nations Advisory Committee on Administrative and Budgetary Questions (ACABQ) and is afterwards submitted to the Fifth Committee of the General Assembly. It is finally adopted by the General Assembly in plenary meeting, within the framework of the resolutions concerning the budget of the United Nations.

C. Financing of appropriations and accounts

245. The Registrar is responsible for executing the budget, with the assistance of the Head of the Finance Division. The Registrar has to ensure that proper use is made of the funds voted and must see that no expenses are incurred that are not provided for in the budget. He alone is entitled to incur liabilities in the name of the Court, subject to any possible delegations of authority. In accordance with a decision of the Court, adopted on the recommendation of the Sub-Committee on Rationalization, the Registrar now communicates every three months a statement of accounts to the Administrative and Budgetary Committee of the Court.

246. The accounts of the Court are audited every year by the Board of Auditors appointed by the General Assembly and, periodically, by the internal auditors of the United Nations. At the end of each biennium, the closed accounts are forwarded to the Secretariat of the United Nations.

D. Budget of the Court for the biennium 2006-2007

247. Regarding the budget for the 2006-2007 biennium, the Court is pleased to note that its two requests for new posts have been accepted. With an experienced grade P-4 official heading up its IT Department, the Court will certainly now be in a better position to respond to the General Assembly's wish that it have greater recourse to new technology. Additionally, the Court now has a P-3 official to assist the President, who, over and above his or her judicial duties, performs a whole series of tasks of a diplomatic or administrative nature.

248. However, there are only five law clerks available to carry out research for the other 14 Members of the Court and the 22 judges *ad hoc* chosen in the 12 cases pending before the Court. Given the Court's sustained activity and the need to respond as rapidly as possible to pending cases, the question of increasing the number of law clerks presents itself in ever more acute terms. The Court is of the view that, like members of all leading international courts and national courts, its Members are entitled to individualized legal assistance so that they can work more rapidly and efficiently in their deliberating and adjudicatory tasks. A request to increase the number of law clerks from five to 14 will be included in the Court's budget submission for the biennium 2008-2009.

Budget for 2006-2007

Programme: Members of the Court	
0311025 Education Grants/Travel to Court sessions/ Home leave	664,200
0311023 Pensions	2,459,500
0242504 Duty allowance: judges *ad hoc*	383,800
2042302 Travel on official business	44,200
0393902 Emoluments	4,725,200
	8,276,900
Programme: The Registry	
0110000 Established posts	11,344,500
0170000 Temporary posts for the biennium	2,175,300
0200000 Common staff costs	6,424,600
0211014 Representation allowance	7,200
1210000 Temporary assistance for meetings	1,491,500
1310000 General temporary assistance	146,400
1410000 Consultants	41,700
1510000 Overtime	86,000
2042302 Official travel	38,900
0454501 Hospitality	18,300
	21,774,400
Programme: Programme Support	
3030000 External Translation	259,300
3050000 Printing	656,200
3070000 Data processing services	127,600
4010000 Rental/maintenance of premises	2,385,600
4030000 Rental of furniture and equipment	39,900
4040000 Communications	325,000
4060000 Maintenance of furniture & equipment	228,00
4090000 Miscellaneous services	40,200
5000000 Supplies & materials	250,100
5030000 Library books & supplies	163,800
6000000 Furniture & equipment	84,100
6025041 Acquisition of office automation equipment	96,400
6025042 Replacement of office automation equipment	194,700
6040000 Replacement of Court's vehicles	54,700
	4,905,600
TOTAL	34,956,900

XII. Examination by the General Assembly of the previous Report of the Court

249. At the 39th Plenary Meeting of the Sixtieth Session of the General Assembly, held on 27 October 2005, at which the Assembly took note of the Report of the Court for the period from 1 August 2004 to 31 July 2005, the President of the Court, Judge Shi Jiuyong, addressed the Assembly on the role and functioning of the Court (A/60/PV.39).

250. In his address President Shi stated that, as it approached its sixtieth anniversary, "the popularity of the Court as a dispute resolution mechanism continue[d] to grow". "More and more States are beginning to realize how the Court can serve them", said the President, adding, "experience has shown that recourse to the Court is a pacifying measure". "The Court", the President continued, "is . . . ideally equipped to settle quickly and durably, at minimal costs, any type of legal dispute, whatever its nature and the type of solution pursued, and no matter what the status of the relationship between the litigant parties".

Still a heavy caseload, but a reduced backlog

251. The President reminded the Assembly of the "tremendous efforts" made by the Court "in the last decade to increase its judicial efficiency while maintaining its high quality of work". In particular, he stressed "how much [had] been accomplished since those not so distant times when there was talk of a serious backlog of cases at the Court". "[T]he total number of 21 cases on the docket of the Court . . . a year ago had dropped to 11 at the end of the period under review", though there were now in fact 12 cases on the List, following the institution of proceedings by Costa Rica against Nicaragua on 29 September 2005. "Although it still represented a substantial amount of work, 12 cases was indeed a perfectly reasonable number of cases to have on the docket of an international court", said the President.

252. The President explained that between 1 August 2004 and 31 July 2005 the Court had held hearings in three cases (*Armed Activities on the Territory of the Congo (Democratic Republic of the Congo* v. *Uganda), Armed Activities on the Territory of the Congo (Democratic Republic of the Congo* v. *Rwanda)* and *Frontier Dispute (Benin/Niger)*) and handed down ten judgments (the eight cases concerning *Legality of Use of Force* between Serbia and Montenegro and various member States of NATO; the case concerning *Certain Property (Lichenstein* v *Germany)* and the *Frontier Dispute (Benin/Niger)*).

253. President Shi pointed out that "the achievement of the Court during the review period reflecte[d] its commitment to dealing with cases as promptly and efficiently as possible, while maintaining the quality of its judgments and respecting the consensual nature of its jurisdiction".

Renewed appeal to the General Assembly for financial support

254. In his address the President of the Court urged the General Assembly to maintain its financial support for the Court, whose budget represented less than 1 per cent of the Organization's total budget. "In its budgetary request for the biennium 2006-2007, which is currently under consideration, the Court", stated President Shi, "has made every effort to restrict itself to proposals which are financially modest, but also of the utmost significance for the implementation of key aspects of its work". "The Court hopes that these budgetary proposals will meet with your agreement, thereby enabling the principal judicial organ of the United Nations better to serve the international community", added the President.

255. Following the President's presentation of the Court's Report, addresses were made to the Assembly by the Representatives of Cameroon, China, Costa Rica, Egypt, Japan, Kenya, Malaysia, Mexico, New Zealand, Nigeria, Pakistan, Peru, Republic of Korea, Russian Federation, Sri Lanka and Syria.

256. More comprehensive information on the work of the Court during the period under review will be found in the *I.C.J. Yearbook 2005-2006*, which will be issued at a later date.

Rosalyn HIGGINS,
President of the International
Court of Justice.

The Hague, 1 August 2006.

---

[1] By letter of 7 June 2006, the Office of Legal Affairs of the United Nations informed the Court that the Permanent Representative of Serbia and Montenegro to the United Nations in New York had requested on 3 June 2006 that the name "Serbia" be used as the official name of the Republic of Serbia within the United Nations. The Office of Legal Affairs also transmitted to the Court a copy of a letter dated 3 June 2006 whereby the President of the Republic of Serbia informed the Secretary-General of the United Nations that, following the Declaration of Independence adopted by the National Assembly of Montenegro on 3 June 2006, "the membership of the state union Serbia and Montenegro in the United Nations, including all organs and organizations of the United Nations system, [would be] continued by the Republic of Serbia on the basis of Article 60 of the Constitutional Charter of Serbia and Montenegro". By a Note Verbale dated 6 June 2006, the Secretary-General transmitted to the Permanent Representatives of all Member States of the United Nations a copy of the communications from the Permanent Representative of Serbia and Montenegro and from the President of the Republic of Serbia. In his Note Verbale, the Secretary-General apprised Member States of the steps that were being taken to inform all organs and organizations of the United Nations system of the situation.
On 21 June 2006, the Office of Legal Affairs transmitted to the Court a letter dated 16 June 2006 whereby the Minister for Foreign Affairs of the Republic of Serbia informed the Secretary-General, inter alia, that "[t]he Republic of Serbia continue[d] to exercise its rights and honour its commitments deriving from international treaties concluded by Serbia and Montenegro" and requested that "the Republic of Serbia be considered a party to all international agreements in force, instead of Serbia and Montenegro". Furthermore, on 28 June 2006, by its resolution 60/264, the General Assembly admitted the Republic of Montenegro as a new Member of the United Nations.
On 19 July 2006, the Office of Legal Affairs transmitted to the Court a letter dated 30 June 2006 addressed to the Secretary-General by the Minister for Foreign Affairs of the Republic of Serbia under cover of a Note Verbale of 3 July 2006 from the Permanent Mission of the Republic of Serbia to the United Nations. By his letter, the Minister confirmed the intention of the Republic of Serbia to continue to exercise its rights and honour its commitments deriving from international treaties concluded by Serbia and Montenegro, with effect from 3 June 2006; he specified that all declarations, reservations and notifications made by Serbia and Montenegro would therefore continue in force with respect to the Republic of Serbia, unless the Secretary-General, as depositary, were notified otherwise.

[2] The Court delivered its Judgment in the case concerning *Armed Activities on the Territory of the Congo (Democratic Republic of the Congo* v. *Uganda)* in December 2005. The case nevertheless

technically remains pending, in the sense that the Parties could again turn to the Court to decide the question of reparation if they are unable to agree on this point.

[3] See note 2 above.
[4] See note 1 above.
[5] See note 1 above.
[6] See note 1 above.
[7] See note 1 above.
[8] See note 2 above.
[9] See note 1 above.
[10] See note 1 above.
[11] See note 2 above.
[12] See note 1 above.
[*] Amendment having entered into force on 29 September 2005.

CHAPTER 6

Secretariat: Annual Reports

1. United Nations: Report of the Secretary-General on the Work of the Organization for 2005/2006

Note

Symbols of United Nations documents are composed of capital letters combined with figures. Mention of such asymbol indicates a reference to a United Nations document.

Chapter I

Introduction

1. In this, my tenth and last annual report, I have sought to provide an overview of the Organization's main achievements and challenges during the past 12 months in the light of the critical developments in the decade since I took office at the beginning of 1997. I have also subsumed in a single report both the work of the Organization as such and the progress made in implementing the Millennium Declaration, which in previous years has been the subject of a separate report.

2. The report is arranged under headings that readers will recognize as corresponding to the four main sections of the outcome document of the 2005 World Summit of September 2005, which in turn followed the structure of my "In larger freedom" report: development; peace and security; human rights, rule of law and humanitarian affairs; and strengthening the United Nations. To these I have added a fifth, "global constituencies", to cover an area that has not previously been classified as central to the Organization's work but has become increasingly important—and will, I believe, become even more so as the new century advances.

3. Over its lifetime the United Nations has changed from being principally a conference-servicing Organization to become a truly global service provider working on the ground in virtually every corner of the world to improve the lives of people who need help. This transformation has occurred in a dramatic way during the past decade. More than 70 per cent of our $10 billion annual budget now relates to peacekeeping and other field operations, compared to about 50 per cent of a budget less than half that size 10 years ago. Over 50 per cent of our 30,000 civilian staff now serve in the field. The number of humanitarian offices increased from 12 offices with 114 staff members in 1997 to 43 offices with 815 staff members in 2005. Human rights work at the country level has grown significantly; in 1996 the Office of the United Nations High Commissioner for Human Rights (OHCHR) was present in 14 countries, and currently OHCHR-supported human rights personnel are deployed in over 40 countries. We have been called upon to support over 100 national elections. In addition, the Millennium Development Goals have become an operational template for use by Governments and peoples around the world to advance the well-being of all. The Joint United Nations Programme on HIV/AIDS (UNAIDS) is leading the charge to combat existential threats such as HIV/AIDS by bringing together the efforts and resources of 10 United Nations system organizations to the global AIDS response, and the UNAIDS secretariat works on the ground in more than 75 countries.

4. If any one phenomenon can be said to have dominated the decade we have just lived through, it must surely be globalization. This term has been variously defined, but to me it

conveys above all an era in which international relations are no longer almost exclusively about relations between nation-States, but also relations among people of different nationalities who interact with each other in a whole host of ways as individuals or as members of self-constituted groups across national boundaries, indeed across continents and oceans, often without needing to refer to the State at all. While the United Nations is constituted by Member States, these "non-State actors" on the international stage form new global constituencies with which the United Nations is increasingly called upon to interact.

5. The United Nations is having to learn how to work with global business and global civil society in all their manifold forms. The Organization must encourage partnerships with these vital actors to promote desirable changes and deliver growth, security and services, especially in the field.

6. But while nation-States are no longer the sole players in international relations, they are still the most important. And they face collective challenges that no single State can solve by itself.

7. Certainly, the State has not withered away or become redundant. On the contrary, the role of the State as regulator (though not administrator) of economic activity and mediator between different interest groups becomes all the more important as society becomes more complex. The more deadly weapons proliferate, the more essential is the State's monopoly on the means of coercion. To convince oneself of this, one has only to look at those unhappy countries where States are weak or are said to have failed. Many of them are countries that the United Nations knows all too well, since it is often where States are weak or have failed that we are summoned to assist.

8. That, too, is an important change. Our founders conceived of the Organization as working mainly to preserve the peace *between* States. They even forbade the Organization, in Article 2.7 of its Charter, a living document that remains vitally relevant today, to intervene "in matters which are essentially within the domestic jurisdiction of any state", though with the sensible reservation that this principle should not prejudice the application of enforcement measures under Chapter VII when the Security Council takes action with respect to threats to the peace, breaches of the peace or acts of aggression.

9. In recent years the Council has made use of this reservation many times, because it has found that breaches of the peace and acts of aggression most often begin *within* States, yet swiftly develop into threats to the peace of a whole region, if not the whole world. Thus the United Nations comes increasingly to see the security of its Member States as inseparable from that of the populations who inhabit them and are represented by them. That is why the world's heads of State and Government felt it necessary, at last year's historic summit, to reaffirm that "each individual State has the responsibility to protect its populations from genocide, war crimes, ethnic cleansing and crimes against humanity", and to affirm that the international community also has the responsibility to take timely and decisive action for this purpose, through the Security Council, when peaceful means prove inadequate and national authorities are manifestly failing to do it.

10. States, in short, are the servants and instruments of human beings, and not the other way round. Once this fundamental principle is understood and accepted, it becomes easy to see why the three cardinal purposes of the Organization—development, security and human rights—are so indissolubly interconnected.

11. In order to develop and prosper, human beings must be able to look to the State for security and protection and be able to exercise their individual rights—not only civil and political but also economic, social and cultural—under the rule of law.

12. Likewise, human beings can feel truly secure only if they enjoy economic as well as political or military security and if they can be confident that their basic rights and human dignity will not be violated.

13. Human beings will enjoy meaningful human rights only if they can escape from grinding and degrading poverty and if they can rely on a strong and just State—one in which their views and interests are truly represented—to protect them from violence and crime.

14. In carrying out its mission on all three fronts, one of the Organization's greatest assets is its idealistic and courageous staff, many of whom serve in situations of hardship and danger. During the past decade United Nations personnel have been increasingly targeted in places of strife and conflict. Our mission to build a safer, better world for all people is no longer a guarantee of protection. The United Nations has suffered a real loss of innocence in recent years. Consequently, we have had to learn how best to advance our mission to help others without excessively endangering our own.

15. But our commitment must never change. The United Nations, founded in the name of "We the peoples", must be able to advance their interests effectively in all three areas—development, security and human rights. Indeed, my millennium report "We the peoples" and my 2005 report "In larger freedom" reflect my own vision of this global responsibility, which has underpinned my tenure as Secretary-General. This report shows how the Organization has sought to do so in the past year and in the light of the past 10 years. I believe there is much in it that we can be proud of. But I am also fully conscious of the alarming extent to which, on all three fronts, our capacities fall short of the challenges we face. That is why I am convinced that the task of strengthening the United Nations is no mere bookkeeping exercise, but an imperative that directly concerns the interests of all Member States and should, much more than it appears to do at present, engage their urgent attention.

Chapter II

Development

Internationally agreed development goals and the Millennium Development Goals

To spare no effort: the millennium promise

16. In the Millennium Declaration of 2000 (General Assembly resolution 55/2), world leaders set forth a bold and inclusive new vision for humanity. Pledging to channel the fruits of globalization to benefit all people, leaders committed themselves "to spare no effort to free our fellow men, women and children from the abject and dehumanizing conditions of extreme poverty". Since 2000, the United Nations, together with eminent voices from Government, civil society, business and science, has given spirit to this commitment in a manner that many would have deemed impossible only a few years ago. The result has been dramatically increased global attention for the full one sixth of humanity who still live in the most extreme form of poverty, measured as income of less than one dollar per day.

17. Such political momentum offers the opportunity to build on the world's considerable recent development successes. As highlighted in the statistical annex to the present report, from 1990 to 2002, the developing world's proportion of people living in extreme poverty dropped from 28 per cent to 19 per cent, driven mostly by gains in eastern and southern Asia. Average child mortality rates in developing countries fell from 95 deaths per 1,000 live births in 1990 to 79 in 2004. More than 1.2 billion people gained access to improved sanitation over the same period. From 1991 to 2004, average net primary enrolment ratios in developing regions increased from 79 per cent to 86 per cent.

18. But progress has been uneven and the ongoing levels of human deprivation remain staggering. Each year, more than 10 million children die before their fifth birthday, mostly from preventable causes. Women in the developing world are more than 45 times more likely, on average, to die during pregnancy and childbirth than women in the developed world. More than 800 million people remain chronically undernourished. Half the developing world still lacks access to sanitation, a fifth has no access to safe water, and slum populations are growing steadily. The environment on which livelihoods depend is suffering degradation in all developing regions. The world missed the international goal for gender parity in education by 2005, and the epidemic of violence against women remains a scourge on humanity.

19. Prior to the Millennium Declaration, the foundations for tackling these challenges were consolidated through the major conferences and summits of the 1990s. At the 2002 International Conference on Financing for Development, held in Monterrey, Mexico, world leaders committed themselves to a new global partnership to achieve the internationally agreed development goals, including the Millennium Development Goals. The Monterrey Consensus reasserted each country's primary responsibility for its own economic and social development through sound governance and policies to fully mobilize domestic resources. These national efforts were to be supplemented by the commitment from developed countries to provide improved access to international markets, more and more effective, stable and predictable official development assistance and private capital flows and a better international architecture to prevent and manage financial crises. As an essential contribution to this process, developed countries also pledged to make concrete efforts towards the target of 0.7 per cent of gross national income as official development assistance and to pursue innovative sources of financing for development. Increased national responsibility was also to be accompanied by a greater voice and greater representation for developing countries in international economic decision-making. In the same year, at the World Summit on Sustainable Development, held in Johannesburg, South Africa, Member States focused on the implementation of sustainable development goals and added partnerships as a major new dimension to achieving those goals. The Summit reinforced the Millennium Development Goals by agreeing to specific, time-bound sustainable development targets, including particular targets for Africa.

20. In implementing this vision of global partnership, many developing and developed countries are leading by inspirational example. But many of them, despite their best efforts, simply remain too poor to make the investments needed to escape the trap of extreme poverty. It is these countries that require the most urgent international support if we are to fulfil the promises of the Millennium Declaration.

21. Recent global political debates have rightly shifted the emphasis from principles to practicalities. In January 2005, the Millennium Project presented to me its report entitled *Investing in Development: A Practical Plan to Achieve the Millennium Development Goals*, stressing the need for practical measures and the feasibility of major success. I welcomed the analysis and the recommendations of the Millennium Project. In March of the same year, I submitted to the General Assembly my report entitled "In larger freedom: towards development, security and human rights for all", which set out a strategic vision for collective action to achieve universal freedom from want, as well as freedom from fear and the realization of dignity for all. Both reports stressed that breakthrough action was required at all levels if implementation were to proceed at a scale commensurate with countries' development needs. Other Secretariat reports, such as the *Report on the World Social Situation 2005* and the *World Economic and Social Survey 2006*, have focused on the growing inequalities that are emerging both within and among countries and that make it challenging, but all the more imperative, to reach the Millennium Development Goals.

2005—a year of commitments

22. As the first major checkpoint since the Millennium Summit, 2005 saw a number of important commitments to a global development agenda, culminating at the 2005 World Summit. All Member States emphasized the vital role played by the major United Nations conferences and summits in shaping a broad development vision and in identifying commonly agreed objectives, and strongly reaffirmed the Millennium Development Goals as the shared, time-bound, integrated and measurable framework for development cooperation. For the United Nations system, it has been extremely encouraging to see the Goals gain political momentum with each passing year. Citizens around the world are rightfully calling upon their Governments to be ever bolder in following through on the Goals. As a result, international development efforts have regained ambition, fusing the possibility for success with a heightened sense of urgency.

23. At the 2005 World Summit (see General Assembly resolution 60/1), Member States agreed to a practical framework for decade-long action when they committed to embedding the global goals into the country-level processes where operational and budgetary decisions are made. In particular, Member States agreed to adopt, by the end of 2006, comprehensive national strategies to achieve the internationally agreed development goals and objectives, including the Millennium Development Goals, supported by the global partnership for development agreed in Monterrey. Member States also committed to launching "quick-impact initiatives", immediate steps that can save and improve millions of lives within the span of only a few years. These include actions to distribute anti-malaria bed nets, free of charge, to eliminate user fees in basic education and health and to expand school meal programmes using locally produced food.

24. World leaders further agreed to several other important targets at the 2005 World Summit. I am therefore recommending the incorporation of these commitments into the set of targets used to follow up on the Millennium Declaration. This includes: a new target under Millennium Development Goal 1: to make the goals of full and productive employment and decent work for all, including for women and young people, a central objective of our relevant national and international policies and our national development strategies; a new target under Goal 5: to achieve universal access to reproductive health by 2015;

a new target under Goal 6: to come as close as possible to universal access to treatment for HIV/AIDS by 2010 for all those who need it; and a new target under Goal 7: to significantly reduce the rate of loss of biodiversity by 2010. The existing target on developing decent and productive work for youth, now under Millennium Development Goal 8, would be encompassed by the new target (under Goal 1). Technical work to select the appropriate indicators would be undertaken by the Inter-agency and Expert Group on Millennium Development Goal Indicators. In this work, the system will be able to build on the Ministerial Declaration on Employment Generation and Decent Work adopted at the 2006 session of the Economic and Social Council, which calls for the development of 10-year action plans and assigns the Council a clear role in monitoring progress in its implementation.

25. As emphasized in Monterrey, commitments can be implemented only if backed by adequate international financing, another realm of significant breakthroughs in 2005. The Multilateral Debt Relief Initiative endorsed the cancellation of debts to the African Development Bank, the International Monetary Fund and the World Bank for those countries that completed the enhanced Heavily Indebted Poor Countries Initiative. Worth approximately $50 billion in face value, this debt relief is projected to save qualifying countries more than $1 billion per year in debt-servicing payments over the coming decade. This agreement marks unambiguous progress and highlights the need for relief for other deserving countries too.

26. Of much greater quantitative importance for development finance, 16 of 22 members of the Organization for Economic Cooperation and Development (OECD) Development Assistance Committee have now either met the official development assistance target of 0.7 per cent of gross national income or set timetables for doing so by 2015. In May 2005, the 15 Development Assistance Committee members that are members of the European Union each agreed to meet a minimum target of 0.51 per cent of gross national income by 2010, en route to 0.7 per cent by 2015. Admirably, Member States that joined the European Union after 2002 set a development assistance target of 0.33 per cent of gross national income by 2015. The Group of Eight summit held in Gleneagles, United Kingdom of Great Britain and Northern Ireland, built on this momentum with an agreement to augment total annual development assistance by $50 billion by 2010, with half of the increase directed to Africa. An increasing number of donors are meeting the target to provide at least 0.15 to 0.20 per cent of their gross national income to assist the least developed countries, and official development assistance to least developed countries has thus increased sharply in recent years. Innovative sources of financing have also been explored and various initiatives are being implemented.

2006—translating commitments into action

27. If history judges 2005 for its promises, then 2006 must be judged on implementation. Are we on course to look back, in 2015, and say that no effort was spared? So far the record is mixed. The words of 2005 have yet to have a direct impact on the lives of the poor people they are meant to help. Nor have they produced the implementation breakthroughs required to achieve the Millennium Development Goals. The challenges remain most pressing in Africa, particularly sub-Saharan Africa, where the proportion of people living in extreme poverty is essentially unchanged since 1990 and the absolute number has increased dramatically.

28. There has been progress, however. For example, the Multilateral Debt Relief Initiative has followed a prompt timetable towards completion; international malaria control efforts are gathering speed, backed by increased donor assistance; momentum is under way to launch the African Green Revolution agreed upon at the 2005 World Summit; and recent global commitments have also prompted new notions of investment scale-up to tackle broader development priorities. To ensure that Member States can respond to their countries' development priorities, last year I personally wrote to all Heads of State and Government offering United Nations assistance and support. I am heartened to note that the United Nations country teams are currently helping many countries to prepare and implement Millennium Development Goal-based national development strategies.

29. Putting the Millennium Development Goals into action, the United Nations has collaborated with Governments and other stakeholders to support so-called millennium villages throughout Africa. The project began with a single village in Sauri, Kenya, in August 2004 and has expanded to 12 sites in Ethiopia, Ghana, Kenya, Malawi, Mali, Nigeria, Rwanda, Senegal, Uganda and the United Republic of Tanzania. Among other successes, the villages are transforming themselves from areas of chronic hunger, tripling their crop production in a short time. Using scientific technology and understanding the agro-ecological zones of the areas, villagers are now able to sell their produce in nearby markets.

30. Thanks to efforts by the World Health Organization (WHO), the United Nations Children's Fund (UNICEF) and others, progress is being made to slow the spread of infectious diseases and provide assistance to those suffering from them. Aid is increasing throughout Africa and other areas to provide insecticide-treated mosquito nets, which can save as many as 20 per cent of children who would otherwise die from malaria. Policies regarding artemisinin-based combination therapy for malaria are now in place, helping to stem the burden of resistance to former malaria treatments and helping many to overcome the disease. A large campaign to eradicate polio over the past decade has nearly been completed, with only four polio-endemic countries left. It is suspected that transmission of the disease could be halted throughout the world by the end of 2006, with the possibility of the world being certified polio-free by the end of 2010.

31. From the work of the Permanent Forum on Indigenous Issues to ensure that policies to attain the Millennium Development Goals reach out to indigenous people to the likely conclusion of the first ever convention on protection and promotion of the rights and dignity of persons with disabilities this year, progress towards policy implementation is evident. Another key issue from the 2005 World Summit—how to realize the great potential of migration to advance worldwide development—will be addressed at the forthcoming high-level dialogue in the General Assembly. This offers a unique opportunity for the Organization to move policies towards economic and social progress for migrants and their countries of origin and destination.

32. The Economic and Social Council has been called upon to play a critical role in the systematic follow-up and monitoring of progress of various programmes. The annual ministerial reviews can become the major mechanism for strengthening accountability for international commitments to the Millennium Development Goals and the other agreed development goals. The Council's high-level development cooperation forum will provide a global platform where all will be able to discuss key policy issues that affect development cooperation in all its forms. I trust that the Council will rise to this major challenge.

33. In spite of these advances, progress remains much too incomplete. Most fundamentally, international financial commitments remain inadequate in terms of timing, volume and quality for achieving the internationally agreed development goals, including the Millennium Development Goals. Many of the new promises will take years to materialize, so it is difficult for low-income countries to begin real investment scale-up. Aggregate official development assistance reached a record high of $106 billion in 2005, up from $69 billion in 2003, but only a small fraction of this nominal increase actually represented additional finance to support real ground-level investments in the countries that need them most. Even multilateral debt relief yields little immediate gain for qualifying countries, since benefits are backloaded and additional financing is still necessary to ensure that multilateral development banks are adequately resourced to finance scale-up programmes. It therefore remains as important as ever for developed countries without timetables for achieving the 0.7 per cent aid target to set them as soon as possible. Moreover, aid delivery mechanisms require dramatic improvement, building on the 2005 Paris Declaration on Aid Effectiveness.

34. Another cause for concern is the suspension of negotiations of the World Trade Organization's Doha Development Round. Developing countries require greater market access and support for capacity development in order to develop the long-term competitiveness that sustains economic development. Following the Ministerial Conference held in Hong Kong, China, in December 2005, which produced few areas of agreement and little momentum, the talks were stalled in July 2006. In the coming months, leadership will be required from all sides, particularly the developed countries, if negotiations are to be saved. It is also important that the Aid for Trade Initiative endorsed at Hong Kong be pursued.

35. The costs of delay and inaction are borne globally, not just locally. One need only consider the challenges posed by emerging diseases such as avian influenza to understand the shared and urgent global interest in supporting practical development steps in all countries. We must recognize the nature of global trust at stake and the danger that many developing countries' hopes could be irredeemably pierced if even the greatest anti-poverty movement in history is insufficient to break from "business as usual". As we move towards implementation in 2006 and beyond, we still must spare no effort.

HIV/AIDS

36. In the 25 years since the first cases of AIDS were reported, AIDS has killed more than 25 million people, orphaned 15 million children and exacerbated hunger and poverty. It has become the leading cause of death among both men and women aged 15 to 59, and women now represent 50 per cent of people living with HIV worldwide. After a tragically late and slow start, the world's response has gathered strength. The adoption of the Declaration of Commitment on HIV/AIDS in June 2001 marked a watershed moment when the world recognized the challenge posed by AIDS and pledged to take action.

37. A great deal of progress has been achieved since then. The Global Fund to Fight AIDS, Tuberculosis and Malaria was established in 2002 to provide low- and middle-income countries with additional financing. More domestic and international resources have been mobilized. The prices of some AIDS medicines have been greatly reduced and the "3 by 5 Initiative", launched by UNAIDS and WHO, has helped to generate a substantial increase in the number of people receiving antiretroviral treatment. Yet, the pace of the epidemic

continues to outstrip current efforts. An estimated 38.6 million people worldwide were living with HIV in 2005. An estimated 4.1 million people became infected with HIV and an estimated 2.8 million lost their lives to AIDS. The global impact of AIDS has already been so devastating that the *Human Development Report 2005* of the United Nations Development Programme (UNDP) concluded that the HIV/AIDS pandemic had inflicted the single greatest reversal in human development.

38. In the 2005 World Summit Outcome, world leaders committed to a massive scaling up of HIV prevention, treatment and care with the aim of coming as close as possible to the goal of universal access to treatment by 2010 for all who need it. The impact is starting to be seen in some areas, with trends in national HIV prevalence showing recent declines in two sub-Saharan African countries, namely Kenya and Zimbabwe, in urban areas in Burkina Faso and Haiti, nationally in Cambodia and Thailand and in four states in India. More than 1.3 million people were receiving antiretroviral therapy in low- and middle-income countries by December 2005, and in sub-Saharan Africa the number of people receiving treatment increased more than eightfold (from 100,000 to 810,000) between 2003 and 2005 and more than doubled in 2005 alone. The number of people receiving antiretroviral therapy in Asia increased almost threefold, to 180,000, in 2005.

39. In response to the request of the General Assembly contained in its resolution 60/224, UNAIDS and its co-sponsors helped to facilitate inclusive country-driven processes to develop practical strategies for moving towards universal access. The report entitled "Towards universal access: assessment by the Joint United Nations Programme on HIV/AIDS on scaling up HIV prevention, treatment, care and support", provides a summary of these country-driven processes and contains practical recommendations on setting and supporting national priorities; ensuring predictable and sustainable financing; strengthening human resources and systems; removing the barriers to ensure affordable commodities; protecting the AIDS-related human rights of people living with HIV, women and children and people in vulnerable groups; and setting targets and accountability mechanisms.

40. The high-level meeting and review of progress on HIV/AIDS, which was held in New York from 31 May to 2 June 2006, provided world leaders with an opportunity to assess progress made in achieving the targets set out in the Declaration of Commitment on HIV/AIDS and to strengthen the global response against the epidemic. In the Declaration of Commitment on HIV/AIDS: five years later, Member States: (a) committed to taking specific actions to scale up nationally driven, sustainable and comprehensive AIDS responses—including the full and active participation of civil society—towards the goal of universal access to HIV prevention, treatment, care and support by 2010; (b) recognized the UNAIDS estimate that $20 billion to $23 billion would be required annually by 2010 to fund sufficiently scaled-up responses; (c) committed to setting up ambitious national targets and costed national plans; and (d) agreed to focus on the key drivers of the epidemic, in particular gender disparity, challenges for young people and stigma and discrimination.

41. The HIV/AIDS epidemic demands an exceptional response. Among the main challenges ahead are the need to work more closely and openly with populations most affected by HIV and AIDS, such as men who have sex with men, sex workers and injecting drug users, and moving from short-term emergency response to a longer-term response that recognizes the exceptionality of AIDS and is integrated with national development

planning and implementation. We need an ambitious and balanced strategy of both prevention and treatment and adequate urgent funding. A real difference can be made in a very short time.

The special needs of Africa

42. World leaders made an unprecedented commitment in the Millennium Declaration to recognize and provide for the special needs of Africa. The need for urgent and concerted action was compelling, as Africa continues to suffer more than its share of the hardships caused by violent conflict, poverty and disease.

43. It must be recognized, however, that encouraging developments have taken place in Africa during the past 10 years. The number of democratically elected national Governments in Africa has increased significantly, and economic growth in some African countries is relatively strong and sustained. There has been a marked resolve by African leaders to take control of the continent's destiny. The Organization of African Unity has been transformed into the African Union, which continues to strengthen its peacekeeping and mediation capacities and its peer-review mechanism, and implementation of the New Partnership for Africa's Development (NEPAD) is moving ahead.

44. Yet major challenges remain. Sub-Saharan Africa lags behind the rest of the developing world in achieving the Millennium Development Goals. About half of the world's armed conflicts, and the vast majority of United Nations peacekeepers, are in Africa. There is a high prevalence of HIV/AIDS in many countries.

45. Providing support for the development of Africa has become a top priority of the United Nations. Regional actions and international initiatives have further strengthened impetus for progress in conflict resolution, economic growth, consolidation of democracy and implementation of NEPAD. With a recent agreement, the Multilateral Debt Relief Initiative has helped Nigeria to shift approximately $1 billion a year from debt servicing to poverty-reduction programmes. Ghana and the Netherlands recently launched a partnership to support Ghana's nationwide school meals programme using locally produced food. Many African countries are preparing 10-year education plans, while Kenya, Malawi, Uganda and the United Republic of Tanzania continue to show the benefits for primary-school enrolment of abolishing user fees for education. Earlier this year Zambia cancelled fees for basic rural health services and Burundi introduced free medical care for mothers and children.

46. The Africa Fertilizer Summit held in June 2006 in Abuja mapped out a common strategy for the continent to achieve food self-sufficiency and launch the rural economic transformation required to overcome extreme poverty. African leaders set targets for 2007 and 2008 en route to a 2015-based plan of action to help farmers move to higher-yielding land practices, with increased use of improved seeds, fertilizers and irrigation.

47. Meanwhile, the Millennium Project launched the Millennium Villages initiative, which aims to identify how recent global commitments can be translated to Government-and community-led development efforts to further the Millennium Development Goals. Ten countries so far are partnering with UNDP in the initiative.

48. The United Nations system offered further assistance in a wide range of areas. The independent panel of experts that I established two years ago has submitted its second

report on the theme "From commitments to results: moving forward NEPAD implementation". The report includes a number of proposals for advancing the NEPAD agenda.

49. In 2005, the Office of the Special Adviser on Africa released a report entitled "Resource flows to Africa: an update on statistical trends". The report found that while official development assistance remained the main external resource flow to Africa, remittances from Africans working abroad had overtaken foreign direct investment in the period 2000-2003. Consequently, public policy should aim to facilitate an increase in remittances, in particular by reducing the cost of transfers so as to achieve the key objective of greater resource flows to households in Africa.

50. Other contributions of the Office of the Special Adviser on Africa include a conference organized in collaboration with the Government of Sierra Leone on disarmament, demobilization, reintegration and stability in Africa in Freetown, in June 2005. It brought together African practitioners and their international partners to share experiences and ideas about ways to improve the design, operation and implementation of disarmament, demobilization and reintegration programmes to better promote sustainable peace on the continent. A similar round table of experts was convened in Cairo in June 2006 on the theme "Natural resources and conflict in Africa: transforming a peace liability into a peace asset" in an effort to promote socially responsible and economically sound resource management in post-conflict countries in Africa.

51. In the years ahead, the United Nations must respond even better to Africa's needs and aspirations. This is consistent with the Organization's ideals, and the people of Africa deserve nothing less.

Ensuring environmental sustainability

52. In 1992 the United Nations Conference on Environment and Development was held in Rio de Janeiro, Brazil, to address pressing issues regarding environmental protection and socio-economic development. Over 100 world leaders signed the United Nations Framework Convention on Climate Change and the Convention on Biological Diversity, endorsed the Rio Declaration and adopted a strategic plan for preventing environmental degradation and achieving environmental sustainability in the twenty-first century, the so-called Agenda 21. The Commission on Sustainable Development was created to monitor and report on implementation of the Earth Summit agreements. Five years later, in 1997, the General Assembly met in special session in New York to reaffirm the Earth Summit compact and review the implementation of Agenda 21 by countries, international organizations and civil society.

53. During my tenure, I have seen a greater understanding among Governments that human security is also threatened by environmental degradation. The continuing increase in the number of ratifications of major multilateral environmental agreements shows the growing commitment of countries to address global environmental issues. Ensuring environmental sustainability is one of the main pillars of the global fight against poverty, and it is essential for achieving the Millennium Development Goals. The United Nations has been active in seeking ways to improve and sustain the environment.

54. The Millennium Ecosystem Assessment, which I launched in 2001 and a report on which was released in March 2005, highlighted the urgency of making more progress towards environmental sustainability. It found that 60 per cent of the world's ecosystems,

such as drylands, forests, fisheries and even the air we breathe, are being degraded or used unsustainably. The United Nations system must continue to help countries to integrate environmental concerns effectively into national policy frameworks for development and poverty reduction. The Bali Strategic Plan for Technology Support and Capacity-building, adopted by the Governing Council of the United Nations Environment Programme (UNEP), is aimed at strengthening the capacity of Governments of developing countries and countries with economies in transition to achieve their environmental goals and targets, as well as the environment-related development goals agreed internationally, thus enhancing the environmental sustainability of their countries' development. UNEP, UNDP and their relevant partners are intensifying their activities as envisaged in the Bali Strategic Plan.

55. At the 2005 World Summit, world leaders decided on a number of measures aimed at protecting our common environment, including a call for a more coherent institutional framework to address the environmental challenges of today. While the General Assembly has started its consideration of these matters, I have established the High-level Panel on United Nations System-wide Coherence that will present its proposals on how to ensure and enhance coordination of United Nations activities in the areas of development, humanitarian affairs and the environment. In the meantime, UNEP and UNDP, two of the main implementing agencies of the Global Environment Facility, have integrated their respective poverty and environmental projects into the Poverty and Environment Initiative, which was announced at the "Environment for the Millennium Development Goals" high-level event during the Summit in September.

56. Action on climate change is particularly urgent, and implementing a global response to it is a priority of the United Nations. The entry into force of the Kyoto Protocol in February 2005 represented a historic moment in the international response to climate change. Yet this is just one step. There is a need to build a stronger international consensus for setting goals beyond the first Kyoto commitment period of 2008-2012. As at July 2006, 164 countries had ratified the Protocol, representing over 60 per cent of emissions from industrial countries. The wider United Nations Framework Convention on Climate Change remains the multilateral framework for action.

57. A major challenge for all countries in the years ahead is the development of new and sustainable energy sources. Governments, businesses and communities around the world have an important role to play in this endeavour and in the broader effort, in the words of the Millennium Declaration, to free all of humanity from the threat of living on a planet irredeemably spoiled by human activities, and whose resources would no longer be sufficient for human needs.

Chapter III

Peace and security

Conflict prevention and peacemaking

58. The United Nations was founded on a commitment to prevent war and to strengthen means for conflict resolution. The Millennium Declaration reaffirmed that preventing deadly conflicts and protecting people from violence is a priority of the Organization. We continue to be reminded of the importance of peacemaking and attempting to prevent

conflict before it develops. Early action to address the root causes of potentially violent conflict, as well as diplomatic initiatives to bring parties together to bridge their differences, are less costly than waiting until conflicts erupt or run their destructive course.

59. During the past decade, the Organization has begun taking prevention more seriously. Efforts to live up to the Charter and the Millennium Declaration have brought improvements around the world. In Africa, the United Nations has been instrumental in peacemaking, as well as in peacekeeping and peacebuilding, in Sierra Leone, Liberia, Angola, Mozambique, Cameroon, Nigeria and elsewhere. In Europe, United Nations-mediated final status talks on Kosovo are under way, and in Cyprus United Nations efforts have been aimed at encouraging a resumption of negotiations for a comprehensive settlement. In Asia, the United Nations has been lending support to reconciliation efforts in Iraq and peace processes in Nepal. In Central Asia I initiated the establishment of a regional United Nations centre for preventive diplomacy, an initiative that enjoys the support of five countries in the region. In the Americas, the General Assembly discontinued its annual review of Central America in 2005, marking the end of over 20 years of successful United Nations peacemaking efforts in the region. Meanwhile, conflict-prevention activities are under way in the Andean region and in Guyana. In countless other cases, through development programming, good offices and other means, United Nations officials shore up fragile situations and help national counterparts to avoid the scourge of war.

60. The Organization has seen institutional progress in peacemaking over the past decade. I warmly welcomed the decisions of the 2005 World Summit with respect to conflict prevention and mediation and can report several steps towards implementation of those decisions. A dedicated mediation support capacity is being established within the Department of Political Affairs, which will serve as a repository of lessons and experiences and will offer more systematic support to United Nations mediators and to mediation partners outside of the United Nations. There has also been important normative, political and institutional progress in the area of conflict prevention. Unfortunately, however, we still have a long way to go to ensure that effective preventive action is taken when the opportunity arises. At the systemic, structural and operational levels, more understanding, resources, cooperation and will are needed to make armed conflict less viable and less likely.

Peacekeeping

61. Over the past decade, we have been reminded that United Nations peacekeeping plays a crucial role in securing States and individual political freedoms. Missions such as those in Sierra Leone, Timor-Leste, the Democratic Republic of the Congo and the Balkans have been central to my tenure. When I became Secretary-General, the United Nations had fewer than 13,000 troops deployed worldwide and was recovering from the setbacks of the early 1990s. Today 65,500 troops and military observers, 7,500 police and more than 15,000 international and local civilian personnel serve in 15 peacekeeping operations and 3 special political or peacebuilding missions, in Afghanistan, Sierra Leone and Timor-Leste. The annual budget for United Nations peacekeeping has increased from approximately $1 billion in 1997 to approximately $5 billion today—totalling 0.5 per cent of global military spending. In 1997 military and police personnel were drawn from about 70 countries versus over 100 countries currently. In 1998 4 out of the top 10 contributors of troops were developing countries, whereas today all 10 are developing countries.

62. The past year has witnessed the successful transition from peacekeeping to peacebuilding in Sierra Leone and support for the organization of fair and largely calm elections from the Democratic Republic of the Congo, Liberia, Burundi and Haiti. In the particularly challenging environments of Afghanistan and the Democratic Republic of the Congo, peacekeeping operations have facilitated complex transitional political processes.

63. But the year has also brought harsh reminders that the risk of failure is high. We withdrew our peacekeepers from Sierra Leone in December 2005. However, while we pulled our last soldiers from Timor-Leste in May 2005, within just one year an international force had returned to the country as it slipped back towards violence. Meanwhile, progress in the Democratic Republic of the Congo was tempered by violent incidents in the eastern part of the country, which highlighted the challenging and often hostile environment in which our peacekeeping operations take place.

64. The transformation of United Nations peacekeeping is not only numerical. Our traditional role of monitoring ceasefires remains very important, but we have become deeply engaged in facilitating political processes to give countries and territories emerging from conflict the opportunity for legitimate Government. This has been particularly important in, for example, Kosovo, where the United Nations has served as the interim administration and is now leading the political process to determine Kosovo's future status. In addition, in 2005 alone, over 50 million registered voters had the chance to participate in elections and referendums overseen by United Nations peacekeeping missions. Because we recognize that voting alone does not bring stable politics, we are increasingly engaged in helping Governments to reform their security sectors and in providing social services to all. In Liberia and Haiti, our missions are also paying particular attention to the way in which State services are provided and, together with partners, assisting national authorities to enhance the accountability of Government finances.

65. Building these capacities requires significant resources. Over the past year I have been grateful to the Security Council for strengthening the mandates of our missions in Burundi, the Democratic Republic of the Congo and Haiti and for permitting the transfer of personnel from Liberia to Côte d'Ivoire and from Burundi to the Democratic Republic of the Congo. I recall my earlier statements that fulfilling complex mandates requires the highest-calibre civilian staff, drawn from across the United Nations system, other multilateral organizations and Member States. This year, we made important progress in approving and staffing the initial operating capability for a standing police capacity. We must continue to work to get the best professionals, civilian and uniformed, in the field on the shortest possible notice.

66. But building peace takes not only strong personnel but time. Observing the setback in Timor-Leste, we have been reminded that, while the concerns of the Organization's financial and personnel contributors must always be taken into account, it is important that the international community does not withdraw too hastily from conflict-scarred countries. I am hopeful that the new Peacebuilding Commission, which has, with the support of the two Governments, identified Burundi and Sierra Leone for attention, will play an important role in coordinating the rebuilding of post-conflict societies.

67. We also need strong partners. This year we have continued to develop our relationships with other international organizations. I welcome the European Union's decision to provide a standby force to support the United Nations Operation in the Congo during national elections in the Democratic Republic of the Congo, and am grateful to the North Atlantic Treaty Organization, the European Union and the Organization for Security and Cooperation in Europe for their continued collaboration in ensuring stability and political progress in Kosovo. Meanwhile, the United Nations has made marked progress in cooperating with the African Union, as demonstrated by the joint United Nations-African Union assessment mission to Darfur, Sudan, in June. This allowed the two organizations to develop a consolidated plan for strengthening the current African Union Mission in the Sudan and to provide recommendations for the transfer from that mission to a United Nations peacekeeping operation in the region.

68. Yet we must also recognize that, in spite of this cooperation and considerable effort by the international community, the Government of the Sudan has yet to approve a United Nations peacekeeping operation in Darfur. Alongside the constraints placed on the operations of the United Nations Mission in Ethiopia and Eritrea by the Government of Eritrea and the request of the Government of Burundi that the United Nations Operation in Burundi withdraw, this is a potent reminder that we can build peace and stability only where there is sustained local political support and raises very hard questions about why we sometimes fail to win that support from parties when we need it most. The answers are primarily political. The parties to a conflict may not always perceive an effective peacekeeping operation as being in their interest. There are also often misperceptions about the agenda of our peacekeeping operations. However, once the parties have recognized that United Nations peacekeeping has no other goal than that of promoting international peace and security, we must ensure that our peacekeepers meet the highest standards and that the necessary resources are made available.

69. We have recognized that we sometimes lose local support because of our operational failings, most obviously in the case of sexual exploitation and abuse, which we have worked hard to eradicate in recent years. We also accept that we lose credibility when we lack the full range of resources necessary to address multiple challenges, such as localized violence by politically motivated spoilers and organized crime. Too often, our stature is eroded by disenchantment with the often slow processes of development or institution-building. Our own morale also suffers badly in these circumstances.

70. But we must understand above all that the deployment of peacekeepers, under direct United Nations command or otherwise, will bring real peace only where the international community maintains close involvement in finding political solutions with local actors and in creating conditions for effective reconstruction and development. At a time when our peacekeeping forces are so overextended, and often taking significant risks, it must be remembered that their presence can ease dialogue and succeed only where there is political will, and cannot act as an easy long-term alternative to it.

71. As we approach the end of my term of office and as we continue to search for a settlement to the great crises of our time, such as those in the Middle East and the Sudan, it is crucial that we continue to muster the political will that can translate our investment of financial and human resources into peace.

Peacebuilding

72. In the course of the past decade, ever more focus at the United Nations has been devoted to post-conflict peacebuilding—that is, in the aftermath of conflict, the restoration of State authority, the revitalization of State-society relations and of civil society and the reconstruction of the institutional foundations of economic and social development.

73. The track record of peacebuilding efforts is decidedly mixed. By some counts between a third and half of those countries that emerge from war relapse into it within five years. This phenomenon was illustrated in recent years by the relapse into violence in Haiti and a resurgence of tension in Timor-Leste, in both cases requiring the return of international peacekeepers. In these and similar cases, too little had been done to re-establish the institutional and economic conditions that can sustain political competition within a framework of constitutional order and law.

74. That peacebuilding often fails is not a source of surprise. The political fractures, social and economic inequalities, resource scarcities and other tensions that generate conflict are exacerbated, not diminished, by war. The mere fact of the signing of a peace agreement does not signify an end to these sources of conflict; peace agreements are at best merely a long-term road map for overcoming them. Implementation of those agreements and the wider process of restoring political and economic relationships is the harder part of the battle.

75. A source of surprise, no; but a source of deep concern, certainly. For not only does relapse into war squander national and international investments in peacemaking and recovery, the fighting that occurs after the collapse of a peace agreement is sometimes far more deadly than in earlier rounds, as parties' belief in the prospects of reconciliation is shattered, the possibility of power-sharing seems more remote, and thus a winner-take-all mentality pervades. In such circumstances parties often commit to total war and the mass killing it can entail.

76. Parties themselves are often conscious of this risk, and thus sometimes take the necessary tough decisions to forge the necessary political compromises, build the necessary institutional restraints and make the necessary sacrifices to restore the populations' faith in the prospects of recovery and lead people away from war. Where peacebuilding succeeds it is always the leadership of domestic actors that is the essential ingredient of success. No amount of international engagement can substitute for domestic political leaders shouldering their responsibilities and leading their people towards peace and development.

77. Domestic leadership is the essential condition of peacebuilding, but it is rarely a sufficient condition. Rather, substantial international support has often made a crucial difference. Indeed, notwithstanding important failures, the fact is that over the past decade international assistance for the implementation of peace agreements and for wider peacebuilding processes has made a critical contribution to an overall decline in the level of civil war in the world—an achievement of historic significance.

78. And when peacebuilding efforts have succeeded—as they have in El Salvador, Guatemala, Mozambique, Cambodia, Rwanda and Eastern Slavonia and show every sign of doing in Burundi, Sierra Leone and Liberia—they show the United Nations system at its best and in all of its facets.

79. The United Nations is first and foremost, of course, a membership organization. And peacebuilding highlights this not only because of the irreducible role of national leadership, but also in that the major contributors to peacebuilding efforts are Member States—both regional Governments that can vitally help to stabilize emergent national authorities and donor Governments that provide the bulk of financial resources to the reconstruction process and an additional layer of political support.

80. The United Nations is also a network of capacities. Some of these, such as the World Bank, the International Monetary Fund and UNDP, play central roles in economic and institutional reconstruction, while others, such as the Office of the United Nations High Commissioner for Refugees (UNHCR), OHCHR, the World Food Programme and UNICEF play vital roles in humanitarian and social recovery.

81. The United Nations is also a source of operational capacity. The deployment of such capacities—particularly in the form of peacekeeping operations, which are now routinely structured to integrate within them all of the various aspects of United Nations operational engagement—has proved vital to helping parties overcome their divisions, provide a secure space within which they can resolve tensions and serve as a channel for resources for the rehabilitation of State and social infrastructure.

82. Bringing all of these roles together has been a major challenge in the past decade. But it is precisely this role that the Peacebuilding Commission was established to play. By creating a forum that links the General Assembly, the Economic and Social Council and the Security Council; by bringing a wider range of States, especially regional actors and the major financial and troop contributors, into the deliberations of the Security Council; by creating a body with an interest in long-term, sustained engagement beyond the normal period of a peacekeeping operation; by creating a forum in which the United Nations system as a whole, including the international financial institutions, can meet with a core set of the most engaged Member States; and, most importantly, by creating a platform for national authorities to set out their own vision and their own priorities for reconstruction—in all of these ways, the establishment of the Peacebuilding Commission holds the promise of more effective, more reliable peacebuilding results.

83. The Peacebuilding Commission has been slow to start and has yet to show its full promise. But good things take time, and we should not be discouraged by the fact that this new body is still trying to find effective ways of working. The creation of a Peacebuilding Support Office and the establishment of a Peacebuilding Fund will add critical tools to its repertoire. Over the next decade, I anticipate that the Peacebuilding Commission will be at the core of the work of the United Nations and the international community in peacebuilding—rightly recognized by the 2005 World Summit as a vital role for the Organization.

Combating terrorism

84. The threat of terrorism to international peace, security and development has taken on new importance during the past 10 years. Consequently, the international community has taken a number of important steps to provide a solid legal basis for common actions against terrorism, including the adoption of 13 universal instruments and their protocols and amendments, the latest of which—the Convention for the Suppression of Acts of Nuclear Terrorism—was opened for signature during the World Summit in September 2005.

In the Millennium Declaration world leaders resolved to take concerted action against international terrorism. At the World Summit they strongly condemned, for the first time, terrorism in all its forms and manifestations, committed by whomever, wherever and for whatever purposes. I trust that the conclusion of a comprehensive convention on international terrorism will be forthcoming.

85. United Nations counter-terrorism activities have expanded dramatically in order to address the growing challenge of terrorism. The milestone Security Council resolutions, 1267 (1999), 1373 (2001), 1540 (2004) and 1624 (2005), and expert groups that support the three counter-terrorism subsidiary bodies have made States more responsible for taking practical steps to prevent terrorist financing, travel and access to weapons of mass destruction, as well as the incitement of terrorism. A remarkably wide array of organizations, departments and agencies in the United Nations system, including the International Atomic Energy Agency (IAEA), the United Nations Office on Drugs and Crime, Interpol, the United Nations Educational, Scientific and Cultural Organization, the International Civil Aviation Organization, the International Maritime Organization, WHO and many others, are actively involved in different aspects of preventing and combating terrorism.

86. However, the increasing demand by Member States for technical assistance in implementing universal instruments and the corresponding need for coordination among the growing number of United Nations entities involved in countering terrorism have demonstrated the need for a comprehensive, coherent and consistent counter-terrorism strategy.

87. At the 2005 World Summit, world leaders welcomed my identification of the five elements of a counter-terrorism strategy that I set out in Madrid in March 2005 and agreed to develop them further to fashion a strategy that makes the international community stronger and terrorists weaker. In addition, they requested that I submit proposals to strengthen the capacity of the United Nations system to assist States in combating terrorism and to enhance the coordination of United Nations activities in this regard.

88. In April 2006 I submitted my report entitled "Uniting against terrorism: recommendations for a global counter-terrorism strategy". My proposals stem from the fundamental conviction that no cause, no matter how just, can excuse terrorism. These proposals are focused around five main elements: dissuading groups from resorting to terrorism or supporting it; denying terrorists the means to carry out an attack; deterring States from supporting terrorist groups; developing State capacity to prevent terrorism; and defending human rights in the context of terrorism and counter-terrorism.

89. Throughout the report I have highlighted operational actions to enable Governments, the United Nations and other international organizations, civil society and the private sector—all using their comparative advantages—to work together to counter terrorism while respecting the rule of law and human rights. Over the years, the international community has come to realize that effective counter-terrorism measures and the protection of human rights are not conflicting goals, but complementary and mutually reinforcing ones. The importance of a culture of peace and the fact that terrorism does not emanate from any particular region, ideology or religion—nor is it directed only at certain groups of countries or people—have also become increasingly clear. In this regard, efforts to promote a dialogue among civilizations serve an increasingly useful purpose.

90. I am confident that the United Nations system has vital contributions to make in many aspects of counter-terrorism—from promoting the rule of law and effective criminal justice systems to ensuring that countries have the means to counter the financing of terrorism to strengthening capacity to prevent terrorists from acquiring nuclear, biological, chemical or radiological materials. Biological terrorism in particular poses a formidable challenge and acutely requires new thinking on the part of the international community. For this reason I proposed in my report the need for a multi-stakeholder dialogue in order to ensure that advances in biotechnology are not used for nefarious purposes. We must also never forget that victims are the true face of terrorism: protecting their rights, ensuring that their voices are heard and providing assistance to facilitate their reintegration are of utmost importance. While the primary responsibility for this lies with individual States, the relevant United Nations entities can help.

91. To achieve these goals, I am taking steps to institutionalize the Counter-Terrorism Implementation Task Force that I created one year ago, which brings together 23 United Nations system entities that address different aspects of terrorism, to ensure overall coordination and coherence in United Nations counter-terrorism efforts. I am also establishing a focal point in the Secretariat to help coordinate a civil society campaign to counter terrorism, and I have suggested the creation of an informal group of United Nations technical assistance providers, donors and recipients to exchange information and coordinate efforts.

92. I am pleased that the General Assembly has used my recommendations to foster discussions on a global counter-terrorism strategy. The adoption of such a strategy will enhance operational measures to counter terrorism and will mark a historic step, bringing together all 192 Member States to demonstrate their resolve—and ability—to defeat this scourge. I trust that agreement on a strategy will be forthcoming without delay. All States—large or small, strong or weak—are vulnerable to terrorism and its consequences. They all stand to benefit from a strategy to counter it.

Disarmament and non-proliferation of weapons of mass destruction

93. The elimination of weapons "adaptable to mass destruction" has been on the United Nations agenda since 1946. Over the past decade, we have witnessed at first rising and then diminishing expectations concerning weapons of mass destruction. In 1995, parties to the Treaty on the Non-Proliferation of Nuclear Weapons agreed to extend the treaty indefinitely. A year later, the Comprehensive Nuclear-Test-Ban Treaty was signed. In 2000 the Review Conference of the Parties to the Non-Proliferation Treaty adopted new political commitments to advance the treaty's aims. In 2005 Member States had two opportunities to strengthen the foundations of the treaty, first at the Review Conference in May and then at the World Summit in September. On both occasions, failure to reach consensus on non-proliferation and disarmament sent a terrible signal of a growing international rift on what is potentially the most dangerous threat to international peace and prosperity. At the same time, the world has made remarkable progress in forging a global taboo against chemical weapons. Since its entry into force in 1997, membership in the Chemical Weapons Convention has grown to 178. The treaty is the first to provide for a robust international system to verify the destruction of an entire class of weapons of mass destruction. Since 1995, membership in the Biological Weapons Convention has grown to 155 with the

addition of 21 parties. However, concerns persist over the lack of means to verify compliance and the need to expand membership even further.

94. Today the United Nations continues to play an active and influential role in efforts to stem the proliferation of lethal weaponry. In several major speeches this year, I have drawn attention to my overriding concern that the international community is presently facing two very divergent courses. One path, that of active engagement by all Member States, can take us to a world in which the proliferation of nuclear weapons is restricted and reversed through trust, dialogue and negotiated agreement. The other more dangerous course could lead to a world of fearful instability where such weapons are the currency of international relations and in which non-State actors acquire the means to carry out terrorism with potentially catastrophic consequences.

95. If ever there was a time to break the deadlock in multilateral negotiations and bring disarmament back into the limelight of the international agenda, I believe that it is now. At such a moment, we should remember what the Treaty on the Non-Proliferation of Nuclear Weapons has achieved. With near-universal membership, it has entrenched a norm against nuclear proliferation. The success of the treaty, the global support it enjoys and its resilience too often pass unacknowledged.

96. I have also drawn attention to the need to resolve two specific issues of concern. The continuing impasse on the Korean peninsula is especially disappointing given the agreement reached in September 2005 in the Six-Party Talks, which included a set of principles for a verifiable denuclearization of the peninsula. The Islamic Republic of Iran, for its part, needs to enable IAEA to assure the world that its nuclear activities are exclusively peaceful in nature. In both cases, there is a need for solutions that are not only peaceful, but that buttress the integrity of the Treaty on the Non-Proliferation of Nuclear Weapons.

97. While there has been some progress towards disarmament, nuclear weapons worldwide still number in the thousands, many of them on hair-trigger alert. Moreover, new missile testing in 2006 underscores the absence of a multilateral instrument regulating missiles. If we want to avoid a cascade of nuclear proliferation, then there must be a more concerted international effort to build a common understanding of the most immediate nuclear threats. The debate between those who insist on disarmament before taking further non-proliferation measures and those who argue the opposite is in my view self-defeating. Both are essential for security.

98. During a visit to Geneva in June 2006, I was heartened by the fact that the Conference on Disarmament appeared much readier than it has been in recent years to move forward on a programme of work. For the first time in a decade, the Conference is working to an agreed schedule, with particular efforts to reflect the security concerns of all States. In Geneva, I acknowledged the importance of proposals from China and the Russian Federation on preventing the weaponization of outer space and called attention to the elements of a ground-breaking instrument for halting the production of fissile materials for weapons purposes proposed by the United States of America. I hope that these steps represent the beginnings of a new period of productivity.

99. IAEA continues its outstanding work of verifying and assuring compliance with the practical aspects of implementing the Treaty on the Non-Proliferation of Nuclear Weapons. The award of the Nobel Peace Prize to the Director General, Mohamed ElBaradei,

on behalf of the Agency was further evidence of the indispensable role that he and the Organization currently play.

100. I am also pleased to report that in April 2006 the Security Council renewed its resolution 1540 (2004), requiring all Member States to enact and enforce effective national legal and regulatory measures, inter alia to prevent non-State actors from acquiring weapons of mass destruction.

101. In my April 2006 report "Uniting against terrorism", I emphasized the likely devastating impact of a nuclear, biological, chemical or radiological terrorist attack. In that report I suggested that bioterrorism—the misuse of biological agents and toxins by non-State actors—was one of the most important under-addressed threats relating to peace and security. I therefore proposed a forum that would bring together key biotechnology stakeholders to provide momentum for a global initiative to minimize the dangers of misuse of biotechnology.

102. The proliferation of small arms continues to pose a serious threat to peace and security in many regions of the world. These weapons may be small, but they cause massive destruction. In 2001 Member States made a commitment to urgently address the illicit trade in small arms and light weapons. I am encouraged by the General Assembly's adoption in December 2005 of an international tracing instrument to identify and trace illicit small arms. However, I am disappointed that the 2006 United Nations conference to review progress made in the implementation of the Programme of Action on Small Arms ended without agreement on further measures. Still, it did succeed in drawing the issue to the attention of the international community, which clearly remains committed to the Programme of Action as the main framework for measures to curtail the illegal trade in those weapons.

103. The various challenges we presently face have never been greater, more varied or, in many respects, more dangerous. They will demand a shared level of commitment, innovative thinking and practical action on the part of all Member States if we are to prove ourselves equal to the challenge. My vision for the United Nations of the twenty-first century is one in which we are increasingly determined to move forward on three fronts—security, development and human rights—simultaneously. These issues are all inextricably linked precisely because they depend upon and reinforce one another. We cannot afford to fail.

Chapter IV

Human rights, rule of law and humanitarian affairs

Rule of law

104. The United Nations was established in the aftermath of a terrible war to ensure that relations among nations would be grounded in international law, including human rights and the dignity of the human person. "Rule of law" is the core concept at the heart of the Organization's work and mission. Those principles apply at the international level as well as within States. Indeed, the Millennium Declaration reaffirmed the commitment of all nations to the rule of law as the all-important framework for advancing human security and prosperity.

105. At the international level, the most striking development over the past decade has occurred in the area of international criminal justice. The International Tribunals for the former Yugoslavia and Rwanda established by the Security Council in 1993 and 1994 respectively marked the first generation of tribunals since the International Military Tribunal established in Nuremberg. They demonstrated the collective will not to allow grave violations of international law to go unpunished. It will be important to continue to ensure that the two tribunals work effectively and efficiently to complete their work. I encourage Member States to cooperate fully with them and to surrender indictees to them upon request.

106. One of the greatest and possibly most lasting achievements of the tribunals was to make the vigorous prosecution of such crimes an accepted practice. Indeed, those ground-breaking efforts contributed to the establishment of the Special Court for Sierra Leone and the Extraordinary Chambers in the courts of Cambodia. In the development of the new tribunals, the Organization applied important lessons learned from the experiences of the first two. Both of the second-generation tribunals, unlike their predecessors, provide for the participation of national judges and prosecutors and the application of national as well as international law.

107. As 2005 came to a close, the Security Council, in its resolution 1644 (2005), requested me to begin a process aimed at the establishment of a tribunal of an international character for Lebanon as a result of the bombing on 14 February 2005 that killed former Lebanese Prime Minister Rafik Hariri and other persons. As we move towards the establishment of this tribunal, the Secretariat will ensure that it applies the highest standards of international justice as it carries out its work. In addition, in Burundi, pursuant to Security Council resolution 1606 (2005), the Secretariat is undertaking an approach that combines judicial and non-judicial accountability mechanisms through discussions with the Burundian authorities regarding the legal framework for both a truth and reconciliation commission and a tribunal. In these efforts, the Secretariat will seek to build on the lessons learned from the previous tribunals.

108. The establishment of the International Criminal Court in 2002 was the realization of a long effort to end impunity and undertake through the rule of law that those who commit the crime of genocide, crimes against humanity and war crimes will no longer be beyond the reach of justice. This important step demonstrated the international community's commitment to a permanent and universal mechanism to ensure that as regards those most serious of crimes, impunity will not be tolerated. One hundred Member States have become parties to the Rome Statute of the International Criminal Court. Importantly, the Statute provides for action by national legal authorities before the exercise of international jurisdiction. Since 2004, the Court has opened investigations into situations in the Democratic Republic of the Congo, Uganda and Darfur, the latter being referred to the Court by the Security Council. One suspect alleged to have committed war crimes, a Congolese national, was arrested and transferred to the Court in March 2006. In October 2005, the Court's pre-trial chamber unsealed arrest warrants for five senior leaders of the Lord's Resistance Army for crimes against humanity and war crimes committed in Uganda since July 2002. Extending the participation of Member States in the International Criminal Court will be a further challenge in the area of international justice.

109. Justice, especially transitional justice in conflict and post-conflict societies, is a fundamental building block of peace. In the face of pressures to the contrary, the international community should ensure that justice and peace are considered to be complementary requirements. Indeed, we must never choose between justice and peace, even if it is not possible to pursue both goals in parallel. This is particularly important because it remains our firm position that there should be no amnesty for international crimes.

110. As I pointed out in my report of 23 August 2004 to the Security Council on the rule of law and transitional justice in conflict and post-conflict societies, the rule of law, in this context, refers to a principle of governance in which all persons, institutions and entities, public and private, including the State itself, are accountable to laws that are consistent with international human rights norms and standards. Many parts of the United Nations system work to varying extents on expanding the rule of law, including transitional justice. We have tried, at least in the area of peacebuilding, to ensure coherence and effectiveness in our efforts. As a result, I am encouraged by the recent establishment of the Peacebuilding Commission, which will assist States to ensure that in troubled areas of the world the rule of law is upheld.

111. The rule of law should also apply in the work of the organs of the United Nations. I am pleased that the Security Council has recently renewed its commitment to ensure that fair and clear procedures exist for placing individuals and entities on sanctions lists, for removing them and for granting humanitarian exceptions.

112. In 2004 I spoke to the General Assembly about the need to restore and extend the rule of law throughout the world. I characterized it as a framework in which rather than might making right, right would make might. I warned that the rule of law was at risk around the world, with laws being disregarded in too many quarters. The United Nations as a collective, and each of its Member States individually, must commit to ensuring that at all levels and in all situations we adhere to and promote those legal principles that constitute our Organization's foundation.

Human rights

113. Over the past decade, we have seen a significant and welcome elevation of the importance of human rights in the work of the Organization. The Millennium Declaration and the 2005 World Summit Outcome reaffirmed the basic premise that human rights formed a central pillar and were the shared responsibility of the United Nations system as a whole.

114. Mainstreaming all human rights, including the right to development, has been central to the series of United Nations reform efforts I have initiated since 1997. It has been an important focus of the work of OHCHR in strengthening the linkages between the normative and operational work of the United Nations system. Progress has been made in this regard across the system in many areas. Building on this progress, I argued in my 2002 and 2005 reports on United Nations reform that more focused attention was needed to support Member States in their efforts to build stronger national systems for the promotion and protection of human rights. The 2005 World Summit gave unprecedented political backing to strengthening the capacity of the High Commissioner and her office to integrate the promotion and protection of human rights into national policies.

115. At the World Summit, Member States accepted my suggestion that, in order to establish human rights at its proper level within the system, they should create a Human Rights Council, directly elected by the General Assembly, to work alongside the Security Council and the Economic and Social Council. In March 2006 the General Assembly adopted a resolution establishing the Council to replace the Commission on Human Rights. One of the features of the Council is that it will review, on a periodic basis, the fulfilment of the human rights obligations of all countries through a universal periodic review mechanism. On 9 May 2006, the 47 members of the Council were elected, and they committed to fully cooperating with the Council and to upholding the highest standards in the promotion and protection of human rights. Together with many other dignitaries, I addressed the opening of the first session on 19 June 2006. Among the important actions taken, the Council adopted the International Convention for the Protection of All Persons from Enforced Disappearances and the United Nations Declaration on the Rights of Indigenous Peoples. It also decided to establish two intersessional open-ended intergovernmental working groups: one to develop the modalities of the universal periodic review mechanism and the other to formulate concrete recommendations on the issue of reviewing and, where necessary, improving and rationalizing all mandates, mechanisms, functions and responsibilities in order to maintain a system of special procedures, expert advice and a complaint procedure.

116. The 2005 World Summit Outcome represented a clear and unambiguous acceptance by all Governments of the collective international responsibility to protect populations from genocide, war crimes, ethnic cleansing and crimes against humanity. For the first time ever, Member States expressed a willingness to take timely and decisive collective action for that purpose, through the Security Council, when peaceful means prove inadequate and national authorities are manifestly failing to do it. The decision represents a renewal of the United Nations promise of "never again", but we must match our rhetoric with a real willingness to take action.

117. Following my report "In larger freedom", the High Commissioner for Human Rights released her plan of action (May 2005), presenting an overall vision for the future direction of OHCHR. In early 2006, she launched her first biennial strategic management plan, which articulates how OHCHR aims to implement the vision in the plan of action and provides a comprehensive overview of the areas of work on which OHCHR will focus and the resources that will be required. In the autumn of 2005, the General Assembly supported the implementation of the new plan by resolving to double the regular budget of the Office over five years. In the biennium 2006-2007, this means an additional 91 posts and a further $20 million in available funding.

118. The plan of action calls for attention to be paid to a range of implementation gaps on the ground and points to the need for concerted action by OHCHR and the United Nations system to work with countries to close those gaps for the effective protection and realization of human rights. The "action 2 programme" I established as a follow-up to my 2002 report "Strengthening of the United Nations: an agenda for further change", is led by OHCHR with participation by the United Nations Development Group and Executive Committee on Humanitarian Affairs agencies. As country-level implementation of action 2 intensifies, increased attention will be needed to direct the wider efforts of the United Nations system at the country level to ensure that they effectively contribute to greater

development of national capacity for more effective and sustainable protection of human rights.

119. The treaty bodies made progress in harmonizing their working methods and considering means to assist States parties to fulfil their substantive commitments and meet their reporting obligations. Guidelines for a common core document now exist and are available for States parties to use. In March 2006, the High Commissioner prepared a concept paper that elaborated on the proposal in the plan of action for a unified standing treaty body. It provides a basis on which options for reform could be explored.

120. Special procedures mechanisms fulfilled an important role in the protection of human rights. In the period from September 2005 to June 2006 they undertook fact-finding missions to over 40 countries. During the same period they sent over 900 communications to 125 countries in all regions of the world, covering almost 2,500 individuals. They also undertook a number of ground-breaking studies in thematic areas related to their mandates.

121. In line with my reform programme and the High Commissioner's plan of action, OHCHR is enhancing its country engagement efforts and increasing its field operations. In 2005, OHCHR opened three new offices, in Nepal, Guatemala and Uganda.

122. The OHCHR office in Nepal has a broad mandate to protect and promote human rights, including by conducting monitoring activities throughout the country. During the demonstrations and protests in April 2006, OHCHR monitoring teams throughout the country documented events, helped deter violence and visited over a thousand people who were detained. With regional offices around the country and monitoring on the street, OHCHR was uniquely placed to contribute to the protection of human rights on the ground.

123. Against the background of violent incidents that took place in Timor-Leste in April and May 2006, the Government of Timor-Leste requested the United Nations to establish an independent commission to review the incidents. I then asked the High Commissioner to establish and support an independent special commission of inquiry for Timor-Leste. The commissioners began their work in Timor-Leste in July 2006 and will report to me by October 2006.

124. In my 2005 report "In larger freedom", I argued that together with development and security, human rights formed the third pillar of the Organization's work. The cause of human rights has entered a new era—an era of implementation. The reforms adopted in the past year, as well as those still under way, reflect this evolution and will better equip the United Nations to fulfil the promise of the Charter.

Democracy and good governance

125. The last decade has witnessed substantial progress for democratic governance. Today more Governments have been chosen by competitive elections than at any time in history. This symbolizes important gains in human rights, freedom and choice. Inclusive public participation and competitive multi-party elections are essential for empowering the poor and for building lasting peace settlements, although they are not sufficient by themselves.

126. The past year witnessed several landmark elections in countries emerging from conflict. The United Nations played a key role in providing assistance with elections in Afghanistan, Burundi, Côte d'Ivoire, the Democratic Republic of the Congo, Haiti, Iraq, Liberia and Palestine—registering voters, administering polling places, facilitating the establishment of electoral laws and strengthening independent electoral commissions. One important outcome of the first legislative elections for the 249-seat Wolesi Jirga ("House of the People") in Afghanistan in September 2005 was the election of 68 women. The United Nations mounted its most ambitious programme ever when aiding elections in the Democratic Republic of the Congo, costing an estimated $432 million. The Democratic Republic of the Congo had not held a multi-party election since 1965 and the country was emerging from an extended period of crisis. The complicated political and electoral situation in Côte d'Ivoire led to a new form of United Nations electoral support: the appointment of a High Representative for Elections to facilitate solutions to electoral disagreements.

127. The United Nations has also assisted dozens of countries that have requested advice or support with more routine electoral administration processes, such as training of professional electoral officials, assisting with electoral dispute resolution, advising on electoral system design, supporting voter education programmes, training journalists in campaign coverage and assessing the costs of registration and balloting.

128. Despite these positive developments, many important challenges remain. Organizing inclusive and competitive elections is only one step—though a necessary one—in building democracy. Elections raise expectations that governing institutions and processes will be responsive to the needs and concerns of all citizens, including the poor and marginalized. To fulfil these hopes, work at the United Nations has gradually shifted during the past decade from a traditional emphasis on public administration towards challenging new issues in democratic governance.

129. To strengthen the efforts of Governments, civil society and non-governmental actors and regional and international organizations that are striving to build and consolidate the pillars of democracy, the World Summit decided in September 2005 to establish the United Nations Democracy Fund. The Fund has attracted $49 million in pledged or contributed funds. The Fund will finance projects designed to empower civil society, strengthen the rule of law, increase popular participation and ensure that people are able to exercise their democratic rights.

130. The United Nations works today with countries to ensure that parliaments are effective and representative, human rights are respected, judges are fair and impartial, the media are independent and free and decision-making is responsive to local concerns. Democratic participation and Government capacity-building need to go hand-in-hand. If people vote but experience no real improvement in their daily lives, then they may become disillusioned. If Governments are strengthened but are not accountable to the people, then this process may benefit the few and not the many. This long-term twin challenge lies at the heart of the work of the United Nations on strengthening democratic governance.

131. To achieve these ends, the United Nations provides a wide range of services, policy advice and technical assistance designed to strengthen justice systems and human rights, parliamentary representation, local governance and decentralization, public administration

reform and anti-corruption efforts, gender equality, e-governance and access to information, civil society and public opinion. In these programmes, the United Nations collaborates closely with many partners and donor organizations, as well as with parliamentary networks, civil society organizations and other entities.

132. Parliaments can play a critical role by linking citizens and the State, as well as by reducing conflict. The United Nations has worked to strengthen these institutions in more than 50 countries, especially in West African and Arab States. Decentralizing governance is also important for delivering services and achieving the Millennium Development Goals. Improving communities and reducing poverty requires public sector management to be efficient and responsive and for corruption to be eradicated.

133. The International Conference of New or Restored Democracies, working with the United Nations, is a forum especially suited to supporting democracy among approximately 120 countries from the developing and developed world. The sixth conference will take place in Doha in October 2006, the first time it will have been held in the Arab world. Together with the Conference, the Community of Democracies also works with the United Nations to widen acceptance of democratic governance within the international community.

134. The last decade has seen important advances in building effective democratic institutions in many countries, including in some of the poorest nations in the world. The United Nations has contributed substantially towards those developments. Yet in many places the quality of democratic governance continues to need further strengthening and in some, democratic progress has stalled and even moved backwards. Unless international commitment and support is maintained well after polling day, elections may generate empty promises and democratic governance and human development may fail to be sustained.

Humanitarian affairs

135. Humanitarian assistance serves as a tangible demonstration of the United Nations commitment to save lives and alleviate suffering by providing urgently needed help to communities devastated by violent conflict or natural disaster. Emergency relief aid serves as the first rung on the ladder of development, helping vulnerable populations survive catastrophes as they move towards ever-greater self-reliance. In the past 10 years, the humanitarian community has provided assistance and protection to tens of millions of civilians, who tragically continue to be the primary victims of conflict and civil strife. Multiple crises now occur simultaneously across the globe, with humanitarian access and insecurity a growing challenge, especially in fragile or failing States. In 1996 the United Nations issued 13 consolidated appeals totalling $1.8 billion to assist 17 million people in crises around the world. Ten years later, consolidated appeals sought $4.7 billion to fund 18 humanitarian programmes serving 31 million people in 26 countries.

136. As part of my reform programme in 1998, the Department of Humanitarian Affairs was reorganized into the Office for the Coordination of Humanitarian Affairs in an effort to strengthen the coherence and overall effectiveness of humanitarian action. The mandate was expanded to include the coordination of humanitarian response, policy development and humanitarian advocacy. In the past decade, the United Nations has intensified inter-agency coordination, improved field-level coordination and bolstered resource mobilization efforts.

137. As I noted in my report "In larger freedom", no country, weak or strong, can remain isolated from or immune to threats of man or nature that transcend borders. Now more than ever we need a revitalized, effective and accountable United Nations that is capable of meeting the humanitarian challenges ahead. To that end, in 2005 the United Nations launched a comprehensive reform of the global humanitarian system that is already demonstrating life-saving results for some of the world's most desperate and destitute communities.

Humanitarian achievements

138. In 2005 the United Nations embarked on a series of reforms aimed at strengthening the global humanitarian system to ensure a more predictable, coordinated, efficient and effective response. In March 2006 I launched the Central Emergency Response Fund, one of the first reform proposals announced at the 2005 World Summit, marking a critical improvement of the capacity for humanitarian response by the United Nations. To date, more than 40 donors have pledged $264 million to the new Fund, which upgrades the former Central Emergency Revolving Fund with a grant facility of up to $450 million added to the $50 million loan component already in place.

139. Using the Fund, United Nations agencies can now jump start relief operations in the earliest days of a crisis when most lives are on the line and timely resources are most needed. The Fund also redresses some of the current inequities in humanitarian funding by dedicating one third of its resources to core, life-saving activities in chronically neglected crises. Launched five months ago, the Fund has provided more than $100 million to 10 organizations for more than 150 projects in 20 countries, the majority of them in Africa. Most importantly, the Fund has helped save lives and alleviate the suffering of millions.

140. The second element of reform addresses the need for improved accountability and predictability of response. With humanitarian resources stretched; multiple, simultaneous crises on several continents; and ever-more aid actors in the field, response coordination is not a luxury but a necessity. The newly launched "cluster leadership" provides more systematic predictability by clearly identifying roles and responsibilities within United Nations agencies in nine key areas of response, from relief to early recovery, to help fill gaps in assistance needs.

141. The third element of humanitarian reform underscores the need for strengthened United Nations country-level representation, as endorsed by the Economic and Social Council and reaffirmed in the 2005 World Summit Outcome.

Humanitarian response: results

142. In 2005, the world saw the number of natural disasters increase in frequency and severity. Bracketed by the Indian Ocean tsunami in late 2004 and the South Asian earthquake in October, United Nations humanitarian agencies were stretched to their limits in providing emergency assistance to all those in need.

143. To meet global relief and protection requirements, in 2006 the United Nations issued a consolidated humanitarian appeal for $4.7 billion to fund 18 programmes serving 31 million people in 26 countries. By mid-year, the appeal was 35 per cent funded. The 2005 consolidated appeal sought nearly $6 billion to assist 30 million people in 29 countries, and 67 per cent was funded by year's end.

144. Last year, United Nations humanitarian agencies provided food aid to 97 million people in 82 countries, including 6.5 million in the Sudan; vaccinated over 30 million children in emergency situations against measles; supported hundreds of health facilities; provided access to shelter, suitable land, safe drinking water and sanitation to hundreds of thousands of people; created hundreds of emergency education facilities; provided protection and assistance to some 20 million refugees and displaced persons; and supported child protection activities in some 150 countries.

Natural disasters

145. While recovery from the tsunami tragedy and efforts to "build back better" proceeded apace, humanitarian actors struggled to cope with an 18 per cent increase in the number of large-scale natural disasters in 2005; 157 million people were affected and 92,000 killed in those disasters. As always, poor communities were at greatest risk—and least able to withstand—nature's destructive potential.

146. Floods, droughts and windstorms accounted for more than 96 per cent of those affected by natural disasters in 2005. Twenty-seven tropical storms, thirteen of which became hurricanes, devastated populations in twelve countries, killing more than 1,000 people and displacing hundreds of thousands.

147. Earthquakes, volcanoes and tsunamis were the deadliest natural hazards last year. The worst of these tragedies occurred in October 2005 when a massive earthquake in South Asia killed more than 73,000 people, injured 69,400 and left 3.3 million homeless. Despite unprecedented logistical challenges and harsh Himalayan weather, relief efforts assisted upward of 3 million people with winterized shelter, medical care, food, water and sanitation.

148. In the Horn of Africa, recurring cycles of drought have exacerbated food insecurity and affected 15 million people. In April 2006, I launched a regional appeal for the Horn of Africa addressing both immediate needs for more than 8 million people as well as underlying causes of vulnerability. Of the $855 million requested, less than 40 per cent of this emergency appeal has been met.

Refugees and displaced persons

149. As 2005 drew to a close, the world saw the number of refugees decline for the fifth straight year, while the number of new refugees was the lowest in nearly 30 years. Globally, there are now 12.7 million refugees registered by the United Nations (of whom 4.3 million are Palestine refugees in the Occupied Palestinian Territory, Jordan, Lebanon and the Syrian Arab Republic). In Afghanistan, Burundi and Liberia, hundreds of thousands of people who had been forced from their homes have been able to return to their countries.

150. Sadly, however, there has been a significant rise in the number of internally displaced persons. Worldwide some 23 million people remain displaced as a result of violence and armed conflict. Millions more have been displaced by natural disasters.

Complex emergencies

151. Conflicts in the Democratic Republic of the Congo, the Sudan and northern Uganda, among others, continue to claim hundreds of thousands of lives, deprive people of land and property, destroy livelihoods, and foment instability. Regional spillover of localized

conflicts in Chad and northern Uganda pose challenges to humanitarian operations, as do the issues of access and security.

152. In Darfur, currently the world's largest relief operation, some 13,000 aid workers are struggling to assist 3 million destitute people—half of Darfur's population—despite daily acts of hideous violence and harassment. In large pockets of Western and Northern Darfur, limited access threatens to sever the humanitarian lifeline for hundreds of thousands of civilians. Overall funding is insufficient to the region's massive humanitarian needs.

153. Humanitarian needs are also acute in the Democratic Republic of the Congo, where 3.9 million people have perished from hunger and disease during the country's civil war. Some 1,200 people continue to die each day—a silent tsunami death toll every six months. Despite these grim statistics, only 51 per cent of the country's $212 million humanitarian appeal was funded in 2005.

154. As we see all too plainly in Darfur, aid cannot be a substitute for political solutions or remain an excuse for political inaction. We must address both symptoms and causes of crises if we are to staunch the world's haemorrhage of human suffering.

The road ahead: humanitarian challenges

155. Significant progress has been made in strengthening our global humanitarian system. However, we need to focus more attention on protecting civilians and establishing safe access to asylum. Thousands of women are still raped and violated as a matter of course, and defenceless civilians continue to be killed. We need earlier conflict mediation efforts, increased access for humanitarian workers and, most importantly, well-trained and-financed peacekeepers with strong mandates to protect civilians.

156. Funding inequities remain as persistent as they are pervasive; some neglected crises receive barely 20 per cent of funds required. We also need to improve the speed of humanitarian funding so that monies arrive when they can do the most good. Currently, United Nations emergency "flash appeals" receive on average only 16 per cent of funds during the critical first month of a crisis.

157. Humanitarian crises exact a terrible toll on children, who are at grave risk of violence, exploitation, abuse and recruitment into fighting forces. Each year hundreds of thousands of children die from malnutrition, hunger and preventable disease.

158. In the last decade, the number of people affected by disasters was three times higher than in the 1970s. As our climate changes we need to strengthen our disaster risk reduction and preparedness measures, drawing on inter-agency early warning and contingency planning efforts.

159. The need for a reformed, strengthened global humanitarian system has never been more apparent or necessary. We need to work together, harnessing the world's generosity, strength and attention, to tackle the most pressing humanitarian challenges of our day. The Millennium Development Goals represent a shared vision of how to tackle some of these challenges. Our generation has no more worthy goal and no more important aspiration. Let us seize this opportunity. Lives depend on it.

Chapter V

Strengthening the United Nations

The intergovernmental machinery

160. As I have said on several occasions, as the world changes, the United Nations must continue the process of renewal and adaptation. The effort to make the United Nations a more effective instrument of its members' collective will is one that is of vital importance for people around the world who look to the Organization for help in defeating poverty, preserving peace, easing humanitarian emergencies and protecting human rights. At the Millennium Summit in 2000, Member States clearly recognized that all the principal organs of the United Nations were in need of reform. At the 2005 World Summit they reaffirmed their commitment to a more efficient and effective United Nations, including with a call for a strengthened intergovernmental machinery.

Security Council

161. I have always maintained that no reform of the United Nations will be complete without the reform of the Security Council. The Council should be more representative of today's geopolitical realities and more efficient and transparent in its working methods. The Millennium Declaration called for an intensification of Member States' efforts "to achieve a comprehensive reform of the Security Council in all its aspects". At the 2005 World Summit, world leaders stated that Security Council reform was "an essential element of our overall effort to reform the United Nations". Enhancing the Council's legitimacy through such reform will enable it to better fulfil its primary responsibility for the maintenance of peace and security in the world.

162. The High-level Panel on Threats, Challenges and Change, which I commissioned to recommend practical measures for ensuring effective collective responses to global security challenges, proposed two models for an equitable enlargement of the Security Council. In my report "In larger freedom", I urged the membership to consider the options and reiterated the need for reform of the Council's working methods. Member States responded actively, by taking initiatives and engaging in debate on both the expansion of the Council and on possible ways to improve the Council's methods of work.

163. There is broad support within the membership on the need for reform of the Security Council. It is important to find common ground for action on this fundamental piece of overall United Nations reform. Indeed, decisions on such reform, taken sooner rather than later, will ensure that the United Nations machinery to promote the establishment and maintenance of peace and security will remain relevant and credible to meet today's and tomorrow's challenges.

General Assembly

164. The Millennium Declaration and the 2005 World Summit Outcome reaffirmed the General Assembly's central position as the chief deliberative, policymaking and representative organ of the United Nations. In recent years much has been achieved on improvement of the Assembly's working methods. For example, presidents of the Assembly are now elected several months in advance of the opening of the session, as are the Main Committee chairs and bureaux, thereby dovetailing the transitions between sessions and ensuring the

maximum passage and retention of institutional memory. Progress also continues to be made on shortening the agenda, on institutionalizing interactive discussions and question periods with senior Secretariat officials on specific programmes, mandates and activities and on working to ensure maximum coordination and minimum duplication in the subjects and areas covered by different bodies.

165. However, much remains to be done to increase the Assembly's effectiveness and its contribution to the Organization's activities. I am encouraged to see that the Ad Hoc Working Group on the Revitalization of the General Assembly has devoted a number of general debates and thematic meetings to these issues during the current session.

166. While everyone agrees on the need for General Assembly revitalization, there remain contending views on the ways in which this goal might best be achieved. Some Member States focus on the rationalization of the Assembly's working methods, while others advocate a more substantive reinforcement of its role and authority, I continue to believe that many of the elements of these approaches and others could contribute to the greater effectiveness and efficiency that so many Member States wish to see the General Assembly regain.

Economic and Social Council

167. In my report "In larger freedom", I called for a revived role for the Economic and Social Council in shaping, implementing and coordinating the development agenda. During the course of its work, the Council has initiated various relevant initiatives to promote coherence and harmonization, however more could be done to enhance its functions of coordination, policy review and policy dialogue in the economic and social areas mandated by the Charter.

168. At the 2005 World Summit, world leaders recognized the need for a more effective and efficient Economic and Social Council. In response to my proposals to revamp the unique functions of the Council, they agreed to strengthen it by reconceiving its function of serving as a platform for high-level dialogue on global economic and social affairs but also assigning some new functions. In particular, Member States decided to establish a high-level development cooperation forum, to be held every two years, for the purpose of reviewing trends in development cooperation, promoting greater coherence in the various development interventions and better linking the normative and operational work of the Organization. Member States further agreed to hold every year an assessment of progress in the achievement of the internationally agreed development goals, including the Millennium Development Goals, at the ministerial level. I am confident that these functions will contribute to our efforts to strengthen the role of the United Nations in the area of development. In order to allow the Council to respond effectively and efficiently, world leaders also agreed to review and adapt its methods of work.

169. In the follow-up to the World Summit, the President of the General Assembly launched a negotiating process to define the details of the decisions made by world leaders. A draft resolution was tabled by the co-chairs and informal consultations have been held. Member States will resume consultations at the end of August, and I am confident that a final agreement can be reached expeditiously. The strengthening of the Economic and Social Council has long been needed. It is my hope that a strengthened Council will be able to assert its

leadership in driving a global development agenda and providing direction to the efforts of the intergovernmental bodies of the Organization working in this field.

The Secretariat

170. Reforming the United Nations has been a priority of mine since I assumed office in 1997. In the past 10 years I have proposed and implemented numerous ideas and changes to bring the United Nations up to best international practices. This has included changes to work programmes, structures and systems, at headquarters locations and in the field. Much of my reform agenda has been implemented, however, not all the reforms were accepted by Member States. Understanding that the Organization needs to continue to improve, in March 2006 I released a final reform package in my report "Investing in the United Nations: for a stronger Organization worldwide". Much of the agenda contained in the report will be for my successor to implement over the coming years. It is my hope that the Organization will continue to move towards enhanced efficiency and effectiveness.

171. The 1997 reform package included a number of changes to the Secretariat structure, most notably the creation of the Department of Economic and Social Affairs from three existing departments and the consolidation of two programmes into the Office for Drug Control and Crime Prevention (now the United Nations Office on Drugs and Crime). The Centre for Human Rights was also merged into the Office of the United Nations High Commissioner for Human Rights. Three important new structures were introduced to improve United Nations management: the post of Deputy Secretary-General was created, a cabinet in the form of the Senior Management Group was established and four sectoral committees were formed to bring coherence to the work of the United Nations on peace and security, humanitarian affairs, development and economic and social affairs. In 2002 I proposed a second major reform package, which contained proposals for a major overhaul of the Department of Public Information and the Department of General Assembly Affairs and Conference Services (now the Department for General Assembly and Conference Management). In 2005, two senior management committees were created to improve executive decision-making and a Management Performance Board was established to improve senior managerial accountability.

172. Efforts to improve the overall efficiency of the Organization also moved on several other fronts. Approximately 1,000 staff posts were permanently eliminated in the 1998-1999 budget. In the 2004-2005 budget cycle, nearly 1,000 reports and activities were consolidated or discontinued and resources were redeployed to higher-priority areas of work. Asked to do more with less, the Organization has had in fact only very limited real growth in its regular budget. Much has been invested in information technologies since the late 1990s. One visible benefit is that all United Nations official reports and publications can now be retrieved for free through the Official Document System, which is available over the Internet. The United Nations website provides extensive materials in multiple languages, making up-to-date information and images available through multimedia sources. Open debates of the Security Council are now webcast along with other important meetings.

173. More broadly, following the findings of an internal staff survey and in response to reported shortcomings in the management of the oil-for-food programme, I introduced at the beginning of 2005 a series of measures to strengthen accountability and improve ethical conduct. In particular, an Ethics Office was established in December 2005, which is now

administering new policies of protection for reporting of misconduct and financial disclosure. The Ombudsman, whose office was established in 2002, has been facilitating the informal resolution of disputes between United Nations staff and management. At the request of the General Assembly, I have also commissioned a multidisciplinary panel to analyse and review all aspects of the existing internal justice system. The panel will report to the Assembly at its sixty-first session.

174. Reforms on procurement were initiated in 1999, and the United Nations has undergone significant transformation since then. To ensure more effectiveness, annual procurement plans now are posted on the United Nations website, which, in addition to providing advance information, allows vendors not registered with the Procurement Division to register and participate. Furthermore, all purchasing requirements are now posted on the website, progress on a transaction can be traced and details of the awards are posted in accordance with international standards. These and other procurement reform efforts were validated by an independent review conducted by the United States National Institute of Government Purchasing in mid-2005. Following a revelation of criminal misconduct concerning a United Nations procurement official, later that year I ordered a comprehensive review of internal and financial controls. The General Assembly approved emergency funding in July 2006 to increase the professional capacity in this area. Further reforms are to be discussed by Member States at the sixty-first session of the Assembly.

175. The budgeting system has been transformed from one focusing on a detailed description of inputs and resources to one that identifies intended outcomes and measurable indicators of achievement. The long-range planning cycle has been reduced from four years to two and a duplicative intergovernmental review eliminated. In addition, the Financial Regulations and Rules of the United Nations have been updated and consolidated to delegate more authority but make managers more accountable. In the reform package set out in "Investing in the United Nations", I propose more comprehensive strengthening of the financial management and budgetary processes.

176. My latest reform proposals recognize the need for an integrated and mobile global workforce that draws on and develops the experience and talent existing both at Headquarters and in the field. A host of improvements to the United Nations system of managing its people has been introduced in recent years. First, a new web-based recruitment system for hiring, reassigning and promoting staff to ensure greater transparency in advertising vacancies was put in place in 2002. Managers are now empowered to select their own staff, subject to appropriate checks and balances. Second, incentives to encourage staff mobility between duty stations and functions were introduced. Training and learning programmes for all staff are now more widely available. Third, a new performance appraisal system was introduced. Finally, a number of "staff-friendly" benefits were introduced to bring the United Nations in line with major corporations offering similar incentives, including the introduction of flexible working hours, telecommuting possibilities and paternity leave entitlements. However, more can and should be done, and I have appealed to Member States for a significant infusion of resources for this purpose.

177. Facing a sharp escalation in threats against United Nations personnel, the staff security procedures were reviewed, first in 2000 and again in 2003, following the tragic loss of 22 United Nations staff in Baghdad. In late 2004 I recommended a major overhaul of the United Nations security system. This included a request for a sizeable increase in resources

allocated for protection of staff and proposals to strengthen and clarify the chain of command. A new Department of Safety and Security was subsequently created, consolidating functions previously performed by separate offices. It now provides timely, professional advice on security-related matters, including through more thorough threat and risk assessment. The new department is responsible for the security of some 100,000 United Nations staff and 300,000 dependants in 150 duty stations throughout the United Nations system, many of which are in crisis and post-conflict risk situations.

The mandates of the Organization

178. In 1954, Dag Hammarskjöld conducted the first review of mandates, at the request of the membership. Since then there has been no other attempt to review the mandates adopted by Member States to guide the work of the Organization. I therefore proposed in my report "In larger freedom" that Member States undertake a review of all mandates older than five years to see whether activities concerned were still genuinely needed or whether the resources assigned to them could be reallocated in response to new and emerging challenges. I stressed the need for "a capable and effective" Secretariat that could change in response to changing needs of the Organization. I underlined that Member States had a central role to play in ensuring that the Organization's mandates stayed current.

179. In September 2005 at the World Summit, world leaders responded by requesting the General Assembly and other relevant organs to review all mandates older than five years originating from resolutions of the General Assembly and other organs in order "to strengthen and update the programme of work of the United Nations". They further requested me to facilitate this process with analysis and recommendations. In response to that request, I provided an analytical framework for review of the Organization's mandates in my report "Mandating and delivering: analysis and recommendations to facilitate the review of mandates". That report addressed key challenges in the mandate generation cycle, including the lack of evaluative information on the effectiveness of mandates, burdensome reporting requirements, overlap between and within organs and the gap between mandates and resources. The report also made recommendations in relation to each of the Organization's programme priorities. It was supplemented by an online inventory of mandates, designed to facilitate Member States' review.

180. The General Assembly began reviewing its mandates through a series of informal consultations, which also saw the participation of senior programme managers. Member States responded to the recommendations in my report and provided additional proposals of their own aimed at strengthening the programme of work of the Organization. The Assembly also authorized an ad hoc working group to review in the first stage of the exercise mandates older than five years that have not been renewed. Work is ongoing, and the Secretariat will continue to assist and facilitate the exercise throughout the process.

181. Concurrently with the consultations in the General Assembly, the Economic and Social Council and the Security Council have begun the process of reviewing their own mandates. The review of the Economic and Social Council has been following a process similar to that in the Assembly. The Security Council has focused on an initial set of mandates for its first phase. As I have mentioned on several occasions, the review of mandates is a historic opportunity to renew and strengthen the work of the Organization. Member States should seize this opportunity to ensure that our Organization can respond effectively to today's needs.

Cooperating with regional organizations

182. Over the past decade there has been a significant increase in the range of partnerships between the United Nations and regional organizations in such areas as peacekeeping and peacemaking, strengthening good governance and the rule of law, promoting respect for human rights and responding to humanitarian emergencies. I have stressed the importance of a new vision of global security that draws upon the resources and legitimacy of effective regional and global institutions that are both flexible and responsive to the complex challenges of today's world.

183. To support those efforts, I have engaged the heads of regional organizations in regular exchanges of views on issues of common concern. The high-level meetings with the heads of regional organizations and other intergovernmental organizations have now been made an annual event so that we can focus on practical cooperation on key issues and follow up more effectively. At the sixth high-level meeting, which I convened in July 2005, we established a standing committee to provide overall guidance to the process of creating a more structured relationship between the United Nations and regional organizations so a genuine agreement based on comparative advantages can be realized.

184. At the World Summit last September, world leaders supported a stronger relationship between the United Nations and regional and subregional organizations, as envisaged in Chapter VIII of the Charter, and resolved to expand cooperation with such organizations through practical means, such as formalized agreements between their respective secretariats. The implementation process will be reported to the seventh high-level meeting, which I will convene in September 2006. Also, a report capturing the past, present and future of our evolving joint work is being submitted to the Security Council for its meeting on 20 September under the presidency of Greece. This is an important opportunity to consolidate institutional relationships and look to the future.

185. Our joint working groups have also decided to enlist the support of the United Nations University's comparative regional integration studies programme to study the organizational, operational and resource capacities of partner organizations in the maintenance of peace and security. Meanwhile, I have moved to ensure that the Secretariat itself is adequately resourced to service the strengthening partnership.

System-wide coherence

186. The fragmentation of the United Nations system and the consequent inability of United Nations support to generate maximum impact at the country level has been an issue of concern to Member States for many years.

187. In response to this concern, I have introduced several important initiatives, which together have made a significant difference in the way the United Nations works, especially at the country level. Four Executive Committees were established in 1997—on development, humanitarian affairs, peace and security, and economic and social affairs—to provide a forum where United Nations departments and programmes could discuss specific issues on a regular basis and plan more coherent approaches to each issue. As they began to be effective, most of the specialized agencies asked to join, resulting in greatly increased communication and understanding among the various entities working on those issues.

188. At the same time, as I noted earlier, I established a cabinet structure, the Senior Management Group, wherein the heads of the key departments of the Secretariat could interact and, by inviting the chairs of the four Executive Committees, provided a link to the wider United Nations system. The Policy and Management Committees are enhancing decision-making at the most senior level.

189. These Headquarters coordination and decision-making mechanisms have complemented the pre-existing United Nations System Chief Executives Board for Coordination, which I chair twice a year, bringing together the heads of all United Nations entities to further cooperation on a range of substantive and management issues.

190. While addressing the need for better coordination at Headquarters, I have also focused most of my efforts on country-level coordination. The resident coordinator system has been improved, including through an expanded United Nations Development Group and a toolkit that includes operational tools and procedures agreed upon across the development agencies, thus providing for much more coherent action at the country level. Furthermore, the humanitarian coordinators can count on strong technical support and guidance, an emergency fund at his or her disposal and agreed leadership roles to play to ensure a fast and effective humanitarian response. Progress has also been made in ensuring synergy and coherence between the activities of peacekeeping operations and country teams, both during and after the mission period, through the establishment of a post under the Special Representative of the Secretary-General charged with bridging the two United Nations presences in the field and leading joint planning at the country level.

191. At the 2005 World Summit, leaders called for stronger system-wide coherence across the United Nations system and in particular across development-related organizations, agencies, funds and programmes of the United Nations system. To this end, the Summit Outcome specifically invited me "to launch work to further strengthen the management and coordination of United Nations operational activities", while continuing ongoing efforts to strengthen the governance, management and coordination of the Organization.

192. In February 2006, I created a High-level Panel on United Nations System-wide Coherence. The Panel brings together 15 eminent persons, whose extraordinary experience and authority are a measure of the importance that I attach to the Panel's work and are a reflection of the wish of all Member States to create a more coherent and effective Organization.

193. The objective of the Panel is to propose recommendations that will lead to a revitalized United Nations system that is better equipped to help achieve the internationally agreed development goals, including the Millennium Development Goals. In particular, the Panel's aim is to help create a United Nations system that provides more effective support for plans and priorities defined at the country level to address development, humanitarian, environmental and other critical challenges, including gender issues, human rights and sustainable development. The Panel is expected to deliver its recommendations to me by September 2006 to allow for a formal presentation to the General Assembly at its sixty-first session and possible implementation in 2007.

194. In order to ensure the engagement and commitment of all key stakeholders, the Panel has undertaken a broad consultative process including country, regional and thematic consultations, as well as meetings with Member States and United Nations organizations and

hearings with civil society organizations. Moreover, the work of the Panel is enriched by research, analysis and insights from inside and outside the Organization, and takes into account other complementary United Nations reform efforts.

Chapter VI

Global constituencies

Strengthening ties to civil society

195. Since the early 1990s, and particularly during my term as Secretary-General, the relationship of the United Nations with civil society has greatly deepened and expanded. This has been the case even though the United Nations is and will remain an intergovernmental organization, where decisions are taken by its Member States. This process of increasing engagement with civil society and other non-State actors has strengthened both the institution and the intergovernmental debate and has been part of the ongoing process of modernization and institutional change that the Organization has undergone in the past decade. As I wrote in "In larger freedom: towards development, security and human rights for all", the goals of the United Nations can be achieved only if civil society and Governments are fully engaged.

196. Civil society has been a key partner of the United Nations since its inception, whether at the country level delivering humanitarian assistance or at the global level participating in debates in the Economic and Social Council. But in the past two decades or so, there has been an enormous transformation in the nature and importance of the role of civil society, at the national level and in the international arena, including at the United Nations. The growth of civil society at the international level has paralleled the globalization process. Globalization, and the technologies that partly propelled it, has led to a broadening of horizons, the multiplication of global issues, a widening of interests and increased opportunities for participatory democracy.

197. Where once representative democracy was at the core of democratic forms of governance, today participatory democracy is increasingly important. Representative democracy is under stress in many countries, as demonstrated by low turnouts for elections and disillusioned citizens. The ability of civil society organizations to represent the interests of citizens, to interact directly with Governments and to participate directly in policy debates at the national and international levels contributes to the legitimacy of democratic ideals.

198. Where once large intergovernmental meetings and conferences were mainly the realm of Governments, today it would be unthinkable to stage such events without the policy perspectives, unique advocacy and mobilization of civil society. The engagement of civil society has clearly enhanced the legitimacy, accountability and transparency of intergovernmental decision-making. A recent example is the global mobilization of civil society around debt, trade and aid issues and the Millennium Development Goals by the Global Call to Action against Poverty in 2005.

199. Where once agendas were set by Governments, today civil society has brought new issues to the table and has been instrumental in, for instance, the establishment of the International Criminal Court and the adoption of the Convention on the Prohibition of the Use, Stockpiling, Production and Transfer of Anti-personnel Mines and on Their Destruction.

200. Where once governance was limited to Governments, today various non-State actors, including civil society, are part of various governance structures. Recent examples are the Programme Coordinating Board of UNAIDS and the Internet Governance Forum, which will have its first meeting from 30 October to 2 November 2006 in Athens.

201. Where once monitoring and enforcement were largely the role of Governments, today civil society has an important role in making sure that commitments are implemented, for example in timber certification, the fight against child labour, corporate social responsibility and human rights.

202. Where once checks and balances in democratic societies were largely the domain of national parliaments, today civil society plays its part.

203. Given the increasing importance of civil society, the United Nations has found several ways to engage with it. Many United Nations entities, including funds, programmes and specialized agencies, consult with civil society on a regular basis through various mechanisms, such as forums, hearings, consultations, advisory committees and the like. This is, of course, critical given the fact that civil society has become an essential partner for different kinds of humanitarian, development and peacebuilding operations of the United Nations. The number of operational activities of the United Nations where civil society has played an increasingly important role has expanded, and now also includes such areas as electoral support and conflict prevention.

204. In July, the High-level Panel on United Nations System-wide Coherence in the areas of development, humanitarian assistance and the environment that I appointed in February and the High-level Group for the Alliance of Civilizations held hearings with civil society in Geneva.

205. Throughout my term as Secretary-General, I have consistently encouraged a deeper relationship between the United Nations and civil society. I have myself actively engaged with civil society on many occasions—including at the major United Nations conferences and summits, during my travels and at Headquarters. One recent example is my visit to Darfur in March 2005, where I met with representatives of non-governmental organizations, who work in Darfur under very dangerous circumstances, to underline the crucial role of non-governmental organizations in the international community's efforts there.

206. The exponential growth in both numbers and influence prompted me to establish a Panel of Eminent Persons on United Nations-Civil Society Relations, chaired by the former president of Brazil, Fernando Henrique Cardoso, to assess and draw lessons from interactions between the United Nations and civil society and recommend ways to improve them. The Panel submitted its report in June 2004 and I presented my response to it in September of the same year.

207. The Panel argued very convincingly that the United Nations must become an even more outward-looking organization. That means using its unique convening power to reach out to diverse constituencies, especially where such actors command great expertise or resources relevant to a particular issue. Facilitating the participation of different stakeholders in relevant debates of global significance can only enhance the quality and depth of policy analysis and implementable outcomes, including in the form of partnerships. In that

way, the United Nations will expand its global reach and influence, ensuring that its decisions will be better understood and supported by a broad and diverse public.

208. Unfortunately, the Member States have not taken any formal action on the Cardoso Panel's recommendations and my response to them. Nevertheless, a number of actions have been taken. For example, the United Nations Development Group is strengthening the capacity of United Nations resident coordinators to engage with civil society at the country level. A number of country offices have appointed a civil society focal point in the United Nations country team to strengthen engagement of the United Nations system with civil society, pursuant to my recommendations. Work is also under way to establish a trust fund to support the country teams in their work with civil society.

209. In addition, at the intergovernmental level, the General Assembly has held four informal interactive hearings with representatives of non-governmental organizations, civil society organizations and the private sector. The first one was held during the lead-up to the 2005 World Summit, and three additional ones were held in 2006 as inputs to the high-level meetings to review the Declaration of Commitment on HIV/AIDS, on the midterm comprehensive global review of the implementation of the Programme of Action for the Least Developed Countries for the Decade 2001-2010 and on international migration and development. These hearings have been an important innovation for interaction between civil society and the Assembly.

210. The President of the sixtieth session of the General Assembly appointed in May 2006 the Permanent Representatives of Indonesia and Norway as his personal advisers on the relationship between Member States and civil society, including non-governmental organizations. The advisers conducted a series of consultations with non-governmental organizations, Member States and United Nations staff. The President sent their report to all Member States on 7 July 2006.

211. The report acknowledges that there are clear differences in expectations between Member States and civil society on the relationship between them. Yet, it suggests that there is sufficient ground to explore better interaction and more meaningful inclusiveness, for example, through meetings between the President of the General Assembly and civil society at the beginning of his or her term or at other key moments, and between the chairs of the Main Committees of the Assembly and civil society.

212. Civil society is now such a powerful force in the world that the United Nations will have to continue exploring new mechanisms and formats for engaging with it. As we move forward on this together, it is important that we collectively address some Member States' lingering concerns about, and sometimes mistrust of, civil society. Our civil society partners must ensure that they comply scrupulously with the responsibilities and obligations that accompany their rights at the United Nations and continue to improve their overall transparency and accountability to others. I am aware that many civil society organizations, associations, networks and bodies are rising to these challenges in a variety of creative ways, and this bodes well for the future.

213. One other area that requires attention is the frequent underrepresentation of civil society from developing countries at United Nations meetings. Establishing a better regional balance would require changes both within civil society and by Member States. International

civil society organizations, for example, could make more of an effort to include organizations from developing countries in their networks, choose citizens from developing countries as their representatives at the United Nations and base their headquarters more often in developing countries. Member States could help by generously supporting travel and related expenses of participants from developing countries in United Nations events. At the same time, we should use modern communication technologies to explore how civil society organizations from different regions can make contributions to global policy debates and discussions without having to be physically present.

Engaging the business community

214. For the first time in over 60 years of United Nations history, we are making business and other social actors vital partners in pursuit of our goals. This new relationship has had two fundamental implications for the work of the Organization.

215. First, it has furthered progress in achieving the Millennium Development Goals, ultimately improving the lives of the poor by facilitating support in critical areas, ranging from simple advocacy of United Nations goals to the provision of humanitarian assistance and the formation of partnerships in information technology, microcredit and health. Hundreds of projects in support of the Millennium Development Goals have resulted from this engagement, including those initiated under the Growing Sustainable Business for Poverty Reduction initiative, which aims to stimulate profitable foreign investment in the world's poorest countries to foster sustainable economic opportunities on the ground.

216. Second, new forms of engagement with businesses also advance United Nations reform by providing the Organization with exposure to improved management practices and better ways of leveraging its moral authority and convening power, thus becoming a powerful catalyst for institutional innovation across the system.

217. At the centre of these efforts is the Global Compact, which I launched in July 2000. It is the world's largest corporate citizenship initiative today, with over 3,000 participants from more than 100 countries, over half from the developing world. Through learning, dialogue and partnership projects, the Global Compact has brought about far-reaching changes. The alignment of corporate activities with broader United Nations goals has also brought about significant improvements in governance and capacity-building for suppliers and small enterprises. By advocating universal principles as an integral part of business strategies and operations, global markets have become more robust and inclusive.

218. Through the Global Compact Office, many United Nations organizations have found a new entry point for engaging businesses and improving their own ability to work with the private sector. The Organization itself, through the United Nations Joint Staff Pension Fund and the procurement process, is internalizing the Global Compact's principles, thus gaining credibility and ethical strength. Overall, these changes are bringing greater efficiency and innovative ways of leveraging institutional advantages throughout the Organization.

219. The other main entry point for the business community is the United Nations Fund for International Partnerships (UNFIP), which has provided vital support to a wide array of United Nations programmes, generated nearly $1 billion in new resources for United Nations causes, and has evolved into the United Nations Office for Partnerships. While our engagement of businesses is firmly rooted in the understanding that the goals of business

and the United Nations are very distinct, there are increasingly overlapping objectives. Nonetheless, this cooperation requires clear rules of engagement in order to protect the United Nations while forging partnerships that advance practical implementation. Today, the Organization has in place integrity measures and policy frameworks to define the rules of engagement. The Global Compact Office has spearheaded many of these developments, and I am confident that it will continue to lead this promising reform from within the Organization. It is my hope that Member States will continue to support these efforts and that engagement with the business community and other societal actors will continue to evolve as an integral part of organizational change to make the United Nations fit for the twenty-first century.

Chapter VII

Conclusion

220. The themes of good governance and accountability run through this report like golden threads. The Member States need to be well governed and accountable to their citizens if they are to nourish economic and social development, if they are to achieve lasting security and if they are to uphold human rights under the rule of law. The Organization, for its part, can become stronger and more effective only if it is better managed and more clearly accountable to the Member States.

221. Let me conclude by observing that these principles are also valid for the global order. The United Nations is not a world government, and therefore ensuring good governance and accountability at the global level is not simply a matter of improving the efficiency of the United Nations. It goes far beyond that. It is a matter of ensuring that governors are responsible to the governed and that world Powers remember their responsibility to those whose lives may be transformed, for better or worse, by their decisions.

222. That implies a need for greater accountability and transparency, and fairer representation, in all global institutions. More than that, it implies that all global institutions need to be transformed into an effective expression of an emerging global community, underpinned by shared values, held together by bonds of human solidarity and inspired by mutual respect and understanding among people of different cultures and traditions. If we continue to move in this direction, the human species will not simply survive on this small planet but will in fact thrive. The fact that the destinies of all the world's inhabitants are so closely interlinked will no longer be simply a reality, but indeed a source of hope.

Statistical annex

Millennium Development Goals, targets and indicators, 2006

			Africa			Asia					CIS							
	World	Developing regions	Northern	Sub-Saharan	Latin America & Caribbean	Eastern	Southern	South-Eastern	Western	Oceania	All	Europe	Asia	Developed regions	T.C. of south-eastern Europe	LDC	LLDC	SIDS
GOAL 1 I Eradicate extreme poverty and hunger																		
TARGET 1 - Halve, between 1990 and 2015, the proportion of people whose income is less than one dollar a day																		
Indicator 1. Population below $1 purchasing power parity per day (percentage)[a]																		
1990		27.9	2.2[b]	44.6	11.3	33.0	39.4	19.6	2.2[b]	19.6	0.4				0.4			
2002		19.4	2.4[b]	44.0	8.9	14.1	31.2	7.3	2.4[b]	7.3	2.5				1.8			
TARGET 2 - Halve, between 1990 and 2015, the proportion of people who suffer from hunger																		
Indicator 4. Prevalence of underweight children under five years of age (percentage)																		
1990		33	10	32	11	19	53	39	11									
2004		28	9	30	7	8	47	28	8									
Indicator 5. Proportion of population below minimum level of dietary energy consumption (percentage)																		
1990-1992		20	4	33	13	16	25	18	6	15	7[c]	4[c]	16[c]	<2.5[c]		22	38	23
2001-2003		17	4	31	10	12	21	12	9	12	7	3	20	<2.5		19	36	19
GOAL 2 I Achieve universal primary education																		
TARGET 3 - Ensure that, by 2015, children everywhere, boys and girls alike, will be able to complete a full course of primary schooling																		
Indicator 6. Net enrolment ratio in primary education (primary-level enrolees per 100 children of enrolment age)[d]																		
1991	81.2	78.8	80.6	53.0	85.8	97.7	72.2	92.3	79.7	74.4	88.8	91.0	84.1	96.4		52.1	51.7	66.5
2004	87.0	85.8	94.0	64.2	94.9	94.1	89.3	92.9	82.9	79.6	90.9	90.1	91.8	95.6		69.0	69.4	82.8
Indicator 8. Literacy rate of 15-24 year-olds (percentage)																		
1990	84.3	80.9	66.3	67.4	92.7	95.5	61.5	94.3	80.1	73.5	99.2	99.8	97.7	99.7		56.3	65.0	84.8
2000-2004[e]	87.2	85.0	84.3	73.1	96.0	98.9	72.2	96.2	91.3	72.8	99.7	99.7	99.8	99.3		63.7	70.3	85.3
GOAL 3 I Promote gender equality and empower women																		
TARGET 4 - Eliminate gender disparity in primary and secondary education, preferably by 2005, and to all levels of education no later than 2015																		
Indicator 9a. Ratio of girls' gross enrolment ratios to boys' gross enrolment ratios in primary education																		
1991	0.89	0.87	0.82	0.84	0.97	0.93	0.76	0.96	0.83	0.92	0.99	1.00	0.99	0.99		0.79	0.82	0.96
2004	0.94	0.94	0.94	0.89	0.97	1.00	0.91	0.97	0.89	0.91	0.99	0.99	0.98	0.99		0.88	0.86	0.95
Indicator 9b. Ratio of girls' gross enrolment ratios to boys' gross enrolment ratios in secondary education																		
1999	0.92	0.88	0.93	0.82	1.07	0.95	0.74	0.97	0.79	0.93	1.03	1.05	0.96	1.01		0.77	0.81	1.05
2004	0.94	0.92	0.97	0.79	1.08	1.00	0.83	1.00	0.80	0.93	0.98	0.99	0.96	1.01		0.81	0.81	1.04

	World	Developing regions	Africa: Northern	Africa: Sub-Saharan	Latin America & Caribbean	Asia: Eastern	Asia: Southern	Asia: South-Eastern	Asia: Western	Oceania	CIS: All	CIS: Europe	CIS: Asia	Developed regions	T.C. of south-eastern Europe	LDC	LLDC	SIDS
Indicator 9c. Ratio of girls' gross enrolment ratios to boys' gross enrolment ratios in tertiary education																		
1999	0.97	0.78	0.69	0.69	1.12	0.55	0.63	0.99	0.82	0.67	1.20	1.27	0.89	1.19		0.57	0.73	1.15
2004	1.03	0.87	0.93	0.63	1.17	0.81	0.70	1.04	0.89	0.90	1.28	1.32	1.02	1.27		0.63	0.83	1.25
Indicator 10. Ratio of literate women to men, 15-24 years old																		
1990	0.91	0.88	0.73	0.80	1.00	0.96	0.72	0.97	0.81	0.87	1.00	1.00	1.00	1.00		0.72	0.80	0.97
2000-2004[e]	0.93	0.91	0.87	0.88	1.01	0.99	0.79	0.99	0.92	0.94	1.00	1.00	1.00	1.00		0.80	0.86	1.00
Indicator 11. Share of women in wage employment in the non-agricultural sector																		
1990	35.9		20.1	32.4	38.3	37.9	13.1	37.3	16.6	28.4	48.5			43.4				
2004	39.1		20.3	35.0	43.2	41.2	17.3	38.3	20.1	37.3	51.1			46.4				
Indicator 12. Proportion of seats held by women in national parliament (single or lower house only, percentage)																		
1990	12.4	10.4	2.6	7.2	11.9	20.2	5.7	10.4	4.6	1.2				15.4		7.3	14.0	14.4
2006[f]	16.6	15.3	7.0	16.2	20.4	19.5	12.8	15.8	7.6	3.2	10.8	11.0	10.6	21.1		15.6	16.3	17.8
GOAL 4 I Reduce child mortality																		
TARGET 5 - Reduce by two thirds, between 1990 and 2015, the under-5 mortality rate																		
Indicator 13. Under-5 mortality rate (deaths per 1,000 live births)																		
1990	95	106	88	185	54	48	126	78	69	87	50	28	83	12	29			
2004	79	87	37	168	31	31	90	43	58	80	44	20	78	7	17			
Indicator 15. Proportion of 1-year old children immunized against measles (percentage of children aged 12-23 months who received at least one dose of measles vaccine)																		
1990	73	71	85	56	76	98	58	71	80	70	85			84	93			
2004	76	73	94	65	92	85	62	81	88	48	98			92	96			
GOAL 5 I Improve maternal health																		
TARGET 6 - Reduce by three quarters, between 1990 and 2015, the maternal mortality ratio																		
Indicator 17. Proportion of births attended by skilled health personnel																		
1990	47	43	40	42	72	51	30	38	60		99	99	97		96			
2004	58	56	71	46	88	79	36	68	66		99	99	99		96			
GOAL 6 I Combat HIV/AIDS, malaria and other diseases																		
TARGET 7 - Have halted by 2015 and begun to reverse the spread of HIV/AIDS																		
Indicator 18a. HIV prevalence (estimated adult, 15-49, percentage)																		
1990		0.37	<0.1	2.7	0.3	<0.1	0.1	0.1	<0.1	<0.1		<0.1	<0.1	0.2				
2005		1.1	0.1	5.8	0.6	0.1	0.7	0.5	<0.1	1.5		1.1	0.2	0.5				

	World	Developing regions	Africa: Northern	Africa: Sub-Saharan	Latin America & Caribbean	Asia: Eastern	Asia: Southern	Asia: South-Eastern	Asia: Western	Oceania	CIS: All	CIS: Europe	CIS: Asia	Developed regions	T.C. of south-eastern Europe	LDC	LLDC	SIDS
Indicator 18b. HIV prevalence (percentage of adults living with HIV who are women)																		
1990			<20	54	33	<20	<20	<20	<20	<20		<20	<20	<20				
2005			22	59	34	27	28	33	<20	59		31	27	28				
Indicator 19a. Condom use at last high-risk sex (percentage of population 15-24 that used a condom during last high-risk sex,[g] 1998-2004; number of countries covered by the surveys provided in parentheses)																		
Women				27 (26)			51 (1)											
Men				43 (25)			59 (1)						54 (3)					
Indicator 19b. Percentage of population aged 15-24 with comprehensive correct knowledge[h] of HIV/AIDS (percentage, 1998-2004; number of countries covered by the surveys provided in parentheses)																		
Women				24 (34)			21 (·)	18 (3)					6 (5)					
Men				31 (18)			17 (·)											
Indicator 20. Ratio of school attendance of orphans to school attendance of non-orphans aged 10-14[i] (number of countries covered by the surveys provided in parentheses)																		
1998-2004				0.85 (39)														

	World	Developing regions	Africa: Northern	Africa: Sub-Saharan	Latin America & Caribbean	Asia: Eastern	Asia: Southern	Asia: South-Eastern	Asia: Western	Oceania	CIS: All	CIS: Europe	CIS: Asia	Developed regions	T.C. of south-eastern Europe	LDC	LLDC	SIDS
TARGET 8 - Have halted by 2015 and begun to reverse the incidence of malaria and other major diseases																		
Indicator 22a. Population in malaria-risk areas using effective malaria prevention measures (percentage of children under 5 who sleep under insecticide-treated bed nets)																		
1999-2004				4														
Indicator 22b. Population in malaria-risk areas using effective malaria treatment measures (percentage of children under 5 with fever who are appropriately treated)																		
1999-2004				37				3										
Indicator 23a. Incidence and death rates associated with tuberculosis (number of cases per 100,000 population, excluding HIV infected)																		
1990	122	149	59	148	98	116	173	272	68	203	51	48	60	28				
2004	128	151	49	281	59	102	166	217	50	166	103	104	117	16				
Indicator 23b. Prevalence and death rates associated with tuberculosis (number of deaths per 100,000 population excluding HIV infected)																		
1990	28	35	5	38	14	25	45	67	11	53	9	9	9	3				
2004	23	27	4	56	8	16	31	36	8	29	17	17	17	2				
Indicator 24a. Proportion of tuberculosis cases detected under DOTS (percentage)																		
2000	28	29	82	36	43	30	15	39	27	13	11	3	36	22				
2004	53	54	83	47	58	63	51	65	26	26	22	13	46	44				
Indicator 24b. Proportion of tuberculosis cases cured under DOTS (percentage)																		
2000	82	82	88	72	81	94	83	86	81	76	76	68	78	77				
2003	82	83	86	72	83	93	85	86	83	67	72	62	76	76				

	World	Developing regions	Africa: Northern	Africa: Sub-Saharan	Latin America & Caribbean	Asia: Eastern	Asia: Southern	Asia: South-Eastern	Asia: Western	Oceania	CIS: All	CIS: Europe	CIS: Asia	Developed regions	T.C. of south-eastern Europe	LDC	LLDC	SIDS
GOAL 7 I Ensure environmental sustainability																		
TARGET 9 – Integrate the principles of sustainable development into country policies and programmes and reverse the loss of environmental resources																		
Indicator 25. Proportion of land area covered by forest (percentage)																		
1990	31.3		1.3	29.2	49.9	16.5	14.0	56.3	3.3	68.3	38.6	46.6	3.9	30.4				
2005	30.3		1.5	26.5	46.0	19.8	14.2	46.8	3.5	63.4	38.6	46.7	3.9	30.8				

	World	Developing regions	Africa: Northern	Africa: Sub-Saharan	Latin America & Caribbean	Asia: Eastern	Asia: Southern	Asia: South-Eastern	Asia: Western	Oceania	CIS: All	CIS: Europe	CIS: Asia	Developed regions	T.C. of south-eastern Europe	LDC	LLDC	SIDS
Indicator 26. Area protected to maintain biological diversity (percentage of total territorial area, including terrestrial and marine)																		
1990	8.7	9.0	3.5	10.5	12.8	10.4	4.8	6.1	4.0[j]	1.2	6.5	7.3	3.0	12.4		8.5	9.0	2.0
2005	11.6	12.2	4.7	11.2	17.7	14.4	6.0	9.5	18.7[j]	1.6	7.7	8.6	3.9	16.3		9.5	11.6	3.4
Indicator 27. Energy use per $1,000 GDP (consumption of kg oil equivalent)[k]																		
1990	235	266	164	360	167	419	245	203	250		658[l]	625[l]	985[l]	216	415	258		
2003	212	218	165	363	162	219	201	211	287		531	519	627	189	261	260		
Indicator 28. Carbon dioxide emissions (per capita, in metric tons)[m]																		
1990	4.0	1.6[n]	1.9[n]	0.8[n]	2.4[n]	2.4[n]	0.8[n]	1.0[n]	4.7[n]	1.4[n]	13.2[n]	12.6[o]	7.2[o]	12.6[p]				
2003	4.0	2.2[n]	2.8[n]	0.7[n]	2.4[n]	3.4[n]	1.2[n]	1.7[n]	5.8[n]	1.4[n]	8.1[n]	9.1[n]	5.1[n]	12.9[p]				
Indicator 28b. Consumption of ozone-depleting substances (CFC in millions of ODP tonnes)																		
1990		113.4	9.1	8.9	32.6	41.8	2.5	16.1	6.1	0.04	105.9	104.5	1.4	514.7	3.5	1.0	1.5	
2004		63.4	4.3	3.9	13.6	22.9	7.1	8.2	4.2	0.02	0.7	0.5	0.2	1.9	0.6	2.7	0.9	
TARGET 10 - Halve, by 2015, the proportion of people without sustainable access to safe drinking water and basic sanitation																		
Indicator 30. Proportion of population with sustainable access to an improved water source, urban and rural (percentage)																		
1990 Total	78	71	89	49	83	71	72	76	85	51	92			100				
Urban	95	93	95	82	93	99	90	93	94	92	97			100				
Rural	64	60	82	36	60	59	66	68	70	39	84			99				
2004 Total	83	80	91	56	91	78	85	82	91	51	92			99				
Urban	95	92	96	80	96	93	94	89	97	80	99			100				
Rural	73	70	86	42	73	67	81	77	79	40	80			95				
Indicator 31. Proportion of population with access to improved sanitation, urban and rural (percentage)																		
1990 Total	49	35	65	32	68	24	20	49	81	54	82			100				
Urban	79	68	84	52	81	64	54	70	97	80	92			100				
Rural	26	17	47	24	36	7	8	40	55	46	63			99				
2004 Total	59	50	77	37	77	45	38	67	84	53	83			99				
Urban	80	73	91	53	86	69	63	81	96	80	92			100				
Rural	39	33	62	28	49	28	27	56	59	43	67			98				
TARGET 11 - By 2020, to have achieved a significant improvement in the lives of at least 100 million slum dwellers																		
Indicator 32a. Access to secure tenure (slum population in millions)																		
1990	721.6	660.9	21.7	101.0	110.8	150.8	198.7	49.0	28.6	0.4		9.2	9.7	41.8		81.9	46.5	5.7
2001	924.0	860.1	21.4	166.2	127.6	193.8	253.1	56.8	40.7	0.5		8.9	9.8	45.2		140.1	47.3	7.3
Indicator 32b. Access to secure tenure (percentage of urban population living in slums)																		
1990	31.6	47.0	37.7	72.3	35.4	41.1	63.7	36.8	34.4	24.5		6.0	30.3	6.0		76.3	48.4	24.0
2001	31.6	43.3	28.2	71.9	31.9	36.4	59.0	28.0	35.3	24.1		6.0	29.4	6.0		78.2	56.5	24.4

	World	Developing regions	Africa: Northern	Africa: Sub-Saharan	Latin America & Caribbean	Asia: Eastern	Asia: Southern	Asia: South-Eastern	Asia: Western	Oceania	CIS: All	CIS: Europe	CIS: Asia	Developed regions	T.C. of south-eastern Europe	LDC	LLDC	SIDS
GOAL 8 I Develop a global partnership for development																		
TARGET 12 - Develop further an open, rule-based, predictable, non-discriminatory trading and financial system																		
TARGET 13 - Address the special needs of the least developed countries																		
TARGET 14 - Address the special needs of landlocked countries and small island developing States																		
TARGET 15 - Deal comprehensively with the debt problems of developing countries through national and international measures in order to make debt sustainable in the long term																		
Indicator 33a. Net ODA to all developing and least developed countries (annual total assistance in billions of United States dollars)																		
1990		52.7														15.2		
2004		106.5[q]														23.5		
Indicator 33b. Net ODA, to all developing and least developed countries (percentage of OECD/DAC donors' gross national income)																		
1990		0.33														0.09		
2004		0.33[q]														0.08		
Indicator 34. Proportion of bilateral, sector allocable ODA of OECD/DAC donors to basic social services - basic education, primary health care, nutrition, safe water and sanitation (percentage)																		
1995-1996	8.1																	
2003-2004	16.0																	
Indicator 35. Proportion of bilateral official development assistance of OECD/DAC donors' that is untied (percentage)																		
1990	67.6																	
2004	91.3																	
Indicator 36. ODA received in landlocked developing countries as a proportion of their gross national incomes (percentage)																		
1990																	6.5	
2004																	7.3	
Indicator 37. ODA received in small island developing states as a proportion of their gross national incomes (percentage)																		
1990																		2.8
2004																		1.1
Indicator 38a. Proportion of total developed country imports (by value, excluding arms) from developing countries and least developed countries, admitted free of duty (percentage)																		
1996		52														67		
2004		75														81		
Indicator 38b. Proportion of total developed country imports (by value, excluding arms and oil) from developing countries and least developed countries, admitted free of duty (percentage)																		
1996		53														77		
2004		75														79		

	World	Developing regions	Africa: Northern	Africa: Sub-Saharan	Latin America & Caribbean	Asia: Eastern	Asia: Southern	Asia: South-Eastern	Asia: Western	Oceania	CIS: All	CIS: Europe	CIS: Asia	Developed regions	T.C. of south-eastern Europe	LDC	LLDC	SIDS
Indicator 39a. Average tariffs imposed by developed countries on agricultural products from developing countries (percentage)																		
1996		9.8														4.3		
2004		8.4														3.4		
Indicator 39b. Average tariffs imposed by developed countries on textiles from developing countries (percentage)																		
1996		8.1														5.7		
2004		5.7														1.5		
Indicator 39c. Average tariffs imposed by developed countries on clothing from developing countries (percentage)																		
1996		14.5														11.4		
2004		10.4														2.5		
Indicator 40. Agricultural support estimate for OECD countries as a percentage of their gross domestic product																		
1990														1.90				
2004[s]														1.16				
Indicator 41. Proportion of ODA provided to help build trade capacity (trade-related technical assistance/capacity-building as a percentage of total sector allocable ODA)																		
2001	4.0																	
2004	3.6																	
Indicator 42a. Total number of countries that have reached their HIPC completion points																		
2000	1			1														
2006	18			14	4													
Indicator 42b. Total number of countries that have reached their HIPC decision points (but not completion point)																		
2000	21			17	4													
2006	11			11														
Indicator 42c. Total number of countries that have yet to be considered for HIPC decision points																		
2000	16																	
2006	9			7				2										
Indicator 42d. Total number of countries eligible for HIPC																		
2000	38																	
2006	38																	
Indicator 43. Debt relief committed under HIPC (to countries that have reached their decision or completion point, in billions of United States dollars, cumulative)																		
2000	34																	
2006[t]	59																	
Indicator 44. Debt service as a percentage of exports of goods and services																		
1990		16.4	39.8	11.5	20.5	4.7	17.7	16.7		14	3.9[u]	3.9[u]	3.5[u]		9.4	16.8		
2004		7	10.9	5.8	14.6	0.9	14.7	9.2		1.2[v]	5.5	5.6	4.4		8.9	8.2		

	World	Developing regions	Africa: Northern	Africa: Sub-Saharan	Latin America & Caribbean	Asia: Eastern	Asia: Southern	Asia: South-Eastern	Asia: Western	Oceania	CIS: All	CIS: Europe	CIS: Asia	Developed regions	T.C. of south-eastern Europe	LDC	LLDC	SIDS
TARGET 16 - In cooperation with developing countries, develop and implement strategies for decent and productive work for youth																		
Indicator 45. Unemployment rate of young people aged 15-24 years																		
1995	12.1		33.9	18.0	14.2	7.2	9.4	9.7	20.8	7.9	19.4			15.8				
2005	13.7		34.5	18.3	15.2	7.8	11.3	17.0	23.6	6.6	18.1			13.8				
TARGET 17 - In cooperation with pharmaceutical companies, provide access to affordable, essential drugs in developing countries																		
TARGET 18 - In cooperation with the private sector, make available the benefits of new technologies, especially information and communications																		
Indicator 47. Telephone lines and cellular subscribers (number of telephone lines and cellular subscribers per 100 population)																		
1990	10.1	2.3	2.9	1.0	6.4	2.4	0.7	1.4	10.0	3.4	12.5			45.4	13.8	0.3	2.3	7.3
2004	46.4	31.7	27.6	8.2	50.0	54.1	8.4	27.4	52.5	10.1	57.1			130.1	73.8	3.2	7.4	37.8
Indicator 48a. Personal computers and Internet users (number of personal computers per 100 population)																		
1990	2.5	0.3	0.1	0.3	0.6	0.3	0.0	0.3	1.2	0.0	0.3			11.1	0.2	0.1	0.0	3.9
2004	13.0	4.9	2.6	1.6	9.0	6.9	1.7	3.5	10.8	6.5	9.6			55.9	8.1	0.8	1.3	13.3
Indicator 48b. Personal computers and Internet users (number of Internet users per 100 population)																		
1990	0.3	0.0	0.0	0.0	0.0	0.0	0.0	0.0	0.0	0.0	0.0			0.3	0.0	0.0	0.0	0.0
2004	13.7	7.0	6.3	1.8	11.9	10.3	3.4	7.4	10.5	4.7	8.9			51.4	16.5	0.7	1.4	12.9

Source: United Nations Inter-Agency and Expert Group on the Millennium Development Goal Indicators and Millennium Development Goal indicators database (http://mdgs.un.org).

Abbreviations: CDIAC, Carbon Dioxide Information Analysis Center (United States of America); CFC, chlorofluorocarbons; CIS, Commonwealth of Independent States; DOTS, directly observed treatment strategy; GDP, gross domestic product; HIPC, heavily indebted poor countries initiative; LDC, least developed countries; LLDC, landlocked developing countries; ODA, official development assistance; ODP, ozone-depletion potential; OECD/DAC, Organization for Economic Cooperation and Development/Development Assistance Committee; SIDS, small island developing States; TC, transitional countries.

(Footnotes on following page)

Given the limited space available, indicators for which no new data are available are not presented here, with the exception of indicator 32, Proportion of households with access to secure tenure, which is the only indicator to monitor the target. Also, indicator 14, Infant mortality rate, is not presented because trends can be assessed by the indicator on child mortality. The complete statistical annex, including all indicators used in monitoring progress towards the Millennium Development Goals, is available at http://mdgs.un.org.

Except where indicated, regional groupings are based on United Nations geographical regions with some modifications to create to the extent possible homogenous groups of countries for analysis and presentation. The regional composition adopted for the 2006 reporting of Millennium Development Goal indicators is available at http://mdgs.un.org under "Data".

The Commonwealth of Independent States (CIS) comprises Belarus, the Republic of Moldova, the Russian Federation and Ukraine in Europe, and Armenia, Azerbaijan, Georgia, Kazakhstan, Kyrgyzstan, Tajikistan, Turkmenistan and Uzbekistan in Asia. "Developed regions" comprises Europe (except CIS countries), Australia, Canada, Japan, New Zealand and the United States of America. Developed regions always include transition countries in Europe unless the latter are presented separately as "transition countries of south-eastern Europe".

Indicator 1

[a] Estimates by the World Bank in May 2006. High-income economies, as defined by the World Bank, are excluded.

[b] Combined estimates for North Africa and Western Asia.

Indicator 5

[c] Data refer to the period 1993-1995.

Indicator 6

[d] The net enrolment ratios in primary education correspond to school years ending in the years displayed.

Indicators 8 and 10

[e] Data refer to the latest literacy estimates and projections released by the United Nations Educational, Scientific and Cultural Organization Institute for Statistics for the period 2000-2004.

Indicator 12

[f] As at 1 January 2006.

Indicator 19a

[g] Percentage of young women and men aged 15-24 reporting the use of a condom during sexual intercourse with a non-regular sexual partner in the past 12 months among those who had such a partner in the past 12 months.

Indicator 19b

[h] Percentage of young women and men aged 15-24 correctly identifying the two major ways of preventing the sexual transmission of HIV (using condoms and limiting sex to one faithful, uninfected partner) who reject two common local misconceptions and who know that a healthy-looking person can transmit the AIDS virus.

Indicator 20

[i] Ratio of the current school attendance rate of children aged 10-14 both of whose biological parents have died to the current school attendance rate of children aged 10-14 both of whose parents are still alive and who currently live with at least one biological parent.

Indicator 26

[j] The figures from 1995 to 2005 are due to the establishment of a new large protected area in Saudi Arabia.

Indicator 27

[k] Data are not directly comparable with earlier series because constant price GDP has been rescaled to year 2000 international (purchasing power parity) dollars.

[l] Figures are for years other than that specified.

Indicator 28

[m] Total CO_2 emissions from fossil fuels (expressed in millions of metric tons of CO_2) includes CO_2 emissions from: solid fuel consumption, liquid fuel consumption, gas fuel consumption, cement production and gas flaring (CDIAC).

[n] Based on data provided by CDIAC.

[o] Based on data provided by CDIAC. The 1990 rows show 1992 data for CIS countries.

[p] Based on the annual national emission inventories of annex I countries (with the exception of Belarus, the Russian Federation and Ukraine, which are included under CIS) that report to the United Nations Framework Convention on Climate Change; non-annex I countries do not have annual reporting obligations. In order to assess trends for annex I countries as a group, the aggregate figures for 2003 include data referring to a previous year for countries where 2003 data were not available. Data refer to 2002 for Poland. Emissions/sinks from land-use change and forestry are excluded.

Indicators 33a and 33b

[q] Data are preliminary and are for 2005.

Indicator 35

[r] Based on only some 40 per cent of total ODA commitments from OECD/DAC member countries, as it excludes technical cooperation and administrative costs, as well as all ODA from Austria, Luxembourg, New Zealand and the United States that do not report the tying status of their official development assistance.

Indicator 40

[s] Preliminary data.

Indicator 43

[t] As at March 2006.

Indicator 44

[u] Data are for 1994.

[v] Data are for 2003.

2. Report of the Executive Director of the United Nations Children's Fund: Annual Report to the Economic and Social Council (E/2007/6-E/ICEF/2007/3)

Summary

The present report, which is prepared annually, covers a range of issues arising from the decisions of the Economic and Social Council and the General Assembly, and provides the perspective of the United Nations Children's Fund (UNICEF) on these topics of system-wide interest. It describes UNICEF actions to contribute to the implementation of the Millennium Development Goals and to respond to the outcome of the 2005 World Summit. It provides information about the direction UNICEF is taking to work in closer partnership with other members of the United Nations system to ensure that development assistance produces sustainable results for children.

This report, together with an addendum containing the comments made by the members of the Executive Board during its first regular session of 2007, will be submitted to the Economic and Social Council for consideration at its substantive session of 2007.

I. Introduction

1. Achieving the Millennium Development Goals will only be possible with special efforts to reach the 49 per cent of the developing world's population who are children. UNICEF took numerous steps in 2006 to ensure that this will happen, by putting more emphasis on partnerships; by increasingly integrating its programmes; and by working more effectively and efficiently, especially through harmonized work with other parts of the United Nations. Such strategic, inclusive approaches are the path to measurable and sustainable results.

Partnerships

2. The scope of the Millennium Development Goals and its related targets is so great that one of the most critical roles of UNICEF is to deepen its alliances with others whose work will affect children, and to engage other collaborators for children both in the field and in policy dialogues.

3. New partnerships were created to "Unite for Children" and ongoing partnerships were deepened and broadened. UNICEF continues to work with, contribute to and provide leadership in major global organizations and coalitions that share a focus on children, including the Global Alliance for Vaccines and Immunization; the Global Fund to Fight Aids, Tuberculosis and Malaria; Roll Back Malaria; Health Metric Network; the Partnership on Maternal, Newborn and Child Health; and the United Nations Girls' Education Initiative. To address the needs of 146 million undernourished children under five years of age, UNICEF and the World Food Programme (WFP) have collaborated with the World Bank, the United Nations Standing Committee on Nutrition and other partners in shaping the Ending Child Hunger and Undernutrition Initiative, which focuses on Millennium Development Goal 1, to halve by 2015 the proportion of people who suffer from hunger and undernutrition. The Executive Director also participated in the Clinton Global Initiative and in the World Economic Forum in Davos, joining with others to place the concerns of children in the centre of the global agenda.

4. In the area of sports, the Executive Director initiated the "Unite for Children, Unite for Peace" campaign with the Fédération Internationale de Football Association (FIFA) at the opening of the World Cup in June 2006. This campaign took advantage of a global spotlight on sports to promote nonviolence, tolerance and peace for children and for all. In addition, at the second regular session of the Executive Board in September, Fútbol Club Barcelona expanded its philanthropic tradition to address the problems of children affected by HIV/AIDS. And in the United States, the National Basketball Association launched a public service campaign in support of "Unite for Children, Unite against AIDS", which was launched in 2005 with participation of the Joint United Nations Programme on HIV/AID and other United Nations agencies.

5. Partnerships with children and young people continue to be an important means for UNICEF and other agencies to include the most direct and most immediate perspectives on programme directions. At the "Junior 8" youth forum held in conjunction with the G8 Summit in July in Saint Petersburg, the Executive Director interacted with youth delegates from the eight member countries, who then presented their recommendations to the G8 leaders. Another major process during the year depended greatly on young people's involvement and perspectives. The United Nation Study on Violence against Children, supported by the Office of the United Nations High Commissioner for Human Rights, Save the Children Foundation, the World Health Organization (WHO) and UNICEF, reached out to children who had experienced violence through nine regional forums. Children contributed their insights and participated in the preparation of recommendations for the study. In addition, children and young people—helped by Save the Children—played a large part in producing a special children's version of the report and an educational booklet designed to provide children and young people over the age of 12 years with information about violence and ideas for actions they can take to prevent and respond to violence. It is clear that this innovative involvement of children throughout, from preparation to published materials, contributed to the success and usefulness of the study.

Greater programme integration

6. Another UNICEF strategy for increasing the effectiveness of its programmes to reach the Millennium Development Goals involves greater integration of programmes so that results are mutually reinforcing. In West Africa, UNICEF is scaling up a community-based programme known as the Accelerated Child Survival and Development (ACSD) programme, which combines high-impact health and nutrition interventions and which has resulted in significant decreases in pilot districts of as much as 20 per cent in child mortality in only two years. UNICEF will use this model for results-driven strategies in other sectors and regions, and is sharing it widely with other partners.

7. Over the course of the year, UNICEF also continued to strengthen its partnerships within, and to harmonize its work processes with, other parts of the United Nations system. Many of these results are detailed in the following sections.

A. Funding for operational activities for development of the United Nations system

8. The seventh pledging event in the context of the multi-year funding framework took place in January 2006. Details were provided in the annual report to the Executive Board, presented at the annual session of 2006 (E/ICEF/2006/11).

9. For the current year, as of 30 September 2006, UNICEF had recorded regular resources income of $452.5 million from government donors and intergovernmental agencies against medium-term financial plan projections of $488 million. Total regular resources income from all sources for 2006 is projected to be $962 million, with the level of government regular resources contributions in line with financial plan estimates. Other resources contributions recorded from Governments were $886 million. Of this, $614 million went to other resources-regular against a financial plan of $581 million, while $272 million went to other resources-emergency against a financial plan of $394 million. Total other resources income from all sources was $1,338 million, against the 2006 plan target of $1,403 million.

10. UNICEF requires a predictable, long-term and increased base of core resources to enhance effectiveness and to better engage partner countries in capacity development, technical advice and a normative agenda in a systematic and responsive manner. UNICEF encourages all Member States to increase their annual voluntary contributions to core resources and, for those in a position to do so, to provide multi-year commitments and payment schedules at the pledging event held at the first regular session of the Executive Board.

B. Capacity-building

11. National capacity development continues to be a key focus of UNICEF cooperation. In a trend that is continuing as part of the 2006-2009 medium-term strategic plan (MTSP), the organization is making a gradual and relative shift from an approach that is based mainly on support to project implementation to one that is more strategic, policy-oriented and focused on support to national programmes and partner institutions, including strengthening their systems and capacities to scale up basic service delivery.

12. One of the major areas in which UNICEF has engaged in capacity-building is through technical and financial support provided to the implementation of national-level household surveys, especially the multiple indicator cluster surveys (MICS). The MICS have become the single most important source of data for monitoring progress towards the Millennium Development Goals, as they provide data on more than half of the indicators for the Goals. MICS currently are being conducted in 54 countries.

13. To meet the increased demand for data at more frequent intervals, MICS will be conducted every three years rather than every five years. This will provide a solid and more up-to-date statistical base for national partners to use to improve their programme planning and policy formulation. The data derived from MICS are a critically important source of information for both national and global tracking of progress toward a range of international goals and targets, including the forthcoming assessment of progress towards the goals established by the General Assembly Special Session On Children, entitled *A World Fit for Children*, in September 2007, as well as the Abuja Targets on malaria, and the General Assembly Special Session on HIV/AIDS. In this way, more frequent surveys will lead to more accurate planning, more effective programming and, therefore, to measurable results for children.

14. In 2006, a new version of *DevInfo* was released with UNICEF support. This new version operates both as a desktop application and on the internet. To support users of this new

version, since May 2006 workshops are under way to reach professionals from United Nations agencies, government statistical offices, academic institutions and non-governmental organizations, representing 120 countries. Eighty countries have now adopted the *DevInfo* technology to support their national socio-economic database.

15. Urban Info, a customized version of *DevInfo* developed by the United Nations Centre for Human Settlements (Habitat), was launched at the World Urban Forum in June 2006. Another *DevInfo* adaptation, Millennium Development Goals Info 2006, was presented at the General Assembly in September 2006. It contains the official Millennium Development Goals data set published by the United Nations Statistics Division in coordination with all other United Nations agencies. Since September 2006, the United Nations System Avian Influenza Coordinator's office has adopted the *DevInfo* database system to monitor the global situation of the H5N1 virus. The system will help with quick and efficient data collection and support both global and national teams to formulate effective preparedness and response plans to the virus.

16. EmergencyInfo, a powerful decision support system based on *DevInfo* database technology, was developed with UNICEF support to bridge information gaps within the first days of an emergency and provide support for rapid data collection, situation assessment, standard monitoring reports and disaster preparedness. By combining the advanced data access and presentation features of *DevInfo* and making it accessible on handheld digital devices, it will help humanitarian agencies to respond faster and more accurately in emergencies.

17. A new enhanced website (www.devinfo.org) offers access to information about *DevInfo* implementation and provides a forum for the global sharing of experiences in the monitoring of the Millennium Development Goals using this technology.

18. UNICEF has also supported thematic south-south cooperation. This has been especially important over the course of the past year in the area of HIV and AIDS. Brazil, for example, has reached out to Bolivia, Cape Verde, Guinea-Bissau, Paraguay, San Tome and Principe and Timor-Leste to expand care and support to children, adolescents and pregnant women affected by HIV/AIDS as well as other sexually transmitted diseases. Among the main outputs for this cooperation have been the sharing of experiences, supplies of antiretroviral drugs and test kits, and capacity-building for health professionals.

C. Transaction costs and efficiency

19. In the area of financial management, reforms made over the past three years have created new efficiencies. The benefits of other work now in progress will be available in the near future. All of these efforts are being done in close collaboration with other funds, programmes and agencies.

20. The integrated enterprise resource planning system implemented in 1999 has continued to bring new efficiencies in the areas of financial management, with benefits at the headquarters and field levels and for donors, development partners and staff. There is a seamless system for financial transactions from New York to the smallest field office, which is updated every 10 hours and handles more than 10 million transactions per year from 234 sites and in 147 currencies. With this system, UNICEF operationally closed its

financial books of accounts for 2005 by the end of January 2006, four months earlier than the previous biennium and the earliest it has ever been done. As a result, accurate financial reports to government partners and donors were generated from early February with a ripple effect of efficiencies. Concomitant with this, field offices now have increased authority in the area of payments to partners and in administering their support budgets.

21. In the area of human resources administration, including payroll, the SAP human resources module has been in place since mid-2005. This system is now being extended to regional offices, including any co-located country offices, enabling more rapid and accurate input of data.

22. In 2006, UNICEF harmonized its cost-recovery policies with those of the United Nations Development Group (UNDG) members, making it much easier for partners, both donors and programme countries, to plan programmes and encourage partnerships. The harmonization of other financial practices among the funds and programmes has accelerated, with benefits for all parts of the system and for partners. The harmonized approach to cash transfers has now been launched and a simplified means of transferring funds to partners is now available to all UNICEF field offices. A roll-out of this harmonized policy by the United Nations country team (UNCT) members is under way.

23. Discussions are under way among the funds and programmes in a number of other areas. Now that basic financial reporting has been harmonized, the United Nations Development Programme (UNDP), the United Nations Population Fund (UNFPA) and UNICEF are looking at revising the presentations of their biennial support budgets in a results-based format. When this is done, all of the UNICEF budget will be results-based, as 85 per cent of the UNICEF budget is already results-based with a results framework in the country programmes linked to the focus areas of the MTSP and national priorities based on the Millennium agenda. In addition, the Comptrollers of the United Nations, UNDP, UNFPA, UNICEF and WFP are discussing the creation of one standard set of Financial Rules and Regulations. This will facilitate the adoption in 2010 of the International Public Sector Accounting Standards (IPSAS), for which work is well under way to ensure shared interpretations and strategies. The adoption of IPSAS will further strengthen a coherent approach in financial management throughout the United Nations.

24. The first United Nations joint office has been established in Cape Verde, and the UNDG Executive Committee agencies currently are undertaking a review to identify its benefits, including any demonstrated efficiencies in administration, management and programme effectiveness, which have been brought about by the common country programme. UNICEF continues, with the other funds and programmes, to work for common premises by regularly reviewing proposed and active shared premises. UNICEF also works closely with a network of United Nations organizations to increase efficiencies in administrative procedures, finding areas for common services. One example is harmonizing travel processes and procedures, where UNICEF has taken steps to simplify its procedures in ways that conform with best practices in other agencies.

D. Coherence, effectiveness and relevance of operational activities for development

25. The report of the Secretary-General's High-level Panel on United Nations System-wide Coherence had just been issued at the time of finalization of the present report. UNICEF was engaged in the discussions held by the Panel, both bilaterally and as part of the consultations organized in various locations. It is clear that the directions expected to be proposed by the Panel are consistent with the work already being carried out as part of the ongoing reforms of the UNDG, Executive Committee on Humanitarian Affairs (ECHA) and the Chief Executives Board for Coordination machinery, and the implementation of the previous triennial comprehensive policy review. UNICEF will continue to work in these areas and, pending decisions by the inter-agency and intergovernmental bodies on the implementation of reforms stemming from the Panel's report, will report to the Executive Board in accordance with the established mechanisms as well as any new ones that may be established.

26. The cost-recovery policy mentioned in paragraph 22 above is facilitating the ability of UNICEF to collaborate with partners, including through participation in joint United Nations programmes. These programmes are now done in the context of United Nations Development Assistance Frameworks (UNDAFs). Thirty-eight UNDAFs were completed in 2006, bringing the total to date to 112. The guidelines for Common Country Assessments (CCAs) and UNDAFs have now been used for four years, and the circulation of experienced senior staff and improved training have helped country teams use these instruments more effectively for their planning. One measure of this is that UNDAFs are increasingly commonly directly related to national development plans, including poverty reduction strategies (PRSs).

27. Originally, the UNDAF was to be based on the needs identified by the CCA, but there has been an increase in nationally-produced analyses, usually associated with a PRS. Therefore, the requirement for a CCA has evolved and in some cases, country teams and national partners have agreed that a separate CCA would be duplicative. This trend needs to be monitored to ensure that the national analysis adequately covers such areas of concern as human rights and child protection. UNCTs are also involved in Joint Assistance Strategies, which integrate the support strategies of all (signatory) donors and agencies, in countries where they have been developed, including Ghana, the United Republic of Tanzania and Zambia.

28. An evaluation of the role and quality of UNDAFs carried out for the UNDG during 2006 concluded that UNDAFs have become more focused over the past years, that the United Nations in the field is now better aligned with national processes and that UNDAFs have strengthened the United Nations' collective identity and team-building. At the same time, the transaction costs of the UNDAF process are still high. The United Nations is not yet fully reflecting new aid modalities in its work and there is scope for the United Nations to better exploit its comparative advantage in programming. The current revision of the CCA/UNDAF guidelines is taking these findings into account.

29. The planning of country programmes involves the preparation and approval of cumulative documentation from the CCA (in most cases), the UNDAF and, based on the UNDAF and for each agency, a country programme document (CPD) for approval by the Executive Board and a country programme action plan (CPAP). In order to streamline this process,

UNDP, UNFPA, UNICEF and WFP prepared a common proposal that was initially presented to the UNICEF Executive Board at the annual session in June. The proposal was that one single document be prepared which would incorporate elements of the CCA, UNDAF, CPD and CPAP. A portion of this would be presented to the Executive Boards for approval, as CPDs are currently. The proposals were not fully adopted by the respective Executive Boards. Efforts to streamline the planning process and increasing the coherence of United Nations programmes will continue in 2007.

30. The Regional Directors of the UNDG Executive Committee agencies and of other agencies and organizations have met with increasing frequency to support the ability of country teams as they cooperate with national partners to deliver development results. The Regional Directors' Team in Southern Africa, which was started to support UNCT responses to the "triple threat" of HIV, food insecurity and governance problems, has continued to mature. The team now covers both Southern and Eastern Africa and has a full Programme Support Group which coordinates responses to UNCT requests for support. The Latin America and Caribbean region also has a very active Regional Directors' Team that is supporting the development of CCAs and UNDAFs, resolving implementation issues and supporting the development of UNCTs. There is now agreement that a regional hub should be established in Panama, to increase the ability of regional staff to support country teams. All Regional Directors' Teams were requested to make a joint assessment of the performance of Resident Coordinators in 2005. For some countries, a "180-degree assessment" tool was introduced on a pilot basis, through which the members of a UNCT provide an opinion of other UNCT members, including the Resident Coordinator. The assessment meetings have been frank, constructive and useful to the UNDP Regional Directors in making a more balanced report on Resident Coordinator performance to the chair of the UNDG.

31. UNICEF fully supports the enhancement of the role of the Resident Coordinator/Humanitarian Coordinator as an objective leader of a UNCT who speaks for the United Nations with one voice. As a result of strong encouragement from the Executive Director, an additional four UNICEF staff have been appointed as Resident Coordinators, bringing to nine the number of UNICEF staff who are currently serving as Resident Coordinators. An additional UNICEF staff member is serving as a deputy Resident Coordinator/Humanitarian Coordinator. This brings to 18 the number of UNICEF staff who have ever served as Resident Coordinator, Deputy Special Representative of the Secretary-General or deputy Resident Coordinators.

E. Evaluation of operational activities

32. As noted in last year's report, evaluations in the United Nations system are being strengthened by inter-agency collaboration. In this regard, a Tsunami Evaluation Coalition of 40 organizations, including the Food and Agricultural Organization of the United Nations, UNDP, UNICEF, the United Nations Office for the Coordination of Humanitarian Affairs and WHO, has prepared a consolidated document which assessed the impact of the Indian Ocean tsunami on local and national capacities, the role of needs assessment, the coordination of international humanitarian assistance, the links between relief, rehabilitation and development, and the funding of the tsunami response. UNICEF was a member of the Coalition's core management group.

33. A Real-Time Evaluation Initiative is now under way to agree on an interagency approach for real-time evaluation of humanitarian actions. UNICEF has prepared a concept paper for the Inter-Agency Standing Committee (IASC). The Horn of Africa (Somalia, Kenya and Ethiopia) formed the first pilot case.

34. In the area of evaluation, UNICEF is taking steps to prepare for the 2007 triennial comprehensive policy review of operational activities for development (TCPR). UNICEF is leading the task group of the United Nations Evaluation Group on country-led evaluation. A first pilot is under way in South Africa. The exercise consists in assessing from a country perspective the contribution of the United Nations and other external support. UNICEF, with UNDP, is co-leading an assessment of the quality of the current UNDAFs. The findings will be included in the TCPR report to be reviewed by the Economic and Social Council at its substantive session of 2007.

35. UNICEF is gathering lessons and good practices from the ACSD programme through systematic weekly updates, regional network meetings, country annual reports and independent evaluations. The knowledge generated through these processes is used to formulate policies and update strategies in real time for ACSD.

UNICEF is also working to develop more general knowledge management strategies for widespread and decentralized application in UNICEF programmes. This will help to develop and document a strong evidence base to improve both implementation and policy advocacy in all programmes.

F. Gender mainstreaming

36. UNICEF continues to seek innovative approaches to reaching Millennium Development Goal 3, promoting gender equality and empowering women and girls, by infusing its programmes with a gender perspective as part of the human rights-based approach to programming. UNICEF is also taking steps to improve gender balance within the organization.

37. All country offices have been asked to undertake a gender self-assessment and review of UNICEF-assisted country programmes during the programme cycle, using the specific gender assessment tools available in the Programme Policy and Procedure Manual. UNICEF currently is conducting an organization-wide evaluation to assess implementation of the policy on gender equality and women's rights adopted in 1994 as well as implementation of General Assembly resolution 59/250 of 22 December 2004 on the TCPR.

38. UNICEF is an active member of the UNDG Task Team on Gender Equality, which aims to strengthen accountability for gender equality among UNCTs. As noted in this report last year, the United Nations Development Fund for Women (UNIFEM) and UNICEF conducted a study on the extent to which gender equality is reflected in the latest generation of CCA/UNDAFs. The review showed that the link between analysis and corresponding action and investment in gender equality remains weak, and noted that UNCTs have demonstrated insufficient capacity to undertake holistic, rights-based programming for gender equality and women's empowerment. The review proposed launching a process through which self-selected UNCTs would generate replicable means of undertaking rights-based, change-oriented programming to increase the capacity of government and civil society to promote gender equality and women's empowerment. This process will be well-documented and best practices would be disseminated widely for adoption by

other countries. This recommendation was endorsed in June 2006 by the Executive Heads of the UNDG Executive Committee and the initiative will be led by UNICEF and UNIFEM.

39. For many years, United Nations agencies have been presenting individual reports to the Committee on the Elimination of Discrimination against Women on the status of implementation of the Convention on the Elimination of all Forms of Discrimination against Women in areas falling within the scope of their activities. The Committee has recently requested United Nations entities to explore means of enhancing the flow of information from the United Nations system to the Committee. As planned, UNICEF, in partnership with UNFPA, UNIFEM and WHO, presented a joint report to the Committee at its thirty-fourth session dealing with reproductive health and violence for four countries: Cambodia, Eritrea, Mali and Thailand. The report for Eritrea was prepared by the UNCT. This practice was subsequently expanded at the Committee's thirty-sixth session, at which another six reports were prepared by UNCTs, and will continue at the thirty-seventh session. The Committee expressed its appreciation for this coordinated and comprehensive presentation of information. These are the first instances of UNCTs preparing a report to a treaty body and this precedent is under consideration as a best practice for adoption by other such bodies.

40. The Legislative Reform Initiative which UNICEF is conducting continues to produce programming tools to promote the implementation of the Convention on the Rights of the Child and the Convention on the Elimination of All Forms of Discrimination against Women through comprehensive, holistic and participatory legislative reforms, and the development of a rights-based legislative framework. UNICEF is also developing a handbook to serve as a reference on harmonizing national legislation with international instruments, particularly these two Conventions, to be used by legislators, parliamentarians, jurists, lawyers, judges, line ministries, government officials, human rights and children's rights advocates and policymakers.

41. UNICEF continues to work at national, provincial and community levels to prevent gender-based violence in conflict situations and to respond to the needs of survivors in emergency situations.

42. UNICEF has participated in the creation and dissemination of field guidelines and tools for implementation of existing policies, and has promoted inter-agency collaboration in addressing sexual and gender-based violence in emergencies. The IASC Guidelines for Gender-based Violence Interventions in Humanitarian Settings are now ready for field testing.

43. UNICEF, as co-chair of the ECHA-Executive Committees on Peace and Security Working Group on Assistance to Victims of Sexual Exploitation and Abuse by United Nations staff and related personnel, has finalized the drafting of the Secretary-General's Strategy on Victim Assistance, which is due for discussion by the General Assembly in 2007.

44. UNICEF is committed to attaining the United Nations system-wide goal of gender parity in staffing at all levels by 2010. The report of a study on gender imbalance in UNICEF, presented to the Global Management Team in January 2006, indicated that steady progress has been made and that UNICEF ranks among the top three United Nations agencies in terms of gender parity (46 per cent). However, gender imbalance at the senior levels has been quite persistent. The study concluded that gender parity can be achieved by 2010 if senior management takes a clear and accountable lead, models the desired management culture and invests in human resources management.

45. The Executive Director moved quickly to address these recommendations. She appointed a Special Adviser for Gender and Diversity to report on follow-up to the recommendations and attainment of the goals laid out in the report. She ensured that the steering committee and its reference group which support the comprehensive organizational review are gender balanced. She has established a policy that one half of all committee members should be women. She requested that the organizational review and the supporting strategic review of human resources management incorporate the findings of the gender report in their work.

46. Further progress has been seen in the implementation of the first-ever Senior Staff Review and Rotation Exercise, which was initiated by the Executive Director. Positive action was taken to increase the gender balance in senior management and there was an increase in the number of female staff at the D-2 level from 19 per cent in 2005 to 30 per cent in September 2006.

47. The global action plan for implementation of the gender parity study is in place. It is derived from a strategy of policy commitment, qualitative and quantitative measurement, institutionalized human resources management procedures and an organizational culture of respect and accommodation. The plan proposes action in six key areas: recruitment; retention; talent development; work culture; accountability; and monitoring and reporting.

48. Managers will be accountable for the action plan. The Special Advisor, Gender and Diversity, supported by a review group, will be the advocate and link for monitoring the implementation of the plan and will report periodically on progress to the Global Management Team.

II. Follow-up to international conferences and panels

49. The commitments set out in the final document of the General Assembly Special Session on Children, entitled *A World Fit for Children*, are being implemented in the context of follow-up to other major international conferences and summits. Notable among them are the World Summit on Sustainable Development and the International Conference on Financing for Development, both held in 2002. The goals of *A World Fit for Children* are also firmly grounded in the resolutions of the 2005 World Summit and the 2006 High-Level Meeting on AIDS.

50. The four major goal areas of *A World Fit for Children* strongly reinforce the United Nations Millennium Declaration and the Millennium Development Goals. The building of a world fit for children would be a major step in fulfilling the commitments of the Millennium Summit of 2000.

51. Some 177 countries are now engaged in follow-up activities to the Special Session on Children which include incorporating the goals of *A World Fit for Children* into their planning processes, either by developing National Plans of Action on children's issues (NPAs) or by integrating the goals into mainstream national plans and/or PRSs. Several countries have used both mechanisms. In some countries, subnational follow-up has been a major focus of activity, including the development of provincial or local plans of action.

52. There is also increased attention to the Convention on the Rights of the Child. The majority of NPAs make reference to the Convention or to the concluding observations of the Committee on the Rights of the Child on the respective state party reports. Other human rights instruments, such as International Labour Organization (ILO) Convention 138 con-

cerning the minimum age for admission to employment and ILO Convention 182 concerning the prohibition and immediate action for the elimination of the worst forms of child labour, and the two optional protocols to the Convention on the Rights of the Child, are also increasingly recognized as part of the framework for NPAs. Almost all the NPAs prepared since the Special Session anticipate the need to review national legislation in relation to the provisions of the Convention. A number also propose strategies to increase the attention given to the views of children.

53. A total of 47 countries had completed NPAs by end of 2005, an increase from 25 in 2003. In addition, 99 countries had incorporated the goals of *A World Fit for Children* into national development plans and/or poverty reduction strategies by end of 2005, an increase from 68 in 2003. These goals are also explicitly targeted in sectoral plans of 90 countries.

54. At its fifty-eighth session, the General Assembly decided to convene a commemorative plenary meeting in 2007, devoted to the follow-up to the outcome and the progress made in implementing the Declaration and the Plan of Action, based on a report to be prepared by the Secretary-General. UNICEF was asked to prepare and disseminate information on the progress made in the implementation of the Plan of Action. UNICEF is now working closely with Governments to support their reviews of progress. Because they are so closely linked, national reporting may take the form of a distinct section of the national report on the Millennium Declaration and Millennium Development Goals. This work is taking place through local UNICEF offices, National Committees for UNICEF and UNCTs.

55. UNICEF actively participated in the fiftieth session of the Commission on the Status of Women in 2006 and played a fundamental role in ensuring the visibility of the situation and rights of the girl child. As the Commission's fifty-first session in early 2007 will focus on the elimination of all forms of discrimination and violence against the girl child, UNICEF is a central partner of the Division of Advancement of Women in the preparations and will support participation from country offices and young people from all regions. UNICEF has worked closely with the Division, the NGO Committee on UNICEF, the Working Group on Girls and the Innocenti Research Centre in organizing the expert group meeting that will feed into the Secretary-General's report on the girl child to the Commission. The report of the expert group meeting is being translated into a youth-friendly version by UNICEF for discussion and sharing with young people.

Conclusion

56. A culture of continual improvement is being established at UNICEF, in harmony with the processes of United Nations reform. UNICEF has reached out to other partners, within and outside the United Nations system, more inclusively and more dynamically over the past year. Steps are being made in knowledge management so that best practices, programme data and evaluation results are shared and used for programme adaptations.

57. This is leading to more efficient and effective programming and advocacy for children, and to the creation of measurable results. This is essential to reaching the Millennium Development Goals and the provisions of the Millennium Declaration. In doing so, UNICEF is fully working in the spirit of cooperation and collaboration laid out by the TCPR by continuing to improve its effectiveness, efficiency, coherence and impact.

3. Joint Report of the Administrator of the United Nations Development Programme and of the Executive Director of the United Nations Population Fund (E/2007/5)

I. Joint UNDP/UNFPA section

A. Implementation of the reform programme of the Secretary-General and the provisions of the triennial comprehensive policy review

Capacity development

1. In July 2006, the UNDG programme group provided guidance to resident coordinators and United Nations country teams on how to mainstream capacity development in national development strategies through the United Nations Development Assistance Framework. Based on feedback from United Nations country teams, the UNDG task team on capacity development, in which both UNDP and UNFPA participate, is finalizing a position statement on capacity development. The position statement includes a matrix of optional United Nations roles in mainstreaming capacity development as well as an inventory of tools available in the United Nations system.

2. Using this position statement, UNFPA expects to complete in 2006 its national capacity development strategy. Based on country experiences as well as the UNDG matrix on capacity development, the strategy will: (a) assist national counterparts in assessing the national capacity that is necessary to develop and maintain population programmes; (b) prioritize ways to fill gaps; and (c) support monitoring and learning as part of results-based management. The UNDP and UNFPA partnership on the harmonized approach to cash transfers analyses the gaps and needs in the management capacity of implementing national partners and seeks to address them, in collaboration with the United Nations World Food Programme (WFP) and the United Nations Children's Fund (UNICEF).

3. UNDP work in capacity development focused on two goals: (a) mainstreaming capacity assessments and strategies into the Millennium Development Goal support services programme; and (b) developing evidence-based policy guidance on key cross-cutting elements of capacity development strategies. For the first goal, UNDP has integrated capacity diagnostic expertise into the Millennium Development Goal teams in the Asia and the Pacific and the Africa regions to ensure that Millennium Development Goal-based national development strategies, including needs assessments and policy choices, reflect capacity assets and gaps. For the second goal, UNDP is articulating seven priority strategies for capacity development within its overall capacity development policy. This work covers capacity diagnostics, knowledge services and learning, leadership development, institutional reform and change management, multi-stakeholder engagement processes, mutual accountability mechanisms and incentive systems. The work of UNDP in strengthening national capacity to manage aid in the context of the Paris Declaration on Aid Effectiveness is also reflected in policy guidance on aid management and aid management instruments; on capacity development of national procurement systems; and in direct budget support and sector-wide approaches.

4. During the past year, UNFPA initiated a process of consultation with Member States to regionalize its operations. One of the motivating factors for the proposed regionalization is to leverage technical expertise to develop capacity in the countries and regions UNFPA serves by strengthening technical support to country offices and government partners. By combining existing regional technical capacity with the UNFPA Technical Advisory Programme, UNFPA seeks to anchor technical capacity-building in regional experiences as well as in global best practices. This will ensure that the capacity-building initiatives in UNFPA programming are coordinated, coherent and region-specific.

5. South-South cooperation is an important element of the UNFPA strategy on capacity development. UNFPA is developing an inventory of South-based expertise in population issues, which it will make available to all countries.

Information technology and knowledge sharing

6. In order to support the development of global knowledge sharing and networking among United Nations agencies on the Millennium Development Goals, the UNDG is developing a policy network that will bring together the expertise of the United Nations system and other partners to support countries in implementing Millennium Development Goal-based national development strategies. The UNDG has set up a network of United Nations system colleagues on knowledge networking, in which both UNDP and UNFPA participate. Over 10 United Nations organizations are now building on the UNDP model of knowledge networks. Several global networks have been established in the areas of human rights and debt management. UNDP and UNFPA are working with the knowledge management working groups in the UNDG and in the United Nations Chief Executives' Board. UNDP is working with several of the United Nations regional economic and social commissions to develop new approaches to knowledge sharing to support the Millennium Development Goals. UNDP is also preparing a knowledge management and communications strategy to support the Millennium Development Goals, initially in 18 countries.

Simplification and harmonization of rules and procedures, transaction costs and efficiency

7. Through active participation in the UNDG, UNDP and UNFPA continued efforts to simplify and harmonize their processes and procedures to reduce transaction costs for themselves and for their national partners. With regard to the common country programming process, a recent independent review revealed that the United Nations Development Assistance Framework has contributed to this goal, although much still remains to be done. The ongoing revision of the guidelines for the common country assessment and the United Nations Development Assistance Framework is facilitating these improvements by strengthening national ownership as well as alignment with and involvement in national development plans and processes, and better positioning the United Nations in the new aid environment.

8. In response to paragraph 49 of General Assembly resolution 59/250 on the triennial comprehensive policy review of operational activities for development of the United Nations system, and in order to better align United Nations programming instruments with national planning processes, the UNDG developed a proposal to simplify the programming process and programming tools. The proposal called for combining several programming instruments (the United Nations Development Assistance Framework and the results matrix, the

country programme documents and the country programme action plans) into a single, consolidated United Nations Development Assistance Framework. The heads of the UNDG Executive Committee agencies agreed to submit a joint proposal to their respective Executive Boards to revise the approval process of their agency-specific contributions to the consolidated United Nations Development Assistance Framework, in accordance with the UNDG proposal. In September 2006, the Executive Boards of UNDP/UNFPA and UNICEF adopted a decision to shorten the time frame for country programme approval (UNDP/UNFPA Executive Board decision 2006/36 and UNICEF Executive Board decision 2006/19).

9. To facilitate the work of United Nations country teams, the UNDG working group on programme policy is developing a manual on programme policies for the United Nations system and is updating the learning kit on the common country programming process.

10. UNFPA has been actively engaged in sector-wide approaches and has contributed to sector funding baskets in several countries. As a follow up to the Paris High-level Forum on Joint Progress toward Enhanced Aid Effectiveness, UNFPA issued internal guidelines on engagement in sector-wide approaches and poverty reduction strategies, and is strengthening its internal guidance on the new aid environment.

11. UNDP, UNFPA and UNICEF presented to the annual sessions 2006 of their respective Executive Boards a joint report on their experiences in implementing joint programming and joint programmes since 2004 (DP/2006/33-DP/FPA/2006/11 and E/ICEF/2006/13 and Add.1). The UNDG is reviewing the guidance note on joint programming to reflect recent changes. One such change is the 2006 UNDG management group endorsement of the proposal to harmonize cost-recovery rates for UNDG Executive Committee agencies participating in multi-donor trust funds, joint programmes and joint offices. The UNDG is providing support through joint programme training and learning modules on programme and operational issues. In 2006, the UNDG Executive Committee agencies developed and deployed to their country offices a harmonized, joint programme reporting format for donors. The UNDG established a joint programme database utilizing information provided by country offices and headquarters on more than 300 joint programmes. It also conducted a review and collated lessons learned from joint programme development and implementation in 14 countries as a key input for the 2006 revision of the joint programming guidance note.

12. In January 2006, the United Nations established the first joint United Nations office—the Office of United Nations funds and programmes in Cape Verde. By the end of 2006, the UNDG will conduct an interagency review of the Cape Verde experience to provide information on progress and challenges, and to build on lessons learned in the first year. The lessons learned from the joint office initiative will enable the UNDG Executive Committee agencies to implement the initiative more effectively. Though the joint office was originally thought to be more appropriate for countries with modest United Nations operations, larger countries such as Viet Nam have come forward. The joint office initiative in Viet Nam is progressing rapidly. The challenge is to find different models to meet different country situations, a task that has now been assigned to the Boston Consulting Group.

13. The recommendations of the High-level Panel on United Nations System-wide Coherence in the areas of development, humanitarian assistance and the environment are expected to provide a major momentum to increase coherence and effectiveness at the country level.

Coherence, effectiveness and relevance of operational activities for development

Common country assessment and the United Nations Development Assistance Framework

14. The UNDG is seeking to further improve guidelines and training on the common country assessment and the United Nations Development Assistance Framework. The proposed revisions to the guidelines are expected to: (a) enhance the participation of non-resident agencies; (b) strengthen country ownership; (c) enhance engagement in poverty reduction strategies; and (d) provide criteria to determine when a separate common country assessment is the most appropriate United Nations contribution to analytical work in a country. UNDP and UNFPA are also working to improve the alignment of their country programmes with the United Nations Development Assistance Framework, within the current common country programming process.

15. To improve inter-agency collaboration, UNDP and UNFPA have encouraged the participation of the United Nations specialized agencies and the regional economic commissions in the common country programming process, thereby capitalizing on their comparative advantages and enriching the quality of the common country assessments and the United Nations Development Assistance Frameworks. The regional economic commissions are providing data and analyses to United Nations country teams. Country analytical work has become a responsibility that is shared with both national and international development partners.

16. Recognizing the importance of ensuring the quality of the common country programming process, UNFPA has increased the level, quality and intensity of its participation in all stages of the country programming process—in the United Nations country teams; in the regional directors' teams; in the country programme support group and in other UNDG working groups. UNFPA seeks to leverage its comparative advantage in the areas of data, gender, reproductive and sexual health, and population and development.

Resident coordinator system and United Nations country teams

17. As called for in General Assembly resolution 59/250, the UNDG has developed a mutual performance appraisal system for resident coordinators and United Nations country teams. The performance appraisal system reinforces resident coordinator and United Nations accountability for the resident coordinator system. It supports the authority of the resident coordinator as the principal United Nations representative in a country, while recognizing the mandates and representational needs of each member of the United Nations country team. The UNDG is launching globally a pilot programme for a web-based, reciprocal 180 degree assessment tool for resident coordinators and United Nations country team members, which it will implement in 2007. The UNDG is also refining the job description and accountability framework for resident coordinators.

18. Beginning in 2006, the resident coordinator induction programme has included representatives from and partnership with relevant United Nations funds, programmes and specialized agencies. The UNDG is undertaking efforts to improve the quality of resident coordinator/humanitarian coordinator candidates; the gender and regional balance; the selection process; training; and resident coordinator/humanitarian coordinator capacity through strengthened professional staff support. At the regional level, dedicated support by the regional directors' teams will further strengthen the resident coordinator system and

United Nations country teams. UNDP is redoubling its efforts to introduce country directors in countries with large and medium-sized United Nations country teams.

19. The UNDG working group on common premises and services continued to guide and assist United Nations country teams in establishing United Nations houses and United Nations common premises. Proposed projects include the construction of new premises; the renovation or alteration of existing premises; and more complex projects, such as 'design, build, operate and transfer arrangements' with developers. There are currently 36 projects worldwide. In order to encourage the sharing of office premises at the subnational level, the UNDG took an inventory of the subnational offices of each UNDG Executive Committee agency. To better manage the common premises and services programme, the UNDG rolled out a common services management system in 22 countries.

Gender

20. In October 2006, the UNDG reviewed and made recommendations to improve the gender equality accountability mechanisms of UNDP, UNFPA, UNICEF, WFP and the International Labour Organization. The review examined key strategy documents (such as the multi-year funding framework (MYFF) and reports to the respective Executive Boards and to the Economic and Social Council) to analyse the extent to which these documents included gender-related targets and indicators. The study also analysed reporting, evaluation and audit functions; staff performance appraisal; and development and budget functions. The review included an analysis of a number of indicator systems and scorecards on gender equality and other areas.

21. UNDP and UNFPA have played important roles in the UNDG and at the national level on gender mainstreaming, as individual entities and in the context of the resident coordinator system. UNDP facilitated the first-ever United Nations country team harmonized reporting on the status of the implementation of the Convention on the Elimination of All Forms of Discrimination against Women to the thirty-sixth session of the Committee on the Elimination of Discrimination against Women in August 2006.

22. UNDP has responded positively to the findings and recommendations of the 2005 independent evaluation of gender mainstreaming in UNDP. The findings and recommendations are included in the corporate gender action plan, 2006-2007, which the Executive Board endorsed at its first regular session 2006. The gender action plan responds to the four "Cs", which are the main concerns of the evaluation: (a) commitment and accountability; (b) capacity; (c) communication and visibility; and (d) core resources. UNDP relies on the United Nations Development Fund for Women (UNIFEM), its associated fund, for technical services in areas where UNIFEM has expertise and capacity, especially at the regional level.

23. Through its corporate strategy, UNFPA also seeks to build a stronger internal accountability system and to enhance its capacity to improve programming on gender mainstreaming. In collaboration with UNIFEM, UNFPA developed capacity-building tools on gender budgeting for reproductive rights and other gender-related priorities, to ensure that sufficient budget allocations are available to implement national gender-equality policies and programmes.

24. In 2006, UNFPA responded to emerging issues such as international migration, focusing on female migrants and gender-based violence, in partnership with the International

Organization for Migration and the Division for the Advancement of Women of the United Nations Department of Economic and Social Affairs.

25. Because women's leadership is critical to advancing reproductive rights, UNFPA continues to support women's networks, including women parliamentarians, women's rights groups and indigenous people's movements to implement the recommendations of the ten-year review of the Beijing Platform for Action. UNFPA is also one of the founding members of a global initiative, the Women Leaders Intercultural Forum, which brings together women leaders to advance the role of women in promoting intercultural understanding and fosters inter-generational partnerships to groom young women leaders.

South-South cooperation

26. Following Executive Board endorsement of the third UNDP cooperation framework for South-South cooperation, 2005-2007, UNDP has worked to promote South-South cooperation throughout the United Nations system. An analysis of data on South-South cooperation submitted by country offices suggests that in Africa, South-South cooperation is most prominent in efforts to combat HIV/AIDS and to support democratic governance. In the Asia and the Pacific region, it is most prominent in crisis prevention and recovery, and in energy and the environment. In Latin America, the priority areas for South-South cooperation are in crisis prevention and recovery, and in support to democratic governance.

27. UNDP has supported the development of partnerships and other mechanisms that bring together southern centres of excellence, the private sector and civil society organizations, in order to foster the implementation of South-South action plans in priority areas such as science capacity-building, technology transfer, remittances and creative industries. UNDP is developing a programme that links technology exchange centres in middle-income countries with their counterparts in poorer countries, particularly in Africa. UNDP is also supporting the sharing of southern development knowledge and increasing the visibility of southern experts and institutions throughout UNDP and in the UNDG office through the use of its internet-based information system, the Web of Information for Development, known as WIDE.

28. In response to the 2004 tsunami, UNDP launched a South-South grants facility that enables countries to pool resources to quickly fund short-term, community-based recovery efforts. Brazil, India and South Africa have established a fund in UNDP that supports efforts to meet the Millennium Development Goals. The Second South Summit (Doha, June 2005) established the South Fund for Development and Humanitarian Assistance.

29. UNFPA is committed to South-South cooperation within the framework of capacity development, in accordance with the UNDG position statement. In line with the Programme of Action of the International Conference on Population and Development (ICPD) and the outcomes of the other major United Nations conferences and summits, including the 2005 World Summit, UNFPA work in South-South cooperation in 2005 and 2006 has supported the development of census and population surveys, the planning and delivery capacity for reproductive health services, women's empowerment and the application of a 'culture lens' to national population programmes.

30. Four patterns of population assistance within South-South cooperation activities are discernible. The first pattern relates to bilateral support for countries in similar stages of

development, within the same region or subregion. Often taking the form of study tours, this type of South-South activity has been implemented in African countries, particularly in West Africa, and to a lesser extent in East Africa, as well as in South Asia and South-East Asia. The second pattern relies on regional 'pivot' countries that have region-specific experience in planning and delivering population programmes, and that provide technical assistance to other countries in the region and subregion. Brazil, Egypt, India, Senegal, Thailand and Tunisia often provide this type of technical assistance. Also noteworthy are the recently established reproductive health networks in East Africa and in West Africa, and the Mediterranean network on gender-based violence.

31. The third pattern of South-South cooperation involves countries such as Brazil, China and India that provide support beyond their regions in research and analysis, training and the development of new products. Finally, there are South-South cooperation modalities that are culture-centred, including those among Muslim countries that support each other's efforts to foster commitment to a rights-based approach to reproductive health service delivery and gender equality.

Transition from relief to development

32. In order to strengthen coordination arrangements for transitions from relief to development, the UNDG and the Office for the Coordination of Humanitarian Affairs (OCHA) have jointly reviewed coordination practices in the recovery phase of crises or disasters and have established joint modalities to provide transition support. As in the tsunami-affected regions, the United Nations has established joint United Nations offices or offices of the resident coordinator/humanitarian coordinator in Pakistan, Sudan and other countries. UNDP has assisted United Nations country teams in preparing draft transitional strategies that delineate United Nations support for recovery and reconstruction plans, such as those in Lebanon and Pakistan. OCHA has agreed to permit UNDP and other United Nations organizations to include early recovery activities and resource requirements for recovery coordination in the consolidated appeals processes.

33. UNDP continued to develop modalities for joint programming with the United Nations Department of Peacekeeping Operations in areas such as disarmament, demobilization and reintegration, and the rule of law. In 2006, the Department of Peacekeeping Operations and UNDP jointly established the first post-peacekeeping United Nations integrated office—in Sierra Leone—which is designed to ensure the most effective return to development in a post-crisis situation. The United Nations will establish a similar office in Burundi in 2007.

34. As the lead agency for the early recovery cluster in the Inter-Agency Standing Committee for Humanitarian Affairs, UNDP leads efforts to strengthen the capacity of United Nations resident coordinators/humanitarian coordinators to initiate early recovery activities. OCHA put into practice the cluster approach, which involves multi-agency collaboration, in the aftermath of the 2005 earthquake in Pakistan. This approach is viewed as the way forward.

Evaluation of operational activities for development

35. The new UNDP evaluation policy that the Executive Board approved at its annual session 2006 seeks to establish a common institutional basis for the UNDP evaluation function, thereby increasing the transparency, coherence and efficiency of evaluation in

generating and using evaluative knowledge for organizational learning and in supporting accountability. The policy affirms the UNDP commitment to human development and human rights, national ownership and managing for development results.

36. UNDP is the chair of the United Nations evaluation group that brings together the professional units and individuals responsible for evaluation within the United Nations system. Through the United Nations evaluation group, UNDP has taken the lead in the first country-led, country-level joint evaluation with the Government of South Africa, seeking to evaluate the relevance and effectiveness of the United Nations system in South Africa over the past decade. It is also leading the study on ways to evaluate the United Nations Development Assistance Framework.

37. In 2006, the UNDP Evaluation Office published six evaluations of country-level assessments of development results in Bangladesh, Ethiopia, Honduras, Montenegro, Serbia and Syria. UNDP will complete five more evaluations by the end of 2006. In addition, UNDP completed two strategic evaluations on gender mainstreaming in UNDP and on the UNDP role in and contribution to the HIV/AIDS response in Ethiopia and in Southern Africa. In 2006, UNDP will complete five more strategic evaluations on a range of activities, including UNDP work in conflict-affected countries, governance-policy linkages and the national human development report system.

38. In September 2005, UNFPA conducted—for technical advisers, UNFPA representatives and other programme staff in West Africa—a subregional dialogue on results-based monitoring and evaluation in the context of United Nations reform. This resulted in a medium-term action plan to strengthen results-based monitoring and evaluation in country offices and among national counterparts. In 2006, UNFPA focused on the performance assessment of offices through oversight missions undertaken by evaluators and auditors. UNFPA assessed the performance of eight country offices, one UNFPA Country Technical Services Team and the Humanitarian Response Unit at headquarters on the relevance of UNFPA assistance and quality issues related to monitoring and evaluation systems.

39. UNFPA presented to the annual session 2006 of the Executive Board the results of its evaluation of quality assessment, conducted in 2005. UNFPA developed a follow-up action plan that included updating the programme policies and procedures manual, developing additional guidance, such as a new set of minimum evaluation standards, and improving the linkage between evaluation and knowledge sharing.

B. Follow-up to international conferences and the Millennium Development Goals

40. A key focus for UNFPA and UNDP in 2006 was to continue consultations in the UNDG and in the United Nations country teams to promote United Nations reform as outlined in the 2005 World Summit Outcome, the triennial comprehensive policy review of operational activities for development of the United Nations system and the Paris Declaration on Aid Effectiveness. The emphasis is on achieving 'one United Nations' as a way to enhance programme results and accountability and to promote capacity development and ownership of national development strategies to achieve the international development goals. The UNDG is currently implementing its 2006-2008 action plan on the follow-up to the 2005 World Summit. The plan addresses the scaling up of actions and results to help countries

achieve the Millennium Development Goals, to reduce risks and to preserve the results achieved thus far.

41. UNDP, in partnership with the UNDG, United Nations organizations, the Bretton Woods institutions and other development partners, has launched a Millennium Development Goal support initiative to assist countries in preparing Millennium Development Goal-based national development strategies. The initiative has three dimensions: (a) Millennium Development Goal diagnostics and investment planning; (b) widening policy options; and (c) strengthening national capacities to achieve the Millennium Development Goals. While the primary focus is on Africa, the initiative will also be rolled out in priority countries in other regions. By 2007, the initiative is expected to cover 60 countries.

42. During the fiftieth session of the Commission on the Status of Women, UNFPA successfully advocated and supported the commitment to achieve universal access to reproductive health by 2015 and to strengthen policy and programme linkages between HIV/AIDS and reproductive health in resolution 50/2 on women, the girl child and HIV/AIDS. In May/June 2006, UNFPA participated in the High-level Meeting on AIDS and in the comprehensive review of the progress achieved in realizing the targets set out in the Declaration of Commitment on HIV/AIDS, which the General Assembly adopted at its twenty-sixth special session in June 2001. UNFPA inputs in the Political Declaration on HIV/AIDS adopted at the meeting stressed the linkages between HIV/AIDS and reproductive health.

43. In August 2006, the Ad Hoc Committee on a Comprehensive and Integral International Convention on the Protection and Promotion of the Rights and Dignity of Persons with Disabilities included, as advocated by UNFPA, sexual and reproductive health in the draft International Convention on the Rights of Persons with Disabilities, the first time this issue had been included in an international human rights instrument.

44. Maternal heath remains a priority pillar for UNFPA. In cooperation with the Government of Belgium and the European Commission, UNFPA organized the International Symposium on Sexual Violence in Conflict and Beyond (Brussels, 21-23 June 2006). The UNFPA Campaign to End Fistula is now active in 35 countries in sub-Saharan Africa, Asia and the Arab region – a remarkable achievement in a short time. In September 2006, in Maputo, Mozambique, UNFPA, along with the Government of Mozambique, the African Union and the European Commission, supported the special session of the African Union Ministers of Health, which focused on scaling up sexual and reproductive health services throughout Africa to achieve the goal of universal access to reproductive health. UNFPA released its 2006 *State of World Population* report, which focused on women and international migration, and its special youth edition, *Moving Young*, to coincide with the General Assembly High-level Dialogue on International Migration and Development in September 2006. Both publications contributed to raising awareness and building global consensus on the women-and-youth dimensions of the problem.

45. UNFPA continues to strengthen partnerships with civil society organizations, both globally and at the country level, to implement the international development goals. UNFPA has supported the participation of its non-governmental organization (NGO) partners in various civil society hearings in the General Assembly. The 2006 global consultation between NGOs and UNFPA served as a mechanism to exchange information and strengthen communications on emerging ICPD issues. Partnerships with civil

society focus on knowledge sharing and capacity-building at local, national and global levels. The UNDG is currently promoting two initiatives as a follow-up to the Report of the Secretary-General in response to the report of the Panel of Eminent Persons on United Nations-Civil Society Relations (A/59/354). These initiatives, which UNFPA supports, include the identification by all United Nations country teams of civil society focal points and the creation of a trust fund to strengthen partnerships with civil society at the country level.

II. UNDP section

A. Implementation of the reform programme of the Secretary-General and the provisions of the triennial comprehensive policy review

Funding for operational activities for development of the United Nations system

46. Total UNDP resources reached $4.8 billion in 2005, up from $4.1 billion in 2004. This represents an increase in nominal terms of $700 million or 17 per cent over 2004. When adjusted for price changes and exchange rate fluctuations, the real increase is about $460 million or 11 per cent. UNDP regular resources increased for the fifth consecutive year after reversing their six-year downward trend in 2001. Compared to 2004, income to regular resources grew nominally by 10 per cent to $921 million or by approximately 7 per cent in real terms. For the first time in a decade, gross regular resources surpassed the level of $900 million and thus exceeded the 2004-2007 UNDP MYFF interim target set for 2005. Thirteen members of the Development Assistance Committee of the Organization for Economic Cooperation and Development (OECD) increased their core contributions in local currency terms to UNDP regular resources—four by more than 10 per cent and three by 20 per cent or more in nominal terms.

47. This level of contributions is consistent with the objectives set forth in the 2004-2007 UNDP MYFF. It also signals renewed support from Member States for a United Nations development arm that benefits from adequate and predictable funding. However, UNDP continues to rely heavily on a limited number of donors. The top ten donors provided about 82 per cent of regular resources in 2005. While regular resources income remained volatile with respect to exchange rate fluctuations, adherence to multi-year funding mechanisms is enhancing income predictability. Nine members of the OECD Development Assistance Committee have made multi-year contribution commitments.

48. Other (non-core) resources experienced a higher growth than regular resources in 2005. Non-core or earmarked contributions from bilateral donor governments slightly exceeded $1 billion. Nearly all OECD Development Assistance Committee donors are active in co-financing UNDP programmes. Non-core resources entrusted to UNDP by non-bilateral partners, such as the European Commission, the World Bank and the Global Fund to Fight Aids, Tuberculosis and Malaria exceeded $1.4 billion. Local resources, channelled through UNDP by programme country governments and other local partners to support their own national development, amounted to $1.1 billion. As aid mechanisms available at the country level diversify and multiply, UNDP is increasingly being called upon to support governments in obtaining, directing and managing different types of funding in accordance with national priorities.

Crisis prevention and recovery

49. Through the Bureau for Crisis Prevention and Recovery, UNDP supports Member States in: (a) achieving a peaceful and lasting management of conflicts and disputes, before the emergence of violence; (b) reducing risks posed by natural disasters; (c) achieving lasting recovery from violent conflict; and (d) achieving swift recovery from the impact of natural disasters. To better accomplish this, the Bureau designed a five-year strategy for the period 2007-2011, following extensive consultations with development partners. A key element of this strategy is the active promotion of women as central partners in crisis prevention and recovery efforts.

Conflict prevention

50. In order to assist Member States in building their capacity to manage conflicts, UNDP provided assistance in four areas in 2005-2006:

(a) Mainstreaming conflict analysis into development plans and programmes. Burundi, Colombia, Fiji and Indonesia have received such support.

(b) Building indigenous mediation capacity through credible modern and traditional governmental and civil society institutions and processes. Beneficiaries include the ethnic relations commission in Guyana, the political parties' registration commission in Sierra Leone, the newly established national peace council in Ghana and similar initiatives in Kenya, Nigeria and Zimbabwe.

(c) Building consensus on divisive social and economic issues. UNDP provided support for national and civic dialogue initiatives in Argentina, Côte d'Ivoire, Guinea, Guyana, Lesotho, Mauritania and Togo, among others.

(d) Building an infrastructure for peace within which local disputes over land, resources, religion or ethnicity, chieftaincy succession and elections can be identified and addressed before they lead to violent conflict. In this regard, UNDP has supported initiatives in Ghana, Guyana, the Niger Delta, Nigeria and Sierra Leone.

51. In 2005 and 2006, UNDP continued to provide much of this assistance: (a) in collaboration with other United Nations system partners, especially with the Departments of Political Affairs and Economic and Social Affairs of the United Nations; and (b) in the context of systematic efforts to strengthen the United Nations Interdepartmental Framework for Coordination on Early Warning and Preventive Action, an internal United Nations mechanism to coordinate preventive action.

Post-conflict recovery

52. UNDP support for post-conflict recovery focuses on early recovery and on longer-term post-conflict peacebuilding. In 2005 and 2006, UNDP supported Member States in the following areas:

(a) Transitional recovery. UNDP implemented systematic and large-scale efforts to generate economic livelihoods and opportunities for communities, especially for internally displaced persons and refugees, in the following countries: Afghanistan, Democratic Republic of the Congo, Haiti, Indonesia, Iraq, Sri Lanka, Sudan and Uganda.

UNDP also supported an innovative joint effort by Colombia and Ecuador to address the needs of conflict-affected communities along their shared border.

(b) Security sector reform and transitional justice. UNDP supported: (i) access to justice, especially for rural communities, in Haiti, Sierra Leone and Sudan; (ii) the reform and strengthening of the penal system in Haiti and Sierra Leone; (iii) multi-stakeholder dialogues on the reform of the security sector in Haiti and Sudan, and on transitional justice in Bosnia and Herzegovina, Montenegro and Serbia; and (iv) the strengthening of police capabilities for conflict management and community policing in Albania and Sierra Leone.

(c) Small arms reduction, disarmament and demobilization. UNDP efforts targeted the perceptions of insecurity and the factors that fuel the demand for weapons. Beneficiaries of UNDP support in 2005-2006 included Afghanistan, Burundi, Democratic Republic of the Congo, El Salvador, Haiti, Liberia and Sudan.

(d) Mine action. UNDP has placed particular emphasis on developing joint methods with other United Nations partners, especially the United Nations Department of Peacekeeping Operations, for mine action in post-conflict situations. The joint mine action centre established in Sudan is an important example. In 20052006, UNDP provided technical and advisory services to more than 30 mine-affected countries. A central focus of UNDP support has been to strengthen South-South cooperation on this issue, including through the mine action exchange programme.

(e) Special initiatives for countries in transition. In 2006, UNDP took systematic steps to strengthen its 'surge' capacity—the ability to rapidly support its country offices in providing prompt and effective responses to early recovery needs.

Natural disaster risk reduction

53. UNDP recently launched a global initiative to mainstream disaster risk reduction into development programming. The initiative focuses on producing tools and increasing programme capacities to include disaster concerns in United Nations as well as UNDP development planning processes. Recognizing the importance of regional and subregional collaboration in reducing disaster risks, UNDP launched programmes in Africa, the Caribbean and Central Asia in 2005 and 2006 to assist regional organizations and to develop regional frameworks, in order to better address risks such as droughts and hurricanes.

Natural disaster recovery

54. In addition to coordinating and directly implementing important aspects of the international response to the 2005 earthquake in Pakistan, UNDP continued to provide support in 2005 and 2006 to the tsunami-affected countries, especially Indonesia, Maldives, Sri Lanka and Thailand. The international community has recognized the need for more comprehensive and predictable approaches in post-disaster recovery. To address this need, UNDP, with the support of Japan and other partners, launched in 2005 the International Recovery Platform to increase global capacity for post-disaster recovery planning.

B. Strategic partnerships, including cooperation with the World Bank

55. UNDP has worked extensively with United Nations partner organizations to strengthen existing partnerships and to develop new ones. UNDP continues to work closely with the

World Bank on a wide range of issues. In 2006, UNDP and the World Bank set up a joint task force on scaling up support for the Millennium Development Goals as a basis for future collaborative work. The task force produced a paper and an agenda for action at the third meeting of the OECD Development Assistance Committee and the World Bank on scaling up for results (June 2006). UNDP continues to widen and strengthen its partnerships with the private sector, civil society and foundations.

III. UNFPA section

A. Implementation of the reform programme of the Secretary-General and the provisions of the triennial comprehensive policy review

Funding for operational activities for development of the United Nations system

56. In 2006, regular resources are expected to reach $360 million, a 3 per cent increase compared to 2005. This growth is due primarily to increases in local currency pledges from Australia, Austria, Finland, Ireland, Luxembourg, New Zealand, Norway, Spain and Sweden. As of 1 September 2006, 140 countries had contributed $215.4 million to regular resources. In 2005, 172 countries made pledges to UNFPA; a similar number is expected for 2006. UNFPA has received 64 multi-year pledges so far, up from 55 in 2005.

57. In 2005, income to other resources was provided through co-financing arrangements ($157.7 million) and other arrangements ($36.1 million), including the junior professional officer programme and third-party procurement services. Co-financing projections for 2006 so far indicate a lower income compared to 2005, which included generous contributions in response to the 2004 tsunami and the 2005 earthquake in Pakistan.

Country-level capacity of the United Nations system and regional support

58. As reported last year, UNFPA is pursuing its regionalization strategy in the context of United Nations reform efforts. UNFPA believes that this process offers an opportunity to further strengthen the capacity of country offices to support the needs of programme countries. The UNFPA Technical Advisory Programme continues to support capacity-building at country and regional levels and has been instrumental in supporting country office implementation of United Nations reform processes.

B. Strategic partnerships, including cooperation with the World Bank

59. UNFPA collaborates closely with the World Health Organization (WHO) and UNIFEM within the framework of the UNFPA strategic partnerships programme. The aim of the strategic partnerships programme is to provide coordinated technical assistance to countries in priority areas. UNFPA works with WHO to improve sexual and reproductive health through the adoption of evidence-based guidelines that are updated regularly to reflect international scientific consensus. In June 2006, UNFPA and WHO issued a joint communiqué that identified a number of priority areas for cooperation in sexual and reproductive health. With UNIFEM, the initial aim is to strengthen national capacity in gender-responsive budgeting.

60. Over the past months, UNFPA and the World Bank have revived the World Bank-UNFPA joint action plan and have identified concrete steps and areas of collaboration. To strengthen this collaboration, UNFPA has published an action guide on contributing to

national poverty reduction strategies and is planning to organize a workshop with the World Bank on how to mainstream youth issues into poverty reduction strategies.

IV. Joint UNDP/UNFPA recommendation

61. The Executive Board may wish to take note of this report (E/2007/5) and transmit it to the Economic and Social Council, together with the comments and guidance provided by delegations at the present session.

4. Report of the United Nations High Commissioner for Human Rights for 2006 (A/61/36)

Note

Symbols of United Nations documents are composed of capital letters combined with figures. Mention of such asymbol indicates a reference to a United Nations document.

Chapter I

Introduction

1. The present report is submitted pursuant to General Assembly resolution 48/141 and focuses on developments since the sixtieth session of the Assembly, including in relation to implementation of my Plan of Action and the Strategic Management Plan of the Office of the United Nations High Commissioner for Human Rights (OHCHR), the establishment of the Human Rights Council and treaty body reform. This report should be read in the context of my report submitted earlier this year to the Commission on Human Rights and the Human Rights Council (E/CN.4/2006/10).

Chapter II

Country engagement

2. In line with the Secretary-General's report to the General Assembly, "In larger freedom: towards development, security and human rights for all" (A/59/2005), my Plan of Action emphasizes that "engagement and dialogue with countries will be the primary means through which OHCHR works to ensure the implementation of human rights".

3. Country engagement, in its various forms, aims to assist States to address protection gaps through a consultative process which involves Government, civil society and other relevant national counterparts as well as international ones—including within the United Nations. OHCHR is not an arbiter or judge, but sees its work as an ongoing dialogue, bringing duty-bearers and rights-holders together towards more effective promotion and protection of human rights. To this end, the monitoring of human rights developments at the country level and relevant collection of information are indispensable tools for an objective analysis of the human rights situation which, in turn, is fundamental in order to devise the most adequate form of technical cooperation.

4. The first area of action anticipated in my Plan of Action is "greater country engagement through an expansion of geographic desks, increased deployment of human rights staff to countries and regions, the establishment of standing capacities for rapid deployment, investigations, field support, human rights capacity-building, advice and assistance, and work on transitional justice and the rule of law".

A. Strengthening Headquarters capacity to support country engagement

1. Enhancing geographic desks' capacity

5. In order to pursue a more effective country engagement strategy at all levels, the strengthening of Headquarters capacity is essential. In my Plan of Action, it is foreseen that

geographic desks will be strengthened at headquarters through a substantial increase in staffing levels. This will allow OHCHR to follow more closely and analyse more thoroughly human rights-related developments in the various regions and, on this basis, to engage more efficiently. This will also enable best advantage to be taken of the work of the whole range of international human rights mechanisms—treaty bodies, special procedures and the Human Rights Council—and to monitor the implementation of their recommendations.

2. Establishment of a Rapid Response Unit

6. A Rapid Response Unit was established to strengthen and coordinate the Office's response to human rights crises. One of the key components of a rapid response capacity is to deploy human rights officers at short notice. In the case of Lebanon, since the beginning of the crisis on 12 July, I have taken measures to deploy a human rights officer on the ground despite a very difficult environment and severe security constraints. This has enabled my Office better to analyse the situation, identify priority human rights concerns and propose responses.

7. The strengthening of the Unit is also crucial as, over the past years, OHCHR has increasingly been called upon to support the establishment of, and to take part in, rapid response initiatives, such as fact-finding missions, commissions of inquiry, start-up missions, and operations requiring strengthening due to unforeseen needs. The Unit assists in the planning, design and execution of such initiatives and is in the process of establishing partnerships with United Nations agencies and an internal and external stand-by roster of qualified staff to secure adequate stand-by resources.

8. In 2005, the International Commission of Inquiry on Darfur, as well as a fact-finding mission on Togo and the OHCHR mission to Kyrgyzstan concerning the events in Andijan, Uzbekistan, were successfully supported. In 2006, OHCHR has supported similar initiatives, namely the Independent Special Commission of Inquiry for Timor-Leste and the High-Level Commission of Inquiry into the situation in Lebanon.

9. Some preparatory work has also been undertaken with a view to strengthening OHCHR capacity in the area of investigation as far as the development of methodological tools to guide OHCHR work and delivery of training are concerned. Contacts have been made with expert institutions for possible collaboration in this area. A study on the work of OHCHR in fact-finding and inquiry missions has been prepared (E/CN.4/2006/89).

3. Support to national human rights institutions

10. National human rights institutions (NHRIs) are a key element of the OHCHR country engagement strategy as indispensable actors for any long-term human rights approach in a country or region. OHCHR has helped establishing and strengthening NHRIs as important partners in its work. During 2006 OHCHR has provided advice on the establishment or strengthening of NHRIs on: appointments procedures (in Sierra Leone, in cooperation with the United Nations Mission in Sierra Leone; Sri Lanka); enabling legislation to establish an NHRI (The Comoros; Iraq; Mauritania, in cooperation with UNDP; Pakistan, with the Pakistani Parliamentarians Commission for Human Rights; Nepal; Scotland; United Kingdom; Uruguay; Chile).

B. Strengthening OHCHR presence in the field

11. It is through its expanded presence in the field, both at country and regional levels, that OHCHR will be able to achieve the greatest impact. Indeed, our presence on the ground enables first-hand knowledge, comprehension and analysis of human rights issues and developments, facilitates the establishment of stronger relationships with all counterparts including rights-holders, and thus fosters institutional credibility and trust. A monitoring presence can have a significant preventive and protective impact. Field presence therefore remains a preferred form of OHCHR country engagement. However, in order to play an effective role, country and regional offices need to be able to pursue the whole of the High Commissioner's mandate as set out in resolution 48/141 and should be adequately staffed and resourced.

12. Thus, my Plan of Action and Strategic Management Plan envisage an increase in operational deployment at the country and regional levels.

1. Establishment of new Regional Offices

13. I intend to strengthen the seven existing regional and subregional offices of OHCHR. In particular, the Regional Office for the Middle East and the Gulf, in Beirut, is being revitalized and restructured following the crisis in Lebanon.

14. The establishment of four new regional offices, and of a human rights training and documentation centre, is progressing:

- In June 2006, a Regional Representative was deployed to Kyrgyzstan to cover Central Asia;
- OHCHR has undertaken preparations for the opening of a Regional Office for West Africa in Dakar, with an annex in Abuja;
- My Office has conducted consultations regarding the establishment of a Regional Office for Northern Africa in Cairo. A draft host country agreement, as well as a concept paper regarding the mandate, functions, and activities of the Regional Office have been provided to the Government of Egypt;
- An assessment has been conducted to identify a location of our future Regional Office in Central America and a decision should be made by October 2006;
- As requested by the General Assembly in resolution 60/153 of 16 December 2005, consultations with the Government of Qatar are ongoing to establish a United Nations human rights training and documentation centre for South-West Asia and the Arab region, which is expected to start operations in 2006.

15. Regional offices will allow OHCHR to constructively collaborate with Governments in the region, relevant regional and subregional intergovernmental and non-governmental organizations in the area of human rights, national human rights institutions, as well as United Nations Country Teams (UNCTs). Regional offices would thus facilitate the development and implementation of engagement strategies for all countries concerned.

2. Expansion of country offices

16. An expansion of country offices is foreseen, but on a modest scale for 2006-2007 as the objective is to strengthen existing presences. OHCHR currently has 10 country offices, and two new offices will be established, in Togo and Bolivia. Consultations with the

Government of Togo have advanced significantly and it is expected the office of OHCHR there will be established by the end of 2006. As for Bolivia, a technical assessment mission of OHCHR was conducted in La Paz in early September 2006 to initiate negotiations with the Government.

17. Last year, I established offices in Nepal, Guatemala and Uganda. In these three countries, our engagement has been fruitful and the Governments' cooperation promises an improvement of the human rights situation.

18. In Nepal, our presence throughout the country has been credited with contributing to the protection of vulnerable populations. It has also been praised for promoting restraint by all parties to the conflict. Both parties have requested the assistance of OHCHR to continue monitoring the human rights situation. My Office is determined to pursue its engagement.

19. In Guatemala, the office of OHCHR is strongly engaged, together with the Government, the Ombudsman, the judiciary, Congress and civil society, in addressing long-standing human rights issues, including discrimination faced by indigenous peoples, poverty and public insecurity. The Office is firmly committed to further assist the Government in conducting and implementing reforms stemming from the peace agreements.

20. In Uganda, my Office is engaged in an open dialogue with the Government and security sector institutions for the prevention of human rights violations.

21. At the same time, OHCHR is phasing down in Bosnia and Herzegovina, Serbia, and in The former Yugoslav Republic of Macedonia, where it has been present for more than 10 years. OHCHR will remain present in the region, strengthening its Office in Kosovo in light of serious human rights concerns and upcoming challenges.

C. Strengthening partnerships within the United Nations

22. Our country engagement will undoubtedly have a stronger impact through the strengthening of partnerships with other parts of the United Nations—in line with my objective of exercising greater leadership within the organization.

1. Increased engagement with peace missions

23. My Plan of Action states that the protection of human rights must be at the core of policies to address conflicts. It also foresees a review of the support for Human Rights Components of Peace Missions with a view to making it more effective and increasing its capacity to provide advice and training to their civilian, police and military component. In 2005, OHCHR coordinated interdepartmental consultations which culminated in a Secretary-General's decision on human rights in integrated missions, adopted in October 2005. This decision constitutes a significant step in bringing human rights to the heart of the work of peace missions and is a cornerstone of a consolidated cooperation between the Department of Peacekeeping Operations and the Department of Political Affairs and OHCHR as well as UNCTs.

24. This decision sets out the responsibility of all United Nations entities to ensure the integration of human rights into field operations and the consolidation of core human rights functions in field missions. It provides that all core human rights functions in an integrated mission will be coordinated by one human rights component and reaffirms the role of OHCHR as the "lead agency" for human rights operations. Importantly, heads of human rights components of peace missions become my Representatives and, as such, are also

full-fledged members of the United Nations country team—thereby potentially enabling a more systematic human rights engagement of UNCTs in peacekeeping contexts and allowing a broader range of capacity-building activities. OHCHR is working closely with the Department of Peacekeeping Operations, the Department of Political Affairs, individual peace missions, as well as other partners, to implement the decision, and an Action Plan has been developed.

25. The Secretary-General's decision also emphasizes the importance of public human rights reporting and efforts will be made, increasingly, towards joint human rights reporting—including thematic reporting—and wider dissemination. A number of missions are issuing regular public human rights reports, including the United Nations Organization Mission in the Democratic Republic of the Congo, the United Nations Stabilization Mission in Haiti, the United Nations Operation in Burundi, the United Nations Operation in Côte d'Ivoire, the United Nations Mission in Liberia, the United Nations Assistance Mission for Iraq and the United Nations Mission in the Sudan—the latter two jointly with OHCHR.

26. OHCHR assisted in developing guidelines on the Integrated Mission Planning Process (IMPP) and has taken part in a number of technical assessment missions (Sudan/Darfur, Timor-Leste). OHCHR has also advanced work on developing the human rights-related sections of the DPKO Peacekeeping Guidance Project. In this context, a project was started to consolidate and develop policy and methodological guidance for human rights components of peace operations, as well as human rights guidance for military, police and rule of law components of missions. Some activities were undertaken in cooperation with the Department of Peacekeeping Operations to disseminate concepts and materials on rights-based approaches to the work of military peacekeepers among member States, and a basic module on human rights for inclusion in a training series for all peace operations personnel was updated. An inter-agency project (UNMIS, OHCHR, UNDP, UNICEF, UNFPA) to assist the African Union Mission in Darfur in strengthening its human rights capacity, including through the development of training, was started.

2. Stepping up cooperation with humanitarian actors

27. The strengthening of collaboration with humanitarian actors is a major objective of OHCHR, not only in the context of conflicts or in post-conflict times, but also in relation to natural disasters. Over the past year OHCHR continued to build partnerships with humanitarian agencies and engage with humanitarian-related mechanisms, including the Inter-Agency Standing Committee (IASC). OHCHR also takes an active role in the development of the inter-agency Protection Standby Capacity (PROCAP). Moreover, we have actively engaged on the Protection Cluster Working Group in the reform and strengthening of the humanitarian coordination system including, through the design of profiles, assessment criteria and training modules.

28. We have equally supported the development of tools for humanitarian response, and have taken the lead in the drafting of the recently published Human Rights Guidance Note for Humanitarian Coordinators.

29. My Office has also recently become part of important initiatives to mainstream human rights into humanitarian assistance/relief in the aftermath of natural disasters. Since 2004, a senior human rights adviser has been deployed to Sri Lanka to work under the Resident

Coordinator system to mainstream human rights in the work of the United Nations in support of the peace process but also to provide advice to the United Nations country team on rights-based approaches to the humanitarian response following the tsunami. Also, since October 2005, a human rights adviser has been posted to Pakistan following the earthquake. In both cases, the work of the advisers has been praised as a valuable contribution to improve the conception and delivery of humanitarian assistance.

3. Improving partnerships with the United Nations Resident Coordinator System

30. Cooperation with the Resident Coordinator System and United Nations country teams is becoming more structured and systematic. In compliance with the mandate of OHCHR to coordinate the human rights promotion and protection activities throughout the United Nations system, and in follow-up to the Secretary-General's request for OHCHR to work through the Resident Coordinator System to ensure that human rights are incorporated into country-level analysis, planning and programme implementation, OHCHR has strengthened its cooperation with UNCTs, deploying human rights advisers to assist resident coordinators in responding to complex human rights issues, when these arise.

31. OHCHR has also initiated discussions with United Nations partners such as the United Nations Development Group Office (UNDGO) and UNDP towards strengthening the effectiveness of human rights advisers to UNCTs, in line with system-wide efforts to strengthen coherence in the developmental and humanitarian work. As part of this effort, OHCHR is seeking to standardize the basic conditions and operating procedures in place for the deployment of human rights advisers to United Nations country teams, in a manner consistent with the objectives of the Office. OHCHR has human rights advisers in four countries: Georgia, Pakistan, Somalia and Sri Lanka funded either by the OHCHR Voluntary Fund for Technical Cooperation or in collaboration with other United Nations agencies and departments. Further human rights advisers are envisaged in different regions throughout 2006 and 2007.

D. Overcoming the closed-door policy

32. Despite the wide range of country engagement tools, my Office as well as special procedures mandate-holders still encounter difficulties in accessing a number of countries and I would like to continue or initiate a dialogue with the Governments of these countries to assist them in addressing the important protection gaps they face. I would also like to reiterate that closed-door policies and denial of access are grave concerns as they impede both on accurate assessment of the human rights situation in the country and any possibility of relevant technical assistance.

Chapter III

Developments in strategic thematic areas

A. Development, poverty reduction and the Millennium Development Goals

33. My Office is strengthening its capacities and consolidating expertise in the areas of the right to development and the Millennium Development Goals (the Goals), in order to more effectively support Member States in making the right to development a reality in practice. On the basis of work by the High-Level Task Force on the Implementation of the Right to

Development, the Working Group on the Right to Development, at its seventh session in January 2006, adopted a set of criteria to evaluate, through the lens of the right to development, global partnerships as contained in Goal 8, with a recommendation to pilot these criteria to selected global partnerships. The Working Group's recommendations were endorsed by the Human Rights Council at its first session in June 2006, and OHCHR is presently supporting the High-Level Task Force in preparing first steps towards piloting of the above-mentioned criteria.

34. OHCHR has set working towards poverty reduction with other partners as one of its priorities for the 2006-2007 biennium programme, and to date I can report on progress in a few selected areas.

35. OHCHR has continued to support the Social Forum under the Sub-Commission on the Protection and Promotion of Human Rights, or any successor advisory body the Human Rights Council may decide upon. It will be instrumental in advancing a shared conceptual understanding of the linkages between human rights and extreme poverty, and in ensuring that the voices of the poorest are heard in United Nations discussions on these issues.

36. Consistent with the World Summit Outcome resolution, my Office is presently exploring the prospects of deeper collaboration with the World Bank. At the invitation of the World Bank's Nordic/Baltic donors, OHCHR has contributed actively to the Nordic/Baltic Executive Directors' Human Rights Initiative, which led to the establishment in July 2006 of the World Bank's Justice and Human Rights Trust Fund. Discussions are under way with World Bank officials to identify areas of collaboration under the Trust Fund, including in capacity development and integrating human rights in poverty-reduction strategies at the national level.

37. Building on conceptual work launched in 2002, OHCHR will publish a set of "Principles and guidelines for a human rights approach to poverty reduction strategies" in October 2006. The guidelines are intended as a tool to assist countries, international agencies and development practitioners to translate human rights norms, standards and principles into policies and strategies in favour of the poor. Internal capacity-building efforts within OHCHR have been strengthened and re-oriented towards a stronger country and regional focus, enhancing OHCHR dialogues with national partners and multilateral and bilateral development agencies on these issues.

38. I have chosen "Poverty and human rights" as the theme for this year's Human Rights Day on 10 December 2006. It is hoped that the Human Rights Day would serve as a reminder of our commitment to the universality of human rights and the elimination of poverty. A range of media events and country level activities will take place highlighting—through people's own stories—the impact of poverty as the gravest human rights challenge in all countries of the world, and how strategies grounded in the human rights framework can help individuals and communities to challenge entrenched patterns of discrimination and lift themselves from the poverty trap.

39. There are also a number of important partnership initiatives under way that support OHCHR contributions to United Nations system-wide poverty reduction goals. Notable among them is OHCHR's continued leadership in the Action 2 reform initiative of the Secretary-General, aimed at enhancing system capacity in supporting Member States'

efforts to strengthen human rights protection systems at the national level. As country-level implementation of Action 2 intensifies, the programme is scaling up its support to United Nations country teams with seed funding for capacity-building activities. It is envisaged that, by the end of 2006, some 30 United Nations country teams will benefit from support offered by the Action 2 programme.

B. Economic, social and cultural rights

40. In line with the objectives set out in my Strategic Management Plan for 2006-2007, OHCHR has embarked on efforts to strengthen its expert capacity in the area of economic, social and cultural rights, with a focus on legal protection and advocacy—a theme for my report to the 2006 session of the Economic and Social Council (E/2006/86).

41. OHCHR has supported the intergovernmental discussions on the drafting of an optional protocol to the International Covenant on Economic, Social and Cultural Rights, which would establish an individual communications procedure to the Covenant. OHCHR serviced and provided substantive support to the third session of the Open-ended Working Group on an Optional Protocol (6-17 February 2006) (E/CN.4/2006/47). OHCHR attended and contributed to regional consultations on the optional protocol convened by the Governments of Mexico and Finland (Mexico City, 30-31 May 2006, and Helsinki, 27-28 July 2006), and it is planning to support further regional consultations. OHCHR will also support an experts' meeting convened by the Chairperson-Rapporteur (Lisbon, 29 September-1 October 2006).

42. OHCHR is in the process of elaborating a strategy for its work on economic, social and cultural rights, in consultation with various partners. One key objective is to enhance OHCHR's capacity, including through its field presences, to assist States, at their request, in strengthening national protection of economic, social and cultural rights, and to provide thematic support to the United Nations human rights treaty bodies and special procedures as well as United Nations agencies, funds and programmes.

C. Women's rights

43. OHCHR is in the process of establishing a new Women's Human Rights and Gender Unit, as part of our efforts to strengthen the Office's thematic expertise and our work for greater protection and empowerment of women. The Unit will focus on issues such as overcoming discrimination against women, including by addressing laws and practices that discriminate against women, violence against women, and combating impunity for violations of women's human rights.

44. OHCHR participates in a number of inter-agency bodies working on women's human rights. In the reporting period, OHCHR has, inter alia, contributed to the work of the Inter-Agency Network on Women and Gender Equality (IANWGE), supporting the work of task forces dealing with women, peace and security, and indigenous women as well as IANWGE cooperation with the Organization for Economic Cooperation and Development/ Development Cooperation Directorate Network on Gender Equality. OHCHR also participates in the Inter-Agency Standing Committee Taskforce on Gender and Humanitarian Action, where we, among other things, have contributed to the development of "A Handbook for Gender Equality in Humanitarian Action", and in the Joint United Nations Executive

Committee on Humanitarian Affairs (ECHA)/United Nations Executive Committee on Peace and Security (ECPS) Taskforce on Protection from Sexual Exploitation and Abuse.

45. OHCHR worked bilaterally with a number of United Nations partners, including with DPKO to integrate a gender and women's human rights perspective in peacekeeping operations, with the Office of the United Nations High Commissioner for Refugees (UNHCR) and World Health Organization (WHO) supporting efforts to mainstream gender and women's human rights in their work. OHCHR has also participated in a range of activities of the Division for the Advancement of Women under the annual joint workplan submitted to the Commission on the Status of Women and the Commission on Human Rights.

D. Issues of equality and non-discrimination

46. Notable progress has been made in our efforts to promote equality and non-discrimination. My Office has provided substantive expertise and support in contribution to the adoption by the Ad Hoc Committee of the General Assembly on a draft international convention on the rights of persons with disabilities. After its adoption by the General Assembly, I believe that this Convention will offer genuine protection to the estimated 10 per cent of the world's population who have a disability and who are exposed to the most extreme forms of denial of human rights. I look forward to collaborating with States and civil society to support the new Committee on the Rights of Persons with Disabilities that will be established under the Convention.

47. Another landmark is the adoption by the Human Rights Council of the long-negotiated United Nations Declaration on the Rights of Indigenous Peoples. My Office has continued its work on the promotion and protection of the human rights of indigenous peoples by supporting, at the substantial and organizational levels, the existing human rights mechanisms relating to indigenous peoples, standard-setting processes, advocating for inter-agency cooperation, mainstreaming indigenous peoples rights within the United Nations system and UNCTs, empowering indigenous organizations and communities, and assisting States on these issues. OHCHR is strengthening its capacity-building work aimed at indigenous peoples through the Indigenous Fellowship Programme, as well as OHCHR/UNDP Human Rights Strengthening (HURIST) project activities in Bolivia, Ecuador, Guatemala and Kenya.

48. The struggle against racism, racial discrimination and xenophobia constitutes a priority for my Office. The principal focus of OHCHR has been on the effective implementation of the Durban Declaration and Programme of Action. We continue to provide substantive and organizational support to the work of the Intergovernmental Working Group on the Effective Implementation of the Durban Declaration and Programme of Action, the Working Group of Experts on People of African Descent and the group of Independent Eminent Experts.

49. The Office extended support to the Regional Conference of the Americas against racism, racial discrimination, xenophobia and related intolerance organized by the Governments of Brazil and Chile and held in Brasilia from 26 to 28 July 2006, on progress made and challenges remaining with regard to the effective implementation of the Durban Programme of Action.

50. My Office initiated and organized a number of activities in commemoration of the International Day for the Elimination of Racial Discrimination on 21 March 2006, including panel discussions on the theme "Fighting everyday racism" in collaboration with the International Labour Organization (ILO) and the United Nations Educational Social and Cultural Organization (UNESCO).

E. Issues of migration and trafficking

51. Migration is high on the international agenda of 2006, and rightly so. The High-Level Dialogue on International Migration and Development of the General Assembly scheduled in September 2006 triggered an important debate on migration within the United Nations system and the international community at large.

52. My Office has actively contributed to the preparation of the High-Level Dialogue and has aimed at bringing human rights to the forefront of the debate. Respecting human rights is not only a legal obligation. It is also a precondition for our societies to grow and prosper in peace and security. OHCHR provided comments on the outline and drafts of the Secretary-General's report on international migration and development (A/60/871). A paper on the interlinkages between migration, development and human rights, a set of key messages as well as a compilation of findings and observations by the United Nations human rights system relating to the human rights of migrants are available on OHCHR's website, as its contribution to the High-Level Dialogue.

53. A human rights approach to migration includes a recognition that migrants are holders of rights which States of origin, transit and destination have an obligation to respect—the International Convention on the Protection of the Rights of All Migrant Workers and Members of Their Families offers States the most comprehensive framework for the protection of the rights of migrants. It also calls on States, inter alia, to recognize that development is more than an economic parameter and encompasses human rights; that human rights deficits must be addressed in order to make migration an informed choice; and that discrimination is an underlying factor of migrants' vulnerability, which limits or nullifies migrants' contribution to development and thus needs to be addressed forcefully. Measures to protect the human rights of victims of human trafficking and smuggling are urgently needed, and information on safe and legal migration is to be made available and accessible. There is also a need for migration policies and programmes to be gender-sensitive to ensure that adequate attention is given to the special circumstances of migrant women.

54. From December 2005 to March 2006, OHCHR chaired the Geneva Migration Group (GMG), which became the Global Migration Group during the OHCHR chairmanship. We continue to be an active member of GMG, which aims to enhance the overall effectiveness of inter-agency response to the opportunities and challenges posed by migration.

55. OHCHR, together with the *Defensoría del Pueblo of Bolivia* and the International Coordinating Committee of National Institutions (ICC), is organizing the Eighth *International Conference of National Human Rights Institutions*, on "Migration: the role of National Human Rights Institutions". The purpose of the Conference, to be held 23-27 October 2006 at Santa Cruz, Bolivia, is to develop and strengthen cooperation between NHRIs with regard to migrant and human rights issues; promote the adoption of strategies with regard to migration and human rights; establish guidelines for NHRIs in dealing with migrant issues; and adopt a Declaration and a Plan of Action on NHRIs and migration.

56. OHCHR supports human rights mechanisms, including those specifically dealing with the human rights of migrants, the Committee on Migrant Workers and the Special Rapporteur on the human rights of migrants. In July 2006, the Committee issued its contribution to the High-Level Dialogue on Migration and Development[1] based on the day of general discussion held on 15 December 2005. On 28 April 2006, the Committee adopted concluding observations on the initial report of Mali.[2] They are the first concluding observations on a State-party's report submitted under article 73 of the Convention on Migrant Workers.

57. The escalating dimension of human trafficking globally, its growing complexity including its connections with migration and transnational organized crime, are the focus of OHCHR Trafficking Programme. Prevention of trafficking involves identifying the linkages with development issues, including the rule of law, irregular migration, forced labour, and gender discrimination. Protection to victims of trafficking entails strengthening legal and policy initiatives, including shelters, skills training and reintegration schemes that provide assistance to and protect the victims of trafficking. By coordinating the Intergovernmental (IGO) Contact Group on Human Trafficking and Migrant Smuggling—which includes as members UNHCR, ILO, the International Organization for Migration, the United Nations Children's Fund, WHO and the NGO Caucus—OHCHR has continued to support effective human rights-based advocacy on the issue of trafficking within the United Nations system and in cooperation with civil society organizations.

F. Rule of law and democracy

58. My Office has responded to the demands for policy guidance, advisory services, methodology and expertise in the area of transitional justice and rule of law. OHCHR Rule of Law Tools for Post-Conflict States were published, outlining the basic principles involved in mapping the justice sector, prosecution initiatives, truth commissions, vetting, and monitoring legal systems. OHCHR further initiated development of additional two policy tools on the legacy of hybrid courts, and on reparations programmes. OHCHR has been also collaborating with DPKO in the development of a performance measurement system for the justice sector in post-conflict States. In March 2006, my Office took part in the negotiations in Bujumbura between the United Nations and the Government of Burundi on the establishment and operation of a Truth and Reconciliation Commission and a Special Tribunal in Burundi as provided for in Security Council resolution 1606 (2005).

59. OHCHR has continued to examine the question of the protection of human rights and fundamental freedoms while countering terrorism and to make recommendations about the obligations of States in this regard, including through my annual reports to the General Assembly and the Commission on Human Rights. The Office supports the work of the Human Rights Council and its special procedures mandates, as well as the human rights treaty bodies and the Subcommission on the Promotion and Protection of Human Rights, in addressing a broad range of issues related to the impact of terrorism on human rights. OHCHR has worked with UNODC to deliver a specialized training programme for judges and prosecutors, and is developing a number of tools such as fact sheets on terrorism and human rights, and on the relationship between international humanitarian law and human rights law. The Office participated in a meeting organized by UNODC for West and Central African Governments in May 2006 on national legal frameworks for countering terrorism.

OHCHR together with OSCE-ODIHR is organizing an expert workshop, which will aim to enhance understanding and awareness of human rights norms and standards in international cooperation in relation to counter-terrorism, in particular among security experts and legal advisers from relevant national ministries, law enforcement and the judiciary.

60. In my Plan of Action, I identified democratic deficits as a main challenge to human rights. OHCHR provides dedicated support to the United Nations Democracy Fund (UNDEF) established by the Secretary-General in July 2005. OHCHR plays an active role in the Programme Advisory Group advising on programme funding criteria and on project proposals. OHCHR also seconded one senior staff member to work in the UNDEF secretariat.

G. Human rights responsibilities of business

61. I am pleased to note that the United Nations Global Compact initiative has now been endorsed by all Heads of State and Government of the United Nations as well as by the General Assembly. Over the past year, OHCHR worked closely with the Global Compact Office and with members of the business community to enhance the understanding of human rights and to develop tools for companies committed to incorporate human rights into the core of their operations.

62. OHCHR also assisted the work of the Special Representative of the Secretary-General on the issue of human rights and transnational corporations and other business enterprises. The interim report of the Special Representative contained a persuasive analysis of the broad contextual factors framing the issue of human rights and business.

Chapter IV

Establishment of the Human Rights Council, Universal Periodic Review and review of mandates and mechanisms

63. Following the decision to establish a Human Rights Council, my Office played a central role in ensuring the smooth transition from the Commission on Human Rights to the Human Rights Council and provided substantive and technical support to the Council at its inaugural session held from 19 to 30 June 2006, as well as its first two special sessions on the situation of human rights in the Palestinian and other occupied Arab territories (5-6 July 2006) and in Lebanon (11 August 2006).

64. The Council has quickly acted in accordance with the mandate entrusted to it by the Assembly—that of promoting universal respect for the protection of all human rights and fundamental freedoms—with such notable achievements as the adoption of the Convention for the Protection of All Persons from Enforced Disappearance and the United Nations Declaration on the Rights of Indigenous Peoples.

65. The Council has also taken initial, yet critical, steps towards addressing the many complex procedural issues that accompany the establishment of a new and strengthened intergovernmental human rights body: the development of a programme of work for the first year; the extension for one year of all mandates, mechanisms, functions and responsibilities of the former Commission on Human Rights to prevent any gap in human rights protection during this transitional period; and the establishment of two intersessional

open-ended intergovernmental working groups to review all such mandates and mechanisms above and to develop the modalities of the universal periodic review (UPR).

66. OHCHR will support the work of those two intergovernmental working groups. including through preparing background information on the functioning of the mandates and mechanisms of the former Commission, and on existing review mechanisms in other international or regional organizations for UPR. It is also compiling the contributions of all stakeholders as an input to both working groups.

67. In relation to the review of mandates and mechanisms, it should be noted that special procedures constitute an essential element of the United Nations efforts to protect and promote human rights, as well as a unique mechanism to monitor the human rights situation worldwide. The foundation of this system is the independence and expertise of special procedures mandate-holders. Another unique feature of the special procedures system is the direct accessibility of mandate-holders, as supported by OHCHR, including through the communications mechanism. Mandate-holders are also frequently and directly in contact with Governments and other stakeholders. A number of violations faced by individuals have been successfully addressed and remedies initiated accordingly.

68. Notwithstanding the achievements of the special-procedures system, various stakeholders, including the OHCHR, have identified ways to strengthen it. It is expected that the limitation of the terms of tenure of mandate-holders to a maximum of six years would continue, as this was a major step taken to reinforce independence. My Office can maintain and regularly update a roster of suitable and experienced experts who possess the relevant expertise. It could also constitute an advisory panel chaired by me and composed of experts from all regions which would establish a shortlist of candidates for submission to the Chairperson of the Council.

69. The Human Rights Council will want to ensure, to the fullest extent possible, universal coverage of human rights issues while focusing on those human rights situations and countries that warrant special attention. Thematic mandates can broadly reflect the equal importance of civil and political, and economic, social and cultural rights and attempt to ensure that there is balanced geographic coverage. At the same time, there is a need to help identify potential gaps in protection, for example in relation to specific groups of persons, or specific countries that face major challenges. In order to support this universal coverage and close any protection gap, the Human Rights Council could encourage States to increase their cooperation, and to regularly extend invitations, in particular standing invitations, to mandate-holders.

70. Confidence-building measures among special procedures and Governments and other stakeholders can lead to more comprehensive interactive dialogue, better sharing of information and views with stakeholders and the timely preparation of visits with the involvement of all concerned parties.

71. Further interaction among different mandate-holders could also be facilitated between different mandate-holders.

72. My Office has already supported measures that ensure maximum efficiency of the system. To facilitate internal communication and collaboration, mandate-holders established a Coordination Committee at their annual meeting in 2005. OHCHR developed

communication tools for, and with, the mandate-holders, and created a centralized quick-response desk for communications with Member States. Mandate-holders are also in the process of revising their Manual, which includes guidelines and agreed methods of work and OHCHR is coordinating a public consultation process in this regard. My Office has also enhanced its website, including on good practices and positive developments.

73. I share the view of many States that, in addition to the outcome of the review of mandates and mechanisms, the ultimate test for the Council will be the establishment of the UPR mechanism by which all States will be subject to a periodic review of the fulfilment of their human rights obligations and commitments. The international community has high expectations of UPR, including that it will redress the selectivity and over-politicization, particularly in the consideration of human rights situations in countries, which had plagued the former Commission. Whether this will be the case depends very much on whether two critical elements, universality of coverage and the equal treatment of all Member States, are guaranteed and fully integrated into the new mechanism from the outset.

74. Much thought has already been devoted to the possible modalities and process of UPR and efforts in this area will intensify over the next few months. A range of options have already been presented on such issues as periodicity of review, sources of information for review, process, mechanism and actors to conduct the review, as well as outcomes and follow-up. All the options and formulas on the table have their merits and present a number of challenges. Whatever modalities are developed for UPR, the process that will be agreed upon in the end should be inclusive, results-oriented, well-structured, manageable and transparent. In this regard, several key elements should be emphasized.

75. The willingness of countries under review to open themselves to genuine scrutiny which, in turn, might prompt remedial action, is crucial for the success and effectiveness of UPR. Countries should be assessed on the basis of human rights instruments to which they are parties and other obligations, as well as the 2005 Summit Outcome Document and States' voluntary pledges and commitments to the Council, if any. The result should both yield a full picture of a country's human rights situation, and help to identify gaps that may require concerted action to improve protection capacity.

76. Further, while UPR should be made an integral component of the United Nations human rights system, it is important to maximize resources and methods so as to attain synergy and complementarity, rather than overlap and duplication, with other human rights mechanisms, in particular the special procedures and treaty bodies. Collectively, the interaction and combined outcomes of these three sets of protection mechanisms are designed to help—and when necessary to persuade—States to fulfil their human rights obligations and responsibilities, and to offer a comprehensive understanding of country situations.

77. The Council should benefit from the reports and findings of the special procedures, including with respect to responses to urgent situations. The periodicity of Council sessions should allow for the development of new modalities for enhanced interaction with special procedures. For this purpose consideration might be given to the establishment of a special segment devoted to the discussion of key concerns with mandate-holders at each of the sessions envisaged by the Council throughout the year. Special procedures could, directly or through their Coordination Committee, also contribute through prioritizing countries pending UPR in their plan of work; or through considering to issue an update for those

countries already visited, which are being reviewed. Not only could UPR make use of their findings, conclusions and recommendations, but mandate-holders could be involved in its deliberations. The discussions and outcome of UPR could provide an incentive for States to follow up on recommendations by special procedures.

78. UPR should not undermine or make less effective the reporting procedures of the seven human rights treaty bodies. States should not reduce cooperation with the treaty-based procedures when they are under review through UPR. It should not become a means to challenge the decisions and recommendations of the treaty bodies, but should place emphasis on the follow-up to such decisions and recommendations. To the extent that countries appear before the Council on a regular basis, the follow-up procedures of the treaty bodies could be significantly strengthened. Thus, a Council recommendation requesting a State to implement a particular treaty body recommendation with immediate effect would contribute to reinforcing the efficacy of the treaty-based mechanisms.

79. I remain confident that the UPR mechanism will develop into a significant, constructive and highly visible activity of the Council.

Chapter V

Treaty body reform

80. In my Plan of Action, I indicated that I would develop proposals for a unified standing treaty body and invite all States parties to the seven principal human rights treaties to consider holding an intergovernmental meeting.

81. My proposal is based on the premise that, in spite of its achievements, the system currently faces serious challenges. Some are linked to its success, and stem from the increase in human rights instruments and the increasing number of States assuming new legal obligations. New bodies to monitor the draft treaties on disappearances and disability as well as the Subcommittee on Prevention established under the Optional Protocol to the Convention against Torture, which entered into force on 22 June 2006, were recently created. Many States accept the treaty body system on a purely formal level, but do not engage with it, or do so in a superficial way, either because of insufficient resources or absence of political will. Many States parties consider that the reporting procedures of the treaty bodies are overly burdensome and duplicative, and many reports remain overdue. I consider a unified standing treaty body to be a solution, which could address these challenges.

82. OHCHR has convened, or participated in, a number of consultations on the proposal for a unified standing body. In March 2006, I circulated a concept paper on the proposal to all stakeholders, and solicited feedback. The Fifth Inter-Committee Meeting and the Eighteenth Meeting of Chairpersons of treaty bodies discussed the concept paper in some depth. Further discussion on the concept paper and other possible solutions to achieve a more unified treaty body system took place at an informal brainstorming meeting convened in Liechtenstein from 14 to 16 July 2006.

83. The concept paper will be complemented by several option papers. An informal paper detailing the legal options for, and obstacles to, a unified standing body was prepared with inputs from the Office of Legal Affairs. The legal options paper was discussed in Liechtenstein in a preliminary way.

84. Some treaty body members welcomed my proposal; others have opposed it, mostly on the basis that a unified standing body could undermine the specificity of the seven major human rights instruments. A similar division of opinion on my proposal exists among States and in the NGO community.

85. A proposal for the creation of a single body for consideration of individual complaints only, put forward by the Committee on the Elimination of Racial Discrimination has attracted some support, while most reform options essentially focus on the harmonization of working methods.

86. While it is premature to draw definitive conclusions, it appears that the proposal for a unified standing treaty body that would unify both reporting and complaints procedures may not be achievable in the short term.

87. In the meantime, OHCHR has continued to support harmonization of the reporting guidelines of all treaty bodies, with a view to rationalizing reporting for States parties. A working group composed of one member of each of the seven treaty bodies met in December 2005 and February 2006 to finalize the harmonized reporting guidelines. The Fifth Inter-Committee Meeting considered the revised draft guidelines for a Common Core Document and targeted treaty-specific reports and recommended that all treaty bodies apply the guidelines in a flexible way, review their own respective guidelines for initial and for periodic reports, and signal indications of any difficulties with their implementation. The experience of each treaty body with the implementation of the Consolidated Guidelines will be reviewed by the Seventh Inter-Committee Meeting in 2008.

88. Several States parties have indicated their interest in training on the Common Core Document and to date OHCHR has conducted courses in Angola, Nicaragua and Panama.

Chapter VI

Country engagement

89. The period under review marks a landmark in the development of the capacity of the United Nations to protect and promote all human rights for all. The establishment of the Human Rights Council has given practical expression to the Charter's recognition of human rights as an equal aspect of the Organization's functions and responsibilities, alongside security and development. The establishment of the Council raises numerous implications for the conduct of its future work, its methodology and ultimately its results. The period of transition poses particular challenges in ensuring that the successes of past experience are retained and strengthened, and that the failings of the past do not weaken the new and upgraded architecture of protection and promotion of human rights.

90. My Office is closely involved in these issues and the reform and review processes emerging from them, drawing on the full range of its experience in the areas of country engagement, thematic expertise and servicing of the special procedures and human rights treaty bodies.

91. The period under review has highlighted a variety of country-specific concerns, where OHCHR's engagement with Governments and civil society has provided appropriate support and assistance to States seeking to enhance the protection and promotion of human

rights enjoyed by persons in those countries. OHCHR has continued to strengthen its capacities in a variety of areas posing particularly stark human rights challenges in the contemporary world.

92. Finally, the very welcome recent additions to the catalogue of international human rights instruments require OHCHR to play its part in making the rights recognized therein a reality.

93. In this report I have sought to inform members of the General Assembly of the progress made over the last year in implementing my Plan of Action and the OHCHR Strategic Management Plan. I urge members of the Assembly to join in our efforts over the coming years to enable a stronger and better equipped Office, able to meet the human rights needs of States, institutional partners and civil society, but first and foremost those of the rights-holders, in particular victims of human rights violations everywhere.

---

[1] A/61/120.

[2] CMW/C/MLI/CO/1.

5. Report of the United Nations High Commissioner for Refugees, 2005–2006 (A/61/12)

Note

Symbols of United Nations documents are composed of capital letters combined with figures. Mention of such asymbol indicates a reference to a United Nations document.

I. Introduction

1. On World Refugee Day in June 2006, the High Commissioner reported that global refugee numbers are now the lowest they have been for over 25 years, and that in 2005, mass outflows of new refugees into neighbouring States were the lowest for 29 years.

2. More than 6 million refugees have been able to go home since 2002. Yet for many repatriating populations, return may be even more of a struggle than exile if the international community does not continue to nurture their reintegration and support the receiving communities. A cooking pot and a few seeds do not go far when a family returns home to rebuild its life in the midst of widespread devastation. UNHCR will continue to call on governments and development agency partners to include refugees and returnees in reconstruction strategies and thereby help ensure that return is a lasting solution.

3. One of the weightiest questions today for the international community is how to tackle the plight of millions of internally displaced persons. While the Office has helped hundreds of thousands of internally displaced individuals and families go home, tens of millions more are still living like refugees within their own borders. They need much more help than they have traditionally received, and UNHCR intends to do its share.

4. Motivated by a mutual desire for more predictable and effective response to situations of internal displacement, the Inter-Agency Standing Committee (IASC) has steered concerned member agencies towards a new framework for collaborative action under the cluster leadership approach. Ironically, as if nature echoed the need for the world to unite its efforts to improve the lot of vulnerable people, two major natural disasters in the past 18 months also brought nations and agencies together in an unprecedented joint relief response. However, UNHCR's key role is where displacement is caused by conflict; and this is where the Office will more systematically take the lead on protection, camp coordination and management, and emergency shelter.

5. In other situations across the world, as migration flows grow ever more complex, there is a tendency for the general public to confuse economic migrants and asylum-seekers fleeing persecution. And so long as desperate people depart on hazardous voyages, whether by land or across the seas, UNHCR must ensure that asylum-seekers have access to proper status determination procedures and to find appropriate responses. Protection is at the core of the Office's humanitarian mandate.

II. Focus and objectives of report

6. This report provides an account of activities undertaken by UNHCR between January 2005 and mid-2006 in response to the needs of a global population of 20.8 million[1] persons

of concern. It describes major developments with respect to protection, assistance and the search for durable solutions for refugees and others of concern. It also reviews partnerships and coordination within and beyond the United Nations system and provides an update on current management and oversight issues. More detailed information on regional and country activities and global priorities may be found in UNHCR's Global Report 2005 and Global Appeal 2006, and in the various reports presented to UNHCR's governance body, the Executive Committee of the High Commissioner's Programme, and its Standing Committee. All of these reports are available on the Office's website: *http://www.unhcr.org*.

III. International protection

7. While the protection environment improved in many areas in 2005-2006, UNHCR continued to face significant challenges in filling gaps in protection. Sexual and gender-based violence (SGBV) and exploitation remained pervasive problems for populations of concern globally and were often linked to restricted livelihood alternatives and sub-standard food rations. Despite dramatic drops in the number of asylum applications, people in need of international protection continued to encounter restrictive practices with regard to reception and access to asylum procedures. In some regions, there were instances of detention and *refoulement* in countries that previously had a good record of respect for refugee rights.

8. UNHCR has taken a number of steps to "operationalize protection" to ensure that it can continue to strengthen its protection capacity in the light of changing developments. These steps include systematizing dialogue on cross-cutting issues at the most senior levels of management within UNHCR, establishing a Field Reference Group on Protection Policies, developing a protection monitoring tool, and creating an innovative age, gender and diversity mainstreaming (AGDM) accountability framework.

9. At its October 2005 session, UNHCR's Executive Committee adopted two thematic Conclusions, in addition to the General Conclusion on International Protection (A/AC.96/1021, paras.20-22). One sets out the general principles upon which complementary forms of protection should be based, the other framework considerations for implementing local integration. In its General Conclusion, the Committee encouraged States, UNHCR, other intergovernmental and non-governmental organizations (NGOs) to cooperate and to redouble their efforts to implement the Agenda for Protection (A/AC.96/965/Add.1), to provide information on their follow-up activities and to explore with UNHCR the merits of a consolidated report to the Executive Committee on its implementation.

10. A detailed overview of developments from mid-2005 to mid-2006 is contained in UNHCR's annual Note on International Protection (A/AC.96/1024). The following paragraphs give a brief overview of challenges encountered and measures undertaken in relation to these developments, broadly following the six goals of the Agenda for Protection.

A. Strengthening implementation of the 1951 Convention and 1967 Protocol

11. With the accession of Afghanistan to the 1951 Convention and its 1967 Protocol, 146 States were parties to one or both of these instruments; yet there remain regions where accession is rare. UNHCR continued its efforts to promote accession, including through refugee law courses for government officials.

12. To facilitate a more harmonized interpretation of the 1951 Convention, UNHCR issued Guidelines on International Protection on the eligibility of victims of or persons at risk of trafficking, clarifying the application of the refugee criteria to individuals based on actual or feared trafficking experience and elaborating procedural standards for handling asylum claims of female and child victims of trafficking. UNHCR also made legal interventions in the courts of a number of asylum countries and at the European Court of Human Rights.

13. The reporting period witnessed further restrictions on access to and enjoyment of asylum against a backdrop of growing national concerns with security issues. In a number of asylum countries, UNHCR advocated the proper use of the exclusion clauses of the 1951 Convention as an appropriate means of dealing with individuals not deserving of international protection. Incidents of *refoulement* were reported while in some countries access to territory or asylum procedures was limited by practical measures or new legal restrictions. UNHCR intensified its advocacy on these issues, notably through training activities with border officials and the police.

14. The Office was involved in refugee status determination (RSD) in 78 countries, rendering decisions for some 60,000 people in 2005. The challenge remains to pursue a timely and properly resourced transfer of responsibility to national authorities. UNHCR expanded training and capacity building of its staff and protection partners and initiated a revision of its various protection learning programmes.

15. UNHCR's recently published Operational Protection Reference Guide provides a compendium of good practices on field-level protection in camps and settlements, covering issues ranging from the administration of justice to prevention of and response to SGBV. A Note on HIV/AIDS and the Protection of Refugees, IDPs and Other Persons of Concern has also been issued to help address a number of specific protection problems, including threats of *refoulement* based on HIV status as well as discrimination and breaches of confidentiality.

B. Protecting refugees within broader migration movements

16. The continuing loss of lives of people attempting to cross the seas in various parts of the world such as the Mediterranean, the Gulf of Aden, the coast of West Africa, and the Caribbean, demanded increased focus on the complexities of managing large-scale mixed population movements and combating smuggling and human trafficking. The relatively large numbers of maritime arrivals tested the capacities of some coastal States and, in some situations, countries of transit and destination reacted to increased migration pressures through interceptions and expulsions risking *refoulement* of refugees and asylum-seekers. UNHCR sought to engage governments at both regional and national levels to raise awareness of international protection needs and responsibilities, and to promote regional cooperation for comprehensive approaches to the problem.

17. As a founding member of the Global Migration Group, comprised of 10 organizations actively involved in international migration and related issues, UNHCR contributed to preparations for the 2006 General Assembly High-Level Dialogue on International Migration and Development. Pursuant to its mandate for refugee protection, UNHCR also undertook activities to build the capacity of States to identify asylum-seekers and

refugees amidst broader migration movements and to protect them in line with international standards.

18. UNHCR and the International Organization for Migration (IOM) continued efforts to strengthen cooperation with regard to broader migration movements. A bilateral working group has been established to encourage closer cooperation between the two organizations in addressing the "asylum-migration nexus" in the North African region. One successful example of collaboration has been the establishment, with the support of the Italian Government, of a joint IOM/Italian Red Cross/UNHCR monitoring and screening mechanism on the Mediterranean island of Lampedusa, where 22,000 spontaneous arrivals were recorded in 2005.

19. UNHCR worked within the United Nations system, with other organizations, including IOM, the International Centre for Migration Policy Development (ICMPD), the Organization for Security and Cooperation in Europe (OSCE), and with NGO partners, to ensure that legislation to criminalize trafficking includes measures to protect and support victims of trafficking.

C. Sharing burdens and responsibilities more equitably and building capacities to receive and protect refugees

20. In a significant example of burden and responsibility sharing, 439 Uzbeks who had fled to the Kyrgyz Republic in July 2005 were evacuated by UNHCR to Romania, where status determination and resettlement procedures were carried out in a safe environment while other countries rallied to realize protection for this group through resettlement. By early May 2006, 359 of the refugees had been resettled.

21. UNHCR's Strengthening Protection Capacity Project (SPCP) consolidated and expanded its work to develop and pilot a comprehensive and sustainable capacity-building methodology with practical and long-term deliverables. Within the United Nations system, UNHCR collaborated with other entities to maximize synergies capitalizing on respective competencies, such as in reintegration activities in post-conflict situations where UNHCR is increasingly working within the United Nations Development Assistance Framework (UNDAF) to ensure that the specific needs of returnees are incorporated into national development plans. At the national level, partnerships with civil society included, in particular, local NGOs, many of which are implementing partners.

D. Addressing security-related concerns more effectively

22. Whether through armed attacks or military infiltration, the security of refugees and IDPs in many countries was threatened. Nowhere was this more daunting than in the Darfur region of Sudan and in eastern Chad. In northern Central African Republic, banditry and lawlessness prompted Chadian refugees to repatriate despite earlier intentions to integrate locally. SGBV remained prevalent in many camps. Security of staff and beneficiaries remained a concern: in Southern Sudan a staff member and a guard were killed in an attack on the UNHCR office in Yei. In Cairo, a three-month protest by Sudanese asylum-seekers beside the UNHCR office was forcibly broken up by local authorities, resulting in the death of 27 people.

23. Of particular concern was the forced military recruitment of children, in response to which UNHCR stepped up its interventions, including through joint advocacy and monitoring

with the United Nations Children's Fund (UNICEF). Strengthening response and preventive mechanisms to address SGBV, including domestic violence, also remained one of UNHCR's top priorities. Efforts were made to sensitize refugee and local communities, as well as relevant government officials, police, lawyers, and the judiciary on how best to address SGBV issues.

E. Redoubling the search for durable solutions

24. Large-scale voluntary repatriation movements which took place during the reporting period attested to UNHCR's invigorated focus on finding durable solutions. Unfortunately, the displacement of all too many refugees and IDPs remained protracted. Nearly 5 million refugees were living in such circumstances during the reporting period. Major populations included Afghans (1.7 million), Burundians (394,000), Congolese (DRC) (308,000), Somalis (229,000) and Sudanese (364,000).

25. Working with States to identify comprehensive approaches for specific caseloads, making complementary use of all three durable solutions, remains a major challenge. The protracted confinement of refugees to camps and closed settlements is a severe restriction of their rights. It is important, however, to acknowledge the concerns of refugee-hosting States. Countries of asylum need help to overcome numerous obstacles that prevent them from finding alternatives to closed camps. They need to be assisted and encouraged to allow refugees greater freedom of movement, access to social services and the right to earn a living. As part of ongoing efforts to give focus to comprehensive approaches to durable solutions, the restructuring of UNHCR's Department of International Protection included the creation of a Solutions and Operations Support Section charged primarily with reviewing protracted refugee situations; the restructuring also provides an enhanced Resettlement Service.

26. Voluntary repatriation or return continued to be the durable solution which benefited the largest number of refugees and IDPs while resettlement remained a key instrument of international protection and responsibility sharing, and an important durable solution for refugees. New opportunities opened up for the pursuit of local integration. Self-reliance enhanced the protection of a number of refugees pending a durable solution and also brought benefits to local communities.

F. Meeting the protection needs of refugee women and refugee children

27. The protection of women and children of concern remained a core activity and an organizational priority for UNHCR. The Office adopted a two-pronged approach of AGDM and targeted action to empower women to realize their rights, as well as to increase children's participation and respect for their rights (see also Chapter V.H below). A rights and community-based approach underpins UNHCR's work to ensure partnership with the community through mobilizing all members and building on their capacities and resources to strengthen the protection of women and children. While the High Commissioner's Five Commitments to refugee women continued to guide prioritization, the issuance of the Secretary-General's action plan (S/2005/636) on women and peace and security implementing Security Council resolution 1325(2000) further reinforced the Office's strategic directions within a United Nations system-wide framework.

28. Various initiatives were also taken during the reporting period to enhance the protection of refugee and asylum-seeking children, including those who were unaccompanied or separated. In May 2006, in collaboration with the International Committee of the Red Cross (ICRC), UNICEF and the Committee on the Rights of the Child as well as various NGOs, UNHCR released guidelines on the Formal Determination of the Best Interests of the Child, which outline the standards to follow when dealing with unaccompanied and separated children, in particular to identify a durable solution. Major concerns included forced military recruitment of children in camps, exploitation and abuse, child labour and school dropout rates, particularly of girls. Efforts were made to address these issues by sensitizing the community, reinforcing vocational training, providing psychosocial support and organizing more recreational facilities.

IV. Populations of concern

29. Table 1 at the end of this report reflects end-of-year figures for the populations of concern to UNHCR in 2005 across the world. For more detailed statistical information, please refer to UNHCR's 2005 Global Refugee Trends report published on 9 June 2006 and available at *http://www.unhcr.org/statistics*. All data presented should be considered provisional.

30. For the second year running, the total population of concern to UNHCR increased, from 19.5 million persons at the beginning of 2005 to 20.8 million by the end of 2005. By the end of the year, refugees[2] constituted 40 per cent of the total population of concern to UNHCR, down from 49 per cent at the beginning of 2005. IDPs were the second largest group, accounting for 32 per cent of the total number, followed by stateless persons[3] at 11 per cent.

31. Thus, while refugees still constitute the largest group of people for whom the Office is responsible under its mandate, the current trend indicates that in future, UNHCR's involvement with internally displaced populations is likely to expand, as the international community hones its approach to addressing the needs of IDPs.

32. The number of other persons of concern categorized in the table under the heading "Various" increased by 58 per cent in 2005 to over 960,000. This increase primarily reflected the newly included persons of concern from Colombia in Ecuador (250,000) and in the Bolivarian Republic of Venezuela (an increased estimate from 26,400 to 200,000). These persons had not formally applied for asylum for various reasons, including security concerns, despite being in need of international protection.

V. Operations, durable solutions and global priorities

33. This section of the report describes and comments on key operational developments and strategic responses to ongoing challenges, notably UNHCR's global priorities. It does not attempt to elaborate on details of the different operational situations and responses, which are covered more comprehensively in the Global Report 2005 and the Global Appeal 2006.

A. New refugee outflows

34. The level of new refugee outflows in 2005 was the lowest since 1976. A total of 136,000 *prima facie* refugee arrivals were recorded in 19 asylum countries, notably Chad (32,400), Benin (25,500), Uganda (24,000), Ghana (13,600) and Yemen (13,200).

35. The ongoing conflict in the Darfur region of Sudan continued to cause particular concern during the reporting period. The steady decline in the security situation in the Chad/Darfur area included instances of military recruitment in the refugee camps in eastern Chad, which also triggered the displacement of 15,000 Chadians into west Darfur as well as tens of thousands of Chadians within Chad itself. Instability in the north of the Central African Republic continued to cause further refugee movements into Chad. In parts of Somalia, Côte d'Ivoire and the Democratic Republic of the Congo, violence continued to drive people from their homes. In the first half of 2005, some 40,000 persons fled from Togo, but a recent verification exercise in Benin and Ghana revealed that half of the refugees had returned spontaneously or moved to other African countries.

B. Internally displaced persons

36. Under the IASC's cluster leadership initiative, UNHCR assumed the global cluster lead for conflict-induced internal displacement situations in the areas of protection, camp management/coordination and emergency shelter. Thus, while estimated numbers of IDPs worldwide amount to some 24 million, at the end of 2005, UNHCR offices reported on some 6.6 million IDPs protected and assisted by the Office in 16 countries. This represents an increase of 22 per cent from the previous year, reflecting in particular the newly reported IDP situations in Iraq (1.2 million) and in Somalia (400,000). Several countries reported a decrease in IDP numbers, including Liberia (-261,000), the Russian Federation (-164,000) and Bosnia and Herzegovina (-126,500). No significant change, however, was recorded in Colombia[4] (over 2 million IDPs) or in Azerbaijan (almost 580,000).

37. In January 2006, UNHCR undertook its cluster leadership roles in Uganda, Liberia, the Democratic Republic of the Congo and later in Somalia. In the Darfur region of Sudan, the number of IDPs recorded by UNHCR increased to 842,000. Security problems restricted access, leaving serious protection problems. In Côte d'Ivoire, access constraints have also arisen, highlighting the need to be attentive to maintaining humanitarian space. In Timor-Leste, the situation remains very volatile and the political uncertainty has given rise to continuing waves of violence and some hesitance on the part of IDPs to return. In mid-2006 in Lebanon, UNHCR began leading the protection and emergency shelter clusters during the crisis which led to the displacement of some 700,000 persons.

C. Voluntary repatriation

38. An estimated 1.1 million refugees repatriated voluntarily to their country of origin during 2005. The main returns were to Afghanistan (752,100), Liberia (70,300), Burundi (68,300), Iraq (56,200) and Angola (53,800).

39. Recent years have seen extraordinary levels of voluntary repatriation, mainly due to the return of over 4.2 million Afghans from neighbouring countries. In 2005, half a million Afghans returned home; however in 2006 there has been a decrease in the number of returns, and repatriation of the remaining 3.5 million Afghans is likely to pose different challenges. Insecurity in parts of Afghanistan and poverty amongst the resident populations will have to be addressed and policy interventions will be required to manage continuing cross-border migration. The support and solidarity of the international community has played a very important role in addressing these challenges to date and its continued engagement in recovery support, in close consultation with the States of the region, will be

equally critical in the future. The London Compact of January 2006 signals an important commitment in this respect, and further progress in security, governance and human rights will also help support return and reintegration.

40. However, UNHCR is keenly aware that the achievement of return home for large numbers of refugees or IDPs is only possible when adequate conditions of peace exist—usually brokered through a combination of determined political leadership and sustained international support. In Sri Lanka, the escalation of violence in mid-2006 has brought renewed internal displacement and the suspension of the return programme for Sri Lankan refugees from southern India.

41. New voluntary repatriation operations launched or expanded during the year included those to Southern Sudan and to the Democratic Republic of the Congo. In Liberia and Burundi, the Office shifted from facilitating repatriation operations to actively promoting returns once conditions were judged adequate to enable return in safety and dignity. Nevertheless, the sustainability of repatriation remains particularly vulnerable when there is neither infrastructure nor any livelihood opportunities to go back to—as is the case in Southern Sudan. It is thus paramount to have strategies and development actors involved early enough so that a recurrence of conflict and renewed flight can be mitigated.

D. Local integration

42. Local integration is a legal, economic, social and cultural process offering a durable solution for refugees which can also be beneficial to host populations. The Executive Committee adopted a Conclusion on Local Integration in October 2005 which set out a framework for facilitating local integration. Naturalization is the final step in achieving local integration. However, statistical data on naturalized refugees is only available on a limited scale, primarily because national statistics generally do not differentiate between naturalized refugees and non-refugees. Such information should be considered as indicative only. During 2005, UNHCR was informed of the following significant numbers of refugees being granted citizenship by the host country: United States (58,900 from January to September); Turkmenistan (10,000); Kyrgyzstan (3,400); Armenia (2,300); Belgium (2,300); Mexico (1,200) and Ireland (580).

E. Resettlement

43. In 2005, some 30,500 refugees were resettled with the assistance of UNHCR. The main nationalities benefiting from UNHCR-facilitated resettlement were refugees from Somalia (5,900); Liberia (4,700); Sudan (3,200); Afghanistan (3,200) and Myanmar (2,900). The largest numbers of resettlement departures were from Kenya (6,800); Thailand (2,500); Guinea (1,900); Ghana (1,800) and Egypt (1,300). During 2005, a total of 16 countries reported the admission of resettled refugees: these included the United States (53,800 during the US fiscal year and including family reunification); Australia (11,700); Canada (10,400); Sweden (1,300), Finland (770); Norway (750) and the Netherlands (420).

44. UNHCR is pursuing its efforts to expand the use of resettlement as a tool of international protection, as a durable solution, and as a burden and responsibility sharing mechanism, inter alia by further diversifying the nationalities of refugees being resettled and the number of countries receiving resettled refugees. In some cases it has used a group referral methodology. One concrete outcome of these efforts was the emergency resettlement operation for Uzbek

refugees initiated in July 2005. Another encouraging example was the resettlement of a number of emergency cases in Morocco to two western European countries.

F. Prevention and reduction of statelessness and protection of Stateless persons

45. Senegal and Romania acceded to the 1954 Convention on the Status of Stateless Persons and to the 1961 Convention on the Reduction of Statelessness, bringing the number of States Parties to these Conventions to 59 and 31 respectively. UNHCR provided advice on the drafting of the Council of Europe Convention on the Avoidance of Statelessness in relation to State Succession as well as a Resolution on legal identity and statelessness of the Asian-African Legal Consultative Organization. UNHCR and the Inter-Parliamentary Union launched a new Handbook on nationality and statelessness to provide guidance for parliamentarians to prevent and reduce statelessness when revising citizenship laws as well as practical examples of initiatives to do so. UNHCR continued to provide specific advice to States on the drafting and amendment of nationality laws. The Office worked with specific States to prevent new cases of statelessness arising, particularly in situations of State succession and to protect the rights of stateless persons.

46. In pursuit of its mandate to contribute to the prevention and reduction of statelessness, UNHCR has expanded its data collection mechanism with the aim of identifying stateless persons more systematically. In 2005, available data indicated an estimated 1.5 million people in 30 countries. At the end of 2005, the numbers reported in 47 countries had risen to 2.4 million, and it is expected that figures will continue to increase as new data becomes available. At the same time, the Office assisted concerned States in reducing protracted situations of statelessness by resolving the nationality status of statelessness populations on their territories.

G. Linking humanitarian assistance to longer term development

47. UNHCR continues to promote and implement the strategies outlined in its May 2003 Framework for Durable Solutions: Development Assistance for Refugees (DAR); Repatriation, Reintegration, Rehabilitation and Reconstruction (4Rs) and Development through Local Integration (DLI).

48. In 2005 the 4Rs approach was reviewed in Afghanistan, Eritrea, Sierra Leone and Sri Lanka. This experience is now influencing the design, implementation and evaluation of voluntary repatriation programmes in the Democratic Republic of the Congo, Liberia, Somalia and Southern Sudan and is being complemented by the introduction of AGDM participatory assessment in further attempts to empower refugees to play an active role in rebuilding their lives and livelihoods. To promote livelihood strategies, UNHCR has been building networks and seeking partnerships in order to expand livelihood opportunities, notably in relation to youth employment and microcredit schemes. Nevertheless, in some situations, the slow implementation of rehabilitation and reconstruction initiatives threatens the sustainability of the reintegration of those who have repatriated.

49. In the same spirit, efforts are being focused on mainstreaming a self-reliance approach in assistance programmes. In Ecuador, for example, a DAR programme has been established in areas hosting Colombian refugees pursuant to the 2004 Mexico Declaration and Plan of Action. In Africa, an evaluation of the Zambia Initiative, designed to encourage donors and development partners to contribute to the development of refugee-hosting areas

in the western part of the country, was completed and will be available later in 2006. Other countries in Africa, including the United Republic of Tanzania and the southern part of Chad, as well as several eastern European countries, are also being considered as potential areas for the development of self-reliance and livelihood strategies for refugees, IDPs and returnees.

H. Global priorities and responses to operational challenges

Identifying and measuring progress on global priorities and strategic objectives

50. Standards and indicators are among the systems and tools being developed to enable UNHCR to measure progress against strategic and operational objectives and to improve its ability to report on results. The second edition of UNHCR's practical guide on using this measurement framework has been produced with the inclusion of additional indicators, notably those covering situations of return and urban refugees, and the Office will continue to build on this as a basis for future results-based reporting. The Annual Protection Report has been redesigned to better capture baseline data relating to the protection of asylum-seekers, refugees, IDPs, returnees and stateless persons.

Registration

51. UNHCR's software registration tool "*proGres*" has now been implemented in over 120 individual sites in over 40 country operations. Work continues on mainstreaming key registration activities into field operations, including the use of biometrics; the issuance of identity documents; and the development of standardized reports to further enhance delivery of protection and durable solutions.

Refugee women, refugee children, community development and education

52. In 2005 UNHCR continued to focus on implementing the action plan to address the critical areas highlighted by the three evaluations on refugee women, refugee children and the role of the community services through a parallel approach of mainstreaming and targeted action to support discriminated groups. By the end of 2006, over 90 countries should be participating in the AGDM project. Part of the AGDM strategy is to develop an accountability framework with a reporting mechanism for senior managers to provide clear feedback on the completion of agreed actions to create the right conditions for promoting AGDM; the prevention of and response to SGBV; gender equality; and children's rights. This will be supported by participatory research with the direct involvement of refugee and returnee girls and boys.

53. In June 2006, the Standing Committee encouraged UNHCR to enhance its partnership with child protection agencies to build common understanding and an implementation strategy for child protection in all operations.

54. Implementation of UNHCR's education policies was strengthened in 2005 through regional workshops on the application of field guidelines and strategic partnerships on education (INSPIRE) in Colombia, and on Education and a Community Approach in Senegal. The Office is encouraging the establishment of national education committees to promote greater access for refugees to quality education. Some 1,000 students continue to receive university scholarships under the Albert Einstein German Refugee Initiative (DAFI).

Nutrition

55. To counter increasing trends of acute malnutrition and micronutrient deficiencies among refugee children and refugee women, the Office is working in collaboration with WFP to reduce the acute malnutrition rates to less than 10 per cent (measured by Z-score[5]). In June 2006, the Standing Committee adopted a decision encouraging UNHCR to pursue its efforts to meet acceptable standards related to the nutrition and health status of refugees and calling for the inclusion of all persons of concern to the Office in relevant national, regional and international initiatives, notably the Ending Child Hunger and Undernutrition Initiative (ECHUI).

Environmental concerns

56. Efforts to integrate environmental issues into field operations, in accordance with UNHCR's Environmental Guidelines revised in 2005, include a range of handbooks on Forestry, Livestock and Sustainable Agriculture. Repatriation operations in Africa will be helped to develop country-specific rehabilitation strategies in partnership with government authorities, NGOs, the World Conservation Union, UN-Habitat, the United Nations Environmental Programme and other concerned agencies.

HIV/AIDS

57. In the past year, UNHCR has introduced a planning mechanism to ensure that HIV is adequately considered as a cross-cutting issue in programme development, and a separate HIV unit has been created to expand HIV programmes in Africa and Asia. Since becoming a UNAIDS cosponsor, the Office has intensified its partnerships with several United Nations agencies andNGOs. In March 2006, the Standing Committee adopted a decision endorsing the recommendations of the Global Task Team on Improving AIDS Coordination among Multilateral Institutions and International Donors and all the related decisions of the Programme Coordinating Board.

VI. Coordination and partnerships

58. This part of the report covers some key aspects of the Office's work in partnership with coordination bodies within the United Nations system, with non-governmental organizations (NGOs) and other bilateral partnerships.

A. Coordination bodies within the United Nations system

59. UNHCR is actively supporting the current initiatives towards reform of the United Nations system and improvements to the global humanitarian response capacity. These include discussions on policy and implementation notably with regard to peace and security, system-wide coherence, development, and strengthening the Resident Coordinator and Humanitarian Coordinator (RC/HC) systems. UNHCR's involvement with the Secretary-General's High-level Panel on System-wide Coherence focuses on issues such as transition from relief to development and the RC system. The Office is also engaged in the Peacebuilding Commission, whose work should play a crucial role in supporting the sustainable reintegration of returning refugees and internally displaced populations.

60. With the support, advice and encouragement of the Executive Committee, the Office has contributed to the conceptual development and practical roll-out of the inter-agency cluster leadership approach, and has accepted to undertake the lead role in protection, in camp coordination and management, and in emergency shelter for IDPs in situations of conflict-generated displacement.

61. The Office continues to participate actively in other key coordination bodies such as the Chief Executives Board for Coordination (CEB) and its subsidiary bodies, the High-Level Committees on Programmes (HLCP) and on Management (HLCM), as well as the United Nations Development Group (UNDG) and the Executive Committee on Humanitarian Affairs (ECHA). Together with UNAIDS cosponsors and other partners, UNHCR has continued to work to combat HIV and AIDS among refugees and other persons of concern, and to ensure the inclusion of persons of concern within host country national and regional policies and programmes. It has also worked in close partnership with the United Nations common system to implement a joint structured programme to address the issue of HIV/AIDS in the workplace. UNHCR continues to function as the Secretariat of the United Nations sub-cluster on humanitarian response and post-conflict recovery in the African Union's New Partnership for Africa's Development (NEPAD) programme.

B. Bilateral partnerships

62. Bilateral collaboration is helping render UNHCR's interventions more effective in areas such as food security and nutrition (with the World Food Programme); the upholding of human rights (with the Office of the High Commissioner for Human Rights and the newly formed Human Rights Council); advocacy in combating restrictive asylum measures in response to perceived risks of terrorism (with the United Nations Office on Drugs and Crime); the rights of internally displaced persons (with the Representative of the Secretary-General on the Human Rights of Internally Displaced Persons) and in respect of the many challenges posed by the asylum-migration nexus (with IOM). Also of particular importance in many situations are UNHCR's partnerships with the Food and Agricultural Organization, the International Labour Organization, UNICEF, the United Nations Volunteers, and with ICRC and the International Federation of Red Cross and Red Crescent Societies.

C. Non-governmental organizations

63. UNHCR's partnerships with NGOs continue to evolve towards more comprehensive collaboration and involvement in the assessment, planning, implementation and evaluation phases of operations, as well as in revising various guidelines and policies. In 2005, over 20 per cent of the Office's budget was channelled through partnerships with nearly 650 NGOs, almost 80 per cent of which were national NGOs. The bulk of the funding covered education, legal assistance/protection, health and nutrition, shelter/other infrastructure, community services and transport/logistics.

VII. Management and oversight of programmes

A. Financial management

64. Financial management in UNHCR is challenged by constantly evolving demands for assistance, notably in emergency situations; unpredictable levels of voluntary contributions; and chronic underfunding of approved budgets. When currency markets are volatile, as in

2005, the difficulties of financial planning and control are further accentuated. In response, the Office has pursued careful monitoring of projected income, expenditure and fund balances throughout the financial year. At the same time, new financial monitoring and projection tools have been developed to analyse past cost trends and project future income and expenditures as well as associated risks.

65. Financially, 2005 was the most challenging year since the inception of the Unified Budget in 2000. The gap between total funds available for the 2005 Annual Programme and the Executive Committee-approved budget was US$ 102.2 million, compared to US$ 28.9 million in 2004, and unfortunately this prevented the implementation of US$ 78 million worth of planned activities.

66. At the beginning of 2005, as a precaution against potential shortfalls in the Annual Programme, spending authority was reduced for programme budgets, and non-staff administrative costs were "capped" even further. However these initial measures were not sufficient to offset currency exchange losses. While strenuously endeavouring to preserve beneficiaries from the impact, during the last quarter of the year management again reduced spending authority for both the Field and Headquarters. Although UNHCR ended the year having to borrow some US$ 12 million from the Working Capital and Guarantee Fund, with the carry-over of earmarked funds of US$ 9 million, the net deficit for 2005 was finally brought down to US$ 3 million.

67. The Supplementary Programme Budget was almost 50 per cent higher than in 2004 as there were many more situations requiring the creation of a supplementary programme in 2005. New and major supplementary programmes in 2005 included: emergency assistance to Sudanese refugees in eastern Chad and Darfur; the Indian Ocean tsunami emergency; the Iraq operation; repatriation and reintegration of Burundian refugees; return and reintegration of Sudanese refugees to Southern Sudan; the South Asia earthquake; and the UNHCR/MINURSO Western Sahara Confidence Building Measures operation.

68. Total income for 2005 amounted to just over US$ 1,216 million. Contributions and miscellaneous income (including a carry-over from 2004) provided US$ 843.6 million for the Annual Programme Budget and US$ 317.2 million for the Supplementary Programme Budgets. US$ 39.3 million was received from the United Nations Regular Budget and US$ 16.1 million was provided for Junior Professional Officers (JPOs). Expenditure in 2005 totalled US$ 1,141.6 million as shown in Table 2. Broken down by region and type of assistance, expenditure in 2005 was highest in Africa (some US$ 529 million), followed by CASWANAME (some US$ 165 million).

B. Oversight and audit

OIOS Audit Service

69. During the period 1 July 2005 to 30 June 2006, the UNHCR Audit Service of the United Nations Office of Internal Oversight Services (OIOS) covered operations and activities with expenditure amounting to US$ 172 million. OIOS audited processes and activities in over 20 UNHCR operations in the Field as well as several units at Headquarters.

70. OIOS continues to apply a measurement system to rate the effectiveness of the application of key internal controls in audited operations. This facilitates benchmarking between country operations; provides management with assurances that activities are well or adequately

administered; and assists in identifying operations where prompt corrective action is required. Since 2005, following recommendations by the United Nations Board of Auditors, all audits rated as "below average" or "deficient" are brought to the attention of the Oversight Committee where the main control failures and emerging risks are highlighted. With the assistance of an external consultancy, UNHCR has initiated a Risk Management Framework which will help develop a risk-based audit plan for UNHCR's activities starting in 2008.

Inspection and Investigation

71. In November 2005, the High Commissioner issued revised terms of reference on the role, functions and modus operandi of the Inspector General's Office (IGO), providing a new charter with the aim of strengthening provisions for ensuring the independence of the IGO; introducing a policy of wider dissemination of inspection reports; and updating the IGO's operational policies and procedures in line with relevant recent administrative instructions from the Secretary-General. A Memorandum of Understanding (MOU) with OIOS has also been drafted, specifically aimed at enhancing cooperation and collaboration in the conduct of investigations and inspections. The IGO has continued to increase investigation capacity through the training of 80 UNHCR staff members in the Investigation Learning Programme (ILP) in 2005.

C. Policy development and evaluation

72. A Policy Development and Evaluation Service (PDES) was established in 2006, replacing the former Evaluation and Policy Analysis Unit. In addition to policy development, PDES will assume responsibility for the formulation, development and implementation of UNHCR's evaluation activities. A review of UNHCR's existing evaluation policy will take account of the Norms and Standards for Evaluation adopted by the inter-agency United Nations Evaluation Group.

D. Building performance-related accountability

73. Significant efforts have been made in the reporting period to build UNHCR's performance and accountability. In early 2006 UNHCR launched a comprehensive review of both Headquarters and Field operations under the leadership of a Director for Structural and Management Change, as well as measures to institute a system to support the development of results-based management (RBM), budgeting and reporting, and to strengthen field operations. The Office has made substantial progress in designing a software tool for the institutionalization of RBM through the Operations Management Support Software (OMSS), which will link operations plans at the country, regional and corporate strategic levels. It will be fully integrated with the PeopleSoft database and the Project Profile software so as to allow registration data to serve as the basis for programme planning.

74. Additional efforts include moves to shift the decision-making process for resource allocation closer to the point of delivery in the Field and to simplify procedures and reporting; new workforce management strategies; progress with the Management Systems Renewal Project (MSRP); measures to strengthen oversight and accountability in UNHCR; and restructuring of the Department of International Protection and the Division of Operational Support to sharpen their focus and support to field operations.

75. In June 2006, the Director for Structural and Management Change reported to the Standing Committee on developments under the change process which aimed to align

UNHCR's structures, processes and workforce management with current needs and challenges. A framework plan and budget are to be presented in September 2006, including an assessment of impact on both beneficiaries and staff.

Information management

76. The Division of Information Systems and Telecommunications (DIST) commenced implementation of the approved DIST Information and Communications Strategic Plan, with the aim of achieving significant cost savings by optimizing UNHCR's computing infrastructure and improving the quality of service to users.

77. Following the successful implementation at Headquarters of the financial and supply chain components of MSRP, the team commenced a progressive roll-out of the system to field locations. At the same time, design and development of the human resources (HR) management and global payroll modules was completed and the first delivery of the new HR system is anticipated in the course of 2006. The hosting arrangements for MSRP were transferred to the United Nations International Computing Centre, resulting in significant cost savings and increased service standards.

78. Field support has included the provision of assistance for the roll-out of the Project Profile registration system: over 5 million refugees are now registered in "*proGres*", enabling UNHCR to apply new registration standards, improve protection activities and enhance monitoring and reporting.

VIII. Conclusion

79. As this report has illustrated, UNHCR is committed to discharging its core mandate even more effectively and to rising to new challenges in a rapidly evolving operational environment. Its strong support for the cluster leadership approach to addressing internal displacement more predictably is but one example; the structural and management changes set in motion by the High Commissioner are another. Ultimately, it is intended to devote a larger share of UNHCR's resources to field operations and to improve the quality of life-sustaining, protection and other services provided to refugees and other persons of concern to the Office. The involvement of beneficiaries in needs identification and programme design remains essential, as does a human resources strategy which places greater emphasis on quality management and individual performance, as well as accountability. Protection will remain at the core of UNHCR's work, but also hinges on deeper partnership and teamwork with a range of actors, especially the beneficiaries themselves, and the unwavering commitment of the international community.

---

[1] See Table 1 and Chapter IV.

[2] Persons recognized as refugees under the 1951 UN Convention relating to the Status of Refugees and its 1967 Protocol, the 1969 Organization of African Unity (OAU) Convention, in accordance with UNHCR's Statute, persons granted a complementary form of protection and those granted temporary protection.

[3] Persons who are not considered nationals by any country under the operation of its laws. It is estimated that there may be over 11 million stateless persons worldwide, but despite renewed efforts by UNHCR, many stateless persons have yet to be identified and statistical data remains incomplete.

[4] The Government estimates that there are between 2.5 and 3 million IDPs in the country, of whom some 1.8 million are registered. According to non-governmental organizations, the figure may be as high as 3.3 million.

[5] Z-score: a means of measuring and analyzing heights and weights in a nutrition survey.

Table 1

Refugees, asylum-seekers, internally displaced persons (IDPs) protected/assisted by UNHCR, returnees (refugees and IDPs), stateless persons, and others of concern to UNHCR by country/region of asylum (end-2005)

Data are provisonal and subject to change. Status as at 2 June 2006.

Region/Country/Territory[1]	Refugees[2]	Asylum-seekers[3]	Returned refugees[4]	IDPs[5]	Returned IDPs[6]	Stateless persons[7]	Various[8]	Total
Benin	30,294	1,695	-	-	-	-	-	31,989
Burkina Faso	511	784	-	-	-	-	-	1,295
Cameroon	52,042	6,766	-	-	-	-	-	58,808
Côte d'Ivoire	41,627	2,443	2	38,039	-	-	-	82,111
Gambia	7,330	602	-	-	-	-	-	7,932
Ghana	53,537	5,496	1	-	-	-	-	59,034
Guinea	63,525	3,808	3	-	-	-	-	67,336
Guinea-Bissau	7,616	166	-	-	-	-	-	7,782
Liberia	10,168	29	70,288	237,822	260,744	-	34	579,085
Mali	11,233	1,833	-	-	-	-	-	13,066
Niger	301	48	-	-	-	-	-	349
Nigeria	9,019	420	7,401	-	-	-	3,000	19,840
Senegal	20,712	2,629	-	-	-	-	-	23,341
Sierra Leone	59,965	177	210	-	-	-	-	60,352
Togo	9,287	420	3	3,000	6,000	-	-	18,710
Total West Africa	**377,167**	**27,316**	**77,908**	**278,861**	**266,744**	**-**	**3,034**	**1,031,030**
Djibouti	10,456	19	-	-	-	-	-	10,475
Eritrea	4,418	1,591	1	-	-	-	31	6,041
Ethiopia	100,817	209	147	-	-	-	-	101,173
Kenya	251,271	16,460	-	-	-	-	-	267,731
Somalia	493	98	11,952	400,000	-	-	-	412,543
Sudan	147,256	4,425	18,525	841,946	-	-	36,110	1,048,262
Uganda	257,256	1,809	24	-	-	-	-	259,089
Total East & Horn of Africa	**771,967**	**24,611**	**30,649**	**1,241,946**	**-**	**-**	**36,141**	**2,105,314**
Burundi	20,681	19,900	68,248	11,500	-	-	-	120,329
Central African Republic	24,569	1,960	74	-	-	-	-	26,603
Chad	275,412	68	1,447	-	-	-	-	276,927
Congo	66,075	3,486	346	-	-	-	-	69,907
Dem. Rep. of the Congo	204,341	138	39,050	-	-	-	-	243,529
Equatorial Guinea	-	-	-	-	-	-	-	-
Gabon	8,545	4,843	-	-	-	-	-	13,388
Rwanda	45,206	4,301	9,854	-	-	-	-	59,361
Sao Tome and Principe	-	-	-	-	-	-	-	-
United Rep. of Tanzania	548,824	307	-	-	-	-	-	549,131
Total Central Africa & the Great Lakes	**1,193,653**	**35,003**	**119,019**	**11,500**	**-**	**-**	**-**	**1,359,175**
Angola	13,984	885	53,771	-	-	-	-	68,640
Botswana	3,109	47	-	-	-	-	-	3,156
Comoros	1	-	-	-	-	-	-	1
Lesotho	-	-	-	-	-	-	-	-
Madagascar	-	-	-	-	-	-	-	-
Malawi	4,240	5,331	-	-	-	-	-	9,571
Mauritius	-	-	-	-	-	-	-	-
Mozambique	1,954	4,015	-	-	-	-	-	5,969
Namibia	5,307	1,073	53	-	-	-	-	6,433
South Africa	29,714	140,095	-	-	-	-	-	169,809
Swaziland	760	256	-	-	-	-	-	1,016
Zambia	155,718	146	-	-	-	-	-	155,864
Zimbabwe	13,850	118	-	-	-	-	-	13,968
Total Southern Africa	**228,637**	**151,966**	**53,824**	**-**	**-**	**-**	**-**	**434,427**
Total Africa	**2,571,424**	**238,896**	**281,400**	**1,532,307**	**266,744**	**-**	**39,175**	**4,929,946**

Region/Country/Territory[1]	Refugees[2]	Asylum-seekers[3]	Returned refugees[4]	IDPs[5]	Returned IDPs[6]	Stateless persons[7]	Various[8]	Total
Afghanistan	32	14	752,084	142,505	17,044	-	-	911,679
Algeria[9]	94,101	306	1	-	-	-	-	94,408
Bahrain	-	15	-	-	-	-	-	15
Egypt	88,946	11,005	-	-	-	96	-	100,047
Iran (Islamic Rep. of)	716,403	140	68	-	-	-	-	716,611
Iraq	50,177	1,948	56,155	1,200,000	196,000	130,000	-	1,634,280
Israel	609	939	-	-	-	-	-	1,548
Jordan	965	16,570	-	-	-	9	-	17,544
Kazakhstan[10]	7,265	65	-	-	-	50,576	-	57,906
Kuwait	1,523	203	-	-	-	80,000	21,000	102,726
Kyrgyzstan	2,598	498	-	-	-	100,000	-	103,096
Lebanon	1,078	1,450	-	-	-	-	19	2,547
Libyan Arab Jamahiriya[11]	12,166	200	-	-	-	-	-	12,366
Mauritania	632	92	-	-	-	-	29,500	30,224
Morocco	219	1,843	-	-	-	4	-	2,066
Occupied Palestinian Territory	-	-	3	-	-	-	-	3
Oman	7	4	-	-	-	-	-	11
Pakistan[12]	1,084,694	3,426	1	-	-	-	-	1,088,121
Qatar	46	28	-	-	-	-	-	74
Saudi Arabia	240,701	212	-	-	-	70,000	-	310,913
Syrian Arab Republic[13]	26,089	1,898	19	-	-	300,000	-	328,006
Tajikistan	1,018	22	40	-	-	-	-	1,080
Tunisia	87	26	-	-	-	-	-	113
Turkmenistan	11,963	2	-	-	-	-	-	11,965
United Arab Emirates	104	79	-	-	-	-	-	183
Uzbekistan	43,950	587	-	-	-	-	-	44,537
Yemen	81,937	798	6	-	-	-	-	82,741
Total CASWANAME	**2,467,310**	**42,370**	**808,377**	**1,342,505**	**213,044**	**730,685**	**50,519**	**5,654,810**
Australia	64,964	1,822	-	-	-	-	-	66,786
Bangladesh	21,098	58	-	-	-	250,000	-	271,156
Cambodia	127	68	-	-	-	-	31	226
China	301,041	84	-	-	-	-	-	301,125
Hong Kong SAR, China	1,934	1,097	-	-	-	-	-	3,031
India	139,283	303	-	-	-	-	-	139,586
Indonesia	89	58	135	-	-	-	246	528
Japan	1,941	533	-	-	-	-	-	2,474
Lao People's Dem. Rep.	-	-	-	-	-	-	-	-
Malaysia	33,693	10,838	-	-	-	-	61,552	106,083
Mongolia	-	2	-	-	-	581	-	583
Myanmar	-	-	92	-	-	236,495	-	236,587
Nepal	126,436	1,272	-	-	-	400,000	10,928	538,636
New Zealand	5,307	396	-	-	-	-	-	5,703
Papua New Guinea	9,999	4	-	-	-	-	-	10,003
Philippines	96	42	-	-	-	-	766	904
Republic of Korea	69	519	-	-	-	-	-	588
Singapore	3	1	-	-	-	-	-	4
Sri Lanka	106	121	2,700	324,699	27,185	-	-	354,811
Thailand	117,053	32,163	-	-	-	-	135	149,351
Timor-Leste	3	10	-	-	-	-	-	13
Viet Nam	2,357	-	179	-	-	15,000	-	17,536
Total Asia & the Pacific	**825,599**	**49,391**	**3,106**	**324,699**	**27,185**	**902,076**	**73,658**	**2,205,714**

Region/Country/Territory[1]	Refugees[2]	Asylum-seekers[3]	Returned refugees[4]	IDPs[5]	Returned IDPs[6]	Stateless persons[7]	Various[8]	Total
Albania	56	35	-	-	-	-	-	91
Armenia	219,550	70	-	-	-	-	-	219,620
Austria	21,230	40,710	-	-	-	500	-	62,440
Azerbaijan	3,004	115	1	578,545	-	2,300	327	584,292
Belarus	725	56	-	-	-	9,983	2,414	13,178
Belgium	15,282	18,913	-	-	-	237	-	34,432
Bosnia and Herzegovina	10,568	215	1,273	182,747	5,164	-	-	199,967
Bulgaria	4,413	805	-	-	-	-	-	5,218
Croatia	2,927	8	5,261	4,804	2,736	20	-	15,756
Cyprus	701	13,067	-	-	-	1	-	13,769
Czech Republic	1,802	924	-	-	-	-	-	2,726
Denmark	44,374	509	-	-	-	446	-	45,329
Estonia[14]	7	8	-	-	-	136,000	-	136,015
Finland	11,809	-	-	-	-	726	-	12,535
France	137,316	11,700	-	-	-	835	-	149,851
Georgia	2,497	8	41	234,249	398	1,289	-	238,482
Germany[15]	700,016	71,624	-	-	-	9,476	-	781,116
Greece	2,390	8,867	-	-	-	-	3,000	14,257
Hungary	8,046	684	-	-	-	49	-	8,779
Iceland	293	29	-	-	-	53	-	375
Ireland	7,113	2,414	-	-	-	-	-	9,527
Italy	20,675	-	-	-	-	886	-	21,561
Latvia[16]	11	9	-	-	-	418,638	-	418,658
Liechtenstein	150	60	-	-	-	-	-	210
Lithuania	531	55	-	-	-	8,708	-	9,294
Luxembourg	1,822	-	-	-	-	-	-	1,822
Malta	1,939	149	-	-	-	-	-	2,088
Netherlands	118,189	14,664	-	-	-	6,500	-	139,353
Norway	43,034	-	-	-	-	941	-	43,975
Poland	4,604	1,627	-	-	-	74	-	6,305
Portugal	363	-	-	-	-	-	-	363
Republic of Moldova	84	148	-	-	-	1,530	-	1,762
Romania	2,056	264	-	-	-	400	-	2,720
Russian Federation[17]	1,523	292	162	170,544	1,677	71,155	237,676	483,029
Serbia and Montenegro	148,264	33	5,828	246,391	2,482	-	85,000	487,998
Slovakia	368	2,707	-	-	-	-	-	3,075
Slovenia	251	185	-	-	-	445	-	881
Spain	5,374	-	-	-	-	18	-	5,392
Sweden	74,915	15,702	-	-	-	5,299	-	95,916
Switzerland	48,030	14,428	-	-	-	28	-	62,486
The fYR of Macedonia	1,274	723	-	-	-	2,200	123	4,320
Turkey	2,399	4,872	21	-	-	-	1,400	8,692
Ukraine[18]	2,346	1,618	1	-	-	70,077	2,809	76,851
United Kingdom	293,459	13,400	-	-	-	205	-	307,064
Total Europe	**1,965,780**	**241,697**	**12,588**	**1,417,280**	**12,457**	**749,019**	**332,749**	**4,731,570**

Region/Country/Territory[1]	Refugees[2]	Asylum-seekers[3]	Returned refugees[4]	IDPs[5]	Returned IDPs[6]	Stateless persons[7]	Various[8]	Total
Argentina	3,074	825	-	-	-	-	-	3,899
Belize	624	14	-	-	-	-	-	638
Bolivia	535	3	-	-	-	-	-	538
Brazil	3,458	195	-	-	-	91	4,000	7,744
Canada	147,171	20,552	-	-	-	-	-	167,723
Chile	806	107	-	-	-	-	-	913
Colombia	155	41	5	2,000,000	-	9	-	2,000,210
Costa Rica[19]	11,253	223	-	-	-	-	-	11,476
Cuba	706	32	1	-	-	-	-	739
Ecuador	10,063	2,489	-	-	-	-	250,000	262,552
El Salvador	49	1	-	-	-	-	-	50
Guatemala	391	3	-	-	-	-	-	394
Haiti	-	-	-	-	-	-	-	-
Honduras	22	50	-	-	-	-	-	72
Mexico	3,229	161	-	-	-	-	-	3,390
Nicaragua	227	1	44	-	-	-	-	272
Panama	1,730	433	-	-	-	6	10,265	12,434
Paraguay	50	8	-	-	-	-	-	58
Peru	848	336	3	-	-	-	-	1,187
Suriname	-	-	-	-	-	-	-	-
United States[20]	379,340	169,743	-	-	-	-	-	549,083
Uruguay	121	9	-	-	-	-	-	130
Venezuela (Boliv. Rep. of)	408	5,912	-	-	-	-	200,000	206,320
Total Americas	**564,260**	**201,138**	**53**	**2,000,000**	**-**	**106**	**464,265**	**3,229,822**
Various	-	-	20	-	-	-	-	20
Grand Total	**8,394,373**	**773,492**	**1,105,524**	**6,616,791**	**519,430**	**2,381,886**	**960,366**	**20,751,862**

The data are generally provided by Governments, based on their own definitions and methods of data collection.

A dash (-) indicates that the value is zero, not available or not applicable

1 UNHCR region and country or territory of asylum or residence. In the absence of government figures, UNHCR has estimated the refugee population in many industrialized countries, based on recent refugee arrivals and recognition of asylum-seekers. For Canada, the United States, Australia and New Zealand, estimates are based on arrivals/recognition during the past five years whereas, for most European countries, a 10-year period has been applied. These periods reflect the different naturalization rates for refugees.

2 Persons recognized as refugees under the 1951 UN Convention/1967 Protocol, the 1969 OAU Convention, in accordance with the UNHCR Statute, persons granted a complementary form of protection and those granted temporary protection.

[3] Persons whose application for asylum or refugee status is pending at any stage in the procedure.

[4] Refugees who have returned to their place of origin during the calendar year. Source: Country of origin and country of asylum.

[5] Persons who are displaced within their country and to whom UNHCR extends protection and/or assistance.

[6] IDPs of concern to UNHCR who have returned to their place of origin during the calendar year.

[7] The table refers mainly to de jure stateless persons (persons who are not considered as nationals by any country under the operation of its laws) but also de facto stateless persons as well as persons who have difficulties establishing their nationality. The table includes countries with reliable official statistics, as well as countries where estimates of stateless populations exist, including Bangladesh, Iraq, Kuwait, Kyrgyzstan, Nepal, Saudi Arabia, the Syrian Arab Republic, The fYR of Macedonia and Viet Nam.

[8] Persons of concern to UNHCR not included in the previous columns.

[9] According to the Government of Algeria, there are an estimated 165,000 Sahrawi refugees in Tindouf camps.

[10] Apart from 4,932 persons officially registered as stateless, the figure includes ethnic Kazakhs with foreign citizenship who move to Kazakhstan and who may find themselves in a stateless situation for a period of time while applying for Kazakhstan citizenship.

[11] 2004 data for the Libyan Arab Jamahiriya (refugees and asylum-seekers).

[12] UNHCR figures for Pakistan only include Afghans living in camps who are assisted by UNHCR. According to a 2005 Government census of Afghans in Pakistan and subsequent voluntary repatriation during the year, there are an additional 1.5 million Afghans living outside camps, some of whom may be refugees. Those Afghans living outside camps receive no UNHCR assistance except access to UNHCR-facilitated voluntary repatriation.

[13] Figures are based on estimates from international NGO sources.

[14] The large majority of persons recorded as stateless have permanent residence and enjoy more rights than foreseen in the 1954 Convention relating to the Status of Stateless Persons. Among those persons with undetermined citizenship, 120,431 hold permanent residence permits and 15,569 temporary residence permits.

[15] With the introduction of the new Immigration Act in 2005, the Central Aliens Register now encompasses new residence categories and simultaneously refines previous ones, allowing for a better differentiation of refugee statistics. The refugee data included in this table refer to 15 December 2005.

[16] Includes 418,440 non-citizens and 198 stateless persons. The Republic of Latvia enacted a Law on Stateless Persons on 17 February 2004, which replaced the Law on the Status of Stateless Persons in the Republic of Latvia of 18 February 1999, and which determines the legal status of persons who are not considered as citizens by the legislation of any State and whose status is not determined by the 25 April 1995 Law on the Status of those Former USSR Citizens who are not Citizens of Latvia or of Any Other State. The latter granted a transitional legal status to permanently residing persons (non-citizens) entitling them to a set of rights and obligations beyond the minimum rights prescribed by the 1954 Convention relating to the Status of Stateless Persons, and identical to those attached to the possession of nationality, with the exception of certain limited civil and political rights. Therefore, the exclusion clause provided by Article 1.2.2 (ii) of the 1954 Convention is applicable to the non-citizens of Latvia.

[17] Includes an official figure of 16,741 stateless persons who hold a temporary residence or residence permit in the Russian Federation, 14,414 de facto stateless Meskhetians in Krasnodar krai registered by IOM, and an estimated 40,000 other stateless persons.

[18] The figure of stateless persons is based on an extrapolation from the number of stateless persons registered in the 2001 census in Ukraine. It includes 6,735 stateless persons officially registered with the Ukrainian Ministry of Interior and 6,500 Formerly Deported Persons.

[19] 2004 data for Costa Rica (asylum-seekers).

[20] UNHCR's method of estimating the refugee population in the United States is currently under review due to newly available information. As a result, the estimated refugee population in the country may increase significantly as of 2006.

Table 2

UNHCR expenditure in 2005 by regional bureau and type of assistance activity

(All sources of funds - in thousands of US Dollars)

Region/ Country/Territory	Type of Assistance					Support		
	Emergency Assistance	Care and Maintenance	Voluntary Repatriation	Local Settlement	Resettlement	Programme Support	Management & Administration	Total
1. West Africa								
Benin	198.9	-	-	409.3	-	1,303.6	-	**1,911.8**
Cameroon	-	666.8	383.8	696.3	-	571.1	-	**2,317.9**
Côte d'Ivoire	61.9	5,608.7	2,534.5	471.4	-	2,166.2	-	**10,842.7**
Gambia	-	23.9	-	281.0	-	343.2	-	**648.2**
Ghana	152.6	2,730.6	528.6	1,944.9	-	3,089.6	-	**8,446.2**
Guinea	-	11,265.7	3,084.2	992.9	-	3,061.2	-	**18,404.0**
Liberia	-	861.2	39,076.1	233.5	-	5,870.8	-	**46,041.6**
Nigeria	-	438.9	1,104.3	589.5	-	711.0	-	**2,843.8**
Senegal	-	-	-	722.0	-	1,130.7	-	**1,852.7**
Sierra Leone	-	4,828.9	13,695.4	451.0	-	3,136.8	-	**22,112.1**
Regional Activities	2,079.3	96.1	153.6	2,675.5	137.4	-	-	**5,141.8**
subtotal (1)	**2,492.7**	**26,520.8**	**60,560.4**	**9,467.3**	**137.4**	**21,384.2**	-	**120,562.8**
2. East and Horn of Africa								
Djibouti	-	1,597.1	995.8	-	-	942.8	-	**3,535.7**
Eritrea	-	1,630.4	7,460.4	-	-	1,281.1	-	**10,371.9**
Ethiopia	-	7,139.2	3,593.0	2,756.6	-	2,570.6	-	**16,059.4**
Kenya (incl. Regional Support Hub)	-	22,412.9	5,078.2	-	65.4	7,838.3	-	**35,394.8**
Somalia	1,301.8	156.0	5,788.7	-	-	587.0	-	**7,833.5**
Sudan	-	3,842.8	45,909.3	7,345.1	76.6	5,669.1	-	**62,842.9**
Uganda	986.6	379.9	4,868.1	9,543.0	-	2,477.8	-	**18,255.4**
subtotal (2)	**2,288.4**	**37,158.3**	**73,693.5**	**19,644.7**	**142.0**	**21,366.7**	-	**154,293.6**
3. Central Africa and the Great Lakes								
Burundi	-	1,700.4	32,346.1	-	82.1	3,607.8	-	**37,736.4**
Central African Republic	-	682.5	945.0	677.4	-	1,030.4	-	**3,335.3**
Chad	3,543.8	54,790.6	153.8	2,334.8	-	11,213.2	-	**72,036.2**
Congo (Republic of)	-	3,953.3	1,939.8	707.5	-	1,581.4	-	**8,182.0**
Democratic Republic of the Congo	-	1,628.4	22,112.1	3,826.3	-	4,609.8	-	**32,176.6**
Gabon	-	1,779.2	228.9	-	-	925.5	-	**2,933.6**
Rwanda	-	4,344.7	1,880.9	-	-	1,223.8	-	**7,449.4**
United Republic of Tanzania	-	13,772.6	13,368.4	-	-	2,316.6	-	**29,457.6**
Regional Activities	-	8,061.9	-	831.0	85.9	-	-	**8,978.8**
subtotal (3)	**3,543.8**	**90,713.6**	**72,975.0**	**8,377.0**	**168.0**	**26,508.5**	-	**202,285.9**
4. Southern Africa								
Angola	-	-	17,095.7	544.3	-	3,363.9	-	**21,003.9**
Botswana	-	1,567.3	-	-	-	437.3	-	**2,004.6**
Malawi	-	1,847.5	66.6	26.9	-	516.8	-	**2,457.8**
Mozambique	-	-	-	1,949.2	-	462.0	-	**2,411.2**
Namibia	-	2,266.4	64.6	-	-	725.1	-	**3,056.1**
South Africa	-	489.7	184.8	-	-	2,380.9	-	**3,055.4**
Zambia	-	2,934.3	4,275.2	3,326.3	-	2,648.1	-	**13,183.9**
Zimbabwe	-	852.0	-	543.0	-	404.0	-	**1,799.0**
Regional Activities	224.2	289.2	-	2,270.7	71.5	-	-	**2,855.6**
subtotal (4)	**224.2**	**10,246.4**	**21,686.9**	**8,660.4**	**71.5**	**10,938.1**	-	**51,827.5**
SUBTOTAL AFRICA (1-4)	**8,549.1**	**164,639.1**	**228,915.8**	**46,149.4**	**518.9**	**80,197.5**	-	**528,969.8**
5. Central Asia, South West Asia, North Africa and the Middle East - CASWANAME								
Afghanistan	-	168.7	51,076.0	-	-	5,091.5	-	**56,336.2**
Algeria	-	4,063.7	-	-	-	488.5	-	**4,552.2**
Egypt	-	546.9	54.3	2,436.0	60.3	1,172.8	-	**4,269.3**
Iran (Islamic Republic of)	-	391.9	8,013.0	2,641.4	-	2,851.8	-	**13,898.1**
Iraq	-	274.1	23,629.4	-	-	1,528.1	-	**25,431.6**
Israel	-	101.4	-	-	-	15.5	-	**116.9**
Jordan	-	1,064.1	2,584.9	-	-	816.4	-	**4,465.4**
Kazakhstan	-	839.3	2.0	-	-	450.1	-	**1,291.4**
Kyrgyzstan	982.4	541.2	-	163.8	-	525.4	-	**2,212.8**
Lebanon	-	1,454.7	300.5	-	84.2	1,202.6	-	**3,042.0**
Libyan Arab Jamahiriya	-	355.0	3.5	-	-	361.9	-	**720.4**
Mauritania	-	250.5	-	-	-	359.7	-	**610.2**
Morocco	-	184.2	-	-	-	300.3	-	**484.5**
Pakistan	10,458.1	10,910.1	9,281.3	-	-	2,781.6	-	**33,431.1**
Saudi Arabia	-	520.7	-	-	-	1,332.9	-	**1,853.6**
Syrian Arab Republic	-	1,100.2	213.0	-	26.8	488.4	-	**1,828.4**
Tajikistan	-	279.0	410.0	-	-	563.0	-	**1,252.0**
Tunisia	-	131.0	-	-	-	134.0	-	**265.0**
Turkmenistan	-	393.9	-	214.8	-	388.3	-	**997.0**
Uzbekistan	49.4	574.5	-	-	-	591.9	-	**1,215.8**
Western Sahara Operation (Conf Bld Measures)	-	388.0	-	-	-	122.8	-	**510.8**
Yemen	-	3,821.0	28.9	-	-	643.7	-	**4,493.6**
Regional Activities		273.6	1,389.3	216.5				**1,879.4**
subtotal (5)	**11,489.9**	**28,627.7**	**96,986.1**	**5,671.5**	**171.3**	**22,211.2**	-	**165,157.7**

Region/ Country/Territory	Type of Assistance					Support		
	Emergency Assistance	Care and Maintenance	Voluntary Repatriation	Local Settlement	Resettlement	Programme Support	Management & Administration	Total
6. Asia and the Pacific								
Australia and New Zealand	-	261.4	-	-	-	744.5	-	**1,005.9**
Bangladesh	-	1,342.6	929.6	-	-	605.6	-	**2,877.8**
Cambodia	-	765.3	398.5	-	-	350.6	-	**1,514.4**
China	-	1,844.0	-	1,514.2	-	439.8	-	**3,798.0**
India	-	2,214.4	133.9	-	-	983.2	-	**3,331.5**
Indonesia	19,617.4	846.9	-	2,126.1	-	1,481.8	-	**24,072.2**
Japan	-	143.0	-	338.0	-	1,961.1	-	**2,442.1**
Malaysia	-	1,556.8	-	-	-	1,153.7	-	**2,710.5**
Mongolia	-	153.1	-	-	-	41.6	-	**194.7**
Myanmar	-	-	3,365.6	-	-	975.4	-	**4,341.0**
Nepal	-	6,598.4	-	-	2.6	813.9	-	**7,414.9**
Papua New Guinea	-	-	301.6	154.5	-	-	-	**456.1**
Philippines	-	53.2	-	72.8	-	63.5	-	**189.5**
Republic of Korea	-	23.5	-	-	-	491.1	-	**514.6**
Singapore	-	52.6	-	-	-	-	-	**52.6**
Sri Lanka	9,256.9	107.7	2,782.7	3,873.1	-	1,749.4	-	**17,769.8**
Thailand	-	7,136.9	-	-	-	1,715.1	-	**8,852.0**
Timor-Leste	-	189.1	-	-	-	333.7	-	**522.8**
Viet Nam	-	-	-	238.7	-	250.8	-	**489.5**
Regional Activities	-	54.7	-	48.8	-	-	-	**103.5**
subtotal (6)	**28,874.3**	**23,343.6**	**7,911.9**	**8,366.2**	**2.6**	**14,154.8**	**-**	**82,653.4**
7. Europe								
Albania	-	457.8	-	693.8	-	803.6	-	**1,955.2**
Armenia	-	-	-	1,301.2	-	546.1	-	**1,847.3**
Austria	-	-	-	726.3	-	524.5	-	**1,250.8**
Azerbaijan	-	1,577.0	-	1,107.9	-	797.0	-	**3,481.9**
Belarus	-	166.0	-	495.4	-	252.0	-	**913.4**
Belgium	-	-	-	512.6	-	2,365.6	-	**2,878.2**
Bosnia and Herzegovina	-	5,480.5	2,772.8	-	-	2,385.3	-	**10,638.6**
Bulgaria	-	189.6	-	393.8	-	445.0	-	**1,028.4**
Croatia	-	824.7	2,218.5	287.3	-	1,256.0	-	**4,586.5**
Cyprus	-	80.1	-	155.8	-	392.6	-	**628.5**
Czech Republic	-	-	-	447.3	-	424.3	-	**871.6**
France	-	-	-	1,657.5	-	882.5	-	**2,540.0**
Georgia	-	1,110.0	-	2,468.2	-	1,044.3	-	**4,622.5**
Germany	-	-	62.6	1,037.1	-	825.7	-	**1,925.4**
Greece	-	-	-	621.6	-	807.5	-	**1,429.1**
Hungary	-	421.2	-	652.6	-	973.2	-	**2,047.0**
Ireland	-	-	-	139.5	-	399.6	-	**539.1**
Italy	-	-	-	829.8	-	1,075.5	-	**1,905.3**
Malta	-	-	-	35.2	-	-	-	**35.2**
Poland	-	-	-	269.4	-	534.7	-	**804.1**
Portugal	-	-	-	56.1	-	-	-	**56.1**
Republic of Moldova	-	35.7	-	302.0	-	293.4	-	**631.1**
Romania	784.9	207.5	-	429.2	-	513.8	-	**1,935.4**
Russian Federation	-	2,962.4	-	10,373.7	-	1,668.0	-	**15,004.1**
Serbia and Montenegro	-	18,238.8	1,282.8	1,397.8	-	1,792.3	-	**22,711.7**
Slovakia	-	-	-	216.9	-	496.2	-	**713.1**
Slovenia	-	50.6	-	224.8	-	237.5	-	**512.9**
Spain	-	-	-	676.4	-	585.0	-	**1,261.4**
Sweden	-	-	-	820.0	-	1,084.9	-	**1,904.9**
Switzerland	-	-	-	350.1	-	385.1	-	**735.2**
The former Yug. Rep. of Macedonia	457.1	2,082.2	36.0	-	-	901.4	-	**3,476.7**
Turkey	-	-	619.2	4,050.9	-	3,329.5	-	**7,999.6**
Ukraine	-	260.9	-	1,567.7	-	932.6	-	**2,761.2**
United Kingdom	-	-	36.4	289.0	-	1,591.4	-	**1,916.8**
Regional Activities	-	263.8	-	518.0	-	-	-	**781.8**
subtotal (7)	**1,242.0**	**34,408.8**	**7,028.3**	**35,104.9**	**-**	**30,546.1**	**-**	**108,330.1**

Region/ Country/Territory	Type of Assistance					Support		
	Emergency Assistance	Care and Maintenance	Voluntary Repatriation	Local Settlement	Resettlement	Programme Support	Management & Administration	Total
8. The Americas								
Office of UNHCR in New York						2,509.5		**2,509.5**
Argentina	-	-	-	91.8	-	746.9	-	**838.7**
Brazil	-	170.1	-	760.2	586.9	330.5	-	**1,847.7**
Canada	-	-	-	661.8	-	665.8	-	**1,327.6**
Colombia	-	-	-	7,359.0	-	1,365.7	-	**8,724.7**
Costa Rica	-	-	-	709.3	-	665.1	-	**1,374.4**
Cuba	-	268.9	46.8	-	-	-	-	**315.7**
Ecuador	-	-	-	2,562.7	-	816.8	-	**3,379.5**
Mexico	-	-	-	729.2	-	878.1	-	**1,607.3**
Panama	-	27.8	-	393.6	-	424.4	-	**845.8**
United States	-	-	-	1,925.6	-	1,371.1	-	**3,296.7**
Venezuela (Bolivarian Rep. of)	-	486.4	-	-	-	1,232.1	-	**1,718.5**
Regional Activities	-	-	-	3,360.6	258.8	-	-	**3,619.4**
subtotal (8)	**-**	**953.2**	**46.8**	**18,553.8**	**845.7**	**11,006.0**	**-**	**31,405.5**
9. Global Programmes	1,941.7	10,577.8	47.0	10,069.6	3,030.9	35,708.2	-	**61,375.3**
SUBTOTAL FIELD (1 - 9)	**52,097.0**	**262,550.2**	**340,935.9**	**123,915.4**	**4,569.4**	**193,823.8**	**-**	**977,891.7**
10. Headquarters								
Programme support						69,451.5		**69,451.5**
Management and administration								**-**
- Annual Budget fund							47,040.1	**47,040.1**
- Regular budget fund							38,534.0	**38,534.0**
subtotal (10)	-	-	-	-	-	**69,451.5**	**85,574.1**	**155,025.6**
11. Junior Professional Officers							**8,715.0**	**8,715.0**
TOTAL UNHCR (1 - 11)	**52,097.0**	**262,550.2**	**340,935.9**	**123,915.4**	**4,569.4**	**263,275.3**	**94,289.1**	**1,141,632.3**

6. Report of the Commissioner-General of the United Nations Relief and Works Agency for palestine Refugees in the Near East (A/61/13)

Note

Symbols of United Nations documents are composed of capital letters combined with figures. Mention of such a symbol indicates a reference to a United Nations document.

Letter of transmittal

28 September 2006

I have the honour to submit to the General Assembly my annual report on the work of the United Nations Relief and Works Agency for Palestine Refugees in the Near East (UNRWA) for the period 1 January 2005—31 December 2005. The report is submitted in compliance with the request contained in paragraph 21 of resolution 302 (IV) of 8 December 1949 and with paragraph 8 of resolution 1315 (XIII) of 12 December 1958.

For the first time, the report covers a calendar year—a departure from the previous practice of reporting on events in a July-to-June cycle. This change was prompted by the need to synchronize the report with annual budgeting and planning processes. The first section of the report summarizes significant internal developments; our operational context, which spans five fields of operation and includes the occupied Palestinian territory; and the Agency's financial status. The latter part of the report is devoted to overviews of the four programme areas: education, health, relief and social services, and microfinance and microenterprise.

As the Agency's working environment is subject to rapid—often unforeseen—change, new realities have imposed themselves upon the matters addressed in the 2005 report. Therefore, I would like to take this opportunity to draw your attention to some critical aspects of events in Lebanon and the occupied Palestinian territory during the first seven months of 2006.

Lebanon

Hostilities in Lebanon have precipitated a complex emergency that engages the mandates of many humanitarian actors. Of the 405,000 Palestine refugees registered with UNRWA in Lebanon, 104,000 reside in camps in and around Saida and a further 99,000 are registered in the vicinity of Tyre. These communities were most directly affected by the armed conflict that raged until a cessation of hostilities entered into force on 14 August 2006. While focused on the plight of Palestine refugees within its mandate, UNRWA extended its support to anyone who needed help within the wider Lebanese population. Twenty-five health clinics were open to all with 600 health-care workers in attendance. In Saida, Tyre, Beirut and North Lebanon, UNRWA teams cared for displaced persons who took refuge in

UNRWA schools. The Agency played an active role in organizing the evacuation of United Nations staff and dependants to safety in the Syrian Arab Republic and Jordan and has continued to assist sister United Nations agencies with logistics, transport, lodging for emergency staff and other support. Sadly, we lost one staff member. Abdul-Rahman Atieh Sagher was killed in an Israeli air strike just minutes after he had begun his shift as a sanitation labourer in Ein el Hilweh Camp and hours before the cessation of hostilities took hold. He worked for UNRWA for 21 years.

UNRWA participated in an inter-agency United Nations flash appeal launched on 24 July 2006. The Agency asked for $7.2 million, including $1 million for emergency activities in the Syrian Arab Republic. The appeal covered resources needed for emergency food rations, household items, emergency health-care kits, hospitalization costs and measures to protect staff and secure installations. Emergency activities also addressed the urgent task of repairing disrupted water supplies.

Prior to the outbreak of hostilities, Prime Minister Siniora had taken a very welcome initiative to improve the living conditions in Palestinian refugee camps in Lebanon, and UNRWA was working closely with the Lebanese Government to advance this initiative. The conflict caused greater hardship in the camps, where Lebanese civilians sought refuge in large numbers. Continuing our efforts to improve camp conditions is more critical than ever. In its plan for recovery, the Government of Lebanon has included an appeal for $3 million for critical projects in the camps, again demonstrating its commitment to improving the lives of refugees.

The occupied Palestinian territory

Living conditions in the occupied Palestinian territory have deteriorated rapidly over the course of 2006, resulting in substantially increased demands for the Agency's services. By the end of 2005, the effects of the second intifada already weighed heavily on the occupied Palestinian territory and its residents. Poverty, unemployment and economic stagnation were at high levels and coping mechanisms were exhausted. The election of a new Government in January 2006, led by Hamas, brought on a de facto sanctions regime under which Israel and major donors cut off the flow of funds to the Palestinian Authority and virtually froze banking transactions. This brought socio-economic and living conditions to new lows. With the Palestinian Authority unable to pay the salaries of its 152,000 employees from March 2006, public services for health, water, sanitation and energy were severely disrupted, causing a steep decline in living conditions. Unemployment, poverty and food insecurity rose steeply as the closure regime was tightened, as small businesses and shops were forced to close for lack of credit and as Palestinian access to Israeli labour and markets was blocked. These conditions were not conducive to stability and the rule of law in the occupied Palestinian territory.

In response to rapidly deteriorating conditions, UNRWA increased its 2006 emergency requirements from $95 million to $171 million in May. Activities foreseen under this appeal included an expansion of the emergency job creation and cash assistance programmes to partly meet sharply increased demand. The Agency also expanded its assistance to include support for some 23,000 Palestine refugees employed by the Palestine Authority and therefore bereft of income.

In May 2006, the Quartet endorsed a proposal by the European Union to establish a Temporary International Mechanism to ensure the direct delivery of limited assistance to the Palestinian people. Fuel and spare parts were delivered to one public utility in Gaza during the last week of July, and the first payments to some health sector workers were announced on 27 July 2006. However, by the end of August, there was no indication as to when allowances to the poor would be paid.

On 25 June 2006, Palestinian militants attacked an Israel Defense Forces (IDF) military post at Kerem Shalom, killing two IDF soldiers, injuring four and taking one captive. This action caused the armed conflict to reach new levels of intensity, with refugees and civilians in the Gaza Strip bearing the brunt of the violence. The human toll at the end of July stood at 161 dead, 605 injured and thousands displaced from their homes. Palestinian militants increased the firing of rockets into Israel and frequent IDF incursions into Gaza were met with armed resistance. Shelling and aerial bombardment by IDF destroyed homes, small businesses and vital infrastructure, including the Gaza airport, two ministries, six bridges and all six transformers of the Gaza Strip's power plant, which supplied 43 per cent of Gaza's electricity. The consequent disruption of electricity and water supplies served to further worsen humanitarian conditions. Some 3,000 displaced persons from the Beit Hanoun, Meghazi, Beit Lahia and Rafah areas, who were not taken in by family or friends, were given temporary refuge and care in six UNRWA schools. With the 2006-07 school year due to commence in September, UNRWA was exploring alternative ways to accommodate the displaced.

From January through July 2006, Karni crossing was closed for 42 per cent of the time, compared to 18 per cent in 2005 and 19 per cent in 2004. The closures, which Israeli authorities have ascribed to security reasons, resulted in severe shortages of medicines and basic food items such as flour and protein sources. Closures of Karni crossing in the same period caused UNRWA to incur storage, demurrage and transport charges of $736,490.

At Erez crossing, starting in May 2006, procedures on the ground became very restrictive and unpredictable. Restrictions have also increased on the movement of UNRWA staff members within the West Bank, including to and from East Jerusalem, largely as a result of the continued construction of the barrier in the occupied Palestinian territory.

Internal developments

During the first seven months of 2006, a critical phase of the process of organizational reform was successfully completed with the help of consultants and under the leadership of my deputy, Filippo Grandi. The Agency underwent a period of intensive reflection and discussion on the question of how best its management could be enhanced to enable the Agency to fulfil its mandate more effectively. The resulting initiatives cover critical areas of improvement, including programme cycle management, strategic planning, resource mobilization and public information. Together they constitute the spectrum of measures required to modernize and strengthen the management of UNRWA. Stakeholders were consulted at every stage of the process. The entire organizational development package was presented to a meeting of the UNRWA Advisory Commission in June, at which it was broadly welcomed. The Agency is in the process of raising funds to meet the $30 million three-year budget. Our donors and host countries acknowledge that improving the way the Agency functions will make it better able to address the needs of the Palestine refugees.

The humanitarian crises in Lebanon and the Gaza Strip have, meanwhile, created new demands on donor funds. Nevertheless, the Agency hopes that it will be able to implement these critical reforms, which will enable it to more effectively reach those most in need.

Following established practice, the annual report in draft form was distributed in advance to the members of the Advisory Commission, whose comments and observations were given careful consideration. The draft report was discussed with the Commission at a meeting held in Amman on 27 and 28 September 2006. The views of the Commission are contained in a letter addressed to me from the Chairperson of the Advisory Commission. A copy of the letter follows.

I have maintained the practice of showing my report in draft form to representatives of the Government of Israel. Pursuant to the General Assembly decision that the Advisory Commission establish a working relationship with the Palestine Liberation Organization (PLO) (decision 48/417 of 10 December 1993), a representative of PLO participated as an observer at the meeting of the Commission on 27 and 28 September 2006 and a copy of the draft report was shared with him. The report was discussed during the meeting of the Advisory Commission, held on 27 and 28 September and comprising 24 members and observers, including the delegation of Palestine, which participated fully as an observer. A representative of the European Community also attended the meeting.

(*Signed*) Karen **Koning AbuZayd**
Commissioner-General
United Nations Relief and Works Agency
for Palestine Refugees in the Near East

Letter dated 28 September 2006 from the Chairperson of the Advisory Commission of the United Nations Relief and Works Agency for Palestine Refugees in the Near East addressed to the Commissioner-General of the Agency

At its regular session of 26 September 2006, the Advisory Commission of the United Nations Relief and Works Agency for Palestine Refugees in the Near East (UNRWA) considered your draft annual report on the Agency's activities and operations during the period from 1 January 2005 to 31 December 2005, which is to be submitted to the General Assembly at its sixty-first session. The Commission commends your decision to start providing reports to the General Assembly in a calendar year format, noting that this decision should help establish more direct linkage between the Agency's strategic and financial planning by synchronizing its annual reporting with its budget planning process, which is already based on the calendar year. However, the Commission notes that this change has necessarily forced you to report again on the Agency's activities for the period January to June 2005. To avoid unnecessary duplication, the Commission has focused on the last six months of your report and on your letter of transmittal.

The Commission is committed to supporting you in discharging your duties and has also implemented a number of internal organizational changes since the General Assembly decided to expand the number of the Commission's members last December, during its sixtieth session. On 19 June 2006, the members of the expanded Commission adopted formal rules of procedure and developed an annual workplan to more effectively support your efforts to develop the enhanced strategic response to the significant challenges described in your report.

The Commission is particularly concerned with the deteriorating situation in the Gaza Strip, the West Bank and Lebanon. The unilateral disengagement by Israel in 2005 from the Gaza Strip and the northern West Bank did not bring the hoped-for stabilization and subsequent phasing out of UNRWA emergency operations. On the contrary, early in 2006, UNRWA was compelled to once again expand its emergency operations in the West Bank, the Gaza Strip and Lebanon, where Israeli military operations had severe consequences on the situation of Palestine refugees and Lebanese civilians, many of whom were displaced. The Commission commends UNRWA for its efforts in addressing the urgent needs of Palestine refugees and of those displaced Lebanese civilians who sought the Agency's assistance. The Commission commends the Agency's staff who remained in the Gaza Strip and Lebanon during hostilities in order to ensure continuation of all regular programme and emergency operations. The deteriorating economic situation and increased poverty in the West Bank and especially in the Gaza Strip have created additional demand on the Agency's services. This makes the role of UNRWA in providing essential services and humanitarian assistance to the Palestine refugees even more important during the current crisis and necessitates a vital role of donor support to the Agency's appeals. In addition, the Commission urges UNRWA to continue to closely monitor and report to its stakeholders on violations of international humanitarian law.

The Commission is concerned that the separation wall/fence, closures, curfews and other restrictions imposed by the Israeli authorities in both the West Bank and the Gaza Strip, will lead to further hardship for the affected Palestinian population. These restrictions obstruct access to employment, income and essential goods and services. They have, moreover, seriously restricted the ability of the Agency to move staff and humanitarian assistance to those in urgent need. The Commission therefore reiterates the urgent need to remove restrictions regarding the movement of Agency staff and goods, in keeping with international law, the November 2005 Agreement on Movement and Access and the agreements between UNRWA and the Government of Israel. In this connection, the Commission reaffirms the need to respect the integrity of the United Nations and the immunities of its staff operating in areas of conflict, as stated in Security Council resolution 1502 (2003) on the protection of United Nations personnel, associated personnel and humanitarian personnel in conflict zones.

The Commission is concerned about the costs emanating from the various restrictions imposed by Israel, such as $492,934 in relation to problems with the movement of UNRWA employees and some $1,355,149 for excess storage and demurrage charges in 2005. The Commission opposes Israel's continued efforts to impose a direct tax charge on Agency containers passing through Karni, amounting to $98,396, as this violates the exemption granted to UNRWA under the 1946 Convention on the Privileges and Immunities of the United Nations. The Commission endorses the Agency's demands for compensation for damaged UNRWA installations from the Israeli authorities and the reimbursement of all outstanding port charges ($25,764,820) and to be henceforth exempted from such charges, in accordance with the 1967 Comay-Michelmore Agreement between Israel and UNRWA. The Commission moreover invites the General Assembly to examine this issue at its sixty-first session and to consider including a call for reimbursement of these charges by the Israeli authorities in its resolution dealing with UNRWA operations.

The Commission commends the Lebanese Government on their June 2005 announcement to ease restrictions on obtaining work permits for Palestine refugees in Lebanon and steps taken by the Government to improve the conditions of Palestine refugees living in camps. The Commission encourages the Government of Lebanon to support this announcement with further concrete measures.

The Commission commends the Palestinian Authority for its efforts in making payments on outstanding value-added tax (VAT) due to UNRWA and notes the Agency's efforts in following up on this matter. It urges the Agency to continue to pursue with the Palestinian Authority the objective of VAT exemption for UNRWA and the reimbursement of the remaining outstanding VAT.

The Commission commends the Agency's management and, in particular, its area staff for their resolute and effective response to the deteriorating emergency situation in the West Bank, the Gaza Strip and Lebanon. The dedication, commitment and unrelenting engagement of the Agency's staff members, often under life-threatening conditions, have contributed to the relief of grave humanitarian needs.

The Commission welcomes the organizational reform that is now being implemented in UNRWA. The reform is soundly based on the 2004 Geneva conference and builds upon the external review of UNRWA in 2005 and on intensive reflection and discussion on the question of how to improve on the Agency's effectiveness. The Commission commends the management and staff of UNRWA on this comprehensive and consultative process.

The Commission, which discussed the organizational development package during its regular session in June 2006, is confident that this endeavour will yield a comprehensive and strategic approach building on the revision of the medium-term plan to guide the development of the regular budget. Such an approach is indispensable if the Agency is to respond adequately to the evidenced and prioritized needs of refugees in the five fields of operations. Utilizing the data collected through the survey by the University of Geneva's Graduate Institute of Development Studies and other initiatives on the living and socio-economic status of the refugees in the strategic planning of programmes and budgets is essential for substantiating these needs and priorities. Moreover, the medium-term plan projects and priorities should be consolidated within the main programmes of UNRWA (health, education, relief and social services). In this connection, the Commission calls upon donors to contribute adequate resources in a timely manner.

The Commission welcomes the efforts made by UNRWA to improve the structure of its annual report and to base its reporting on programmes in the subprogramme overview (section II of the report) against performance indicators. The Commission believes this is a step in the right direction and encourages UNRWA to pursue its efforts in this regard. The Commission hopes that the establishment of a permanent monitoring and evaluation section, as described in the organizational development package, will contribute to transparent reporting based on these indicators and the development of other indicators. Data collected through the refugees' needs field survey of 2005 and the analytical reports from this survey to be completed by the end of 2006 should also help in better defining targets and indicators. The Commission recognizes progress made by UNRWA in achieving a substantial number of its objectives and encourages UNRWA to make additional efforts to address areas in which the actual performance is far below targets.

The Commission requests an update on the implementation of the Agency's strategy to mainstream gender in its operations that was presented at the hosts and donors meeting held in November 2005.

The Commission notes that the UNRWA regular budget for 2005 was set at $396.4 million, against which the Agency received $378.6 million. It also notes that the Agency launched an emergency appeal for the West Bank and the Gaza Strip for $185.81 million for the year 2005. As at 31 December 2005, $110.7 million had been pledged and $70.15 million was received. The Commission notes that contributions to the Agency's emergency appeal in 2006 improved considerably. In light of the deteriorating humanitarian situation in the West Bank and the Gaza Strip, the Commission appeals to the donor community to fully support the Agency's emergency programmes, while UNRWA is urged to develop a comprehensive resource mobilization strategy for both its regular and emergency activities. In this regard, the Commission would like to stress the importance of initiatives for coordination between UNRWA, donors and host countries and of striving for a maximum degree of aid harmonization to increase aid effectiveness.

The Commission notes that, in 2005, UNRWA commissioned an external review of its emergency programme for the West Bank and the Gaza Strip. The Commission welcomes the intention of UNRWA to share this report before 1 December 2006 and looks forward to the opportunity to discuss it at one of its future sessions.

The Commission greatly appreciates the host Governments and donors for their continuing support and services provided to Palestine refugees. However, the Commission also urges the international community to maintain adequate levels of funding consistent with the needs of refugees and calls on UNRWA to continue its efforts to reach out to non-traditional donors.

The Commission recognizes the vital role of the Agency in providing refugees with essential services and in contributing to regional stability until a just settlement to the refugee issue is implemented in accordance with the relevant United Nations resolutions, especially General Assembly resolution 194 (III) of 11 December 1948.

The Commission expresses its warm appreciation for your personal commitment and activities in the service of the refugees and the effective leadership you are providing to the Agency.

Frans **Makken**
Chairperson of the Advisory Commission
of the United Nations Relief and Works Agency
for Palestine Refugees in the Near East

I. Overview

1. The United Nations Relief and Works Agency for Palestine Refugees in the Near East (UNRWA) was established pursuant to General Assembly resolution 302 (IV) of 8 December 1949. The Agency became operational on 1 May 1950, responding to the humanitarian needs of about 880,000 Palestine refugees in the region. Over the past five decades, the Agency has grown into one of the largest United Nations programmes, employing over 26,000 staff members.

2. The purpose of UNRWA is to contribute to the human development of Palestine refugees in the Gaza Strip, the West Bank, Jordan, Lebanon and the Syrian Arab Republic until a just solution is found to the refugee issue. It does this by providing basic services and other support within the framework of international human rights law and other relevant standards. Among United Nations agencies, it is unique in delivering a variety of services directly to refugees.

3. UNRWA works in a particularly complex and fast-changing political environment and is able to react quickly and flexibly to changes that take place in the regional and operational environment. The Agency strives to be strategic, focused, innovative, dynamic and agile. It bases its work on refugee needs, assets and aspirations, works in partnership with other organizations and builds synergies among its programmes.

4. UNRWA is an advocate of—and seeks to safeguard—the rights of Palestine refugees and acts as a witness and a protecting presence in areas of humanitarian crisis and conflict.

5. Through its education programme, UNRWA provides Palestine refugees with opportunities to acquire knowledge, life skills, experiences and values in an environment that is conducive to learning. Its educational services include education at the elementary, preparatory and (in Lebanon only) secondary level, technical and vocational education and training, teacher training and placement and career guidance.

6. Through the health programme, UNRWA protects and promotes the health status of Palestine refugees by providing access to comprehensive, quality basic health care, consistent

with the policies and strategies of the World Health Organization (WHO). Its health services include medical care (laboratory services, outpatient services, maternal and child health, disease prevention and control, physical rehabilitation, oral health, school health and hospital services), environmental health (sewage and drainage, solid waste management and water supply) and supplementary feeding.

7. Through the relief and social services programme, UNRWA provides a social safety net for—and promotes the self-reliance of—the most disadvantaged Palestine refugees, especially women, the aged, youth and persons with disabilities. Its relief and social services include food support; shelter rehabilitation and cash assistance to families living in conditions of special hardship; the development of community-based social services for women, the disabled, children and youth; and community support through access to subsidized credit.

8. Through the microfinance and microenterprise programme, UNRWA promotes economic development and poverty alleviation by providing credit for microenterprise, household consumption and housing needs. This credit improves the quality of life of householders, small business owners and microentrepreneurs; sustains jobs; decreases unemployment; reduces poverty; empowers women; and provides income-generating opportunities for Palestine refugees and other poor and marginal groups. Specific services include microenterprise credit, solidarity-group lending, small-scale enterprise, consumer lending, housing loans and small and microenterprise training.

A. Political, economic and security developments

9. The environment in which UNRWA carried out its operations in 2005 was again dominated by events in the occupied Palestinian territory and Israel. The year began with a period of relative calm following the election of President Mahmoud Abbas and the declaration of a ceasefire by the main Palestinian groups in January. In February, at a meeting in Sharm El-Sheikh between President Abbas and Israeli Prime Minister Ariel Sharon, both sides declared a ceasefire.

10. The most significant political development in the occupied Palestinian territory was the build-up to, and implementation of, Israel's evacuation of its settlements in the Gaza Strip and parts of the northern West Bank. The Quartet responded by establishing the Office of the Special Envoy of the Quartet for Gaza Disengagement. UNRWA worked closely with the envoy, James Wolfensohn, and his team in areas where the Agency could bring concrete benefits that could be implemented in the short term. These included the expansion of the Agency's emergency job creation scheme, a capital injection into the Agency's microfinance and microenterprise programme to facilitate increased lending and an acceleration of the programme to reconstruct Palestinian homes demolished during the intifada.

11. UNRWA hoped that the disengagement from the Gaza Strip would bring a relaxation of the closure regime and unfettered access for Palestinian goods to the outside world and so lead to an economic recovery, thereby enabling the Agency to wind down its emergency operations. However, the only sign of such a relaxation has been the agreement in November to open the Rafah terminal to allow people, but not goods, to travel between the Gaza Strip and Egypt. Following the Gaza disengagement, Palestinian labourers wanting to work in Israel and Palestinian exporters using the commercial crossings out of the Gaza Strip into

Israel faced increasing difficulties, further exacerbating the dire economic situation. In early 2006, the situation in the occupied Palestinian territory has compelled the Agency to expand its emergency operations. This followed the Palestinian elections of January 2006, the consequent suspension of international aid and tax revenues to the Palestinian Authority and the non-payment of salaries to Palestinian Authority employees.

12. Despite the improvement in the political situation in the first half of 2005, low levels of violence continued, with regular Palestinian deaths and injuries caused by shooting from Israeli settlements and border posts in the Gaza Strip and during IDF arrest and demolition operations in the West Bank. There were also suicide bomb attacks on civilian targets inside Israel in February, July, August, October and December of 2005, responsibility for which was claimed by Palestinian factions not committed to the ceasefire. In the months following the Gaza disengagement, the firing of rockets from the north of the Gaza Strip and the extensive use of artillery in the area by IDF increased the numbers of deaths and injuries and the level of destruction.

13. The modest easing in the political situation was reflected in a slight improvement in Palestinian economic indicators. The World Bank estimates that real gross domestic product growth in the West Bank and the Gaza Strip reached 8 to 9 per cent in 2005, continuing the weak recovery that began in 2003. However, the Palestinian economy still operated at well below its potential, with real gross domestic product per capita almost 30 per cent lower than in 1999. According to the World Bank, the inability of the Palestinian economy to fully realize its productive potential was chiefly the result of restrictions on the movement of people and goods.

14. The socio-economic situation remained precarious. Unemployment during the third quarter of 2005 was at 23 per cent (20 per cent in the West Bank and 29 per cent in the Gaza Strip), more than double pre-intifada levels. Youth unemployment was even more acute, with a 35 per cent rate among 20 to 24 year-olds. Furthermore, the official unemployment figures did not include the large numbers of Palestinians forced into subsistence-level self-employment in the informal sector. The World Bank reported that about 43 per cent of the Palestinian population still fall below the poverty line, with perhaps 15 per cent living in deep poverty, i.e., not able to meet subsistence needs.

15. Significant political and security developments also took place in the Lebanon field of operations. On 14 February 2005, a bomb killed former Prime Minister Rafik Hariri, who had resigned in September 2004. The assassination triggered widespread, and sometimes opposing, popular and political protests. A United Nations team was assigned to investigate the assassination.

16. Syrian troops had withdrawn from Lebanon by 26 April. In the period between the assassination and the withdrawal, thousands of Syrian workers left Lebanon. In July 2005, elections brought to power a new Government headed by Prime Minister Fouad Siniora.

17. In June 2005, the Minister of Labour, Trad Hamadeh, announced the easing of work permit restrictions on Palestinians in Lebanon, and visits by a Minister of the Palestinian Authority led to a new Lebanese/Palestinian dialogue. This revolved around four issues: improvement in humanitarian conditions for refugees; disarmament of Palestinian militias outside the refugee camps; control of arms within the camps; and diplomatic relations between Lebanon and the Palestine Liberation Organization (PLO).

18. In Jordan, in November 2005, three hotels in Amman were targeted by suicide bombers, resulting in the deaths of 59 people and injuries to 100.

B. Internal developments

19. Peter Hansen, Commissioner-General of UNRWA, retired in March 2005, after nine years in office. The Secretary-General appointed Karen Koning AbuZayd as the new Commissioner-General for a three-year term beginning on 28 June 2005. Ms. AbuZayd came to the post with the benefit of five years' experience as Deputy Commissioner-General. In October, the Secretary-General appointed Filippo Grandi as Deputy Commissioner-General. Mr. Grandi previously served as Deputy Special Representative of the Secretary-General responsible for political affairs at the United Nations Assistance Mission in Afghanistan.

20. In February 2005, in a major statement on the Agency's future direction, UNRWA launched its medium-term plan for 2005-2009. The plan is aimed at restoring the quality of the Agency's operations to levels attained before being undermined by many years of underfunding. The plan, which is under constant review and will be revised as developments affecting refugees evolve, has four main objectives: to achieve parity of UNRWA services with host authority and international standards; to address the needs of the most vulnerable refugees; to maximize the economic potential of refugees; and to build capacity within UNRWA.

21. In keeping with the medium-term plan's fourth objective, in 2005 UNRWA took a number of steps to streamline the operations management function, including separating the previously combined post of Director of UNRWA Operations in Gaza and Director of Operations; placing a Department of Operational Support at headquarters in Amman; strengthening the Management Committee and the Programme and Budget Committee; and establishing a Human Resources Task Force.

22. In late 2005, the Agency vigorously continued a process of management reform that had been in process for several years. UNRWA benefited from two external reviews. One, carried out by the Overseas Development Institute's Humanitarian Policy Group, focused on the Agency's emergency programmes, while the other, led by consultants engaged by the United Kingdom's Department for International Development on behalf of a group of donor Governments, examined management issues more broadly. The Department for International Development reviews comprehensively identified the Agency's strengths and weaknesses and presented recommendations on how the management function could be enhanced. UNRWA took these recommendations one step further and embarked on a process of organizational development with the assistance of Swiss-based consultants and with support from the Governments of Switzerland and Canada.

23. The organizational development process was announced at the meeting of UNRWA host authorities and donors in November 2005 in Jordan. The process began with a rapid organizational assessment at the beginning of 2006, and led to the production in May 2006 of an organizational development package, entitled "Serving Palestine refugees more effectively—strengthening the management capacity of UNRWA". That document constitutes the blueprint for comprehensive management reform over the next three years.

24. As part of its capacity-building process, the Agency, in partnership with the University of Geneva's Institut Universitaire d'Etudes du Développement has also been pursuing a project of data collection and analysis that will enable it to better understand the profile and needs of refugees. In 2005, UNRWA completed survey fieldwork involving interviews of over 10,000 registered refugees in all five fields. The analytical reports from the survey are due to be completed at the end of 2006 and will be utilized to enhance the Agency's transition towards needs-based planning and outcome-based monitoring of programmes.

25. In keeping with its goal of more accurately targeting its services, UNRWA embarked on a study which should lead to a new approach to poverty analysis in its relief and social services programme. This is in line with the Agency's move from a status-based to a needs-based approach in all of its budgeting and programming activities.

26. A new approach to public information and non-traditional fund-raising was begun in 2005 when UNRWA established two Friends of UNRWA associations in Spain and the United States of America. Both associations will work to raise awareness of the Agency's activities in their local media and endeavour to raise funds from private donors and other untapped sources. Each association's incorporation as a non-profit organization will allow donors to make tax-deductible contributions to the Agency's work.

27. In 2005, UNRWA formalized the provision of services to needy family members of refugee women married to non-refugees, a category previously ineligible for services. This was the result of the Commissioner-General's decision to introduce gender-neutral registration guidelines (determining eligibility for services), in line with United Nations norms.

28. The groundwork has been laid for advancing the Agency's strategy of mainstreaming gender in the Agency's operation. In November 2005 the Agency presented the initial findings of the consultancy report entitled "UNRWA gender study—a review of programme experience" to its host countries and donors meeting. This review of the experience of UNRWA with gender issues in its major programmes is intended to feed into the formulation of a gender mainstreaming strategy for the Agency's internal employment policies and practices.

29. Likewise, the Agency has committed to developing an operationally oriented policy framework for addressing the protection needs of Palestine refugees and other UNRWA beneficiaries. In November 2005, a senior protection policy adviser was appointed.

C. Operational context

1. Emergency operations

30. Since 2000, UNRWA has implemented an extensive emergency assistance programme for refugees affected by the conflict in the occupied Palestinian territory. Its largest-scale emergency activities during 2005 were the provision of food aid to over 1.3 million refugees and the creation of 2.3 million workdays for 33,000 unemployed breadwinners. Emergency operations also include the provision of mobile medical clinics in the West Bank and cash assistance and replacement accommodation for those whose shelters have been demolished during Israeli military operations. By the end of 2005, UNRWA had completed 925 new shelters for homeless refugees in the Gaza Strip and had over 1,000 under construction.

2. Refugee access

31. Israel's disengagement from the Gaza Strip in August 2005 had the immediate effect of allowing freedom of movement for Palestinians within the Strip. The signing, on 15 November 2005, of the Agreement on Movement and Access and the Agreed Principles for the Rafah Crossing led to hopes of a major improvement in the ability of Palestinians to leave and re-enter the Gaza Strip through Rafah.

32. However, with the exception of the opening of the Rafah terminal, which during the last months of the year saw between 500 and 800 travellers per day, few of the undertakings made in the agreement have been implemented, reportedly for security reasons. The Karni commercial crossing out of the Gaza Strip was closed for long periods of time and has not seen the capacity improvements included in the agreement; the Erez crossing for workers and businesspeople allowed only an average of between 1,500 and 3,000 people to cross for a period of a few months and then closed completely to Palestinians in March 2006; no bus or truck convoys between the Gaza Strip and the West Bank were established; and there has been no progress towards reducing obstacles to movement inside the West Bank. Indeed, according to the United Nations Office for the Coordination of Humanitarian Affairs, the 376 barriers in the West Bank in August 2005 had increased to 519 by May 2006.

33. Curfews in the West Bank, combined with checkpoints, the barrier and its associated regime, have had the effect of cutting the territory into three distinct areas—northern, central and southern—and have impeded refugees from accessing their families, places of work, schools, medical services and farmland. Furthermore, access to the Jordan Valley in the east of the West Bank, has been completely cut and permits are required to enter the 10 per cent of the land that sits between the barrier and the 1949 armistice line. UNRWA and the Office for the Coordination of Humanitarian Affairs have documented the tightening of the permit regime, which has had severely detrimental effects on the economic productivity of farmers in the "seam zone".[1]

34. In the Gaza Strip, the firing of rockets by Palestinians from the northern end of the Strip during October 2005 led to Israel declaring a "no-go zone" north of the towns of Beit Lahia and Beit Hanoun. This zone affects several thousand inhabitants of nearby villages. Israeli shelling in this area makes it dangerous to travel and interferes with access to schools, clinics and other services.

3. Staff security

35. The Gaza Strip returned to United Nations security phase III on 21 December 2004, and the international employees of UNRWA headquarters in Gaza, who had been relocated to Amman and Jerusalem since July 2004, returned to their duty stations.

36. However, a deterioration in the internal Palestinian security situation in August 2005 and the brief kidnapping of two United Nations Development Programme and then three UNRWA staff members led to an extended relocation of Gaza-based international staff, with the exception of those directly concerned with emergency or humanitarian relief operations or security matters, out of Gaza headquarters. At the end of the reporting period, the staff remained relocated in Amman and Jerusalem.

37. Another occurrence of internal violence, the bombing of the United Nations Reporting and Evacuation Centre in Gaza City on 1 January 2006, led to a brief relocation, also of

international staff, from the UNRWA Gaza field office. In spite of these extensive relocations, all programme and emergency operations continued. The Agency is indebted to its staff and acknowledges their dedication and loyalty in such difficult and often dangerous circumstances. It notes with regret that the 12,000 local staff of UNRWA in the occupied Palestinian territory are the only United Nations staff members working in the area who do not receive hazard pay. The Agency continues to discuss this anomaly with United Nations Headquarters, but had not resolved the matter by the end of the reporting period.

4. Palestine refugees in Lebanon

38. On 15 October 2005, Prime Minister Siniora announced his Government's intention to improve humanitarian conditions for Palestinian refugees in Lebanon. The Prime Minister requested UNRWA to submit a report to him on the conditions of Palestinian refugees in Lebanon, on what UNRWA could do to alleviate conditions and on what the Government could do to facilitate this work. This approach marks a major change in Lebanese official policy towards the Palestinian refugees and their humanitarian conditions.

39. UNRWA submitted a report to the Government of Lebanon on 19 October 2005, outlining the camp improvement needs of refugees in Lebanon. The report listed $50 million worth of projects critical to improving refugee living conditions. The Prime Minister's office and UNRWA have met with donors to promote this plan.

D. Legal matters

40. During the reporting period, restrictions on the freedom of movement of Agency staff, vehicles and goods continued to be imposed, particularly in the occupied Palestinian territory and by the Israeli authorities. These restrictions undermined the ability of UNRWA to provide its essential and emergency services. Although security concerns are cited as the reason for imposing the restrictions, in the Agency's view, many are in violation of applicable international law and have caused serious financial loss to the Agency in addition to their human impact on refugees.

41. The Agency has also suffered financial loss owing to the levying of extra charges in respect of its supplies, physical damage to its installations from IDF military operations, and the continuing non-remittance to the Agency by the Palestinian Authority of all value-added tax sums owed.

1. Agency staff

42. The Israeli authorities, citing security concerns, have continued to impose restrictions on the freedom of movement of UNRWA personnel in the occupied Palestinian territory. The restrictions have included: the external closure of the West Bank and the Gaza Strip; the imposition of curfews and internal closures; the prohibition of local staff travelling in United Nations vehicles across the Erez crossing, across the Allenby Bridge, in Israel and in portions of the occupied Palestinian territory annexed by Israel; and the maintenance of excessively cumbersome procedures for obtaining often-denied permits for local staff who live in the West Bank and the Gaza Strip to enter Israel and East Jerusalem.

43. The Israeli authorities have also continued to impose other restrictions on the travel of UNRWA personnel and vehicles across borders and crossing points. Restrictive procedures

at Erez crossing often resulted in lengthy delays on the Gaza side of the crossing, in the unprotected area of the Palestinian checkpoint, which endangered staff members' safety. National staff were often barred from using Erez or Rafah crossings. The restrictions are inconsistent with established principles of international law, the Charter of the United Nations, the 1946 Convention on the Privileges and Immunities of the United Nations and the 1967 exchange of letters between the Agency and the Government of Israel (the Comay-Michelmore Agreement). The Comay-Michelmore Agreement, inter alia, requires the Government of Israel to "facilitate the task of UNRWA to the best of its ability, subject only to regulations or arrangements which may be necessitated by considerations of military security".

44. In the Agency's view, many measures did not relate to military security but were rather matters of police or administrative convenience. The Israeli authorities however, maintained that the restrictions were necessary for military security or self-defence, including against terrorist attacks. The Agency continued to make representations to the Israeli authorities at all levels to have the constraints affecting its operations removed.

45. Both in the West Bank and the Gaza Strip, enhanced coordination through IDF liaison officers led to some improvement in staff movement in the last six months of the reporting period, particularly in the light of the disengagement from the Gaza Strip. However, there was no substantial overall improvement, and the freedom of movement of UNRWA staff members remained unpredictable. Following the Israeli disengagement from the Gaza Strip in mid-September 2005, internal movement restrictions were lifted in the Gaza Strip. Movement of staff members through Rafah became easier following the partial implementation of the 15 November 2005 Agreement on Movement and Access but became even more restricted after the attack by Palestinian militants on IDF at Kerem Shalom crossing in June 2006.

46. Movement restrictions in the West Bank and the Gaza Strip have resulted in lost staff days, labour replacement costs and associated administrative costs totalling $492,934 for the period.

47. During the reporting period, no significant movement restrictions were imposed on UNRWA staff by the Governments of Jordan, Lebanon and the Syrian Arab Republic or by the Palestinian Authority.

48. At the end of the reporting period, 47 staff members were being detained, of whom 34 were held by the Israeli authorities, 10 by the Palestinian authorities, and one each by the authorities of Jordan, Lebanon and the Syrian Arab Republic. Despite requests in accordance with General Assembly resolution 36/232 of 18 December 1981, the Israeli authorities did not permit access to, or provide in many cases all relevant information and documents concerning, detained UNRWA staff. The Agency was therefore unable to ensure that rights and obligations flowing from the Charter of the United Nations, the 1946 Convention and the relevant Agency Staff Rules and Regulations were respected. Further, the lack of access and documentary information materially hampered the Agency's ability to consider disciplinary measures in accordance with established United Nations standards.

2. Agency services and premises

49. UNRWA is required to route its shipments of humanitarian goods and supplies into the Gaza Strip through the Karni crossing, except for construction materials which enter the Gaza Strip through the Sofa crossing. The Israeli authorities continued to impose transit charges on containers moving through Karni, forcing UNRWA to pay $98,396 in 2005. In the Agency's view, the charge is a direct tax, from which it ought to be exempted under the 1946 Convention.

50. Owing for the most part to closures of Karni crossing by the Israeli authorities, UNRWA incurred excess storage and demurrage charges of $1,355,149, including demurrage charges of $788,115 for empty containers that were stranded in the Gaza Strip. Although restrictions on movement of goods through Karni crossing remained closely linked by the Israeli authorities to security incidents and alerts, and the movement of goods through Karni was adequate in the months immediately prior to Israel's disengagement from the Gaza Strip, the Agency considers that for substantial periods the throughput was not consistent with Israel's obligations under the Comay-Michelmore Agreement and under article 59 of the 1949 Geneva Convention relative to the Protection of Civilian Persons in Time of War.

51. With respect to the importation of vehicles, the Government of the Syrian Arab Republic has reaffirmed that there is no limitation on the number of vehicles that UNRWA may import. In practice, however, the Syrian authorities continue to make the importation of new vehicles contingent on the deletion of the records of existing vehicles on a one-for-one basis. This represents a de facto limitation and resulted in a two-week delay in the importation of 19 vehicles.

52. During the reporting period, 24 Agency construction projects in the West Bank and Gaza Strip with an overall budget of $3,575,267 were delayed or stopped altogether due to the restrictions on the movement of personnel, vehicles and construction materials. In Lebanon, the entry of construction materials to camps is subject to approval from the Lebanese army, but this has not caused delays during the reporting period.

53. The Operations Support Officer programme continued in both the West Bank and the Gaza Strip. The programme played an invaluable role in facilitating access of staff members and UNRWA vehicles, including ambulances and humanitarian convoys, through checkpoints in the West Bank and into areas affected by ongoing IDF military operations in the Gaza Strip; in monitoring and reporting on the developing humanitarian crisis among the Palestinian population; in the regular monitoring and inspection of UNRWA installations; and in providing a measure of protection to Palestine refugees.

54. The 1946 Convention guarantees that "the premises of the United Nations shall be inviolable" and the Comay-Michelmore Agreement obliges the Government of Israel to "ensure the protection and security of the personnel, installations and property of UNRWA". Contrary to these provisions, IDF entered and/or threw tear gas into UNRWA premises on seven reported occasions. Seven UNRWA schools were hit by shelling or gunfire from the direction of Israeli positions on 10 occasions, which is additionally in violation of the 1989 Convention on the Rights of the Child and international humanitarian law. The Agency has submitted to Israel claims for damage to its installations totalling $5,970 for

the reporting period, bringing the total amount of claims submitted to Israel since the beginning of the current intifada to $951,646. Israel has not responded to these claims for damages, although in response to some protests, Israel has denied or disputed responsibility for causing damage.

55. UNRWA installations in the West Bank and the Gaza Strip, including schools, were subjected to 11 incursions by Palestinian militants on eight occasions, and by Palestinian Authority security forces on three occasions. In each instance the Agency protested to the Palestinian Authority.

56. There were no incursions into UNRWA premises in Jordan, Lebanon or the Syrian Arab Republic.

3. Other legal matters

57. During the reporting period, the Agency was reimbursed by the Palestinian Authority some $8.9 million for value-added tax paid by the Agency in prior years. As at 31 December 2005, the total amount of value-added tax still due to the Agency from the Palestinian Authority was approximately $8.2 million. The Palestinian Authority has acknowledged that it should reimburse the Agency, but has not yet done so.

58. The issue of reimbursement by the Government of Israel of port and related charges incurred by the Agency in connection with goods imported to the Gaza Strip and the West Bank through Israel is unresolved. The Agency's position is that the obligation to pay port and related charges remains with the Government of Israel pursuant to the terms of the Comay-Michelmore Agreement. The total amount of port charges due to the Agency as at 31 December 2005 was $25,764,820, for which the Agency has filed a claim with the Government of Israel. This claimed amount includes the cost of container transit charges and excessive storage and demurrage charges referred to in paragraphs 49 and 50 above.

59. The Agency continued to be required to pay to the Syrian authorities port fees and charges totalling $22,781 for the reporting period, which the Agency maintains is contrary to the 1948 Agreement between the United Nations and the Government of the Syrian Arab Republic. While the Ministry of Foreign Affairs has indicated it would consider the matter, it remained unresolved at the end of the reporting period.

60. In the Syrian Arab Republic, the Agency continued to be required to submit its customs declaration forms with commercial invoices for endorsement by the Boycott Office. While no imports have been refused as a result of this requirement, the Agency has protested the requirement to the Syrian authorities on the grounds that imports by UNRWA should not require such endorsement under the 1946 Convention.

4. Legal status of Palestine refugees in the Agency's fields of operation

61. The movement of Palestinians, including Palestine refugees, within, to and from the occupied Palestinian territory was tightly controlled and subject to a complex permit regime implemented by the Israeli authorities as well as various agreements, including the 15 November 2005 Access and Movement Agreement. Palestine refugees may obtain identification documents, but the Israeli authorities administer the population and register and control the issue of identity documents for the West Bank, Jerusalem and the Gaza Strip.

Palestine refugees have access to Palestinian Authority services equal to that of other Palestinians in the occupied Palestinian territory. Palestine refugees also had the same rights as other Palestinian residents to vote in elections.

62. The largest number of Palestine refugees resides in Jordan. Most enjoy Jordanian citizenship, are able to work in government offices and throughout the local economy and have access to governmental institutions and other assistance. Palestinians who left the Gaza Strip in 1967 and their descendants, on the other hand, have only temporary Jordanian passports valid for two years and without national identity numbers. The 1996 Labour Law requires non-Jordanians to have legal residency and valid passports and permits in order to work. Access to social security benefits depended on reciprocal privileges in the worker's country of origin, rendering stateless Palestine refugees ineligible. The Government of Jordan provided to Palestine refugees and displaced persons services and benefits such as education, rent and utilities, subsidies and rations, camp services, health care, public security and social services.

63. In June 2005, the Lebanese Labour Ministry allowed Palestinian registered refugees born in Lebanon to work at manual and clerical jobs and to obtain work permits, both of which were previously denied. Palestinians were still effectively prohibited from practising several professions, including medicine, law, journalism and engineering. Unemployment among refugees was high and living conditions poor. All Palestine refugees registered with UNRWA and their descendants received identity documents attesting to their right to be in Lebanon and could acquire renewable travel documents valid from three to five years. According to a 1957 decree still in force, Palestine refugees who are registered with the Directorate of Political and Refugee Affairs of the Ministry of the Interior but who do not reside in refugee camps can freely change their residence, but those who reside in camps have to apply for a permit before moving to other camps. Palestinian refugees have limited access to government services and have to depend almost entirely on the Agency for basic services. Legislation preventing Palestine refugees from buying immovable property remained in force.

64. Palestinian refugees in the Syrian Arab Republic continued to have full access to government services and to the labour market, with the exception that, under Law No. 260 of 1956, Palestinian refugees who took refuge in the Syrian Arab Republic on or after 10 July 1956, are not allowed to occupy civil posts in the Government. According to Syria's 1957 law on the legal status of Palestinians, Palestinian refugee residents have almost the same legal protection as Syrian citizens but have no right to be naturalized or to vote. The Government of the Syrian Arab Republic provided to Palestinian refugees services such as education, health, housing, utilities, security and social services.

E. Financial overview

1. Sources of funding

65. With the exception of the regular international staff posts funded by the General Assembly through assessed contributions, UNRWA operations, projects and emergency appeals are funded by donors' voluntary contributions. The Agency's project expenditure mainly consists of non-recurrent costs funded by earmarked contributions for specific activities. Project funding supports, complements and enhances the Agency's regular activities and programmes.

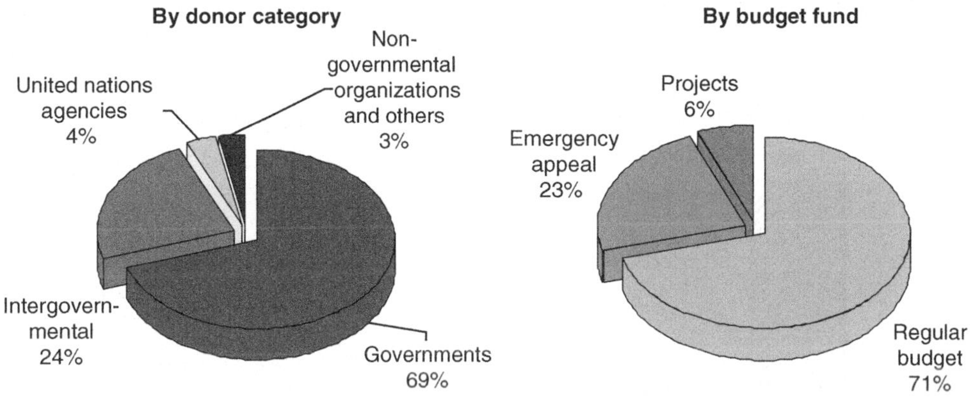

Figure I Distribution of sources of funding by donor category and budget fund

2. Expenditure

66. The Agency expended $484.2 million during 2005 against a budget of $537.7 million on its regular, project and emergency appeal activities. The largest component was an expenditure of $377.2 million under the regular budget, accounting for nearly 78 per cent of total expenditures. Emergency appeal activities and projects accounted for 18 per cent and 4 per cent, respectively. The microfinance and microenterprise programme made up less than 1 per cent of total expenditures.

67. As in the past, education remained the largest programme in 2005, with a budget accounting for almost 60 per cent of the annual total. Health, relief and social services, common services and operational and technical services followed, with 18 per cent, 10 per cent, 8 per cent and 5 per cent, respectively.

TABLE 1 REGULAR BUDGET 2005

(In millions of United States dollars)

	Budget	*Expenditure*		*Variance*
Education	215.6	224.6	(60 per cent)	9
Health	70	68.3	(18 per cent)	1.7
Relief and social services	38.9	35.9	(10 per cent)	3
Operational and technical support	23.6	19.3	(5 per cent)	4.3
Common services	35.3	29.1	(8 per cent)	6.2
Other	13	—		13
Total	**396.4**	**377.2**	**(100 per cent)**	**19.2**

68. The level of budget implementation was constrained by the fragile security situation, especially in the two largest areas of operation, the Gaza Strip and the West Bank. Some of the $19.2 million positive variance is thus due to the fact that certain earmarked activities could not be implemented during the year.

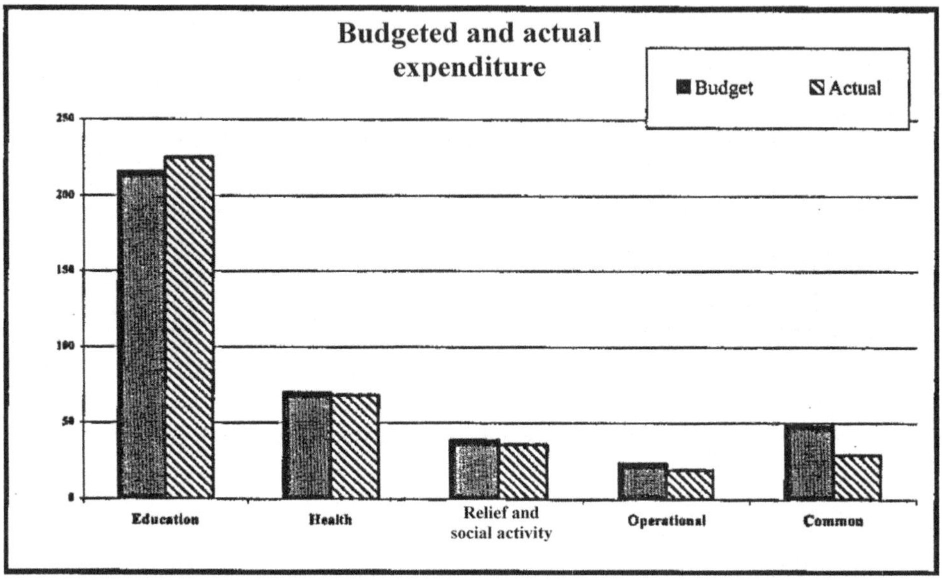

Figure II **Comparison of the budget and actual expenditure** (In thousands of United States dollars)

3. Audit activities

69. The Department of Inspection and Oversight Services conducted its activities under the terms of the Agency's Organization Directive No. 14, which is reviewed by the Audit and Inspection Committee. There were 42 assignments, of which 37 were concluded. Reports produced in 2005 related to audit, inspection, investigation, fraud prevention and fraud detection. They contained 259 recommendations/conclusions for management action.

70. UNRWA management responded by fully accepting 228 recommendations (88 per cent) and had implemented 81 of these (36 per cent) by the end of the reporting period.

71. Assignments were undertaken in all five field offices and headquarters to ensure adherence to internal controls and to establish an anti-fraud environment in the Agency. The activities audited were in domains such as health and education, registration of refugees, payroll systems, microfinance and microenterprise lending, financial statements, cash and food assistance to refugees, camp rehabilitation projects, emergency appeal implementation, poverty alleviation and procurement of sugar, flour and school supplies.

72. The Department of Inspection and Oversight Services also sought and obtained the support of United Nations Headquarters in New York to conduct a highly technical audit of the Agency's management of its information technology systems. In 2005, the audit committee recommended the appointment of three external members to provide a wider range of perspective and professional input.

II. Subprogramme overview

A. Performance report for sub-goal I: education

73. The goal of the Agency's education programme is to provide Palestine refugees with opportunities to acquire knowledge, life skills, experiences and values in an environment that is conducive to learning. The programme includes education at the elementary, preparatory and (in Lebanon only) secondary level for almost 500,000 children, technical and vocational education and teacher training, placement and career guidance. Highlights include:

(a) The implementation and completion of the staff training, community involvement and strategic development plan known as the "School as a focus for development" project;

(b) The establishment of a new quality assurance framework as a planning, self-assessment and continuous improvement tool;

(c) The expansion and integration of the "Human rights, conflict resolution and tolerance" teaching programme;

(d) The implementation in the Gaza Strip of the "Information and communications technology as tool for learning" project;

(e) Close cooperation with the education authorities in Jordan, the Syrian Arab Republic and the occupied Palestinian territory on curriculum and other educational development issues;

(f) The proportion of UNRWA school buildings operating on a double shift (two schools in one building) at 77 per cent. Additionally, 17 per cent of schools inadequately housed in rented buildings;

(g) A total of 1,091 teacher workdays lost in the occupied Palestinian territory because of closures, curfews and armed conflict;

(h) The launching of a psychosocial support programme (currently in the early stages of development), designed to reach some 90,000 pupils in the occupied Palestinian territory.

TABLE 2 PERFORMANCE BY INDICATORS

Expected accomplishments	*Performance indicators*	*Achievements*
Maintenance and improvement of the quality of education provided to the Palestinian refugee population at all levels by maintaining an environment conducive to learning; meeting the needs arising from the natural growth in the refugee population through upgrading and construction of facilities; and enhancing the skills and competencies of the Agency's teaching and training staff.	(i) Maintenance of relatively high pupil pass rate in the elementary cycle	Unit of measure: per cent Target (2005): 96 per cent Result (2005): 94.9 per cent
	(ii) Maintenance of relatively high pupil pass rate in the preparatory cycle	Unit of measure: per cent Target (2005): 98 per cent Result (2005): 96.1 per cent
	(iii) Maintenance of relatively low dropout rate in the elementary cycle	Unit of measure: per cent Target (2005): 0.5 per cent Result (2005): 0.48 per cent

Expected accomplishments	*Performance indicators*	*Achievements*
	(iv) Reduction in the dropout rate in the preparatory cycle	Unit of measure: per cent Target (2005): 2.8 per cent Result (2005): 2.69 per cent
	(v) Number of additional educational facilities or other infrastructure facilities constructed or renovated	Unit of measure: number of facilities Target (2005): 384 Result (2005): 293
	(vi) Number of education staff from various categories (teaching and non-teaching) trained	Unit of measure: number of staff Target (2005): 1,800 Result (2005): 2,096
	(vii) Improvement in the pupil/ teacher ratio in the elementary cycle	Unit of measure: ratioTarget (2005): 36:1 Result (2005): 33.1:1
	(viii) Improvement in the pupil/ teacher ratio in the preparatory cycle	Unit of measure: ratioTarget (2005): 27:1 Result (2005): 25.8:1
	(ix) Number of schools operating on a double-shift basis	Unit of measure: number of schoolsTarget (2005): 470Result (2005): 514
Adaptation and improvement of course content and curricula in the general and technical education programmes in order to match developments in host countries.	Percentage of the curricula adapted/ improved relative to the total number of modifications required	Unit of measure: per cent Target (2005): 100 per cent Result (2005): 100 per cent
Adaptation and improvement of course content and curricula in vocational training institutions to meet changing market conditions.	Percentage of the curricula adapted/ improved relative to the total number of modifications required	Unit of measure: per cent Target (2005): 100 per cent Result (2005): 100 per cent

Significant activities

74. The "School as a focus for development" programme is a master plan to improve the strategic development of schools in five areas: school planning, staff development, teaching and learning, school and the community and quality assurance. Training in all five areas has been completed in all UNRWA schools, and each school has established a development team and formulated its own strategic development plan. Each school has also established school councils on which parents work together with teaching staff and has made major shifts in culture to promote autonomy and opportunities for creativity and innovation.

75. The quality assurance framework is a unique programme to monitor and improve standards in UNRWA schools. In the 2004-2005 academic year, training on the framework was completed in five fields, with special workshops being held to iron out problems. Documents and support materials are now available in Arabic and English, and eight standards, composed of 40 performance indicators, have been established.

76. In 2005, the "Human rights, conflict resolution and tolerance" programme reached all UNRWA schools, with 350,000 students in grades 4 to 10 and in all subject areas involved. The programme is aimed at introducing students to societal, democratic and global values

and developing their skills for the peaceful resolution of conflicts. About 20,000 UNRWA teachers, head teachers and school supervisors have been trained and all schools now have their own student parliaments, storybooks in Arabic and workbooks for students, each with about 50 activities and teachers' training guides.

77. Violence in schools was identified as an area deserving study and urgent intervention. While acknowledging the complexity of this issue and its close relationship to economic hardship, the unrelenting armed conflict and related community-level violence in the occupied Palestinian territory, the Agency took some initial steps towards a comprehensive, interdepartmental response.

78. The "Information and communications technology as tool for learning" project has provided Internet access for all Agency schools in the Gaza Strip; installed 115 working computer laboratories; provided training for 1,000 teaching and administrative staff and seen the appointment of 180 additional information and communications technology teachers. The programme has also seen UNRWA forge partnerships with key information and communications technology companies such as Intel, Microsoft and the International Computer Driving Licence of the United Nations Educational, Scientific and Cultural Organization in Cairo.

79. In 2005, 9 UNRWA students were killed and 20 were injured by Israeli military activity in the Gaza Strip. One of the children was killed by gunfire in the playground of an UNRWA school. The disruption and loss of teaching time caused by closures and clashes have fragmented the learning process for many children. Eighty per cent of children in the occupied Palestinian territory are believed to suffer from some level of post-traumatic stress disorder. In addition to psychosocial support, UNRWA provides after-school remedial learning, extra-curricular activities in partnership with non-governmental organizations and distance learning for children who face difficulties reaching schools.

B. Performance report for sub-goal II: health

80. The goal of the health programme is to protect, preserve and promote the health status of the registered Palestine refugees within the Agency's five areas of operation. It pursues this goal within the available means and in a manner consistent with the principles of the United Nations, the basic concepts and strategic approaches of WHO, the health-related Millennium Development Goals and the standards set out in the Convention on the Rights of the Child. Highlights include the following:

(a) Medical consultations provided to refugees rose by 2.4 per cent, to 8.4 million. The number provided with hospital treatment grew by 7.8 per cent, to 61,895, while dental consultations increased by 6.1 per cent, to 655,493;

(b) The number of newly registered pregnant women increased by 3.5 per cent, to 87,668, those receiving post-natal care rose by 4.3 per cent, to 74,316 and the number of family planning acceptors grew by 8.5 per cent, to 109,244;

(c) The number of patients with non-communicable diseases under supervision at UNRWA health facilities increased by 11.4 per cent, to 135,496;

(d) The management health information system on family planning and maternal health care was expanded;

(e) Five postgraduate fellowships were sponsored fully or partially by UNRWA during 2005;

Utilization of curative medical services 1995-2005

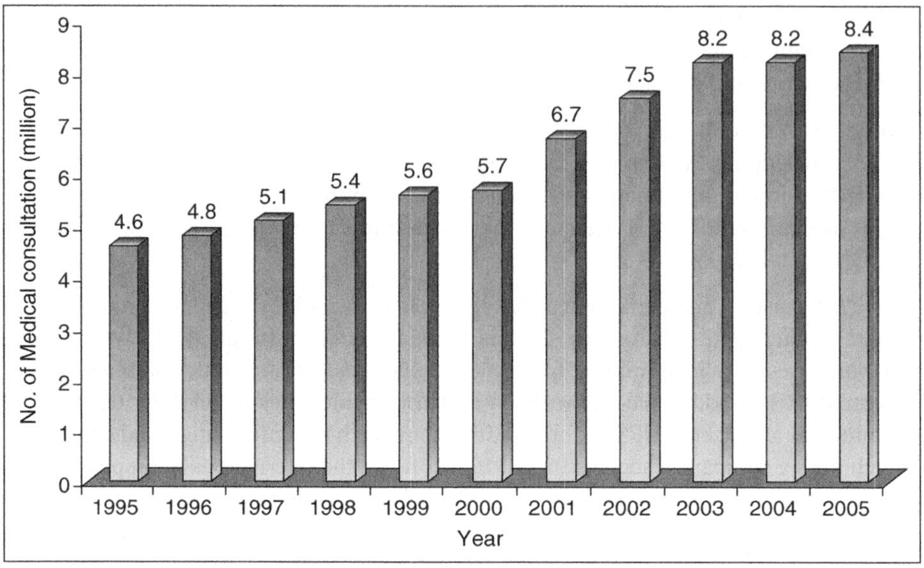

Figure III **Utilization of curative medical services 1995-2005**

Correlation between number of pregnant women and family planning acceptors 1995-2005

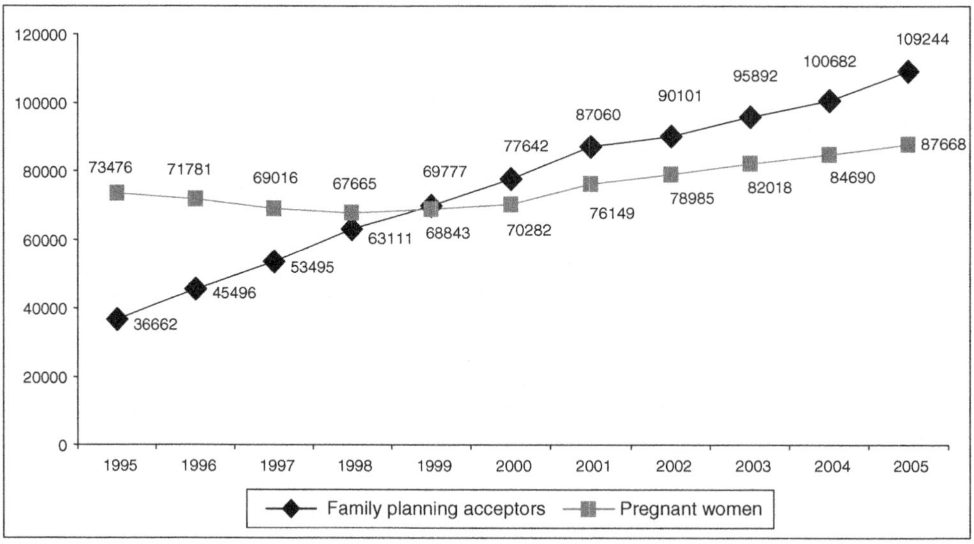

Figure IV Correlation between number of pregnant women and family planning acceptors 1995-2005

(f) Three new technical medical instructions were introduced during 2005 and four technical instructions were revised;

(g) Three agency-wide research studies were conducted to assess the health status of Palestine refugees;

TABLE 3 PERFORMANCE BY INDICATOR

Performance indicator	*Actual*	*Target*
Infant mortality rate per 1,000 live births	22	22
Child mortality rate per 1,000 live births	24.4	25
Pregnant women registered at UNRWA maternal and child health clinics during first trimester (out of all pregnant Palestine refugee women)	57.5 per cent	50 per cent
Pregnant women who paid at least four visits to clinics during the antenatal period	89.1 per cent	90 per cent
Babies delivered by trained personnel	99.5 per cent	98 per cent
Women receiving post-natal care	93.3 per cent	96 per cent
Prevalence of contraceptive methods among mothers of infants 0 to 3 years of age attending UNRWA maternal and child health clinics	55.4 per cent	55 per cent
Total fertility rate	3.2	3.2
Pregnant women protected against tetanus	99.5 per cent	Above 95 per cent
12-month-old infants fully immunized	99.2 per cent	Above 95 per cent
18-month-old infants receiving all booster doses	98.4 per cent	Above 95 per cent
Incidence of neonatal tetanus and poliomyelitis	None	None
Cure rate of smear positive TB cases	100 per cent	100 per cent
Average daily medical consultations per doctor	110	70
Camp shelters with access to safe water	99.7 per cent	98 per cent
Refugee shelters connected to underground sewerage system	84 per cent	85 per cent
Female medical personnel	29.3 per cent	50 per cent

Significant activities

81. During 2005, the management health information system on family planning and maternal health care was expanded into all 125 UNRWA health centres. The management health information system is an ongoing process to allow the entry of all related health data onto a new information and communication technologies system. It facilitates the interpretation of results, the analysis of performance indicators and the evaluation of medical outcomes.

82. A technical instruction was introduced during 2005 on screening for cervical and breast cancers. This was done to improve primary prevention activities that help avoid the development of cancer by reducing or eliminating exposure to cancer-causing factors. The instruction seeks to improve health education and counselling; management of sexually transmitted infections; effective treatment for precancerous lesions; early detection of cancers through frequent medical check-ups of individuals at risk; and targeted screening activities.

83. A second set of technical instructions was issued on the prevention and control of thalassaemia and sickle-cell anaemia by following up on haemoglobinopathies found among registered

refugees. The instruction also sought to update the established database on all known cases and carriers of hereditary anaemias, including Beta-thalassemia and sickle-cell anaemia.

84. A third set of technical instructions was issued to improve the procedures for estimating access and utilization rates of UNRWA health services by registered refugees. It will allow for better human resource allocation based on more reliable estimates of budget and expenditure per user.

85. Four technical instructions were revised, including those on school health, the issuing of rations to pregnant women and nursing mothers, hospital services and guidelines for handling formalities at health centre dispensaries. The Agency's technical instructions are revised on a regular basis to ensure their consistency with evolving WHO technical guidelines and procedures.

86. In 2005, UNRWA conducted three major pieces of health research to assess the health status of Palestine refugees. These comprised a study of the prevalence of anaemia among schoolchildren, which revealed an overall rate of anaemia of 15.8 per cent Agency-wide. An additional study on the current contraceptive practices among mothers of children 0 to 3 years attending UNRWA health clinics revealed contraceptive use at 55.4 per cent. The third study was conducted to assess oral health status among school children using the Decayed, Missing, Filled Teeth (DMFT) index and the prevalence rate of dental calculus.

C. Performance report for sub-goal III: relief and social services

87. The goal of the Agency's relief and social services programme is to provide a social safety net for the most impoverished Palestine refugees and to promote the self-reliance of less advantaged members of the refugee community, especially women, the elderly, youth and those with disabilities. Services provided by the relief and social services programme include food support; shelter rehabilitation and cash assistance to families in special hardship; community-based social services; access to subsidized credit; and the maintenance, updating and preservation of records and documents of 4.3 million registered refugees. Highlights include the following:

(a) Eligibility for special hardship relief services was extended to the children of 674 refugee women married to non-refugee men. These family members constitute a new category of beneficiaries;

(b) The tendering process for software development for the new refugee registration information system of the Palestine Refugee Records Project was completed. Two and a half million of the over 13 million historical documents from the Agency's registration and family files were scanned and preserved;

(c) Major reform of the special hardship assistance programme commenced through an in-depth survey of the client population and revision of the eligibility criteria and poverty thresholds for Jordan;

(d) Funding shortfalls necessitated a reduction in refugee food packages. The value of food assistance in Jordan, Lebanon and the Syrian Arab Republic fell from $110 to $86.4 per refugee per annum;

(e) Some 374 special hardship case shelters were rehabilitated (including those rehabilitated in southern Lebanon after a six-year wait). This represented 3.4 per cent of the total 10,894 shelters identified as being in need of rehabilitation;

TABLE 4 PERFORMANCE BY INDICATOR

		Achievements	
Expected accomplishment	*Performance indicator*	*2005 target*	*2005 result*
Improved quarterly delivery of food rations and cash subsidy "safety net" support to special hardship case families	Percentage of food rations and cash subsidies distributed in relation to the projected ceiling	100 per cent	A quarterly average of 228,971 beneficiaries (5.7 per cent of the registered refugee population) received their rations and cash subsidies, representing 99.8 per cent of the yearly projected ration/cash subsidy ceiling (917,272)
Increased provision of selective cash to refugee families facing emergency financial crisis or lacking basic economic necessities within a timely manner	Percentage of increase in number of special hardship case and non-special hardship case families receiving cash assistance in relation to the previous reporting period	Special hardship case families: 3.5 per cent Non-special hardship case families: 1 per cent	12,030 special hardship case families (19.4 per cent) of the total special hardship case families benefited; 158 non-special hardship case families were assisted, representing 1.3 per cent of the special hardship case families; achievement above target was due to the additional funds received under the medium-term plan (2005-2009); 205 per cent increase in available funds over 2004 levels
Ability to keep up-to-date computerized registry of all registered refugees through timely verifications and modification transactions	Percentage of modification transactions and verification requests processed in relation to those requested by refugees and Governments, United Nations agencies or the relevant officials	100 per cent	100 per cent: 513,917 modification transactions completed and 182,886 verification requests processed
	Percentage of new registrations (new inscription cases) in relation to total received applications	11 per cent	248 new inscription cases were approved by the relief and social services programme, representing 39 per cent of total pending applications; achievement above target due to clearing the backlog of pending cases in the Jordan field during 2005
Increased development opportunities for women	Number of women benefiting from skills training activities	11,400	12,100 (6 per cent increase)
Increased access to services and opportunities for persons with disabilities	Number of persons with disabilities receiving direct rehabilitation services	12,700	18,300 (44 per cent increase)
Improved access of children and youth to educational, cultural, social, recreational and sports activities	Number of children and youth participating in cultural, social, recreational and sport activities	9,000	20,000 (122 per cent increase)
Increased provision of credit and skills training opportunities to Palestine refugees	Number of clients benefiting from loan products	2,300	3,600 (56.5 per cent increase)

(f) Selective cash assistance was provided to 12,188 special hardship and non-special hardship families. This represented a 104 per cent increase over the figures for 2004;

(g) A microcredit community support programme manager was hired to guide and monitor credit operations;

(h) Reduction of social worker caseload norms (from 250 to 200 families per social worker) was approved, a prerequisite for introducing best practices in social work and improving quality of services;

(i) Three hundred relief and social services programme staff and refugee volunteers in UNRWA community-based organizations benefited from gender training courses.

Significant activities

88. UNRWA field offices began to provide services to family members of refugee women married to non-refugees. Revised consolidated eligibility and registration instructions will ensure that assistance is gender-neutral and that it reaches those most in need, and registration software is being adapted to guide staff in the application of this policy.

89. In an effort to address the weaknesses of the current registration system and introduce the benefits of new technologies, the system is being redesigned through the Palestine Refugee Records Project to create an Intranet registration system that will allow centralized updating of refugee information from 39 registration offices Agency-wide. The tendering process for the outsourcing and development of the software for the new system was completed and a vendor identified.

90. UNRWA laid the foundations for major reform of the special hardship assistance programme, which provides a social safety net for the most impoverished families, by conducting a socio-economic survey of 3,603 special hardship case families. Analysis of the results led to the establishment of abject and absolute poverty lines for Jordan and the development of a proxy means testing formula (to revise eligibility criteria), as a first step to moving the Special Hardship Assistance Programme from a status-based to a needs-based approach.

TABLE 5 BASIC SOCIAL AND ECONOMIC INDICATORS FOR SPECIAL HARDSHIP FAMILIES

Indicator	*Total*
Education Drop-out rates (children ages 6-15 years of age) Illiteracy rates	14.3 per cent 16.6 per cent
Health Families supporting a person with a disability Families supporting a person with a chronic illness Individuals with health insurance	11.5 per cent 21.8 per cent 41.7 per cent
Expenditures and income Individuals with expenditures of less than $1 per day Individuals with expenditures of less than $2 per day Average annual per capita income Average annual family income	46.7 per cent 85.8 per cent $449$1,800

Indicator	*Total*
Housing	12.63 per cent 64.1 per cent
Dwellings with asbestos roofs	42.6 per cent 24.09 per cent
Dwellings that are cold and difficult to heat	
Dwellings that are poorly ventilated	
Dwellings without heat	

91. By July 2005, distribution of flour to special hardship case families was phased out in Jordan, Lebanon and the Syrian Arab Republic and mixed pulses were introduced as a substitute. This step was necessitated by funding shortfalls; by the realization that the distribution of flour was no longer an effective intervention; and by the desire to introduce commodities with richer protein content. UNRWA was also obliged to freeze its annual special hardship case assistance ceiling (instead of increasing the ceiling annually by the customary 3.5 per cent) due to shortage of funds, thereby decreasing the percentage of impoverished refugees receiving safety net assistance.

92. The social services programme continued to provide tens of thousands of women, persons with disabilities, children and youth with the assistance and the skills needed to encourage their personal and economic development. This was achieved through a network of 104 community-based organizations managed by dedicated community volunteers. In Lebanon, 151 unemployed refugee women gained access to training and employment opportunities through the expansion of an apprenticeship programme. In the West Bank, three centres introduced programmes that allowed 73 women to obtain high school diplomas through structured education classes. A new Women's Programme Centre with a kindergarten was established in Jenin Camp and opportunities for women to gain access to information was increased through the newly established Internet café at the Women's Programme Centre in Madaba, Jordan. The disability programme constructed a new school in Rafah in the Gaza Strip for refugees with hearing impairments, with an audiology centre and vocational training facilities. In the West Bank, an Artificial Limbs and Prosthetic Devices Unit was inaugurated in Jenin Camp. In the Syrian Arab Republic, a comprehensive survey was conducted in all camps in coordination with the United Nations Children's Fund and the General Authority for Palestine Arab Refugees, to establish a disability database to improve planning and service delivery. Another survey was conducted in Lebanon in cooperation with the Palestinian Disability Forum, targeting children aged 3 to 18 years of age.

93. Social workers and their immediate supervisors participated in the second phase of a certified education training programme, developed in collaboration with Southern Illinois University, Carbondale, United States of America, in order to learn how to implement a best practice generalist approach to social work. In 2005, 223 staff in Jordan, the Syrian Arab Republic, Lebanon and the West Bank successfully completed four out of the eight required courses, while 91 social workers and their immediate supervisors from the Gaza Strip completed only two courses due to repeated closures and travel restrictions.

94. Difficulties continued in planning for the shelter rehabilitation programme, since it relies on project funding. The ability to implement a more developmental approach, in which refugees contribute their own labour or resources, is constrained because donors require a quick turnaround time for shelter project implementation—which leaves insufficient time for staff to work with families on a self-help basis.

D. Performance report for sub-goal IV: microfinanceand microenterprise

95. The goal of the Agency's microfinance and microenterprise programme is to promote economic development and alleviate poverty. This is achieved through the provision of credit for small enterprises, household consumption and housing needs. The aim is to improve the quality of life of small business owners, sustain jobs, reduce unemployment and poverty, create household assets, improve housing stock and empower women. Highlights include the following:

(a) In 15 years, the programme has financed over 106,000 loans totalling $109 million and is now the largest microfinance provider in the occupied Palestinian territory;

(b) The programme's base loan capital increased by $5.23 million thanks to donations made in the context of the Gaza disengagement. It was also able to develop its small-business-training subprogramme and expand its credit operations;

(c) The programme expanded its branch office network to 10 offices, which will increase by an additional three offices in the West Bank, Jordan and the Syrian Arab Republic in 2006;

(d) With financial support obtained at the time of the Gaza disengagement, the programme was able to secure funding to pilot a new housing loan product, which will be expanded to the West Bank, Jordan and the Syrian Arab Republic once it has been successfully tested in the Gaza Strip in 2006;

(e) The programme successfully administered the PalFund, a new development-financing trust fund supported by the Organization of Petroleum Exporting Countries Fund for International Development to support businesses in the occupied Palestinian territory. UNRWA financed 2,629 PalFund loans totalling $2.38 million;

(f) In order to benchmark its performance, the programme is participating in the MIXmarket and MicroBanking Bulletin, in which its performance is compared and scaled with another 631 microfinance institutions. In order to further improve its transparency, the programme contracted an institutional rating to be conducted on its performance in 2005. This rating will assess, inter alia, the governance, risk management, activities and services of the programme.

TABLE 6 PERFORMANCE BY INDICATOR

		Achievements	
Expected accomplishment	*Performance indicator*	*2005 target*	*2005 result*
Microenterprise credit			
Increased business development and income-generating opportunities	Number of loans disbursed Total value of loans financed	15,000 $13 million	14,826 $15.66 million
Improved outstanding portfolio and number of active loans	Number of active loans Total value of outstanding loans Repayment rate	10,000 $6.50 million 97 per cent	9,500 $6.46 million 96.6 per cent

Expected accomplishment	Performance indicator	Achievements	
		2005 target	2005 result
Solidarity group lending			
Increased capacity of women microentrepreneurs	Number of loans disbursed to women	4,100	4,852
	Total value of loans financed	$3 million	$3.04 million
Improved outstanding portfolio for women clients	Number of active loans to women	3,150	3,338
	Total value of active loans	$1.49 million	$1.29 million
	Repayment rate	97 per cent	95 per cent
Consumer lending			
Increased financial services to poor people that are unable to access bank credit	Number of loans disbursed	2,500	2.210
	Total value of loans financed	$1.10 million	$1.32 million
Improved outstanding portfolio for consumer clients	Number of active loans	1,860	1,616
	Total value of outstanding loans	$0.53 million	$0.63 million
	Repayment rate	97 per cent	94 per cent
Small-scale enterprise			
Increased business development opportunities for small-scale enterprises	Number of loans disbursed	150	51
	Total value of loans financed	$1.50 million	$0.47 million
Improved outstanding portfolio	Number of active loans	200	94
	Total value of outstanding loans	$2.50 million	$0.71 million
	Repayment rate	96 per cent	80 per cent

Significant activities

96. Although the programme grew significantly in 2005, it continued to suffer from risks associated with the continuing intifada, the rise in inter-Palestinian strife and an intensified closure regime. This resulted in the programme not being able to achieve full operational self-sufficiency in 2005. Thus, the operational self-sufficiency rate of the programme was just 86 per cent and the programme ran a loss of $491,614 on operations during the year. Operational self-sufficiency performance in the West Bank was lowest, at 72 per cent, followed by the Gaza Strip at 86 per cent. While the programme has taken significant risk-mitigation measures, the current performance is the inevitable result of maintaining microfinance operations during conflict.

97. After just over two years, the offices in Jordan and the Syrian Arab Republic are operating profitably. The programme in the Syrian Arab Republic is a model of efficiency, with high staff productivity and a very low portfolio-at-risk rate. In 2005, the operational self-sufficiency rate was 110 per cent. The operation in Jordan, although less productive, has achieved a very profitable operational self-sufficiency rate of 163 per cent. Given that, it has been unfortunate that UNRWA has been unable to raise the donor funding needed to match the strategic objectives and outreach targets in the Agency's medium-term plan for 2005 to 2009. As a result, the programme lacked resources to expand its network of offices.

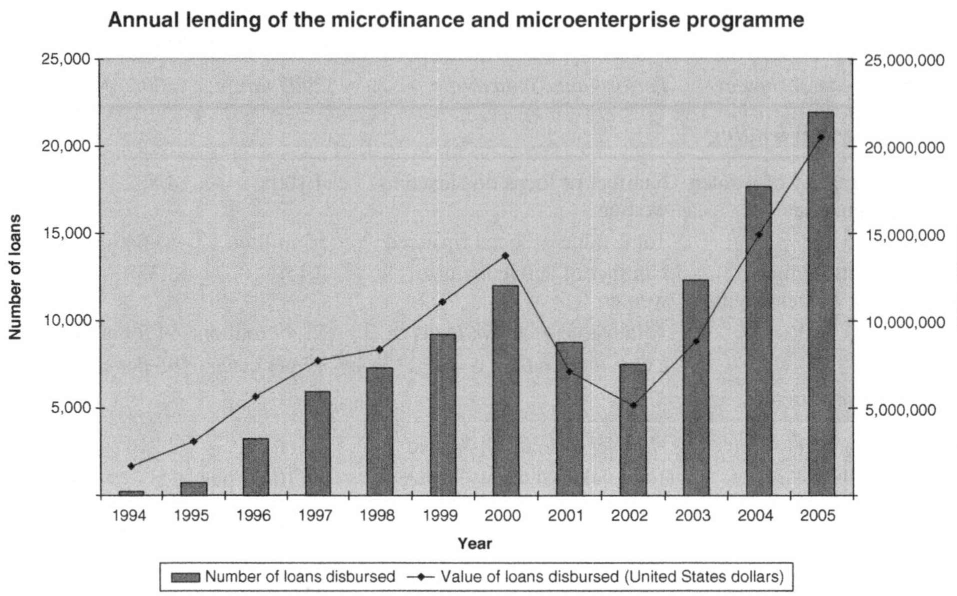

Figure V Annual lending of the microfinance and microenterprise programme

98. In 2005, the programme experienced its highest level of outreach since the start of the intifada. The declining outreach of the two years following 2000 appears to have halted—although the programme is not immune to further economic shocks. The programme produced record outreach in 2005, when it financed 22,000 loans totalling $20.49 million. Half of this financing was in the Gaza Strip, 31 per cent in the West Bank, 12 per cent in Jordan and 7 per cent in the Syrian Arab Republic.

99. A key to improving the programme as it grows is to modernize its management information system. For three years, the programme has been planning to replace its four outdated loan management information databases. These were developed in-house when the programme was structured quite differently and are no longer able to provide the required level of financial and managerial reporting. They are also inefficient, expensive and time-consuming to use. These systems need to be replaced with a new online, centralized database that will allow the programme to streamline management reporting, decentralize decision-making and rationalize staffing. To achieve this, a 700-page user requirement document was developed and used as the basis for two (so far unsuccessful) bidding processes. The current inability to find an appropriate and cost-effective information system is hindering the effectiveness of the programme.

100. The crisis in the occupied Palestinian territory and the chronic shortfall in project funding in Jordan and the Syrian Arab Republic caused the programme to fall short of the loan financing goals presented in the medium-term plan. Nevertheless, it was more

successful in achieving the modified, results-based indicators that took account of these risks. It achieved just 69 per cent of the medium-term plan loan outreach objectives in the Gaza Strip, 67 per cent in both the West Bank and Jordan and 53 per cent in the Syrian Arab Republic. Overall, it achieved just 60 per cent of its loan financing objective and has not had sufficient financing to expand its network of branch offices as rapidly as desired.

[1] The Office for the Coordination of Humanitarian Affairs and UNRWA, "Humanitarian impact of the West Bank barrier, Special focus, Crossing the barrier: Palestinian access to agricultural land", January 2006.

7 Annual Report of the Executive Director of the World Food Programme for 2006

Annual report of the Executive Director of the World Food Programme for 2006

Note by the Secretary-General

The Secretary-General has the honour to transmit to the Economic and Social Council the annual report of the Executive Director of the World Food Programme for 2006, as approved by the Board of the Programme in its decision 2007/EB.1/2, which is also attached.

Decision 2007/EB.1/2 of the Executive Board of the World Food Programme adopted by the Board at its first regular session of 2007 (19-22 February 2007)

Annual report for 2006 to the Economic and Social Council and the Council of the Food and Agriculture Organization of the United Nations

The Board approved the annual report for 2006 to the Economic and Social Council and the Council of the Food and Agriculture Organization of the United Nations (FAO) (WFP/EB.1/2007/4). In accordance with its decision 2004/EB.A/11 of 24 May 2004, the Board requested that the annual report be forwarded to the Economic and Social Council and to the FAO Council, along with the Board's decisions and recommendations for 2006 and the present decision.

20 February 2007

Executive Summary

In response to increased inter-governmental and inter-agency interest in United Nations reform, this report focuses on WFP's progress in implementing reform measures and the challenges WFP faces in continuing the reform agenda.

In 2006, WFP's work in United Nations reform and inter-agency cooperation included the achievements set out below.

(i) Leadership of the humanitarian logistics cluster and co-leadership of the emergency telecommunications cluster, under which the principles governing relationships among United Nations and Inter-Agency Standing Committee logistics bodies were reviewed to increase their effectiveness and clarity.

(ii) WFP was the largest appealing agency in the 2006 Common Appeals Process, accounting for 42 percent of all requirements. As of 30 November 2006, WFP had received 88 percent of requirements against appeals.

(iii) WFP intensified its participation in joint programmes in 27 countries on HIV/AIDS, education, the Millennium Development Goals, nutrition, disaster management and the environment.

(iv) Collaboration among the Rome agencies ensured that food security, hunger reduction, rural and social development, and safety nets became focus areas in the United Nations Development Group action plan for achieving the Millennium Development Goals.

This report is in accordance with streamlined corporate reporting to the Board and WFP parent bodies (WFP/EB.A/2004/5-F). It is consistent with the United Nations Economic and Social Council format for annual reporting by United Nations agencies, based on provisions of the 2004 General Assembly resolution on the Triennial Comprehensive Policy Review of Operational Activities for Development. This report takes account of comments from the Board on the 2005 Annual Report and from the Bureau in September 2006. The timing for submitting it to the Board's First Regular Session of 2007 does not allow inclusion of complete statistical information for all of 2006. Partnership statistical data in the Section on Collaboration with Partners refer to 2005, because 2006 data are not yet available. Complete statistical information will be available in the 2006 Annual Performance Report, submitted to the Board's Annual Session.

Structures and Mechanisms

Inter-Agency Standing Committee (IASC)

1. IASC continued to improve humanitarian response by rolling out and refining the cluster system; WFP guided implementation of the system, focusing on results. WFP's leadership of the logistics cluster and co-leadership of the emergency telecommunications cluster was further strengthened. WFP and IASC partners reviewed the principles governing

relationships among IASC logistics bodies to increase their effectiveness. WFP contributed to other clusters, especially nutrition, protection, health and early recovery. WFP is also leading the developing of a rapid nutrition assessment toolkit.

Executive Committee on Humanitarian Affairs (ECHA)

2. Through ECHA, WFP highlighted the situation of its staff who work in insecure and difficult environments. Working with the United Nations Development Group (UNDG)/ECHA group on transitions, WFP helped to bring United Nations development and humanitarian actors together to develop common approaches to post-conflict transition policies and programmes.

Consolidated Appeals Process (CAP)

3. WFP was the largest appealing agency in the 2006 CAP, accounting for 42 percent of all requirements. As of 30 November 2006, WFP had received 88 percent of requirements against appeals.

4. As part of inter-agency implementation of needs analysis frameworks (NAFs), WFP and the Food and Agriculture Organization of the United Nations (FAO) led the food-security NAFs in Côte d'Ivoire, Somalia, the Occupied Palestinian Territory and Uganda. Food security working groups led by WFP and FAO analysed needs and priorities, providing a basis for a food-security analysis by the Common Humanitarian Action Plan (CHAP).

United Nations Development Group (UNDG)

5. WFP chaired the Programme Group (PG) in 2006, guiding working groups on (i) national development strategies based on the Millennium Development Goals (MDGs), (ii) aid effectiveness and (iii) programming policy. For the first time, UNDG Executive Committee (ExCom) regional directors were consulted about the most effective support that the PG could provide to regional and country structures.

6. The PG prepared an action plan for realizing the objectives endorsed by the 2005 World Summit, using an operational framework based on the MDGs. This allows country-level efforts to be scaled up and ensures alignment with national priorities and development strategies. The UNDG principals endorsed the action plan, which now provides a reference for gauging achievement of the MDGs.

7. The Rome-based agencies ensured that food security, hunger reduction, rural and social development and safety nets were focus areas for the action plan. WFP encouraged country offices to refer to the action plan during discussion in United Nations country teams—particularly in the Common Country Assessment (CCA)/United Nations Development Assistance Framework (UNDAF) process – and to advocate for food security, nutrition and education, including WFP food-based interventions where appropriate.

Funding and Resources

8. WFP's fundraising ensured increased and stable funding from major donors, attracted new donors—including private corporations and individuals—and encouraged occasional donors to become regular contributors. WFP's fundraising strategy aims to increase

the impact of donations through greater flexibility and predictability—larger proportions of multilateral contributions, more cash donations, twinning arrangements and fewer restrictions.

9. As of 30 November 2006, contributions to WFP amounted to US$2.4 billion: emergency operations (EMOPs) and protracted relief and recovery operations (PRROs) received approximately 80 percent; development operations 9 percent; and special operations and others, including the Immediate Response Account (IRA), the remaining balance. Approximately 10 percent of these funds were multilateral, and 90 percent were directed multilateral; 82 public-sector donors contributed to WFP operations, including ten new donors contributing US$97 million.

10. WFP benefited from private sector support, with US$47 million confirmed as of 30 November 2006. WFP is preparing an innovative strategy to consolidate and institutionalize its private fundraising activities; this includes seeking cash from a balanced portfolio of corporations, individuals, foundations and community-based organizations.

Central Emergency Response Fund (CERF)

11. The new centralized funding mechanisms for humanitarian operations had the greatest effect on WFP operations of any of the current United Nations reforms. As of November 2006, the United Nations, including CERF and the common humanitarian funds, was WFP's third largest donor, contributing US$126.5 million, compared with US$7 million in 2005.

12. The CERF and WFP's internal rapid response funding mechanism, the Immediate Response Account (IRA), operate collaboratively to augment WFP's emergency response capacity. The IRA supplements the CERF grants, which have a maximum allocation of US$30 million per crisis for all United Nations agencies. The IRA is used to address timing issues, because these funds are accessed within 24 hours; CERF grant approval takes longer. The CERF contributions to WFP in 2006 as of 30 November 2006 amounted to US$67 million.

Implementation of United Nations Reform Measures

Harmonization of Programmes

13. In 2006, ExCom members and WFP improved country programming by making it more results-based and linking planning and implementation to the MDGs. Cape Verde experimented with a Common Country Programme (CCP) and a country programme action plan (CPAP); collaboration achieved results that were in line with national development goals. The CCA/UNDAF guidelines were updated to reflect joint programming that emphasizes national planning, capacity-building and inter-agency frameworks for disaster prevention and post-conflict recovery.

14. WFP will increase its participation in poverty reduction strategies (PRS). With FAO, the International Fund for Agricultural Development (IFAD), the United Nations Children's Fund (UNICEF) and the World Bank, WFP provides information about food-insecure people, helping to ensure that food security remains a high priority. Food security was incorporated into Mali's national Poverty Reduction Strategy Paper (PRSP) thanks to joint efforts by FAO and WFP.

Joint Programmes (JPs)

15. WFP participated in 46 JPs in 27 countries in various sectors. These included two HIV/AIDS JPs in Lesotho. One, with the Joint United Nations Programme on HIV/AIDS (UNAIDS), the United Nations Development Programme (UNDP) and FAO, involves and empowers people living with HIV/AIDS by emphasizing capacity-building. The second, with FAO and UNICEF, aims to improve the nutritional status of children living with HIV/AIDS. In Malawi, WFP is the lead agency for coordinating food security and nutrition support of HIV/AIDS-affected people, partnering FAO, UNICEF and the World Health Organization (WHO). In Rwanda, WFP, UNICEF and UNDP support improved self-reliance for HIV-affected people, including co-production of a weekly radio programme on nutrition and HIV, with local radio and government support. The programme will be in the local Kinyarwanda language, and be available throughout the Great Lakes Region.

16. With UNICEF and WHO, WFP is implementing the Healthy Schools Initiative in Afghanistan, benefiting 1.5 million schoolchildren. WFP also leads the national deworming campaign, which helps 6 million schoolchildren and will be handed over to the national authorities as part of capacity-building. WFP leads the deworming campaign in Haiti, with WHO and UNICEF.

17. WFP is promoting girls' education in Cameroon, with UNICEF, the International Labour Organization (ILO), UNDP, UNESCO, the United Nations Population Fund (UNFPA) and WHO; in Pakistan, with UNICEF and the United Nations Office for Project Services (UNOPS); and in Egypt, with, ILO, UNDP, UNESCO, UNFPA, UNICEF, the United Nations Development Fund for Women (UNIFEM). In Burkina Faso, WFP, UNICEF, UNDP and FAO designed a girls' education programme and provide a minimum essential package for schoolchildren, especially girls.

18. In Bhutan, WFP, UNDP, UNFPA, United Nations volunteers (UNVs) and UNICEF are implementing the Human Security Fund, addressing rural hunger and poverty, illiteracy, school enrolment, unemployment and youth, child and maternal mortality and HIV/AIDS. WFP contributes food-for-education (FFE) programmes.

19. In Bolivia, WFP is involved in the Contigo Avanzar campaign advocating for and disseminating MDGs, with FAO, UNDP, UNFPA and UNICEF. For each MDG the initiative uses musical compositions, departmental workshops and other audiovisual media.

20. In the United Republic of Tanzania, WFP, UNICEF, UNDP, the United Nations Industrial Development Organization (UNIDO), the Office of the United Nations High Commissioner for Refugees (UNHCR) and FAO are implementing a pilot programme supported by the United Nations Trust Fund for Human Security. The project targets refugee host areas in north-western Tanzania, and aims to improve food and environmental security, reduce the small arms and light weapons trade, and strengthen host area capacities in vulnerability analysis. WFP and UNHCR lead this transition programme, with WFP leading the humanitarian and transport sectors.

21. In Peru, WFP, UNDP, FAO, UNICEF and WHO collaborate to respond to natural disasters. WFP-led activities include improving the nutritional and health status of local communities to reduce their vulnerability.

22. WFP, the United Nations Assistance Mission in Afghanistan (UNAMA), the United Nations Environment Programme (UNEP), FAO, UNOPS, UNDP, UNIFEM, UNFPA, UNICEF, UNESCO, the International Organization for Migration (IOM), UNHCR, the United Nations Office on Drugs and Crime (UNODC), the United Nations Mine Action Centre for Afghanistan, and the United Nations Human Settlements Programme (Habitat) cooperate on the Green Afghanistan Initiative, which focuses on the environment.

Paris Declaration on Aid Effectiveness

23. WFP participates in the Paris Declaration agenda in Cambodia, Mozambique, Nicaragua, Rwanda and the United Republic of Tanzania. WFP developed guidelines for country offices engaged in harmonization and alignment processes. In December 2006, WFP and the other UNDG ExCom funds and programmes signed a CPAP for the Joint Assistance Strategy for Tanzania. The Tanzanian government's preference for general budget support, however, is a challenge to programme implementation for many development partners, including United Nations agencies. The aid environment in Tanzania is changing rapidly, and WFP needs to adopt sector-wide approaches and management.

Resident Coordinator (RC)/Humanitarian Coordinator (HC) System

24. In 2006, WFP increased its participation in RC and HC issues. A new accountability framework for the RC system is being introduced. This will increase the involvement of regional directors, who will oversee and support UNCTs' promotion of United Nations reform in countries. Regional directors will prepare "team opinions" of RCs and United Nations country teams (UNCTs), based on representatives' assessments of UNCTs. WFP regional and country directors piloted a feedback tool, which WFP regional human resources officers have been trained to use.

25. WFP seeks to attract and retain top-quality individuals as RCs or HCs, and to increase their impact on United Nations work at the country level. To increase the number of WFP staff in RC/HC rosters, six people from WFP attended the RC Assessment Centre during 2006. Four WFP staff members currently serve as RCs, including one in the Sudan who also serves as Deputy Special Representative of the Secretary-General.

26. WFP helped to improve the training and selection of HCs. Three WFP country directors are in the HC pool, established in 2006 to provide qualified candidates for quick selection.

Joint Offices (JOs)

27. WFP and the other ExCom agencies initiated a pilot JO in Cape Verde in January 2006. One CCP was approved by the Boards of all four agencies. WFP's Board also noted that a development project it had already approved was subsumed in the CCP. The RC was designated to represent the ExCom agencies, and UNDP was designated as support agency to implement the JO model. UNDP business processes, based on the Atlas Enterprise Resource Planning system, were therefore applied. Staff employment contracts with the four agencies were terminated, and new contracts were offered to those selected for the JO through a job fair. The full JO started on 1 April 2006. An inter-agency team selected a WFP professional as the deputy representative in charge of programme aspects of the JO. She joined in September 2006.

28. WFP chaired the JO Working Group (JOWG) of UNDG in 2006. The group will support the creation of additional JOs in 2007, though this may not follow the Cape Verde model. Supported by JOWG, a UNDG internal review of implementation of the Cape Verde JO will be completed in the first quarter of 2007. WFP supports UNDG's development of additional JO model offices through consultation from its corporate partner, the Boston Consulting Group.

29. WFP and the Secretary-General's High-Level Panel on United Nations System-Wide Coherence believe that the main goal of JOs should be more coherent and improved United Nations country programming. There is a risk that the JO process focuses too much on administrative coordination and not enough on the impact of programming.

Common Premises

30. In August 2006, WFP became chair of the Working Group on Common Premises. WFP evaluated potential common premises and United Nations House initiatives, and funded projects where the financial, operational, safety and security aspects of common premises would benefit country offices. Using its United Nations reform fund for 2006, WFP managed design and construction of the Bhutan United Nations House, carried out a seismic assessment of the United Nations House in Armenia, and supported a working group to evaluate 21 United Nations House or common premises projects.

United Nations Joint Logistics Centre (UNJLC)

31. WFP is responsible for the administrative and financial management of UNJLC. In 2006, IASC agreed that UNJLC would be a tool for the WFP-led Logistics Cluster; the precise arrangements will be worked out and approved by IASC in 2007. In 2006, UNJLC was involved in the Pakistan earthquake relief operation, providing logistics coordination and information management services to the humanitarian community; this operation was phased out in August. In July 2006, UNJLC deployed staff to Lebanon, to support the Logistics Cluster team, WFP logistics and the rest of the humanitarian community with logistics information and mapping services, reporting, and tracking of non-food items (NFIs); this operation was phased out in October. UNJLC assisted the HC and the Logistics Cluster team in the Democratic Republic of the Congo (DRC), and continued to coordinate and manage NFIs in Darfur.

32. Declining donor support for the UNJLC core unit in Rome is a major challenge. The unit initiates and supports UNJLC field operations, and reduced support is preventing it from responding efficiently through the rapid deployment of staff.

United Nations Humanitarian Air Service (UNHAS)

33. UNHAS provided assistance in major emergencies in Pakistan and Lebanon, initiated common services in the Central African Republic and Sri Lanka, and continued its operations in Afghanistan, Angola, Burundi, Chad, DRC, West Africa, Somalia, the Sudan and the United Republic of Tanzania. A large-scale special project in DRC transported demobilized soldiers by air, on behalf of the World Bank/*Commission nationale de la démobilisation et réinsertion*.

34. As of November 2006, the 64 aircraft and heavy-lift helicopters chartered by WFP/UNHAS had transported 359,000 passengers and 29,600 mt of cargo for the relief

operations of United Nations agencies and more than 200 non-governmental organizations (NGOs). Drastically improved road access to beneficiaries in southern Sudan considerably reduced cargo deliveries by air.

35. The aviation management structure was strengthened in response to recommendations in the International Civil Aviation Organization's recent audit report.

Collaboration with Partners

36. In 2005, WFP collaborated with 13 United Nations agencies, the World Bank, the International Committee of the Red Cross (ICRC), the International Federation of Red Cross and Red Crescent Societies (IFRC), IOM and ILO in 230 projects in 80 countries. Statistical data on partnerships for 2006 will be available in the Annual Performance Report at the Board's 2007 Annual Session.

UNICEF

37. With collaboration on 138 projects in 68 countries in 2005, UNICEF remained WFP's main partner, primarily in education, mother-and-child health (MCH), nutrition and technical assistance.

38. In Uganda, WFP and UNICEF implement the Nutrition Work in Conflict-Affected Districts JP, addressing child and maternal nutrition, and are developing a global partnership for capacity-building. WFP and UNICEF implemented a nutrition project in Bhutan for the Multiple Indicator Cluster Survey, and developed a strategy and action plan for double fortification of salt. In Pakistan, UNICEF and WFP initiated the MCH JP, with WFP providing fortified food to encourage positive health behaviour and increased target group attendance at common target health facilities.

39. In line with their 2005 Memorandum of Understanding (MOU), WFP and UNICEF are cooperating to eliminate child hunger and undernutrition and achieve MDG 1 target 2—reduce by half the prevalence of underweight among children under 5. The Ending Child Hunger and Undernutrition Initiative (ECHUI) is a global partnership to ensure coherent global and national efforts. United Nations partners in ECHUI include UNICEF, the World Bank, UNHCR, UNDP, FAO and UNFPA.

40. In West Africa, WFP and UNICEF are implementing a joint nutrition strategy, especially through MCH programmes. Joint advocacy with donors was established, in which WFP and UNICEF—in discussions with the World Bank—advocate to make nutrition a PRS priority. In a similar initiative for education, WFP and UNICEF promote the Essential Learning Package within the Sahel Alliance.

41. In Latin America and the Caribbean, the UNICEF/WFP Regional Strategic Partnership Meeting in May 2006 recognized that UNICEF/WFP partnership is critical to ending child hunger. WFP and partners influenced policy and put child hunger and undernutrition high on government agendas. In Peru, WFP, UNICEF, the World Bank, the Pan-American Health Organization (PAHO), WHO, the United States Agency for International Development (USAID), NGOs and the government collaborated in a national initiative to combat chronic malnutrition, which the government declared a priority. WFP and UNICEF foster South–South cooperation; WFP, UNICEF, PAHO/WHO and other partners have established

a regional knowledge management initiative for policy-makers, to strengthen national policies to eradicate child undernutrition.

42. A joint WFP/UNICEF project in the Occupied Palestinian Territory provides salt producers with potassium iodide to increase the percentage of iodized salt, and includes iodized salt in WFP rations. In Timor-Leste, WFP and UNICEF jointly employed a nutritionist to recommend ways of strengthening their joint programming. In Cambodia, collaboration with UNICEF started in 73 schools and has now expanded to 654 child-friendly schools.

43. The "essential package" of 12 school-based interventions was established with UNESCO, UNICEF, WHO and other partners and is based on the Focusing Resources on Effective School Health framework. It delivers complementary nutrition, health and basic education inputs in all WFP-assisted schools, to improve the health and nutritional status of schoolchildren. There are WFP/UNICEF partnerships in 38 countries; the most comprehensive being those in Afghanistan and Pakistan, where deworming campaigns reached more than 11 million children. Expected approval for an additional 13 million deworming tablets will benefit Afghanistan, Angola, Bangladesh, Cameroon, Ecuador, Uganda, the United Republic of Tanzania and Zambia.

FAO

44. In 2005, FAO was WFP's second largest partner, cooperating in 87 projects in 53 countries, mainly in promoting agricultural and crop production, FFE and joint assessments.

45. In the context of the Comprehensive Africa Agriculture Development Programme, supported by WFP, the New Partnership for Africa's Development (NEPAD) launched the Home-Grown School Feeding Programme (HGSFP), which links school feeding to agricultural development by expanding local markets through the purchase of home-grown food commodities.

46. In Ghana, HGSFP was integrated into the WFP country programme (CP); the governments of Ghana and the Netherlands, WFP and the business community linked to the University of Berkeley used locally purchased foods to support the National School Feeding Programme. An MOU between WFP and the National Ghana School Feeding Programme will ensure joint targeting, a sustainable exit strategy and harmonized inputs, strategies and monitoring mechanisms.

47. FAO and WFP joint crop and food supply assessment missions (CFSAMs) are very valuable to humanitarian food security interventions. By September 2006, CFSAMs had been conducted in Angola, Cameroon, Liberia and Burundi; additional missions are planned for Burkina Faso, Ethiopia, Mauritania and the Sudan.

48. Following a technical consultation in December 2005 on issues such as the relationship between national food gaps and household food needs, and improved estimation of commercial imports, WFP and FAO are revising CFSAM guidelines.

49. The challenge is to develop a standard food security classification system that consolidates inter-sectoral data and facilitates comparisons of humanitarian needs among countries. In Somalia, WFP and FAO are using the Integrated Phase Classification (IPC) system and guidance developed by the FAO Food Security Assessment Unit. IPC is also being piloted in

Côte d'Ivoire, the Occupied Palestinian Territory and Somalia as part of CAP/NAF. WFP plans to extend the pilot to other countries before revising the IPC guidelines with FAO.

50. WFP and FAO continued the twin-track approach in the Junior Farmer Field and Life School (JFFLS) programme in Mozambique, Namibia, Swaziland and Zambia.

51. In September 2006, WFP and FAO signed a local MOU in the Philippines to build peace and improve food security among conflict-affected farmers in the first joint food-for-work (FFW) project in Mindanao. This aims to improve the agricultural productivity and livelihoods of poor farmers affected by conflict and internal displacement.

52. The Emergency Relief Coordinator and Special Envoy for the Horn of Africa requested FAO and WFP to start a regional consultative process addressing long-term food security challenges in the region, to mitigate the effects of future droughts in the Horn of Africa.

IFAD

53. In 2005, WFP and IFAD cooperated on nine projects in eight countries, mainly on agricultural production, land and water development, road development and disaster recovery. WFP provided food aid to communities benefiting from IFAD micro-credit schemes, to improve infrastructure or develop skills in income-generating activities.

54. In 2001, WFP/IFAD collaboration in India addressed poverty eradication and food security. WFP hosts IFAD's Field Presence Unit in India. The benefits of this collaboration include improved project design, cost efficiency and joint advocacy. Combining the agencies' food and cash resources has developed sustainable livelihoods for 600,000 of the most food-insecure tribal people.

55. In Mali, WFP, IFAD and the government signed a Letter of Understanding (LOU) for rural development through asset creation. In the United Republic of Tanzania, WFP has partnered IFAD since 1999, supporting the government's Participatory Irrigation Development Programme; WFP's food-for-asset-creation activities have constructed/rehabilitated 328 km of access roads and excavated 461 km of canals. WFP, IFAD and government interventions created 36 irrigation schemes for paddy irrigation land.

Rome-Based Agency Cooperation

56. A senior-level working group of the Rome-based agencies met for the first time in August 2006 to discuss improvements in joint working. Areas where increased collaboration was proposed included the integration of food security and rural development into national PRS, regional approaches to combating food insecurity, and needs assessment.

57. In November 2006, WFP, FAO, IFAD and Habitat collaborated during the International Forum on the Eradication of Poverty held in New York to mark the end of the first United Nations Decade for the Eradication of Poverty. The agencies co-sponsored a panel and produced a joint paper on "Reducing Hunger and Extreme Poverty: Towards a Coherent Strategy", highlighting the need for a twin-track approach to hunger and poverty reduction.

58. The heads of the three Rome-based agencies visited Ghana in December 2006 to reaffirm their determination to strengthen joint efforts to reduce hunger and poverty in Ghana's food-insecure northern regions.

59. The Rome-based agencies continued to cooperate in the International Alliance Against Hunger (IAAH). During the FAO Committee on World Food Security, a special event, Alliances Against Hunger, Today and Tomorrow, brought about national alliances such as the Jordanian National Alliance. WFP and Jordan are strengthening this alliance's institutional capacity.

60. IAAH was among the first partners WFP contacted in 2005 when it launched the Walk the World event. This initiative stimulated activities such as the Germany—Jordan Drive Away Hunger rally, in 2006.

61. The Rome-Based Management Development Centre – a joint WFP, IFAD and FAO initiative – was launched in 2004. Simulations, competency-based interviews and assessment results increased participants' awareness of their own management and leadership skills. Since its inception, 114 senior managers from the three organizations—42 from WFP—have participated. Other United Nations agencies recognize this programme's effectiveness in developing senior managers, and the Rome-based agencies are exploring ways of expanding partnerships with these agencies. Women in leadership, negotiation skills and Myers Briggs training sessions were attended by 92 participants—15 from WFP.

UNAIDS

62. As a co-sponsor of UNAIDS, WFP is the lead agency for nutrition and dietary support of people with HIV, and provides guidance to national governments and the other nine co-sponsors of UNAIDS.

63. In March 2006, the Global Task Team on Improving AIDS Coordination among Multilateral Institutions and Donors was established in accordance with the Three Ones principles. WFP advocates for food, nutritional and dietary support to be included in comprehensive care and support packages for governments. The role of food and nutrition in maintaining the health and quality of life of people living with HIV and AIDS is now widely recognized. In July 2006, WFP became chair of the UNAIDS Committee of Coordinating Organizations.

64. In August 2006, at the International AIDS conference in Toronto, WFP called on all stakeholders in the fight against AIDS to include food and nutritional support in the essential package of care for people affected by HIV. As Stephen Lewis stated: "… it is now accepted as unassailable truth that people in treatment need nutritious food supplements to maintain and tolerate their treatment".

65. WFP operates in 21 of the 25 most severely affected countries, and has HIV/AIDS-related activities in 51 countries. WFP interventions focus on three areas: care and treatment, support to orphans and vulnerable children affected by AIDS, and awareness and prevention education.

UNHCR

66. WFP and UNHCR continued their joint support to 1.9 million refugees and 2 million returnees in 30 countries. Collaboration includes a global work plan, joint plans of action at the country level, regular high-level meetings, WFP's participation in the UNHCR Executive Committee, and UNHCR's in the WFP Executive Board, a high-level working group to review joint issues related to internally displaced people (IDPs), and collaboration at the field and headquarters levels.

67. More than 15 joint assessment missions (JAMs) were carried out, and training for JAMs was provided in Geneva in October 2006. UNHCR participated in WFP's training of staff and counterparts on protection issues in the delivery and distribution of food aid.

68. WFP and UNHCR are partners on IDP issues in countries where UNHCR is the global cluster lead for protection and emergency shelter and camp management/coordination for people displaced as a result of conflict. Both agencies collaborated on repatriating refugees to Angola, Burundi, DRC, Liberia and the Sudan.

69. WFP and UNHCR joint advocacy continues. For the first time, the heads of WFP, UNHCR and UNICEF visited DRC, Burundi and Rwanda together in February and March 2006 to highlight the needs of people in the Great Lakes Region.

70. WFP and UNHCR issue joint press releases and statements, particularly for under-funded operations where food pipeline breaks are expected. Both agencies collaborate on ending child hunger and improving the nutritional status of refugees. UNHCR has made nutrition one of its Global Strategies for 2006–2009.

71. In the United Republic of Tanzania, UNHCR, UNICEF and WFP lead monthly Development Partners Group refugee sub-group meetings, organize donor missions and conduct annual nutritional surveys with other partners.

United Nations Volunteers

72. United Nations Volunteers (UNV) collaboration with WFP is growing: 257 UNVs—190 international and 67 national—contributed to WFP's field operations in 2005. As of 30 September 2006, 210 UNVs were serving with WFP.

73. This partnership was strengthened by joint support of WFP's and the UNV International Volunteer Day. In Trinidad and Tobago, two UNV doctors organized an 11 km Walk Against Child Hunger.

WHO

74. WFP/WHO cooperation grew over the past year. WHO became one of WFP's main partners in 2005, with 69 projects in 42 countries. Health and nutrition—52 projects—and HIV/AIDS—17 projects—featured prominently; 70 percent of joint activities were in emergency and recovery operations.

75. In 2006, high-level meetings were held to enhance cooperation in humanitarian issues. A technical logistics agreement is being finalized, in which WHO will tap WFP's expertise in logistics and use its Humanitarian Response Depots, while WFP benefits from WHO's technical experience in health and nutrition. From early 2007, WFP plans to involve WHO in its preparedness and contingency planning, assessments and vulnerability mapping activities in countries that include DRC.

World Bank

76. In 2005, WFP and the World Bank collaborated in 26 projects in primary schools, MCH, and nutrition and HIV/AIDS in 17 countries. Collaboration is growing, especially in post-conflict and post-emergency countries, as both organizations develop more efficient food systems and recognize each other's strategic guidelines for poverty reduction.

77. Following WFP missions to Niger in the aftermath of the food crisis in late 2005, the World Bank invited WFP to participate in the mid-term evaluation of a nationwide irrigation project. This led to the extension of benefits to poor, food-insecure farmers who had been excluded. Within the 2006 budget support project, Rural and Social Sector Reform Credit, WFP helped to draft a policy document identifying actions that the government needs to implement to trigger the release of World Bank funds. WFP highlighted the importance of food security as an element in Niger's national development strategy, and identified policy actions to this end.

78. WFP, the World Bank and FAO are discussing development of the grain market in Africa. WFP will analyse the effects and consequences of food aid distribution and local food aid procurement on underlying grain markets, and the effects of inadequate infrastructure on grain markets.

79. WFP and the World Bank are collaborating on a weather-based insurance pilot project to provide monetary compensation to Ethiopian farmers and protect them against rainfall risk.

Collaboration with NGOs

80. In 2005, a record 2,274 NGO partners handled 42 percent of WFP's food aid in 73 countries and 209 projects. Most of these partnerships—involving 170 NGOs—were in conflict areas such as Afghanistan, Burundi and DRC.

81. Consultations in Europe and the United States aimed to engage NGOs in ECHUI and public awareness raising on hunger-related issues. NGOs were briefed about participation in the global Partners Group.

82. The Office for the Coordination of Humanitarian Affairs (OCHA) and three NGO consortia organized a meeting on enhancing the effectiveness of humanitarian action, in Geneva in July 2006. WFP's Executive Director attended the meeting, which was valuable in fostering relationships between the United Nations and NGOs. WFP is a member of the inter-agency working group to follow up on this meeting. Partnerships between WFP and NGOs also benefited from WFP's role as lead agency for the logistics cluster, as funding was channelled directly to NGOs and international organizations. In Lebanon, WFP provided NGOs with a common transport system.

83. The regional NGO strategy in southern Africa focused on linking partners and United Nations teams through the Regional Inter-Agency Coordination Support Office process, and identified programming and technical gaps in the regional portfolio. Two staff members from the Cooperative for Assistance and Relief Everywhere (CARE) and Action Aid were seconded to help improve regional capacity to collect outcome data, develop HIV/AIDS programmes and strengthen field-level collaboration. WFP established NGO consortia to respond to the relief and recovery needs of country offices. Swaziland uses the Coordinating Assembly of NGO Consortia, and Zimbabwe's flexible umbrella/nodal NGO management and delivery system can scale up or down at short notice.

84. In October 2006, WFP and 25 NGOs co-chaired WFP's annual NGO consultation on Partnerships in Food Aid Interventions in the 21st century. Issues included cost sharing, the Sudan operation, WFP targeting, humanitarian reform, local/regional procurement, future levels of food assistance, and protection. On 1 December 2006, WFP and the NGO Islamic Relief signed an MOU for global cooperation, which will lead to new collaborations to assist WFP beneficiaries, more than half of whom live in Muslim communities.

Follow-Up to International Conferences

Secretary-General's High-Level Panel on United Nations System-Wide Coherence in the Area of Development, Humanitarian Assistance and the Environment.

85. The High Level Panel's report which was released in November 2006, was a major follow-up to the 2005 World Summit. In May 2006, WFP hosted in Rome the High-Level Panel consultations on humanitarian and transition issues, and seconded a staff member to the panel secretariat for several months. WFP, FAO and IFAD will implement the report's recommendation for closer cooperation among the Rome-based agencies to address long-term food security needs, particularly in sub-Saharan Africa. Action on most of the panel's recommendations will require broader inter-agency cooperation, guidance from the new Secretary-General and in some cases inter-governmental action among Member States. WFP will participate in the interagency and intergovernmental bodies, and will regularly inform the Board of developments.

High-Level Meeting on the Mid-Term Comprehensive Review of the Implementation of the Programme of Action (Brussels Programme of Action) for the Least-developed Countries (LDCs) for the decade 2001–2010)

86. WFP participated in consultations for the mid-term comprehensive global review of implementation of the Brussels Programme of Action, making statements in Addis Ababa and at the ministerial-level meeting in Cotonou. In September 2006, the Executive Director participated at the high-level meeting of the General Assembly to review the Brussels Programme of Action and reaffirm commitment to LDCs. Through the review WFP highlighted its focus on LDCs, and its commitment to delivering the bulk of its resources to LDCs, to reduce hunger, malnutrition and poverty. In 2005, US$1.9 billion—three quarters of WFP's expenditures—were allocated to LDCs. WFP targeted a greater portion of its resources to LDCs than any other United Nations agency, far exceeding average bilateral official development assistance (ODA). At the high-level meeting in New York, WFP and FAO stressed the Rome agencies' important role in addressing hunger and food insecurity in LDCs.

Other Issues Relevant to Implementation of the Triennial Comprehensive Policy Review (TCPR)

Transition from Relief to Development

87. In April 2006, WFP disseminated field guidelines on exiting emergencies, including tools for shifting from emergency response to longer-term programmes that protect and improve livelihoods and resilience, and for phasing out WFP assistance from a transition setting or country. On the Board's request, WFP presented a discussion paper on "WFP Thinking and Experience on Programming in Transition Settings" at the informal consultation in October 2006. Although 90 percent of WFP food is directed to emergencies and 10 percent to development, in PRROs the tonnages for relief and for recovery are roughly 50:50. WFP will ensure that best practices for exiting emergencies and transitions are included in all future EMOPs and PRROs. Next steps include developing guidance on targeting in emergencies, developing comprehensive training on programming in emergencies and transitions, and continuing to participate in inter-agency fora, such as the IASC Early Recovery Cluster and the UNDG/ECHA Working Group on Transition Issues.

Capacity-Building

88. WFP's Strategic Objective 5 is to strengthen the capacities of countries and regions to establish and manage food assistance and hunger reduction programmes. There are regional capacity development projects in Latin America and the Caribbean and southern Africa. Afghanistan, Bangladesh, Egypt, Senegal and Yemen have capacity development as a main objective. At least 30 country offices have mainstreamed capacity-building activities within food assistance interventions. In 2006, capacity development components for new CPs were appraised in Bangladesh, Egypt, India and Yemen. WFP technical assistance is a major feature of capacity development, with thousands of government and NGO participants being trained. Technical services and cooperation with governments were established in 20 areas.

89. WFP partnered the Economic Commission for Latin America and the Caribbean to pilot the economic model and methodology for regional cost of hunger studies that estimate the economic impact of undernutrition. Methodology for the Nutrition and Food Security Atlas was developed with Tufts University and tested in the Dominican Republic.

90. The southern Africa project highlighted the importance of ensuring local ownership: participation from Southern Africa Development Community (SADC) partners led to adoption of a five-year programme on Strengthening Vulnerability Assessment and Analysis in the SADC Region. There is a full-time WFP staff member at the SADC/Vulnerability Assessment Committee in Gaborone, co-funded by WFP and FAO. Another WFP staff member is stationed in the Ministry of Agriculture in Pretoria, supporting development of the national Food Insecurity and Vulnerability Information and Mapping Systems process.

91. WFP provided technical training on early-warning systems (EWS), emergency preparedness and response to technical departments of the African Union Commission (AUC) and some regional economic communities. WFP and AUC jointly developed: (i) Alert Africa, and Africa-Wide EWS; and (ii) the Building Africa-Wide Vulnerability Analysis and Mapping (VAM) Network. WFP and other United Nations agencies developed a post-conflict reconstruction and development strategic framework for AU, as a blueprint for intervening in countries emerging from conflict. WFP provides technical support on gender policy to AUC's Directorate for Women and Gender.

92. In Ethiopia, WFP's capacity-building is based on its experience in local-level participatory planning, in which communities lead the management of their natural resources. In Indonesia, WFP collaborated with UNDP, UNESCO and WHO to build the capacity of central, provincial and district government officials in emergency management and contingency planning. In Liberia and the Dominican Republic, UNICEF and WFP built the Ministry of Health's capacity to establish a nutrition surveillance system.

Gender Mainstreaming

93. Implementation of WFP Gender Policy 2003–2007: Enhanced Commitments to Women (ECW) to Ensure Food Security continues through (i) guidelines on implementation of the ECWs, (ii) collection and analysis of baseline survey data to produce a global report in 2005 and a follow-up study in 2007, (iii) regional and country-level training, completed in early 2006, for 60 country offices and 1,400 WFP and partner staff, and (iv) field-based research on implementation of the ECWs.

94. WFP has mainstreamed gender in:

- the operational sectors of CPs;
- the updated Programme Guidance Manual (online), and Food Distribution Guidelines;
- a training manual on *Leadership Skills, Gender and HIV/AIDS*, for which the links between gender and HIV/AIDS were explored; a recent publication *Getting Started: HIV, AIDS and Gender in WFP Programmes*, describing how WFP's efforts to achieve gender equality and empowerment contribute to reducing the vulnerability of women and girls to HIV/AIDS;
- the 2006 food security and nutrition assessment in Darfur;
- field studies in DRC, Colombia, Liberia and Uganda in 2006 on the impact of humanitarian crises on both sexes, food aid protection challenges and gender-based violence; WFP activities, such as protection rations, contributed to beneficiaries' safety;
- programme evaluations and reports such as those on Ethiopia, India, the Sudan and Indonesia; and WFP's overall results-based monitoring system;
- a chapter on Food Security, Distribution and Nutrition in *Women, Girls, Boys and Men: Different Needs – Equal Opportunities. A Gender Handbook for Humanitarian Action*, in collaboration with FAO and UNICEF, as a member of the IASC task force on gender and humanitarian assistance.

Challenges

95. There is need to mainstream gender in all conflict prevention and early warning tools, so more efforts are needed in needs assessment, contingency planning and early warning. Although WFP does not have a treaty-based protection mandate, it is well-placed to promote protection. More efforts are needed to increase understanding of how WFP can contribute to protection concerns, including gender-based violence, however.

Evaluation

96. During 2006, WFP presented 13 evaluation reports to the Board. Of particular interest were (i) an evaluation of WFP's Business Process Review, which seeks to maximize resource use and improve food pipelines, particularly in relief operations, (ii) a joint UNHCR/WFP evaluation of pilot food distribution projects, (iii) the Tsunami Evaluation Coalition synthesis report and (iv) the inter-agency real-time evaluation of the application of the IASC Cluster Approach in the South Asia Earthquake.

97. The Niger evaluation report distinguished between the period before the humanitarian crisis (harvest 2004 to July 2005) when the assessment and response by stakeholders proved to be inadequate and the acute phase of the crisis, when WFP's strategic reorientation was fully relevant, if somewhat late.

98. WFP is a member of the United Nations Evaluation Group (UNEG), which it anticipates will facilitate a peer review of the evaluation function in WFP in 2007.

Activities of the Executive Boards

Participation in the 2006 Joint Meeting of the Boards of UNDP/UNFPA, UNICEF and WFP

99. UNFPA coordinated the joint meeting of the Boards of UNDP/UNFPA, UNICEF and WFP, which took place in New York in January 2006. For the second consecutive year, WFP coordinated the Transitions from Relief to Development theme, highlighting recovery from the 2005 Pakistan earthquake. To reflect the field perspective, WFP invited UNDP's Pakistan country director and the Pakistan's Secretary of the Ministry of Economic Affairs to make statements on United Nations inter-agency and government cooperation. Board Members' reactions were positive, and they encouraged the United Nations agencies to foster capacity-building, preparedness and national leadership.

Participation in Joint Field Visits of the Boards

100. The Boards of UNDP/UNFPA, UNICEF and WFP visited Indonesia in March 2006, coordinated by UNDP. The purpose was to help Board Members understand the extent and ways in which United Nations organizations, collaborating with government and other partners, contributed to the transition from a humanitarian disaster of unprecedented scale—the December 2004 tsunami—to reconstruction and recovery. The visit also demonstrated how multilateral agencies support governments' achievement of goals. Particular attention was paid to issues relevant to United Nations reform and donor coordination. The mission concluded that the Indonesia UNDAF had strong country ownership, and noted that joint programming is an important tool.

TABLE 1: GENERAL ASSEMBLY RESOLUTIONS THAT MENTION WFP AS A FOLLOW-UP AGENCY

Resolution	*Timing*	*Title*	*Action by WFP*
A/Res/60/123 (A/60/ L.3)	Ongoing	Safety and security of humanitarian personnel and protection of United Nations personnel	Information Note on Funding of Security Management Arrangements, WFP/EB.1/2006/13-C.
A/Res/60/125 (A/60/ L.39)	Ongoing	International cooperation on humanitarian assistance in natural disasters, from relief to development	WFP's follow-up on humanitarian assistance is reported in the 2005 Annual Report to the Economic and Social Council (ECOSOC) and the FAO Council, section 6.
A/Res/60/195 (A/60/488/Add.3)	Ongoing	International Strategy for Disaster Reduction (ISDR)	WFP is a member of the Platform for Promotion of Early Warning. It is also involved in the ISDR initiative, which deals with the Kyoto Framework for Action.
A/Res/60/218 (A/60/496)	Ongoing	Humanitarian assistance and rehabilitation for Ethiopia	WFP provides inputs on its achievements to the report of the Secretary-General through the RC.
A/Res/60/219 (A/60/496)	Ongoing	Assistance for humanitarian relief and the economic and social rehabilitation of Somalia	See above
A/Res/60/128 (A/60/499)	Ongoing	Assistance to refugees, returnees and displaced people in Africa	WFP/UNHCR Joint Evaluation of the Pilot Food Distribution Projects, WFP/EB.1/2006/7-D. See also the Paragraphs on UNHCR in the section on Collaboration with Partners in this report.
A//Res/60/141 (A/60/505 and Corr.1)	Ongoing	The girl child	WFP provides inputs on its achievements, three times a year, to reports of the Commission on the Status of Women, ECOSOC and the General Assembly. WFP's Gender Policy (2003–2007)—Enhanced Commitments to Women to Ensure Food Security, WFP/EB.3/2002/4-A.
A/Res/60/165 (A/60/509/ Add.2) (Part II)	Ongoing	The right to food	WFP and the Voluntary Guidelines to Support the Progressive Realization of the Right to Adequate Food in the Context of National Food Security, WFP/EB/2/2005/4-B.

TABLE 2: ECOSOC RESOLUTIONS THAT MENTION WFP AS A FOLLOW-UP AGENCY

Resolution	*Title*	*Action by WFP*
2005/42	United Nations Public–Private Alliance for Rural Development	The Rome-based agencies support IAAH and work together in the twin-track approach. See below for more details.
2005/45	Promoting an integrated approach to rural development in developing countries for poverty eradication and sustainable development	WFP, FAO and IFAD focus on achieving MDG 1. They encourage investment in rural development and agriculture to support developing countries creating vibrant economies where people can provide for themselves. The Rome-based agencies are strengthening efforts to make the twin-track work. They highlighted food security, hunger reduction and rural development in the outcome document of the September 2005 World Summit. In August 2006, the three agencies formed a senior-level working group on cooperation to integrate food security and rural development into national PRS and regional approaches to combating food insecurity, among others.
2006/4	Sustained economic growth for social development, including the eradication of poverty and hunger	All WFP policies governing the use of food aid aim to eradicate hunger and poverty (WFP Mission Statement). WFP, its United Nations partners, NGOs and other organizations implement initiatives to achieve MDG 1. Details are in this report.
2006/10	Ad Hoc Advisory Group on Haiti	WFP provides inputs on its achievements to the report of the Secretary-General through the RC.
2006/11	Ad Hoc Advisory Group on Guinea-Bissau	See above

Annex I

Points Raised at the 33rd Session of the Fao Conference

"65. The Conference *commended* and *reiterated* its support to WFP for its performance in responding to both man-made and natural disasters. Many Members considered that more attention should be paid to development activities. Members also expressed support for WFP management.

66. Some Members recognized the importance of continuing WFP/FAO cooperation, especially with regard to food security, needs assessment, emergency responses in the provision of agricultural inputs, and nutrition. Cooperation with other UN agencies, civil society, governments and other partners in promoting comparative advantage and effectiveness was also stressed.

67. Some Members commended WFP's focus on women as regarded mother and child nutrition and school feeding programmes. There was some concern, however, over diminishing development programmes that were crucial in addressing hunger as a result of the increase in emergency activities. It was important for development activities to remain intact for capacity-building efforts of developing countries. Some Members stressed that emphasis should be on the traditional core activity of food aid.

68. Most Members recognized the importance of WFP's call for an expansion in its multilateral donor base, and called for the flexibility that more multilateral cash donations would provide.

69. Some Members expressed concern about the capacity of WFP staff to cope with an ever increasing number of emergency situations. While welcoming the concern expressed about staff well-being, the WFP noted that several mechanisms were in place to assist staff in coping with stress such as Rest and Relaxation (R&R), staff rotation, peer support volunteers, and that management was paying continued attention to this matter.

70. A concern was raised that the contributions of small non-traditional donors should not result in decreasing support by the traditional donors. A few Members also addressed the need for strategic food stocks to be available in disaster-prone areas.

71. Some Members praised WFP's business process review, and further encouraged innovative approaches."

(Source: FAO Conference, 33rd Session, Rome, 19-26 November 2005.

http://www.fao.org/docrep/meeting/010/j6321e/j6321e00.htm)

Acronyms used in the Document

AIDS	auto-immune deficiency syndrome
AU	African Union
AUC	African Union Commission
CAP	Consolidated Appeals Process
CARE	Cooperative for Assistance and Relief Everywhere
CCA	Common Country Assessment
CCP	Common Country Programme
CERF	Central Emergency Response Fund
CFSAM	crop and food supply assessment mission
CHAP	Common Humanitarian Action Plan
CP	country programme
CPAP	country programme action plan
DRC	Democratic Republic of the Congo
ECHA	Executive Committee on Humanitarian Affairs
ECHUI	Ending Child Hunger and Undernutrition Initiative
ECOSOC	United Nations Economic and Social Council
ECW	Enhanced Commitments to Women
EMOP	emergency operation
EWS	early-warning system
ExCom	UNDG Executive Committee
FAO	Food and Agriculture Organization of the United Nations
FFE	food for education
FFW	food for work
Habitat	United Nations Human Settlements Programme
HC	Humanitarian Coordinator
HGSFP	Home-Grown School Feeding Programme
HIV	human immuno-deficiency virus
IAAH	International Alliance Against Hunger
IASC	Inter-Agency Standing Committee
ICRC	International Committee of the Red Cross
IDP	internally displaced person
IFAD	International Fund for Agricultural Development
IFRC	International Federation of Red Cross and Red Crescent Societies
ILO	International Labour Organization
IOM	International Organization for Migration
IPC	Integrated Phase Classification
IRA	Immediate Response Account
ISDR	International Strategy for Disaster Reduction
JAM	joint assessment mission

JFFLS	Junior Farmer Field and Life School(s)
JO	joint office
JOWG	Joint Office Working Group
JP	joint programme
LDC	least-developed country
LOU	Letter of Understanding
MCH	mother-and-child health
MDG	Millennium Development Goal
MOU	Memorandum of Understanding
NAF	needs analysis framework
NEPAD	New Partnership for Africa's Development
NFI	non-food item
NGO	non-governmental organization
OCHA	Office for the Coordination of Humanitarian Affairs
ODA	official development assistance
PAHO	Pan-American Health Organization
PDE	External Relations Division
PG	Programme Group
PRRO	protracted relief and recovery operation
PRS	poverty reduction strategy
PRSP	Poverty Reduction Strategy Paper
RC	Resident Coordinator
SADC	Southern Africa Development Community
TCPR	Triennial Comprehensive Policy Review
UNAIDS	Joint United Nations Programme on HIV/AIDS
UNAMA	United Nations Assistance Mission in Afghanistan
UNCT	United Nations country team
UNDAF	United Nations Development Assistance Framework
UNDG	United Nations Development Group
UNDP	United Nations Development Programme
UNEG	United Nations Evaluation Group
UNEP	United Nations Environment Programme
UNESCO	United Nations Educational, Scientific and Cultural Organization
UNFPA	United Nations Population Fund
UNHAS	United Nations Humanitarian Air Service
UNHCR	Office of the United Nations High Commissioner for Refugees
UNICEF	United Nations Children's Fund
UNIDO	United Nations Industrial Development Organization
UNIFEM	United Nations Development Fund for Women

UNJLC	United Nations Joint Logistics Centre
UNODC	United Nations Office on Drugs and Crime
UNOPS	United Nations Office for Project Services
UNV	United Nations volunteer
USAID	United States Agency for International Development
VAM	vulnerability analysis and mapping
WHO	World Health Organization

The manufacturer's authorised representative in the EU for product safety is Oxford University Press España S.A. of El Parque Empresarial San Fernando de Henares, Avenida de Castilla, 2 - 28830 Madrid (www.oup.es/en or product.safety@oup.com). OUP España S.A. also acts as importer into Spain of products made by the manufacturer.
Printed and bound by CPI Group (UK) Ltd, Croydon, CR0 4YY
30/03/2026
02080869-0020